Christm

To
Carolyn
from
Sam & Eva

The Illustrated Bible
and Church Handbook

The Illustrated Bible

and Church Handbook

edited by Stanley J. Stuber

GALAHAD BOOKS · NEW YORK CITY

Published by Galahad Books, a division of A & W
Promotional Book Corporation, 95 Madison Avenue, New York, N.Y. 10016, by arrangement with
Association Press, 291 Broadway, New York, N.Y.
10007

Library of Congress Catalog Card No.: 73-79814
ISBN: 0-88365-024-X

Manufactured in the United States of America.

INTRODUCTION

The outstanding quality of *The Illustrated Bible and Church Handbook* is that it combines a number of features to make an exceptional resource for the Church school teacher, the young Christian, the pastor, and the concerned layman. For example, in addition to the nearly 4,000 basic reference items, it contains almost 2,000 illustrations, 1,692 Scripture references, 18 full-page charts and diagrams, and an index of eighteen pages. Thus it provides quick reference on most matters pertaining to the Bible and to the Christian Church.

This unique handbook is in no sense exhaustive; much more could be written on each of the subjects. But bringing within one cover such a range of Bible information and Church-related items — including Christian symbols and hymns — provides a treasury of reference material that should be of great value to the active Christian worker and learner.

In this introduction, we have two chief purposes. The first is to give, in outline form, the nature of the *contents* of the book. Secondly, we wish to explain briefly how these contents may be *used* to good advantage in the home, the Church and Church school, in the library, and by the pastor and his various assistants.

CONTENTS

This book is divided into three parts: one dealing with facts about the Bible, a second giving a brief outline of Church history in topic form, and a third opening up the fascinating area of Christian hymns — their writers and their background stories.

Bible study is essential if we are to understand the Christian way of life and to follow Christ in Christian action. *The Illustrated Bible and Church Handbook* offers the basic facts as a beginning to further investigation by the Bible student or teacher. It covers a wide area of biblical information in brief, concise, introductory form, and by hundreds of specific references linking each particular item to a much wider field of exploration. It is the hope of the editor that this book will not only serve an immediate need — that of giving information — but will also lead into areas of serious Bible study. It is when we "dig in" that Bible topics and characters really come to life.

In regard to Chapter I, it is important to keep in mind: That the letters O.T. and N.T. indicate whether the biblical person is in the Old Testament or New Testament and that the letters M and F indicate male or female.

Church history spans a period of nearly two thousand years. Hundreds upon hundreds of books have been written about the early beginnings of the Church, about its expansion, missionary program, theology, great conferences, divisions, leaders, service activities, and councils. While the reading of Church history is important, the making of it is far more important. Therefore, while we always have to remember that the names and faces we see in Part II were once living people, we also must keep in mind that we too, as modern Christians in the twentieth century, are writing pages of Church history by what we say and do. In this sense, we wish to learn more about our Church Fathers in order to become better Christians ourselves in our own day and generation.

Part II presents in capsule form a "Who's Who" of outstanding leaders, a section on the hundreds of symbols that have been created to illustrate certain functions of Christianity, explanations of a long list of ecclesiastical terms (which might be difficult to find in one place outside this volume), and a chapter on the practices and events related to Christmas.

Living persons are not included in Chapter III. These abbreviations are used: c.—about or approximately (for a date); d.—died; q.v.—(whom see) see elsewhere in the book; r.—ruled.

Because of its broad range of material, the book inevitably reflects the wealth of diversities within the Christian Church. Readers will be enriched by their encounter with words and interpretations that may be unfamiliar to them but are full of meaning for other Christians. This characteristic is possibly most apparent in the chapter on "Facts about the Church." Its contents are derived from the practices of both liturgical and nonliturgical churches. Thus it speaks of both the Lord's Supper and the Eucharist, pastor and priest, font and baptistry, sacrament and ordinance. It combines distinctive theological interpretations of such subjects as baptism, confirmation, and the physical elements of the Lord's Supper. Referring to the Lord's Supper, for example, it defines the "Host" as the word used for the consecrated bread in some liturgical churches.

Some words will be completely strange to some readers. Others will be defined in unexpected ways. Thus the use of this selection of brief, comprehensive, diverse definitions will lead readers to a new understanding of the Church.

There are, of course, many books dealing with the authors and the background stories of Christian hymns. *The Illustrated Bible and Church Handbook* is unique in providing a handy listing. Enough information is given here to bring new light, new insights, new appreciation of these hymns. The paragraphs make fascinating little stories by themselves. They may often be used to illumine a talk, a sermon, or a class session. These brief, illustrated facts about familiar, and not so familiar hymns can prove to be the most useful part of the whole book. The chapter is particularly valuable because of the illustrations. The collection of portraits is noteworthy; some of the pictures have not been published before.

It is impossible to know for certain how many hymns have been written in the history of the Church. Some authorities say more than three million. Others say over five million. But we do know that Isaac Watts alone wrote

200 in less than two years, that 6,500 are attributed to Charles Wesley, and that Fanny Crosby completed at least 8,000. Naturally, the selection in this book has to be very limited.

Another valuable aspect of *The Illustrated Bible and Church Handbook* is found in the hundreds of illustrations. Facts may often seem dull, but when they are well illustrated, they can take on entirely new significance. The multitude of facts presented here have double value because of the illustrations that enliven them. With the addition of the illustrations, the Bible or Church material can be read with greater understanding. The illustrations thus add a new perspective to the entire book.

USE OF THE BOOK

The way to get the most from this reference book is to use it constantly. Daily use is strongly recommended. It should be considered as a daily companion — like a dictionary — and should, therefore, be kept in a place that is easily accessible.

Although it is hoped that readers will find enjoyment in browsing through the pages of *The Illustrated Bible and Church Handbook,* the chief object of the book is to serve as a ready, handy, quick reference. Do you want to know a certain date? Or a particular event in the life of the Church? Do you want to know a few facts about a leader of Christendom? Or do you want to match a Christian symbol to a certain event, or even find an explanation of a symbol you have noticed in the daily newspaper or in a magazine?

There are various ways to get quick answers to such questions. For example:

1. Make use of the Table of Contents. Here you will find the scope of the book in outline form. You may want to read an entire section rather than to get information on a word or two. By taking a section at a time, you will receive more in the way of continuity.

2. Within each part there are chapters and sections that will give you, in the large, what you want to know. A section may, therefore, be used for background information.

3. Note that in the section on Christmas, there is not only the alphabetized collection of pertinent facts, customs, traditions, songs, and stories but also a Christmas supplement including Christmas verses from the Bible, a listing of Christmas paintings, and the complete poem, "A Visit from St. Nicholas", by Clement C. Moore.

4. For quick, ready reference, the three-way Index should be used. Much attention has been given to this Index because it is the "tool of discovery" that serves as a guide to the word-explorer. First of all, there are hundreds of *names* in alphabetical order. This makes it easy to find the name for which you are looking. Along with the name, a page reference (or references) is given. It then becomes an easy step to turn from the Index to the page where the material may be found. This also applies to the *subject or topic* part of the

7

Index. Although you will not find here everything pertaining to the Bible and the Church in the hundreds of topics listed, most of your normal needs will be met. The third part of the Index is a listing of hymns with their reference page number.

It is strongly recommended that the owner of this book take time, as soon as possible, to become familiar with its contents and come to know its possibilities and limitations. Discover how it can be a constant source-book, a guide in time of need. Learn how its frequent use can help to make you a better teacher, a more interesting preacher, or a keener student.

One of the greatest needs in the Christian Church today is a well-informed constituency. Christians ought to know, in some detail, about their own faith, the practices of their own religious organization, the leadership it has developed, and the hymns that express the courage of its convictions and the message of its soul. Christians need to know more of their own Christian heritage in order to make better current Christian history. Therefore, it is our hope that this reference book will serve as a treasury from which may be drawn from time to time pieces of valuable information that will contribute by its use to the glory of the Christian way of life.

STANLEY I. STUBER

ACKNOWLEDGEMENTS

A large book of the nature of *The Illustrated Bible and Church Handbook* necessarily requires the talents of many persons in its creation and production.

The editor wishes to express his appreciation to the following contributors: The Rev. David W. Thompson for "Who's Who in the Bible" and "Facts About Christmas"; Frederick L. Fay for "Facts About the Bible"; the Rev. John W. Brush for "Who's Who in Church History"; the late Rev. Frederick L. Eckel, Jr., for "Facts About the Church"; Mildred C. Whittemore for "Who's Who of Hymn Writers"; and Helen Salem Rizk for "Stories of Favorite Hymns." A like measure of gratitude is expressed to William Duncan for the drawings; to Carroll E. Whittemore for "Symbols of the Church" and for collecting the material in its original form; to Fred Becker for suggesting its development as a book; and to Dr. Helen Hill Stuber for compiling the Index.

TABLE OF CONTENTS

Introduction by STANLEY I. STUBER   5

What the book contains and how to derive the greatest benefit from its various sections

Acknowledgements   9

An expression of appreciation to those who have helped to write this reference book

Part I — The Bible

I.   *Who's Who in the Bible*   13

All of the principal personalities of the Bible . . . Who they were . . . How to pronounce their names . . . Their significance . . . Main Scripture references to them . . . Illustrations of events in their lives

II.   *Facts About the Bible*   77

A treasury of definitions and explanations . . . Ideas, beliefs, ways of life, places of importance, history, geography, clothing, everyday facts of the Bible narrative . . . Old Testament and New Testament references . . . Drawings that dramatize their meaning

Part II — The Church

III.   *Who's Who in Church History*   141

Biographies-in-brief of the great men and women of the Church . . . Saints and scholars, martyrs and missionaries, contemporary and ancient . . . Where and when they lived . . . Their contributions to Christianity . . . Graphically portrayed in paintings and photographs

IV.   *Facts About the Church*   205

Traditions and practices of the Church, particularly in relation to worship . . . Church architecture and furniture . . . A cross section of both liturgical and nonliturgical forms . . . Charts, diagrams, drawings

V.   *Symbols of the Church*   269

Symbols of the Old Testament and the New Testament . . . The Apostles and the Saints . . . Glossary of terms . . . Forms of ecclesiastical salutation

VI. *Facts About Christmas*   327

Carols, stories, names, events, symbols, festivals, and celebrations related to Christmas . . . Scripture passages for the day . . . Lists of
songs, stories, paintings . . . Greetings from around the world . . . A
Christmas chronology

Part III — Hymns of The Church

VII. *Who's Who of Hymn Writers*   389

Sharply drawn, comprehensive word portraits . . . The men and women
who gave the Church its greatest songs of worship . . . A listing of
some of their works . . . Illustrated by an unusual collection of photographs and drawings

VIII. *Stories of Favorite Hymns*   451

How 180 favorite hymns came to be written . . . Excerpts from them
. . . What they reveal of their authors . . . What they mean to Christians
today . . . Drawings that express their themes

Index: Names (Persons and Places) . . . Topics (Church and Theological) . . .
Hymns and Carols

Part I—The Bible

Chapter I
Who's Who in the Bible

A

AARON (ar'on) O.T. A son of Amram and Joche-bed, elder brother of Moses and Miriam. First mentioned in Exodus 4:14. He was appointed by God to be the interpreter of his brother Moses (Exodus 4:16) and became the instrument through which many of the miracles of the Exodus occurred. Together with Hur, he held up the weary arms of Moses in the military victory over Amalek. (Exodus 17:10) He became the first High Priest of the Israelite nation, and served the latter part of his life in that capacity. He died on Mount Hor after the transference of his robes and office to Eleazar. (M) (Numbers 20:28)

AARON

AARONITES (ar'on-ites) O.T. Priestly descendants of Aaron. (1 Chronicles 12:27)

ABAGTHA (a-bag'tha) O.T. One of the chamberlains of King Ahasuerus in Persia. (M) (Esther 1:10)

ABEDNEGO (a-bed'ne-go) O.T. One of the three friends of the prophet Daniel, saved miraculously from the flames of the burning fiery furnace during the reign of Nebuchadnezzar of Babylon. (M) (Daniel 3)

ABEDNEGO

ABEL (a'bel) O.T. The second son of Adam and Eve, brother of Cain, and a keeper of sheep. Abel became the world's first murder victim, according to the Bible account. His sacrifice of the firstlings of his flock was respected and received by God, while Cain's offering of the fruit of the ground was rejected. Motivated by jealousy and stirred by anger, Cain slew Abel. (M) (Genesis 4:1-10)

ABI (a'bi) O.T. The mother of King Hezekiah, 25 year old King of Judah. (F) (2 Kings 18:2)

ABIATHAR (a-bi'a-thar) O.T. A high priest. descendant from Eli. He was the only one of the sons of Ahimelech, the high priest, who escaped death at the wrath of Saul. (1 Samuel 22:20) Abiathar supported David throughout his life, and remained faithful to him through Absalom's rebellion. (2 Samuel 15:35) However, when Abiathar suported Adonijah, who had set himself up as a successor to the throne in opposition to Solomon, he was deprived of his position as high priest. (M) (1 Kings 1:7; 2:27)

ABEL

ABIDAN ((a-bi'dan) O.T. Chief of the tribe of Benjamin at the time of the Exodus. (M) (Numbers 1:11)

ABIGAIL (ab'i-gal) O.T. A beautiful woman, wife of a wealthy sheep owner named Nabal. She supported David with food and drink during his exile, at a time when her husband refused to help him. At Nabal's death, David called for Abigail and made her his wife. (F) (1 Samuel 25:2-42)

ABIGAIL

15

ABIMELECH (a-bim'e-lek) O.T. A son of Gideon. After his father's death, he slew his seventy brothers with the exception of the youngest, Jotham. Abimelech persuaded the people of Shechem to appoint him King. His reign over Israel was short and bloody, ending in his own death at the hand of a woman of Thebez who struck him on the head with a piece of millstone. (M) (Judges 9)

ABISHAG (ab'ish-ag) O.T. A beautiful woman who took care of King David in his old age. (F) (1 Kings 1:1-4)

ABNER (ab'ner) O.T. First cousin to King Saul, and commander-in-chief of his army. After serving under Saul, Ish-bosheth, and David, Abner was treacherously murdered by Joab at the gates of Hebron. (M) (2 Samuel 3)

ABNER

ABRAHAM (a'bra-ham) O.T. The founder of the Hebrew nation. He was born in Ur of the Chaldees. At the age of 75, following the command of God, he travelled with all his household to the land of Canaan. Here Abraham received a promise from God that the land would be the inheritance of his descendants. The life of the great patriarch was marked by experiences of faith, courage, generosity and patience. His generosity was seen when he offered his nephew, Lot, first choice of the new land. His courage was shown when he accepted without fear the challenge of a new and strange land. His faith was proved when he was willing to sacrifice Isaac, his son of promise. His patience was revealed as he waited without doubt for the fulfillment of the will of God. Abraham lived a long and successful life with rich possessions and many children. The most noted of his family were: Sarah, his wife, and son Isaac; Hagar, his wife, and son Ishmael; and his grandsons, Jacob and Esau. Abraham died at the age of 175 years. (M) (Genesis 12-24)

ABRAHAM

ABSALOM (ab'sa-lom) O.T. King David's third son, and famed for his personal beauty. He plotted against his father to gain his throne and almost succeeded. But in a decisive battle at Gilead, Absalom's forces were totally defeated and he himself, while riding to escape, was caught by the hair of the head and left hanging in a tree. (M) (2 Samuel 18)

ACHAICUS (acha'icus) N.T. An early Christian in the church at Corinth. (M) (1 Corinthians 16:17)

ABSALOM

ACHAN (a'can) O.T. A member of the tribe of Judah who participated in the destruction of Jericho. He disobeyed the command to utterly destroy all that was in the city, when he hid clothes, silver and gold in his tent. For this sin, Achan, and his family, were stoned to death. (M) (Joshua 7)

ACHISH (a'kish) O.T. A Philistine king who helped David escape from Saul. (M) (1 Samuel 21:10)

ACHAN

ACHSAH (ak'sah) O.T. One of the daughters of Caleb. She married Othniel, the first judge of Israel. (F) (Joshua 15:17)

ADAH (a'dah) O.T. One of Esau's three wives and the mother of Eliphaz. (F) (Genesis 36:2,3)

ADAM (ad'am) O.T. The name of the first man, according to the Bible account. He was created from the dust of the earth, in the image of God. Into his nostrils was breathed the breath of life, and he became a living soul. He was placed in the garden of Eden as the keeper of living things. He was permitted to eat of the fruit of every tree in the garden with the exception of one, "the tree of the knowledge of good and evil." When Adam, tempted of the evil one, ate of this tree, he was expelled from the garden for his disobedience. Adam lived 930 years, according to the Bible, and was the father of many children, the most famous of whom were Cain, Abel, and Seth. (M) (Genesis 1,2,3)

ADAM

ADMATHA (ad-ma'tha) O.T. One of the seven princes of Persia. (M) (Esther 1:14)

ADNAH (ad'na) O.T. Captain of over a quarter million men in the army of Jehoshaphat. (M) (2 Chronicles 17:14)

ADONIZEDEK (a-do'ni-ze'dek) O.T. A king of Jerusalem at the time of the invasion of the promised land by Joshua. (M) (Joshua 10:1-27)

ADONIJAH (ad-o-ni'jah) O.T. Fourth son of King David who attempted unsuccessfully to occupy his father's throne. Solomon was proclaimed the new king. (M) (1 Kings 1,2)

ADONIJAH

AGABUS (ag'a-bus) N.T. A Christian prophet in the time of the early church. (M) (Acts 11:28; 21:10)

AHAB (a'hab) O.T. Seventh king of Israel and husband of Jezebel. His interest in pagan worship drew warnings from the prophet Elijah. Another prophet, Micaiah, successfully foretold his death in a military venture againt Ramoth in Gilead. (M) (1 Kings 21)

AHAB

AHASUERUS (a-has-u-e'rus) O.T. King of Persia, recognized by most to be Xerxes of history. After Vashti, the queen, had been exiled, Esther the Jewess was selected to become the queen. Ahasuerus was friendly to the Jewish people and rewarded the courage of Esther and the wisdom of Mordecai, her cousin, with legislation which allowed the Jews to defend themselves against all their enemies. (M) (Esther 1-10)

AHAZ (a'haz) O.T. Twelfth king of Judah. He is remembered as a weak king who depended upon the heathen ceremonies. He consulted wizards and magicians. He made his own son pass through the fire to Molech, the heathen God. He practiced numerous forms of idolatry. At his death he was refused burial with the kings. (M) (2 Chronicles 28:27)

AHAZIAH (a-ha-zi'ah) O.T. Son of Ahab and Jezebel, the eighth king of Israel. He was an idolater and worshipped Baal. Bible records say that he was an evil king. He died after a serious fall through the lattice of an upper chamber in his Samaritan palace. (M) (2 Kings 1:1-17)

AHIKAM (a-hi'kam) O.T. An influential officer at the court of Josiah and a protector of the prophet Jeremiah in the days of Jehoiakim, King of Judah. (M) (Jeremiah 26:24)

AHIMAAZ

AHIMAAZ (a-him'a-az) O.T. Son of Zadok, the high priest, in the time of King David, and a swift runner who served as an important messenger to the King. (M) (2 Samuel 18:19)

AHIMAN (a-hi'man) O.T. One of the giants driven from Hebron by Caleb. (M) (Joshua 15:14)

AHIMELECH (a-him'e-lek) O.T. High Priest at Nob in the days of King Saul, who was killed because he gave shrewbread and Goliath's sword to David. (M) (1 Samuel 22:11)

AHINADAB (a-hin'a-dab) O.T. One of King Solomon's 12 officers of provision. (M) (1 Kings 4:7,14)

AHIO (a-hi'o) O.T. A son of Ahinadab and brother of Uzzah, who helped guide the ark of God. (M) (2 Samuel 6:3,4)

AHITHOPHEL

AHITHOPHEL (a-hith'o-fel) O.T. A man of great wisdom and a counselor to King David. He is considered by many authorities to be the grandfather of Bathsheba. Ahithophel joined the group who followed Absalom in a revolt against David. However, when Ahithophel's counsel was ignored, he realized the folly of the venture and committed suicide. (M) (2 Samuel 17:1-23)

AHOLIAB

AHOLIAB (a-ho'li-ab) O.T. A weaver and embroiderer of such great skill that Moses appointed him, with Bezaliel, to erect the tabernacle. (M) (Exodus 35:30-35)

ALEXANDER (al-ex-an'der) N.T. 1. A son of Simon the Cyrene, the Simon who was compelled to carry the cross of Christ. (M) (Mark 15:21)
2. Alexander the defender, a man selected by the Jews at Ephesus to plead their cause with the mob. N.T. (M) (Acts 19:33)
3. Alexander the Great. Son of Philip of Macedonia, and one of the great rulers of the early world. Born in B.C. 356, he conquered Greece, Persia, Syria, Palestine, Egypt, and all the known Mediterranean area. He died in Babylon at the young age of 33. Alexander the Great is supposed by many to be intended in the prophecy of Daniel. (M) (Daniel 2:39,40; 7:6; 11:3,4)
4. Alexander the coppersmith. N.T. One who did the apostle Paul and his fellow-workers much injury. (M) (2 Timothy 4:14)

ALEXANDER THE
GREAT

ALEXANDRIANS (al-ex-an'dri-ans) N.T. The Jewish colonists of Alexandria. (Acts 6:9)

ALPHAEUS (al-fe'us) N.T. 1. Father of James the Less, one of the 12 disciples of Jesus, and son of one of the Marys. (M) (Mark 15:40; Matthew 10:3)
2. The father of Matthew (or Levi), one of the 12 disciples of Jesus. (M) (Mark 2:14)

ALEXANDER THE
COPPERSMITH

AMALEKITES (am'a-lek-ites) O.T. Descendants of Esau, who lived in the Sinai Peninsula. A nomadic race, their wealth was in their flocks and herds. They were an important people in the time of Moses (Numbers 24:20), but became almost extinct after battles with Saul (1 Samuel 14:48) and David. (1 Samuel 30:1-17)

AMAZIAH (am-a-zi'ah) O.T. Son of Joash, and the ninth king of Judah. He began his reign at the age of 25 years. (2 Kings 14:1,2) Amaziah undertook a successful military venture against the Edomites; but was himself defeated and captured by the armies of Israel.

AMMIEL

AMBASSADOR (am-bas'sa-dor) A person of high rank hired by one government to represent it with another. Messengers from one country to another. (Isaiah 18:2) One of the earliest forms of ambassadors is found in Numbers 20:14; 21:21.

AMMIEL (am'miel) O.T. One of the twelve spies sent by Moses into the land of Canaan. (Numbers 13:1,2) He perished by the plague for his evil report. (M) (Numbers 14:37)

AMNON

AMON

AMOS

ANANIAS

ANDREW

AMMONITES (am'mon-ites) O.T. The people descended from Ben-Ammi, a son of Lot. (Genesis 19:38) They were a nomadic race generally located west of the Jordan. The Ammonites were always bitter enemies of the Israelites, and were idol worshipers, with Molech, their tribal divinity. (Deuteronomy 2:19-21)

AMNON (am'non) O.T. The eldest son of David, murdered by his half-brother, Absalom. (M) (2 Samuel 13:1-29)

AMOK (a'mok) O.T. A chief of priests returning with Zerubbabel from captivity in the land of Babylon. (M) (Nehemiah 12:20)

AMON (a'mon) O.T. One of the eight chief gods of Egypt, sometimes called Amen. (Nahum 3:8) (Jeremiah 46:25)

AMORITES (am'or-ites) O.T. One of the chief tribes of Canaan before its conquest by the Israelites. They lived in the mountain areas of Old Testament Palestine. (Deuteronomy 1:44)

AMOS (a'mos) O.T. An inhabitant of Tekoa in Judah, six miles south of Bethlehem. He was a shepherd called by God to be a prophet to the northern kingdom of Israel during the reign of Jeroboam II. (M) (Amos 1:1)

AMOZ (a'moz) O.T. The father of Isaiah the prophet. (M) (2 Kings 19:2)

AMRAM (am'ram) O.T. Father of Moses, Aaron, and Miriam. (M) (Numbers 26:59)

ANAKIM (an'a-kim) O.T. A tribe of giants who lived in the southern part of Palestine. They were driven from their land by Caleb. Goliath was probably one of the Anakim. (Joshua 15:14)

ANAMMELECH (a-nam'me-lek) O.T. One of the idols worshipped by the Babylonians with rites similar to Molech, where the children were burned as a sacrifice. (2 Kings 17:31)

ANANIAS (an-a-ni'as) 1. Ananias of Damascus. N.T. A Jewish Christian who restored the sight of Paul and received him into the Church. (M) (Acts 22:12)
2. Ananias of Jerusalem. N.T. A disciple at Jerusalem, who with his wife Sapphira sold his possessions for the benefit of the Church, and laid only a portion before the altar as the whole. When Peter denounced the fraud, Ananias fell down and died. (M) (Acts 5:1-11)

20

ANDREW (an'dru) N.T. One of the twelve apostles of Jesus, (John 1:40) and brother of Peter. He was a native of Bethsaida and a disciple of John the Baptist, leaving him to follow Jesus. In the listing of the Apostles, he seems to occupy fourth place following Peter, James and John. Tradition says that Andrew was crucified in Achaia on a cross shaped like the letter X. (M) (Mark 3:18; Acts 1:13)

ANDRONICUS (an-dron'i-kus) N.T. An important Christian in the early church at Rome. (M) (Romans 16:7)

ANNAS

ANGELS (an'gels) Angels are spiritual beings a little higher in order than man. From their worship of God, they are called sons of God; (Job 38:7) from their character they are called holy ones; (Psalms 89:5) and their office is that of a messenger from God to man.

ANNA (an'na) N.T. A prophetess who visited the temple daily in Jerusalem and who was present at the dedication of Jesus. She recognized and proclaimed Him to be the Messiah. (F) (Luke 2:36)

APOLLOS

ANNAS (an'nas) N.T. A high priest appointed by the Governor of Syria before whom Jesus was brought for his first hearing during his trial in Jerusalem just before his crucifixion. (M) (John 18:13)

ANTIPAS (an'ti-pas) N.T. 1. Herod Antipas. The son of Herod the Great. (see Herod) 2. Antipas of Pergamum. A Christian martyr of the early church in Pergamum. (M) (Revelation 2:12,13)

APELLES (a-pel'les) N.T. An approved Christian of Rome, saluted by the apostle Paul. (M) (Romans 16:10)

AQUILA

APOLLOS (a-pol'los) N.T. A Christian Jew of Alexandria who was famed for his oratory. He was first instructed in the ways of the Lord according to the teaching of John the Baptist, but later more perfectly taught by Priscilla and Aquila. He was a teacher and preacher in the area of Corinth, and an acquaintance of the missionary Paul. (M) (1 Corinthians 16:12)

APOSTLE (a-pos-el) The official name for the first twelve disciples Jesus chose to send forth to preach the gospel and to be with Him during the course of his earthly ministry. The Apostles were simple and uneducated, coming from the more humble stations of life. They accompanied Jesus on his travels, witnessed his miracles, heard his teachings, and proclaimed his messiahship. The twelve apostles

ARABIANS

ASA

ASHTORETH

ASSYRIANS

ATHALIAH

were: Peter, James, John, Andrew, Philip, Bartholomew, Thomas, Matthew, James the Less, Thaddaeus, Simon the Canaanite, and Judas Iscariot. (Matthew 10:2)

APPHIA (af'fi-a) N.T. A Christian woman member of the household of Philemon. (F) (Philemon 2)

AQUILA (ak'wi-la) N.T. A Jew of Rome, who was forced to flee the city with his wife Priscilla because of a law passed by the Emperor Claudius. He was a tentmaker by trade and a good friend of Paul. (M) (Acts 18:2; 18:18,19)

ARABIANS (a-ra'bi-ans) The nomadic tribes who lived in the area east and south of Palestine. They were known in early days as Ishmaelites. (2 Chronicles 17:11)

ARIEL (a'ri-el) O.T. One of the leaders, under Ezra, of the caravan returning from Babylon to Jerusalem. (M) (Ezra 8:16)

ARISTARCHUS (ar-is-tar'kus) N.T. A companion of Paul on his third missionary journey. (M) (Acts 19:29)

ARISTOBULUS (ar-is-tob'u-lus) N.T. A Christian resident at Rome, and by tradition a missionary to Britain. (M) (Romans 16:10)

ARTAXERXES (ar-ta-xerx'es) O.T. The King of Persia, 465 B.C., who allowed the rebuilding of the walls of Jerusalem. (M) (Ezra 7; Nehemiah 2)

ARTEMAS (ar'te-mas) N.T. A friend and companion of St. Paul. (M) (Titus 3:12)

ASA (a'sa) O.T. The third king of Judah, who reigned for 40 years. His rule was marked by peace, reformation, building of fortified cities, destruction of false idols, and the raising of a great army of 580,000 men. (2 Chronicles 14:8) He died in the 41st year of his reign, highly honored and respected. (M) (2 Chronicles 15:8)

ASENATH (as'e-nath) O.T. Wife of Joseph, and mother of Manasseh and Ephraim. (F) (Genesis 41:50)

ASHER (ash'er) O.T. The eighth son of Jacob, and the leader of one of the twelve tribes of Israel which settled in the northwestern part of Palestine near Mt. Carmel. (M) (Genesis 30:13; Joshua 19:24-31)

ASHTORETH (ash'to-reth) O.T. The Phoenician goddess of love and fertility. She also appears as a war-goddess in Assyria and Babylonia. The worship of Ashtoreth became identified with Venus and Aphrodite, Greek and Roman goddess of love and beauty. It spread to the Hebrews in the time of the judges and kings. (F) (1 Kings 11:5, 33; Judges 10:6)

ASRIEL (as'ri-el) O.T. Son of Gilead, and great-grandson of Manasseh. (M) (Numbers 26:31)

ASSHUR (ash'ur) O.T. The second son of Shem, and the country where the descendants of Shem settled. (M) (Genesis 10:22; Ezra 4:2)

ASSYRIANS (as-syr'i-ans) O.T. Members of a large and powerful nation located on the Tigris River. The capital city was Nineveh, the place where Jonah went to preach the message of God. The most famous of the Assyrian Kings was Sennacherib. The worship of the Assyrians was centered around thirteen major and numerous minor divinities, the head of which was Asshur, chief god. The great empire came into being before the time of Moses, and lasted until the rise of the Medes about 607 B.C. (Genesis 2:14; Isaiah 10:5)

ATHALIAH (ath-a-li'ah) O.T. Daughter of Ahab and Jezebel. She introduced the worship of Baal into the kingdom, and ruled six evil years, until the elevation of Joash to the throne, when she was killed. (F) (2 Chronicles 22:11)

ATHENIANS (a-the'ni-ans) N.T. Inhabitants of Athens, the famous Greek city of culture and learning in early civilization. The city itself was located approximately five miles from the sea and was the gem, the jewel of the Golden Period of Greek history. Athenians saw daily such superb sights as the Acropolis, citadel of Athens; the Parthenon, temple to the goddess Athene; the Acropolis with all its temples of gods and heroes, and Mars Hill, where Paul preached a famous sermon. Athens became the center of science, literature and art in the ancient world. (Acts 17:21,22)

AUGUSTUS CAESAR (au-gus'tus) N.T. The first Roman Emperor. The title Augustus was conferred upon him after a victorious struggle for control of the Roman Empire with Mark Antony, just prior to the birth of Christ. His name is a familiar part of the eternal Christmas story. (M) (Luke 2:1)

AVITES (a'vits) O.T. People sent from Avva, a city in Assyria, to re-populate captured Israelite cities. Although they served their own gods and images, they learned to know the Lord and to serve Him. (2 Kings 17:24-41)

AZAREL (az'a-rel) O.T. One of the musicians in the great temple orchestra in the time of David. (M) (1 Chronicles 25:18)

AZARIAH (az-a-ri'ah) O.T. A common name in Hebrew families, particularly among the priests. Some of the principal persons who had this name were: 1. The son of Ahimaaz. He was the apparent successor to Zadok, the high priest. (1 Chronicles

ATHENIANS

AUGUSTUS
CAESAR

AZAREL

BAAL

BALAAM

BARABBAS

BARAK

BARNABAS

6:9) 2. Tenth king of Judah, also called Uzziah. (2 Kings 14:21) 3. Son of Oded, unusual prophet in the days of King Asa. (2 Chronicles 15:1) (M)

AZAZIAH (az-a-zi'ah) O.T. One of the musicians appointed by King David to play at the procession of the ark of God. (M) (1 Chronicles 15:21)

AZMAVETH (az'ma-veth) O.T. One of the mighty men of David. (M) (1 Chronicles 11:33)

AZUBAH (a-zu'bah) O.T. Mother of King Jehoshaphat. (F) (1 Kings 22:42)

B

BAAL (ba'al) O.T. The supreme god of the Phoenician and Canaanite nations. The worship of Baal attracted the Israelites during the time of the Judges. (Judges 3:7-11) Temples were constructed and ceremonies conducted in recognition of the heathen god. (1 Kings 16:32) Elijah the prophet warned Israel against allegiance to Baal and exposed its false power in a dramatic contest with the prophets of Baal on Mt. Carmel. (1 Kings 18:17-40)

BAALIS (ba'al-is) O.T. Ammonite King at the time of the destruction of Jerusalem by the armies of Nebuchadnezzar. (M) (Jeremiah 40:14)

BAALZEBUB (ba'al-ze'bub) O.T. A form of Baal, and the name by which Baal was worshipped as Lord of the flies. Ancient peoples called upon him to control this pest. (2 Kings 1:16)

BAASHA (ba'a-sha) O.T. Third King of the northern kingdom of Israel. He reigned for 24 years. (M) (1 Kings 15:17)

BABYLONIANS (bab'y-lon'i-ans) O.T. The people who lived in the land of Babylon located in the vicinity of the Persian Gulf and extending northward along the Tigris and Euphrates rivers. The city of Babylon, situated on both sides of the Euphrates about 250 miles from the gulf, was approximately an area of 100 square miles enclosed by lofty, huge walls. The Bible indicates that the history of Babylon began in the time of Nimrod. (Genesis 10:6-10) It flourished until the conquest of Cyrus, King of Persia. (Jeremiah 51:37)

BALAAM (ba'lam) O.T. A man who possessed the gift of prophecy. (Numbers 22:5) He was requested by Balak, the King of Moab, to curse Israel. He refused after a prohibition by God, the second refusal following an experience with a speaking donkey. (Numbers 22:28) Instead of cursing Israel, Balaam prophesied magnificent blessings from God. (M) (Numbers 22-25)

24

BALAK (ba'lak) O.T. The King of the Moabites, who hired Balaam to curse the people of Israel. Balak's plans were never fulfilled. (M) (Numbers 22)

BARABBAS (ba-rab'bas) N.T. A robber, prisoner in Jerusalem at the time of Jesus' trial before Pilate, guilty of murder, who was released to freedom at the request of the people, instead of the Saviour, who was then crucified. (M) (Mark 15:7)

BARAK (ba'rak) O.T. A son of Abinoam. He was inspired by the prophetess Deborah to deliver Israel from the bondage of the Canaanites. He defeated their armies on the plain of Jezreel. (M) (Judges 4)

BARBARIAN (bar-bar'i-an) N.T. The term used to describe all people who were not Greeks. (Romans 1:14)

BAR-JONA (ba-jo'na) N.T. A name used by Jesus in reference to his disciple Peter, "Simon Barjona." (M) (Matthew 16:17) It means son of Jona.

BARNABAS (bar'na-bas) N.T. An early Christian, born on the isle of Cyprus, who introduced Paul to the Church, and helped him on his first missionary journey. (M) (Acts 9:27; Acts 13)

BARTHOLOMEW (bar-thol'o-mew) N.T. One of the 12 Apostles. He is considered by many to be identical with Nathaniel. Little mention is made of him in the Bible, but tradition says that he travelled as far as India and Armenia in his missionary work. (M) (Matthew 10:3)

BARTIMAEUS (bar-ti-me'us) N.T. A blind beggar of Jericho, who by his faith was healed of his blindness. (M) (Mark 10:46)

BARUCH (ba'ruk) O.T. Faithful friend and helper of the prophet Jeremiah. (M) (Jeremiah 43:1-6)

BARZILLAI (bar-zil'la-i) O.T. A wealthy man of Gilead who befriended David during his flight from Absalom. (M) (2 Samuel 17:27)

BASEMATH (bas'e-math) O.T. A daughter of Solomon, who married Ahimaaz. (F) (1 Kings 4:15)

BATHSHEBA (bath'she-ba) O.T. The wife of Uriah the Hittite, who attracted King David with her unusual beauty. After Uriah's death she became the wife of the King and the mother of four sons including Solomon. Bathsheba assisted Solomon in his quest for the throne of Judah by urging David to select him instead of Adonijah. Bathsheba was one of the ancestors of Jesus. (M) (2 Samuel 11; 1 Kings 1:11; Matthew 1:6)

BARTHOLOMEW

BARTIMAEUS

BATHSHEBA

BEELZEBUB

BENJAMIN

BERNICE

BEZALEL

BOAZ

BEDAN (be'dan) O.T. A judge of Israel following Gideon. (M) (1 Samuel 12:11)

BEELZEBUB (be-el'ze-bub) A name for Satan, the prince of the devils. (Matthew 10:25)

BELSHAZZAR (bel-shaz'zar) O.T. Famous king of Babylon, who held a grand feast in his palace during the exile of Daniel, using the sacred vessels of the temple of Jerusalem. (Daniel 5:1-29) He was a witness to the miraculous appearance of the "handwriting on the wall" interpreted by Daniel to mean the overthrow of the kingdom. Belshazzar was the last Babylonian king and was succeeded at his death by Darius the Mede. (M) (Daniel 5:31)

BENAIAH (be-na'iah) O.T. One of the mighty men of King David's bodyguard. (2 Samuel 23:20) Among the feats of strength and courage for which he is remembered, is the slaying of a lion in a pit of snow. Benaiah remained faithful to Solomon during his reign and was promoted to commander-in-chief of the whole army. (M) (1 Kings 2:35; 4:4)

BEN-HADAD (ben-ha'dad) O.T. The name of three kings of Damascus. Ben-hadad II lived during the time of Elisha the prophet. Long wars with Israel characterized his 30 year reign. (M) (2 Kings 8:7-15)

BENJAMIN (ben'ja-min) O.T. The youngest son of Jacob and Rachel, and the young brother of Joseph. During the famine of Judah when the sons of Jacob travelled into Egypt seeking food at the Pharaoh's court over which Joseph presided, Benjamin was used as a hostage to guarantee the return of the Canaanite brothers. The name Benjamin was adopted by a whole tribe of Israelites who settled in the southern part of Palestine. (M) (Genesis 44)

BERNICE (ber-ni'ce) N.T. Daughter of Herod Agrippa I, and wife of Herod, King of Chalcis. She was present with her brother Agrippa II at Paul's defense before Festus in Caesarea. (F) (Acts 25:23)

BEROEANS (be-re'ans) N.T. Inhabitants of the city of Beroea in Macedonia who are remembered because of their thorough studies of the Scriptures. (Acts 17:10,11)

BETHUEL (beth-u'el) O.T. Nephew of Abraham, and father of Rebekah. (M) (Genesis 22:22,23)

BEZALEL (bez'a-lel) O.T. An architect of the tribe of Judah, who helped construct the tabernacle. He was responsible chiefly for all works "of metal, wood and stone." (M) (Exodus 31:1-6)

BIGTHA (big'tha) O.T. One of the seven chamberlains of King Ahasuerus. (M) (Esther 1:10)

BILDAD (bil'dad) O.T. One of Job's friends who had explanations for Job's many difficulties. (M) (Job 2:11)

BILHAH (bil'hah) O.T. Handmaid of Rachel, and mother of Jacob's sons, Dan and Naphtali. (F) (Genesis 30:3-8)

BILSHAN (bil'shan) O.T. One of the companions of Zerubbabel on his expedition from Babylon to Jerusalem. (M) (Ezra 2:2)

BISHOP (bish'op) N.T. One who is an overseer of the spiritual well being of others. (1 Timothy 3:2)

BIZTHA (biz'tha) O.T. The second of the seven chamberlains of King Ahasuerus. (M) (Esther 1:10)

BLASTUS (blas'tus) N.T. A chamberlain of Herod Agrippa I. (M) (Acts 12:20)

BOAZ (bo'az) O.T. A wealthy Bethlehemite who married Ruth the Moabitess. He saw her first when she was gleaning wheat in his fields. Boaz is mentioned as one of the ancestors of Christ. (M) (Matthew 1:5; Ruth 4:1-12)

CAESAR

CAIAPHAS

C

CAESAR (se'zer) N.T. Title given to all the Roman Emperors. (John 19:12, 15)

CAIAPHAS (ka'ya-fas) N.T. High priest of the Jews and son-in-law to Annas. Caiaphas was high priest during the ministry of John the Baptist; and he was in the middle of the plot to destroy Jesus. It was at his palace that the elders, scribes, and chief priests met to discover ways of arresting Jesus. When the Galilean was seized by the soldiers, it was to Caiaphas that he was first taken. Much of the responsibility of the death of the Saviour rests upon him. (M) (Luke 3:2; John 11:49-53)

CAIN

CAIN (kan) O.T. The oldest son of Adam and Eve, and the world's first farmer, according to the Bible. In a violent outburst of jealousy and anger he killed his brother Abel. (See Abel) For this crime he lived a life of exile in the land of Nod. (M) (Genesis 4)

CALEB (ka'leb) O.T. One of the spies sent by Moses into Canaan. He, with Joshua, gave a good report of the land. Later he claimed possession of the land of the Anakim and the hill country around Hebron. With fearless courage he drove out the giants and inhabited the area. (M) (Joshua 14)

CALEB

CHLOE

CLAUDIUS

CLEOPAS

COLOSSIANS

CANAAN (ka'nan) O.T. The fourth son of Ham, and the ancestor of the Phoenicians and other races that lived in Palestine before its conquest by the Israelites. (M) (Genesis 10:6)

CANAANITES (ka'nan-ites) O.T. The people who lived in the land of Canaan, descendants of Ham. The Canaanites were doomed to destruction because of their wickedness. (Deuteronomy 20:17)

CARCAS (kar'kas) O.T. One of Ahasuerus' chamberlains. (M) (Esther 1:10)

CARSHENA (kar-she'na) O.T. A prince of Persia and Media. (M) (Esther 1:14)

CHALDEANS (kal-de'ans) O.T. All the people of the Babylonian empire.

CHENANIAH (ken-a-ni'ah) O.T. A leader of the Levites in music and law. (M) (1 Chronicles 15:22; 26:29)

CHILEAB (kil'e-ab) O.T. A son of David and Abigail. (M) (2 Samuel 3:3)

CHILION (kil'i-on) O.T. Naomi's son and the husband of Orpah. (M) (Ruth 1:2-5)

CHLOE (klo'e) N.T. A Christian woman who lived in Corinth. (F) (1 Corinthians 1:11)

CHRIST (krist) N.T. The annointed one. A term conferred upon Jesus meaning Messiah. (See Jesus) (M) (Matthew 16:16; Mark 8:29; Luke 3:15)

CHRISTIAN (kris'chan) N.T. A follower of Jesus Christ. The name was first used in Antioch. Strangely enough, it was devised by the enemies of the Church, and used as a term of contempt. It is used only three times in the Bible: Acts 11:26; Acts 26:28; 1 Peter 4:16.

CLAUDIA (klo'di-a) N.T. A Christian woman who joined with Paul in sending greetings to Timothy. (F) (II Timothy 4:21)

CLAUDIUS (klo'di-us) N.T. Fourth Roman emperor, 41 to 54 A.D. During his reign there were several severe famines. (Acts 11:28-30) A decree from Claudius exiled all the Jews from Rome. (Acts 18:2) He died as the result of poison administered by his fourth wife, Agrippina, mother of Nero. (M)

CLEMENT (klem'ent) N.T. An early Christian who worked with Paul at Philippi. It is believed by some authorities that he became later bishop of Rome. (M) (Philippians 4:3)

CLEOPAS (kle'o-pas) N.T. One of the two disciples who were on the way to Emmaus at the time of the resurrection. (M) (Luke 24:18)

28

CLEOPHAS (kle'o-fas) N.T. Clopas in the R.S.V. A man who was the husband of one of the Marys who stood at the cross when Jesus was crucified. (M) (John 19:25)

COLOSSIANS (ko-losh'anz) N.T. The Christians in the city of Colossae located in Phrygia, Asia Minor, who received a letter from the Apostle Paul warning them against the false doctrines that were corrupting their faith. (Colossians 1:2)

CORINTHIANS (ko-rin'th-anz) N.T. The Christians in the church at Corinth established by the missionary Paul, and to whom he wrote two letters. (1 Corinthians 1:2; 2 Corinthians 1:2)

CORNELIUS (kor-nel'yus) N.T. A Roman centurion of Caesarea. A kind man full of good works. Baptized by Peter, he became one of the first Gentile converts of the Christian faith. (M) (Acts 10:1-48)

CRISPUS (kris'pus) N.T. Chief ruler of the Jewish synagogue in Corinth, and baptized together with his family by Paul. (M) (Acts 18:8)

CYRUS (si'rus) O.T. The greatest of the Persian kings and founder of the empire. His courage and military genius enabled him to extend the boundaries of the Persian empire to its greatest extent. From the Biblical records he is remembered as the king who was host to the prophet Daniel, and as the one who sponsored an edict for the rebuilding of the temple at Jerusalem. (M) (Daniel 6:28; Ezra 1:1-4)

D

DAGON (da'gon) O.T. The national god of the Philistines. One of the famous temples of Dagon was at Gaza in the time of Samson. Some authorities say that Dagon is represented with the face and hands of a man and the tail of a fish. (Judges 16:21-30)

DAMARIS (dam'a-ris) A woman of Athens converted to Christianity by Paul. (F) (Acts 17:34)

DAN O.T. One of the twelve sons of Jacob, and whose mother was Bilhah, Rachel's maid. In the division of the land of Palestine, Dan and the descendants of Dan received the lowlands along the seacoast near Joppa, and a very small section of the hill country. They were never able to drive out the Philistines, so they migrated northward and became the northern-most point of the Jewish kingdom. (M) (Genesis 30:6)

CORNELIUS

CRISPUS

CYRUS

DAGON

DANIEL

DARIUS

DAVID

DELILAH

DANIEL (dan'yel) O.T. Famed Jewish prophet at the court of Babylon. He had been captured with others and carried off from Palestine by Nebuchadnezzar. At Babylon, Daniel with three of his friends, obtained permission to substitute simple food for the rich fares of the palace court. He thus retained his Jewish faith even though he became an expert in Babylonian knowledge. Daniel gained prominence through a succession of dream interpretations: the great image of Nebuchadnezzar, the vision of the approaching madness of Nebuchadnezzar, the vision of the 4 successive empires represented by animals including a ram trampled by a goat, and the vision of the final conflict of the kingdoms of the world against the Kingdom of God. Daniel was appointed to influential governmental positions. Jealousy of Daniel because of his success resulted in plots to destroy him. He was cast into a den of lions, but protected miraculously from their powerful jaws. (M) (Daniel 1:3-7; 2:1-45; 4:1-37; 6:3-23; Ezekiel 14:14)

DANITES (dan'ites) O.T. Descendants of Dan and members of one of the twelve tribes of Israel. (Judges 13:2)

DARIUS (da-ri'us) O.T. King of Persia when Daniel was thrown into the lions' den. (Daniel 6:1) (M)

DAVID (da'vid) O.T. Shepherd boy of Bethlehem who became the King of the Israelites, succeeding Saul. His early life was filled with adventure including the defeat of the giant Goliath with only a sling, five pebbles, and faith. His courage against the Philistines earned him a place in the palace of Saul, the King, where his skill with the sword and the harp made him a favorite. Jealousy because of his power drove David into exile for many years, but he returned to take over the throne of Israel. His reign was marked with periods of great victory, but also bitter defeat. He united Israel into a great kingdom, but he experienced deep despair in the death of his friend Jonathan, and his son Absalom, and remorse over his murder of Uriah, husband of Bathsheba. He was considered to be Israel's greatest King. (M) (1 Samuel 16:1-13; 14-23; 17:41-54; 2 Samuel 2:4; 11:2-27; 1 Kings 2:1-9)

DEBIR (de'ber) O.T. King of Eglon, one of the five hanged by Joshua. (M) (Joshua 10:3)

DEBORAH (deb'o-ra) O.T. A prophetess of Israel who inspired Barak to deliver Israel from bondage in the era of the Judges. (F) (Judges 4:4-6)

DELILAH (de-li'la) O.T. A Philistine woman who persuaded Samson to reveal the secret of his great strength and was influential in his capture. (F) (Judges 16:4-18)

DEMETRIUS (de-me'tri-us) N.T. A silversmith at Ephesus who made silver shrines of Diana. (M) (Acts 19:24)

DEMETRIUS

DEMON (de'mon) N.T. Generally referring to spiritual beings at enmity with God. They were thought of as evil spirits. (Luke 10:17-20; 8:29)

DIANA (di-an'a) N.T. The mother goddess of Asia Minor. Her image is supposed to have fallen from heaven. Ephesus was one of the centers of this heathen worship, where Demetrius and other silversmiths made images of her and her temple. (F) (Acts 19:24)

DINAH (di'na) O.T. Daughter of Jacob and Leah. She married Shechem, the son of Hamor the Hivite. Her brothers, Simeon and Levi, were so disturbed by the union of their sister with Shechem, that they attacked the Hivite city, killed all the men, including Shechem and his father, and laid waste the entire city. (F) (Genesis 34:1-31)

DIANA

DISCIPLES (dis-ci'p'ls) N.T. A name given to the followers of Jesus. (See Apostle) (Luke 14:26; John 13:23)

DORCAS (dor'kas) N.T. A Christian disciple of Joppa, known as Tabitha. Because of her kindness and almsdeeds, she was greatly missed at her death. Peter was informed, and upon arriving at Joppa, and kneeling in prayer, brought about the miracle of her coming to life again. (F) (Acts 9:36-43)

DRUSILLA (droo-sil'a) N.T. Daughter of Herod Agrippa I. A beautiful girl and sister to Bernice. She married Felix, procurator of Judea, and had a son named Agrippa. Both Drusilla and her son died in the eruption of Mt. Vesuvius. (F) (Acts 24:24)

DORCAS

E

EDOM (e'dum) O.T. The name given to Esau after he sold his birthright to Jacob. (See Esau) (M) (Genesis 25:30)

EDOMITES (e'dum-its) O.T. The descendants of Esau or Edom. Because of the hatred between Esau and his brother Jacob, the Edomites were always bitter enemies of the Israelites. (Genesis 36:9)

EGLON (eg'lon) O.T. A king of Moab who crossed the Jordan and captured Jericho from the Israelites and took tribute for 18 years. He was finally killed by Ehud, judge of Israel. (M) (Judges 3:12-30)

EGLON

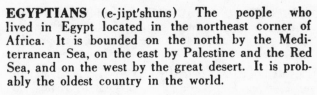

EGYPTIANS (e-jipt'shuns) The people who lived in Egypt located in the northeast corner of Africa. It is bounded on the north by the Mediterranean Sea, on the east by Palestine and the Red Sea, and on the west by the great desert. It is probably the oldest country in the world.

EHUD (e'hud) O.T. The second judge of Israel. He was left handed and a man of great strength. (M) (Judges 3:15)

ELAH (e'la) O.T. The son of Baasha king of Israel, and his successor. He ruled for only two years. He was killed while drunk, by Zimri a captain of his chariots. (M) (1 Kings 16:8-10)

ELAMITES (e'lam-its) O.T. The inhabitants of the country called Elam, located near the Persian gulf. Some authorities say they were not a Semitic race, but one of the pre-Sumerian populations of Babylonia. (Ezra 4:9)

ELDAD (el'dad) O.T. One of the elders of the Israelites who received the power of the Spirit of God from Moses. (M) (Numbers 11:26-29)

ELEAZAR (e-le-a'zer) O.T. 1. Aaron's third son and his successor as High Priest. (M) (Numbers 20:28) 2. One of the three mighty men of David's army. (M) (2 Samuel 23:9)

ELI (e'li) O.T. A high priest and a judge of Israel. His long and faithful service was marred by the weakness of his two sons, Hophni and Phinehas, who were responsible for the loss of the Ark of God to the Philistines. Eli died when he was 98 years old. (M) (1 Samuel 1:9)

ELIAKIM (e-li'a-kim) O.T. Overseer of King Hezekiah's household. He was a good man of high character and chosen as one of the three representatives to confer with leaders of Sennacherib at a time when the gates of Jerusalem were surrounded by the Assyrian armies. The prophet Isaiah spoke of him so highly that he must be regarded as a type of the Messiah. (M) (2 Kings 18:18; Isaiah 22:20-25)

ELIAM (e-li'am) O.T. Bathsheba's father. (M) (2 Samuel 11:3)

ELIEZER (e-li-e'zer) O.T. 1. The servant of Abraham. (M) (Genesis 15:2) 2. The second son of Moses and Zipporah. (M) (Exodus 18:4)

ELIHU (e-li'hu) O.T. One of the advisors of Job who reproved Job and his three friends and defended the justice of God. (M) (Job 32-37)

EGYPTIANS

ELEAZAR

ELI

ELIAKIM

ELIJAH (e-li'ja) O.T. An Old Testament prophet, one of the most colorful of all the people in the
Bible. He warned, exhorted, encouraged, challenged,
and prophesied without fear of man or the power of
men. He was a man of strong words and positive
action. His miracles are some of the greatest of the
Old Testament. Standing on the summit of a hill,
hands heavenward, long, thick hair hanging down his
back, clothed in natural skin loin cloth and sheep-
skin mantle, Elijah made one of the outstanding
pictures of the Hebrew race. He prophesied during
the reigns of Ahab and Jezebel, Ahaziah, and Jehoram in the vicinity of 850 B.C. According to the
Bible account he ascended into heaven, escorted by
fiery horses and chariot and carried by a whirlwind.
(M) (1 Kings 18:46; 19:9-18; 2 Kings 1:1-18; 2
Kings 2:1-12)

ELIJAH

ELIMELECH (e-lim'e-lek) O.T. Husband of
Naomi. (M) (Ruth 1:2)

ELIPHAZ (el'i-faz) O.T. The wisest of the three
friends of Job. He had the best explanation of Job's
difficulty. His answer was the answer of common
sense. (M) (Job 15)

ELISHA (e-li'sha) O.T. The attendant and disciple of Elijah; and his successor as prophet of
Israel. His ministry was a long and colorful demonstration of faith and practice. Among his unusual
miracles were: the purification of Jericho springs
(2 Kings 2:19-22), the multiplication of the widow's
oil (2 Kings 4:1-7), the restoration of life to the
Shunem woman's son (2 Kings 4:8-37), increasing
loaves (2 Kings 4:42-44), and the cleansing of
Naaman, Chief Captain of the King of Syria. (2
Kings 5:1-14) His prophetic ministry was sixty years
in length. (M)

ELIZABETH

ELISHEBA (e-lish'e-ba) O.T. Aaron's wife. (F)
(Exodus 6:23)

ELIZABETH (e-liz'a-beth) N.T. Zacharias' wife
and mother of John the Baptist. She was also a
relative of Mary, the mother of Jesus. (F) (Luke
1:11-13, 36)

ELISHA

ELKANAH (el-ka'na) O.T. The father of Samuel. (M) (1 Samuel 1:1)

EMMANUEL (em-man'u-el) N.T. A term referring to the Messiah, and meaning God with us.
(Matthew 1:23) (See Immanuel)

ENOCH (e'nuk) O.T. The father of Methuselah.
It is said of Enoch, he "walked with God three
hundred years . . . and he was not, for God took
him." (Genesis 5:22-24) Like Elijah, he was translated without seeing death. (M)

ENOCH

EPICUREANS

ERASTUS

ESAU

ESTHER

ENOSH (e'nosh) O.T. The son of Seth. (M) (Genesis 4:26)

EPAPHRAS (ep'a-fras) N.T. A fellow worker with the Apostle Paul, and teacher at the Christian Church in Colossae. (M) (Colossians 1:7)

EPHESIANS (e-fe'zhanz) The people who lived in the city of Ephesus, capital of the Roman province of Asia. Realizing its strategic position and political importance, Paul established a Christian church there. His later letter to the Ephesians is one of the important books of the New Testament.

EPHRAIM (e'fra-im) O.T. Son of Joseph and Asenath, daughter of an Egyptian priest. He was born during Joseph's reign as Prime Minister in Egypt. At the time of his grandfather Jacob's death, Ephraim received the right hand of blessing with the prophecy that he would become the ancestor of a great multitude of peoples and tribes. (M) (Genesis 41:45-52)

EPICUREANS (ep-i-ku-re'anz) N.T. A leading philosophic group who got their name from Epicurus, an Athenian philosopher born in 341 B.C. The doctrines of Epicurus, widely accepted in Asia Minor and surrounding areas, stressed true pleasure and experience rather than absolute truth and reason. It was one of the influential philosophies during the time of Paul the Apostle.

ERASTUS (e-ras'tus) N.T. One of the helpers of Paul at Ephesus. He was sent with Timothy into Macedonia just prior to the Ephesian riot. (M) (Acts 19:22)

ESAU (e'saw) O.T. Isaac's oldest son, and twin-brother of Jacob. He was the heir to his father but sold his birthright to his brother for some pottage. The loss of his covenant blessing through the craft of his mother Rebekah (Genesis 27) stirred Esau to vengeful anger against his brother Jacob. However, they were later reconciled and lived in peace. The descendants of Esau were called the Edomites. (M) (Genesis 33)

ESSENES (e-senz') N.T. A Jewish sect in the time of Christ. They were about 4000 in number and lived a more-or-less separated life in the wilderness of Judea. Each colony had common provisions, simple habits, plain food and clothing, and lived their lives according to the laws of Moses.

ESTHER (es'ter) O.T. A beautiful Hebrew maiden brought up in the Persian city of Susa by her cousin Mordecai. She became the wife of Xerxes, (Ahasuerus) King of Persia. The story of her courage, love, and devotion to her people, and her struggle to protect her race, is one of the most beautiful of the Old Testament. (F) (Esther 2:7)

ETHIOPIAN EUNUCH N.T. A minister of Queen Candace of Ethiopia. He had complete charge of her treasure. While returning from a journey to Jerusalem, the Ethiopian Eunuch was met and converted by Philip, the evangelist. (M) (Acts 8:26-40)

ETHIOPIANS (e'thi-o'pi-anz) The people who lived in the land located in the upper regions of the Nile River, south of Egypt in Africa. This country is called in Hebrew Kush (Cush). (Isaiah 20:4)

EUNICE (u-ni'se) N.T. A Christian Jewess, mother of Timothy. (F) (Acts 16:1; 2 Timothy 1:5)

ETHIOPIAN
EUNUCH

EUODIA (u-o'di-a) N.T. A Christian woman of Philippi rebuked by the Apostle Paul for her bickering. (F) (Philippians 4:2)

EUTYCHUS (u'ti-kus) N.T. A young man of Troas who fell asleep during one of Paul's sermons. He fell from the third loft to the floor and was considered dead; but he was miraculously restored by the great missionary. (M) (Acts 20:9,10)

EUTYCHUS

EVE (ev) O.T. The name given to the first woman by Adam. Eve meant ("the mother of all living." Eve, with Adam, was a part of the garden of Eden. The Bible narrative says that Eve, under Satanic influence, tasted of the forbidden fruit, and persuaded Adam to do the same. Because of this disobedience to the command of God, they were both expelled from the garden. Eve was the mother of many sons and daughters, foremost of whom were Cain, Abel, and Seth. (F) (Genesis 3:1-24; 4:1; 5:3)

EZEKIEL (e-zek'yel) O.T. One of the major Jewish prophets. He was taken captive by the Babylonians and moved from Judah to the banks of the Chebar, a river in Babylonia. (Ezekiel 1:1) He lived in high esteem and honor with his companions in captivity; and his prophecy, if not always understood, received the highest consideration. (M) (Ezekiel 37:1-14)

EZRA

EZRA (ez'ra) O.T. A famous scribe and priest who lived in Persia. He obtained permission from the Persian King to lead a company of men back to Jerusalem. Ezra was one of the primary leaders of the movement to rebuild the Jerusalem walls and restore the Law of Moses. (M) (Ezra 7:1-10)

F

FELIX (fe'liks) N.T. A mean, cruel ruler appointed Roman procurator of Judea in A.D. 53 by Claudius the Emperor. The Apostle Paul was brought to trial before Felix in Caesarea; and was kept in prison two years, in the hope of extorting money from him. (M) (Acts 24:26,27) (Acts 24:24)

FELIX

FESTUS (fes'tus) N.T. The successor to Felix as procurator of Judea. (M) (Acts 24:27)

GABRIEL (ga'bri-el) A high ranking angel who visited the prophet Daniel, announced the birth of John the Baptist, and hailed Mary the Mother of Jesus. (Daniel 8:15-17; Luke 1:11-22, 26-38)

GABRIEL

GAD (gad) O.T. A son of Jacob and Zilpah. He was one of the leaders of the twelve tribes of Israel. (M) (Genesis 30:10,11)

GADDI (gad'i) O.T. One of the spies sent into Canaan by Moses. (M) (Numbers 13:11)

GAIUS (ga'yus) N.T. A companion of Paul. He was dragged into the amphitheater at Ephesus during a riot. (M) (Acts 19:29)

GALATIANS (ga-la'shanz) N.T. The people who lived in the district of Asia Minor called Galatia, and to whom Paul wrote one of his letters.

GADDI

GALILEANS (gal'i-le'anz) N.T. Inhabitants of the province of Galilee in Palestine.

GALLIO (gal'i-o) N.T. Proconsul of Achaia in the time of Paul. (M) (Acts 18:12)

GAMALIEL (ga-ma'li-el) A famous Jewish doctor of law who was a teacher of Paul. (M) (Acts 22:3)

GEHAZI (ge-ha'zi) O.T. Elisha's servant who was smitten with leprosy because he received money and garments as a reward for Naaman's healing. (M) (2 Kings 5)

GAMALIEL

GENTILES (jen'tilz) All people in the world other than the Jews. (Romans 2:14)

GIBEONITES (gib'e-un-its) O.T. The inhabitants of Gibeon, chief city of the Hivites. (2 Samuel 21:1)

GIDEON (gid'e-un) O.T. Great deliverer and judge of Israel. He is remembered for his unusual calling, the miracle of the fleece, (Judges 6:36-40) and his famous night attack on the Midianite camp, accompanied with but 300 men. (Judges 7:2-23) He is mentioned by the author of Hebrews as one of the great men of faith. (M) (Hebrews 11:32)

GIDEON

GITTITES (git'its) O.T. The 600 men of Gath who followed David, led by Ittai the Gittite. (2 Samuel 15:18-21)

GOD (god) The supreme Creator and Ruler of all the Universe, who was from the very beginning and is everlasting. He is the Maker and the Maintainer of all that is life. (John 1:1-18)

GOLIATH (go-li'ath) O.T. The Philistine giant who was slain by David. He was said to have been nine feet nine inches in height. When he defied the armies of Israel, David accepted his challenge to battle and defeated him, armed with faith and a sling shot. (M) (1 Samuel 17) A second Goliath, called the Gittite, whose spear's shaft was like a "weaver's beam," was slain by Elhanan of Bethlehem. (2 Samuel 21:19)

GOLIATH

GOOD SAMARITAN N.T. The hero of a story told by Jesus. A traveller on the road to Jericho was attacked by robbers and left as dead. Both a Priest and a Levite passed by without helping, but a "certain Samaritan" took pity on the wounded traveller and gave him aid. With this story Jesus was teaching the meaning of love and neighborliness. (Luke 10:33-36)

GOOD
SAMARITAN

GREEK (grek) A native of Greece, or one of the Greek race. Frequently when the word Greek is used in contrast to Jew, it refers to all foreigners in general. (Acts 16:1; 17:4)

H

HABAKKUK (ha-bak'uk) O.T. One of the minor prophets of Judah. He probably lived during the reigns of Josiah, Jehoahaz, and Jehoiakim, however it is not certain. (M) (Habakkuk 1:1)

HADAD (ha'dad) O.T. The supreme deity of Syria.

HADADEZER (had'ad-e'zer) O.T. A Syrian king defeated by David. (M) (2 Samuel 8:3)

HADASSAH (ha-dash'a) O.T. The original Jewish name of Queen Esther. (See Esther) (F) (Esther 2:7)

HADAD

HAGAR (ha'gar) O.T. An Egyptian woman, handmaid of Sarah. Hagar was the mother of Abraham's son Ishmael. She was expelled, with her son, from the family of Abraham by Sarah; and saved from death by the appearance of an angel of God in the wilderness of Beersheba. (F) (Genesis 16:1-16; 21:15-21)

HAGGAI (hag'a-i) O.T. A prophet of Jerusalem in 520 B.C. His prophecies concerned the reconstruction of the Temple of Jerusalem after the period of the Israelite captivity in Babylonia. He was a contemporary with Zechariah. (M) (Haggai 1:1)

HAGAR

HAM

HAMAN

HANNAH

HEROD

HAM (ham) O.T. The youngest son of Noah. (Genesis 9:18-24) His descendants were the people of Arabia, Ethiopia, Egypt, and Canaan. (M) (Genesis 10:6-14)

HAMAN (ha'man) O.T. A favorite of the court of Xerxes, King of Persia. Because of Mordecai's refusal to pay respect, Haman plotted the destruction of all the Jews; but his plans were thwarted by Esther. (M) (Esther 8:3; 7:10; 9:7-10)

HAMMEDATHA (ham'e-da'tha) O.T. Father of Haman. (M) (Esther 3:1)

HAMUTAL (ha-mu'tal) O.T. Wife of King Josiah, and mother of Jehoahaz and Zedekiah. (F) (2 Kings 23:31; 24:18; Jeremiah 52:1)

HANANI (ha-na'ni) O.T. Father of Jehu and himself a seer. He was placed in stocks in prison for rebuking Asa, King of Judah. (M) (1 Kings 16:1; 2 Chronicles 16:7-10)

HANNAH (han'a) O.T. Wife of Elkanah and mother of Samuel. She vowed that if she had a son she would devote him to the service of God. Samuel was born, and the vow was kept. Hannah gave her son into the hands of Eli, where he was trained in the ways of the prophet. (F) (1 Samuel 1; 2:1-10)

HANNANIAH (han'a-ni'a) O.T. The name of fourteen different men of the Old Testament, most important of whom was Hannaniah, the false prophet who opposed Jeremiah, and who received the penalty of death because of his false prophecy. (M) (Jeremiah 28:5-17)

HARAN (ha'ran) O.T. Brother to Abraham, and father of Lot. (M) (Genesis 11:27)

HAZAEL (haz-a'el) O.T. A Syrian King anointed by Elijah the Prophet at Damascus. His reign extended from about 842 to 796 B.C. (M) (1 Kings 19:15)

HEBER (he'ber) O.T. The husband of Jael, the woman who slew Sisera. (M) (Judges 4:11-22)

HEMAN (he'man) O.T. The son of Joel and grandson of Samuel. He was a famed musician in the temple orchestra of David. (M) (1 Chronicles 6:33; 15:16-22)

HENADAD (hen'a-dad) O.T. The head of a family of Levites who had an important part in the rebuilding of the temple at Jerusalem. (M) (Ezra 3:9)

HERMAS (hur'mas) A Christian resident at Rome to whom Paul sends salutations in his letter to the Romans. Many of the early church fathers attribute the work called "The Shepherd" to him. It was never received as an authoritative book of the New Testament Canon. (M) (Romans 16:14)

HERMES (hur'mez) N.T. The Greek god corresponding to the Roman god Mercury, and to whom Paul was likened in the city of Lystra. (M) (Acts 14:12)

HERODIAS

HEROD (her'ud) N.T. The name of several rulers over Palestine. Herod the Great, ruler at the time of Jesus's birth in Bethlehem; Herod the Tetrarch, son of Herod the Great, ruler at the time of the death of John the Baptist; Herod the King, or Agrippa, who slew James, the brother of John; Herod Agrippa II, before whom the Apostle Paul was tried. (M) (Matthew 2:1; 14:1-12; Acts 12:1,2; 25:13)

HERODIANS (he-ro'di-anz) N.T. A group of influential Jews who supported the Herods. (Mark 3:6)

HERODIAS (he-ro'di-as) N.T. Wife of Herod, son of Herod the Great. She was influential in attaining the death of John the Baptist. (F) (Matthew 14:3-12)

HEZEKIAH

HEZEKIAH (hez'e-ki-'a) O.T. The thirteenth king of Judah, son of Ahaz. Hezekiah is considered one of the most perfect kings of Judah. He reigned for twenty-nine years, and was influential in inspiring his followers to destroy the false idols and restore the temple worship. (M) (2 Kings 18:5)

HILKIAH (hil-ki'a) O.T. A priest, the father of Jeremiah. (M) (Jeremiah 1:1)

HIRAM (hi'ram) O.T. King of Tyre who sent workmen and materials to Jerusalem to build a palace for David and a temple for Solomon. (M) (2 Samuel 5:11; 2 Chronicles 2:11-16)

HIRAM

HITTITES (hit'its) O.T. Founders of a great nation that flourished in Asia Minor between 1900 and 1200 B.C. The Hittites are often mentioned in the lists of people inhabiting Canaan before the conquest by Israel. (Genesis 15:20; Exodus 3:8)

HIVITES (hi'vits) O.T. One of the races of Canaan before the conquest by the Hebrews. (Genesis 10:17; Exodus 3:17)

HOLY GHOST or HOLY SPIRIT The Spirit of God, the third person of the Trinity. The Spirit is sent forth by God, given by God, and has fellowship with the spirit of men, teaching, rebuking, inspiring, and illumining. (John 16:7-15; Matthew 28:19)

HOSEA

HUR

HOSEA (ho-ze'a) O.T. A prophet, son of Beeri, who prophesied during the reigns of Uzziah, Jotham, Ahaz, and Hezekiah, kings of Judah, and Jeroboam II, king of Israel. His message emphasized God's love for men. (M) (Hosea 1:1; 14:4-7)

HOSHEA (ho-she'a) O.T. The nineteenth and last King of Israel. During his reign Israel was invaded by the armies of Shalmaneser and made a tributary of Assyria. (M) (2 Kings 15:30; 17:3)

HULDAH (hul'da) O.T. A prophetess who lived in Jerusalem during the reign of Josiah. (F) (2 Kings 22:14-20)

HUR (hur) O.T. A man of Judah who with Aaron held up the arms of Moses during a victorious fight with the Amalekites. (M) (Exodus 17:10-12)

ISAAC

I

ICHABOD (ik'a-bod) O.T. Grandson of Eli, so named because "the glory has departed from Israel." (M) (1 Samuel 4:19-22)

IMMANUEL (i-man'u-el) O.T. A name ascribed to Jesus meaning "God with us." The birth of Immanuel was foreseen by the Prophet Isaiah. (Isaiah 7:14)

ISAIAH

IRA (i'ra) O.T. A native of Tekoa, one of the mighty men of David's army. (M) (1 Chronicles 11:28)

ISAAC (i'zak) O.T. The son of Abraham and Sarah. He was the promised heir of Abraham, and the object of his father's great sacrificial act of faith. (Genesis 22:1,2) Ishmael was his half-brother, Rebekah was his wife, and Jacob and Esau his most famous children. (M) (Genesis 24,26,27)

ISAIAH (i-za'ya) O.T. The greatest of the prophets of the Old Testament. He was a man of wisdom, eloquence and literary genius, with divinely inspired prophetic vision. (M) (Isaiah 1:1; 9:2-7)

ISCAH (is'ka) O.T. Abraham's niece and sister of Lot. (F) (Genesis 11:27-29)

ISCARIOT (is-kar'i-ot) N.T. The name included with Judas the traitor which distinguished him from Judas the other Apostle. (M) (Matthew 10:4)

ISHBOSHETH

ISHBAK (ish'bak) O.T. Son of Abraham and Keturah. (M) (Genesis 25:2)

ISHBOSHETH (ish'bo'sheth) O.T. One of Saul's younger sons. At the death of his father, Ishbosheth was proclaimed king in opposition to David, sovereign over Judah. He reigned for two troubled years at his capital city Mahanaim east of the Jordan. His attempt to destroy the forces of David were unsuccessful. Ishbosheth was assassinated in approximately 1050 B.C. and the dynasty of Saul came to an end. (M) (2 Samuel 2:10; 2:12-3:1)

ISHMAEL

ISHMAEL (ish'ma-el) O.T. Son of Abraham and Hagar, and half-brother to Isaac. A misdemeanor of mocking Isaac led to the expulsion of Ishmael and his mother from the family of Abraham. They wandered in the wilderness of Beersheba until they nearly died, but the angel of the Lord saved them. Ishmael lived to become the ancestor of a great tribe of people. (M) (Genesis 16:15; 21:14-21)

ISHMAELITES (ish'ma-el-its) O.T. The descendants of Ishmael who were nomadic tribes dwelling in the deserts of Africa and Asia, and who were famed for their skill with the bow. (Genesis 17:20; 25:12-16; 37:25)

ITTAI

ISRAEL (iz'ra-el) O.T. The name given to Jacob at the time of his reunion with his brother Esau. (M) (Genesis 32:22-32)

ISRAELITE (iz'ri-el-it) O.T. A descendant of Jacob (Israel), and thus an heir to the promise of God. (Exodus 9:7) (Romans 9:4-13)

ISSACHAR (is'a-kar) O.T. The ninth son of Jacob, and father of one of the twelve tribes of Israel. (M) (Genesis 30:17,18; Numbers 26:23)

ITHAMAR (ith'a-mar) O.T. The youngest son of Aaron, and successor with Eleazar, to the high priestly office. He was an ancestor of Eli. (M) (Exodus 6:23; 28:1; Numbers 4:28)

JABAL

ITTAI (it'ta-i) O.T. A native of Gath, the commander of 600 men, who was a faithful follower of David. (M) (2 Samuel 15:18,19)

J

JABAL (ja'bal) O.T. Son of Lamech. He was the father of such as dwell in tents and have cattle. (M) (Genesis 4:20)

JABIN (ja'bin) O.T. The name of two Canaanite kings of Hazor in Galilee. The first was defeated by Joshua at the waters of Merom. (Joshua 11:1-14) The second was an oppressor of Israel in the time of the Judges. (M) (Judges 4:2-24)

JACOB

41

JAEL

JAMES, SON
OF ZEBEDEE

JASON

JEHOIACHIN

JACOB (ja'kub) O.T. The second son of Isaac and Rebekah, and twin brother to Esau. He bought the birthright from his brother for porridge, and acquired, deceitfully, the patriarchal blessing from Isaac. He married Rachel and Leah, and became the father of twelve famous sons for whom the twelve tribes of Israel were named. Joseph, his favorite son, was sold into slavery in Egypt. Later Jacob lived in that country for seventeen years and died there, 147 years old. His body was carried from Egypt to Canaan during the Exodus, and buried in the cave of Machpelah with his fathers. (M) (Genesis 25:21-26; 29-34; 27:1-41; 29, 30, 47:9; 50:1-14)

JAEL (ja'el) O.T. A woman who killed Sisera, Commander-in-chief of Jaban's army, by hammering a tent pin through his head. (F) (Judges 4:17-22)

JAIR (ja'er) O.T. Jair the Gileadite, judge of Israel for twenty-two years. He had thirty sons and thirty cities. (M) (Judges 10:3-5)

JAIRUS (ja'i-rus) N.T. A ruler of the synagogue, probably in Capernaum, whose daughter was restored to life by Jesus. (M) (Mark 5:22)

JAMES (jamz) N.T. The name occurs a number of times in the New Testament. 1. James the son of Zebedee — One of the twelve Apostles, brother of John. 2. James the son of Alphaeus — Another one of the twelve Apostles. 3. James, the Lord's brother— Head of the church at Jerusalem in the Apostolic age. 4. James, known as the father of the Apostle Judas. (M) (Matthew 10:3; Luke 6:15; Matthew 13:55; Luke 6:16)

JAPHETH (ja-feth) O.T. One of the three sons of Noah. The descendants of Japheth occupied the "isles of the Gentiles" around the Mediterranean sea. (M) (Genesis 10:5)

JARED (ja'red) O.T. The father of Enoch. (M) (Genesis 5:18)

JASON (ja'sun) N.T. A Christian of Thessalonica who gave lodging to Paul and Silas in his home while they were visiting that city. He was dragged out of his home by the Jews and brought before the rulers for his hospitality toward these objectionable men. (Acts 17:5-9) Jason may have been a relative of Paul. (M) (Romans 16:21)

JEBUSITES (jeb'u-zits) O.T. A mountainous tribe of Canaan before the conquest by the Hebrews. (Joshua 18:16)

JEDIDAH (je-di'da) O.T. Mother of King Josiah. (F) (2 Kings 22:1)

42

JEDIDIAH (jed'i-di'a) O.T. The name given to Solomon by Nathan the prophet. (M) (2 Samuel 12:25)

JEHOAHAZ (je-ho'a-haz) O.T. Son and successor of Jehu. He reigned seventeen wicked years in Samaria, as King of Israel. (M) (2 Kings 13:1-9)

JEHOIACHIN (je-hoi'a-kin) O.T. Son and successor of Jehoiakim as King of Judah. His reign was for three months and ten days, after which Jehoiachin, the queen-mother, all the servants, captains, and officers gave themselves up to the armies of Nebuchadnezzar and were carried away captive to the land of Babylon. (M) (2 Kings 24:10-12; 2 Chronicles 36:9,10; Jeremiah 52:28)

JEHOIAKIM

JEHOIADA (je-hoi'a-da) O.T. A high priest during the usurpation of Athaliah. When Athaliah destroyed all of the royal seed, Jehoiada and his wife stole the young boy Joash and hid him for six years in the temple, and eventually restored him to the throne. (M) (2 Chronicles 22:10-24)

JEHOIAKIM (je-hoi'a-kim) O.T. Son of Josiah, king of Judah. At the beginning of his reign 608 B.C., he was subject to Egypt. When Nebuchadnezzar defeated the Egyptians, Jehoiakim became subject to him. After three years Jehoiakim broke his allegiance and rebelled against him. The Babylonian king sent forces to Jerusalem, captured Jehoiakim, bound him and put him in a cage to be carried to Babylon. (M) (2 Kings 23:34; 24:1)

JEHOSHAPHAT

JEHORAM (je-ho'ram) O.T. Son of Ahab and king of Israel in 853 B.C. His reign was one of wickedness like his father. (M) (2 Kings 3:1)

JEHOSHAPHAT (je-hosh'a-fat) O.T. Son of Asa, and one of the best, most pious and prosperous kings of Judah. The history of his 25 years reign is found in 1 Kings 15:24-2 Kings 8:16. (M) (2 Chronicles 17:1-21:3)

JEHU

JEHOVAH (je-ho'va) One of the names of God. It means "I am; the Eternal Living One." The Jews, out of reverence, avoided mention of this name, and substituted "Lord" or "God."

JEHU (je'hu) O.T. Son of Jehoshaphat, and a king of Israel in 842 B.C. (M) (2 Kings 9, 10)

JEPHTHAH (jef'tha) O.T. A judge of Israel for six years. (M) (Judges 11:1-12:7)

JEREMIAH (jer'e-mi'a) O.T. A great prophet, son of Hilkiah . . . He is sometimes called the "weeping prophet" because he foretold the destruction of Jerusalem, and lamented the absence of moral strength in his people. (M) (Jeremiah 1:1; 1:4-19)

JEREMIAH

JEROBOAM

JEROBOAM (jer'o-bo'am) O.T. The first king of the divided kingdom of Israel in 987 B.C. He instigated the false worship of God by erecting golden calves at each end of his kingdom. He died in the 22nd year of his reign. (M) (1 Kings 11:26; 12:25-33)

JESSE (jes'e) O.T. A sheep-herder of Bethlehem, David's father. (M) (1 Samuel 16:1, 18, 19)

JESUS

JESUS (je'zus) N.T. The name of our Lord, given to Him by the angel to Joseph (Matthew 1:21) and to Mary. (Luke 1:31) He was born in Bethlehem, according to leading authorities, about the year 4 B.C. His early life was lived in Nazareth, a town in the hills of Galilee. He began his public ministry at the age of 30; and he travelled the length and breadth of Palestine with his 12 disciples, healing, teaching, performing miracles, and showing the people how to know God. His popularity, his simple interpretation of religion, and his open claims to divinity, created bitter enemies among the Jewish religious leaders. They plotted his death, and with the help of Judas Iscariot, one of the twelve, they accomplished it at Jerusalem, three years after his ministry had begun. The third day after his crucifixion on a Roman cross, and burial in a sealed tomb of stone, Jesus arose from the dead and was seen by many of his followers. Scores watched him ascend into heaven and heard his last commandment, "Go ye into all the world!" His teachings of love and truth have been life and hope to every generation. (M) (Matthew, Mark, Luke and John)

JETHRO

JETHRO (jeth'ro) O.T. A priest of Median and Moses' father-in-law. He was deeply sympathetic with the burden of Moses, rejoiced over his victories, and had intelligent suggestions for the administration of tribal government. (M) (Exodus 3:1; 18:1-27)

JEW (joo) Originally one belonging to the tribe of Judah; however, later use included anyone of the Hebrew race. (2 Kings 25:25)

JEWESS (joo'es) A woman of the tribe of Judah, or of the Hebrew race. (F) (Acts 24:24)

JEZEBEL

JEZEBEL (jez'e-bel) O.T. Wife of Ahab, king of Israel. She was a worshiper of Baal and influenced her husband in building a temple and an altar to Baal in Samaria. Her life was selfish and cruel, filled with intrigue and murder. She died a violent death under the wheels of the chariot of Jehu. (F) (1 Kings 16:31; 18:4-13; 21:23; 2 Kings 9:7; 9:30-37)

JOAB (jo'ab) O.T. Loyal friend and commander-in-chief of King David's army. Joab remained faithful to David until the close of his life when he followed Adonijah. Solomon, David's son, with his ascension to the throne, suspected Joab of treachery, and forced him to flee to the shelter of the altar at Gibeon, where he was slain by Benaiah. (M) (2 Samuel 2:12-32; 1 Kings 2:28)

JOB

JOASH (jo'ash) O.T. King of Judah for forty years. (836 to 796 B.C.) He was the son of Ahaziah, king of Judah, and the only one of his children to escape the murderous purge of Athaliah. 2. Son and successor of Jehoahaz as the King of Israel in the time of Elisha the prophet. (M) (2 Kings 11:1-3; 12:1-3; 2 Kings 13:14)

JOB (job) O.T. A pious man who dwelt in the land of Uz. He suffered a series of catastrophes that gave rise to the question: Why does God allow the righteous to suffer? (M) (Job 1:1)

JOCHEBED (jok'e-bed) O.T. Wife of Amram and mother to Aaron, Moses, and Miriam. (F) (Exodus 6:20)

JOHN

JOEL (jo'el) O.T. The second of the twelve minor prophets, who prophesied in Judah. His prophecy was an exhortation for the people to turn to God with penitence, fasting, and prayer, so that the plague of drought and locusts might be ended and the blessings of God experienced. (M) (Joel 1:1)

JOHN (jon) N.T. A son of Zebedee and brother of James. He was the youngest of the twelve Apostles, and known as "the beloved." He was always close to Jesus, in his ministry, at the transfiguration, in the garden of Gethsemane, at the last supper, at the foot of the cross. After Jesus' death, John worked actively with Peter in missionary endeavor. Five books of the New Testament are believed to have been written by him: the fourth gospel, three epistles, and the Revelation. (M) (Mark 1:19,20; John 13:23; Mark 14:33; Acts 3:1)

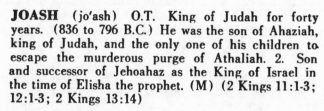

JOHN
THE BAPTIST

JOHN THE BAPTIST N.T. The forerunner of Jesus, whose way he was sent to prepare. Born in the year 5 B.C., he had Zacharias as father and Elizabeth as mother. He dwelt and preached in the wilderness area of the Jordan River. He was the man who baptized Jesus. John's colorful career ended with his death by beheading. (M) (Luke 1:13; 3:2-22; 7:18-28; Mark 6:16-29)

JONAH

JONAH (jo'na) O.T. A prophet of Israel, fifth of the minor prophets, son of Amittai, and a citizen of Gathhepher, a small town in Galilee. According to the book of Jonah, he was bidden by God to go to the city of Nineveh to warn the people about God, but he was unwilling to go. Instead, he took a boat at Joppa to flee away. A great storm arose and Jonah was thrown into the sea by the sailors, to escape the wrath of God. Jonah was delivered from death by the presence of a great fish that swallowed him. Later he was cast out on shore and continued his mission to Nineveh and the fulfillment of God's command. (M) (2 Kings 14:25; Jonah 1:1)

JONATHAN

JONATHAN (jon'a-than) O.T. The oldest son of King Saul, and a famous warrior of great courage and strength. He established one of the world's most famous friendships with David. (M) (2 Samuel 1:23; 1 Samuel 14:6-16; 23:16-18)

JOSEPH

JOSEPH (jo'zef) O.T. 1. The son and favorite child of Jacob and Rachel. His position in the family, and his capacity to receive visions created jealousy in the minds of his brothers. Joseph was sold by his ten brothers to an Ishmaelite caravan, and he was taken as a slave into Egypt. In Egypt, after a series of dramatic experiences, Joseph rose to the station of a great ruler, second only to the Pharaoh. His wisdom and foresight saved the Egyptians from the plight of a severe famine. Later, Joseph was reunited with his brothers, and together with Jacob, they and their descendants, lived in Egypt until the time of the Exodus. (M) (Genesis 30:22-24; 37-50) 2. Joseph the husband of Mary, mother of Jesus. (M) (Luke 3:23) N.T. 3. Joseph of Arimathaea, in whose tomb Jesus was buried. (M) (Matthew 27:57-60)

JOSHUA

JOSHUA (josh'u-a) O.T. The successor to Moses as leader of the Israelites during the Exodus. He is remembered for his good report as one of the twelve spies, (Numbers 14:6) defeat of Jericho where the walls fell down, (Joshua 6) and the division of the conquered Canaan. (Joshua 13) He died at the age of 110 years. (M) (Joshua 24:29)

JOSIAH (jo-si'ah) O.T. The son and successor of Amon as king of Judah. (638 B.C.) He began his reign at the age of 8 years, and was in power 31 years. (M) (2 Kings 22:1-23:30)

JOTHAM (jo'tham) O.T. 1. Youngest son of Gideon who escaped the massacre by Abimelech. (M) (Judges 9:1-21) 2. A King of Judah in the time of Isaiah. (M) (1 Chronicles 5:17)

JUBAL

JUBAL (joo'bal) O.T. The father of all such as handle the harp and pipe. (M) (Genesis 4:21)

JUDAH (joo'da) O.T. The fourth son of Jacob and Leah. He was the founder of one of the twelve tribes of Israel. (M) (Genesis 29:35; 37:26,27; 44:18-34)

JUDAS (joo'das) N.T. 1. Judas of Galilee who raised a revolt in the days of the enrollment. (M) (Acts 5:37) 2. Judas Iscariot, the one of the twelve apostles of Jesus who betrayed our Lord for thirty pieces of silver. (M) (Luke 6:16; Matthew 26:14) 3. Judas, also called Thaddaeus, one of the twelve apostles. (M) (John 14:22) 4. Judas, the brother of Jesus, (Matthew 13:55) and perhaps the author of the book of Jude. 5. Judas, surnamed Barsabbas, a leading man in the early church at Jerusalem. (M) (Acts 15:22,27,32)

JUDAS

JUDE (jood) N.T. An English form of the name Judas, and the name of the author of the Epistle of Jude. This was probably Judas, one of the four brothers of Jesus. (M) (Mark 6:3)

JUDEANS (joo-de'ans) The people of the land of Judah.

JUDGES (ju'giz) O.T. Leaders raised by God to relieve Israel of foreign oppressors. Some of the famous judges were: Samson, Gideon and Samuel.

JUPITER

JUDITH (joo-dith) O.T. A wife of Esau. (F) (Genesis 26:34)

JULIA (jool'ya) N.T. A Christian woman at Rome. (F) (Romans 16:15)

JULIUS (jool'yus) N.T. A Roman centurion responsible for the transport of Paul and other prisoners from Caesarea to Rome. (M) (Acts 27:1)

JUPITER (joo'pi-ter) N.T. The supreme god of the Romans, corresponding to Zeus in the Greek religion. Barnabas was mistaken for Zeus on his missionary journey with Paul to Lystra in Asia Minor. (Acts 14:12,13)

KINGS

JUSTUS (jus'tus) N.T. The surname of Joseph called Barsabbas, who was the unsuccessful candidate for the vacant spot among the twelve disciples after the death of Judas Iscariot. (M) (Acts 1:23) 2. A man of Corinth with whom Paul lodged. (M) (Acts 18:7) 3. The surname of a man called Jesus who was a fellow worker with Paul. (M) (Colossians 4:11)

K

KENITE (ken'ite) O.T. An early Canaanite tribe which dwelt in the rocky, rugged country southeast of Hebron. (Judges 1:16)

KETURAH (ke-tu'ra) O.T. Abraham's second wife. (F) Genesis 25:1; 1 Chronicles 1:32)

LABAN

LAZARUS OF
BETHANY

LAZARUS
THE BEGGAR

LEAH

LEPER

KINGS (kings) O.T. A male sovereign given supreme authority over a nation, usually received through heredity. The three great kings of Israel were David, Saul, and Solomon.

KISH (kish) O.T. A Benjaminite, father of King Saul. (M) (1 Chronicles 8:33)

KORAH (ko'ra) O.T. A Levite who was the leader of a dramatic rebellion against Moses and Aaron at the time of the Exodus. He was jealous because of Aaron's position as High Priest. Korah paid the penalty of perishing in fire and earthquake with all his followers. (M) (Numbers 16; 26:9-11)

L

LABAN (la'ban) O.T. Abraham's brother, and a native of Haran. He was the father of Leah and Rachel. Jacob worked for Laban at least twenty years to win the hands of his daughters in marriage. (M) (Genesis 29:13,14)

LAMECH (la'mek) O.T. 1. A descendant from Cain whose three sons, Jabal, Jubal, and Tubal-cain, were the inventors of useful instruments; introduced and practiced animal-husbandry; made musical instruments, and bronze and iron weapons. (M) (Genesis 4:19-22) 2. The son of Methuselah and father of Noah. (M) (Genesis 5:25,28)

LAODICEANS (la-od'i-se'ans) N.T. The inhabitants of the city of Laodicea in the Roman province of Asia. (Colossians 4:16; Revelation 3:14)

LAZARUS (laz'a-rus) N.T. 1. The beggar in the parable of the Rich Man and Lazarus. (M) (Luke 16:19-31) 2. The brother of Mary and Martha of Bethany, and the good friend of Jesus. Stricken with a grievous disease, Lazarus had fallen sick and died. Mary and Martha sent word to Jesus. Upon receiving their message, Jesus journeyed to Bethany and raised Lazarus from the dead. (M) (John 11:1-44)

LEAH (le'a) O.T. The oldest daughter of Laban. The weakness of her eyes made her less attractive than her sister Rachel. She was married to Jacob by deceitful measures. She was the mother of Reuben, Simeon, Levi, Judah, Issachar, and Zebulun. (F) (Genesis 29:16-35; 30:17-21)

LEMUEL (lem'u-el) O.T. King of Massa in Arabia, whose mother taught him wise sayings recorded in the Book of Proverbs. (M) (Proverbs 31:1-9)

LEPERS (lep'ers) Those persons stricken with a dreadful skin disease, who were required to remain apart from others. (Leviticus 13:45,46)

LEVI (le'vi) O.T. 1. The third son of Jacob and Leah. (M) (Genesis 29:34) 2. N.T. Another name for the disciple Matthew. (M) (Mark 2:14-17)

LEVI

LEVITES (le'vits) O.T. 1. The descendants of Levi, the son of Jacob. (Exodus 6:16-25) 2. The men of Levi set apart for the care of the sanctuary. It was the duty of the Levites to transport the tabernacle during travel and to set it up during rest. (Numbers 1:50-53)

LIBERTINES (lib'er-tines) N.T. Properly translated it means "freedmen." They were probably former prisoners of Roman generals who had been set free. They had a synagogue at Jerusalem, and were enemies of Stephen. (Acts 6:9)

LOT

LOIS (lo'is) N.T. A Christian woman of great faith, grandmother of Timothy. (F) (2 Timothy 1:5)

LOT (lot) O.T. Son of Haran, and nephew of Abraham. He travelled with Abraham from Ur of the Chaldees to Canaan. Given the choice of the new country, Lot settled in the fertile plains of the Jordan River. In character, Lot was just the opposite from Abraham. He was selfish, weak, and worldly; and on more than one occasion saved from disaster by Abraham. (M) (Genesis 11:31; 13:8-12; 19:1-28)

LUCIUS (lu'shi-us) N.T. A Christian of Cyrene, and a teacher in the early church at Antioch. (M) (Acts 13:1)

LUKE

LUKE (luk) N.T. A Christian physician and close companion of the Apostle Paul. He was the author of a history of the life of Christ (the gospel of Luke), where he records in great detail the manner of his birth. (Luke 2) He also wrote an historical account of the early Christian church as established by Paul. (Acts) He remained with Paul, constantly, perhaps as his personal physician. He was with him at the time of his imprisonment in Rome. As a dedicated Christian, and a thorough historian, Luke was one of the most influential persons of the early Christian era. (M) (2 Timothy 4:11)

LYDIA (lid'i-a) N.T. A woman of Thyatira who became the first European convert of Paul. She made her living by selling purple dye and dye goods in Philippi. She was a worshiper of God, and joyfully received the "good news" of the gospel. After her conversion she became a hostess of Paul and his companions, insisting that they stay at her home as long as they wanted. (F) (Acts 16:14,15; 40)

LYDIA

MAGI

MAGICIAN

MALCHUS

MAMRE

MAACAH (ma'a-ka) O.T. 1. Mother of Absalom. (F) (2 Samuel 3:3) 2. Favorite wife of Rehoboam and mother of King Abijah. (F) (2 Chronicles 11:20-22)

MACEDONIANS (mas'e-do'ni-ans) N.T. The inhabitants of the country immediately to the north of Greece. Paul witnessed among the Macedonians on his second missionary journey, in such towns as Neapolis, Philippi, Amphipolis, Apollonia, Thessalonica, and Beroea. (Acts 16:9—17:14)

MAGI (ma'ji) N.T. A religious group to which the Wise Men belonged who came from the east to worship the baby Jesus. They were a priestly caste, who studied the mysteries of astrology and natural sciences.

MAGICIAN (ma-gi'cian) One who pretends to have supernatural powers received by calling upon evil spirits. (Acts 19:19; Daniel 1:20; Exodus 7:11)

MAHALATH (ma'ha-lath) O.T. Daughter of Ishmael and a wife of Esau. (F) (Genesis 28:9)

MAHLON (ma'lon) O.T. Son of Elimelech and Naomi, and the first husband of Ruth. (M) (Ruth 1:2; 4:10)

MALACHI (mal'a-ki) O.T. A prophet, the author of the last book of the Old Testament. His prophecy was during the time of Nehemiah. Malachi believed that a spiritual worship was the one great need of true religion. (M) (Malachi 1:1)

MALCHIAH (mal-ki'a) O.T. A royal prince, into whose dungeon the Prophet Jeremiah was cast. (M) (Jeremiah 38:6)

MALCHUS (mal'kus) N.T. A High Priest's slave who had his ear cut off by Peter in the Garden near Kidron. Judas Iscariot had betrayed Jesus with a kiss, and the Roman soldiers had seized the Lord to take him away, when Peter drew a sword to defend his Master. In the struggle Malchus' ear was cut off, and Jesus healed the ear by touching it. (M) (Luke 22:49-51)

MAMRE (mam're) O.T. An ancient Amorite chieftain, who with his brothers was in alliance with Abraham. Under the shade of an oak grove of Mamre, Abraham lived during the interval between his residence at Bethel and Beersheba. (M) (Genesis 14:13; 18:1)

MANAEN (man'a-en) N.T. A teacher and prophet in the church at Antioch at the time of the appointment of Paul and Barnabas as missionaries to the Gentiles. (M) (Acts 13:1)

MANASSEH (ma-nas'e) O.T. 1. Joseph's oldest son. (M) (Genesis 41:51) 2. The fourteenth' king of Judah, son of Hezekiah. (M) (2 Kings 21:1)

MANOAH (ma-no'a) O.T. A Danite, native of the town of Zorah, and the father of Samson. (M) (Judges 13:2)

MARK

MARK (mark) N.T. One of the evangelists and author of the second book of the New Testament. (Gospel of Mark) His first name was John, and he accompanied Paul and Barnabas on their first missionary journey through the isle of Cyprus. He left them at Perga and returned to Jerusalem. Whatever the reason for his conduct at this time, Paul disapproved of it so much that he refused to take him on a second missionary trip. Mark continued his witness with Barnabas. Later, on request, he joined Paul during the great missionary's imprisonment at Rome. Tradition says that after the death of Paul and Barnabas, Mark visited Egypt where he founded the church of Alexander, and died a martyr's death. (M) (Acts 12:25; 13:5; 2 Timothy 4:11)

MARTHA

MARTHA (mar'tha) N.T. Sister of Mary and Lazarus of Bethany, and close friend of Jesus. She was a sincere believer who desired to make Jesus comfortable in her home. (F) (Luke 10:38-42)

MARY (mar'i) N.T. The name of a number of important women in the New Testament. 1. Mary the mother of Jesus. Mary was a virgin in Nazareth of Galilee, betrothed to a carpenter named Joseph. The angel Gabriel hailed her as the one who would bear a son named Jesus, "the Son of the Most High." (F) (Luke 1,2)

2. Mary of Bethany. The sister of Martha and Lazarus, and a devoted believer and follower of Jesus. When Martha rebuked her for not having more interest in taking care of the physical needs of Jesus, Mary heard the encouraging words, "Mary hath chosen the good part." She was constantly eager to listen to the teachings of Jesus. Her pure devotion to Jesus was shown at a supper in Bethany. During the process of the meal, at which were the Master and the disciples, Mary brought an alabaster box of pure ointment, very costly, and annointed the feet of Jesus, wiping them with her own hair. (F) (Luke 10:38-42) (John 12:3)

MARY MAGDALENE

3. Mary Magdalene. One of the devoted disciples of Jesus, from whom he had cast seven devils. (Mark 16:9) She became one of the group close to Jesus who cared for his immediate needs. She was one of the women who went to the tomb to annoint his body. She was the first person to whom Christ appeared after his resurrection. (F) (Luke 8:1-3; John 20:11-17)

MARY, MOTHER OF JESUS

MATTHEW

4. Mary the wife of Clopas. She was the mother of James the Less, one of the women who went to the tomb, and one of the few at the cross. (F) (John 19:25; Luke 24:10)

5. Mary the mother of Mark. The Christian woman in whose house the disciples gathered to pray for Peter's release from prison. (F) (Acts 12:12)

MATTHEW (math'u) N.T. One of the twelve apostles. His name was originally Levi, and he was a publican or taxgatherer. Christ called him from his work and he immediately followed. His understanding of human nature and experience in business was of great value to the group of disciples. He was the author of the first book of the New Testament. (Gospel of Matthew) (M) (Mark 2:14; Luke 6:15)

MATTHIAS (ma-thi'as) N.T. The follower of Christ chosen by lot to fill the vacancy left by the treacherous Judas Iscariot. (M) (Acts 1:21-26)

MEDES (medes) O.T. Persons belonging to the Median nation south of the Caspian Sea. Media was approximately 600 miles long and 250 miles wide. One of the most famous Medes was King Darius. (Daniel 5:31)

MEPHIBOSHETH

MELCHIZEDEK (mel-kiz'e-dek) O.T. King of Salem and priest of the Most High God. Abraham recognized his true priesthood by meeting him in the valley of Shaveh and giving him tithes. (M) (Genesis 14:18)

MEPHIBOSHETH (me-fib'o-sheth) O.T. The son of Jonathan. When he was five years old his father, Jonathan, and his grandfather, Saul, were killed. His nurse fled in panic carrying him in her arms. She dropped him and Mephibosheth became lame in both feet. David, later, showed kindness to Mephibosheth, because of Jonathan, and restored to him the estates of Saul. (M) (2 Samuel 4:4; 9:1-13)

MERAB (me'rab) O.T. Saul's eldest daughter. She was promised in marriage to David, but the promise was never kept. (F) (1 Samuel 14:49)

MERCURY

MERCURY (mur'ku-ri) N.T. The Roman name of the Greek god Hermes. (See Hermes)

MERES (me'rez) O.T. One of the 7 princes of Persia and Media at the court of Ahasuerus. (M) (Esther 1:14)

MESHA (me'sha) O.T. A king of Moab who sacrificed his oldest son to the fire god Chemosh in an attempt to defend his people against the armies of Jehoram and Jehoshaphat. (M) (2 Kings 3:4-27)

MESHACH (me'shak) O.T. One of the three friends of Daniel who was thrown into the burning fiery furnace but yet was not burned. (M) (Daniel 1:7; 2:49; 3:13-30)

MESHACH

MESSIAH (mes-si'ah) A name applied to Jesus because he is believed to be the fulfillment of God's promise to provide a Deliverer and a Savior for his people. Messiah is applicable in its first sense to anyone anointed with the holy oil. (John 1:41)

METHUSELAH (me-thu'ze-la) O.T. The son of Enoch, and according to the Bible the oldest man who has ever lived. He was 969 years old at his death. (M) (Genesis 5:25-27)

METHUSELAH

MICAH (mi'kah) O.T. One of the minor prophets who prophesied in the reigns of Jotham, Ahaz, and Hezekiah. (M) (Micah 1:1)

MICAIAH (mi-ka'ya) O.T. 1. Wife of Rehoboam and mother of King Abijah. (F) (2 Chronicles 13:2) 2. A prophet who insisted on proclaiming God's message, even at his own discomfort. (M) (1 Kings 22:13-28)

MICHAEL (mi'ka-el) An archangel, one of the chief archangels. (Jude 9; Daniel 10:13; 21; Revelation 12:7)

MICHAL (mi'kal) O.T. The younger of Saul's two daughters who married David. Saul offered Michal to David on the condition that he slay a hundred Philistines; when David doubled his condition, Michal became his wife. Later, Michal saved David from the assassins whom her father had sent to take his life. (F) (1 Samuel 14:49; 18:27,28)

MICAH

MIDIAN (mid'i-an) O.T. A son of Abraham and Keturah. (M) (Genesis 25:1-6)

MIDIANITES (mid'i-an-its) O.T. Arabians dwelling primarily in the desert north of the peninsula of Arabia. One of the most famous Midianites was Jethro, the father-in-law of Moses. (Exodus 3:1)

MILCAH (mil'ka) O.T. A daughter of Haran and sister of Lot. She was the wife of Nahor, by whom she had eight children, and the grandmother of Rebekah. (F) (Genesis 11:29; 22:20-23; 24:15)

MICHAL

MIRIAM (mir'i-am) O.T. Sister of Aaron and Moses. She watched over Moses when he was an infant in the ark of bulrushes in the river Nile. After the crossing of the Red Sea during the Exodus she was known as a prophetess, and assisted Moses and Aaron in the leadership of the children of Israel. She was one of the leaders, with Aaron, in a complaint against Moses for his marriage with a Cushite woman, and for this rebellion was stricken with leprosy. She died and was buried in the wilderness of wandering. (F) (Exodus 15:20; 2:4-8; Numbers 12:1-16)

MIRIAM

MOAB (mo'ab) O.T. The son of Lot. (M) (Genesis 19:37)

MOABITES (mo'ab-ites) O.T. Descendants of Moab, closely related to the Ammonites. (Genesis 19:37,38) Before the Israelite crossing of the Red Sea, the Moabites were numerous in the vicinity of the Dead Sea. One of the most important Bible characters from the Moabite race was Ruth. (Ruth 1:22)

MOLECH

MOLECH (mo'lek) O.T. A fire god worshipped by the Ammonites. One of the terrible practices of the worship of Molech was the sacrifice, by burning, of humans, especially little children. Solomon and Ahaz were influential Israelites who were guilty of encouraging the worship of Molech among the children of God. (1 Kings 11:7; Leviticus 18:21)

MORDECAI

MORDECAI (mor'de-ki) O.T. A Benjaminite who was carried into Babylonian exile in 597 B.C. He adopted and brought up Esther, and directed her in a number of experiences that led to the delivery of the Jews from Persian persecution. Mordecai reached a position of 2nd man in the empire. (M) (Esther 2:5; 3:5-11; 6, 10)

MOSES (mo'zez) O.T. One of the greatest Hebrew leaders. Son of Amram and Jochebed, he was saved from death in his childhood when his mother hid him in the bulrushes of the river Nile. He was brought up in the Egyptian court of the Pharaoh, but was forced to flee to the land of Midian when he became involved in the murder of an Egyptian. He lived 40 years in Midian in the home of Jethro, a Priest, marrying one of his daughters, and tending his flocks. While in Midian, Moses saw the burning bush and heard the voice of God appointing him as a leader to liberate the children of Israel from bondage in Egypt and to lead them to the land of promise in Canaan. After a series of miracles and wanderings, Moses was successful, before his death, in guiding his people to the entrance of the promised land. The outstanding experience in Moses' life was the receiving of the Ten Commandments on Mt. Sinai,—an event that has influenced the history of almost every nation in the world. (M) (Exodus 2 and 3; 20:1-17; Deuteronomy 34:1-8)

MOSES

N

NAAMAH (na'a-ma) O.T. One of the four women whose names are preserved in the records of the world before the flood. (F) (Genesis 4:22)

NAAMAN (na'a-man) O.T. A commander-in-chief of the Syrian army who was healed of leprosy by the prophet Elisha. (M) (2 Kings 5)

NAAMAN

NABAL (na'bal) O.T. A sheep-master of Judea whose wife was Abigail. David was living in the desert near by and levying tribute on the large sheep owners for the protection of his army. Nabal endangered the lives of his whole household by refusing to pay tribute. Abigail, upon learning the situation, hurried to David with the tribute and other supplies, thus saving the lives of the whole family. Nabal, realizing the danger to which he had exposed himself, was seized with a violent heart attack and died. (M) (1 Samuel 25:2-38)

NABOTH

NABOTH (na'both) O.T. An owner of a vineyard in Jezreel who refused to sell to King Ahab. Because of his refusal, a plan was conceived and carried out, by Jezebel, Ahab's wife, whereby Naboth was falsely accused and stoned to death. (M) (1 Kings 21:1-24)

NADAB (na'dab) O.T. The oldest son of Aaron, who was struck dead, with his brother Abihu, while offering a "strange fire" unto God. (M) (Leviticus 10:1-7) 2. Son and successor of Jeroboam, King of Israel. (M) (1 Kings 15:25-31)

NAOMI

NAHASH (na'hash) O.T. An Ammonite king who refused the offer of surrender by the people of Jabeshgilead unless they consented to lose their right eyes. The people were saved by King Saul, who totally defeated Nahash and the Ammonites. (M) (1 Samuel 11:1-11)

NAHOR (na'hor) O.T. Brother of Abraham. (M) (Genesis 11:27)

NAHUM (na'hum) O.T. One of the minor prophets. His area of prophecy was Judah. (M) (Nahum 1:15)

NAOMI (na'o-mi) O.T. Wife of Elimelech and mother-in-law to Ruth. (F) (Ruth 1, 4)

NAPHTALI (naf'ta-li) O.T. Sixth son of Jacob and ancestor of one of the twelve tribes of Israel. (M) (Genesis 30:8)

NATHAN

NATHAN (na'than) O.T. An eminent Hebrew prophet in the reigns of David and Solomon. The proposal for the building of the temple was cleared through Nathan as a prophet of God. Nathan was sent to David to remind him of his great sin with Uriah the Hittite and Bathsheba. He was also the author of a history about David and Solomon. (M) (1 Chronicles 17:1-15; 29:29; 2 Samuel 12:1-15)

NATHANIEL (na-than'a-el) N.T. One of the twelve disciples who was introduced to Jesus by Philip. A native of Cana of Galilee, Nathaniel was declared by Jesus to be an "Israelite indeed in whom was no guile." He was probably the same person as Bartholomew. (M) (John 1:45-51)

NATHANIEL

NEHEMIAH

NAZARENE (naz'a-ren) N.T. One who lived in Nazareth of Galilee. Jesus was frequently referred to by this name. (Matthew 2:23)

NEBUCHADNEZZAR (neb'u-kad-nez'er) O.T. One of the greatest and most powerful of the Babylonian kings. He conquered Jerusalem and took many prisoners into captivity. The whole of the eastern world felt the scourge of his armies. It is said that he was the builder of the famous "hanging garden," in Babylon, one of the seven wonders of the ancient world. (M) (2 Chronicles 36:6; Jeremiah 39:5; Daniel, Chapters 2,3, and 4)

NEHEMIAH (ne'he-mi'a) O.T. The cupbearer of King Artaxerxes in Persia. Nehemiah was a Jewish exile who longed to return to Jerusalem and rebuild the broken city. He obtained permission from the King and led an expedition to Jerusalem. Nehemiah was one of the strongest influences in the restoration of the deteriorating center of the Jewish faith. (M) (Nehemiah 1:1; 2:6; 2:17)

NERO

NERO (ne'ro) The 5th Roman Emperor, Nero was a cruel murderer of Christians in Rome. In A.D. 64 there was a great, destructive fire in Rome believed by many authorities to have been started by the Emperor himself. The Christians of the city were falsely accused of having caused the fire, and many of them were subjected to cruel deaths. Tradition says that Peter and Paul were among the sufferers. The name Nero is not mentioned in the Bible, however, many authorities feel that the Caesar in Acts 25:12; 26:32 and Philippians 4:22 is he. (M)

NICANOR (ni-ka'nor) N.T. One of the first seven deacons of the early church. (M) (Acts 6:5)

NICODEMUS

NICODEMUS (nik'o-de'mus) N.T. A Pharisee and member of the Sanhedrin who came secretly to Jesus to talk about truth. He became a follower of Christ and defended him at the Feast of the Tabernacles. (M) (John 3:1-21; 7:50-52; 19:39)

NICOLAITANS (nik'o-la'i-tanz) N.T. A sect in the churches of Ephesus and Pergamos who followed the doctrine of Balaam, feeling free to eat flesh offered to idols. This practice was condemned by the Church. (Revelation 2:6, 14, 15)

NICOLAUS (nik'o-la'us) N.T. One of the first deacons of the early church. (M) (Acts 6:5)

NIMROD

NIMROD (nim'rod) O.T. A mighty hunter and a powerful leader of early history. He established such great cities as Babel and Nineveh. (M) (Genesis 10:8-10)

NOAH (no'a) O.T. Son of Lamech and grandson of Methuselah. At 500 years of age he had three sons, Shem, Ham, and Japheth. Noah was a just man, and like Enoch, he walked with God, but he lived in days of great evil. Because of the wickedness of the world, the Bible says, God resolved to destroy it. At His command Noah built an ark, into which his family and two each of all living things entered. A great flood covered the land destroying everything but the life in the ark. Noah lived 350 years after the flood and was 950 years old at his death. (M) (Genesis 5:28,29; 6, 7, 8, 9)

NOAH

NUN (nun) O.T. The father of Joshua. (M) (Joshua 1:1)

O

OBADIAH (o'ba-di'a) O.T. A prophet of Judah, the fourth of the twelve minor prophets. (M) (Obadiah 1:1)

OBED (o'bed) O.T. Son of Boaz and Ruth, and grandfather of David. (M) (Ruth 4:17,21,22)

OG (og) O.T. A giant king of the Amorites who had an iron bedstead approximately 14 feet long by 6 feet wide. (M) (Deuteronomy 3:11)

OG

OHOLIAB (o-ho'li-ab) O.T. (M) See Aholiab.

OMRI (om'ri) O.T. King of Israel for twelve years in 885 B.C. (M) (1 Kings 16:15)

ONESIMUS (o-nes'i-mus) N.T. A slave of Philemon converted by Paul and sent back to his master with the plea that he be received not as a slave but as a brother in Christ. (M) (Philemon 10-19; Colossians 4:9)

ONESIPHORUS (on'e-sif'o-rus) N.T. A Christian at Ephesus who showed great kindness to Paul when the great missionary was in prison at Rome. (M) (2 Timothy 1:16-18)

ONESIMUS

ORPAH (or'pa) O.T. The wife of Chilion, and sister-in-law of Ruth, who chose to remain in her native land of Moab rather than to accompany Ruth and Naomi to Palestine. (F) (Ruth 1:4,14,15; 4:10)

OTHNIEL (oth'ni-el) O.T. Young brother of Caleb, Othniel won the hand of Caleb's daughter, Achsah, in marriage by taking the town of Debir. He became the first judge of Israel after the death of Joshua, and delivered the Israelites from the oppression of Cushan-rishathaim, King of Mesopotamia. (M) (Joshua 15:15-17; Judges 3:8,9)

ORPAH

PATRIARCH

PAUL

PERSIANS

PETER

PASHHUR (pash'her) O.T. A Priest who put Jeremiah in the stocks because of his gloomy predictions. (M) (Jeremiah 20:1-6)

PATRIARCH (pat'ri-ark) O.T. A father or chief of a race; a name given in the New Testament to the Hebrew fathers in the Old Testament. (Hebrews 7:4; Acts 2:29)

PAUL (pol) N.T. Born in Tarsus, Paul's original name was Saul. He studied at Jerusalem under the great teacher, Gamaliel. His early life was dedicated to the persecution of the followers of Christ; but on the road to Damascus he received a vision that altered the course of his life and the destiny of the world—, he heard the voice of Jesus appointing him as the apostle to the Gentiles. Paul's life from that moment on became completely dedicated to the purpose of reaching the known world with the "good news" of Christ. He became the first great travelling missionary, establishing churches in Asia Minor, Macedonia, and Greece. He attained the fulfillment of his goal only after his arrest and imprisonment at Rome. From this central city Paul's influence reached out into the whole world. Paul is the author of thirteen New Testament Epistles whose content indicates him to be the greatest of all Christian thinkers. (M) (The Book of Acts)

PEKAH (pe'ka) O.T. The 18th King of the Northern Kingdom of Israel. (M) (2 Kings 15:25-28)

PERSIANS (pur'zhans) O.T. The people who lived in the great land of Persia, an area of about 50,000 square miles. Cyrus the Great united the many tribes into one great kingdom.

PETER (pe'ter) N.T. A disciple of Christ called "the rock." He and his brother Andrew were partners of James and John, in the fishing business, and together they were disciples of John the Baptist until they were called to follow Jesus. Peter's life follows a threefold pattern. 1. The period of training, as seen in the gospels. He learned to know Jesus and himself in the light of the teachings of Christ. 2. The period of early Church leadership, as seen in the early chapters of Acts. After his denial of his Lord, Peter became the most important single figure in the development of the Christian Church. He was bold and strong, preaching sermons and performing miracles, and holding out the message of God to Jew and Gentile. 3. The period of Missionary Work, as seen in the teachings of the Epistles. Few Bible characters have the strength and enthusiasm of Peter. He fulfilled his name of "rock" and became a solid foundation for the building of the early church. (M) (John 1:35-42; Matthew 4:18,19; 16:16; Acts 2:14,38; John 21:15-19; Acts 10)

PETHUEL (pe-thu'el) O.T. Father of the Prophet Joel. (M) (Joel 1:1)

PHANUEL (fan'u-el) N.T. Father of Anna the Prophetess. (M) (Luke 2:36)

PHARAOH

PHARAOH (far'o) O.T. A title used to designate the kings of Egypt. Some of the Pharaohs mentioned in the Bible are: Shishak, (1 Kings 14:25,26) Tirhakah, (2 Kings 19:9) Neco, (2 Kings 23:29) and Pharaoh-Hophra (Jeremiah 44:30)

PHARAOH'S DAUGHTER O.T. The daughter of Pharaoh who saved Moses from the river Nile and brought him up in the court of Pharaoh. (F) (Exodus 2:5-10)

PHARAOH'S DAUGHTER

PHARISEES (far'i-sez) N.T. Together with the Essenes, and the Sadducees, the Pharisees made up the three chief Jewish parties. The Pharisees were strict formalists believing the outward act more important than the inward heart. They were strict adherents to the law; however, its interpretation often led to complicated additions never included in the original Law of Moses. The Pharisees in the time of Christ were enemies both of John the Baptist and Jesus. They took a prominent part in the plot of Jesus' death. (Matthew 15:1-9; 23:1-36; John 11:47-57)

PHILEMON (fi-le'mon) N.T. A convert of Paul who lived in Colossae. Paul wrote a letter to Philemon asking him to receive Onesimus, Philemon's slave, as a brother in Christ. (M) (Philemon)

PHARISEE

PHILIP (fil'ip) N.T. The name of three men in the New Testament. 1. Philip the tetrarch. Philip was appointed by Rome as the ruler of the area east and northeast of Galilee. He married Salome, the daughter of Herod and Herodias, and was the founder of the city of Caesarea Philippi. History says that his character was excellent and his rule was mild and just. (Luke 3:1)

2. Philip the apostle. One of the 12 apostles. He lived in the same town as Peter and Andrew. Bethsaida on the sea of Galilee. Philip was responsible for guiding Nathaniel to Jesus. He was an assistant in the feeding of the five thousand; he was an aid in helping certain Greeks to see Jesus at the triumphal entry; and he was one of the group in the upper chamber after the resurrection. (Matthew 10:3; John 1:43-51; 6:5,6; 12:20-23; Acts 1:13)

PHILIP

PHOEBE

PILATE

POTIPHAR

PRIEST

3. Philip the evangelist. He was one of the seven deacons chosen by the early church. He preached the gospel in Samaria, performed miracles, and won converts, among whom were Simon the sorcerer and the Ethiopian eunuch. (Acts 6:5; 8:4-8; 8:9-40; 21:8)

PHILIPPIANS (fi-lip'i-anz) N.T. The inhabitants of the city of Philippi in Macedonia. Paul established a Christian church among them on his second missionary journey, and wrote a letter to them which has become a book of the New Testament. (Philippians 4:1,2,14,15)

PHILISTINES (fi-lis'tinz) O.T. An ancient race, perhaps migrating from the isle of Crete, settled on the western coast of southern Palestine. They were always bitter enemies to the Israelites. (Exodus 13:17; 1 Samuel 31:1-7; 17:19)

PHINEHAS (fin'é-as) O.T. 1. Son of Eleazar, and grandson of Aaron. Because of his zeal in destroying idolatry he was granted everlasting priesthood. (M) (Exodus 6:25; Numbers 25:1-18) 2. Second son of Eli who was killed by the Philistines when they captured the ark. (M) (1 Samuel 4:11)

PHOEBE (fe'be) N.T. One of the first deaconesses of the Church. (F) (Romans 16:1,2)

PHOENICIANS (fe-nish'i-ans) The inhabitants of Phoenicia, a strip of land about 125 miles long and 20 miles wide on the northwestern coast of Palestine. They were the originators of the alphabet. (Acts 21:2)

PILATE (pi'lat) N.T. The fifth Roman procurator of Judea. Under him Jesus worked, suffered and died. The character of Pilate is shown clearly in his treatment of Jesus. He was willing to act justly as long as it didn't interfere with his own interests. (M) (Matthew 27; Luke 23)

POTIPHAR (pot'i-far) O.T. The captain of Pharaoh's guard who owned Joseph as a slave in Egypt. Potiphar's wife tried to tempt Joseph to forsake the virtuous way, and failing, influenced her husband to cast him in prison. (M) (Genesis 39:1-20)

PRIEST (prest) A person especially appointed to minister at the sanctuary before the Lord, to teach the people the Law of God, and to inquire for them the divine will of God. (2 Chronicles 15:3)

PRISCILLA (or PRISCA) (pri-sil'a) N.T. The wife of Aquila. She accompanied her husband and helped him in advancing the Christian faith. Paul's estimation of Priscilla was high. (F) (Acts 18:1-3; 18:26; Romans 16:3; 2 Timothy 4:19)

PROCHORUS (prok'o-rus) N.T. One of the seven chosen by the disciples to look after the needs of the widows. (M) (Acts 6:5)

PRODIGAL SON

PRODIGAL SON N.T. The main character in a story told by Jesus. He was the youngest of two sons, and repented his foolish living, returning to his father for forgiveness. By this story, Jesus was teaching the true meaning and value of man's repentance and God's forgiveness. (Luke 15:11-32)

PROPHET (prof'et) A spokesman for God. One who announces or brings a message, either of duty or warning, or a prediction of future events, from God. (Deuteronomy 18:18)

PUBLICAN (pub'li-can) N.T. Those men appointed by Rome to be the collectors of customs and taxes. As these men were under contract to give a certain sum to the Roman treasury, and as they could keep anything above that amount for themselves, they were extremely zealous in their search for revenue. The Publicans were hated and despised by the people. (Luke 18:13)

PUBLICAN

PUL (pul) O.T. An Assyrian King. (See Tiglath-Pileser) (M) (2 Kings 15:19)

PURAH (pu'ra) O.T. Gideon's armor-bearer. (M) (Judges 7:10,11)

PUT (put) O.T. An ancient people related to the Egyptians. They were descendants of Ham, the son of Noah. (Genesis 10:6)

QUEEN OF SHEBA

Q

QUARTUS (kwor'tus) N.T. A Corinthian Christian who joins with Paul in sending salutations to the church at Rome. (M) (Romans 16:23)

QUEEN (kwen) The consort of a king, or a woman who reigns in her own right. (Esther 1:9)

QUEEN OF HEAVEN O.T. A false divinity, probably the Phoenician goddess Ashtoreth, to whom the Hebrew women offered cakes in the streets of Jerusalem. (F) (Jeremiah 7:18; 44:15-30)

QUEEN OF SHEBA O.T. A famous queen who visited King Solomon. (F) (1 Kings 10:1-13)

RACHEL

RAHAB

REBEKAH

REUBEN

RHODA

RABBI (rab'bi) A title of respect given by the Jews to their doctors and teachers. It was frequently used in addressing Jesus. (Matthew 23:7)

RACHEL (ra'chel) O.T. The younger daughter of Laban, the wife of Jacob, and the mother of Joseph and Benjamin. The story of Jacob and Rachel is one of the world's famous love stories. (F) (Genesis 29:16-20)

RAHAB (ra'hab) O.T. A woman of Jericho, who hid the spies sent by Joshua to explore the city. She let them down over the wall by a scarlet cord so they escaped to the Israelite camp. Later when the city was captured, her life was spared. (F) (Joshua 2:1-24; 6:22-25)

REBEKAH (re-bek'a) O.T. A daughter of Bethuel, and the wife of Isaac. The story of her marriage to Isaac is one of the beautiful romances of the Bible. The servant of Abraham had journeyed to Nahor in Mesopotamia in search of a wife for Isaac, Abraham's son. Upon reaching the outskirts of the city, he saw a beautiful maiden coming to the well with a pitcher. He asked for a drink, whereupon Rebekah not only gave him water, but offered to draw water for his camels as well. This was just the sign that he had asked from God. He obtained consent from Rebekah and her father to take her with him back to Canaan as Isaac's wife. Rebekah was the mother of Jacob and Esau. (F) (Genesis 24:1-67)

RECHAB (re'kab) O.T. Father of Jonadab, chief of the Rechabites. (M) (1 Chronicles 2:55)

RECHABITES (rek'a-bits) O.T. A Kenite tribe, whose chief, Jonadab, commanded them to drink no wine or intoxicating liquor, live in no houses, plant no vineyards, and live nothing but the simple life. (Jeremiah 35:1-19)

REDEEMER (re-dem'er) One who sets free. A name applied to Jesus because he came to set men free from the power of sin. (Titus 2:14)

REHOBOAM (re'ho-bo'am) O.T. Son and successor to King Solomon as King of Judah. Rehoboam was the first King of the Southern Kingdom, after the revolt of the ten tribes. (M) (1 Kings 11:43; 14:21,31)

REUBEN (roo'ben) O.T. Jacob's oldest son, and the founder of one of the twelve tribes of Israel. (M) (Genesis 29:31,32)

REUEL (roo'el) O.T. One of the names of Moses' father-in-law, Jethro. (See Jethro) (M) (Exodus 2:18)

RHODA (ro'da) N.T. The servant girl of Mary, the mother of Mark. She answered the door at the time of Peter's miraculous deliverance from prison. (F) (Acts 12:13-16)

RICH YOUNG RULER N.T. A ruler who was challenged by Jesus to share his wealth with the poor before he could inherit eternal life. (M) (Luke 18:18-27)

RICH YOUNG
RULER

RIMMON (rim'on) O.T. 1. A Benjaminite whose two sons murdered Ish-bosheth. (M) (2 Samuel 4:2) 2. A Syrian god, who had a temple at Damascus, where Naaman and his master bowed in worship. He was the god of rain, storm, lightning, and thunder. (M) (2 Kings 5:18)

RIZPAH (riz'pa) O.T. A mother of the Old Testament who guarded, with love and endurance, the bodies of her two dead sons, allowing neither the birds nor beasts to molest them for a long period of time. (F) (2 Samuel 21:7-10)

ROMANS (ro'manz) N.T. 1. Inhabitants of the city of Rome where Paul established a Christian group, and to which he wrote an Epistle, now one of the books of the New Testament. 2. Those, of whatever race, who possessed the rights of citizenship in the Roman Empire. (Acts 2:10; 16:21; 22:25-29)

ROMANS

RUFUS (roo'fus) N.T. A son of the Simon who was compelled to carry Jesus' cross. (M) (Mark 15:21)

RULER (rool'er) In a general sense, one who exercises authority. Specific examples of rulers are: 1. Officer of a synagogue. 2. Member of the Sanhedrin. 3. Civil magistrate of a city. 4. Governor of a feast. (Luke 8:41; John 3:1; Acts 16:19; John 2:8)

RUTH

RUTH (rooth) O.T. A Moabitess, wife first of Mahlon who died in Moab and then of Boaz a landowner in Bethlehem. The story of Ruth's devotion to her mother-in-law Naomi is one of the most beautiful stories of the Bible. Ruth's name is included in the genealogy of Jesus. (F) (Ruth; Matthew 1:5)

S

SADDUCEES (sad'u-sez) N.T. A Jewish religious party who were the opponents of the Pharisees. They were few in number, but made up of men who were educated, wealthy and of good position. They held that the word of the written Law was alone binding, and not the tradition of the elders, as did the Pharisees. (Matthew 22:23)

SALOME

SAMSON

SAMUEL

SAPPHIRA

SARAH

SALMON (sal'mon)   O.T.   The father of Boaz. (M) (Ruth 4:18)

SALOME (sa-lo'me)   N.T.   1. The wife of Zebedee, and the mother of James and John. She was a witness of the crucifixion, and present at the tomb on Resurrection morning. (F) (Mark 15:40; 16:1) 2. The daughter of Herodias, who danced before Herod, and received the head of John the Baptist as a reward for her grace and beauty. (F) (Matthew 14:3-11)

SAMARITANS (sa-mar'i-tans)   Found only once in the Old Testament, it meant an individual belonging to the kingdom of Northern Israel. In the New Testament it refers to inhabitants living in the province of Samaria. (2 Kings 17:29; Luke 17:11)

SAMSON (sam'sun)   O.T.   One of the strongest men of the Bible. He was of the tribe of Dan, and a judge of Israel. A Nazirite, his hair was never cut, and he never drank strong drink. His feats of strength were amazing. He burned a Philistine harvest by tying the tails of 300 foxes together, in pairs; he killed a thousand Philistines with the jawbone of a donkey; he carried a city gate, posts and all, to the top of a hill. Samson met disaster in the presence of a Philistine woman named Delilah. He told her the secret of his strength was in his long hair. The Philistines immediately cut his hair and his strength was gone. Samson remained a prisoner of the Philistines the rest of his life; but performed one more feat of strength. He pulled the pillars of the temple of Dagon asunder, and died with thousands of his enemies. (M) (Judges 13:1-24; 14:1-15:8; 16:1-31)

SAMUEL (sam'u-el)   O.T.   Son of Elkanah and Hannah, Samuel was the earliest of the great Hebrew prophets, and the last of the judges. Samuel annointed Saul as the first King of Israel. (M) (1 Samuel 1; 2:1-11; 1 Samuel 12)

SANHEDRIN (san'he-drin)   N.T.   The name given to the highest Jewish body of government in the time of Christ.

SAPPHIRA (sa-fi'ra)   N.T.   The wife of Ananias of Jerusalem. (F) (Acts 5:1-10)

SARAH (sar'a)   O.T.   The wife of Abraham and mother of Isaac. She accompanied her husband in his travels from Ur of Chaldea, through Syria, Canaan, Egypt and Hebron. (F) (Genesis 20:12; 21:1-5; 23:1,2)

SARGON (sar'gon) O.T. A king of Assyria, who succeeded Shalmaneser. He was one of the greatest Assyrian kings, famed as a warrior and a builder. (M) (Isaiah 20:1)

SATAN (sa'tan) The word means adversary and is applied to the Devil, the chief opponent of God and man. Satan was the tempter of Adam and Eve, Jesus, Peter, Job, Paul, and it is his purpose to undo the work of God, attempting to lead men to sin. (Matthew 4:1; Job 2:1-6; Luke 11:18; Matthew 16:23)

SAUL

SATYR (sat'er) A forest deity of the Greeks and Romans, represented with long-pointed ears, snub nose, and a goat's tail. (Isaiah 13:21)

SAUL (sol) O.T. A Benjaminite, son of Kish, and the first king of Israel. He was famed for his strength and military activity, and stood head and shoulders taller than all his people. Under Saul the Israelites began to assemble into a great nation. (M) (1 Samuel 10:1; 13:1; 31)

SAVIOR (sav'yur) One who saves from evil or danger. The name is applied to Jesus because he saves his people, and delivers them from sin. (Matthew 1:21; Romans 5:8-11)

SAVIOR

SCRIBES (scribz) 1. Men who were employed as public writers. They took dictation, and drew up legal documents. (Jeremiah 36:4) 2. A secretary or government clerk. (Ezra 4:8) 3. A copier of the Law and the Scriptures. (Jeremiah 8:8; Matthew 21:15)

SCYTHIANS (sith'i-anz) N.T. The inhabitants of Scythia just north of the Black Sea. (Colossians 3:11)

SENNACHERIB (se-nak'er-ib) O.T. Son of Sargon and his successor on the throne in Assyria, in 705 B.C. He was cruel and destructive, with less administrative ability than his father. (M) (2 Kings 18 and 19)

SCRIBE

SERAIAH (se-ra'ya) O.T. A chief priest of Jerusalem put to death by Nebuchadnezzar. (M) (Jeremiah 52:24-27)

SERGIUS PAULUS (ser'ji-us paw'lus) N.T. Proconsul of Cyprus when Paul and Barnabas made their first missionary journey. (M) (Acts 13:7)

SERUG (se'rug) O.T. Great-grandfather of Abraham. (M) (Genesis 11:20-23)

SETH (seth) O.T. A son of Adam and Eve. (M) (Genesis 4:25)

SHADRACH

SHEPHERDS

SHEVA

SIHON

SHISHAK

SHADRACH (sha'drak) O.T. One of the three faithful Jews saved miraculously from the fiery furnace in Babylon. (M) (Daniel 1:7; 3:12-30)

SHALLUM (shal'um) O.T. The name of thirteen men in the Old Testament including Shallum, ruler of half the district of Jerusalem, who with his daughters repaired part of the wall of Jerusalem in the time of Nehemiah. (M) (Nehemiah 3:12)

SHALMANESER (shal'man-e'zer) O.T. The name of several Assyrian kings who came into conflict with the Israelites. (M) (2 Kings 17:3)

SHAMGAR (sham'gar) O.T. A deliverer of Israel who killed 600 Philistines with an oxgoad. (M) (Judges 3:31)

SHEM (shem) O.T. One of the sons of Noah. He was the ancestor of races in Asia Minor, Assyria, and Arabia. (M) (Genesis 10:1,21)

SHEMA (she'ma) O.T. One of the priests who assisted Ezra in the reading of the Law publicly to the people of Jerusalem. (M) (Nehemiah 8:4)

SHEMAIAH (she-ma'ya) O.T. The name of 27 men of the Old Testament including Shemaiah, a prophet in the reign of Rehoboam, who warned against the attempt of the King to reconquer the revolting ten tribes of Israel. (M) (1 Kings 12: 22-24)

SHEMUEL (she-mu'el) O.T. Another name for Samuel. (M) (1 Chronicles 6:33)

SHEPHATIAH (shef'a-ti'a) O.T. 1. A son of King Jehoshaphat. (M) (2 Chronicles 21:2) 2. A prince of Jerusalem who advised King Zedekiah to put the prophet Jeremiah to death because of his dismal prophecies. (M) (Jeremiah 38:1)

SHEPHERDS (shep-herdz) Those whose occupation it was to take care of sheep. Famous shepherds were David in the Old Testament, and the shepherds in the story of Jesus' birth in the New Testament. Jesus called himself the Good Shepherd. (Psalm 23; John 10:2-5)

SHEVA (she'va) O.T. A royal secretary, or scribe, of David. (M) (2 Samuel 20:25)

SHIMEI (shim'e-i) O.T. The name of 18 men of the Old Testament, including Shimei, a resident of Jerusalem who was killed, at the command of Solomon, because he left the city to recover two of his slaves. (M) (1 Kings 2:36-46)

SHISHAK (shi'shak) O.T. An Egyptian king who invaded the Southern Kingdom in the reign of Rehoboam. (M) (1 Kings 14:25,26)

SHOBAB (sho'bab) O.T. A son of David and Bathsheba. (M) (2 Samuel 5:14)

SHUAH (shoo'a) A son of Abraham and Keturah. An Arab tribe, the Shuhites, descended from them, and lived near the land of Uz. (M) (Genesis 25:2; Job 2:11)

SILAS

SHUNAMMITE WOMAN (shoo'nam-it) O.T. A woman of Shunem, a village of Canaan, whose son was restored to life by Elisha. (F) (2 Kings 4:8-37)

SIHON (si'hon) O.T. A King of the Amorites at the time of the entrance of Israel into the promised land. He refused permission to the Israelites to cross Amorite territory, and was killed in a struggle with them. (M) (Joshua 13:21)

SILAS (si'las) N.T. A companion of the apostle Paul on his second and third missionary journeys into Asia Minor and Greece. (M) (Acts 15:40; 16:19,25,29)

SIMON
THE ZEALOT

SIMEON (sim'e-un) O.T. The second son of Jacob and Leah. When one of Jacob's sons was bidden to remain as a hostage for the return of the others, Simeon was bound by Joseph in Egypt. (M) (Genesis 29:33; 42:24)

SIMON (si'mun) 1. Simon, the brother of Jesus. N.T. One of the four brothers of the Lord. (M) (Matthew 13:55)

2. Simon, the Zealot. One of the 12 Apostles. (M) (Luke 6:15; Acts 1:13) N.T.

3. Simon Peter. Simon was another name for Peter. N.T. (See Peter) (M) (Matthew 10:2)

4. Simon, a Pharisee. N.T. At his home during a feast a sinful woman anointed the feet of Jesus. (M) (Luke 7:36-50)

5. Simon the Leper. N.T. He lived in Bethany. It may be possible that he was cured by Jesus. Some authorities think that in his house Mary anointed Jesus in preparation for his death and burial. (M) (Matthew 26:6; Mark 14:3)

6. Simon the Cyrenian. N.T. He was selected to carry the cross for Jesus, after the Master sank down under the heavy burden. (M) (Matthew 27:32; Mark 15:21; Luke 23:26)

7. Simon Magus. N.T. A Samaritan living in the days of the early church who was called "the sorcerer" or "magician." His art of magic or trickery was so amazing that the people of Samaria called it "the power of God." At the time of his conversion

SIMON
OF CYRENE

SIMON
THE TANNER

SLAVES

by Philip, and baptism, he was so interested in the laying on of hands practiced by Peter and John that he offered to pay money to receive the same power himself. He was severely rebuked. Tradition says that he followed Peter wherever he went as a constant foe, but was soundly defeated at every encounter. He is said to have followed Peter to Rome where he died an unusual death. According to an early authority, Simon requested that he be buried alive, certain he would rise on the third day. (M) (Acts 8:9)

8. Simon the tanner. N.T. A Christian convert who lived at Joppa near the seaside. It was here that Peter lived for some time. (M) (Acts 9:43)

9. Simon Iscariot. N.T. The father of Judas Iscariot. (M) (John 6:71; 13:2,26)

SISERA (sis'er-a) O.T. A Canaanite commander who sought rest in the tent of the wife of Heber the Kenite, and died in his sleep when she drove a tent peg through his head. (M) (Judges 4:17-22)

SOLDIERS

SLAVES The ownership of one person by another. Slaves were acquired: 1. By capture. 2. By purchase from slave traders. 3. By birth from slaves already owned. 4. In payment of debt. 5. The voluntary sale of one's self or one's children because of poverty. One of the most famous slaves of the Bible was Joseph. (Exodus 21:2,7; Matthew 18:25; Nehemiah 5:5)

SOLDIER A person employed in the defense of his country or tribe. (1 Samuel 4:10; Ezekiel 26:7)

SOLOMON

SOLOMON (sol'o-mun) O.T. Son of David and Bathsheba. He was the successor to David as the King of Judah. Solomon was the richest and the wisest of all Israel's kings. During his 40 year reign, the great Temple was built, and the kingdom reached its greatest boundaries. He died about 931 B.C. (M) (2 Samuel 12:24; 1 Kings 10:4,5,21, 23-25; 11:41-43)

SOSTHENES (sos'the-nes) N.T. A ruler of the synagogue at Corinth who was beaten up by a mob before the judgment seat of Gallio as a result of excitement stirred up by Paul's preaching. (M) (Acts 18:12-17)

STEPHEN (ste'ven) N.T. The first Christian martyr, and one of the deacons of the early church. He died by stoning. Stephen's death was influential in the conversion of Paul. (M) (Acts 7:54-8:1)

SOSTHENES

STEWARDS (stoo'urds) The persons who were in charge of large households. The overseer of an estate. (1 Chronicles 28:1)

STOICS (sto'iks) N.T. A group of philosophers whose founder was Zeno of Cyprus. They believed that virtue is the highest good; and that virtue is living in harmony with nature. They were followers of Socrates and produced such leaders as Seneca and the Emperor Marcus Aurelius. The Apostle Paul encountered the Stoics in Athens. (Acts 17:18)

STEPHEN

SUSANNA (su-zan'a) N.T. One of ·the women who provided for Jesus out of her own means. (F) (Luke 8:3)

SYRIANS (sir'i-anz) People belonging to the Syrian race, or residents of Syria, located north of Palestine. The most famous of the Syrian cities is Damascus, where Paul went after his famed conversion. (1 Kings 10:29)

T

TABITHA (tab'i-tha) N.T. Another name for Dorcas. (See Dorcas)

TAMAR (ta'mer) O.T. Absalom's sister, and the daughter of David. She was famous for her unusual beauty. (F) (2 Samuel 13:1-32)

TAMAR

TAMMUZ (tam'uz) O.T. A deity of the Babylonians, originally the sun god. He is identified with Adonis of Greek mythology. (Ezekiel 8:14)

TAPHATH (ta'fath) O.T. The daughter of Solomon who married Ben-Abinadab. (F) (1 Kings 4:11)

TARTAK (tar'tak) O.T. An idol, said to have been shaped in the form of a donkey, worshipped by the Avites of Samaria. (2 Kings 17:31)

TERAH (te'ra) O.T. A resident of Ur of the Chaldees, and the father of Abraham. (M) (Genesis 11:26)

TAMMUZ

TERESH (te'resh) O.T. A chamberlain of King Ahasuerus who plotted his death and was executed along with an accomplice. (M) (Esther 2:21-23)

TERTIUS (tur'shi-us) N.T. Paul's amanuensis (one employed to write from dictation) for the writing of the Epistle to the Romans. (M) (Romans 16:22)

TERTULLUS (ter-tul'us) N.T. A Roman lawyer hired by the Jews to prosecute Paul before the tribunal of Felix. He was a professional orator. (M) (Acts 24:1-8)

TERTULLUS

TETRARCH (te'trark) N.T. One who rules over the fourth part of a country, or province. (Luke 3:1)

THADDAEUS

THADDAEUS (tha-de'us) N.T. One of the twelve apostles, the same as Judas the son of James. (M) (Luke 6:16)

THEOPHILUS (the-of'i-lus) N.T. The person to whom Luke addressed his gospel (Luke) and history. (Acts) (M) (Luke 1:3; Acts 1:1)

THESSALONIANS (thes'a-lo'ni-anz) N.T. The inhabitants of the city of Thessalonica in Macedonia where Paul established a Christian church on his second missionary journey, and to which Paul wrote two letters which have become part of the New Testament.

THEUDAS (thu'das) N.T. The leader of 400 men overrunning the land in the reign of Herod. (M) (Acts 5:36,37)

THIEF

THIEF (thef) Anyone who takes what isn't his own, the pilferer, the robber, and the highwayman. The two thieves on the cross at the time of Jesus' crucifixion were apparently robbers. (John 12:6; Luke 10:30)

THOMAS (tom'as) N.T. One of the twelve apostles. He was the one who was not present at the first appearance of Jesus to the disciples after the resurrection and who said, "Unless I can put my fingers into the nail prints, I will not believe." Jesus, therefore, made a special appearance to convince the "doubting Thomas." (M) (Matthew 10:3; John 20:24-29; Acts 1:13)

THOMAS

TIBERIUS (ti-ber'i-us) N.T. The second Roman Emperor following Augustus, and whose period of rule went from 14 A.D. to 37 A.D. Jesus was crucified during the reign of Tiberius. (M) (Luke 3:1)

TIGLATH-PILESER (tig'lath-pi-le'zer) O.T. A powerful Assyrian king who ruled from 745 B.C. to 727 B.C. He raised the Assyrian Empire to greater glory than any of the kings before him. (M) (2 Kings 16:10; 15:29)

TIMAEUS (ti-me'us) N.T. The father of the blind Bartimaeus of Jericho. (M) (Mark 10:46)

TIMON (ti'mon) N.T. One of the seven deacons of the early church. (M) (Acts 6:5)

TIMOTHY (tim'o-thi) N.T. A companion and helper of Paul. The extent of Paul's feeling for Timothy is shown by these words: "My true child in faith" (1 Timothy 1:2), and "My beloved and faithful child in the Lord." (1 Corinthians 4:17) Timothy was apparently a convert of Paul's on his first missionary journey. He was a resident of

TIBERIUS

Lystra; his mother was a Jewess and his father a Gentile. His early faith and training was the result of the devotion of Eunice, his mother, and Lois, his grandmother. Timothy remained a close companion of Paul throughout his life, and was probably with him at his death. Two letters, so-called pastoral epistles, were written by Paul to Timothy, and are now part of the New Testament. (M) (2 Timothy 1:5; Acts 16:1,2; 2 Timothy 4:9,21)

TIMOTHY

TITUS (ti'tus) N.T. A convert and good companion of Paul. Much younger than Paul, he, like Timothy, was an apostolic deputy, carrying epistles and serving as messenger. Later he was assigned church work in Crete and Dalmatia. Paul's letter to Titus completes the pastoral epistles in the New Testament. (M) (Galatians 2:3; Titus 1:4; 2 Corinthians 12:18; 2 Timothy 4:10)

TOBIAH (to-bi'a) O.T. An Ammonite slave who made trouble with the Jews in their efforts to rebuild the walls of Jerusalem. (M) (Nehemiah 2:10; 4:3,7)

TOBIJAH (to-bi'ja) O.T. One of the captive Jews from whom the prophet Zechariah took silver and gold to make a crown to put on the head of the high priest. (M) (Zechariah 6:10-14)

TYRANNUS

TROPHIMUS (trof'i-mus) N.T. An Ephesian Gentile, companion of Paul, who caused trouble among the Jews by entering the Temple in Jerusalem. (M) (Acts 21:27-29)

TUBAL-CAIN (tu'bal-kan) O.T. Son of Lamech, who was the forger of cutting instruments of brass and iron. (M) (Genesis 4:22)

TYRANNUS (ti-ran'us) N.T. An Ephesian teacher in whose school Paul taught Christianity for two years. (M) (Acts 19:9,10)

URI

U

URI (u'ri) O.T. The father of Bezalel, one of the architects of the tabernacle. (M) (Exodus 31:2)

URIAH (u-ri'a) O.T. One of David's mighty men who was so exposed in battle that he would be killed. He was the husband of Bathsheba. (M) (2 Samuel 11:1-27)

URIJAH (u-ri'ja) O.T. High Priest in the reign of Ahaz. (M) (2 Kings 16:10-16)

URIJAH

UZZAH

UZ (uz) O.T. A tribe of the Aramaeans descendants from Nahor. Job was supposedly a member of this race. (Genesis 22:20,21; Job 1:1; Lamentations 4:21)

UZZAH (uz'a) O.T. A son of Abinadab, who was struck dead when he placed his hand on the sacred Ark of the Hebrews. The team of oxen transporting the Ark stumbled and Uzzah had reached out his hand to steady it. (M) (2 Samuel 6:3-1]; 1 Chronicles 13:7-14)

UZZIAH (u-zi'a) O.T. Son of Amaziah and his successor as the King of Judah about 785 B.C. He was sixteen years old when he ascended the throne. The only black mark in his prosperous reign was when he attempted to burn incense at the altar of God and was, smitten with leprosy. (M) (2 Kings 15:13; 14:21; 2 Chronicles 26:1,3)

VASHTI

UZZIEL (uz'zi-el) O.T. A Levite, founder of the Uzzielite tribe, who were organized by David to transport the Ark of God. (M) (Exodus 6:18,22; Numbers 3:19; 1 Chronicles 15:10)

V

VASHTI (vash'ti) O.T. The Persian Queen of Ahasuerus. When she refused to show herself at a great feast in Susa, Vashti was exiled and divorced, and Esther was made queen in her place. (F) (Esther 1:10-12,19-22)

W

WIDOW OF NAIN N.T. A woman of Nain who had a son that Jesus raised from the dead. (F) (Luke 7:11-15)

WITCH OF ENDOR

WISEMEN N.T. Those men who came from the East bearing gifts to the infant Jesus. (See Magi) (M) (Matthew 2:1-12)

WITCH OF ENDOR O.T. A medium consulted by King Saul. She was a native of Endor, a little city about six miles from Nazareth. (F) (1 Samuel 28:7-14)

WOMAN AT THE WELL N.T. A Samaritan woman of Sychar who was introduced to the deeper meaning of life by Jesus beside a well in that city. It was to her Jesus said, "God is a Spirit; and they that worship him must worship him in spirit and in truth." (F) (John 4:5-26)

X

WOMAN AT THE WELL

XERXES (zurk'sez) O.T. King of Persia in the time of Esther. Another name for Ahasuerus. (See Ahasuerus) (M) (Esther 1:1)

Z

ZACCHAEUS (za-ke'us) N.T. The little man of Jericho who climbed a tree so he could see Jesus. He was a wealthy tax-collector who later became a disciple of Christ. (M) (Luke 19:1-10)

ZACCHAEUS

ZACHARIAH (zak'a-ri'a) O.T. See Zechariah.

ZACHARIAS (zak'a-ri-as) N.T. The father of John the Baptist. He was a priest whose wife Elizabeth was related to Mary the mother of Jesus. Zacharias prayed for a son, his long prayer was heard and an angel announced the coming birth of John the Baptist. When Zacharias asked for a sign, he was stricken dumb until the birth of his son was accomplished. (M) (Luke 1:5-23, 57-80)

ZADOK (za'dok) O.T. A descendant of Aaron, and high priest of Israel in the time of David and Solomon. He served as high priest jointly with Abiathar during most of the reign of King David. (M) (1 Chronicles 24:3; 2 Samuel 15:24-29; 1 Kings 2:26,27)

ZADOK

ZEBEDEE (zeb'e-de) N.T. The father of James and John, and a fisherman on the Sea of Galilee. (M) (Matthew 4:21,22)

ZEBULUN (zeb'u-lun) O.T. Son of Jacob and Leah, and founder of one of the twelve tribes of Israel. (M) (Genesis 30:19,20)

ZECHARIAH (zek'a-ri'a) O.T. The name of 31 men of the Old Testament including the following: 1. Zechariah, fourth son of King Jehoshaphat. (M) (2 Chronicles 21:2) 2. Zechariah, son of Jehoiada, the high priest, and a righteous man like his father. He was stoned to death in the court of the Temple. (M) (2 Chronicles 24:20-22) 3. A King of Israel who reigned six months on the throne in Samaria. (M) (2 Kings 14:29; 15:8-10) 4. Zechariah, the Prophet. A prophet of God, contemporary of Haggai, who exhorted the Jews to rebuild the walls of Jerusalem. (M) (Zechariah 1:1; 8:1-8)

ZEBEDEE

ZEDEKIAH (sed'e-ki'a) O.T. The last king of Judah and Jerusalem, who was bound and carried to Babylon by Nebuchadnezzar. (M) (2 Kings 24:17-20; 25:1-7; Jeremiah 39:1-14)

ZERUBBABEL (ze-rub'a-bel) O.T. The leader of the Jews who returned from Babylonian captivity to rebuild the city of Jerusalem. (M) (Ezra 2:1,2; Nehemiah 12:1)

ZILPAH (zil'pa) O.T. A maidservant of Leah, and the mother of Jacob's sons Gad and Asher. (F) (Genesis 30:9-13)

ZERUBBABEL

Names in the order of their appearance in the Bible

	Genesis		Genesis		Numbers
God	1:1	Esau	25:25	Ammiel	13:12
Spirit (Holy)	1:2	Jacob	25:26	Ahiman	13:22
Adam	3:17	Edom	25:30	Og	21:33
Eve	3:20	Judith	26:34	Sihon	21:21
Cain	4:1	Basemath	26:34	Balak	22:2
Abel	4:2	Shepherds	29:3	Balaam	22:5
Enoch	4:17	Rachel	29:6	Baal	25:3
Lamech No. 1	4:18	Leah	29:16	Asriel	26:31
Adah	4:19	Zilpah	29:24	Jair	32:41
Jabal	4:20	Bilhah	29:29		Deuteronomy
Jubul	4:21	Reuben	29:32	Anakim	1:28
Tubal-cain	4:22	Simeon	29:33	Ammonite	23:3
Naamah	4:22	Levi	29:34		Joshua
Seth	4:25	Judah	29:35	Rahab	2:1
Enosh	4:26	Dan	30:6	Achan	7:1
Jared	5:15	Naphtali	30:8	Gibeon (Gibeonite)	9:3
Methuselah	5:21	Gad	30:11	Debir	10:3
Lamech No. 2	5:25	Asher	30:13	Jabin	11:1
Noah	5:29	Issachar	30:18	Othneil	15:17
Shem	5:32	Zebulun	30:20	Achsah	15:16
Ham	5:32	Dinah	30:21	Arab (Arabian)	15:52
Japheth	5:32	Joseph	30:24	Danites	19:47
Canaan	9:18	Israel	32:28		Judges
Slave	9:25	Israelites	32:32	Adonizedek	1:5
Put	10:6	Benjamin	35:18	Eglon	3:12
Nimrod	10:8	Korah	36:5	Ehud	3:15
Philistines	10:14	Edomites	36:9	Shamgar	3:31
Jebusites	10:16	Ishmaelites	37:25	Sisera	4:2
Amorites	10:16	Midianite	37:28	Deborah	4:4
Hivites	10:17	Potiphar	37:36	Barak	4:6
Canaanites	10:18	Magicians	41:8	Heber	4:11
Asshur	10:22	Manasseh No. 1	41:51	Jael	4:17
Uz	10:23	Ephraim	41:52	Gideon	6:11
Serug	11:20	Steward	43:10	Purah	7:10
Nahor	11:22	Ruler	45:8	Abimelech	8:31
Terah	11:24		Exodus	Jotham	9:5
Abram (Abraham)	11:26	Pharaoh's Daughter	2:5	Jephthah	11:1
Haran	11:26	Moses	2:10	Manoah	13:2
Lot	11:27	Reuel	2:18	Samson	13:24
Chaldeans	11:28	Jethro	3:1	Delilah	16:4
Sarai (Sarah)	11:29	Aaron	4:14	Dagon	16:23
Milcah	11:29	Levite	4:14		Ruth
Iscah	11:29	Amram	6:18	Elimelech	1:2
Egyptians	12:12	Uzziel	6:18	Naomi	1:2
Pharaoh	12:15	Jochebed	6:20	Mahlon	1:2
Mamre	13:18	Elisheba	6:23	Chilion	1:2
King	14:1	Nadab	6:23	Orpah	1:4
Amalekites	14:7	Eleazar No. 1	6:23	Boaz	2:1
Melchizedek	14:18	Ithamar	6:23	Obed	4:17
Priest	14:18	Elkanah	6:24	Jesse	4:17
Eliezer No..1	15:2	Phinehas No. 1	6:25	David	4:17
Kenites	15:19	Miriam	15:20	Salmon	4:20
Hittites	15:20	Joshua	17:9	Samuel	1 Samuel
Hagar	16:1	Hur	17:10	Elihu	1:1
Angel	16:7	Eliezer No. 2	18:4	Hannah	1:2
Ishmael	16:11	Thief	22:2	Eli	1:3
Isaac	17:19	Bezalel	31:2	Phinehas No. 2	1:3
Moab	19:37	Uri	31:2	Soldiers	4:10
Moabites	19:37	Oholiab (Aholiab)	31:6	Ichabod	4:21
Prophet	20:7		Leviticus	Kish	9:1
Bethuel	22:22	Leper	13:45	Saul	9:2
Rebekah	22:23	Satyrs	17:7	Nahash	11:1
Laban	24:29	Molech	18:21	Bedan	12:11
Keturah	25:1		Numbers	Jonathan	13:2
Midian	25:2	Abidan	1:11	Merab	14:49
Ishbak	25:2	Eldad	11:26	Michal	14:49
Shuah	25:2	Caleb	13:6	Ahimaaz	14:50
Hadad	25:15	Gaddi	13:11	Abner	14:50

74

	1 Samuel		1 Kings		Ezra
Goliath	17:4	Jehoram	22:50	Elamites	4:9
Ahimelech	21:1		2 Kings	Haggai	5:1
Achish	21:10	Baalzebub	1:2	Zechariah No. 4	5:1
Abiathar	22:20	Mesha	3:4	Ariel	8:16
Abigail	25:3	Shunammite Woman	4:8		Nehemiah
Nabal	25:3	Gehazi	4:12	Tobiah	2:10
Joab	26:6	Naaman	5:1	Shallum	3:12
Witch of Endor	28:7	Rimmon No. 2	5:18	Shema	8:4
	2 Samuel	Athaliah	8:26	Amok	12:7
Ishbosheth	2:8	Rechab	10:15		Esther
Amnon	3:2	Jehoahaz	10:35	Vashti	1:9
Chileab	3:3	Joash	11:2	Biztha	1:10
Absalom	3:3	Jehoiada	11:4	Bigtha	1:10
Maacah No. 1	3:3	Amaziah	12:21	Abagtha	1:10
Adonijah	3:4	Azariah No. 2	14:21	Carcas	1:10
Rizpah	3:7	Jonah	14:25	Carshena	1:14
Rimmon No. 1	4:2	Zechariah No. 3	14:29	Admatha	1:14
Hiram	5:11	Uzziah	15:13	Meres	1:14
Shobab	5:14	Pul	15:19	Mordecai	2:5
Solomon	5:14	Pekah	15:25	Hadassah	2:7
Uzzah	6:3	Tiglath-pileser	15:29	Teresh	2:21
Ahio	6:3	Hoshea	15:30	Haman	3:1
Gittite	6:10	Ahaz	15:38		Job
Nathan	7:2	Urijah	16:10	Job	1:1
Hadadezer	8:3	Hezekiah	16:20	Satan	1:6
Syrians	8:5	Shalmaneser	17:3	Bildad	2:11
Zadok	8:17	Medes	17:6	Eliphaz	2:11
Benaiah	8:18	Avites	17:31	Redeemer	19:25
Bathsheba	11:3	Tartak	17:31		Proverbs
Eliam	11:3	Anammelech	17:31	Lemuel	31:1
Uriah	11:3	Abi	18:2		Isaiah
Jedidiah	12:25	Sennacherib	18:13	Immanuel	7:14
Tamar	13:1	Eliakim	18:18	Ambassador	18:2
Ahithophel	15:12	Isaiah	19:2	Sargon	20:1
Ittai	15:19	Amoz	19:2		Jeremiah
Barzillai	17:27	Assyrians	19:35	Jeremiah	1:1
Sheva	20:25	Manasseh No. 2	20:21	Hilkiah	1:1
Ira	20:26	Jedidah	22:1	Queen of Heaven	7:18
Saviour	22:3	Huldah	22:14	Pashhur	20:1
Eleazar No. 2	23:9	Jehoiakim	23:34	Malchiah	21:1
Azmaveth	23:31	Nebuchadnezzar	24:1	Ahikam	26:24
	1 Kings	Jehoiachin	24:6	Hannaniah	28:1
Abishag	1:3	Zedekiah	24:17	Rechabites	35:2
Shimei	2:8	Seraiah	25:18	Shephatiah No. 2	38:1
Taphath	4:11	Jews	25:25	Baalis	40:14
Ahinadab	4:14		1 Chronicles		Ezekiel
Queen	10:1	Scribes	2:55	Ezekiel	1:3
Queen of Sheba	10:1	Azariah No. 1	6:9	Tammuz	8:14
Arabia (Arabians)	10:15	Heman	6:33	Daniel	14:14
Ashtoreth	11:5	Azaziah	15:21		Daniel
Jeroboam	11:26	Chenaniah	15:22	Belshazzar	1:7
Shishak	11:40	Azarel	25:18	Shadrach	1:7
Rehoboam	11:43		2 Chronicles	Meshach	1:7
Shemaiah	12:22	Maacah No. 2	11:20	Abednego	1:7
Josiah	13:2	Ethiopians	12:3	Gabriel	8:16
Asa	15:8	Micaich No. 1	13:2		Hosea
Baasha	15:16	Azariah No. 3	15:1	Hosea	1:1
Ben-hadad	15:18	Adnah	17:14		Joel
Jehoshaphat	15:24	Zechariah No. 1	21:2	Joel	1:1
Elah	16:6	Shepatiah No. 1	21:2	Pethuel	1:1
Omri	16:16	Zechariah No. 2	24:20	Greeks	3:6
Ahab	16:28	Persia (ns)	36:20		Amos
Jezebel	16:31	Cyrus	36:22	Amos	1:1
Elijah	17:1		Ezra		Obadiah
Hazael	19:15	Zerubbabel	2:2	Obadiah	1:1
Elisha	19:16	Nehemiah	2:2	Phoenicia	1:20
Jehu	19:16	Bilshan	2:2		Micah
Naboth	21:1	Henadad	3:9	Micah	1:1
Micaiah No. 2	22:8	Darius	4:5		Nahum
Amon	22:26	Ahasuerus	4:6	Nahum	1:1
Ahaziah	22:40	Artaxerxes	4:7		
Azubah	22:42	Babylonians	4:9		

	Habakkuk		Luke		Acts
Habakkuk	1:1	Susanna	8:3	Erastus	19:22
	Zechariah	Samaritan	10:33	Demetrius	19:24
Tobijah	6:10	Good Samaritan	10:33	Diana (Artemis)	19:24
	Malachi	Martha	10:38	Ephesians	19:28
Malachi	1:1	Mary No. 2	10:39	Gaius	19:29
Matthew	Matthew	Prodigal Son	15:11	Aristarchus	19:29
Jesus	1:1	Lazarus No. 1	16:20	Macedonians	19:29
Christ	1:1	Rich Young Ruler	18:18	Alexander No. 2	19:33
Joseph No. 2	1:16	Zacchaeus	19:2	Thessalonians	20:4
Mary No. 1	1:16	Cleopas	24:18	Trophimus	20:4
Emmanuel	1:23		John	Eutychus	20:9
Herod	2:1	Messiah	1:41	Felix	23:24
Wisemen	2:1	Nathaniel	1:45	Tertullus	24:1
Nazarene	2:23	Nicodemus	3:1	Drusilla	24:24
John the Baptist	3:1	Woman at the Well	4:5	Jewess	24:24
Pharisees	3:7	Simon No. 9	6:71	Festus	24:27
Sadducees	3:7	Lazarus No. 2	11:1	Bernice	25:13
Gentiles	4:15	Romans	11:48	Christian	26:28
Simon No. 3	4:18	Malchus	18:10	Julius	27:1
Peter	4:18	Clopas	19:25	Romans	Romans
Andrew	4:18		Acts	Barbarian	1:14
James No. 1	4:21	Justus	1:23	Phoebe	16:1
Zebedee	4:21	Matthias	1:23	Andronicus	16:7
John	4:21	Patriarch	2:29	Apelles	16:10
Disciples	5:1	Barnabas	4:36	Aristobulus	16:10
Demon	9:33	Ananias No. 2	5:1	Hermas	16:14
Apostles	10:2	Sapphira	5:1	Julia	16:14
Philip No. 2	10:3	Gamaliel	5:34	Tertius	16:22
Bartholomew	10:3	Theudas	5:36	Quartus	16:23
Thomas	10:3	Stephen	6:5		1 Corinthians
James No. 2	10:3	Philip No. 3	6:5	Chloe	1:11
Alphaeus	10:3	Prochorus	6:5	Achaicus	16:17
Thaddaeus	10:3	Nicanor	6:5		2 Corinthians
Simon No. 2	10:4	Timon	6:5	Titus	2:13
Judas No. 2	10:4	Nicolaus	6:5		Galatians
Iscariot	10:4	Alexandrians	6:9	Galatians	3:1
Simon No. 1	13:55	Paul (Saul)	7:58	Philippians	Philippians
Tetrarch	14:1	Simon No. 7	8:9	Bishops	1:1
Herodias	14:3	Ethiopian Eunuch	8:27	Euodia	4:2
Bar-jona	16:17	Ananias No. 1	9:10	Clement	4:3
Herodians	22:16	Tabitha	9:36	Colossians	Colossians
Caesar	22:17	Dorcas	9:36	Epaphras	1:7
Rabbi	23:7	Simon No. 8	9:43	Scythians	3:11
Caiphas	26:3	Cornelius	10:1	Onesimus	4:9
Simon No. 5	26:6	Agabus	11:28	Laodiceans	4:16
Galilean	26:69	Claudius	11:28		2 Timothy
Pilate	27:2	Mary No. 5	12:12	Lois	1:5
Barabbas	27:16	Rhoda	12:13	Eunice	1:5
Simon No. 6	27:32	Blastus	12:20	Onesiphorus	1:16
Joseph No. 3	27:57	Lucius	13:1	Alexander No. 4	4:14
Mary No. 3	27:56	Manaen	13:1	Claudia	4:21
Mark	Mark	Sergius Paulus	13:7		Titus
Jairus	5:22	Paul	13:9	Artemas	3:12
Bartimaeus	10:46	Hermes	14:12		Philemon
Timaeus	10:46	Zeus (Jupiter)	14:12	Philemon	1:1
Alexander No. 1	15:21	Silas	15:22	Apphia	1:2
Rufus	15:21	Timothy	16:1		Jude
Mary No. 4	15:40	Lydia	16:14	Jude	1:1
Salome No. 1	15:40	Jason	17:5		Revelation
Luke	Luke	Beroeans	17:10	Nicolaitans	2:6
Theophilus	1:3	Epicurean	17:18		
Zacharius	1:5	Stoic	17:18		
Elizabeth	1:5	Athenians	17:21		
Augustus Caesar	2:1	Damaris	17:34		
Anna	2:36	Aquila	18:2		
Phanuel	2:36	Priscilla	18:2		
Tiberius	3:1	Crispus	18:8		
Philip No. 1	3:1	Corinthians	18:8		
Annas	3:2	Gallio	18:12		
James No. 4	6:16	Sosthenes	18:17		
Widow of Nain	7:11	Apollos	18:24		
Simon No. 4	7:40	Tyrannus	19:9		

Chapter II
Facts About the Bible

A

AARON   The older brother of Moses and Miriam (Numbers 26:59), and the first head of the Hebrew priesthood.

ABBA   An Aramaic word which means, father (Mark 14:36).

ABEL   Mentioned in Genesis 4 as the younger son of Adam and Eve.

ADDER

ABOMINATION   Whatever is wrong according to God's plan for man's right living, such as, worship of idols (I Kings 11:5), dishonesty (Micah 6:10), etc.

ABRAHAM   Originally Abram. Means "father of a multitude." He was the founder of the Hebrew nation and was called the friend of God (II Chronicles 20:7).

ABSALOM   The third son of King David. He tried to seize the throne which David intended for Solomon, but was unsuccessful. Absalom was killed after his head caught in the branches of a tree and pulled him from the mule he was riding (II Samuel 18).

ALABASTER

ACTS OF THE APOSTLES   The fifth book of the New Testament, and presumed to be written by Luke as a sequel to his gospel narrative. The book is the account of the early Christian church, and portrays the apostles proclaiming their message to the Gentiles.

ADAM   The name of the first man, according to the Bible story of creation.

ADDER   The word used in the Bible for any poisonous snake.

ALMOND TREE

ADVERSARY   A word denoting enemy or opponent of God's way of living.

ALABASTER   A whitish stone resembling marble, used in Bible times for making vases and jars.

ALMOND TREE   A nut-bearing tree resembling a peachtree in shape and blossom.

ALMS   Money, or produce from the field and vineyard, given to those in need (Leviticus 19:9, 10).

ALMS

ALPHA   The first letter of the Greek alphabet. With Omega, the last letter of the alphabet, the two words stand for the eternal existence of God (Revelation 1:8).

ALTAR   A single large stone or a structure of stones or other material on which sacrifices were offered (Genesis 35:1).

AMEN   A Hebrew word signifying "So be it," used at the end of a prayer to indicate approval by those present, as though the prayer had been uttered by themselves.

ALPHA

ALTAR

ANGEL

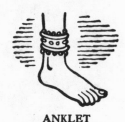

ANKLET

ANNUNCIATION

ANOINT

AMOS   The earliest of the prophets and a great prophet of Judah, who spoke out against the wicked and godless living of his day. He preached that God cared more for right living than for burnt offerings.

ANATHEMA   A Greek word implying that a person or a thing was condemned or accursed.

ANDREW   The brother of Simon Peter and one of the first apostles of Jesus.

ANGEL   The word means "a messenger." The Bible presents angels generally as heavenly beings sent as messengers of God to man on earth.

ANKLET   A metal bracelet worn as an ornament on the leg near the ankle.

ANNA   An aged prophetess living in the Temple (Luke 2:36, 37). She was present at the dedication of the baby Jesus and declared him to be the expected Messiah.

ANNAS   The high priest before whom Jesus was brought for examination after his arrest (John 18:12, 13; 19-24).

ANNUNCIATION   The announcement to Mary by the angel Gabriel that she was to be the mother of a son who should be called Jesus.

ANOINT   To apply oil or ointment to the head. This was done as a sign of hospitality toward a guest, or as an official rite of consecration to certain important offices.

ANTICHRIST   The opponent of Christ, or anyone who stood opposed to Christ.

ANTIOCH   It was at Antioch in Syria that the followers of Jesus were first called Christians (Acts 11:26). Antioch may be considered the birthplace of foreign missions since it was from here that Paul set forth on his first missionary journey (Acts 13:1-3).

APOCRYPHA   Certain books rejected by the early Church but generally not included among the books of our Protestant Bible, yet considered to have some value.

APOLLOS   A Jew from Alexandria who was an enthusiastic and eloquent popular preacher of the gospel. He was a trusted friend of Paul.

APOSTLE   A Greek word meaning "one who is sent." The name "apostles" was applied to the twelve disciples whom Jesus chose to prepare and aid him in his ministry and to send forth to preach the Gospel after he left this earth (Luke 6:13).

APPIAN WAY   A famous road in Italy over which Paul walked on his way to Rome.

APPLE   Not the specie of fruit which we know by that name, but probably the apricot, a common fruit in Palestine.

ARAMAIC The common language of Palestine spoken by Jesus. He undoubtedly knew Greek and Hebrew also.

ARARAT A lofty mountain northeast of Palestine on which Noah's ark is said to have landed after the flood.

APPIAN WAY

ARCHAEOLOGY The scientific study of the remains of past human life, such as fossils, monuments, etc., often carried on by careful digging and uncovering of ancient regions.

ARCHELAUS The son of Herod and the ruler of Judea when Joseph and Mary brought the boy Jesus back from Egypt.

ARCHERS Soldiers using bows and arrows were an important fighting unit in the armies of Old Testament times (I Chronicles 8:40).

AREOPAGUS A rocky hill in Athens where the city court met to consider and pass judgment on criminal, social, and political questions. Paul made a famous speech in this place (Acts 17:22-31).

ARCHER

ARK, NOAH'S The houseboat in which (according to the Bible narrative in Genesis, Chaps. 6-8) Noah with his family and animals were saved from the flood.

ARK OF THE COVENANT A sacred chest in which were kept the Mosaic tables of stone, a pot of manna, and Aaron's rod that budded. The ark was placed in the Holy of Holies of the Tabernacle and later of the Temple, and it was a reminder of God's presence.

ARK, NOAH'S

ARMOR A suit of body coverings, usually metal, for protection in battle.

ARMOR BEARER A young man whose duty was to hold the large shield before a soldier facing attack in battle, and to carry it when not in actual fighting.

ASAPH One of the leaders of David's choir, who founded a guild of singers (I Chronicles 16:4-7). His name is attached to Psalm 50 and Psalms 73-83.

ASCRIBE To give due credit (Deuteronomy 32:3).

ARK OF THE COVENANT

ASHERAH The name of a pagan goddess worshipped in Canaan. Sometimes the word indicated the tree or pole which was her symbol, and sometimes the grove where her image was located.

ASSYRIA A mighty empire on the upper Tigris River. Bible accounts tell of the raiding of Israel and Judah by Assyria, sieges laid to their capitals, and the final carrying away of Israel into captivity.

ARMOR

AX

BABEL, TOWER OF

BAGS

BALANCES

ATONEMENT   The Old Testament belief was that when man offended God by sin, man could be restored only by paying for his wrong by sacrifices, offerings, or by the performance of ritual pleasing to God. This earnest effort to recover favor with God was the atonement man made for his sins.

ATONEMENT, DAY OF   The final day of a most solemn religious celebration, held yearly, when the high priest conducted a ceremonial rite cleansing the people from the defilement of their sins.

AVENGER   The person or persons who returned punishment on one who had done evil to a kinsman. This was approved by Old Testament standards though later this spirit was greatly modified (Numbers 35:19).

AX   A sharp iron instrument with a wooden handle for chopping.

B

BAAL   The heathen god worshipped by the inhabitants of Canaan when the Children of Israel conquered that land.

BABEL, TOWER OF   This tower in Babylon consisted of seven stories, each smaller than the one below, with a shrine on top where the Babylonian god was worshipped. The Bible narrative says it was here God confused the language of man so that they could not understand one another, and were scattered over the face of the earth (Genesis 11:4-9).

BABYLON   The capital city of Babylonia.

BABYLONIA   The country around the lower Tigris and Euphrates Rivers. Many times its rulers harassed the Hebrew kingdoms, and finally carried Judah captive to Babylon.

BAGS   Made of skin or woven material. The shepherd's bag would be used to carry food, or stones to frighten away wild animals, or even to transport a lamb unable to walk. Smaller bags were used to carry money.

BALANCES   Scales used to weigh money and produce. A piece of metal of predetermined weight was placed on one side of the balance and articles to be weighed on the other side until the two sides balanced (Proverbs 11:1).

BALM   The fragrant sap or gum from a bush which grew in Gilead to the east of the Jordan River. It was valued for its healing properties, and was also used by women as a skin cream, and in preparing bodies for burial.

BAPTISM   A rite practiced by John the Baptist who baptized Jesus. Baptism was administered as a symbol of inner cleansing with new members in the early Christian church. The rite has been accepted ever since as evidence of faith in Christ and a pledge of discipleship when entering into membership of the Church. It is one of the two Sacraments of the Church ordained by our Lord himself (Matthew 28:19).

BALM

BAR-   An Aramaic word meaning "son," used as a prefix of a proper name, like Bar-jona (Son of Jona).

BARABBAS   A criminal released by Pilate at the trial of Jesus. Pilate let the crowd choose which prisoner should be released, Jesus or Barabbas, and they chose the latter (Matthew 27:11-26).

BARBARIAN   In New Testament days a barbarian usually meant anyone not a Greek or a Roman.

BARLEY   An important food grain used largely for cattle and horses, although sometimes it was baked into round flat loaves by the village people.

BARNABAS   A member of the early church at Jerusalem and a close friend of Paul. He accompanied the latter on his first missionary journey.

BAPTISM

BATH   Hebrew term for a liquid measure of about 8 gallons.

BATHING   Bathing was a prescribed ceremonial act for a priest or worshipper before approaching the altar, expressing reverence toward God.

BATTERING-RAM   A heavy beam with an iron head sometimes fashioned as the head of a ram; used to batter down gates and walls when a city was besieged.

BATTLEMENT   A low parapet built around the edge of the flat roof of a house to prevent accidents.

BEATITUDE   A Latin word meaning "happy" or "blessed." The term, Beatitudes, refers to the opening of the Sermon on the Mount where nine verses begin with the word "blessed," stating some of the qualities Jesus expected in his followers (Matthew 5:3-11).

BARLEY

BED   Usually a mat of straw or rushes spread on the floor, or a sack filled with straw, which was rolled up and put aside during the day (Luke 5:25).

BEHOLD   Look! See!

BELSHAZZAR   The king of Babylon who gave a great feast, at which the accusing words that appeared on the wall were interpreted by Daniel.

BESEECH   To plead for special favor.

BETH-   A Hebrew word meaning "house." Used in compound proper names, as Beth-el (house of God), Beth-lehem (house of bread).

BATTERING-RAM

BATTLEMENT

BED

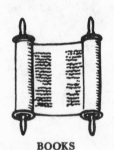

BIER

BOOKS

BOOTHS, FEAST OF

BETHANY   A small village about one and one-half miles from Jerusalem and on the Mount of Olives, the village where Jesus sometimes stayed with his friends Mary, Martha, and Lazarus.

BETHEL   A town about twelve miles north of Jerusalem. Many Old Testament characters were associated with the history of Bethel.

BETHESDA (House of mercy)   A spring-fed pool in Jerusalem, having five porches, where invalids and crippled waited to step into the water. It was said to have healing properties. Here Jesus cured the man sick for 38 years (John 5:2).

BETHLEHEM (House of bread)   A very old town in Palestine, located about five miles south of Jerusalem. It was the home of David, also of Ruth; it is best known, however, as the birthplace of Jesus, the Messiah (Matthew 2).

BIBLE (Greek, meaning "books")   The sacred book of Christians. A collection of 66 books, composed by many different writers over a period of about a thousand years. Included in this volume are laws, history, sacred poems, songs, prayers, proverbs, prophecies, memoirs, letters, speeches, and other literature. The Old Testament was written chiefly in Hebrew and the New Testament in Greek. The Bible is a best seller, and it has been translated into over a thousand languages. A 20-volume Braille Bible and 169 Talking-Book Bible records have been made available for the blind.

BIER   A wooden cot or stretcher on which bodies were transported to the place of burial (Luke 7:14).

BIRTHRIGHT   The special rights, privileges, and inheritance of the oldest son in a Hebrew family (Deuteronomy 21:17).

BISHOP   (From a Greek word meaning, "overseer.") An official in the early Christian Church (I Timothy 3:1-7).

BITTER HERBS   Eaten by Jews at the Passover meal as a reminder of Israel's bitter experience as slaves in Egypt (Exodus 12:8).

BLASPHEMY   Words spoken against the honor of God.

BLEMISH   A mark or defect which prevents something from being perfect.

BLESSING   The bestowing of goodwill or special favor upon another, as when a prayer asks for a blessing from God.

BLINDNESS   Very common in Palestine because of dust, flies, and glare of the sun.

BLOOD   In the Bible, blood was associated with life itself and was never eaten. In worship rites the blood of the sacrificial animals was poured upon the altars as an act of atonement for men's sins.

BOAZ   A wealthy farmer of Bethlehem who befriended and then married Ruth. One of his descendants was David, and he is mentioned in the genealogy of Jesus (Matthew 1:5).

BONDAGE   The same as slavery.

BOOKS   These were long strips of papyrus, or skins, rolled on two sticks. To open such a book was to unroll from one stick to the other.

BOOTHS, FEAST OF   A seven-day fall festival, one of the most joyous and popular of all the year. During this time Hebrew families lived in booths made of the branches of trees and usually built on the roof-tops. The purpose was to serve as a thanksgiving for the harvest and a reminder of the wanderings of the Israelites in the wilderness when they lived in leafy shelters.

BOTTLES   Such containers were commonly made of skins, to hold water, milk, etc., although bottles and jars of earthenware were also used (Matthew 9:17).

BRAMBLES   Thorns and prickly shrubs, of which there were many varieties in Palestine.

BRASEN   Made of brass, a long-lasting metal probably compounded principally of copper and zinc.

BREAD   To make bread, wheat or barley was ground between two round stones. The flour was mixed with milk or water, usually kneaded, formed into flat, round loaves like pancakes, and then baked. Being pliable, the loaves could be bent spoon-shape to dip up gravy and liquids.

BREASTPLATE   The breastplate of the high priest's vestment was made of cloth trimmed with 12 jewels, each bearing the name of a Hebrew tribe. It was worn especially when the priest entered the Holy of Holies once a year (Exodus 28:15-30). The breastplate of a soldier was for protection in battle and was made of heavy leather.

BRICK   Made of clay mixed with water by tramping and kneading and then shaped in molds. Originally they were baked in the sun. Sometimes straw was used to make the clay bind together better.

BULRUSH (Papyrus)   A tall reed which grew in swampy regions in Palestine and along the banks of the Nile in Egypt. The stalks were pliable and could be interwoven to make a small boat or basket. A sort of paper was made by splitting the inner layers of fibers into thin slices, laying them criss-cross, and then pounding them flat.

BURNT OFFERING   An offering placed on the altar and consumed by fire as a gift to a god or idol. With the Hebrews of the Old Testament it symbolized the desire of the sacrificer to submit himself completely to God and to His will.

BRAMBLES

BREAD

BREASTPLATE,
HIGH PRIEST'S

BREASTPLATE,
SOLDIER'S

BRICK

BULRUSH

CALDRON

CAMEL

CANDLESTICK

CAPTIVE

CAESAR   A title of the Roman emperors. Used in the New Testament as the name of the emperor who was ruler of Judea.

CAESAREA   A Roman city on the coast of Palestine nearly 20 miles south of Mt. Carmel. Here lived Pontius Pilate. Paul was imprisoned here for two years before being sent to Rome.

CAESAREA PHILIPPI   A city of northern Palestine near Mt. Hermon. Jesus visited here, and it was the scene of Peter's confession of Jesus as "the Christ, the son of the living God" (Matthew 16:13-16).

CAIAPHAS   High priest in the time of Jesus, before whom Jesus was taken for trial. Later on Caiaphas was antagonistic to the apostles Peter and John.

CALDRON   A large pot for boiling meat, either for ceremonial or for household use.

CALVARY (Skull)   The place outside Jerusalem where Jesus was crucified; the exact location of it is unknown. It is often called Golgotha.

CAMEL   An animal highly prized in the East for transport and other work. He can go longer without food and water than any other beast of burden, and his padded feet adapt him to travel over soft sandy soil.

CANA   A small village in Galilee, near Nazareth, where Jesus performed his first miracle (John 2:1-11).

CANAAN   (Lowland) The land lying westward from the Dead Sea and the Jordan River, to the Mediterranean Sea. This land was given to the Children of Israel by God, who led them out of Egypt to possess it.

CANDLESTICK   More correctly a lampstand of metal holding small lamps, each supplied with oil and a wick (Exodus 25:31-40).

CANON OF SCRIPTURE   The word means a straight rod by which certain things are measured. The canon of the Scriptures refers to those books judged to be worthy of inclusion in the sacred collection (our Bible).

CANTICLES (Song of Songs)   Another title for the Bible book, The Song of Solomon.

CAPERNAUM   A lake port on the northwest shore of the Sea of Galilee, very familiar to Jesus. Many of his recorded activities took place here (Matthew 8:14-17, 9:1-8).

CAPTIVE   One who is taken as a prisoner of war.

CAPTIVITY OF THE JEWS   The period when many thousands of the Jews were deported to Babylonia. See: Exile.

CARAVAN   A company of merchants and travelers making a long trip together for safety.

CARAVAN

CARMEL, MOUNT   A mountain range extending out of Samaria with its headland projecting into the Mediterranean Sea. It was the scene of the contest between Elijah and the priests of Baal (I Kings 18:19-46).

CASTING NET   A net thrown into the water for the purpose of catching fish.

CATHOLIC   A word meaning "universal." It does not signify any established faith or system. As used by the Church, and especially as found in the Apostles' Creed "I believe in the Holy Catholic Church," it refers to the universal, world-wide and age-long faith and practice of the Church.

CATHOLIC EPISTLES   The name given to seven of the New Testament Epistles: James, I and II Peter, I, II, III John, and Jude. These letters were not addressed to a particular person or church but their contents were of a general nature for wide reading. See: Catholic.

CARMEL, MOUNT

CEDAR   The cedar trees of Lebanon were especially sought for building palaces, masts, chests, and musical instruments. The wood is fragrant and very durable, and takes an excellent polish.

CENSER   A small metal vessel usually suspended by chains, made to hold live coals from the altar. When incense was thrown on the coals and the censer swung back and forth fragrant clouds of smoke were produced for religious rites in Tabernacle and in Temple.

CENTURION   An officer in the Roman army who commanded a group of 100 men (Matthew 8:1-13).

CASTING NET

CHAFF   The useless outer husks of threshed grain, which were blown away by the wind when the grain was tossed into the air to winnow it (Psalm 1:4).

CHALDEA   The southernmost of the three countries enclosing the Tigris and Euphrates Rivers. The others were Assyria to the North, and Babylonia in the middle. The term is often used for "Babylonia" (Jeremiah 50:10).

CHARGER   A large shallow dish like a platter, used in connection with the sacrificial offerings. The head of John the Baptist was carried on a charger after his death (Matthew 14:1-12).

CHARIOT   A low two-wheeled cart with high front and sides but open at the back; used principally for war, although high officials sometimes used them for traveling short distances (Acts 8:38).

CENSER

CENTURION

CHARGER

CHARIOT

CITIES OF
REFUGE

CLAY TABLETS

CHASTEN   To punish for the purpose of making better.

CHERUBIM   The plural of CHERUB. Symbolic winged creatures, usually spoken of as being in the presence of Deity, guarding sacred articles or stationed in sacred places. They were purely mythological, but they symbolized the presence of God (Exodus 25:18).

CHEST OF JOASH   A special chest made to receive the money offerings of the people to repair the Temple in the days of King Joash (II Chronicles 24:8-11).

CHILDREN OF GOD   A New Testament conception of those people who have received Jesus Christ by faith and have entered into filial relationship with God the Father (John 1:12).

CHILDREN OF ISRAEL   A term denoting the descendants of Jacob; that is, the whole company of Hebrews, up to the time of King Solomon.

CHRISTIAN   The name borne by followers of Jesus Christ. It was first applied to them in Antioch (Acts 11:26), perhaps in the spirit of scorn.

CHURCH   The name applied to the groups of early Christians who met for consolation and inspiration after Jesus' resurrection. The day of Pentecost is generally considered the birthday of the Church (Acts 2).

CITIES OF REFUGE   Six cities designated as places to which anyone who had killed another unintentionally might flee and find protection from the avenger.

CLAY TABLETS   Soft clay was imprinted with cuneiform writing made by a wedge-shaped stylus and then baked hard. This was one of the chief writing materials of people for thousands of years.

CLOAK   A long, loose outer garment worn by men and women (Matthew 5:40).

CLOUD, PILLAR OF   The pillar of cloud which God placed before the children of Israel by day (a pillar of fire by night), to lead them in their journey to the Promised Land. It was also a comforting visible sign of the continuous presence of God (Exodus 13:21, 22).

COMFORTER   A name for the Holy Spirit, given by Jesus in John 14:16, 26. Another translation is "Counselor."

COMMANDMENT   An order given by one in authority. God's commandments are mentioned in the Bible as laws, statutes, testimonies, etc. Moses was given the Ten Commandments by God on tablets of stone (Exodus 24:12).

CONQUEST OF CANAAN   This refers to the occupation of the land of Canaan when the Children of Israel reached the land promised by God to the descendants of Abraham.

CONSECRATE   To dedicate or devote completely to a specific purpose or service to God.

CONVERSION (A turning to)   A complete about face. In the Bible, usually a turning from false gods to the true God.

COPPER   The most important metal of Old Testament times. It was used in making cups, knives, and many useful and ornamental articles.

CLOAK

CORBAN   An offering dedicated to God, therefore not available for any other use (Mark 7:11).

CORINTH   About 40 miles west of Athens and next after it the most important ancient city of Greece. Paul visited there several times and established a church. Later he wrote several letters to this Christian company.

CORN   A word used to denote the seeds of any of the grains used for food, such as wheat, barley, millet, beans, lentils.

CORNELIUS   A Roman centurion known for his piety and good works. He was the first Gentile convert and was baptized with his family at the command of Peter (Acts 10).

CLOUD, PILLAR OF

CORNERSTONE   A stone at the front angle of the foundation of a wall or building. It was very important as it helped bind together the sides of the structure.

COUNSEL   Advice, as when the young Rehoboam sought counsel from the old men who had been with his father, Solomon (II Chronicles 10:6).

COURT   An open enclosure surrounded by buildings or rooms; often applied to the Temple courts (Psalm 100:4).

CORNERSTONE

COVENANT   A solemn agreement between parties. The Israelites entered into a covenant with God as a means of gaining God's protection (Exodus 34:10). This is spoken of as the Old Covenant, from which we get the name Old Testament for the first part of our Bible. The New Covenant or New Testament is God's promise for salvation to those who believe in Christ and accept him as Savior (I Corinthians 11:25).

COVET   To desire earnestly to possess something which may belong to someone else.

COURT

CREATION   The bringing into existence of something which did not previously exist. The Bible states that God is the Creator of all things, but it does not give details as to the method of creation (Genesis 1).

CROSS   An instrument of execution for criminals used by Phoenicians, Egyptians, Greeks, Romans, and others. The death of Jesus on a cross is told in the Gospel narratives.

CROSS

CROWN

CROWN OF THORNS

CRUSE

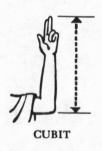

CUBIT

CUNEIFORM WRITING

CROWN   Worn as a symbol of royalty or of high distinction. Victors in the games of Greece were awarded wreaths of laurel or soft branches for their ability (I Corinthians 9:25).

CROWN OF THORNS   Jesus wore a crown of thorns interwoven and placed upon his head in mockery by the Roman soldiers just before his crucifixion.

CRUCIFIXION   A method of capital punishment in the early days. See: Cross. The victim was fastened to a cross by nails driven through hands and feet, and the cross was lifted up and dropped upright in a hole in the ground. Jesus was put to death on Calvary by crucifixion.

CRUSE   A small jar or bottle for holding liquids, such as water, oil, honey.

CUBIT   A measure of length, being the distance from a man's elbow to the tip of his middle finger, or approximately 18 inches.

CUNEIFORM WRITING (Wedge-shaped)   Writing recorded on wet clay tablets by pressing with a stylus of wedge-shaped reed, wood, or bone. The tablets were then baked hard. Many have been preserved to this day, and when deciphered have given much information about peoples and times of long ago.

CUPBEARER   An officer of high rank and importance, whose responsibility was to test the wines, and then to fill the king's cup and present it to him (Nehemiah 1:11-2:1).

CURSE   An utterance calling on Deity to condemn or destroy (Numbers 22:12). The curse was approved and used in Old Testament times. Jesus spoke against it, however, and said, "Bless them that curse you" (Luke 6:28).

CYMBALS   A percussion musical instrument. As used in the Temple worship of David's time, cymbals were round, flat or nearly flat plates of bronze. One plate was fastened to each hand and the two were struck together to accent the rhythm of the music. Cymbals were also used as musical accompaniment for dances.

CYPRUS   A large island in the Mediterranean Sea, about 150 miles northwest of Palestine. The island is about 140 miles long and 60 miles wide, shaped like a fist with the forefinger pointing to the east. On his first missionary journey Paul and Barnabas went across Cyprus preaching in several places (Acts 13).

CYRUS   Founder of the Persian Empire, the largest empire of the world up to that time. After Cyrus conquered Babylonia he encouraged and aided the captive Jews to return to Jerusalem (Ezra 1:1-8)

D

DAMASCUS   Located northeast of Palestine, Damascus was the capital and chief city of Syria and a great trading center. It was while en route to Damascus that Paul had his vision and became a believer in Jesus (Acts 9:1-9).

DANCING   Dancing as mentioned in the Bible was usually part of a religious rite, although it was at times an expression of great joy such as in celebrations of victory.

DANIEL   A young Jew carried as captive to Babylon. According to the narratives in the book of the same name, Daniel had many experiences which showed his trust in God. His example brought comfort and hope to his people in their dark hour of captivity (The Book of Daniel).

DATE   Fruit of the date palm, highly prized as an article of food in Bible times.

DAVID   David was born in Bethlehem, the son of Jesse, and was an ancestor of Jesus, who, centuries later, was also born in Bethlehem. David was the second king of the Hebrew kingdom. Soon after he was anointed king at Hebron he took possession of Jerusalem and made it the capital city. He unified and successfully administered the affairs of the kingdom until it became one of the greatest of ancient times.

DAVID, CITY OF   Jerusalem was called the city of David because he seized it from the Jebusites and made it the capital city of the Hebrew nation.

DAVID, STAR OF   This symbol consists of two equilateral triangles, one over the other, to produce a six-pointed star.

DAY   The Hebrews reckoned a day from sunrise to sunset which they roughly divided into morning, noonday, and evening.

DAYSPRING   Dawn; the first light of day. Also used to indicate the beginning of a new era (Job 38:12; Luke 1:78).

DEACON   An official in the early church whose responsibility was to care for the poor and needy in Christian communities.

DEAD SEA   This body of water, also called the Salt Sea, lies about ¼ mile below sea level. It has no outlet, and so all water flowing in to it can escape only through evaporation. The salt content of the water is five times more than that of the ocean. Fish cannot live in it, and a person will float upon it.

DEBTOR   One who owes a debt, which may be money or an obligation.

DECALOGUE   See: Ten Commandments.

CUPBEARER

CYMBALS

CYPRUS

DANCING

DATE

DAVID, STAR OF

DAYSPRING

DEAD SEA

DESERT

DECAPOLIS Ten cities of Greek population, southeast of the Sea of Galilee, allied for defence against hostile Jews.

DECREE An order from an emperor, political leader, or other person in authority.

DEDICATION The public rite of devoting a place of worship, a shrine, or other structure to a particular purpose.

DEDICATION, FEAST OF A Jewish feast to commemorate the reconsecration of the Jerusalem Temple under Judas Maccabaeus in 165 B.C., after it had been desecrated by foreigners. The festival is perpetuated by Jews today in the Hanukkah, a joyous holiday sometimes spoken of as "The Feast of Lights."

DEFILE To make ceremonially unclean.

DEMON Demons in Bible times were spirits considered responsible for the presence of disease, insanity, and evil in human beings.

DESERT Wild, uninhabited, dry, unproductive country.

DEUTERONOMY (The Second Law) The fifth book of the Old Testament and last book of the Pentateuch. The book contains a re-statement of laws mentioned in other parts of Scripture and they are here attributed to Moses the great Lawgiver. It is believed that a portion of Deuteronomy was the "Book of the Law" (II Kings 22:8) dramatically found in the Temple. Read II Kings 21 and 22.

DEVIL An evil spirit; Satan, the chief of demons; the adversary; the personification of evil.

DEVOUT Religious; spiritually devoted.

DISCIPLE (Learner) People who follow the thinking of another. In the New Testament all those who believed in Jesus and wanted to learn his teachings were considered disciples. See: Apostles.

DISPERSION The Jews who left Palestine and were scattered in distant countries, especially those who were deported to Assyria and Babylonia and who chose to remain there, or to go elsewhere when the majority returned to the homeland.

DONKEY A small tough animal used to carry loads and to ride upon.

DORCAS A Christian woman of Joppa in the early church, who was noted for her kindness to the poor and those in need (Acts 9:36).

DOWRY Money or the equivalent paid to the parents of a bride-to-be as a compensation for the loss of the daughter.

DUNGEON   A dim gloomy room usually underground, to hold prisoners.

DYEING   The Hebrews excelled in this craft, and made use of dyed garments for ordinary wear as well as for ceremonial purposes. They obtained colors from certain shellfish, from bark, plants, and minerals.

DONKEY

E

EAGLE   A very large bird of prey, noted for its strength, keenness of sight, speed, flying range, and ability to attain great height.

EBONY   A hard black, lasting wood from tropical Asia and Africa. It will take a very fine polish.

EDEN, GARDEN OF   A very beautiful fertile region which (according to the Bible story of creation) was the first dwelling place of man (Genesis 2).

EGYPT   A large and very fertile country, southwest of Palestine, through which flows the river Nile. It was to Egypt that the sons of Jacob went for food in a time of famine. To Egypt fled Joseph and Mary and the infant Jesus to escape from King Herod, and there they remained until the king died (Matthew 3:14, 15).

DUNGEON

ELDER   An official title among the early Hebrews for the older and more experienced persons of position and influence in community affairs. In the early Christian church the elders had pastoral supervision of the newly formed groups of believers.

ELIJAH   A remarkable stern prophet of the 9th century B.C. He fearlessly interpreted the will of God to the people in a difficult period of their history.

ELISHA   The young man on whom the prophet Elijah threw his cloak as a sign that Elisha was to carry on with the aged prophet's mission.

EAGLE

ELIZABETH   The mother of John the Baptist and a relative of Mary the mother of Jesus.

EMBALMING   A process practiced by the Egyptians to preserve from decay the bodies of the dead.

EMERALD   A precious stone of a rich green color. One of the stones on the high priest's breastplate. See: Breastplate

EMMANUEL   See: Immanuel.

EMMAUS   A village about 7 miles west of Jerusalem, to which two of Jesus' disciples were walking after the resurrection when Jesus joined them, went to their home for supper, and made himself known to them as the risen Lord (Luke 24:13-35).

ENGINE

EPHOD

EPISTLES

ESDRAELON

FAN

ENCAMPMENT   The resting place for an army or company of travelers. The Bible refers to the places where the Children of Israel stopped on their way from Egypt to Canaan.

ENGINE   In Bible times this was a machine of war used to hurl missiles at the attackers of a besieged town.

EPHAH   A measure of capacity, approximately a bushel.

EPHOD   An apron-like garment worn under the breastplate of the high priest.

EPISTLES   Letters. Most of the New Testament books are letters written by Paul to some of the churches he had started. The letters contain doctrinal instruction, comments on Christian conduct, and pastoral advice.

ESAU   The twin brother of Jacob and slightly the older. Esau traded his rights and privileges as an older son to his brother for a dish of thick soup (Genesis 25:29-34).

ESDRAELON   An extensive and fertile plain in northern Palestine. Through it the caravans passed, and on it were fought many historic battles.

ESSENES   A very early brotherhood or monastic order, the members of which lived most strictly as they aspired to purity and closer communion with God.

ESTHER   A beautiful Jewish woman, queen of a Persian king, who interceded with the king to prevent wholesale slaughter of her people. Her story is told in the Old Testament book that bears her name.

ETERNAL LIFE   Everlasting. But eternal life means more than mere duration; it includes the quality of life that is in harmony with God's eternal purpose for man.

ETHIOPIA   A country in Africa, southeast of Egypt, known to the Hebrews as Cush.

EUPHRATES   A great river nearly 1800 miles long, far to the east of Palestine and serving as the western boundary of Babylonia. At one time the Hebrew Kingdom extended to the Euphrates (II Samuel 8:3).

EVANGELIST   One who proclaims good news. This name was given in the New Testament to men who went from place to place preaching the Gospel.

EVE (Hebrew word meaning "life")   In the Bible story of creation Eve was the first woman, and the name was given her by Adam because she was the mother of all living persons (Genesis 3:20).

EVIL   Bad; wrong; the opposite of good.

EXALT   To raise up; glorify; speak highly of.

EXILE   The period of captivity when the deported Hebrews (an estimated 50,000 of them) lived in Assyria and Babylonia. It began in 597 B.C. and lasted about 50 years; but many of the Hebrews never returned.

EXCOMMUNICATE   Literally, to expel from fellowship. To remove from church membership, and so to forbid the privileges of the Sacraments.

EXODUS (Going out)   The name given to the journey of the children of Israel from Egypt to the Promised Land of Canaan, under the leadership of Moses (about 1200 B.C.). The story is told in the Old Testament Book of Exodus.

EXORCIST   One who claimed to have power to drive out evil spirits by using strange procedures known only to himself. See: Sorcerer.

EZEKIEL   A prophet in Jerusalem who was taken to Babylon at the time of the captivity (597 B.C.). There he did much to encourage his people and help them to retain contact with the Hebrew religious ideal and with its ceremonies.

EZRA   A Jewish priest in Babylon who led a group of 1500 of his people back to Jerusalem to restore the Jewish religious life and state there. The account of his work is given in the Old Testament Book of Ezra.

FARTHING

FERTILE
CRESCENT

F

FAMINE   A period when crops fail and there is very little food.

FAN   A wooden fork or shovel used on the threshing floor to toss grain into the air so that the wind may blow away the chaff and leave the clean grain. See: Winnowing.

FARTHING   A coin of small value in New Testament times, worth somewhat less than one cent.

FASTING   To go without food for an unusual length of time. This was considered by some a discipline pleasing to God because of the hardship involved. When entered upon freely it was considered as having spiritual value.

FATHOM   A measure of depth of water, about six feet.

FEAR OF THE LORD   An expression used in the Bible to indicate reverence and awe when considering the holiness of God.

FEASTS AND FESTIVALS   Important happy occasions in the religious life of the Hebrews, usually to commemorate some important event in their history, or to recognize some significant season or event of the year.

FETTERS

FIGS

95

FIRMAMENT

FLOCK

FOOTMAN

FOUNTAIN

FELIX   Governor of Judea, before whom Paul was taken for trial at Caesarea (Acts 24).

FERTILE CRESCENT, THE   A widely used term to indicate the semicircle of fertile country around the Arabian Desert, beginning with the area of the Tigris and Euphrates Rivers, and extending northwest across Syria and down through Phoenicia and Palestine.

FETTERS   Two bands connected with a short chain, used to fasten the feet so that a person can take only very short steps, and so cannot run away.

FIGS   The pear-shaped fruit of the fig tree; much used in Palestine for food.

FIRE   Considered by Israel as a purifying agent; also represented as a symbol of God's presence and power.

FIRMAMENT   The vault or circle of the sky above us; the heavens. That area above the earth in which God put the sun, moon, and stars (Genesis 1).

FIRST-BORN   The oldest child. The oldest son became the head of the family at the father's death, and received a double portion of the father's estate.

FIRST FRUIT   The Hebrew law required that the first of the fruits should be offered in God's house as acknowledgment that God was the giver of all things.

FISHING   Catching fish for food in Palestine was a common occupation. This was done mostly with nets.

FLOCK   A herd of sheep.

FLOOD   This word is identified with the flood of Noah's day when, according to the story, God sent the deluge to destroy mankind because of their wickedness, saving only Noah and his family (Genesis 6:5-8).

FOOL   One lacking in wisdom and sound judgment.

FOOTMAN   A messenger who ran alongside a chariot to serve the one occupying it. The term footmen is also used to indicate soldiers on foot in contrast to those on horse or in chariots.

FORERUNNER (The meaning of a Greek word signifying "one who goes before")   John the Baptist was called the forerunner of Jesus because he went before Jesus to prepare people for his coming (Matthew 3:11).

FOUNTAIN   A spring of water gushing up out of the ground, as compared with a cistern or a dug well.

FOWL   A general word used in the Bible to indicate any and all kinds of birds.

FOWLER A man who hunts birds, snaring them with a slip cord to entangle their feet and also using a net.

FRANKINCENSE A sweet-scented gummy substance which exudes from certain trees. It is imported from Arabia and India and was used by the Hebrews in worship to make fragrant smoke at the altar (Matthew 2:11).

FRANKINCENSE

FRINGES Borders of twined cord fastened to the edges of garments worn by the children of Israel as a reminder to keep all the commandments of the Lord.

FRONTLETS, OR PHYLACTERIES Strips of parchment on which were written four passages of Scripture, one of which is Exodus 13:2-10. These were then rolled up and put in two leather cases or boxes about 1½ inches on a side and fastened one on the upper left arm and the other on the forehead.

FURLONG A measure of distance; about 600 feet.

FURNACES An enclosure for fire, used for purposes of baking bread or pottery, and also for melting ores.

FRINGES

G

GABRIEL An angel sent as messenger to Mary informing her that she was to become the mother of a son who would be great and do much for his people ('Luke 1:26-33).

GALATIA A Roman province in Asia Minor, northwest of Palestine, where Paul preached and started Christian churches.

GALATIANS, EPISTLE OF PAUL TO THE The first two chapters give the earliest firsthand account of the beginnings of Christianity, and include a vigorous statement by Paul as to his right to be considered an apostle (Chapters 1, 2). The remaining chapters answer some of the Jewish Christians who insisted that Gentiles who would become Christians must do so through obedience to the Mosaic Law. For Paul, Christ had redeemed all men where they were.

FRONTLETS

GALILEE The northern section of Palestine, extending from the Jordan River to the Mediterranean Sea. Jesus spent most of his life in this area.

GALILEE, SEA OF This Sea is on the eastern border of the province of Galilee, and is fed by the Jordan River. It is in the shape of a heart about 13 miles long and 6 miles broad. The Sea of Galilee is about 700 feet below the level of the ocean. It is surrounded by lofty hills, which account for sudden and violent storms.

GALILEE, SEA OF

GATE

GLEANING

GOAD

GOLIATH

GALL   A very bitter tasting herb.

GATE   The gate was an opening in a city wall, with heavy doors which were closed at night and in times of danger or crisis. The open space on the inside was often a gathering place for the people, for the public markets, for men who administered justice, and for others who just came to observe, and discuss public affairs.

GAZA   One of the principal cities of the Philistines in southern Palestine. It was the Temple here in Gaza which Samson destroyed (Judges 16:21-30).

GENERATION   This word usually signified the sum total of people living at the time of speaking. In the plural, it meant ancestors for a long time back, or descendants for many years to come.

GENESIS (Beginning)   The first book of the Bible. It tells the Hebrew story of the beginning of the earth and life upon it.

GENTILES   All people not Hebrews. The Christian Gospel was taken to the Gentile world chiefly by Paul, who was the great missionary to the Gentiles.

GERIZIM   A high mountain in Samaria, the middle province of Palestine. It was the site of the Samaritan temple built after the Captivity as a rival to the Temple in Jerusalem.

GETHSEMANE   A garden at the foot of the Mount of Olives outside Jerusalem, where Jesus went with his disciples to pray after their last supper together. Here it was that Jesus was betrayed by Judas and was seized by the soldiers and led away for trial.

GIANT   A man of unusual size and strength. In Old Testament times a race of giants inhabited Philistia on the shore of the Mediterranean Sea just west of Judea. The giant foe of the Israelites, Goliath, killed by the boy David, was one of these.

GIBEAH   The home of Saul, the first king of Israel.

GIDEON   One of the judges of Israel, who stirred his people to defend themselves against invaders who plundered the country (Judges 7).

GILGAL   The place where the Children of Israel first encamped in the land of Canaan after crossing the Jordan. Here were set up the 12 stones taken from the bed of the river (Joshua 4:20). Gilgal was where Saul was made king (I Samuel 11:15).

GLEANING   The act of gathering the fruit of trees or of grain in the field after the crop had been harvested. This was a privilege reserved for the poor.

GLORIFY   To exalt or praise highly. A term used in the Bible with reference to God.

GLORY Splendor of a very high order; a high degree of quality and character, usually with reference to God (Luke 2:9; Acts 22:6-11).

GOAD (OX-GOAD) A pole with a sharp point for the purpose of pricking the oxen to make them move faster.

GOD The Creator and Maintainer of the universe; the Supreme Being above all created beings and things.

GRANARY

GODLESS Without God, usually through indifference; living and acting without reference to God and so living wickedly.

GODLY The godly are those who try to understand and do the will of God.

GOLGOTHA (Skull) The place outside Jerusalem where Jesus was crucified (John 19:20; Hebrews 13:12). See: Calvary.

GOLIATH A famous giant from Gath, over 9 feet tall, who defied the armies of Israel. He was challenged by David the shepherd boy and was killed by a stone from his slingshot (I Samuel 17).

GRAPES

GOSHEN The name of that part of Egypt along the Nile where Jacob and his family settled when they came at the call of Joseph in time of famine (Gen. 46:28).

GOSPEL The Gospel is the "Good News" about Christ, the Kingdom of God, and the plan of salvation of men's lives which God has made possible through the life and death of Jesus Christ.

GOSPELS, THE These are the four written histories of Jesus Christ, namely, Matthew, Mark, Luke, John, as found in the New Testament. They bear witness to the Gospel message as they serve to make Jesus and his teaching known.

GRASSHOPPER

GOVERNOR A term used to designate a person responsible for something special and important, such as: the head of a tribe, an officer in the king's court, a dispenser of justice. In the time of Christ Rome appointed a governor to rule over Judea.

GRACE The favorable disposition and blessing of God bestowed upon man, even though he may be entirely unworthy and lacking in merit. Such grace is the outright gift of God to undeserving man.

GRANARY A place for storing threshed grain.

GRAPES Grapes grew plentifully in Palestine and were an important food, either eaten fresh from the stems or dried as raisins. Sometimes the juice was boiled down to a honey-like jelly and eaten with bread, but usually the juice was made into wine.

HANDMAIDEN

99

HARP

GRASSHOPPERS or LOCUSTS A destructive pest. They often travel in immense swarms and alight on vegetation and devour it completely.

GRAVEN Carved or engraved with a sharp tool, as on stones, gold, silver, and precious stones.

H

HALLELUJAH (Hallel, praise; jah, Yahweh) An expression found at the beginning or ending of some of the psalms, urging the worshippers to join in praising Yahweh (God) (Psalms 106, 111-113).

HALLOW To make holy. "Hallowed be Thy name" means "May Thy name be regarded as holy, or sacred."

HANDMAIDEN A female servant or attendant.

HARP The harp of Bible times was a small easily carried musical instrument, usually with 8 or 10 strings stretched on a frame and played with the fingers. It was a favorite instrument among the Jews to accompany joyous songs.

HART A male deer.

HART

HATTIN, HORNS OF A two-pointed hill near the Sea of Galilee, said by tradition to be the place where Jesus met the multitudes and taught them, including the Sermon on the Mount (Matthew 5:1).

HEATHEN A word applied to the people and nations who did not worship the God of Israel.

HEAVEN The upper area of the universe. In the Old Testament the Hebrews divided heaven into 3 parts: the lower, where clouds are; the firmament, in which are the sun, moon, and stars; and the upper, the dwelling-place of God and His angels, where the children of God go after death.

HEAVEN

HEBREW (From a word meaning beyond, on the other side) Abram was first called a Hebrew probably because he and his family had come from the other side of the Euphrates (Genesis 14:13). The Hebrews may have originated with the Aramean Semites on the eastern edge of the Arabian desert.

HEBRON A very old city of Palestine, about 20 miles southwest of Jerusalem, and closely associated with early narratives of the Hebrews. For more than 7 years Hebron was the capital city of David, until he captured Jerusalem.

HELMET

HELL   A word used for the place of the dead, without indicating whether or not a place of happiness or misery. The sentence in the Apostle's Creed, "He (Jesus) descended into hell," would therefore mean that Jesus passed into the experience of death. Traditionally the word has been regarded as the place of the condemned wicked after death.

HELMET   A metal head covering to protect from injury in battle.

HERALD   One who speaks for king or other official in a public proclamation.

HERALD

HERD   A group of cattle, such as: oxen, camels, horses.

HERDSMEN   Men who keep or tend cattle, sheep, etc.

HERITAGE   Something valuable passed on to heirs, as from parents to children.

HERMON   The highest mountain (9050 feet) in Syria on the northern boundary of Palestine, whose snow-covered peak all the year made it an important landmark for the Hebrews.

HEROD THE GREAT   The ruler of Judea at the time Jesus was born.

HERD

HEXATEUCH (Six books)   The first six books of the Bible. This includes the Pentateuch (Five books) plus the Book of Joshua which is closely related, being the final stage of the Hebrew conquest.

HEZEKIAH   One of the best kings of Judah, who did much to purify the Temple worship and to strengthen the kingdom.

HIGH PLACES   From earliest times it has been customary for nations to erect places of worship on lofty and prominent spots. The Hebrews followed this same policy, tearing down the signs of idolatrous and heathen worship and devoting the places to the worship of the Hebrew God.

HIGH PRIEST   The spiritual head of the Hebrew congregation and the highest authority in religious matters.

HERMON

HIRAM   The king of Tyre, north of Galilee, who sent workmen, and lumber from the forests of Lebanon, to King David for his palace in Jerusalem and later to King Solomon for the Temple (II Samuel 5:11, I Kings 5:1).

HIRELING   Any lowly servant who worked for pay.

HOLY OF HOLIES   A curtained room at the end of the Tabernacle which contained only the Ark of the Covenant, the symbol of God's presence with the Israelites. No one but the High Priest entered this most holy place, and then only once a year on the Day of Atonement.

HIGH PRIEST

HOLY OF HOLIES

HOLY Separated, set apart, because of being saintly or divine, as "Holy, Holy, Holy, is the Lord God Almighty, who was and is and is to come" (Revelation 4:8).

HOLY SPIRIT One of the manifestations of God in the Trinity, whereby He has fellowship with men, entering into their spiritual experiences, rebuking, inspiring, illumining. After Jesus' death, in some mysterious way, the Holy Spirit was to serve as Helper (John 14:16), as Teacher (14:26), to man.

HOMER A Hebrew measure of capacity, approximately 11 bushels.

HONEY Honey, whether from wild bees or domestic, was abundant in Palestine. It was relished as food and it was sometimes used in the making of cakes, as sugar was unknown (Exodus 16:31).

HOREB, MOUNT Another name for Mt. Sinai, at the foot of which the Israelites encamped for a while, and where Moses received the revelation of the Ten Commandments.

HOSANNA A Hebrew word meaning "Save now," used in the liturgy of the Temple worship. It was also used by the multitude as a greeting at the time of Jesus' Triumphal Entry into Jerusalem (Matthew 21:9).

HOSPITALITY

HOSEA An eighth century prophet. The main emphasis of his message was the forgiving love of God toward man.

HOSPITALITY Hospitality ranked high as a characteristic virtue in Bible times. Strangers as well as guests were welcome, and elaborate measures were taken to minister to their comfort. A first step was to bathe and wipe the hot and dusty feet of guests as they entered the house.

HOST A large number, as of stars (Deuteronomy 4:19), or an army (Genesis 21:22). God is spoken of as the Lord of hosts (I Samuel 17:45) because He was the leader of the armies of Israel.

HOUSE

HOUSE The houses of the poorer people in Bible Lands were usually made of sun-baked mud bricks and were one story in height. Sometimes an enclosed room was built on the flat roof as a guest chamber. The family lived on the raised section of the one-room house and the domestic animals were allowed in the lower part.

HUSBANDMAN A word used in the Bible for a farmer.

HUSKS The sweet pods of the locust tree, probably, which were used for feeding cattle and pigs (Luke 15:16).

HUSBANDMAN

HYMNS   The Psalms were the hymns used in the Hebrew Temple. In New Testament times and since, a variety of compositions have been used by Christians in the worship of God to express spiritual aspirations and to affirm the Christian way of living. A hymnbook today is a good cross-section of spiritual and doctrinal thinking over the centuries, as well as the expression of spiritual ideas and experiences of different groups and individuals.

HYPOCRITE   One who pretends to be what he is not. Jesus sternly denounced those who were insincere in their religious professions (Matthew 6:2, 5, 16).

HYSSOP   A common plant in Palestine having certain cleansing and healing properties.

HUSKS

I

HYSSOP

IDOL   The representation of a person or creature used as the object of worship.

IDOLATRY   The worship of idols.

IMAGES   A likeness, either artistic or offensive, usually representing a human form or an animal or some object, real or imagined.

IMMANUEL (A Hebrew word; Greek, Emmanuel, "God is with us")   The name of a child whom the prophet Isaiah said would be born to a young woman as a sign that God was with Judah (Isaiah 7:14). Because he was with them, the nations threatening Judah would be made desolate before the young child grew to years of maturity (Is. 7:1-16).

IMMORTALITY   Continued existence by man even though he passes through the experience of physical death.

IDOL

INCARNATION (Latin, incarnatio, "to be made flesh")   The Incarnation took place when the Son of God became man in a true human body (John 1:14).

INCENSE   Gums and spices which burned with a fragrant odor, used as a part of the ritual of worship in the Tabernacle and the Temple.

INHERITANCE   See: Heritage.

INIQUITY   Sin or wrongdoing; wicked opposition to the will of God.

INN   A shelter along a road for the lodging of man and beast.

IDOLATRY

103

INCENSE

INN

JACKAL

JACOB'S WELL

INSPIRATION   The action of the Holy Spirit on the minds and hearts of men resulting in a divine revelation and the understanding of divine truth.

INTERCESSION   Speaking on the behalf of another; prayer.

IRON   One of the earlier known metals in Palestine; found plentifully there and used extensively (Deuteronomy 8:9).

ISAIAH   Generally regarded as the greatest of the Hebrew prophets. He enjoyed the confidence of the kings of Judah and spoke of God's will concerning the kingdom and concerning individuals. A book of the Old Testament bears his name.

ISRAEL   The name given to Jacob after he wrestled with the man at the river. It was used to designate the peoples of the twelve tribes and later to include the whole company of Hebrews (Genesis 32:22-32).

ISRAELITE   A descendant of Jacob; any Jew.

IVORY   A hard, white substance taken from the tusks of elephants, hippopotami, and walruses. Used for making delicately carved ornamental objects and for inlay and veneer work on furniture.

J

JACKAL   An animal of the dog family about the size of a fox.

JACOB   Son of Isaac and Rebekah. After wrestling with the man by the river he was renamed "Israel" (Genesis 32:28). Jacob with his sons and their families went to Egypt in a time of famine and remained there (Genesis 46). Jacob had 12 sons, whose households later became the twelve tribes of Israel.

JACOB'S WELL   A very deep well, near the ancient Shechem, probably dug by Jacob. This well was the scene of Jesus' conversation with a Samaritan woman (John 4:5-12).

JAR   A tall container of earthenware used to hold water, oil, and grain.

JASPER   A precious stone radiant and clear as crystal (Revelation 21:11).

JAVELIN   A short light spear intended to be hurled at the enemy.

JEBUS   One of the names of Jerusalem before it was captured by David.

JEHOVAH   One of the Hebrew words for God was YHWH, probably pronounced "Yahweh." Out of reverence for this name, the Jews would not speak it aloud but would use the word "Adonai" (Lord) instead, or "Elohim" (God). Later, vowels were taken from these 2 latter words and were added to the 4 consonants to make the word J(Y)EHOV(W)AH.

JEREMIAH   One of the great prophets of the Hebrews, who lived a century after Isaiah, and was present at the capture and destruction of Jerusalem, 586 B.C.

JERICHO   The ancient city in the Jordan Valley, 5 miles north of the Dead Sea, first to be captured by the Israelites when they entered the Promised Land.

JERUSALEM   This hill city (elevation 2500 feet), the most important town of Palestine, was wrested from the Jebusites by King David and made the capital city of the Israelites. Today it is the capital city of Jews throughout the world. It is the holy city of three world religions, namely Judaism, Christianity, and Islam.

JESUS CHRIST   "Jesus" is our Lord's personal name. "Christ" is his title — the Christ, the anointed one. However, this latter name is commonly used as a proper name either alone or with the name "Jesus."

JEW   Originally this word was used after the time of David and Solomon for a member of the tribe or kingdom of Judah; later it came to mean any member of that race.

JEWELRY   From earliest times articles for personal adornment seem to have been worn. These have included, as with primitive man, ornaments of shell and bone. Later, all sorts of rings, bracelets, amulets, pendants, etc., made of precious stones and metals, were common.

JOHN THE BAPTIST   The man who baptized Jesus. A man of great spiritual strength, he was known as the forerunner of Jesus, the one sent to prepare the way for the coming of the Messiah (Mark 1:1-8).

JONATHAN   The oldest son of King Saul and a very close friend of David, even though Jonathan knew that David was to occupy his father's throne instead of himself.

JORDAN RIVER   The largest and most important river in Palestine. It rises far to the north in the foothills of Mt. Hermon and flows southward more than 100 miles, through Lake Huleh and the Sea of Galilee, descending 3000 feet rapidly until it empties into the Dead Sea 1292 feet below sea level.

JOSHUA   One of Moses' righthand men on the journey from Egypt to Canaan, and the one chosen to succeed Moses after the latter's death on Mt. Nebo.

JAR

JAVELIN

JEHOVAH

JEWELRY

B.C.   EARLY CHRISTIAN

JOT

JOSHUA, BOOK OF   The account of Joshua's leadership of the Israelites and their varied experiences from the crossing of the Jordan to the occupation of Canaan.

JOT   English form of the smallest letter (iota) in the Greek alphabet. Used figuratively to denote the very smallest trifle (Matthew 5:18). See: Tittle.

JOURNEY, A DAY'S   Estimated at four to eight hours' walk, or about 25 miles. This was the unit by which people referred to the distances they traveled. A Sabbath day's journey was limited to 1000 yards. See: Sabbath Day's Journey.

JUBILEE, YEAR OF   Every 50th year was the year of Jubilee, and it was proclaimed by the blowing of trumpets on the Day of Atonement. All Hebrews who were in bondage to their own countrymen were to be set free, and those who had sold their inherited possessions because of poverty had them restored.

JUBILEE,
YEAR OF

JUDAH   The fourth son of Jacob, whose descendants became the tribe of Judah. Later, parts of other tribes joined with them to become the Kingdom of Judah, occupying the greater part of southern Palestine.

JUDAS ISCARIOT   The disciple who betrayed his Master for 30 pieces of silver.

JUDGES   In the early days of the Israelites in Palestine, judges were older men who assumed leadership in times of emergencies, such as an attack by outsiders. The immediate danger passed, the communities naturally looked to these same men for leadership when regular government was lacking.

K

KINE

KIDRON   A valley that borders the eastern slope of Jerusalem, separating it from the Mount of Olives. Jesus and his disciples crossed this valley on their way to Gethsemane (John 18:1).

KINE   Cattle.

KINGDOM   The territory or people ruled over by a king.

KINGDOM OF GOD
KINGDOM OF HEAVEN   These two terms mean the same. Jesus thought of God as father rather than as king, and so the Kingdom of God is really the family of God living together in the spirit of the loving Father.

KINSMEN   Male members of the same family line or race; relatives.

KNIVES

106

KNIVES   In the early days, the Hebrews had knives of shaped flint, although by the time of the Exile they used knives with metal blades.

LAMB

L

LAMB   A very young sheep. Lambs without defects were used as sacrifices for the sins of the people.

LAMB OF GOD   A term used by John the Baptist to denote Jesus, because Jesus was to be sacrificed for a guilt not his own (John 1:29).

LAMENTATION   Wailing and loud cries of grief.

LAMENTATIONS, BOOK OF   A book in the Old Testament containing 5 poems of mourning over the fate of Jerusalem after it was captured in 586 B.C. (II Kings 25).

LAMP   Vessels of clay or of metal to hold oil, from which a wick extended for lighting. Sometimes these lamps were very small to carry in the hand, with an additional supply of oil in a bottle hanging on a string from a finger (Matthew 25:1-13).

LAMP

LATCHET   A narrow leather strap or thong which fastened a sandal to the foot (Luke 3:16).

LAVER   A metal vessel containing water for the priests to wash their hands in before offering a sacrifice. This washing symbolized the holiness required in the service of God.

LAW   In the Bible, law refers to the elaborate system of legislation among the Hebrews, and it covers almost every situation affecting man in relation to others. Much law was established by Moses, but other codes were added later. The first five books of the Bible are commonly spoken of as the Books of the Law.

LATCHET

LAYING ON OF HANDS   An act indicating the bestowing of a blessing, or dedication to a special purpose.

LEATHER   Prepared from skins of sheep and other animals. Used for shoes, clothing, belts, thongs, bottles, shields, helmets, etc. Specially treated skins were used as writing material.

LEAVEN   Something added to dough to cause fermentation and make it rise.

LEBANON (White)   A snow-capped mountain range (about 6000 feet) at the north of Palestine; famous for its beauty, its fruitfulness, and its splendid cedar trees, used for the construction of furniture and buildings (I Kings 5:6).

LAVER

LEBANON CEDAR

LENTIL

LILY

LINTEL

LEGION A division of the Roman army consisting of about 6000 men. The word, however, was commonly used to mean any large number of persons.

LENTIL A plant which bears bean-like seeds that can be boiled for food.

LEPROSY A fearful and loathesome skin disease. In Jesus' day a leper was considered unclean and he was required to live apart from other people. Today medical science knows that this is not necessary, and that the disease can, in many instances, be cured or greatly relieved.

LEVI The third son of Jacob. The tribe of Levites were the people descended from Levi. While the Israelites were on their journey out of Egypt the Levites were assigned to care for the Tabernacle, setting it up, transporting it, etc., and assisting the priests in the religious ceremonies (Numbers 3).

LEVITICUS The third book of the Old Testament. It consists of various priestly codes and ritualistic regulations, together with narratives which touch upon the observance and infractions of these rules. The Levites were responsible for certain duties in connection with the Tabernacle and Temple.

LIBRARIES Libraries in the East were valuable collections of parchment and papyrus scrolls and clay tablets. Several libraries of about 20,000 clay tablets each, along with smaller ones have been unearthed by excavations in Syria and Mesopotamia. These have consisted of temple records, religious, literary, and scientific works, many of which are invaluable to Biblical scholars.

LIGHT In the Bible, light is associated with the presence of God. See: Fire. Jesus is called the Light of the world (John 1:4-9), and Christians who represent him are said to be "the Light of the world" (Matthew 5:14).

LILY Palestine abounded in bright-colored flowers. It is probable that Jesus referred to these in Matthew 6:28 rather than to any particular variety.

LINTEL The beam across the upper frame of a door (Exodus 12:22).

LIZARD A reptile with a long body, a tail, four legs, and a scaly hide. Lizards of many varieties are very common in Palestine.

LO Look! Behold!

LOAF See: Bread.

LOCUST See: Grasshopper.

LORD The owner of property, or a person in authority. When the word begins with a capital letter it refers to God or to Jesus.

LORD'S DAY, THE   The first day of the week was called the Lord's Day by the early Christians because on that day Jesus rose from the dead. It was also the day they assembled for worship in memory of him. See: Sunday.

LIZARD

LORD'S PRAYER, THE   A prayer given by Jesus to his disciples as a model of the true prayer spirit. The first three sentences of the prayer have to do with God's glory, while the next three are concerned with man's needs. A Doxology not found in the oldest Greek manuscripts was probably added during the first century to make the prayer more useful for public worship. This Doxology, "For Thine is the kingdom, and the power, and the glory, forever. Amen," is included as a footnote only in the American Revised Version and the Revised Standard Version.

LORD'S SUPPER, THE   A symbolic rite and sacrament central in the Christian faith, conducted in memory of the Last Supper Jesus had with his 12 disciples in the upper room at Jerusalem. It is sometimes called "The Holy Communion," "The Eucharist," "The Breaking of Bread" (I Corinthians 11:24).

LORD'S SUPPER

LUKE   A Christian physician and companion of Paul on his second missionary journey. Luke has given us an apparently true account of Jesus' life as he was able to get the facts from eye-witnesses (Luke 1:1-4). He was probably also the author of the Book of Acts, in which he gives us the best picture of the early Christian Church (Acts 1:1).

LXX   This abbreviation, consisting of the Roman numerals for 70, is used to denote the Septuagint (70) or Greek version of the Old Testament. Tradition says that this translation was made by about 70 scholars, hence its name.

LXX

LYDIA   A prosperous business woman in Philippi, northern Greece, who was converted under Paul's preaching and was baptized with her whole household. Lydia was the first convert to Christianity in Europe. Later she gave great assistance to Paul and Silas in spreading the Gospel (Acts 16:14).

LYRE   A musical instrument somewhat resembling a small harp.

M

MACCABEES   A patriotic Jewish family that defied the Syrians under Antiochus Epiphanes, who sought to destroy Judaism. The Maccabees recaptured Jerusalem and cleansed the Temple in 165 B.C. See: Dedication, Feast of.

LYRE

MACEDONIA

MACEDONIA   A country north of Greece in which Paul and Silas spent some time successfully establishing the Gospel; their first missionary work in Europe.

MADNESS   A condition of mental derangement or insanity, explained in Bible times as due to the presence of an evil spirit.

MAGI   Men of a priestly cast from the East, who made a study of astrology and mysterious natural sciences. The appearance of a new star sent them, according to the Gospel narrative (Matthew 2:1), to search for the new-born king of the Jews. They are spoken of as Wise Men.

MAGI

MAGIC   The methods by which primitive people try to bring about certain results by apparently supernatural means.

MAGNIFICAT   The beautiful hymn of praise from the lips of Mary when she realized that she was to become the mother of the Messiah (Luke 1:46-55).

MAGNIFY   To praise very highly (Psalm 34:3).

MALEFACTOR   An evil doer; criminal (Luke 23:32).

MAMMON   A word used in the New Testament to indicate trust in wealth and material things rather than in God (Matthew 6:24).

MAN   The Bible regards man as the greatest of God's creatures on earth, because he possesses some of the qualities of God Himself (Genesis 1:26-28).

MANASSEH   One of the two sons of Joseph. In the assignment of land at the occupation of Canaan, Manasseh's descendants were called the "half tribe of Manasseh."

MANGER

MANGER   An open box or trough from which cattle ate their food. Jesus was born in a manger (Luke 2:7,12).

MANIFOLD   Many and varied kinds.

MANNA   Food which was supplied by God to the Children of Israel while on the journey to Canaan (Exodus 16:14,15).

MANTLE   A loose, sleeveless, outer garment worn in Oriental countries.

MARBLE   Limestone which can be given a high polish. A luxury item used for costly buildings, pillars, and flooring. Marble was one of the materials David provided for the building of the Temple (I Chronicles 29:2).

MANNA

MARK   Companion of Paul and Barnabas on preaching tours. He is probably the author of the Gospel bearing his name; it is believed that he obtained much of the matter for the book from Peter.

MARKET PLACE   An open place or square in a town where merchandise may be bought and sold. Sometimes public trials and other assemblies were held in market places.

MARKET PLACE

MARTHA   The sister of Mary and of Lazarus. The members of this family were much loved friends of Jesus and he enjoyed visiting them (John 11:1-6).

MARTYR   A person of strong religious conviction who accepts death rather than give up his faith.

MARY, THE MOTHER OF JESUS   Mary was a common name in New Testament times, as it is today. This Mary was the wife of Joseph, and together they shared the responsibility of bringing up Jesus in the Jewish faith to fulfill his earthly mission.

MARY MAGDALENE   A woman from the village of Magdala, who was healed by Jesus of mental trouble and physical infirmities, and who became one of his followers (Luke 8:2).

MARTYR

MARY OF BETHANY   Sister of Martha and Lazarus. See: Martha.

MASTER   A word used in the Bible to denote a man of authority, such as the head of a house or the owner of slaves. One of the names by which the disciples addressed Jesus. It is a translation of the Greek word for "teacher."

MATTHEW   One of the twelve apostles, evidently a converted Jewish tax collector originally in the service of Rome. While at his place of business near Capernaum Matthew accepted Jesus' invitation to become his follower (Matthew 9:9).

MATTHIAS   The man chosen by lot to be included with the apostles as the successor to Judas who had betrayed Jesus and committed suicide (Acts 1:21-26).

MATTOCK

MATTOCK   A farm tool something like a short-handled hoe, used for breaking up the soil.

MAUNDY THURSDAY   The day in Holy Week before Good Friday. The word "Maundy" is derived from the Latin word "mandare," to command. It is associated with Jesus' words after the Last Supper, "A new commandment I give unto you" (John 13:34).

MEALS   In New Testament times, among the well-to-do, people while eating reclined on the elbow on couches around a low table. The couches were on two or three sides of the table, leaving the fourth side open for attendants to serve the food.

MEALS

MENORAH

MERCY-SEAT

MEZUZAH

MILL

MEDIATOR   One who works to bring together people who are in disagreement. The Bible is concerned with the bringing together of sinful man and God. In the Old Testament the mediator was the priest; in the New Testament he is Jesus (I Timothy 2:5).

MEDITERRANEAN SEA   The body of water between Europe and Africa. Palestine had few good harbors, and the Hebrews did not use the Sea much for commerce. Paul, however, on his missionary journeys, sailed to many ports in the northeastern part of the Mediterranean.

MELITA (Malta)   A small island 60 miles south of Sicily in the Mediterranean, on which Paul was shipwrecked, and where, during his enforced stay of 3 months, he performed miracles of healing and probably preached the Gospel to the natives (Acts 28:1-10).

MENORAH   The Hebrew word for the sacred golden candelabrum of the Jewish Temple. Its seven candlesticks symbolize the seven days of creation (Exodus 37:17-24).

MERCY   In the Bible, mercy is the forbearance and loving-kindness of God toward men, even though they are unworthy of His favor (Psalm 23:6; Psalm 106:1).

MERCY-SEAT   This was the cover of the Ark (See: Ark of the Covenant), the symbolic place of God's eternal presence. Once a year, on the Day of Atonement, the high priest entered the Holy of Holies and burned incense, which enveloped the Ark and the Mercy-Seat. This act represented a petition for God's mercy in the sacrifice of atonement for sin.

MERODACH (Marduk)   The chief god of the Babylonians.

MESOPOTAMIA (Between the rivers)   The land enclosed by the Tigris and Euphrates Rivers.

MESSIAH (One anointed)   A Hebrew word denoting anyone anointed with holy oil and set apart for high office. Jesus is called the Messiah because he is believed to be the one sent by God to fulfill the great expectation of the Jews for a Deliverer and Savior.

MEZUZAH (Doorpost)   A small case containing parchment on which is written Deuteronomy 6:4-9 and 11:13-21 and fastened on the outside door frame. This symbol indicated that this family was trying to live up to the ideals of Judaism. Every devout Jew touched the Mezuzah with his fingers on passing through the doorway, and then kissed his fingers in reverence for the words written within the case.

MICAIAH   A prophet who refused to tone down the message of God to please a king (I King 22).

MIDIANITES   Enemies of the Israelites, living east and south of Palestine, who continually harassed them until finally routed and subdued by Gideon (Judges 6-8).

MILETUS   One of the important towns in Asia Minor where Paul preached (Acts 20:13-38).

MILL   Two circular stones, one upon the other, the upper having a handle by which it may be turned back and forth on the lower, or rotated. Grain put in an opening in the center of the upper stone is ground between the stones, and the meal flows out at the edges upon a cloth.

MINISTER   Sometimes called an "attendant." One who voluntarily serves another. Used thus in the Bible particularly in the conduct of religious services in the synagogue and in the early Christian Church (Luke 4:20).

MINSTREL   A musician, especially one who sings accompanied by a musical instrument (II Kings 3:15).

MIRACLES   Wonderful events or effects which cannot be explained by the operation of any known natural forces and laws. Jesus performed miracles as evidence of his love for mankind.

MIRIAM   The older sister of Moses, who watched her brother as a baby in a basket among the reeds of the river, and who suggested her mother as nurse when the baby was discovered by Pharaoh's daughter.

MIRROR   As used in Bible times, a mirror was of metal usually highly polished copper or bronze.

MITE   The smallest piece of money in the time of Jesus; worth perhaps one-fifth of a cent.

MOAB   A country just east of the Dead Sea, sometimes not friendly to the Israelites.

MOABITE STONE   A stone of black basalt, unearthed in Moab in 1868, which is inscribed in a language similar to Hebrew, and which gives events and places which correspond to some Bible passages.

MOLECH   A god of the peoples east of the Jordan in Old Testament times. Worship of him included sacrifices of small children by fire (Leviticus 18:21).

MOLTEN SEA or BRAZEN SEA.   A huge bronze basin in the court of Solomon's Temple intended for the use of priests in washing their hands and feet before approaching the altar (II Chronicles 4:2-6).

MINSTREL

MIRROR

MITE

MOABITE STONE

MOLTEN SEA

113

MONEY

MONEY-
CHANGERS

MOSES

MOTH

MOURNING

MONEY   From the earliest period of their history in Palestine the Hebrews used metal money (gold, silver, copper), but only in uncoined pieces, the value of which was determined by weighing (Genesis 23:16). Coined money began to be used by them only after their return from the Babylonian captivity (6th century B.C.). In New Testament times none but coins of the Roman Empire were recognized by the Roman government.

MONEY-CHANGERS   Money-changers, present everywhere in Palestine, were also located in the Temple to exchange the money of persons coming from far countries for the currency used in the Temple for the Temple tax. Jesus denounced the money-changers because they charged too much for this service (Matthew 21:12-13).

MONOTHEISM   The worship of one God only.

MOON   The farmers of Bible lands depended on the moon to guide them in the time of planting and in determining the time of religious festivals. The new moon marked the beginning of a new month.

MORIAH, MOUNT   The hill on which was located Araunah's threshing-floor, which David bought on which to build an altar to God (II Samuel 24:18-25).

MOSES   One of the great figures of all time. Moses led the undisciplined, wandering multitude of Hebrews from captivity in Egypt to independence in Palestine, and on the way developed in them a spirit of unity. He was the founder of the religion based on one God. He gave his people the Hebrew Law, which continued practically unchanged until the days of Ezra. His discerning wisdom has influenced all legislation, much of which still exists in orthodox Judaism.

MOST HIGH   A name applied to God (Psalm 7:17).

MOTE   A tiny speck of dirt such as might easily get into one's eye (Matthew 7:3-5).

MOTH   A winged insect extremely common throughout Palestine, which, in the caterpillar state, eats and destroys clothing (Job 13:28; Matthew 6:19).

MOURNING   In Bible times grief was expressed publicly by various actions, which included tearing the clothes, shaving the head, sprinkling ashes on the head, fasting, cutting the flesh. Sometimes professional mourners were hired to lament and wail loudly.

MULTITUDE   A large number of people gathered together (Matthew 5:1).

MURRAIN   An infectious disease or plague of cattle.

MUSIC   Music among the Hebrews found its great encouragement in the Temple worship. Here were large choruses under trained musicians, singing antiphonally; that is, one group responding to another in such volume that they were heard afar off (Nehemiah 12:45-47). Stringed, wind, and percussion instruments were often used to accompany the singing.

MUSTARD SEED   A very small seed, which grows rapidly into a bush 12 or 15 feet in height. Its spreading branches provide alighting space for birds, which feed upon its seeds (Matthew 13:32).

MYRRH   A common shrub in Palestine, with fragrant wood and bark. It gives off a yellowish brown gum used as a perfume, in medicine, in anointing oils, in cosmetics, and in preparing bodies for burial. The Wise Men brought myrrh to the babe Jesus (Matthew 2:11).

MYRTLE   An evergreen shrub, the branches of which were used for making booths at the Feast of Tabernacles (Nehemiah 8:15).

MULTITUDE

MUSIC

MUSTARD SEED

N

NAAMAN   A Syrian general afflicted with leprosy. Healed of his disease by Elisha the man of God, he accepted the God of Israel as the only true God in all the earth (II Kings 5).

NAZARETH   A small village in southern Galilee, halfway between the Sea of Galilee and Mt. Carmel on the Mediterranean, where lived Joseph and Mary. Here Jesus grew from boyhood to manhood.

NAZIRITES   Individuals who took a special vow, and were thus set apart to the service of God in a peculiar way for a specified time. The Nazirite did not use intoxicating drinks, did not cut his hair, and did not touch a dead person.

NEBO, MOUNT   A part of Mt. Pisgah across the Jordan from Jericho. At God's command (Deuteronomy 32:49), Moses ascended to view the Promised Land before he died (Deuteronomy 34:1-6).

MYRRH

MYRTLE

NETS

NETTLES

NILE

NOMADS

NEBUCHADNEZZAR   The Babylonian king who captured Jerusalem and deported many Jews to Babylon 597-588 B.C.

NEHEMIAH   A Jew who was cupbearer to the Persian king during the Exile. He persuaded the king to grant him safe conduct back to Jerusalem, with authority to rebuild the city. This he did in spite of considerable opposition there. The account of his activity is in the Old Testament book that bears his name.

NETS   Cords woven into a mesh and used for catching fish and for snaring small animals and birds.

NETTLES   Thorny plants with sharp points or hairs that enter the flesh easily and cause a stinging pain.

NEW MOON   The first day of the new moon, the beginning of the lunar month, was observed as a holy day, with sacrifices, blowing of trumpets, and abstaining from work (Numbers 10:10; Amos 8:5).

NEW TESTAMENT   The New Testament is the second part of our Christian Scriptures, consisting of 27 books. It contains accounts of the life of Jesus and of the beginnings of the Christian church. The writers did not realize that they were contributing to what would be called "The Holy Scriptures" but were desirous of recording and making public the facts about their Lord and what they had done to proclaim his truth and to reveal his will. See: Bible; Covenant.

NICODEMUS   A Pharisee who paid a night visit to Jesus because he was eager to learn more of Jesus' religious ideas.

NIGHT   The Hebrews divided the night into three watches: dark to midnight, midnight to cockcrow, cockcrow to sunrise. In the New Testament the Roman system of 4 watches was used: twilight to 9 o'clock, 9 to midnight, midnight to 3 o'clock (cockcrow), 3 o'clock to dawn (Mark 13:35).

NILE   The great river of Egypt. The rich fertility of the Nile Valley is due to the river overflowing its banks and flooding the lowlands. Rich silt from northeast Africa is deposited on the land, and when the river recedes to its natural bounds the people sow their seed in the new rich soil.

NINEVEH   Capital and chief city of Assyria. Although the city was totally destroyed in 612 B.C. (Zephaniah 2:13-15), excavations have uncovered portions of it. The king had a vast library of 22,000 inscribed clay tablets. Many of these have been removed and translated, and they give us much information regarding the greatness of Nineveh.

116

NOAH   The tenth in descent from Adam. The Bible narrative says that because of the wickedness of man God destroyed by a Flood every living thing he had created, except Noah and his family, for Noah was a righteous man. Two each of all the lesser creatures were spared and went with Noah into the Ark, and so were saved for a new beginning (Genesis 6:11-22).

OAK

NOMADS   Wandering herdsmen and shepherds who went from one grazing plot to another with their flocks. They were tent-dwellers with no established homes.

NUMBERS   The fourth book of the Old Testament. Its name comes from the census of the people recorded in Chapters 1, 3, 4, 26. The book presents narratives and laws covering the 40 years of Israel's desert wanderings.

O

OBEISANCE

OAK   Oak trees, common in Palestine, frequently reach an advanced age. Because they were greatly venerated in Bible times they were sometimes associated with important events or people (Genesis 13:18; I Kings 13:14).

OATH   An appeal to God to affirm the truth of a statement or one's intention to keep a promise.

OBEISANCE   A bowing of the head, bending of the body, or kneeling to denote reverence or worship (Genesis 24:52).

OBLATION   An offering to God, usually not of animals but of flour, fruit, or even land (Leviticus 2:4, 12; Ezekiel 48:9).

OFFERINGS

OFFERINGS   Offerings to God of many kinds were an important part of Jewish worship. Animal sacrifices were required to be free from blemish. The entire animal must be consumed in the fire as an expression of the complete dedication to God of the one making the sacrifice; other sacrifices were for atonement of sin. See: Atonement.

OINTMENT   Ointment of olive oil base, with other ingredients added, was used to heal cuts and bruises of men and animals and to sooth the skin and perfume the body. A holy anointing oil, stated by Moses, was used in the ritualistic services of the Tabernacle and the Temple (Exodus 30:23-25).

OINTMENT

OLIVE TREE

OLD TESTAMENT   The first and oldest part of our Bible, identical in contents with the Hebrew Bible. The 39 books include historical, legal, devotional, wisdom, and prophetic literature dating from more than a thousand years before Christ. The first 5 books of law are the Hebrew Torah. See: Bible; Covenant.

OLIVE
OLIVE TREE   The olive tree was one of the most plentiful and most highly valued trees of Palestine: its shade was a welcome protection from the hot sun; its nut-like fruit was a staple food; and its oil was used in cooking, for lamp fuel, and as a base for ointments.

OLIVES,
MOUNT OF

OLIVES, MOUNT OF   A ridge of hills just east of Jerusalem, separated by the narrow Kidron Valley. On its lower slope was the Garden of Gethsemane. Jesus sometimes went to the Mount of Olives at evening (John 8:1), from which point he could see the Holy City spread before him.

OMEGA   The last letter of the Greek alphabet. See: Alpha.

OMNIPOTENT   All-powerful.

ONESIMUS   A slave belonging to Philemon of Colossae, in Asia Minor. He ran away from his master and as a fugitive in Rome became a Christian under the influence of Paul. Later he returned to his master with a letter from Paul to Philemon asking that Philemon receive him back, not as a runaway slave but as a beloved brother (Epistle of Philemon).

ONYX   A semi-precious stone of the quartz variety having colored lines or veins through it. Collected by David to be used in the building of the Temple by Solomon (1 Chronicles 29:2).

OMEGA

ORACLE   A person or means by which communications were given to man by God. God's will was made known by means of prophets and priests, dreams (I Samuel 28:6), Urim and Thummim (Exodus 28:30), the Holy of Holies (Psalm 28:2).

ORDAIN   To appoint or designate with authority (I Chronicles 9:22).

ORDINATION   The ceremony, called the "laying on of hands," which set men apart for the Christian ministry (Acts 13:2, 3).

OVEN   A device for baking bread. For home use the oven was something like an earthen jar, with an opening at the bottom for the fire. When the oven was heated the thin cakes of dough were laid or stuck against the outside; or the fire might be raked out and the loaves put inside and the opening sealed while hot.

ORDINATION

OX   The animal most used for farm work (I Kings 19:19) and for sacrifices (I Kings 8:63).

OVEN

P

PALESTINE   A small territory at the eastern end of the Mediterranean Sea. It is about 150 miles long from Dan to Beersheba, and averages about 40 miles in width to the Jordan River—smaller than the state of Massachusetts. The name came from *Philistines*, a people who lived along the southern coast line.

PALM TREE   A tall straight tropical tree ending in a crown of large fan-shaped leaves. The fruit of the date palm was highly valued as food in Bible times.

PALSY   Paralysis. A disease which takes away control of muscles to move parts of the body.

PAPYRUS   See: Bulrush.

OX

PARABLE (Placing beside)   A short narrative by which a moral or religious truth is illustrated by comparison with some well-known experience.

PARADISE (A park)   The word is used in Scripture to indicate the dwelling-place of the righteous after this earthly life (Luke 23:43).

PARCHMENT   The skin of sheep or goats prepared for use as writing material.

PARENTAL BLESSING   Both hands of the father were laid on the head of the child as words of blessing were pronounced. This act was highly valued in Bible days as invoking God's favor and bringing happiness and success to the new generation.

PALM TREE

PASCHAL   Having to do with the Passover celebration, or with Easter.

PASSION   The passion of Christ includes his sufferings from the evening of the Last Supper, through the experiences in the Garden of Gethsemane, in his trial, on the journey to the cross, and during the crucifixion.

PASSOVER   One of the great festivals of the Jews, observed about the time of Easter. Its purpose was to commemorate their deliverance from Egyptian bondage, especially the "passing over" of the homes of the Israelites by the destroying angel when the first-born of Egypt were slain.

PAPYRUS

119

PARENTAL
BLESSING

PEN

PENNY

PHARAOH

PASTORAL EPISTLES　　Grouped as the "Pastoral Epistles" are the New Testament books of I and II Timothy, and Titus. These deal with advice to pastors on the qualifications and conduct of church officers and on other pastoral matters.

PATRIARCH　　A general name given to a Bible character who lived before the time of Moses: for example, Abraham, Isaac, Jacob.

PAUL (Hebrew, Saul)　　A Jew who as a young man, persecuted the early Christians but who became a follower of Christ after a vision he had on the road to Damascus. As an apostle, he was a tireless preacher and promoter of the Christian faith, the first Christian missionary, and the author of about half of the books of the New Testament.

PEN　　Early pens for writing with ink were probably made of reeds, whittled with a penknife to a shape suitable for writing (III John 13; Jeremiah 36:23).

PENNY　　This was the Roman denarius, worth about 20 cents in the time of Christ. This sum was a day's wage of a laborer in the time of Christ.

PENTATEUCH (Five books)　　The first five books of the Bible, known as the Law, and called by the Jews the "Torah." See: Law.

PENTECOST　　This was a solemn one-day festival of the Jews mentioned in the Old Testament. The first Christian Pentecost, on the seventh Sunday after the Resurrection, is significant because of the descent of the Holy Spirit upon the Apostles and the birth of the Christian Church (Acts 2). Pentecost, fifty days after Easter, is Whitsunday.

PERSIA　　A small country southeast of Babylonia. By many conquests it grew in power and size until the Persian Empire extended to Egypt and Asia Minor and became the greatest in western Asia.

PESTILENCE　　Any infectious or contagious disease which spreads rapidly and causes great suffering.

PETER　　A fisherman who became a devoted disciple of Jesus and then an apostle. After Jesus' death, Peter became an outstanding leader of the Christian Church. Tradition says that he suffered martyrdom in Rome by being crucified head downward at his own request.

PETITION　　A request or prayer.

PHARAOH　　An honorary title for the ruler of ancient Egypt. In the Bible the Egyptian king is frequently referred to as "Pharaoh" regardless of which king was meant.

PHARISEES (Separated)   The name given to a sect of the Jews in Jesus' day, probably because their strict insistence on observance of the written Law of Moses and on oral tradition, as they interpreted it, seemed to set them apart from other Jews, and certainly from non-Jews.

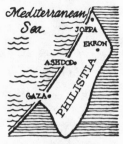

PHILISTIA

PHILEMON   A convert of Paul's, whose runaway slave Onesimus also became a Christian believer under Paul. See: Onesimus.

PHILIPPI   A prominent city in eastern Macedonia. To Philippi Paul went immediately after receiving in a vision the invitation "Come over to Macedonia and help us." This city was the first on the continent of Europe to receive the Christian Gospel (Acts 16).

PHILISTIA   The strip of coast-land along the Mediterranean from Joppa to Gaza, extending inland for 15 miles.

PHILISTINES   The inhabitants of Philistia. They were rivals and enemies of the Israelites, who entered Canaan from the east about the time the Philistines landed in the west.

PHOENICIA

PHOENICIA   The coastal section of Palestine north from Mount Carmel and west of Galilee. The inhabitants, a seafaring people, were fairly highly cultivated. From them came the alphabet, which was the basis for the letters of Hebrews, Greeks, and Europeans.

PHYLACTERIES   See: Frontlets.

PILATE   Governor of Judea, before whom Jesus was tried, scourged, and finally delivered up to be crucified (John 18:28–19:16).

PILGRIMAGE   A journey, usually long, to a religious shrine or holy place by a group of devoted persons.

PHYLACTERIES

PINNACLE   The summit or highest point of the Temple.

PIPE   A wind instrument of reed or wood to produce musical sounds by blowing into one end of it or into a hole in the side. It was in common use by shepherds to call their sheep and by musicians on many joyous or mournful occasions.

PISGAH   A part of Mount Nebo; the mountain from which Moses viewed the Promised Land just before his death. See: Nebo.

PIT   A large deep hole in the ground.

PILGRIMAGE

PINNACLE

PIPE

PIT

PITCHER

PLOW

PITCHER A tall jar of earthenware with one or two handles, used for holding, carrying, and pouring water, wine, and oil.

PLAGUE An affliction or pestilence, very common in Old Testament times especially, considered as being sent by God. The Ten Plagues of Egypt are recorded in Exodus as being visited upon the Egyptians in order that the Pharaoh might let the Israelites go free. See: Pestilence.

PLEDGES A man's personal property given as security for a debt or a promise.

PLOW
PLOWSHARE The plow is a farming implement or tool for turning over the soil in preparation for planting. In primitive days a large long piece of tough wood, sharpened at the end, covered with metal, was used. This dug into the ground as the plow was dragged forward.

POETRY There is much poetry in the Bible, but only in the newer translations is it indicated by the printed form. One of the main characteristics of Hebrew poetry is parallelism; that is, the first line makes a statement and the second line adds to the first idea or states a contrast (Job 3:17; Proverbs 10:11; Psalm 8:4).

POLYTHEISM Belief in more than one god; the opposite of Monotheism.

POMEGRANATE A delicious tropical fruit the size of a small orange (Song of Solomon 8:2).

PORTER The keeper of a city gate, or a doorkeeper in a house or especially the Temple (II Chronicles 23:4).

POST 1. A runner or swift messenger (Esther 3:13). 2. The upright timber (sometimes stone) on the side of a doorway (Deut. 11:20).

POTIPHAR The captain of the Pharaoh's bodyguard who bought the boy Joseph from the Ishmaelites when they brought him down to Egypt (Genesis 39:1).

POTTAGE A stew made of lentils, a plant of the pea family, flavored with other vegetables (Genesis 25:27-34).

POTTER One who made pottery.

POTTER'S WHEEL A horizontal wheel, turned by hand or foot, used by the potter. The clay was put on the revolving wheel, and while in motion it was shaped by the skilful hand of the potter (Jeremiah 18:3).

122

PRAISE To glorify or speak highly of; for example, to glorify or praise God.

PRAYER Prayer is communing with God. It includes confession of wrong doing, giving thanks, praise, making requests on behalf of others or one's self and listening to God.

PRECEPT A commandment, or instruction, or rule intended to improve conduct.

POMEGRANATE

PRESS A machine or device for pressing the juice out of fruit, such as grapes or olives. The press might be a hollowed stone with a hole near the bottom of one side out of which the juice escaped, or it might be a vat. With grapes, the juice was pressed out when barefooted persons trod on the bunches; with olives, a large round stone was rolled over the fruit to break it up.

PRIEST A person appointed or ordained to officiate in religious ceremonies, Jewish or Christian, to perform religious rites, to give moral and religious instruction, and to reveal the will of God.

PRINCE As used in the Bible, not necessarily one of royal descent but a man in a position of authority, such as the head of a tribe, or captain of a body of men; a chieftain.

PRIVILY In a private manner.

POST

PROCURATOR One appointed by the Roman Emperor and directly responsible to him to administer affairs in some part of the empire; often the governor of a province where trouble was present or expected. Some procurators of Judea mentioned in the New Testament are Pontius Pilate, Felix, Festus.

PRODIGAL One who foolishly wastes his money or possessions. Jesus told the parable of the loving father who received back his repentant prodigal son (Luke 15:11-32).

POTTER

PROPHET (Hebrew, one who speaks for another) The Hebrew prophet was not so much a foreteller of what was to occur as he was a "forth-teller" of the will of God, although both ideas might be included in his message. The prophet was a man who felt himself called of God to preach and to speak fearlessly for Him.

PROPHETESS A woman prophet.

PROPHETS, MAJOR These include Isaiah, Jeremiah, and Ezekiel, whose writings consist of utterances of warning and counsel, and incidents in the lives of the three prophets.

PRESS

PRIEST

PRUNINGHOOK

PUBLICAN

PURSE

PROPHETS, MINOR   These twelve prophets are not minor in the importance of their message but only in the brevity of their writing. They are: Amos, Hosea, Micah, Zephaniah, Nahum, Habakkuk, Haggai, Zechariah, Malachi, Obadiah, Joel, Jonah.

PROSELYTE   A person who has been converted or won over from one faith to another.

PROVERB   A short saying expressed in vivid, easily remembered language; a maxim.

PROVERBS, BOOK OF   One of the books of the Old Testament which is a collection of various collections of proverbs, many of which are attributed to Solomon; some to others. The proverbs are bits of wise comment based on keen observations of people and of daily life.

PROVINCES   Geographical divisions of a country made for the purposes of administration.

PRUNINGHOOK   A pole with a curved blade on the end, used to cut off suckers and branches from fruit trees.

PSALMS, BOOK OF   A collection of religious poems used as hymns for the Temple services. The authors of many of the Psalms are unknown, although the name of David is associated with a large number of them. Many of them probably represent Temple hymns which grew out of the religious life of the Jews over a considerable period of time and were brought together as the "Psalms of David" because of his musical gifts and his great contributions to the services of the Temple.

PSALTER   The Book of Psalms. Also a selection of Psalms arranged in a book for church services.

PSALTERY   A favorite musical instrument of the Jews to accompany joyous songs. It was a small stringed instrument, somewhat like a zither or a lyre, the strings of which were plucked with the fingers.

PUBLICAN   In New Testament times, an agent of the Roman governor of Judea employed to collect the Imperial taxes. All that the collector could squeeze from the people above a fixed amount he kept for himself; and so he was hated and treated with contempt.

PULSE   A vegetable something like peas and beans.

PURGE   To cleanse of impurities.

PURIFICATION   A ritualistic observance which cleared a person from the taint of ceremonial uncleanness; such as the house of a leper, a mother after childbirth, the touching of a dead body.

124

PURIM, FEAST OF   A joyous Jewish Festival (March 14 and 15) to commemorate the deliverance of Jews exiled in Persia from wholesale massacre as planned by Haman, chief minister and favorite of the Persian king (Esther 7).

PURSE   A small leather bag or pouch, frequently carried in the girdle and used to hold money. Merchants used such bags for carrying their stone weights for weighing.

QUAIL

Q

QUAIL   A small bird belonging to the partridge family. The Israelites on their journey to Canaan found quail provided by God for food (Exodus 16:13).

QUARTERNION   A squad of four Roman soldiers. Peter was once guarded by four quarternions (Acts 12:4).

QUIVER   A case for holding and carrying arrows.

QUARTERNION

R

RABBI
RABBONI   A term of respect used to address learned men and meaning "Master" or "Teacher." "Rabboni" implies a little more respect than Rabbi. Jesus was addressed both as Rabbi and Rabboni (John 3:2; 20:16).

RACA   Worthless, good-for-nothing! An expression of contempt (Matthew 5:22).

RACHEL   Wife of Jacob and mother of Joseph and Benjamin (Genesis 29:28).

RAIMENT   Clothing, usually of linen or of wool; coarser fabrics of goats' or camels' hair.

RAINBOW   After the Flood God chose the rainbow to be the symbol of His merciful promise that never again would he destroy the earth by flood (Genesis 9:11-17).

RAISINS   Grapes dried in the sun. They were preserved in clusters or were pressed into cakes to keep for food.

RAM   A male sheep. From the ram's horn was made the shophar, a kind of trumpet used to sound signals in battle or at sacred festivals; still used in Jewish synagogues.

QUIVER

RAINBOW

RAM

REAPER

REED

REND

RAMESES   A treasure-city in Egypt built, as was Pithom, by Hebrew slave labor (Exodus 1:11). It was from Rameses that the Israelites set forth on the Exodus from Egypt (Exodus 12:37).

REAPER   One who harvests grain in the field.

REBEKAH   Wife of the patriarch Isaac and mother of Esau and Jacob (Genesis 25:24-26).

RECEIPT OF CUSTOM   The collector's office where people under Roman rule paid their taxes (Matthew 9:9); called also "the place of toll."

RECONCILIATION   Return to harmony after a separation caused by difference of ideas. In the Bible, sinful man has been separated from the righteous God. The Jewish system of sacrifices was planned to bring about this reconciliation with God. In the Christian religion it is through Christ that reconciliation is obtained (II Corinthians 5:18).

REDEEMER   One who sets free, buys back, delivers, or saves. This title is used for Jesus, who came to redeem people from sin and spiritual bondage and to restore them to sonship with God (Titus 2:14).

REED   Any of the tall grasses which grow along low-lying streams. They were used to thatch houses and cover roofs. From tall vigorous reeds with their hollow stalks crude musical pipes were fashioned.

REFINING   The process of separating pure metal from other substances found with it by the use of fire.

REFUGE   A place of safety. Six cities in the early days of the Hebrews in Palestine were set apart as Cities of Refuge. To any one of these a person who had accidentally killed another might flee for safety and receive a fair trial (Numbers 35:9-15).

REHOBOAM   A son of Solomon and the last king of the united monarchy of David and Solomon (I Kings 14:21).

REMISSION   Taking away; forgiving.

REMNANT   Something that remains; a term used to denote that portion of the Jewish people who survived the disastrous experiences of the Exile and remained true to God (Isaiah 10:20-22).

REND   To rip or tear apart violently.

REPENTANT   To feel sorry for something done or not done; to regret very deeply. In the Bible, repentance means forsaking wrongdoing and following God's will completely; it is a condition of salvation (Luke 13:3).

126

RESTITUTION   What is done by an offender to make good for an injury he has caused another.

RESURRECTION   The return of the dead to life. Belief in the resurrection of Jesus after his body was placed in the tomb was central in the faith of the early Christians, as it is with Christians today. This belief is the basis of faith in life after death (I Corinthians 15:12-19).

ROD, SHEPHERD'S

REUBEN   The oldest of Jacob's twelve sons. It was Reuben who persuaded his brothers not to kill Joseph but to put him in a pit from which he might rescue the boy later (Genesis 37:22).

REVELATION, BOOK OF THE   The last book of the Bible. It tells of the bitter conflict between good and evil, and reveals the ultimate triumph of Christ and his Kingdom. The purpose of the book was to give encouragement to faithful Christians in the days of terrible persecution.

ROLL

RIGHTEOUS   Upright; free from wrong in such matters as justice, kindness, sincerity, unselfishness, etc. God alone is righteous; men may only strive to be so.

RITUAL   A carefully prepared style and order of words for use in the conduct of a formal service, such as public worship.

ROD, SHEPHERD'S   A word sometimes used interchangeably with "staff." Usually, however, a rod was a stout club about three feet long with a bulging joint at the end used to strike down wolves when they attacked the sheep.

RUNNERS

ROLL   A book or scroll of ancient times consisted of a long strip of papyrus or parchment, each end of which was fastened to a roller. As one read the book it was unrolled from one roller and wound upon the other.

ROMAN EMPIRE   The expanding Roman Empire extended to include Palestine about 63 A.D. Palestine was ruled by governors and procurators during the lifetime of Jesus, as it was an occupied country.

ROME   The famous capital city of the mighty Roman Empire. At his own request, the apostle Paul was sent to Rome for trial. The early Christians, here persecuted by Roman emperors, sought refuge in the vaults and galleries of the underground quarries of Rome, known as the "catacombs," and here also they buried their dead.

SACKCLOTH

ROOFS The flat roofs of Palestinian houses provided space for recreation, sleeping, drying grain, spinning and weaving, even for the building of a guest room (II Kings 4:10).

RUNNERS Men who went ahead of the king's chariot to test the road or to arrange for improving it (II Samuel 15:1). Runners also brought back reports of the king's battles and ran errands (II Samuel 18:19).

SANDAL

RUTH A young woman of Moab whose Jewish husband died. She went with her sorrowing mother-in-law to Bethlehem, and there met Boaz and married him. Their first child was Obed, who became the grandfather of King David.

SCAPEGOAT

S

SABAOTH, LORD GOD OF Refers to God as the Lord of all the forces operating in His universe.

SABBATH (Day of rest) In the Jews' calendar the seventh day of the week (from Friday evening to Saturday evening), appointed in the fourth Commandment (Exodus 20:8) to be observed as a day of rest as the symbol of the covenant between the children of Israel and God (Exodus 31:12-17).

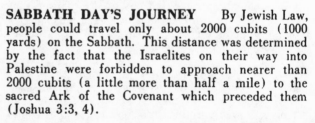

SABBATH DAY'S JOURNEY By Jewish Law, people could travel only about 2000 cubits (1000 yards) on the Sabbath. This distance was determined by the fact that the Israelites on their way into Palestine were forbidden to approach nearer than 2000 cubits (a little more than half a mile) to the sacred Ark of the Covenant which preceded them (Joshua 3:3, 4).

SCEPTER

SACKCLOTH Coarsely woven cloth made of the hair of goats and of camels, and worn as a sign of mourning (Genesis 37:34).

SACRAMENT A religious ceremony in which a certain visible act, accompanied by faith, is believed to impart the blessing of God upon the one who shares in it. The two sacraments of the Protestant church are those authorized by Jesus himself, Baptism, and the Lord's Supper.

SACRIFICE To give up something. In Bible days, offerings were made on altars for the purpose of asking forgiveness of God, for thanksgiving, and for praise.

SCHOOL

SADDUCEES A conservative religious party among the Jews who held that only the written Law was binding. They did not accept oral traditions or the body of interpretation which the Pharisees had developed to supplement the Law.

SAINTS Persons of great holiness and religious devotion (Ephesians 1:1).

SAMARITANS People who lived in Samaria. At the time of the Exile many people from Samaria were carried into Assyria, and from Assyria a variety of colonists were brought to Samaria. The Samaritans were therefore a racially mixed people, scorned by the pure-blooded Jews of Galilee and Judea. They acknowledged as binding only the first five books of the Old Testament.

SAMSON One of the Judges who did good service to Israel by welding the people into a more united group and by defending them from outside foes. His life story, Judges 13-16, seems presented as a series of colorful tales.

SAMUEL The last of the judges of the Israelites, Samuel was also a prophet of God. When the people demanded a king, Samuel selected the young man Saul and anointed him king, a choice later confirmed by the people (I Samuel 10:1, 24).

SAMUEL, I AND II Originally one book called Samuel. The books tell of the Hebrew Monarchy under the leadership of Samuel, Saul, and David.

SANCTUARY A holy place set apart, as for the worship of God; a church. In some Christian churches the enclosure around the altar is called the sanctuary, and it is set apart as an especially holy place for those who serve there.

SANDAL A leather or wooden sole fastened to the foot by a leather thong or shoe latchet (Mark 1:7).

SANHEDRIN The highest judicial council and supreme court of the Jews.

SARAH The wife of Abraham and the mother of Isaac.

SARGON The king of Assyria who captured Samaria and deported many of the people to his own land. The ruins of his high palace have been uncovered and much information gained of that period (II Kings 17:5, 6).

SAUL The first king of the Israelites. His reign brought the Hebrew tribes closer together and paved the way for David, the next king.

SCOURGE

SCRIBE

SCRIP

SCROLLS, THE DEAD SEA

SEAL

SAVIOR   A term applied to Jesus because of his redeeming work in saving people from their sins (Luke 2:11; Luke 19:10).

SCAPEGOAT   At the observance of the Day of Atonement the priest would lay both his hands upon the head of a goat and confess over him all the sins of the people. Then he would send the goat away into the wilderness, thus symbolizing the carrying away of the sins of the people by God (Leviticus 16:20-22).

SCEPTER   A short staff held by a king as the symbol of authority. In the Persian court no one could approach the throne unless the king extended his scepter as a sign of invitation (Esther 4:11).

SCHOOL   In early Bible times mothers and fathers were teachers of their children in the home. After the Exile and in the time of Jesus the synagogue provided a school for the boys; girls were instructed in the home.

SEPULCHRE

SCOURGE   A whip of cords or thongs fastened to a handle, sometimes with pieces of metal attached, or with knots, used as punishment for wrongdoers, and for those who had offended the authorities (II Corinthians 11:24).

SCRIBE   A public letter writer, or copyist, employed by people who could not write.

SCRIBES, THE   A group of people who copied the sacred Scriptures, and interpreted and taught them.

SCRIP   A small leather bag in which shepherds and travelers carried their food or other necessities (I Samuel 17:40).

SCRIPTURE (Writing)   A word used by the Jews to indicate their sacred writings and by Christians for the Old and New Testaments.

SCROLL   See: Roll; Books.

SHEAF

SCROLLS, THE DEAD SEA   A collection of a dozen scrolls of very old manuscripts discovered in the spring of 1947 in a cave near the northwest end of the Dead Sea. Included in the rolls was a practically complete Hebrew manuscript of Isaiah written about the second century B.C., the oldest existing manuscript of this, or any other, Bible book.

SEAL   A device of precious or ordinary stone bearing a design for printing an impression on clay or wax. The impression made was also called a seal. Used to give official sanction to papers, or to protect shipments of grain, wine, olive oil, etc., from being opened by unauthorized persons.

SHEEPFOLD

SELAH A word found only in the poetical books of the Bible, chiefly in the Psalms. Of uncertain meaning, but apparently a Hebrew liturgical or musical direction; possibly an indication of pause.

SENNACHERIB A powerful, boastful Assyrian king whose armies laid waste Judea and besieged Jerusalem (II Kings 18 and 19).

SEPTUAGINT A Greek translation of the Hebrew Old Testament, made at Alexandria in Egypt, probably in the 3rd century B.C. Jesus must have been familiar with this version. It was the Bible of the Christian Church of the first century.

SEPULCHRE A tomb, usually cut out of rock, with the entrance closed by a large rock.

SERMON ON THE MOUNT Some teachings of Jesus given to the disciples on a mountain (Matthew 5:1). It deals with the qualities which are in the true follower, and with the ideal life which he should live.

SHEAF A bundle of grain tied together.

SHEEPFOLD A safe enclosure of stones where sheep were kept at night.

SHEEPGATE An entrance in the wall of Jerusalem through which the animals were taken to the Temple area for sacrifice.

SHEKEL A Jewish silver coin worth about 65 cents; the gold shekel was worth about $10.

SHEMA A Jewish statement of faith, made up of 3 passages in the Old Testament, beginning with Deuteronomy 6:4-9.

SHEWBREAD Twelve large loaves of unleavened bread, corresponding to the twelve tribes of Israel, renewed each Sabbath and placed in two piles on a table in the Tabernacle and the Temple as a symbol of gratitude to God.

SHOES In Old Testament times these were usually simple sandals with a single leather sole bound to the feet with leather thongs. See: Sandal.

SHOPHAR A trumpet made of a ram's horn, used by the Hebrews to sound alarms and to summon to worship in the Tabernacle and the Temple. See: Ram.

SHRINES Sacred places with small images in silver or marble and terra cotta of a god or goddess as a mark of respect and reverence.

SHEKEL

SHEWBREAD

SHOPHAR

SIEGE

131

SILOAM, POOL OF

SIEGE The placing of an army around a city or a fortified place to make it surrender as a result of attack or blockade.

SILAS A companion of Paul on his second missionary journey.

SILOAM, POOL OF
SILOAM, TUNNEL The Siloam Tunnel (1700 feet long) was built in the 8th century B.C. by King Hezekiah to ensure a water supply for Jerusalem in case of a siege. The tunnel supplied water from a spring outside the city to the Pool inside (II Kings 20:20).

SIN Whatever man thinks or does that is contrary to the will of God.

SINAI, MOUNT The mountain where Moses talked with God and received the Ten Commandments (Exodus 20:1-17); sometimes called Mt. Horeb.

SINAI, MOUNT

SLEEPING MAT A long pad or mattress of straw, rushes, or softer material which was spread upon the floor to sleep on. In the daytime it was rolled up and put away.

SLING A weapon of warfare. It usually consisted of a long strip of leather wide at the middle part or of a piece of leather with 2 strings attached to opposite sides. A stone was put in and whirled around the head. When one string was let go the stone went forward with great force. David killed Goliath with a sling (I Samuel 17:40, 48, 49).

SLUGGARD A habitually lazy or indolent person.

SLING

SNARE A trap made by looping a cord to catch birds and small animals by the feet.

SOJOURN, THE This usually refers to the period when the Israelites were in bondage in Egypt (Genesis 15:13).

SOJOURNER A term usually applied to a person not born a Hebrew but living among Israelites on friendly terms.

SOLOMON A son of David and the 3rd king of Israel. Solomon built the Temple and developed the kingdom to its greatest extent. He had a reputation for wealth and wisdom.

SON OF MAN A term used in the Old Testament to indicate a human being. In the New Testament Jesus uses these words to refer to himself (Mark 2:10, 28).

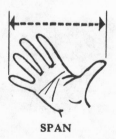

SPAN

SONG OF ASCENTS
SONG OF DEGREES   The Psalms from 120 through 134. These were sung by pilgrims as they ascended the hill to Jerusalem to attend the yearly festivals there.

SONS OF GOD   This expression usually refers to those who are worshippers of God, and who conscientiously strive to live in faith, obedience, and love toward Him.

SOOTHSAYER   A person claiming special power to reveal knowledge not commonly available to everyone (Daniel 2:2).

SOP   In order to gather up the more liquid portion of a meal a thin piece of bread was used as a spoon to dip into a stew or the juice of meat. It was an indication of friendship for several persons to dip the sop into the same dish. Judas made a show of friendship by dipping into the same dish with Jesus (Matthew 26:23).

SORCERER   One who assumes that he possesses supernatural power through the assistance or control of evil spirits.

SOUL   The soul is the individual person who lives in the material body, as in a house and is the life of it; it is that part of man which is immortal and which continues to exist even after the physical body dies and decays. As spirit, the soul draws its life from God (Acts 17:28).

SPAN   A Hebrew unit of measurement, the distance from the tip of the thumb to the tip of the little finger when the hand is expanded — nearly 9 inches.

SPICES   Vegetable substances with fragrant odor and sharp flavor, used for seasoning food, for making cosmetics and ointments, for incense, and in preparation of bodies for burial (Mark 14:1-9).

SPIKENARD   A fragrant plant used in making very expensive perfumes and ointments (John 12:3).

STABLE   A shelter for housing and feeding donkeys and cattle. The stable where Jesus was born in Bethlehem may have been below the guest quarters of the inn.

STAFF   A stick about 6 feet long, used by shepherds in mountain climbing, for leaning upon, and to guide sheep over difficult paths. On entering the fold at night the sheep were "rodded," that is, made to pass under the rod to be counted (Leviticus 27:32).

SPIKENARD

STABLE

STAFF

STEPHEN

STOVES

SUPERSCRIPTION

SWADDLING

SWINE

SYNAGOGUE

STEPHEN   The first follower of Jesus Christ to die as a martyr for his faith. His death led to the conversion of Paul (Acts 7:58-60).

STEWARD   An overseer or person in charge of a large household, as Joseph was for Potiphar (Genesis 39:4).

STONING   Stoning to death was a form of capital punishment declared in the Hebrew Law.

STOVES   Usually made of clay in Bible times. A lower section was for the fire; above there was a lid or other device for holding the cooking vessel.

STRAW   Stalks of grain chopped up into small pieces and used as food for cattle, donkeys, and horses; also used in making bricks to bind the clay together.

SUFFER   To endure pain; also to permit or allow.

SUNDAY   Very early in the Christian Era the first day of the week came to be observed by the followers of Jesus because it was on a Sunday that his Resurrection took place. Each recurring Sunday, therefore, was of special significance to them. Gradually for Christians Sunday took the place of the Jewish Sabbath.

SUPERSCRIPTION (Writing above)   Words written above or upon something, as on a coin (Matthew 22:20), or above the head of one crucified, as above the head of Jesus (Matthew 27:37).

SWADDLING   The method of wrapping up newborn and very young babies. The baby was placed diagonally upon a square piece of cloth and the corners were folded over the body and the feet and under the head. Then the whole bundle was wrapped around with bands of cotton or of silk (Luke 2:7).

SWINE   Pigs. Regarded as unclean by the Hebrews and its flesh unfit for food (Leviticus 11:7).

SYCHAR   A town in Samaria near the land Jacob gave to Joseph. Sychar was where Jesus talked with the Samaritan woman at Jacob's well (John 4:5-26).

SYNAGOGUE   Both a religious congregation and a place of instruction and worship for Jews. While in exile, the Jews were unable to worship in the Temple at Jerusalem, and so they provided lesser places for study and prayer. Upon their return to the homeland they continued to use synagogues, going to the Temple only on the Festival days.

SYNOPTIC GOSPELS Matthew, Mark, and Luke. These three gospel writers seem to have obtained much of their material from the same sources, since they have much in common. The fourth Gospel, John, weaves into his narratives considerable religious interpretations and theology not found in the synoptics.

TABERNACLE

T

TABERNACLE A large movable tent sanctuary which the Israelites used as a place of worship while on their journey from Egypt to Palestine (Exodus 25:1-9).

TABERNACLES, FEAST OF See: Booths, Feast of.

TABLES OF THE LAW The stone tablets on which were written the Ten Commandments which were given to Moses, according to the Bible narrative (Exodus 24:12).

TABLES OF
THE LAW

TABRET A musical instrument like a tambourine or small one-headed hand drum with metal jingles (Genesis 31:27).

TALENT Both a unit of weight and of money. The Hebrew gold talent was worth about $32,640; a silver talent, about $2176.

TALMUD The Talmud is a body of interpretation and commentary on the written Law of the Jews.

TANNER A man who converts skins into leather.

TABRET

TANNING The process of dressing animal skins and converting them into leather.

TARES A poisonous weed closely resembling wheat in appearance until it is fully ripe, when it can be easily recognized and weeded out (Matthew 13:24-30).

TARSUS The large capital city of the Roman province of Cilicia, in Asia Minor, which was the birthplace of Paul (Acts 22:3).

TARES

TAX In New Testament days Rome placed a tax on certain essential commodities such as meat, salt, etc., and on land.

TAX COLLECTOR A man who collected taxes for Rome. See: Publican.

TEMPLE The imposing building of the Jews in Jerusalem for the worship of God. Three Temples have stood on the same site: Solomon's Temple; the Temple of Zerubbabel, built on the return from the Exile; and Herod's Temple, which was the Temple Jesus knew.

TEMPLE

TENTS

TEN COMMANDMENTS, THE   These, as recorded in Exodus 20:3-17, were given by God to Moses on Mount Sinai, who wrote them on two tablets of stone (Exodus 34:27, 28).

TENTS   Tents were made of goats'-hair cloth, a rough, strong dark color fabric.

TERAPHIM   Images of different sizes, commonly small, regarded as household gods; probably thought to possess magical powers.

TESTAMENT   A solemn agreement or covenant. See: Covenant.

TERAPHIM

TESTIMONY   A statement to establish a fact, as that of a witness in court.

THANK OFFERING   An offering to express gratitude to God.

THESSALONICA   A large and important ancient city in Macedonia, capital of the province. Here Paul founded a Christian church. Two letters which he wrote to this church, after leaving the city, are included in the books of the New Testament.

THONG   A narrow strip of leather used to hold a sandal on the foot.

THONG

THRESHING   The process of separating grain from the stalk either by beating the sheaves with a stick while they are spread out on the ground, or if the quantity is large, by driving over it several oxen yoked together and dragging a threshing sledge (Jeremiah 51:33).

THRONE   The seat of a ruling monarch. Sometimes the word signifies royal power rather than a definite seat (II Samuel 3:10).

THRESHING

TIDINGS   News; a message. "Good Tidings" (Luke 2:10).

TILLING   Plowing and preparing the soil for planting.

TIMBREL   A musical instrument like a small tambourine. A tabret.

TIMOTHY   A young Christian, native of Lystra, who was a beloved assistant and companion of Paul on several of his preaching tours.

THRONE

TITHE   A very ancient custom (Genesis 14:20) of giving a tenth part of one's income to God as an expression of thankfulness (Luke 18:12).

TITTLE   A very small mark used in Hebrew writing and printing to distinguish one letter from another. Jesus mentioned it to designate something very small. See: Jot.

TONGUE   Commonly used in the Bible to denote a spoken language.

TONGUES OF FIRE   An expression used to describe the marvelous experience when the Holy Spirit came upon the disciples on the Day of Pentecost (Acts 2:1-21).

TILLING

TORAH   The Jewish Book of the Law: The Pentateuch, or first five books of the Old Testament.

TRANSFIGURATION   A supernatural experience which came to Peter, James, and John, with Jesus on a high mountain. The experience served to increase the confidence and faith of the three in their Lord.

TRANSGRESSION   Something that is done contrary to the law of man or of God; a sin.

TRESPASS   To go on someone else's property. To go beyond the limits of what is right or lawful or just; to sin.

TIMBREL

TRIBE   A group of persons or families descended from a single ancestor, held together by blood ties, and governed by one man regarded as the father. The twelve tribes of Jacob were the families of Jacob's twelve sons.

TRIBULATION   Trouble.

TRIBUTE   Tax of one sort or another (Luke 20:22).

TWELVE, THE   See: Apostle.

TYRE   An important seaport in Phoenicia on the northwest coast of Palestine, famous for its purple dye. It was the home of King Hiram, friend of David and of Solomon, and from him they obtained materials and helpers in constructing David's palace and Solomon's Temple in Jerusalem.

TONGUES OF FIRE

U

UNLEAVENED BREAD   Bread made without yeast.

UPPER ROOM, THE   The large furnished room, chosen by Jesus in which to eat his last Passover with his disciples, was probably on the second floor of a good-sized Jerusalem house (Luke 22:12).

TORAH

137

USURER

USURER   The man who lends money for interest.

USURY   Interest paid on borrowed money.

UTTERMOST   Farthest; to the greatest degree.

V

VALE

VALE   A valley; a ravine.

VEIL   A fabric used by women to conceal their face. Also used by shepherds and farmers to protect the head and neck from the sun's rays. In the Tabernacle and Temple the Holy of Holies was separated from the Holy Place by a large hanging veil. It was this veil in the Temple that was "rent" at the Crucifixion of Jesus (Mark 15:38).

VENGEANCE   Punishment against one who has caused an injury or wrong.

VERILY   Truly.

VEIL

VESSELS   Containers in which food was cooked or kept, such as the bronze and earthen ones used in the home. For the Temple rituals, vessels of gold, silver, and bronze were used (I Chronicles 18:10).

VIA DOLOROSA (The way of sorrow)   A steep, narrow street in Jerusalem. Tradition says that this was the route taken by Christ while bearing his cross from Pilate's judgment hall to Golgotha, the place of his Crucifixion (John 19:17).

VESSELS

VINE   Any slender plant that trails on the ground or climbs some supporting device by means of tendrils. Several kinds of vine are mentioned in the Bible, particularly the grapevine (John 15:1-8).

VINEYARD   A place where grapes are grown. Because of its favorable climate, Palestine from earliest times was a land of countless vineyards.

VISION   Something believed to be real presented to the mind in pictorial form through sleep, trance, or some emotional stimulus. God sometimes spoke to the prophets and holy men through visions (Isaiah 6; Amos 7:7; Acts 10:3).

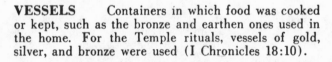

VOW   A solemn promise. In the Bible, a vow to God was a sort of pledge in which a person bound himself to do something if God would grant a special favor (Genesis 28:20, 21).

VINE

138

VULGATE   A famous and important Latin translation of the Bible made by Jerome in the 4th century. For a thousand years it was the standard Bible of the Middle Ages.

VINEYARD

W

WALLET   See: Bag; Scrip.

WASH   The washing of hands before eating was considered very important, as a tradition of old time (Mark 7:3). Besides, everyone put a hand in the common dish of stew or meat. A good host, moreover, made certain that the feet of a guest were bathed on arrival as an act of courtesy and refreshment to the traveler (Luke 7:36-50).

WATCHES OF THE NIGHT   During the Roman occupation of Palestine the Jews recognized four watches of three hours each in the night; they were designated as "even," "midnight," "cock-crowing," and "morning" (Mark 13:35).

WATERPOTS

WATERPOTS   Earthen jars that could be easily borne on head or shoulder were used for carrying water from wells or streams to the house. These were emptied into the large stone waterpots used for storing water (John 2:6).

WAYFARING MAN   A traveler, such as a merchant, metal smith, or ordinary wanderer.

WEDDING   The celebration that accompanied a marriage was a very joyous and festive occasion, lasting perhaps seven days. Great quantities of food and wine were consumed and singing and dancing engaged in (Judges 14).

WAYFARING MAN

WELL   A pit dug about 20 feet into the earth or limestone rock where water would collect in it. The mouth of a well was generally covered by a stone, and sometimes a curb was built around it. Jesus sat beside Jacob's well at Sychar while conversing with the woman of Samaria (John 4:6). The digging of a new well was a time for rejoicing and singing. One of the oldest songs in existence is "The Song of the Well" (Numbers 21:17, 18).

WILDERNESS   The wilderness of Bible days was a desolate, treeless area, with little vegetation except after the rainy season. Only wild animals and occasional groups of wandering people inhabited it.

WELL

WINEPRESS   See: Press.

WINNOWING

WINNOWING   A method of separating the kernels of grain from the chaff after threshing. A shovel, or fan, was used to throw the mixture into the air while the wind blew away the chaff leaving the grain (Psalm 1:4).

WISE MEN   See: Magi.

WORSHIP   Respect, and high honor, and praise to one who possesses divine qualities. The Hebrews could worship only the one true God (Exodus 20:3; Matt. 4:10).

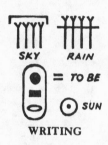

SKY   RAIN

● = TO BE

● SUN

WRITING

WRITING   In Egypt inscriptions in stone have been found dating from about 5000 B.C. The oldest known collection of narrative literature in the world is in the form of clay tablets written in cuneiform (wedge-shaped) characters by Sumerian inhabitants of Babylonia about 4000 B.C. The Egyptians developed a kind of picture writing called "hieroglyphic." See: Phoenicia; Cuneiform Writing.

Y

YOKE (OX)   A wooden crossbar with two bows to go around the necks of two oxen. When yoked together the oxen shared the burden of pulling a heavy load.

YOKE (OX)

Z

ZACHARIAS   The father of John the Baptist. While Zacharias was on duty as priest in the Temple an angel appeared to him and announced that his wife Elizabeth would bear him a son, who would prepare the people for the coming of the Lord (Luke 1:5-23).

ZEAL   Great eagerness; enthusiasm.

ZION

ZION   The head of rock on which stood the Jebusite fortress which was captured by David and renamed by him "Jerusalem." The word Zion came to designate the whole city of Jerusalem.

Part II—The Church

Chapter III
Who's Who in Church History

A

ABELARD, PETER (ab'e-lard) 1079-1142
French theologian and teacher, of astonishing
brilliance, but persecuted for alleged heresy.
The famous monk Bernard (q.v.) was his
special enemy. Abelard is most popularly
remembered for his romantic love affair with
the gifted Heloise, and their love letters are
still treasured.

PETER ABELARD

ALBRIGHT, JACOB (ol'brit) 1759-1808
Brought up a Lutheran, became a Methodist,
but unintentionally effected the foundation of
a new body, the Evangelical Church, in Pennsylvania in 1803. This body merged with the
United Brethren in 1946. Elected first Bishop
in 1807.

JACOB ALBRIGHT

AMBROSE (am'broz) c. 340-397 Imperial
prefect (or governor) of Upper Italy, and
who became Bishop of Milan in 374. His
actions reveal the new power of the Christian
Church after Constantine, but also its intol-
erance of heretics and pagans. Ambrose exerted strong influence over the young Emperor
Gratian and the mighty Emperor Theodosius.
Augustine was converted under his influence
and baptized by him. Ambrose is also
thought to have left his mark on church music.

AMBROSE

ANDREWES, LANCELOT (an'drooz)
1555-1626 Learned and eloquent Bishop in
the Church of England. One of the translators
of King James Bible. Best known for his immortal book of prayers, "Private Devotions".

LANCELOT
ANDREWES

C. F. ANDREWS

ANDREWS, C. F. (an'drooz) 1871-1940 Anglican missionary to India, named by his Indian friends, following his initials, "Christ's Faithful Apostle". Sympathetic friend of Gandhi, who named him Dinabandhu ("Friend of the People").

ANSKAR

ANSKAR (ans'kar) d. 865 Frankish monk who braved mighty perils to bring Roman Catholic Christianity to Denmark and Norway.

ANTHONY

ANTHONY (an'tho-ni) b. c. 250 Egyptian hermit and famous pioneer Christian monk. As a rich young man, he gave all his wealth away, when he heard the words of Jesus, "Go and sell all", and "Take no thought for the morrow." Punished his body severely. The artists have loved to try to depict the demons that so fiercely tempted him. May have lived over a hundred years.

THOMAS AQUINAS

AQUINAS, THOMAS (a-kwi'nas) 1225-1274 Italian Dominican monk and theologian, whose "Summa Theologiae" is considered the most authoritative book in Roman Catholic doctrine. His commentaries on scripture and devotional material have been received with high regard. He has had tremendous influence on theological thought of succeeding ages. His system is named Thomism, and some Twentieth Century theologians are called Neo-Thomists. He brilliantly married reason to revelation.

ARIUS (a-ri'us) d. 336 Pastor in Alexandria, Egypt, whose view of Christ (roughly, half God and half man) aroused Athanasius (q.v.) to spirited opposition, and occasioned the famous debate at the Council of Nicaea, 325 A. D., at which his doctrine was condemned (Arianism).

ARIUS

ARNDT, JOHANN (arnt) 1555-1621 His book, "True Christianity", for generations influenced a host of Germans, in an atmosphere of quarrelsome dogmatism, to a life of prayer and good works.

JOHANN ARNDT

ASBURY, FRANCIS (az'ber'i) 1745-1816 John Wesley's convert and disciple, he came to America to be Methodism's first great leader here. Made bishop by the organizing conference at Baltimore in 1784. A tireless traveller on horseback from Maine to Georgia.

FRANCIS ASBURY

ATHANASIUS (ath'a-na'shi-us) c. 300-373 Born in Alexandria, Egypt, and became Bishop of that city in 328. Though claiming to be its one true bishop as long as he lived, he suffered five exiles, due to the fierce theological and political quarrels of his lifetime. One of the most decisive thinkers in all Christian history, he was the champion of the eternal divinity of Jesus Christ, against the followers of Arius, who even had the Emperor Constantine on their side in his later years. Athanasius was a courageous and resourceful man of action, as well as a brilliant thinker. His view of the eternal Saviorhood of Christ became the regnant view of Christians from the late Fourth Century on.

ATHANASIUS

AUGUSTINE (o'gus-ten) 354-430 Omitting the Apostle Paul, this Bishop of Hippo in North Africa may probably be credited with having lead Christian thinking more powerfully than any other. After a turbulent career as a pagan, he was converted to Christ. His "Confessions" records and reflects this experience memorably. His "City of God" sounds mighty notes in the Christian understanding of history. In his voluminous writing we hear the heavy footbeats of man the sinner, and the more triumphant steps of the sinner saved by God's grace.

JOHN T.
AXTON, SR.

AXTON, JOHN T., SR. (ax'ton) 1870-1934 Congregational minister and first United States Army Chief of Chaplains. He saw service in the Philippines and on the Mexican border. The First World War brought him many decorations. After the War he became the first Chief of Chaplains (1920). His son, John T. Axton, Jr., also served long as an Army Chaplain.

JOHANN
S. BACH

B

BACH, JOHANN SEBASTIAN (bak) 1685-1750 German choir-master, composer of exalted and uplifting church music. His Chorales are of great beauty, depth, and of simplicity-in-subtlety, as are his Oratorios, "St John's Passion" and "St. Matthew's Passion."

BACKUS, ISAAC (back'us) 1724-1806 New England Baptist pastor, historian, and champion of religious liberty.

BALCH, WILLIAM (bolch) 1775-1842 Congregational minister and first United States Navy Chaplain, receiving his commission from President John Adams on October 30, 1799. He served in the United States Navy aboard the USS Congress and the USS Chesapeake. Chaplains served with the Continental Navy prior to Chaplain Balch, but he was the first Chaplain to serve officially in this capacity. His father, Benjamin Balch had previously served as Chaplain in the Continental Navy.

WILLIAM BALCH

BALLOU, HOSEA (ba-loo') 1796-1861 Boston pastor and leading figure in the early years of Universalism, which holds that God will in time save all persons. His thought on Christ was Unitarian.

HOSEA BALLOU

BASIL THE GREAT (baz'l) c. 330-379 Theologian in the succession of Athanasius (q.v.), propagator and law-giver of the monasticism of the East (generally, Greece and Asia Minor). For his last seven years bishop of Caesarea in Cappadocia. With his brother, Gregory of Nyssa, and Gregory of Nazianzus, is made up the trio we call the Cappadocian Fathers, each an important theologian of the Eastern Church (Eastern Orthodox).

BASIL THE GREAT

BAXTER, RICHARD (baks'ter) 1615-1691 English Presbyterian pastor in the stormy 17th Century. He wanted greater breadth in the Church of England. Because of his Puritanism he suffered persecution. Author of "Saints' Everlasting Rest" and "The Reformed Pastor."

RICHARD BAXTER

BEDE

BEDE (bed) c. 672-735 Learned English monk who gave us before his death his very valuable "History of the Church of the English People", which tells us almost all we know about the Christian Church in Britain before his time.

HENRY WARD
BEECHER

BEECHER, HENRY WARD (be'cher) 1813-1887 Eloquent and influential preacher of Plymouth Congregational Church, Brooklyn, New York, son of Rev. Lyman Beecher and brother of Harriet Beecher Stowe. He was a champion of freedom, denounced slavery to an immense congregation, and lead his church in the raising and equipping of a volunteer regiment during the civil war.

BENEDICT
OF NURSIA

BENEDICT OF NURSIA (ben'e-dikt) c. 480-543 Italian monk, founder of the famous monastery at Monte Cassino, between Rome and Naples, and author of the Rule of Saint Benedict, the most influential of all manuals for the conduct of the life of monks living together. The Benedictine Order is still a large one in the Roman Catholic Church.

BERNARD
OF CLAIRVAUX

BERNARD OF CLAIRVAUX (ber-nard) d. 1153 French monk and abbott, eloquent preacher, gifted writer, drawn out very often from his monastery to settle church quarrels, advise popes, to prosecute heretics. Preached the Second Crusade. Outstanding mystic, his soul married to God. Author of hymn, "Jesus, Thou Joy of Loving Hearts."

BEZA, THEODORE (baz') 1519-1605
Brilliant churchman and thinker in the early
generations of French Protestantism. Calvin
(q.v.) died in Beza's arms, and Beza succeeded to the leadership of the reformation
in Geneva.

THEODORE BEZA

BLAIR, JAMES (blar) 1655-1743 Scots-
born, Anglican clergyman. "The grand old
man of Virginia" in colonial days. He
founded, and headed for over fifty years, the
College of William and Mary, our second
American College.

JAMES BLAIR

BOCSKAY, STEPHEN (boc'skay) 1557-
1606 Prince of Transylvania. Hungarian
leader of the Reformation. Champion of
Protestantism in the 16th century in central
Europe. His struggle, together with other
Protestants, with the civic authorities to protect his rights and preserve his properties
ultimately culminated in the peace of Vienna
which guaranteed all the constitutional rights
and religious privileges of the Hungarians
both in Transylvania and imperial Hungary.
Bocskay was important enough to the complete picture of the Reformation in Europe to
be included as one of the ten great Reformation leaders on the wall of the Monument to
the Reformation in Geneva, Switzerland.

STEPHEN
BOCSKAY

BOHME, JAKOB (bu'me) 1575-1624 German (Silesian) shoemaker who has been
called the greatest Protestant mystic. A daring and original thinker who has influenced
poets and theologians from his day to ours.

JAKOB BOHME

BONAVENTURA

BONAVENTURA (bon'a-ven-tu'ra) 1221-1274 Italian Franciscan, mystical theologian, by birth John Fidenza. Later a cardinal. Friendly rival, in theological thought, of the Dominican Aquinas (q.v.).

DIETRICH
BONHOEFER

BONHOEFER, DIETRICH (bon'huffer, dietrick) 1906-1945 German Lutheran pastor and theologian, brilliant in thought and in person. Arrested by Hitler's agents in 1943 for his outspoken opposition to the German tyranny, he was killed by Hitler's agents shortly before the Allied victory would have seen his release.

BONIFACE

BONIFACE (bon'i-fas) c. 670-754 English Benedictine monk, missionary to the Franks, centering in what is now West Germany. Popes made him Bishop, then Archbishop. He worked closely with Popes and Kings to evangelize and educate. Returning at last to Frisia (part of Holland) from which he had earlier been driven, he was killed by a drunken mob.

WILLIAM BOOTH

BOOTH, WILLIAM (booth) 1829-1912 English Methodist preacher who founded the Salvation Army in 1877. Author of "In Darkest England", on his country's awful need of redemption, religious and social. The Gospel for the "down and out" was Booth's strong point. His remarkable wife Catherine helped him mightily, and their children gave their lives to the work.

BOSSUET (bo'su-e') 1627-1704 Silver-tongued French Bishop of Meaux, who sought to sanctify the evil rule of King Louis XIV. Strong opponent of Protestants, earnestly hopeful of winning them back to the Roman Church.

BOSSUET

BRAINERD, DAVID (brai'nerd) 1718-1747 Connecticut Presbyterian minister who became missionary to the Indians in Eastern Pennsylvania. He left behind a journal which influenced scores or hundreds of young men to become missionaries.

DAVID BRAINERD

BRENT, CHARLES H. (brent) 1862-1929 Episcopal Bishop of Philippines, later of Western New York, and a pioneer in the ecumenical movement of the Twentieth Century.

CHARLES H.
BRENT

BRESEE, PHINEAS F. (bre'sa') 1838-1915 Minister, and considered main founder of the Church of the Nazarene. Organized the first local organization (1895) of the fellowship known as the Church of the Nazarene, at Los Angeles. There is a strong accent on the doctrines of holiness and sanctification as taught by John Wesley. The background of this Church is Methodist; they adhere closely to the original Wesleyan ideology.

PHINEAS F.
BRESEE

PHILLIPS BROOKS

BROOKS, PHILLIPS (brooks) 1835-1893
Widely beloved rector of Trinity Church
(Protestant Episcopal) in Boston. Eloquent
preacher. Episcopal Bishop of Massachusetts
(1891-1893). At Christmas, all Christians
sing his words, "O Little Town of Bethlehem."

ROBERT BROWNE

BROWNE, ROBERT (broun) 1550-1633
The pioneer of English Separatism or Congregationalism, although he finally returned to
the Church of England. A man of extreme
temper, he died in jail at eighty years of age,
where he had been sent for an assault on a
constable.

ROBERT
BROWNING

BROWNING, ROBERT (broun'ing) 1812-
1889 English poet who spun many Biblical
and Christian themes with deep insight and
buoyant eloquence. See his "Saul" and
"Death in the Desert".

JOHN BUNYAN

BUNYAN, JOHN (bun'yan) 1628-1688
Self-educated English Baptist preacher who
wrote, in his prison cell at Bedford, the delightful and immortal allegory, "The Pilgrim's
Progress", the greatest classic of Puritanism.
When Bunyan was released from prison, he
served as Pastor at Bedford for sixteen years.
After riding through the rain to London, he
died in the home of a friend in 1688.

BUSHNELL, HORACE (boosh'nel) 1802-1876 Congregational pastor in Hartford, Connecticut. His book, "Christian Nurture", was an important herald of the Christian education movement, as corrective of the great reliance on evangelistic conversion. Other books of his were path-breakers in theology. Pastor of only one church.

HORACE
BUSHNELL

BUTZER (or BUCER), MARTIN (boo'-tser) 1491-1551 Monk who became a Protestant pastor, and gave strong leadership to Protestantism in Strassburg and Alsace. Influenced Calvin.

MARTIN BUTZER

C

CALVIN, JOHN (kal'vin) 1509-1564 French scholar who, though only a layman, became the leading preacher and the dominant force in the newly Protestantized city of Geneva in the Alps. He is the chief builder of the Presbyterian way of thought and church-life, with his "Institutes of the Christian Religion" and his commentaries on the Bible. He has been long criticized for his stern theology and discipline, but today he is winning new appreciation. Yet, his rigid doctrine of election or predestination is rarely held today. Invariably named with Luther as a chief builder of Protestantism.

JOHN CALVIN

CAMPBELL, ALEXANDER (kam'bel) 1786-1866 Born in Ireland, became a Presbyterian minister. The strongest leader in the formation of the Disciples of Christ (1832), aiming to imitate the early Christians and to bring an end to denominationalism.

ALEXANDER
CAMPBELL

WILLIAM CAREY

JOHN CARROLL

PETER
CARTWRIGHT

THOMAS
CARTWRIGHT

CAREY, WILLIAM (kar'i) 1761-1834
English shoemaker, school-teacher, and Baptist minister who became a pioneer of the Protestant world mission. His challenge occasioned the founding of the "Baptist Society for Propagating the Gospel Among the Heathen" (1792). His services in India were remarkable for their range and depth, especially as linguist and Bible translator. Besides his extensive contributions in Bible translations (working with 40 oriental languages) Carey developed grammars and dictionaries in Bengali, Sanskrit, and other native tongues.

CARROLL, JOHN (kar'ul) 1735-1815
Maryland-born, Jesuit-trained, he became the first American bishop in the Roman Catholic Church. He was consecrated in London in 1790. In 1808, his see at Baltimore was made an archdiocese and he its archbishop.

CARTWRIGHT, PETER (kart'rit) 1785-
1872 Rugged Methodist pioneer preacher, son of the Kentucky frontier and its camp-meetings. W. W. Sweet named him "The Friar Tuck of American Methodism." In 1846 he was unsuccessful in an attempt to win an election for Congressman; he was defeated by Abraham Lincoln.

CARTWRIGHT, THOMAS (kart'rit) d.
1603 Puritan professor at Cambridge University. Important proponent of Presbyterianism, before its organization, in the England of Queen Elizabeth. He was relieved of his position, 1570, for his opinions.

CARY, LOTT (kar'i) c. 1780-1828 A Virginia slave, who, after Christian conversion and a purchase of freedom, learned to read, and became a strong Baptist preacher. He went to Liberia as a missionary, and became pastor of the first Baptist Church there, which he helped organize.

LOTT CARY

CHALMERS, THOMAS (cha'merz) 1780-1847 Powerful Scots preacher and social reformer, leader of the Evangelical party that at length seceded from the Church of Scotland (1844).

THOMAS
CHALMERS

CHANNING, WILLIAM ELLERY (chan'-ing) 1780-1842 Eloquent Boston preacher and reformer, the leading voice in the beginnings of Unitarianism in the U. S. A.

WILLIAM E.
CHANNING

CHRYSOSTOM (kris'us-tum) c. 347-407 John of Antioch was the forthright and eloquent preacher in his home city until he was kidnapped and forced to become the Archbishop of Constantinople. In the capital city his preaching was again painfully direct and frank, and the Empress Eudosia banished him because she thought he insulted her. He was soon recalled, but he was not tamed. He applied a strong Gospel to popular evils. Banished again, he died in the desert. Thirty years later, his bones were brought back and buried with great pomp. Later times gave him the name Chrysostom, which means "Golden Mouth".

CHRYSOSTOM

FRANCIS E. CLARK

CLARK, FRANCIS E. (klark) 1852-1927 Congregational minister. Founder, in Portland, Maine, in 1881, of "Christian Endeavor", an interdenominational federation of young peoples' societies. His nickname, "Father Endeavor" came from his first two initials.

JOHN CLARKE

CLARKE, JOHN (klark) 1609-1676 English physician and preacher who led in the founding of the Rhode Island colony, as at first distinct from the settlement at Providence. He secured from King Charles II the Rhode Island charter of 1663 which guaranteed civil and religious liberty. Has been called "the most important Baptist of the 17th Century".

CLEMENT
OF ALEXANDRIA

CLEMENT OF ALEXANDRIA (klem'ent) c. 150-c. 215 Convert from paganism to Christian faith he became the leader in the Christian college ("catechetical school") in the great city of Alexandria in Egypt. Though a philosophical Christian, he wrote: "Philosophers are children until they have been made men by Christ."

THOMAS COKE

COKE, THOMAS (kok) 1747-1814 John Wesley (q.v.) ordained Coke a superintendent to serve in North America. Coke served briefly here, helping in the beginnings of Methodist organization, 1784, in Baltimore (see Asbury).

156

COLET, JOHN (ko'le') 1466-1519 Forerunner of the English Reformation. Bible
lecturer at Oxford, Dean of St. Paul's Cathedral in London, founder of St. Paul's School
for boys. By his teaching and preaching he
made the Apostle Paul live again. Erasmus
said of his friend Colet: "A book was ever
his companion on the road, and his talk was
always of Christ."

JOHN COLET

COLIGNY, GASPARD DE (de ko'le'nye')
1519-1572 French nobleman who became a
devout Protestant, and chief of the military
defense of the Huguenots (as the French Protestants were called) in the fierce "Wars of
Religion". He was murdered in the notorious
St. Bartholomew's Day massacre of Protestants in Paris.

GASPARD DE
COLIGNY

COLUMBA (ko-lum'ba) 521-597 Irish monk
who settled with twelve companions on the
island of Iona, off the west coast of Scotland.
From that place he and his friends brought
the Irish or Celtic (not yet Roman) Catholic
Church to Scotland itself. A powerful person
with winsome Irish characteristics. Sometimes known as Columcille (dove of the cell).

COLUMBA

CONSTANTINE THE GREAT (kon'stan-
tin) 274-337 One of history's most powerful
rulers, as sole emperor of the re-united Roman
Empire from 323 to his death. He attributed
his decisive victory near Rome, in 312, to the
intervention of Christ. From that point on,
he showered the Christian Church with his
favors, and even called and presided over the
first General Christian Council at Nicaea in
325. He was not baptized, however, until he

CONSTANTINE
THE GREAT

JOHN COTTON

MILES
COVERDALE

THOMAS
CRANMER

OLIVER
CROMWELL

knew he was about to die. Shall we call him a Christian Emperor? Was his character Christian in any reasonable sense? The answers are hard to give. At any rate, he marks the end of the terrible persecutions of Christians by the Roman Empire, and the beginning of a very different chapter in the life of the Christian Church.

COTTON, JOHN (kot″n) 1584-1652 Puritan refugee from his pastorate in Boston, England, to his notable pastorate in Boston, Massachusetts, in its first generation. Has been called "the Patriarch of New England".

COVERDALE, MILES (kuv′er-dal) 1488-1568 Translator of the first complete English Bible, 1535. In 1539, he produced the Great Bible, a revision of the Matthew's Bible. His work affected all later English Bibles.

CRANMER, THOMAS (kran′mer) 1489-1556 Father of the Book of Common Prayer and one of the early builders of the Church of England. A Cambridge (fellow) called by King Henry VIII to his government, he became in 1533 Archbishop of Canterbury, highest leader in his church, in the years it was becoming reformed in the Protestant direction. Under the Roman Catholic Queen Mary in 1555, he was put to death, dying with special bravery.

CROMWELL, OLIVER (krom′wel) 1599-1658 English farmer, mighty cavalry leader in the Civil Wars, and at length Lord Protector or dictator of Britain, (1653-1658). Devout Calvinist believer, though not a churchman. As ruler he allowed much religious toleration.

CUSA, NICHOLAS OF (ke'wzz) c. 1400-1464 German scholar, diplomat, bishop, and cardinal. His enduring fame is that of the author and thinker. He wrote "Concerning Learned Ignorance" and "The Vision of God." We may call him a mystic.

NICHOLAS OF CUSA

CYPRIAN (sip'ri-an) c. 200-258 Gifted and wealthy lawyer of Carthage, North Africa, converted to Christ and the Church out of disgust with this evil world. Made Bishop of Carthage. When persecution came, he left, allegedly to administer his church from a point of safety. But ten years later he bravely suffered death for his faith. He believed in the equality of all bishops, as against Rome's exclusive claims. Famous words: "Outside the Church, no salvation," and "He who does not have the Church for his mother cannot have God for his Father."

CYPRIAN

D

DANTE ALIGHIERI (dan'te) 1265-1321 Born in Florence, died as political exile in Ravenna. An outstanding literary creation of all time is his "Divine Comedy", divided into three parts, Hell, Purgatory, Paradise. A long, sharply etched poem by a prophet and a seer. "A medieval miracle of song", said Longfellow.

DANTE ALIGHIERI

DARBY, JOHN N. (dar'bi) 1800-1882 English founder of the Plymouth Brethren (or Darbyites), a wide-spreading movement for restoring simple Christian church practice and faith, with conversion, immersion, premillenialism, and every Christian a minister.

JOHN N. DARBY

PIERRE-JEAN DESMET

DESMET, PIERRE-JEAN (de'smet') 1801-1873 Pioneer Roman Catholic missionary to the American Northwest, beginning in 1840. (See Jason Lee, for the call from the Indians).

DOMINIC

DOMINIC (dom'i-nik) 1170-1221 Spanish monk who founded the Roman Catholic monastic order commonly known as the Dominicans. The original name was the Order of Preaching Brothers. Among famous Dominicans are Aquinas (q.v.), Fra Angelico (q.v.), and Savonarola (q.v.).

JOHN DONNE

DONNE, JOHN (dun) c. 1572-1631 Anglican preacher and poet, through his writings a great favorite in our century. Famous is the passage in his "Devotions" that has the phrase, "For whom the bell tolls", and also his sonnet, "Death, be not proud".

F. M. DOSTOEVSKY

DOSTOEVSKY, F. M. (dos'tu-yei'ski) 1821-1881 Russian novelist who illuminated the strong element of suffering in Christian faith. Greatest work, "The Brothers Karamazov." Other works: "Crime and Punishment," "House of the Dead" and "The Idiot."

DURER, ALBRECHT (du'rer) 1471-1528 Greatest of German artists, his illustrations of the life of Christ and of the Book of Revelation are notable. His painting, "Four Evangelists", has been called the greatest Protestant work of art. Durer was a contemporary and an admirer of Luther.

ALBRECHT DURER

DYER, MARY (di'er) d. 1660 Quaker, hanged in Boston for daring to return from exile. In front of the Massachusetts State House is a new statue (1960) of her.

MARY DYER

E

ECKHART, JOHANNES (ek'hart) c. 1260-1327 Deep German mystic, a Dominican monk, commonly called Meister (Master) Eckhart. He had, and still has through his writings, wide influence. The Roman Catholic Church condemned, in his lifetime, some of his opinions.

JOHANNES
ECKHART

EDDY, MARY BAKER (ed'i) 1821-1910 New England woman who founded "Christian Science" on the basis of her own experience of Christian healing and serenity.

MARY BAKER
EDDY

JONATHAN
EDWARDS

JOHN ELIOT

QUEEN
ELIZABETH

RALPH WALDO
EMERSON

EDWARDS, JONATHAN (ed'werdz) 1703-1758 New England preacher and theologian, one of keenest minds in the history of American religion. As pastor in Northampton, Massachusetts, he preached the need of the second birth with power. He belongs in the stream of the so-called Great Awakening which stirred all the British colonies in America. He died, very shortly after becoming president of New Jersey (now Princeton) College.

ELIOT, JOHN (el'i-ut) 1604-1690 Serving the Congregational Church in Roxbury (now part of Boston), Massachusetts, for sixty years, he gave remarkable service to the Indians within a fifty-mile radius, learning their language, preaching to them, and organizing them into villages of "praying Indians". He translated the Bible into Algonquin.

ELIZABETH, QUEEN (e-liz'a-beth') 1533-1603 Daughter of Henry VIII and Queen of England 1558-1603. Strong defender of the Protestant Church in England. During the 45 years of her reign, the religious struggle between the Protestant and Roman Catholic forces reached its climax. The action of the Queen secured and strengthened the place of Protestantism in England at a critical time in English Church history.

EMERSON, RALPH WALDO (em'er-s'n) 1803-1882 He left his Boston Unitarian pulpit to become America's greatest spiritual teacher apart from the Christian Church and way. He has been called "the high priest of democracy," "the outstanding figure of American letters," and his books "the mirror of the American soul".

ERASMUS (e-raz′mus) d. 1536 Dutch scholar and thinker and wit. Clever and piercing critic of Roman Catholic customs. Someone said of the Protestant Reformation: "Erasmus laid the egg and Luther hatched it." Erasmus never became a Protestant. He wanted the Bible in everyone's hands. Champion of simple ethical Christianity, of moderation and peace. Most famous work, "The Praise of Folly".

ERASMUS

EUSEBIUS OF CAESAREA (u-se′bi-us) d. c. 340 Often called the first Church historian because of his "Ecclesiastical History". A learned bishop and a warm admirer of the Emperor Constantine.

EUSEBIUS
OF CAESAREA

F

FAREL, GUILLAUME (far′el) 1489-1565 Dynamic French Protestant pioneer, who broke ground for the Reformation in many French and Swiss cities. Responsible for getting John Calvin to settle in Geneva.

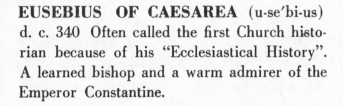

GUILLAUME FAREL

FENELON (fan′lon) 1651-1715 French archbishop especially known for his wise and gentle counsel to persons seeking a more spiritual life, and for his mystical writings. The Pope condemned some of his views. He tried to win Protestants back to the Roman Church by kindness and persuasion.

FENELON

CHARLES G.
FINNEY

FINNEY, CHARLES G. (fin'i) 1792-1875 American evangelist and educator. The young, sceptical but soul-hungry lawyer was converted to strong Christian conviction and ordained to the ministry. A powerful revivalist, he worked, lawyer-like, logically and zealously for a verdict. Author, professor (Oberlin College, Ohio), pastor (same town) and then president of the college.

GEORGE FOX

FOX, GEORGE (foks) 1624-1691 Father of the Society of Friends, commonly called Quakers. A mystic and visionary, a man of steely courage, suffering many hard imprisonments for his faith. The first Quaker meetings were held in the England of the 1650's. Fox also visited the American colonies.

JOHN FOXE

FOXE, JOHN (foks) 1517-1587 English Puritan clergyman who wrote the so-called Book of Martyrs, which burned the tragedy of ages of persecution into the minds of generations of Christians. Under a longer title it appeared in eight volumes in 1563.

FRA ANGELICO

FRA ANGELICO (an-ja'le-ko) 1387-1455 Monastery name of an Italian Dominican monk whose religious frescoes of saints and angels charm us by their freshness and simplicity.

FRANCIS OF ASSISI (a-se'ze) 1182-1226
Undoubtedly, the best-loved of Roman Catholic
saints. Lived out his life almost entirely in
his home town on a beautiful mountainside in
central Italy. Converted from a fun-loving
son of a wealthy merchant into one who craved
at all costs to imitate his Lord Christ. The
way was love, — love of all created things
(see his hymn, "Canticle of the Sun"). Many
followed him and the Franciscan Order was
born. His desire to imitate his Lord was
sealed by the imprintation of the wound-prints
of the Cross in his hands.

FRANCIS OF ASSISI

FRANCIS OF SALES (salz) 1567-1622
French aristocrat who as Bishop of Geneva
won thousands of Protestants back to the
Roman Catholic Church. He is best known
for his writings, especially "Introduction to
the Devout Life".

FRANCIS OF SALES

FRANCKE, AUGUST HERMANN (frang'-
ke) 1663-1727 German Lutheran pastor, a
Pietist (see Spener). Notable for leadership
in founding charitable institutions, with strong
faith that God would provide for every need.
The university of Halle was founded by
Francke and his friends.

AUGUST
HERMANN
FRANCKE

FRAZIER, JOHN B. (fra'zer) 1870-1939
A Southern Methodist. Commissioned as first
Chief of Chaplains of U. S. Navy on November
5, 1917. At this time there were five other
Chaplains on duty that were his seniors, but
his administrative ability and keen judgment
of human nature made him the logical choice.

JOHN B. FRAZIER

It was not until December of 1944, however, that a law was passed giving the rank of Rear Admiral to the Chief of Chaplains.

FREDERICH WILLIAM OF BRANDEN-BURG (wil'yam) 1620-1688 The Great Elector of Brandenburg and staunch champion of the Reformation. During his reign he was a stalwart friend to Education and Religion. When the Edict of Nantes (which had guaranteed religious freedom to the Protestants) was evoked by King Louis XIV of France, and the Huguenot Protestants were forbidden to flee from the country, Frederich William became a saviour and offered freedom and refuge to thousands otherwise destined to be destroyed.

G

GANDHI, MOHANDAS (gan'de) 1869-1948 Lawyer and statesman of India, generally called "Mahatma" (great spirit). Peaceful liberator of his nation from the British imperial yoke. He believed in Love and Truth and Prayer. Never became a professed Christian, but was deeply influenced by the Sermon on the Mount. In prison he often sang "When I survey the Wondrous Cross".

GIBBONS, JAMES (gib'unz) 1834-1921 In 1877 he became Roman Catholic Archbishop of Baltimore, his native city, and in 1886, the second American Cardinal. Friend and advisor of Presidents, and supporter of American democratic ideals.

GLADDEN, WASHINGTON (glad''n) 1836-1918 In Congregational pastorates in

Springfield, Massachusetts, and Columbus, Ohio, he preached and wrote as a gifted prophet of "social Christianity". He sought the practical application of Christian principles to the burning problems of industry, commerce and politics. His hymn, "O Master Let Me Walk With Thee", is very widely sung.

CONRAD GREBEL

GREBEL, CONRAD (gray'bel) c. 1498-1526 The leader of the Swiss Anabaptists in their tragic beginnings in Zurich, Switzerland.

GREGORY THE GREAT

GREGORY THE GREAT—POPE GREGORY I (greg'o-ri) r. 590-604 Possibly the greatest of popes. In a broken and battered Rome he restored order and fed the poor. He improved church music (Gregorian Chant). First to set forth clearly the Roman doctrine of Purgatory. He sent a band of Benedictine monks to Britain, with the end-result that those islands were won to the Rome-led Catholic Church.

SIR WILFRED GRENFELL

GRENFELL, SIR WILFRED (gren'fel) 1865-1940 English medical missionary to Labrador and northern Newfoundland. His services in establishing hospitals, cooperative stores, fox farms, schools, and recreational facilities were invaluable. He was known as "the Apostle to Labrador."

HUGO GROTIUS

GROTIUS, HUGO (gro'shi-us) 1583-1645 Brilliant Dutch thinker in the realms of politics and religion. "The founder of international law".

N. F. S.
GRUNDTVIG

GRUNDTVIG, N. F. S. (groont'vet) 1783-1872 Danish pastor, scholar, author, whose zeal to warm up official Danish Lutheranism may be compared with Kierkegaard's (q.v.). Important in the founding of the Danish Folk High Schools. Author of hundreds of Danish hymns.

MATTHIAS
GRUNEWALD

GRÜNEWALD, MATTHIAS (gru'ne-valt) c. 1445-1528 German artist whose altar-piece in several panels now stands in a museum at Colmar, France. The vivid dramatic power of his depiction of the suffering Christ has won him new and glowing acclaim in our century of tragedy.

GUSTAVUS
ADOLPHUS

GUSTAVUS ADOLPHUS (gus-ta'vus) 1594-1632 Mighty warrior-king of Sweden, and devout Lutheran believer. Killed in his victorious battle at Lutzen, Germany, and remembered by German Protestantism as one of its saviors.

H

GEORGE
FRIEDRICH
HANDEL

HANDEL, GEORGE FRIEDRICH (han'd'l) 1685-1759 German-born composer who gave his best years of musicianship to Britain. His melodious, tender and triumphant "Messiah" has long been the reigning favorite of all religious cantatas. "The Hallelujah Chorus".

HARNACK, ADOLF (har'nak) 1851-1930 One of modern Germany's greatest Christian scholars. A historian of Christian thought. Son of Lutheran theologian Theodosius. Served as professor at Leipzig, Gressen, Marsburg and Berlin. His scholarly writings are on History of Dogma, Gnosticism, Monasticism, Ignatius and old Christian literature. Because of his criticism of the Apostles' Creed, he was suspected by the orthodox of being a heretic.

ADOLF HARNACK

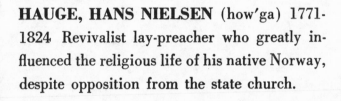

HANS HAUGE

HAUGE, HANS NIELSEN (how'ga) 1771-1824 Revivalist lay-preacher who greatly influenced the religious life of his native Norway, despite opposition from the state church.

HENRY OF NAVARRE, or HENRY IV (hen'ri) 1553-1610 Ruled in France 1594-1610. Protestant-born French noble and warrior who became a Roman Catholic in order to consolidate his kingship. "Paris is worth a mass".

HENRY
OF NAVARRE

ELIAS HICKS

HICKS, ELIAS (hiks) 1748-1830 Long Island Quaker who led the most serious schism (1823) in American Quakerism, a schism now completely healed.

HILDEBRAND

JOHN HENRY
HOBART

RICHARD HOOKER

THOMAS HOOKER

HILDEBRAND (hil′de-brand) c. 1020-1085 Ruled as Pope Gregory VII 1073-1085. Strong-willed and masterful Pope who dared to excommunicate the Holy Roman Emperor Henry IV. The Pope later forgave Henry, but they quarreled again, and Hildebrand died in sad exile as Henry and his soldiers possessed and looted Rome. This reforming Pope greatly strengthened the papacy.

HOBART, JOHN HENRY (ho′bert) 1775-1830 Protestant Episcopal Bishop of New York, a zealous conservative. Active in founding the General Theological Seminary in New York City, where in 1821 he was chosen professor of Pastoral Theology. Author of many books.

HOOKER, RICHARD (hook′er) 1553-1600 Anglican clergyman, author of the "Laws of Ecclesiastical Polity", a great classic of Anglican churchmanship, especially in reply to the Puritans.

HOOKER, THOMAS (hook′er) 1585-1647 Leading figure in early days of the Connecticut Colony, centering in Hartford. Refugee from England, devout believer, eloquent preacher, one of the makers of Congregationalism.

THE REFORMATION WALL

The Reformation Wall, known officially as the International
Monument of the Reformation, is located in Geneva, Switzerland, and was erected in 1917, from funds collected in Protestant countries. On the face of the wall are arranged statues
in high relief of outstanding Protestant Church Reformers.
The main or central group is a series of four figures: Calvin,
Farel, Beza and Knox. On either side of the central group
are other champions of the Reformation. To the left are: Frederick William of Brandenburg, William of Orange, and Admiral
Coligny. To the right are: Roger Williams, Oliver Cromwell
and Stephen Bocskay. Luther and Zwingli have individual
memorials apart from the wall.

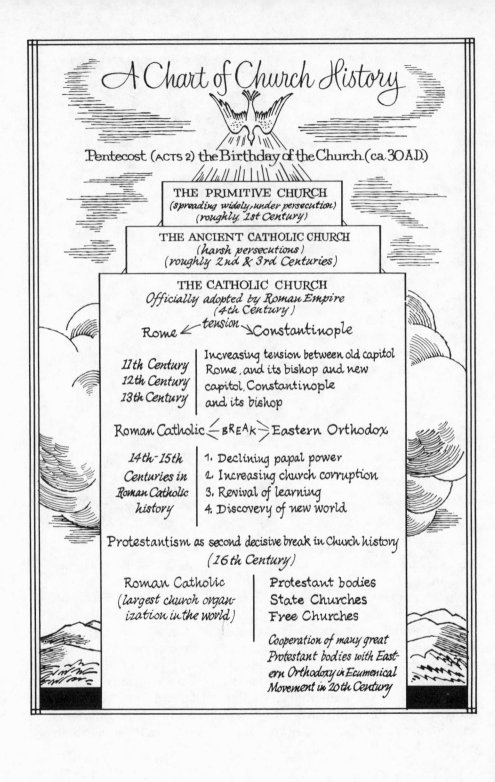

A Chart of Church History

Pentecost (ACTS 2) the Birthday of the Church (ca. 30 A.D.)

THE PRIMITIVE CHURCH
(spreading widely, under persecution)
(roughly, 1st Century)

THE ANCIENT CATHOLIC CHURCH
(harsh persecutions)
(roughly 2nd & 3rd Centuries)

THE CATHOLIC CHURCH
Officially adopted by Roman Empire
(4th Century)

Rome ← tension → Constantinople

11th Century 12th Century 13th Century	Increasing tension between old capitol Rome, and its bishop and new capitol, Constantinople and its bishop

Roman Catholic ← BREAK → Eastern Orthodox

14th–15th Centuries in Roman Catholic history	1. Declining papal power 2. Increasing church corruption 3. Revival of learning 4. Discovery of new world

Protestantism as second decisive break in Church history
(16th Century)

Roman Catholic *(largest church organization in the world)*	Protestant bodies State Churches Free Churches
	Cooperation of many great Protestant bodies with Eastern Orthodoxy in Ecumenical Movement in 20th Century

HUBMAIER, BALTHASAR (hub'myer) 1480-1528 German Roman Catholic priest who became a Protestant, and an Anabaptist preacher. Pastor of a huge congregation in Moravia. He was burned at the stake in Vienna, and his wife- was drowned in the Danube River.

BALTHASAR HUBMAIER

HUGEL, BARON FRIEDRICK VON (hee'gel) 1852-1925 German-born English scholar. Learned and profound Roman Catholic theologian, interpreter of mysticism, friend of Protestants. "The Mystical Quest of Religion."

BARON FRIEDRICK VON HUGEL

HUSS, JOHN (hus) 1373-1415 Heroic and beloved leader of the reform of the Roman Catholic Church in Bohemia. A schoolman and a preacher, he was influenced by older Bohemian (or Czech) reformers and by the writings of John Wycliffe of England. He was burned as a heretic by the Roman Catholic Council of Constance, just about a century before Luther started the great movement of the Reformation.

JOHN HUSS

I

IGNATIUS (ig-na'shi-us) d. c. 117 Bishop (essentially pastor) of the Christian Church in Antioch. Arrested and led to Rome by ten soldiers. Christian churches along the way greeted him with love and visited him in prison. He wrote back to them his well-known letters. He longed to die for Christ, and it is believed that he was thrown to the wild beasts in the Coliseum at Rome.

IGNATIUS

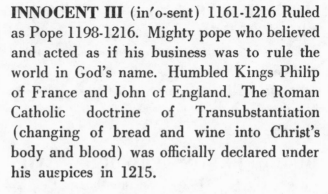

INNOCENT III (in'o-sent) 1161-1216 Ruled as Pope 1198-1216. Mighty pope who believed and acted as if his business was to rule the world in God's name. Humbled Kings Philip of France and John of England. The Roman Catholic doctrine of Transubstantiation (changing of bread and wine into Christ's body and blood) was officially declared under his auspices in 1215.

INNOCENT III

IRENAEUS

IRENAEUS, ST. (i're nay'oos) c. 140-202 Spiritual son of martyr Polycarp, who was Bishop of Smyrna. Went West to settle at Lyons (now in France), where, after the terrible persecution of A.D. 177, he became the Christian bishop. He explained and answered the dangerous Gnostic sects in his great work, "Against the Heresies". Inspiring theologian who made love the gate and Christ the garden.

J

SHELDON
JACKSON

JACKSON, SHELDON (jak's'n) 1834-1909 Of this stout-hearted New York Presbyterian preacher, his biographer sums him up in his sub-title: "Pathfinder and Prospector of the Missionary Vanguard in the Rocky Mountains and Alaska".

JEROME

JEROME (je-rom) c. 340-420 A foremost Christian scholar. He gave the Roman Catholics their Vulgate Bible, the outstanding Latin translation. Died at Jerusalem, where he had spent long years as a monk.

174

JOAN OF ARC (jon uv ark) d. 1431 French peasant girl, visionary who led her King's army against the British invaders. In British hands she was convicted of heresy and burned at the stake. Seven years later the British were driven out of France. Canonized in 1920, she is, above all, the reigning queen of French patriots. Considered one of the most remarkable women of world history. She received no formal education but was so well equipped with common sense, devotion to principle, and natural intelligence that she left the imprint of her courage, faith, and sacrifice on the sands of everlasting time. Tradition says that she was neither beautiful nor cultured, but the beauty of her being far transcended the heights of where mere temporal beauty can ascend.

JOAN OF ARC

FATHER JOHN
OF KRONSTADT

JOHN, FATHER, OF KRONSTADT (kron'shtaht) 1829-1908 Russian Orthodox churchman, preacher of great power, and a healer of many in disease. He also organized many philanthropies.

JOHN
OF DAMASCUS

JOHN OF DAMASCUS (jon uv dam as-kus) c. 676-c. 760 The principal theologian of the Eastern Orthodox side of Christianity.

JOHN OF THE
CROSS

JOHN OF THE CROSS (jon) 1542-1605 Spanish Carmelite monk, a highly revered mystic, and generally called one of Spain's foremost poets.

SAMUEL JOHNSON

JOHNSON, SAMUEL (jon's'n) 1709-1784 English author whose colorful character is revealed so memorably in Boswell's biography of him. But his "Prayers" especially reveal his depth and tenderness as a believing Christian.

RUFUS M. JONES

JONES, RUFUS M. (jo'nz) 1863-1948 Quaker from Maine who became the best beloved Quaker author and leader of his time. Teacher, Haverford College. Interpreter of a sane but warm mysticism. "The American Friends Service Committee", founded 1917, working for compassion and reconciliation, owed much to his leadership.

ADONIRAM
JUDSON

JUDSON, ADONIRAM (jud's'n) 1788-1850 New England-born, pioneer American missionary to the Orient. The vision of Judson and his chums at Andover Theological Seminary led to the founding of the American Board of Commissioners for Foreign Missions, 1810. His service for the Baptists in Burma marked him as a brilliant scholar, Bible translator, a far-visioned, a long-suffering, courageous man.

JUSTIN MARTYR

JUSTIN MARTYR (jus'tin) d. c. 165 A philosopher converted to Christian faith, then a teacher and author who defended his faith against its scornful critics. Justin's First Apology (apology means defense) gives important insights into Second Century Church life and thought. Martyred in Rome, hence the second part of his name in history.

K

KAGAWA, TOYOHIKO (ka-ga-wa) 1888-1960 Outstanding Japanese Christian, gifted evangelist, champion of the poor and the working people, on whose level he sought to live. Protagonist of peace in midst of a war-like Japan.

TOYOHIKO
KAGAWA

KANT, IMMANUEL (kant) 1724-1804 German philosopher, born April 22, 1724, who sparked the Church's return to faith after rationalism of 18th century. Taught that reason had its limits and faith alone could answer the problems of God and immortality. His teachings greatly influenced the motives, beliefs, and actions of both Protestant and Roman Catholic Churches. Greatest contributions were "Critique of Practical Reason" (1788), "Critique of Pure Reason" (1781), and "Religion within the Limits of Reason Alone" (1791).

IMMANUEL KANT

KHOMIAKOV, ALEXEY (kom'yakov) 1804-1860 A widely gifted Russian orthodox layman and theologian who placed authority not in Pope or Bible but in the living, loving fellowship of believers.

ALEXEY
KHOMIAKOV

KIERKEGAARD, SOREN (kir'ke-gor) 1813-1855 Danish Lutheran layman, and probably one of the four or five most influential religious thinkers in the modern world. His fame in the English-speaking world is scarcely thirty years old. Some would speak of his eccentricity as a person, but all acknowledge the depth of his religious insight. There was prophetic fire in his attack on organized Christianity in Denmark.

SOREN
KIERKEGAARD

JOHN KNOX

KNOX, JOHN (noks) 1513-1572 Above all others, the maker of Protestant Scotland. Against great odds, and despite many flights and sufferings, he built Scots Presbyterianism on strong foundations. John Calvin was the greatest influence upon him, and Mary Queen of Scots his most difficult adversary. At his grave one said: "Here lies one who neither flattered nor feared any flesh".

L

BARTHOLOMAS
LAS CASAS

LAS CASAS, BARTHOLOMAS (las ka'-sas) 1474-1566 Spanish Dominican missionary to Mexico. He believed the native Indians were human and had souls, and strongly opposed the brutality of the Spanish conquest.

HUGH LATIMER

LATIMER, HUGH (lat'i-mer) 1485-1555 Bishop of Protestant Church in England who was condemned to burn at the stake by ardent Roman Catholic Queen Mary. His last words, spoken bravely with the flames of death leaping around his body were, "We shall this day light up such a candle, by God's grace in England, as I trust shall never be put out!"

WILLIAM LAUD

LAUD, WILLIAM (lod) 1573-1645 Archbishop of Canterbury in the reign of Charles I, beheaded by order of the Puritan Parliament because of his rigorous persecution of the Puritans. Under his rule of the English Church, thousands of Puritans fled to New England.

LAW, WILLIAM (lo) 1686-1761 Anglican clergyman who gave his life to lonely prayer and to writing and to good works. His book. "A Serious Call to a Devout and Holy Life," was and is a trumpet-call to the life of faith and prayer and godliness.

WILLIAM LAW

LEE, JASON (le) 1803-1845 A famous request of the Nez Perce and Flathead Indians, who came to St. Louis in 1831, for knowledge of the white man's religion, was a large factor in the decision of this stout-hearted missionary to go over the perilous Oregon Trail in 1834. A pioneer Methodist missionary to the Oregon Country.

JASON LEE

LEFEVRE D'ETAPLES (le-fa'vre) d. 1536 French scholar and teacher. Late in a long life, he fell in love with the Bible, and gave utterance to beliefs so close to Protestant that he had to flee for a short time from France. He translated the whole Bible into French.

LEFEVRE
D'ETAPLES

LINCOLN, ABRAHAM (ling'kun) 1809-1865 Sixteenth president of the U. S. A. known to history as "The Great Emancipator" because he officially declared Negro slavery at an end in this land. Though he never joined a Christian Church, he embodied some sterling human qualities, as magnanimity and compassion.

ABRAHAM
LINCOLN

DAVID
LIVINGSTONE

IGNATIUS LOYOLA

RAYMOND LULL

KATHERINE von
BORA LUTHER

LIVINGSTONE, DAVID (liv'ing-stun) 1813-1873 Scot of humble birth, earnest missionary, Christian, intrepid and tireless traveller, he opened up great areas of Africa for missionary work. Sorely troubled by the sufferings of the natives, he sought to bring them not only the Gospel, but the benefits of Western civilization. He died in search of the headwaters of the Nile. His native helpers buried his heart in the heart of Africa. Then his body was carried for burial to Westminster Abbey.

LOYOLA, IGNATIUS (loi-o'la) c. 1491-1556 Spanish soldier wounded in war, converted into zealous "warrior for God", became founder of Society of Jesus (1540), or Jesuits, most powerful order in Roman Catholic Church. His book, "The Spiritual Exercises" is the Christian "soldier's" drill manual. Loyola's men won renown as missionaries (see Xavier), as theologians, as scientists, and as educators, and greatly aided in helping the Roman Catholic Church recover from the shock of Protestant Reformation. Loyola was canonized 1622.

LULL, RAYMOND (lul) d. c. 1316 Unique and colorful Spanish thinker, writer, and missionary to Moslem Island of Mallorca, his home. Wrote over 300 works. Worked hard to establish language schools for missionaries. Stoned by Arab mob in Tunis, and died from his wounds.

LUTHER, KATHERINE von BORA (lu'-ther) 1499-1552 Ex-nun who became the beloved and faithful wife of Martin Luther, his "Katy my rib", as he could call her in fun. She made a monastery into a home.

LUTHER, MARTIN (lu'ther) 1483-1546 Chief builder of the Protestant way, with his conviction on the authority of Scripture and justification (or salvation) by faith, not works. A German monk, he broke decisively with the Church of Rome in 1517-1520 on the basis of profound and life-shaking experience. From Wittenberg, his university center, the teacher-preacher gave dynamic leadership to the new Protestant churches all through Germany. His hymn, "A Mighty Fortress is Our God", has become perhaps the best-loved hymn in the Protestant world.

MARTIN LUTHER

M

MAKEMIE, FRANCIS (ma'ckemee) c. 1658-1708 Scots Presbyterian from Ireland, pioneer leader of the Presbyterians in the American colonies. Organized the first American presbytery in 1706 at Philadelphia.

FRANCIS
MAKEMIE

MARCION (mar'shi-on) c. 110-c. 165 Wealthy ship-owner from the Black Sea region, who later as a Christian in Rome led a break-away from the Church there. He gave his congregations a "canon", i.e., a collection of authoritative books as their Bible, and this was one of the factors leading to the making of our New Testament. In some respects his thinking was twisted, yet he was one of the first to see that love was "the greatest thing in the world".

MARCION

MARQUETTE, JACQUES (mar-ket') 1637-1675 Daring Jesuit missionary who carried the cross through the wilds of New

JACQUES
MARQUETTE

MARTIN
OF TOURS

France. For seven years he served the Indian tribes around the Great Lakes. With French explorer, Joliet, he found the upper Mississippi in 1673. He died in 1675 while preaching on the shores of Lake Michigan.

MARTIN OF TOURS (mar'tin) c. 316-c. 400 Pagan soldier converted to Christian faith and to the life of a monk. His reputation for holiness led to his consecration as Bishop of Tours in Gaul (later France). Thousands of French Catholic churches and hundreds of French villages are named after him.

COTTON MATHER

MATHER, COTTON (math'er) 1663-1728 Son of illustrious pastor, Increase Mather, whom he assisted in a Boston pastorate before he became himself the pastor. Wrote many volumes. He successfully championed vaccination for small-pox, a new thing then.

J. F. D. MAURICE

MAURICE, J. F. D. (mo'ris) 1805-1872 Anglican clergyman and Cambridge professor, author of books on Theology. Friend of the workingmen, spiritual leader of the movement known as Christian Socialism (about 1848).

WILLIAM
McKENDREE

McKENDREE, WILLIAM (m'ken'dre) 1757-1835 Elected in 1808, he became the first American-born bishop of the Methodist Episcopal Church. Born a Virginian "He kept house in his saddle-bags".

182

McPHERSON, AIMEE SEMPLE (mak-fur's'n) 1890-1944 Evangelist, and Founder of the International Church of the Foursquare Gospel. The particular scene of her work was Angelus Temple in Los Angeles with its capacity of more than five thousand.

AIMEE SEMPLE
McPHERSON

MELANCHTHON, PHILIP (me-langk'-thun) 1497-1560 Martin Luther's younger colleague at the University of Wittenberg, and author of the most important Lutheran statement of faith, the Augsburg Confession (1530). He succeeded Luther in the intellectual leadership of the German Reformation.

PHILIP
MELANCHTHON

MENNO SIMONS (men'o se'mons) 1492-1559 Dutch Roman Catholic priest, converted to the Anabaptist position. Pursued by his persecutors, he yet gave strong leadership to the Anabaptists during great troubles. The Mennonites are named for him.

MENNO SIMONS

MILLER, WILLIAM (mil'er) 1782-1849 New York State man, became a Baptist in 1816. Diligent Bible study led him to a strong belief that the Lord would return to earth very soon. People from many churches followed him. His prediction that 1844 would be the date of the Second Advent was not fulfilled, but faithful followers organized in 1845, and more significantly in 1861 as they acquired the name Advent Christian Church.

WILLIAM MILLER

SAMUEL J. MILLS

ROBERT MOFFAT

MOHAMMED

DWIGHT L.
MOODY

MILLS, SAMUEL J. (milz) 1783-1818 Williams College student, leader in the "Haystack Prayer Meeting" that led several students to give their lives in pioneer foreign missionary service. From his zealous labors came many Christian enterprises at home and abroad.

MOFFAT, ROBERT (mof′at) 1795-1883 Pioneer Christian missionary to South Africa. A humble Scot by birth, a gardener by training, he gave a variety of talents to his work. His daughter became the wife of David Livingstone (q.v.).

MOHAMMED (or Mahomet) (mo-ham′ed) c. 570-632 Arabian camel-driver who became the founder of the third and last of the world's three great monotheistic religions, commonly called Islam (meaning submission). In this religion there is a place for Jesus as prophet but not as Saviour or as Person in the Trinity. Islam as a whole still stoutly resists any penetration by Christian propaganda or evangelism. There are hundreds of millions of Mohammedans (Muslims, Moslems, Islam) in the world today.

MOODY, DWIGHT L. (moo′di) 1837-1899 Famous and beloved American evangelist. A layman. When young, a shoe salesman. His simple, direct message brought thousands to Christ in England and America, through Tabernacle meetings which united people from all churches. Moody also founded Northfield School for Girls, Mount Herman for Boys, and Moody Institute for lay religious workers.

MORE, THOMAS (mor) 1478-1535 Gifted London lawyer, author of the famous "Utopia" (1516), Chancellor for King Henry VIII when the monarch was cutting himself, his realm, and the English Church off from the pope. For his conscientious objection to this break, he was beheaded, "The king's good servant", he said, "but God's first". He became Saint Thomas More in 1935.

THOMAS MORE

MOTT, JOHN R. (mot) 1865-1955 American Methodist layman who gave remarkable gifts of leadership and administration to world-wide Christian movements. He presided at Edinburgh, 1910, the missionary conference which helped to spark the Ecumenical Movement.

JOHN R. MOTT

MUHLENBERG, HENRY M. (mu'lenburg) 1711-1787 German-born, he came to the American colonies and became the chief planter of Lutheranism here, with his base in Pennsylvania. Organizer of the first Lutheran synod in America, 1748.

HENRY M. MUHLENBERG

MULLER, GEORGE (mul'er) 1805-1898 German-born founder of orphanages in Bristol, England, famous for his successful reliance on faith and prayer to pay his bills.

GEORGE MULLER

185

JOHN MURRAY

MURRAY, JOHN (mur'i) 1741-1815 A Methodist convert in England who was led to embrace universal salvation, and became the first great leader of Universalism in the new world. Pastor in Gloucester, Massachusetts.

N

NEWMAN, JOHN HENRY (nu'man) 1801-1890 Oxford scholar, brilliant author, and winsome preacher of the Church of England. Startled the world of 1845 by becoming a Roman Catholic. In 1875, he was made a cardinal. Best known for his hymn, "Lead Kindly Light", written in 1834.

JOHN HENRY
NEWMAN

O

OBERLIN, JOHN FREDERICK (o'berlin) 1740-1826 Alsatian rural Protestant pastor, the "patron saint" of rural pastors ever since. He built roads, encouraged sound agriculture, founded classes for children, and in short, renewed a whole needy countryside. A widely tolerant man who extended great kindness and understanding to Catholics and Jews.

JOHN FREDERICK
OBERLIN

ORIGEN (or'i-jen) c. 185-254 A supreme Christian thinker. Son of a Christian martyr of Alexandria, Egypt. At age eighteen, he became head of the famous local Christian school. Lectured and wrote on the Bible and theology, endowed with seven secretaries. He later taught at Caesarea in Palestine. He died at Tyre, due to being tortured and imprisoned in the persecution under Decius. Later generations tried to smirch his name as a heretic.

ORIGEN

OTTERBEIN, PHILIP WILLIAM (ot'er-bin) 1726-1813 German Reformed minister, came to Pennsylvania. Influenced by Asbury (q.v.) and others, with Martin Boehm he began the church body we know as the United Brethren in Christ. (1800) This body merged with another in 1946 to become the present Evangelical United Brethren.

PHILIP WILLIAM
OTTERBEIN

P

PALESTRINA, G. P. (pal'es-tre'na) c. 1524-1594 Probably the chief figure behind modern Roman Catholic religious music, composer of nearly a hundred masses. Bears the surname of the town of his birth.

G. P. PALESTRINA

PASCAL, BLAISE (pas'kal) 1623-1662 French Roman Catholic layman, a genius in mathematics and physics, but most renowned as a Christian mystic, as revealed especially in his "Thoughts" (Pensees), only collected after his death. "The heart has its reasons that the reason cannot know."

BLAISE PASCAL

PATRICK (pat'rik) c. 389-461 Favorite saint of Ireland, and the man who gave definite form to the Church in Ireland. He was British-born. What we read about him is so full of legend that it is almost impossible to extract the truth. He sought to bring the "far western" island into the family of Roman Catholic Christendom, a goal not reached until centuries after his lifetime.

PATRICK

POPE PAUL III

PAUL III, POPE (1534-1549) (pol) 1468-1549 Reform Pope who dedicated his life to the purpose of reconciling factions of Church and State. In 1537, he summoned the Council of Trent, which lasted over a period of twenty-seven years and produced more Church legislation than any other council in Church history.

JOHN MASON PECK

PECK, JOHN MASON (pek) 1789-1858 Illinois counts this Connecticut Baptist preacher one of her leading pioneers and founders. Zealous and resourceful Christian missionary on the frontier.

WILLIAM PENN

PENN, WILLIAM (pen) 1644-1718 English friend (Quaker), son of an admiral, most famous as the founder of the colony of Pennsylvania, a haven for his persecuted co-religionists and for many other persecuted groups. Friend of the Indians. Author and interpreter of the Quaker way.

PETER THE HERMIT

PETER THE HERMIT (pe'ter) 1050-1115? Peter of Amiens, a wandering preacher of the first Crusades who carried to great masses of people the sermon of Pope Urban II where he pled for the defense of Christianity and recovery of Jerusalem. The zealous preacher led a people's division of the Crusades to the Holy Land months ahead of the military, actually reaching Constantinople.

PETRI, LAURENTIUS (pay'tree) 1499-
1573 Laurentius and his brother Olaus were
students at Wittenberg. They became disciples of Martin Luther. Returning to their
native Sweden, Laurentius produced a translation of the N. T. in Swedish at the request
of the king.

LAURENTIUS
PETRI

PETRI, OLAUS (pay'tree) 1493-1552
Olaus preached the new Lutheran doctrines
in Sweden with the full sanction of the king,
though he met with considerable, opposition
from the Bishops. He went further even, and
though he was a priest, defied the mediaeval
church and was publicly married.

OLAUS PETRI

PIUS IX (pi'us) 1846-1878 Italian whose
papal reign was longest on record. Presided
over Vatican Council of 1870 which voted
the infallibility of popes when they officially
declare their mind on faith and morals. He
had earlier proclaimed the Immaculate Conception of the Virgin Mary.

PIUS IX

POLYCARP (pol'i-karp) c. 69-c. 156 Christian Bishop of Smyrna in the Second Century.
He claimed he had been a disciple of Christ's
Apostle John. He visited Rome about 154
A.D., where he disagreed with Bishop Ani-
cetus over the right date to celebrate Easter.
This is our first record of the observance of
that feast-day. As a very old man, Polycarp
was arrested in Smyrna, tried, condemned
and burned to death for his faith, about 156
A.D.

POLYCARP

R

ROBERT RAIKES

RAIKES, ROBERT (raks) 1735-1811 Pioneer of the modern Sunday School, with the establishment in 1789, in his home-town of Gloucester, England, of a Sunday class for the underprivileged children. He was influenced by John Wesley (q.v.) and George Whitefield (q.v.).

WALTER RAUSCHENBUSCH

RAUSCHENBUSCH, WALTER (rou'-schenbush) 1861-1918 German-American Baptist pastor and theological teacher. Earnest and influential exponent of the "Social Gospel", aiming at Christian reform of society. See his books, "Christianity and the Social Crisis" (1907) and "A Theology for the Social Gospel". (1917)

REMBRANDT

REMBRANDT (rem'brant) 1607-1669 Dutch painter of great depth, a profound interpreter of character. The Christ in his paintings and etchings is dignified, strong, and winsome.

MATTEO RICCI

RICCI, MATTEO (re'che) 1552-1610 Italian Jesuit who opened China for Christianity in the 16th century. He founded his first mission at Canton in 1582. Noted scholar, publishing numerous religious volumes in Chinese, the most outstanding of which was the "True Doctrine of God" in 1595. His translation of the 10 Commandments into Chinese, and a Chinese Catechism have been standard tools of missionaries through the years.

ROBERTSON, FREDERICK W. (rob'ert-s'n) 1816-1853 Gifted Anglican preacher, commonly known as Robertson of Brighton, because of his brilliant six-year ministry in that city. A "preacher's preacher".

FREDERICK W.
ROBERTSON

ROBINSON, JOHN (rob'in-sun) c. 1575-1625 English Separatist pastor of the Scrooby Church and then of the congregation in exile at Leyden. Always remembered for his prophecy "that God has yet more light and truth to break forth out of His Holy Word".

JOHN ROBINSON

RUSSELL, CHARLES TAZE (rus'el) 1852-1916 Prophet, teacher, builder of the fast-growing church known as Jehovah's Witnesses. The basis is the expectation of the imminent coming of the Thousand Years when Christ will reign on earth.

CHARLES TAZE
RUSSELL

S

SAVONAROLA, GIROLAMO (sav'o-na-ro'la) 1452-1498 Italian monk of prophetic eloquence, who shook Florence to its foundations by his condemnation of its evils. He hailed the conquering French king who drove out the powerful Medici family. He helped make Florence a Christian republic for a short time, and Christ was named king of the city. The Pope fiercely hated Savonarola, and the people turned against him, and hanged him and burned him.

GIROLAMO
SAVONAROLA

191

PHILIP SCHAFF

SCHAFF, PHILIP (shaf) 1819-1893 May be called the father of church history writing in our country, because of his many volumes on "The History of the Christian Church."

MICHAEL
SCHLATTER

SCHLATTER, MICHAEL (shla′ter) 1716-1790 A Swiss-born German Reformed minister who pioneered for his faith and order in colonial Pennsylvania. There he led in organizing the Reformed churches, under Dutch direction. Often served as chaplain to armed forces.

FRIEDRICH
ERNST DANIEL
SCHLEIERMACHER

SCHLEIERMACHER, FRIEDRICH ERNST DANIEL (shli′er-mak′er) 1768-1834 Influential German theologian who stressed the authority of experience as against more external and dogmatic authorities. To him, religion was the sense of dependence on God. He was both a preacher and a leader; An eminent expounder, and the heart of the movement which united the Lutheran and Reformed Churches of Prussia in 1817.

SAMUEL SIMON
SCHMUCKER

SCHMUCKER, SAMUEL SIMON (shmook′er) 1799-1873 American Lutheran leader, part-founder of Gettysburg Theological Seminary and Gettysburg College, and champion of inter-church co-operation.

SEABURY, SAMUEL (seabury) 1729-1796
A Connecticut man who became the first
bishop in the Protestant Episcopal Church in
the colonies as they were becoming the U. S.A.
He was consecrated in 1784 in Edinburgh,
Scotland. His diocese was Connecticut and
Rhode Island.

SAMUEL SEABURY

SERGIUS OF RADONEZH (sergius of
rad'onesh) 1314-1392 Russian Orthodox
monk, who, though a conspicuous peace-
maker, incited the Muscovites to attack their
overlords the Mongols. The Russians won.
Founder of Russia's greatest monastery, Holy
Trinity, near Moscow. Russia's most famous
saint.

SERGIUS OF
RADONEZH

SERRA, JUNIPERO (ser'a) 1713-1784
Most famous of those Spanish Franciscan
priests who founded the Roman Catholic missions of California.

JUNIPERO SERRA

SERVETUS, MICHAEL (sur-ve'tus) 1511-
1553 Brilliant and erratic Spaniard, famous
among medical men for his pioneering grasp
of the pulmonary circulation of the blood. A
determined and biting critic of the doctrine
of the Trinity, he made the mistake of turning
up in Calvin's Geneva, where he was burned
at the stake as a dangerous heretic: — one of
history's most famous fires.

MICHAEL
SERVETUS

CHARLES M.
SHELDON

SHELDON, CHARLES M. (shel'dun) 1857-1946 Congregationalist pastor at Topeka, Kansas, author of a book, "In His Steps", (1896) which aimed to suggest what Jesus would do if He were here today. The book went round the world in many languages, but may have sold 30,000,000 copies in our language alone.

SIMEON STYLITES

SIMEON STYLITES (sim'e-un sti-li'tez) d. 459 The fanatical Syrian monk who lived 36 years on the top of an increasingly taller pillar, three feet in diameter and finally sixty feet high.

JOSEPH SMITH

SMITH, JOSEPH (smith) 1805-1844 Vermont-born, he became, in Western New York, founder of the Mormon Church (1830), alleging he had found some golden plates containing a new revelation. He led his followers to settle in Illinois, where at length, in trouble with the law, he was killed by a mob entering his jail.

JOHN SMYTH

SMYTH, JOHN (smith) d. 1612 Pastor of the Separatist Congregation at Gainsborough, England, who fled with many followers to Amsterdam. Embraced Baptist principles, and is accounted the pioneer English Baptist. He died in Holland.

SOCINUS, FAUSTUS (so-si'nus) 1539-
1604 Italian Protestant reformer who broke
with Calvinistic theology to build what is
known as Socinianism. Especially successful
in Poland. An important link in the development of Unitarianism. Held the belief that
human reason was the only solid foundation
of Protestantism. Combated the chief Christian dogmas of original sin, human depravity,
and justification by faith.

FAUSTUS SOCINUS

SODERBLOM, NATHAN (su'der-bloom)
1866-1931 Swedish Lutheran Archbishop,
gifted thinker and author, leader in the ecumenical movement. He served as minister of
the Swedish Church in Paris and two years
as Professor of Comparative Theology at
Leipzig. In 1930 he was awarded the Nobel
Peace prize.

NATHAN
SODERBLOM

SPENER, PHILIP JACOB (shpa'ner)
1635-1705 German Lutheran pastor, pioneer
of what is known as Pietism. The Pietists
aimed to thaw out the cold, formal, dogmatic
character of Lutheranism by prayer groups,
Bible study, personal holiness.

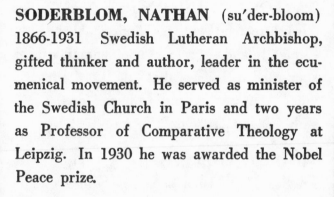

PHILIP JACOB
SPENER

SPURGEON, CHARLES H. (spur'jun)
1834-1892 Eloquent, evangelistic, English
Baptist preacher in London's Metropolitan
Tabernacle (seating 5,000).

CHARLES H.
SPURGEON

EMMANUEL SWEDENBORG

SWEDENBORG, EMMANUEL (swe'den-borg) 1688-1772 Learned Swedish scientist and engineer who, in middle life, was inspired by dreams and visions which he believed carried authentic Divine wisdom. The Church of the New Jerusalem (Swedenborgian) was born of his convictions.

T

J. HUDSON TAYLOR

TAYLOR, J. HUDSON (ta'ler) 1832-1905 Yorkshire man who in 1865 established the China Inland Mission, non-denominational, supported by a faith that "the Lord will provide". The success and influence of the mission was remarkable.

WILLIAM TEMPLE

TEMPLE, WILLIAM (tem'p'l) 1881-1944 Anglican Archbishop successively of York and of Canterbury, a theologian, and a leader in the formative period of the 20th Century Ecumenical movement. An aggressive adherent of social reform, he made the application of Christian philosophy to current problems a main task of his life. He crusaded against slums, usury, dishonesty and greed in business.

GILBERT TENNENT

TENNENT, GILBERT (tennent) 1703-1764 Born in Ireland, became powerful Presbyterian revivalist preacher in the period of the Great Awakening in the American colonies.

TENNYSON, ALFRED (ten′i-sun) 1809-1892 English poet who wrestled hard with the doubts of the new scientific age, and gave splendid expression to the faith that overcomes those doubts. See his "In Memoriam."

TERTULLIAN (ter-tul′i-an) d. c. 230 Sharp, intense, hard-hitting defender of the faith, in Carthage, North Africa. Lawyer by training. First important Christian to write in Latin, and many of his words come through into our English, as Person, Trinity, New Testament. Wrote a long answer to Marcion (q.v.). Late in life joined the sect of Montanists, who represented his very unworldly point of view.

TETZEL, JOHANN (tet′sel) 1465-1519 Dominican friar who was the initial spark that touched off the German Reformation in 1517. It was when Tetzel passed through Saxony selling "indulgences" for the forgiveness of sin that Martin Luther took issue and attacked this practice of the Church.

THEODOSIUS THE GREAT (the′o-do′-shi-us) d. 395 Mighty Roman Emperor, ruling from Constantinople, and called the first great ruler of strong Christian convictions. Under his rule the Second Ecumenical Council was held, setting forth the Nicene faith as the only faith of the Empire. The military fighter against the barbarians was also the Church's battler against Christian heretics and against pagans. Under him the Church and the government were tied so tightly together that only modern times have been able to break the tie, as in the U. S. A.

THERESA OF AVILA

THOMAS a BECKET

LEO N. TOLSTOY

THOMAS DE TORQUEMADA

THERESA OF AVILA (te-re'sa) 1515-1582 Roman Catholic Spain's greatest woman, Carmelite nun, earnest in prayer, a very gifted administrator of convent life, and one of the most brilliant of all Christian mystics.

THOMAS a BECKET (a bek'et) c. 1118-1170 First native Englishman to be Archbishop of Canterbury, the highest Churchman in England. Champion of the Church's rights against King Henry's attempts to rule the Church. Slain in his own cathedral by four knights of the king. King Henry later did penance at Becket's tomb. Two years after the "murder in the Cathedral" (see T. S. Eliot's play), Becket was made a saint.

TOLSTOY, LEO N. (tol-stoi') 1828-1910 Russian count, his chief fame as a novelist ("War and Peace" his masterpiece). Converted to a non-church Christian faith which rejected war and embraced poverty and labor and vegetarianism.

TORQUEMADA, THOMAS DE (tor'ka ma tha) 1420-1498 The Spanish Inquisitor under whom about 2,000 "heretics" were burned to death, and more than 100,000 ruined, and the Jews driven out of Spain. Fanatic for Spanish nationalism.

TYNDALE, WILLIAM (tin'dal) c. 1494-1536 Christian scholar, the genius behind the English Bible, the "John the Baptist" of English Protestantism. Forced out of England by his urge to translate the Bible into his native tongue, he studied in Germany. His translations of the Bible were smuggled into England, but most of them were burned. Finally trapped, imprisoned, tried, condemned and burned as a heretic, near Brussels. His dying prayer, "Lord, open the King of England's eyes", was being answered, for in 1537 an English Bible, largely made from Tyndale's translation, was on sale.

WILLIAM
TYNDALE

V

VINCENT DE PAUL (vin'sent de pol) c. 1576-1660 French Roman Catholic organizer of the Sisters of Charity, a nursing order, also of the Lazarists, who preached to the masses, educated priests, and served as foreign missionaries.

VINCENT
DE PAUL

W

WALDENSTRÖM, P. P. (wal-den'strum) 1838-1917 Swedish preacher, editor, theologian. His strong accent on God's love, as so much greater than God's wrath, led to controversy. He became in 1905 the leader of the Swedish Covenant Church.

P. P.
WALDENSTROM

WALTHER, CARL F. W. (val'ter) 1811-1887 Pioneer organizer and builder of the conservative German Lutherans in the Mississippi valley. The Missouri Synod, his creation, today has over 5,000 congregations.

CARL F. W.
WALTHER

ISAAC WATTS

SIMONE WEIL

CHARLES WESLEY

JOHN WESLEY

SUSANNA WESLEY

WATTS, ISAAC (wots) 1674-1748 The father of English hymnody. Long a Congregationalist pastor in London. By his many wonderful hymns (words) he led the English-speaking Protestant world away from singing only metrical Psalms, which were generally bad poetry set of doleful music. Most famous hymns: "O God Our Help in Ages Past"; "Jesus Shall Reign Where'er The Sun"; "When I Survey the Wondrous Cross".

WEIL, SIMONE (weel) 1909-1943 Brilliant French Jewess, who by choice lived close to the impoverished laborers, sharing their work and life. She became profoundly Christian, close to Roman Catholicism, though never officially embracing that allegiance. Her "Waiting for God" reveals the depth of her mystical faith.

WESLEY, CHARLES (wes'li) 1757-1834 Brother of John (q.v.), Methodist preacher, and author of thousands of hymns, of which some are among the greatest in our language. "Christ The Lord Is Risen Today".

WESLEY, JOHN (wes'li) 1703-1791 Anglican priest, member of "The Holy Club" at Oxford, and unsuccessful missionary to the colony of Georgia. In London in 1738 he knew for sure that Christ was his strong Saviour, and with other members of the club he preached a warm contagious Gospel to the soul-hungry masses of England. Founded the Methodists of the world, even though he claimed no intent of breaking from the Church of England. An organizational genius.

WESLEY, SUSANNA (wes'li) 1669-1742 Mother of John (q.v.) and Charles (q.v.), and doubtless the first "Methodist" and one of the remarkable Christian mothers.

WHITE, WILLIAM (hwit) 1784-1836 Rector of Christ Church, Philadelphia. A chief builder of the Protestant Episcopal body. In 1786 he was elected bishop of the new diocese of Philadelphia, and was consecrated in London, 1787.

WILLIAM WHITE

WHITEFIELD, GEORGE (hwit'feld) 1714-1770 English revivalist preacher, life-long friend and associate of the Wesleys. His astonishing eloquence was the major instrument of the colonial American Great Awakening, a revival movement (c. 1740) from Maine to Georgia.

GEORGE
WHITEFIELD

WHITMAN, MARCUS (hwit'man) 1802-1847 Pioneer Presbyterian missionary to what is now Washington State. Physician, and elder in the first Protestant Church west of Rockies. With wife Narcissa, he was murdered by Indians.

MARCUS
WHITMAN

WHITTIER, JOHN GREENLEAF (hwit'-i-er) 1809-1892 New England Quaker poet and anti-slavery crusader. His "Dear Lord and Father of Mankind" is sung very widely, as is his "We May Not Climb the Heavenly Steeps".

JOHN GREENLEAF
WHITTIER

WILLIAM OF NASSAU, PRINCE OF ORANGE (wil'yam) 1533-1584 The George Washington of the Dutch, the architect of the United Netherlands as a Protestant state. Notable for his championship of religious tolerance.

WILLIAM OF
NASSAU

GEORGE WILLIAMS

ROGER WILLIAMS

JOHN WOOLMAN

SIR CHRISTOPHER
WREN

JOHN WYCLIFFE

WILLIAMS, GEORGE (wil'yamz) 1821-1905 Founder in London, 1844, of the Young Men's Christian Association.

WILLIAMS, ROGER (wil'yamz) c. 1603-c. 1683 English Puritan clergyman who in earliest Massachusetts objected to its restrictions on religious liberty, and fled south to establish Providence Plantation (1636), later united in the colony of Rhode Island. Instrumental in founding the First Baptist Church in America, 1639, but left it very soon to become a "seeker". World-famous as a pioneer exponent of complete separation of Church and State.

WOOLMAN, JOHN (wool'man) 1720-1772 Quaker farmer and tailor in the Colony of New Jersey, who travelled widely in the special interest of getting his fellow Quakers to release their slaves. His Journal, more and more esteemed with the passing generations, reveals one of the most Christlike men in Christian history.

WREN, SIR CHRISTOPHER (ren) 1632-1723 Noted English Architect born at East Knoyle in Wiltshire October 20, 1632. One of the world's most famous designers of Churches and Cathedrals. Best remembered for his restoration of the beautiful St. Paul's Cathedral, London.

WYCLIFFE, JOHN (wik'lif) c. 1324-1384 Oxford scholar, professor and priest who called loudly and earnestly for the reform of the Roman Catholic Church in England, long before the age of Luther. He sent out preachers two by two to reach the people with a simple gospel message, and he guided and inspired a translation of the Bible into English.

X

XAVIER, FRANCIS (za'vi-er) 1506-1552
Spanish Roman Catholic missionary to the
Orient. An original member of the Jesuits
(see Loyola). His abiding popularity is attested by the widespread occurrence of the
name Francis X. in any telephone directory.

FRANCIS XAVIER

Y

YOUNG, BRIGHAM (yung) 1801-1877
Poor Vermont boy who became the most decisive leader of the Mormons, guiding them
on their trek through the desert to the founding of Utah (1847) and the beginnings of a
prosperous city and state under Mormon
auspices.

BRIGHAM YOUNG

Z

ZEISBERGER, DAVID (zis'bur'ger) 1721-
1808 Born in Moravia, a member of the so-
called Moravian Church. Devoted missionary
to Indians in North America, living so closely
with them he came to look like them.

DAVID
ZEISBERGER

ZINZENDORF, COUNT, N. L. VON (fon
tsin'tsen-dorf) 1700-1760 At first the bene-
factor of the religious exiles from Moravia
who settled on his Saxon estate, this devout
Christian became their leader in 1727. These
Moravians went to America, where he named
the town of Bethlehem, Pennsylvania. See his
hymn, "Jesus, Still Lead On".

COUNT N. L.
VON ZINZENDORF

ZWINGLI, HULDREICH or ULRICH
(zwing'gli) 1484-1529 Swiss Roman Catholic
priest, who as preacher in Zurich found himself a Protestant, and gave powerful leadership to the German-speaking Swiss cities who
became Protestant with Zurich.

ULRICH
ZWINGLI

SPECIAL TERMS

ANABAPTIST — means "baptized again", but the Anabaptists of the 16th Century denied that infant baptism was true baptism.

ANGLICAN — describes the Church body that is the officially established Church in England, the Church of the King or Queen.

ASCETIC — describes the person or the life of radical self-denial, especially with respect to the body's cravings.

CANONIZE — to elevate to the rank of saint in the Roman Catholic Church.

ECUMENICAL — adjective descriptive of the world-wide Christian movement; widely revived in our century to describe all our attempts to bring Church bodies together.

HERESY — false or incorrect belief, as opposed to orthodoxy.

HERETIC — in many Christian centuries he has been murdered with the Church's approval.

HOLY ROMAN EMPIRE — the long fumbling attempt to create a civil state in complete accord with the Roman Catholic Church.

INQUISITION — the bitter and murderous attempt of the medieval Church to ferret out and condemn the heretic.

MYSTIC — one who grasps truth by other than purely rational methods; in an extreme sense, one guided by visions and dreams and voices.

ORTHODOX — by Greek derivation, describes right or correct praise, but means generally correct belief. The word with a capital O refers to the Eastern Orthodox Church, the extensive family of church bodies with roots in the Middle East. 1054 A.D. is sometimes given as the decisive date of its separation from the Roman Catholic Church, but the roots of this separation are much older. The ruling patriarch resides in Constantinople.

PURITAN — English church party or member who believed in a stricter interpretation of Christian ethics and simpler forms of worship than did Anglicans generally. Roots especially in reign of Queen Elizabeth I (16th Century).

SAINT — in the New Testament, all Christian believers; in the older Churches, a Christian who achieves unusual holiness of life and conspicuous good deeds, and is officially entitled "saint".

SEPARATIST — Christian person or group that left the Church of England (16th - 17th Centuries) to set up separate congregations. Most Puritans were also Separatists.

Chapter IV
Facts About the Church

ABBEY　The church of a monastery ruled over by an abbot or of a convent for women by an abbess.

ABLUTION　Ceremonial cleansing of the sacred vessels (chalice and paten) after the Eucharist; washing of the priest's hands; a washing or cleansing as a religious rite.

ABSOLUTION　The declaration in a public service or privately by a minister, of God's forgiveness and remission of sins, to those who are repentant and have made a confession of their sins.

ABSTINENCE　The giving up of certain foods or pleasures, such as meat on Fridays, in remembrance of Christ's death on Good Friday, and for the sake of self-discipline.

ACOLYTE　One who assists the minister at the altar in the Eucharist; sometimes called server or altar boy. Originally one of the minor orders of ministers ordained symbolically with cruet and candle.

ACOUSTIC JARS　These were earthenware jars buried beneath, or in the walls of, the choir, with their openings directed toward the interior of the church. They were skillfully designed and so placed as to result in stronger and more resonant tones throughout the church.

ADORATION　The worship given to God in prayer — an outward act and an inward attitude; a type of prayer.

ADVENT　(color: violet)　From Latin advenire, to arrive — the first season of the Church Year, beginning the fourth Sunday before Christmas. The season of preparation for Christ's "Coming" at Christmastide and for his Second Coming to judge the world.

ADVENT SUNDAY　(color: violet) The first Sunday in Advent and the first day of the Christian Year, sometimes called "The Christian's New Year's Day" — always the Sunday nearest November 30th.

AFFUSION　The pouring (not sprinkling) of water upon the head of the person in baptism. (See IMMERSION)

ABBEY

ABLUTION

ACOLYTE

AFFUSION

AISLE

ALB

ALMS BASIN

ALMS BOX

AGNUS DEI　(Lamb of God) An anthem of devotion; a title of Jesus, spoken by John the Baptist, "Behold the Lamb of God, which taketh away the sin of the world" (John 1:29). The Agnus Dei is often a symbol of Christ — a lamb with or without a banner.

AISLE　A division of a church on either side of a nave, often separated by columns or arches. It is incorrectly, although commonly, used to designate a passageway in the nave between pews, properly called a "pace" or alley.

ALB or ALBE　A long white linen basic garment (shoulders to ankles) worn by ministers who celebrate the Holy Communion in Eucharistic Vestments. The alb is always worn with an amice, and is white symbolizing purity. This vestment can be worn by an acolyte or crucifer. (See AMICE)

ALL SAINTS' DAY　(color: white) November 1st — The holy day when we remember all the saints and martyrs of the church. It is also called ALL HALLOW'S DAY; from its eve we get our word Hallowe'en.

ALL SOULS' DAY　(color: black) November 2nd — a holy day in commemoration of the faithful who have died. It is combined with the observance of All Saints' Day in some churches.

ALLELUIA　An exclamation derived from the Hebrew words meaning "praise ye Jehovah."

ALLEY　The passageway between rows of pews. (See AISLE)

ALMS　Originally money or gifts for the poor. It has been extended to mean offerings by congregations or gifts for any religious or charitable purpose.

ALMS BASIN　A large plate, usually of metal, in which are placed the offerings and alms of the worshippers for presentation before the altar.

ALMS BOX　A box or receptacle in the vestibule or narthex for receiving alms.

ALPHA AND OMEGA　The beginning and the end. First and last letters of the Greek alphabet, used in church symbolism to suggest the everlasting nature of Christ's divinity, as in Rev. 1:8, "I am Alpha and Omega."

ALTAR   A table of stone or wood upon which the Holy Communion is consecrated. (See COMMUNION TABLE)

ALTAR

ALTAR BREAD   The bread used in the sacrament of the Lord's Supper. In early days the bread was often unleavened, and may be today; however, since the Reformation, bread as usually eaten is used, but carefully selected of the best and purest quality. (See HOST)

ALTAR COLOR   The seasonal or liturgical color for the day observed in changes of the altar hangings. The dossal and riddles are sometimes neutral and not changed. (See COLOR—LITURGICAL)

ALTAR CROSS   The cross surmounting an altar at the center — sometimes in modern churches hanging above the altar.

ALTAR DESK   Same as MISSAL STAND.

ALTAR DESK

ALTAR HANGINGS   A collective term for frontal, antependia, superfrontal, dossal, and riddles.

ALTAR LIGHTS   A collective term for candles on an altar; sometimes used to designate branch candelabra. See EUCHARISTIC LIGHTS (Communion) and VESPER (Office) LIGHTS.

ALTAR LINEN   A collective term for the cerecloth, altar cloth or fair linen, corporal, chalice veil, purificators, pall, etc. (See separate notes on above.)

ALTAR RAIL   The railing enclosing the sanctuary or surrounding the altar at which communicants kneel to receive the Eucharist; also called sanctuary rail. (See CHANCEL RAIL)

AMBO

ALTAR STEPS   A series of three or more steps often designated as the footpace (top platform), deacon's or gospeller's step (middle), and subdeacon's or epistle step (bottom).

AMBO   A pulpit or platform and reading desk from which Scripture Lessons are read. (See LECTERN)

AMBRY   (See AUMBRY)

AMBULATORY   The passageway found in some churches behind the altar and around the chancel. It is used for choir processionals.

AMBULATORY

AMICE

AMPULLA

ANGELUS

ANTEPENDIUM

AMEN   The response said or sung at the end of prayers, creeds, hymns, and anthems, signifying approval or solemn ratification. ('So be it', 'Verily')

AMICE   A linen neckpiece and collar worn with the alb. It was originally a hood covering the head and neck, symbolizing the helmet of salvation.

AMPULLA   Another name for cruet.

ANATHEMA   A solemn ban or curse pronounced upon a person or thing; a sentence of excommunication.

ANGEL   (Gr. messenger) A spiritual being who serves God; a messenger from heaven. The nine choirs of angels are — seraphim, cherubim, thrones, dominations, virtues, powers, principalities, archangels, and angels. (See ARCHANGEL)

ANGELUS   A form of devotion commemorating the incarnation. It is said at morning (6 a.m.), noon, and night (6 p.m.) accompanying the ringing of a bell in a pattern of 3, 3, 3 and a peal of 9 to 27.

ANGLICAN CHURCH or COMMUNION   Those churches which are in communion with the Church of England and hold the same faith, order, and worship.

ANGLO-CATHOLIC   Meaning universal Church of England — it is used also to designate the High Church group, which emphasizes the ceremonial and catholic approach of churchmanship.

ANOINT   To bless with oil at an ordination, coronation, baptism, etc., or for healing of the sick. (See UNCTION)

ANTEPENDIUM   A cloth which hangs from the pulpit or lectern, usually of silk and embroidered. The hanging on the front of an altar. (See FRONTAL)

ANTHEM   Originally antiphon; it refers to any musical setting of words usually of Scripture or sacred poetry.

ANTIPHON   A verse from Scripture, or an appropriate piece sung before or after the Psalms or Canticles.

ANTIPHONAL   Responsive singing as on alternate verses of Psalms and Canticles between two sides of a choir or a minister or precentor and choir. (See CANTORIS and DECANI)

APOSTLE   Particularly one of the twelve whom the Lord chose to send forth in his name; one sent forth, an ambassador, a missionary.

APOSTLES' CREED   The earliest statement of the Christian faith. Tradition early attributed each article to one of the Twelve Apostles; although improbable, it emphasizes the apostolic nature of its teachings and doctrine.

APOSTOLIC
SUCCESSION

APOSTOLIC   According to the doctrines, teaching, and practice of the Apostles. The Nicene Creed describes the church as "Apostolic," because it seeks to follow the Apostles' teaching and way of life.

APOSTOLIC SUCCESSION   The spiritual authority conferred by the laying on of hands in ordination upon the ministry of the church through a lineal succession of bishops from the apostles.

APPAREL   A colored ornament, richly embroidered, attached on the collar of the amice and upon the cuffs and bottom of an alb.

APPAREL

APSE   A semicircular or polygonal projection or termination to the sanctuary of a church.

ARCHANGEL   The highest ranking angel. Saints Michael, Gabriel, Raphael, and Uriel are the four archangels. Illustration shows St. Michael's symbol.

ARCHBISHOP   A chief bishop who presides over a province or convocation of bishops; a title but not a separate order of the ministry.

APSE

ARCHDEACON   A title given to a minister who presides over an archdeaconry or convocation, or to one who is general missionary of the diocese or has charge of the general missionary work in a diocese.

ASCENSION DAY   (color: white) It commemorates the ascension of Christ to heaven and the end of the resurrection appearances; Holy Thursday or the 40th day after Easter. See Acts 1:9.

ASCRIPTION   Words spoken by a clergyman at the beginning and the end of his sermon.

ASH WEDNESDAY   (color: violet) The beginning of Lent, recalling the Lord's conquering of temptation in the wilderness. The name is derived from the ceremonial practice of placing ashes on the forehead on this day. (See LENT)

St. Michael

ARCHANGEL

ASPERGES

ASPERGES The ceremony of sprinkling altar, clergy, and people with holy water; the anthem "Thou shalt purge me with hyssop and I shall be clean." (Psalm 51:7)

ATHANASIAN CREED A long detailed form of the Christian creed written in the 5th or 6th century setting forth the doctrine of the trinity.

ATONEMENT (at-one-ment, or *at one with God.*) The doctrine that Christ by his incarnation, suffering, and death redeemed man or reconciled man to God. (See REDEMPTION)

AUMBRY

AUMBRY or AMBRY A closed cupboard or receptacle made into or attached to the wall of the chancel or sacristy for the reservation of the Eucharist and the keeping of the holy oils or sacred vessels.

AUMBRY LAMP A light located near the aumbry to indicate the presence of the sacred elements.

AVE MARIA (Hail, Mary) The salutation of Gabriel and of Elizabeth to the Virgin Mary; an early Christian prayer; the title of a well-known anthem based on words of the prayer.

B

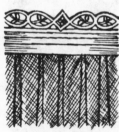

BAGUETTE

BAGUETTE The plain or decorated molding of wood across the top of a dossal, or suspended from a cornice to enhance the beauty of the dossal.

BALDACHIN Usually of stone. An Italian term for the canopy or dome erected above the altar. It may be of metal, wood, or cloth.

BAMBINO A figure of the infant Christ in a crèche or picture.

BANNERS For procession. Banners embroidered with sacred symbols are sometimes carried in church processions. They may be marked to designate classes or organizations within the church. Banners, recognizing faithful class attendance and class offering, are also used in the church schools of many denominations.

BALDACHIN

BANNS The proclamation of an intended marriage in the church.

BAPTISM   A rite associated with membership in the Church; a sacrament (ordinance) representing an act of Christian obedience to be observed after conversion to Christ. Baptism varies from pouring or sprinkling to immersion. Some denominations practice baptism without sacramental implications; other denominations accept baptism as a saving rite.

BAPTISM

BAPTISMAL BOWL   A removable metal or crystal bowl sitting into the baptismal font and holding the water used for baptism by sprinkling or pouring.

BAPTISMAL FONT   A stand or pedestal, either of stone or wood, containing a basin for water used in the rite of baptism.

BAPTISMAL ROBE   A clergyman's robe especially designed to be worn over the baptismal trousers during the sacrament of baptism by immersion.

BAPTISMAL ROBE

BAPTISMAL SHELL   A shell for pouring the water in baptism upon the head of the person to be baptized. It may be real or of precious metal.

BAPTISMAL SLEEVES   Sleeves of waterproof material reaching to the shoulders of the minister, and with tight-fitting cuffs at the wrist to keep the arms dry during the sacrament of baptism by immersion.

BAPTISMAL TROUSERS and BOOTS   Trousers reaching up to the chest, and secured at the bottom to rubber boots. Worn by the clergy when administering the sacrament of baptism by immersion.

BASILICA

BAPTISTRY   The place where the baptismal font is located, usually near the entrance to the church. The baptistry may be in a side chapel or even in a separate building. In some non-liturgical churches the term refers to the large tank in the front of the church for purposes of immersion.

BASILICA   A church built in the style of an ancient oblong Roman hall, often with an apse at one end and a narthex at the other.

BAY   A subdivision between the columns of nave, choir, or transept.

BELFRY   The area or room containing the church bells, usually in an arch, a steeple, or a tower. (See CAMPANILE)

BAY

213

BELFRY

BIER

BIRETTA

BISHOP

BELL   A bell is used to ring from tower or steeple as an invitation for folk to come to the house of God. A chime or carillon of bells sends music and hymns of the church out over the community and reminds of the priority of the things of God over the things of man.

BELL COTE   A small open arched turret on some part of the outside church structure; in it, a single bell may be hung.

BENEDICTION   The blessing pronounced in God's name by the minister upon the congregation at the end of a service.

BETROTHAL   A mutual contract for a future marriage; in ritualistic churches that part of the marriage service in which the man and the woman join hands and give their troth (meaning truth, vow, or promise of faithfulness) each to the other.

BIBLE, THE HOLY   The sacred literature of the Christian religion, containing 39 Old Testament books, 14 Apocrypha (omitted from Protestant versions), and 27 of the New Testament. The Bible is a whole library, containing history, drama, poetry, and letters. There are many versions or translations, as:

DV	Douay Version — Roman Catholic	1610
KJ	King James or Authorized Version	1611
ERV	(English) Revised Version	1885
ASV	American Standard Version	1901
RSV	Revised Standard Version	1952

BIDDING PRAYER   An exhortatory prayer said by the clergyman before the sermon, especially in purely preaching services.

BIER   The carriage or frame upon which a coffin is placed in a church, or borne to a grave or a vault.

BIRETTA   A stiff four-sided cap worn by certain of the clergy in processions and in church services.

BISHOP   (Greek for overseer) In certain churches a clergyman of the highest of the three orders of the ministry (bishops, priests, and deacons). The functions peculiar to the office of a bishop are to preside over his diocese or missionary district, consecrate other bishops, ordain to the ministry, administer confirmation, consecrate church buildings, and administer ecclesiastical discipline. Bishops are successors of the apostles. (See APOSTOLIC SUCCESSION, ORDINARY)

BISHOP, COADJUTOR A bishop who is elected to assist the bishop of a diocese, and who upon the latter's death or resignation succeeds him in office.

BISHOP, SUFFRAGAN A bishop elected to assist the bishop of a diocese, but without the right of succession to his office.

BISHOP'S CHAIR In churches and missions a chair usually placed in the sanctuary for use of the bishop on his visitation. (See CATHEDRA)

BISHOP'S RING A heavy gold signet ring, usually with the seal of the diocese engraved in an amethyst.

BISHOP'S THRONE The seat or cathedra of the bishop, permanently located in a cathedral, usually in the sanctuary.

BOAT (navicula) A vessel for carrying incense for use in a censer as needed; boat boy, one who carries the boat.

BOBECHE A saucer-like receptacle of glass or metal with a hole in the center which fits over a candle and slides to the bottom to catch the melted wax drippings.

BISHOP'S
RING

BOOK OF REMEMBRANCE A book, usually kept in the narthex or vestibule of the church, in which are permanently recorded memorial gifts to the church, such as lectern, windows, cross, candlesticks, pictures. Names of donors, persons memorialized, dates, etc., are included.

BOOKMARK, BIBLE A wide ribbon in the pulpit or lectern Bible, hanging down in front toward the congregation, usually bearing an appropriate symbol.

BISHOP'S
THRONE

BOWING An expression of reverence to Christ in the doxology, gloria, creed, at the name "Jesus," and before the cross on altars and in processionals (Philippians 2:10).

BREAD BOX A covered container, usually of silver, for holding the wafer or bread of the Eucharist.

BREAD PLATE A plate, usually of silver or brass, from which the participant in the sacrament of the Lord's Supper is served the bread. (See PATEN)

BOAT

BREAD PLATE

BROAD CHURCH   A popular name for church people who are liberal in doctrine and in attitude; churchmanship between liturgical (high) and evangelical (low) emphasis; a term often used in the Anglican Church.

BULLETIN   Usually a printed folder with an appropriate picture on the front and on the remaining pages the order of service, announcements for the parish, and messages from the pastor, for distribution at the morning worship and for mailing.

BULLETIN BOARD   Either a large frame set up on a church lawn or wall and sometimes illuminated, stating plainly the name of the church, the clergyman, and his address, or a frame within a church having movable letters to announce Sunday and weekday services or to proclaim pertinent Christian messages or announcements.

BULLETIN BOARD

BURSE   The square pocket or purse which is made to contain the corporal, linen chalice veil, and often extra purificators. It is placed over the veiled chalice and paten on the altar. It is usually of the same material (silk) and color as the chalice veil.

BUTTRESS   A projecting structure or wing built into a wall to strengthen and support the wall or building.

BUTTRESS, FLYING   A masonry beam or bar in arched form from the upper part of a buttress to take the thrust of a roof or vault.

BURSE

C

CALENDAR   The Christian calendar or church calendar (also spelled Kalendar, 'to reckon') is based on the church year beginning with **Advent**, and containing the saints' days and holy days to be observed, depending on denomination or churchmanship. It often includes lections and fast days.

CAMPANILE   A bell tower attached to or separate from a church.

CANDLE FOLLOWERS   (sometimes called Wax Followers) A hood-like covering of glass or metal with hole in the top which is pressed down on candle, permitting the wick to come through and forming an enclosed small puddle which holds the melted wax and eliminates unsightly dripping.

BUTTRESS

CANDLE LIGHTER A stick usually of brass with wooden handle, equipped to hold a wax taper from which the altar candles are lighted. An extinguisher bell is also provided to put out the flame after the service.

CAMPANILE

CANDLEMAS An ancient name given to the feast of the purification of the Virgin Mary, February 2nd, in remembrance of the Lord having been announced by Simeon in the canticle Nunc Dimittis, to be "a light to lighten the Gentiles" (Luke 2:25-32). Tapers and candles are traditionally blessed on this day and carried in procession.

CANDLES The use of candles on the altar is an ancient practice of the church. When the church was driven by persecution underground into the catacombs lamps and candles were the only light. They symbolize Christ as "the Light of the World."

CANDLE

CANON The word canon means rule and is used for:

1. Canon of Scripture — the list of genuine and inspired books of the Bible.

2. The canon laws of the church.

3. The canon of consecration, prayer in the service of the Lord's Supper.

4. A title of certain clergy attached to a cathedral.

CANOPY

CANONICAL According to the canon laws of the church; authoritative, official.

CANONICAL HOURS The daily offices or stated times of the day appointed from ancient times for prayer and devotion. They are: lauds (after midnight); prime (6 A.M.); tierce (9 A.M.); sext (noon); nones (3 P.M.); and compline (bedtime). Matins or morning prayer today is a service made up from lauds, prime, and tierce; vespers or evening prayer from sext, nones, and compline.

CANONIZATION The ceremony by which a deceased Christian is declared by the church to be regarded as a saint; a rite practiced by the Roman Catholic church since the 12th century.

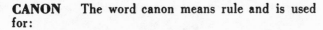

CARDINAL

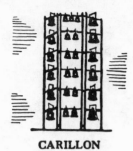

CARILLON

CASSOCK

CATHEDRAL

CELEBRANT

CANOPY (or baldachin) An overhanging cover of a rich fabric of silk and gold or of stone, carved wood, or metal over an altar, pulpit, or bishop's throne.

CANTICLE (little song) A psalm taken from the Scriptures to be said or sung in the services of the church.

CANTORIS (cantor, singer) The side of the choir where the cantor, or precentor, or choir leader sits. For antiphonal singing the opposite side is called the decani. If the altar is at the eastern end, this would usually be the north side of the choir.

CARDINAL A title used in the Roman Catholic church for those appointed by the pope as princes of the church and members of the college of cardinals.

CARILLON A set of at least 23 fixed tuned bells in chromatic order (originally only four), in a tower, on which may be played hymns and tunes by means of an electric keyboard or hand clavier.

CAROL A hymn, joyful in character, sung at the great festivals, such as Christmas, Easter, etc.

CASSOCK A long garment reaching from the shoulders to the ankles, worn by both clergy and choir and all who assist in the services. Cassocks are usually black, but purple for bishops and often red for acolytes; today other colors — white, blue, maroon, etc., — are being used for choirs.

CATECHISM A summary of Christian principles and doctrine in the form of questions and answers to be learned by church members before baptism or confirmation.

CATECHUMEN A convert, or one who is receiving rudimentary instruction in the doctrines of Christianity.

CATHEDRA A chair for the sole use of the bishop in the sanctuary of a cathedral. It is the sign of the bishop's authority.

CATHEDRAL (cathedra Gr. chair) The principal church of the diocese, where the bishop has his *cathedra* or throne.

CATHOLIC   Means universal, all-embracing. The church is described in the creeds as catholic "because it is universal, holding earnestly the faith for all time, in all countries, and for all people, and is sent to preach the gospel to the whole world." It is incorrect to refer to the Roman-Catholic church exclusively as "The Catholic church," for there are other catholic churches — the Uniat, Anglo-Catholic, Greek, etc.

CENSER

CELEBRANT   The minister who celebrates the Eucharist, whether bishop or priest. A deacon may not celebrate the Eucharist, but he may assist the celebrant in administration. The service is often referred to as a "celebration."

CELIBACY   State of being unmarried; required of the clergy of the Roman Catholic church but optional in other churches, except in certain religious orders.

CENSER   A vessel with cover, hung on chains, in which incense is burned. (See THURIBLE)

CERECLOTH   The basic cloth which covers an altar and lies beneath the fair linen. It is waxed, coarse linen (often unbleached) and just the length and breadth of the altar.

CHALICE

CEREMONIAL   The formalities, rules, customs, and usages of worship services.

CHALICE   The cup, usually of silver (or gold), in which the wine is consecrated in the service of the Eucharist. If the chalice is of silver, it often is gold-plated within, and is so required in the Roman Church.

CHALICE VEIL   A silk square veil with matching burse (color of season), used to cover the empty chalice.

CHALICE
VEIL

CHANCEL   The part of the church (the east end) which contains the sanctuary and the choir, usually raised by the chancel steps above the nave.

CHANCEL RAIL or SCREEN   A rail separating chancel from nave, as distinct from altar or sanctuary rail. When a screen separates chancel and nave it is called a chancel screen. (See ROOD SCREEN)

CHANCELLOR   An officer of the diocese whose function is to act as legal advisor; a dignitary of a cathedral; the titular head of a university.

CHANCEL

CHANTRY

CHANT   The musical recitation of parts of the service such as the Psalms and canticles. (See INTONE, ANTIPHONAL)

CHANTRY   A chapel where daily prayers are chanted or said.

CHAPEL   A separate house of worship from the main parish church; a sanctuary with an altar often dedicated to some saint or the Virgin, adjacent to the church or cathedral, as the Lady Chapel; a building or room for worship and devotion with or without an altar, within an institution, as in a school, hospital, monastery, prison, or private dwelling.

CHAPEL

CHAPLAIN   A clergyman whose duty is ministering to the religious needs of a school, fraternity, hospital, legislative body, on board ship, or in military service.

CHAPTER   A main division of one of the books of the Bible; a meeting of the canons of a cathedral presided over by the dean; the governing body of a cathedral; the house in which the canons meet; a branch or unit of an organization.

CHARGE   The people or parish or church over whom a clergyman is placed; an address containing instruction, admonition, and exhortation (as a bishop's or a minister's charge) to the clergy and people at a convention; or a charge to the new minister at his ordination.

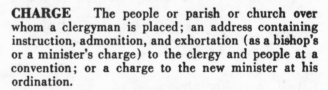

CHAPLAIN

CHASUBLE   A large, oval-shaped vestment (eucharistic) of linen or silk, either plain or colored, without sleeves, worn over the alb, with an opening in the center to go over the head of the celebrant. It is usually decorated on the back with orphreys forming a cross, and, if colored, conforms to the season of the church year. It represents the robe which the Roman soldiers placed on Christ after they had scourged him (John 19:2).

CHIMERE   A bishop's vestment, long, usually of black satin, with armholes but no sleeves, worn over the white rochet.

CHIMES   Bells numbering under 23 but over 6 or 8 constitute a chime.

CHASUBLE

CHOIR   The singers who assist in services of worship; the part of the chancel where the choir sits.

CHOIR GOWN   The gown worn by the choir during divine service. It is usually just a cassock, sometimes with a surplice or stole added.

CHIMERE

CHOIR LOFT   A section of raised pews or stalls, usually within the chancel, which are occupied by the choir during a service of worship.

CHOIR OFFICE   A service which is said or sung in the part of the chancel known as the choir, such as morning and evening prayer.

CHOIR STALLS   The name given to the pews in the section where the choir sings. The stalls are usually deeper, with higher and carved ends, than the usual pews in the nave.

CHORAL SERVICE   A musical service, particularly one where parts are intoned by the minister.

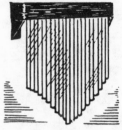

CHIMES

CHORISTER   A singer in a church choir, usually applied to children.

CHRISM   A consecrated oil (olive oil mingled with balsam) for use in ceremonial services and for anointing, as in baptism, confirmation, ordination, etc. In the Eastern Church the priest is allowed to confirm with the chrism consecrated by the bishop.

CHRISOM   A white robe or mantle put over a child in baptism as a sign of innocence.

CHRISTEN   To receive into the church by baptism; to name at baptism; hence, baptism is sometimes called "christening" in some denominations.

CHRISTIAN   One who believes in Jesus Christ and who follows his teaching. A term first used at Antioch as a name for the followers of Christ.

CHOIR

CHRISTIAN NAME   The name or names given and received in baptism.

CHRISTIAN YEAR or CHURCH YEAR   The ecclesiastical calendar of the seasons and holy days, beginning with the first Sunday in Advent (the Sunday nearest St. Andrew's Day, November 30th), the fourth Sunday before Christmas. (See CALENDAR)

CHRISTMAS DAY   (color: white) The feast of the Nativity (or birth) of Christ. It is an immovable feast falling on December 25th. It is a holy day among all Christians.

CHOIR GOWN

CHOIR LOFT

CHORISTER

CHURCH

CIBORIUM

CHRISTMASTIDE The twelve days from Christmas to Epiphany (also called Twelfth-night). The color of the season is white.

CHURCH An edifice or house of worship; the baptized body of Christian believers in and followers of Jesus Christ; a term used as a collective name for all of a denomination or organized group of Christians.

CHURCH EXPECTANT The body of faithful departed from this life awaiting the Last Judgment and the final resurrection; the intermediate state; the church (Christian body of faithful departed) resting in paradise awaiting judgment and resurrection. (See PARADISE)

CHURCH MILITANT The church universal on earth engaged in fighting (hence, militant) against sin.

CHURCH SCHOOL An organization within the church and conducted by it in which all ages of children, youth, and adults study the Bible and the application of biblical teaching to the individual and to his fellows of the community, the nation, and the world.

CHURCH TRIUMPHANT The souls in heaven who have perfect consummation and bliss in God's presence.

CHURCHING (OF WOMEN) A service of thanksgiving of women after childbirth; related to the purification of the Virgin Mary.

CIBORIUM A covered chalice or box, usually of silver, for holding the bread of the Eucharist.

CINCTURE A girdle of cloth worn by the clergy over the cassock.

CIRCUMCISION, THE FEAST OF THE (color: white) January 1st, because it was eight days after birth, according to the Jewish law of circumcision, that the infant Jesus was taken to the temple.

CLERESTORY The upper part of the nave, choir, and transepts of a church or cathedral, which rises above or clear of the aisle and usually contains windows.

CLERGY A collective name for those ordained to the ministry and service of God, as distinct from laity. **CLERGYMAN** One who is ordained.

CLERGY CROSSES These are small crosses usually of sterling silver, sometimes carved or inset with precious stones, and worn with a chain by the clergy.

CINCTURE

CLERICAL COLLAR A stiff white collar which buttons in the rear, worn by clergymen.

CLERK An officer of the church who keeps records of business meetings, membership lists, and attends to official correspondence for the church.

CLOISTER A covered walk or passageway on the grounds of a church or college, monastery, or convent establishment.

CLERESTORY

COLLECT A short prayer for use before a "collection" of people.

COLLECT FOR THE DAY A short prayer appointed for the day of the church year and one which "collects" or sums up the thought of the day or season.

COLLECTION PLATE A large plate made of brass, wood, silver, bakelite, etc., used for the purpose of receiving the offerings of the congregation attending a worship service. (See ALMS BASIN)

COLLECTOR A person chosen to collect the offerings and other money which is turned over to the treasurer.

CLERICAL
COLLAR

COLOR, LITURGICAL The colors of the hangings on the altar, pulpit, and lectern, and of the stoles and Eucharistic vestments worn by the clergy, appropriate to the season of the church year. Each color is symbolic: *white* for purity and joy, used on the great festivals of Christmas and Easter; *red* for blood and fire, used on martyrs' days and Pentecost; *purple* or *violet* for penitence and mourning, used during Advent and Lent; *green* for life, hope, and peace, used for Epiphany and Trinity season; *black* for death, used on Good Friday and for funerals and requiem Eucharists; *rose* used in some churches for 3rd Sunday in Advent and mid-Lent Sunday.

CLOISTER

COMMON PRAYER BOOK

COMMUNION CUP SILENCER

COMMUNION GLASS CUP

COMMUNION TABLE

COMFORTER, THE HOLY The Holy Ghost, Holy Spirit or Paraclete, whom Christ promised to send to his disciples to comfort them in his absence (John 14:25ff).

COMMIXTURE The mixing of water and wine in a chalice; the placing of a piece of the Host into the chalice.

COMMON PRAYER, BOOK OF The official title of the prayer book of the Church of England or the Episcopal Church, so called because it is for use in common as distinguished from private devotions.

COMMUNICANT A baptized member of the church in good standing who is eligible and communicates (or partakes) of the Eucharist regularly.

COMMUNION BREAD The bread or wafer used in the service of the Eucharist; sometimes called altar-bread. (See HOST)

COMMUNION CUP HOLDERS Pieces of wood fastened on the back of pews, with holes bored in them into which communion cups are placed after use.

COMMUNION CUP SILENCERS These are hollow round pieces of flexible rubber inserted in the holes of the cup holders to eliminate noise when empty glasses are placed in the holders after use.

COMMUNION GLASS CUPS Small cups of glass, sometimes of clear plastic, for individual use in the service of the Holy Communion.

COMMUNION, HOLY The sacrament or ordinance of the Lord's Supper, also called the Eucharist, Divine Liturgy, the Mass.

COMMUNION OF SAINTS All members of the church, living and departed, in fellowship and communion with each other in Jesus Christ.

COMMUNION RAIL A rail extending across the front of the chancel, at which communicants kneel to receive the elements in the observance of the Eucharist.

COMMUNION TABLE A table used for the communion service in non-liturgical churches. (See ALTAR)

COMMUNION WAFER (See HOST)

COMMUNION WARE A term referring to individual glasses, communion trays, flagon, and paten used by some churches.

COMMUNION WARE

COMMUNITY, RELIGIOUS A society of men or of women who live together in common, usually under certain vows and a rule of discipline.

COMPLINE The last of the canonical hours or services of the day, said in monasteries, schools, and seminaries at the close of the day; the service often used at conferences in the late evening.

CONFESSION The acknowledgment of sin before God. Private or auricular confession in the presence of a priest is distinguished from public or general confession, which is made in the services of the church.

CONFIRMATION An ordinance of the church. It is administered to those who have been baptized, and is accompanied by the laying on of hands; it is usually performed by a bishop. Note: One joins the church and becomes a member in baptism, and is strengthened (confirmed) in confirmation and admitted to the Lord's Supper.

CONFIRMATION

CONFITEOR A prayer in which confession of sin is made; a confession.

CONGREGATION COUNTER A small device held inconspicuously in the hand of an usher who presses a lever for each person entering the church, as a means of counting attendance at the service.

CONSECRATION The dedication of a person or thing to divine service or holy use; the advancement of a presbyter to the rank of bishop; the setting apart of a church or other place by a bishop to be used for the service of God; the act of the blessing of the elements of bread and wine in the Eucharist.

CONSTANTINE CROSS

CONSOLE The part of the organ where are located the keys, stops, and controls for playing the organ. The same name is given to the keyboard or clavier from which the bells of a chime or carillon are rung.

CONSTANTINE CROSS The cross said to have appeared in a vision to the emperor Constantine before the victory of Milvain Bridge, A.D. 312. It is composed of the two initial Greek letters of the name of Christ, chi (X) and rho (P) entwined as a monogram.

COPE

225

CORPUS

COTTA

CRECHE

CREDENCE

CONSUBSTANTIATION The doctrine held by Lutherans that the bread and wine of the Eucharist are still bread and wine after their consecration, but are also the true body and blood of Christ communicated to the recipients.

CONVENTIONS AND CONFERENCES These terms are variously applied by denominational churches to meetings and/or areas of jurisdiction.

CONVERSION A spiritual and moral change in life associated with the adoption of religious belief with decision and conviction; a change in faith or denomination.

CONVOCATION The territorial divisions in a diocese or a missionary district for promotion of local missionary work; a meeting of the clergy and laity of such a division presided over by a dean; the convention of a missionary district, synod, etc.

COPE A long circular cloke of silk or other rich material, white or varying in color according to the church season, worn over the alb or surplice by some priests and bishops when in processions or services.

CORNICE A decorated wooden strip above the back of the altar from which the dossal is hung.

CORPORAL A napkin of linen embroidered with a cross on the front. It is spread on the altar over the fair linen, and the communion vessels are placed on it.

CORPUS (body) The body of the Lord upon the cross, as on a crucifix.

COTTA (coat) A short white linen (or lace) garment similar to the surplice, worn over the cassock by members of the choir, acolytes, layreaders, etc.

COUNCIL A convention or assemblage of the church meeting to consider business of the church and to legislate (see CANON) regarding matters of doctrine, discipline, and worship; an ecumenical council is a general council of the church. The early ecumenical councils were:

1st Nicaea	325 A.D.
2nd Constantinople	381
3rd Ephesus	437
4th Chalcedon	451
5th Constantinople	553
6th Constantinople	680
7th Nicaea	787

CRÈCHE (crib) The crib or manger containing the nativity scene at Christmastide.

CREDENCE The shelf or table made of wood or stone at the epistle side of the sanctuary where the elements and vessels of the Eucharist are placed before use in the service.

CREDO or CREED (I believe) A statement of faith, such as the historic Apostles, Nicene, and Athenasian Creeds. "Credo" is often used of the Nicene creed when sung in service.

CROSIER

CROSIER or CROZIER A bishop's pastoral staff, a symbol of leadership and pastoral authority; the chaplain or person who carries the bishop's cross or pectoral staff.

CROSS, THE An instrument of shameful execution, which after Christ's crucifixion became the universal symbol of the Christian faith.

CROSSING, THE The portion of a cruciform church where the transepts and the nave intersect.

CROSS

CROWN Used in church symbolism for victory and sovereignty.

CRUCIFER (cross-bearer) One who carries the processional cross, leading a religious processional.

CRUCIFIX A cross bearing the figure of Christ; also the vested figure of Christ the King on a cross.

CROSSING

CRUCIFORM In the form or shape of a cross; used of churches built in the shape of a cross with transepts forming the arms.

CRUETS Two small vessels of glass or metal provided for unconsecrated water and wine and placed upon the credence.

CRYPT An underground portion of a church used as a chapel or a burial vault.

CURATE Originally any minister having charge of the care or cure of souls in a parish; now usually restricted to one who assists the rector or vicar in the parish church; an assistant priest, the holder of a curacy.

CROWN

CRUCIFER

CRUCIFIX

CRUETS

CRYPT

CURE (care)   The spiritual charge of a parish or church congregation.

D

DALMATIC   A vestment of tunic or rectangular shape of rich material (usually matching the material of the chasuble), worn by a deacon at a high celebration of the Eucharist. It is worn over the alb with a stole over the right shoulder.

DEACON (servant)   The first or lowest order of the ministry. St. Stephen was the first deacon (Acts 6:5). Deacons wear a stole crosswise over the left shoulder and under the right arm. They ministered to the poor and the needy in the early church. The title is used in some churches by lay officials who assist the minister.

DEACONESS   A woman trained and set apart by a religious service for the work of the church. In non-liturgical churches the deaconess does not wear a special dress.

DEAN   The presiding minister of a cathedral, originally the head one of ten cathedral canons; the president of a convocation or deanery; the head of the faculty of a college, theological seminary, or department of a university.

DECALOGUE (Gr. ten words)   The Ten Commandments.

DECANI   The side of the choir (originally the dean's side of a cathedral), normally the south (epistle) side opposite the cantoris side.

DEDICATION   A devotional service setting apart to a sacred purpose and use any object, such as a baptismal font, hymnals, a church bell, a memorial window, a private communion set; in churches that do not practice infant baptism, a service of dedication for babies.

DEPOSITION   The suspension or unfrocking of a clergyman from the ministry.

DIACONATE   The office of a deacon, the first order of the ministry.

DIMISSORY LETTER   A letter of transfer for ministers between jurisdictions, or for people transferring from one church to another.

DIOCESAN Pertaining to a diocese; the term also refers to the bishop who is in charge of a diocese.

DIOCESE The area of limits of jurisdiction of a diocesan bishop. A diocese is self-supporting in contrast to a missionary district, which is aided.

DALMATIC

DOCTOR A title, either honorary or earned, awarded by a seminary or a university to a clergyman or to a layman of distinction. The D. D. (Doctor of Divinity) is usually an honorary degree.

DOGMA An article of faith; a truth set forth with and by authority.

DOSSAL, DORSAL or DOSSER (back) The hanging, usually of silk or of tapestry, behind an altar or a throne. The color may be neutral or of the church season.

DOXOLOGY Any liturgical form of words in which glory is ascribed to God or to the Trinity, such as the hymn, "Praise God from whom all blessings flow," or the "Gloria Patri."

DEACON

E

EAST, THE Originally altars were located at the east end of churches because of the sun's rising, symbolizing Christ as the "Sun of our souls"; hence, the term of the East or East End. The eastward position is that of the minister facing the altar regardless of the compass points.

DEACONESS

EASTER A movable feast commemorating the resurrection of Christ; coming in the spring, it symbolizes the resurrection of all nature. Easter is the first Sunday after the first full moon after the vernal equinox (March 21st), except when the full moon falls on Sunday, when Easter is one week later. It controls the Christian year from Septuagesima Sunday through Trinitytide.

EASTER-EVEN The Saturday before Easter and the last day of Lent. Baptism is traditionally administered on Easter-even that the person "being buried with Christ in his death may also be partaker of his resurrection."

DECALOGUE

DOSSAL

EASTERTIDE   The five and one-half weeks following Easter up to Ascension Day (Thursday), commemorating the forty days the Lord spent on earth after his resurrection; commonly called "The Great Forty Days." (color: white)

ELDER   A layman in some churches who shares the government of the local body.

ELEMENTS   The water, wine and bread of the Eucharist.

EMBER DAYS   Days of fasting and prayer for those in holy orders, coming at the four seasons of the year, being the Wednesday, Friday, Saturday after the first Sunday in Lent, the feast of Pentecost, September 14, and December 13. (color: violet)

EASTER

EPIPHANY, THE FEAST OF THE   Twelfth-night or January 6th, a holy day commemorating the manifestation of Christ by a star to the Gentiles; the coming of the Wise Men or Magi. (color: white)

EPIPHANYTIDE   The Epiphany season extends from January 6th to Septuagesima Sunday, and has from one to six Sundays according to the date of Easter. (color for octave: white, for season: green)

ELEMENTS

EPISCOPACY   The type of church government in which bishops are the chief pastors or overseers.

EPISCOPAL CHURCH, THE   The common name of the branch of the Church of England in the U.S.A.; The Protestant Episcopal Church in the U.S.A. It is a church with bishops.

EPISCOPATE   The office of a bishop or the period of time or tenure of a bishop in a jurisdiction. The whole body of bishops of the church.

EPIPHANY

EPISTLE   One of the letters of the New Testament by St. Paul, St. James, St. Peter, St. John, or St. Jude; a portion of an epistle or other Scripture appointed to be read in the communion service.

EPISTLE SIDE   The side of the altar from which the epistle is read; namely, the right (south) side as one faces an altar. (See EAST, DECANI)

EPISTOLER The minister who reads the epistle for the day at the Eucharist.

ESCHATOLOGY (last things) Theology devoted to the study of the Second Coming, death, judgment, and resurrection or life after death.

EUCHARIST (giving thanks) The sacrament of the Lord's Supper, commemorating Christ's sacrifice on the cross.

EUCHARIST

EUCHARISTIC LIGHTS The two candles on the altar used for the service of the Eucharist. They represent Christ as the Light of the World, Christ as Man and God, or the two parts of a sacrament, outward sign and inward grace.

EUCHARISTIC VESTMENTS The special vestments worn in celebrating the Eucharist; viz., alb, amice, girdle, stole, chasuble, and maniple; the dalmatic and tunic also if used.

EUCHARISTIC
VESTMENTS

EVANGELICAL (in the spirit of the gospel) Belonging to or consistent with the four Gospels; applied to Christians or to the church as emphasizing individual salvation by faith.

EVANGELISTS The authors of the four Gospels: St. Matthew, whose symbol is a winged man; St. Mark, a winged lion; St. Luke, a winged ox; and St. John, an eagle.

EVE or EVEN The day preceding a festival, giving an opportunity for preparation for the festival; examples are Christmas Eve and Easter Even.

EVANGELIST

EVENSONG The service of evening prayer, that may be sung (or said). It generally refers to a musical or sung form of the service.

EWER A flagon or pitcher, usually of silver or brass for holding the water for the font in baptism.

EXCOMMUNICATION An exclusion from the fellowship of the church in things spiritual, especially from the sacraments.

EXPECTATION SUNDAY The Sunday after Ascension Day (forty-three days after Easter), referring to the waiting by the apostles for the coming of the Holy Spirit, as commanded by the Lord.

EWER

FAIR LINEN

FAIR LINEN The altar cloth, a long linen cloth covering the altar and hanging over the ends; often embroidered with five crosses. In the plural the term often is applied to all linens used in the Eucharist.

FALD-STOOL A portable folding seat and kneeling desk; the litany desk.

FAST A day or season of penitence and spiritual discipline as: Lent, Ember Days, Ash Wednesday, Good Friday; also the Friday fast or abstinence from meat in remembrance of the Crucifixion.

FALD-STOOL

FATHER First person of the Trinity; a title sometimes used for priests as head of a parish family.

FEAST, FEAST DAY, or FESTIVAL A religious holy day or anniversary set apart for joyful commemoration, as Christmas or Easter. Every Sunday is a "little Easter," a feast honoring the Resurrection.

FERIA An ordinary weekday, which is neither a feast nor a fast; plain or simple music for days marked by no special observance, as opposite of festal.

FILLER, COMMUNION

FESTAL Of or pertaining to a festival or feast; the more elaborate music which is appropriate to such a day or season.

FILLER, COMMUNION GLASS A device for filling the communion glasses in the trays.

FLAG, CHRISTIAN A flag with the same colors as the American flag. The body is white, and in the upper left corner is a square field of blue with a red cross superimposed. It is used in many churches and in processions with the American flag.

FLAG, CHRISTIAN

FLAG, CHURCH, EPISCOPAL A white flag with a red cross extending full height and width. The upper left canton or division is blue, with nine white crosslets arranged in the form of a St. Andrew's cross, recalling the nine original dioceses. This flag was adopted as the Episcopal church flag at the General Convention of October, 1940.

FLAGON A pitcher-shaped vessel, usually of silver or pewter, to hold an extra reserve of wine, from which the chalice may be replenished.

FLECHE A slender church spire above the intersection of the nave and transepts of a church or a cathedral.

FONT The receptacle and pedestal of stone, metal, or wood which holds the water for baptism.

FOOTPACE The platform or base (predella) upon which the altar rests; the place where the priest stands to celebrate the Eucharist.

FRONTAL A cloth, usually of silk or damask, which hangs in front of the altar and reaches to the floor; often decorated with orphreys or bands and used with a frontlet. (See SUPERFRONTAL)

FLAG, CHURCH

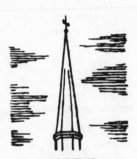

FLAGON

G

GENUFLEXION A bending of the knee as a form of reverence or devotion, made at certain times in services of worship or in church toward the altar.

GHOST, HOLY The third person of the Godhead in the Trinity; the Holy Spirit. The sevenfold gifts of the Holy Ghost listed in Isaiah 11:2 are the spirit of wisdom, of understanding, of counsel, of ghostly strength, of knowledge, of true godliness, of holy fear.

GIRDLE A rope, usually made of white cotton, tied around the waist over the alb. As part of the Eucharistic vestments, it represents the cords with which Jesus was bound in his Passion.

GLORIA IN EXCELSIS (glory be to God on high) One of the most ancient doxologies of the church (4th century). The first verse is the angelical hymn at the nativity of Christ, from Luke 2:13.

GLORIA PATRI (Glory be to the Father) An ascription of praise to the Trinity; a doxology used after the Psalms and Canticles.

GLORIA TIBI (glory be to thee) An ascription of praise before the reading of the gospel.

GODPARENT One who acts as a sponsor at baptism to a godchild and promises to supervise the religious education of the child; godfather and godmother, the parents at the spiritual birth of a child.

FLECHE

FONT

FOOTPACE

FRONTAL

GENUFLEXION

GIRDLE

GOOD FRIDAY (color: black)   The Friday before Easter; the anniversary of the Crucifixion of Christ; "good" because of the atoning sacrifice of the Lord as Saviour of mankind.

GOSPEL   The message or good news proclaimed by Jesus and his church; one of the four books of the New Testament containing the life and sayings of Christ, namely, Matthew, Mark, Luke, John; a portion of gospel Scripture appointed for each Sunday or holy day, called "Gospel for the Day."

GOSPEL SIDE   The side of the altar from which the Gospel is read, the left side as one faces the altar.

GOSPELLER   The minister who reads the gospel at a celebration of the Eucharist.

GOTHIC   A style of architecture characterized by the pointed arch.

GRACE   A supernatural gift of God; divine mercy, forgiveness, and assistance freely given by God for man's regeneration and sanctification; the invocation of divine blessing before a meal.

GRADINE   A shelf on one of a series of shelves behind an altar, on which candlesticks, flowers, etc., may be placed.   (See RETABLE)

GRADUAL   An anthem, sentence, or hymn sung or said between the epistle and gospel in the Communion service.

GRAPE JUICE   Used instead of wine in the observance of the Lord's Supper by non-liturgical churches.

GRATIAS TIBI   (thanks be to thee) An ascription of praise said or sung after the gospel in the Communion service.

GREEK CROSS   A cross having the four extensions of equal length.

GREGORIAN MUSIC   A name for plain song or plain chant, which was improved and established in the church by Gregory the Great in the 6th century. It consists of eight tones with various endings, and is sung in unison. The music is austere and devotional, and is written on a four line staff with square notes.

GUEST BOOK   A book kept on a table in the narthex of the church in which visitors are invited to write their names and addresses.

GOSPEL SIDE

H

HABIT   The special vesture or robes worn by members of religious orders or by the clergy, such as monk's habit, bishop's habit, etc.

HADES   The place of departed spirits, both good and evil.

HASSOCK   A cushion used in place of wooden kneelers.

HEAVEN   The place or state where God dwells; the place or state in which those who love God worship him perfectly in the full light of his presence.

GOTHIC

HELL   The place or state where God is not; hence, the place or state of punishment of the impenitent wicked after death; the intermediate state or abode of departed spirits. (See HADES)

HERESY   A belief contrary to the faith or dogma of the church; denial or perversion of the faith.

HIGH CELEBRATION   The elaborate service of the Eucharist, with vestments, lights, music, and incense; "solemn" if incense is used; usually three clergymen take part.

HIGH CHURCH   A name for those in the Anglican Communion who emphasize the Roman Catholic heritage.

GREEK CROSS

HOLY DAYS OF OBLIGATION   Those principal holy days of the church year on which it is the duty of every communicant to be at the service of the Eucharist. The three great days are Christmas, Easter, and Whitsunday.

HOLY WEEK   The last week of Lent or the week before Easter. (See PALM SUNDAY, MAUNDY THURSDAY, GOOD FRIDAY, EASTER EVEN).

HOMILY   A discourse or sermon; one of the instructions from "The Homilies," written during the Reformation.

HASSOCK

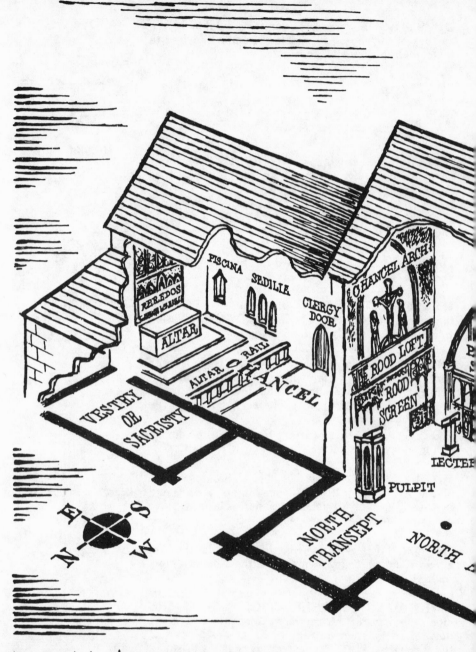

CROSS SECTION OF A CHURCH

HOOD

**HUMERAL
VEIL**

HYMNBOARD

ICON

HOOD, ACADEMIC Vesture given by a college in token of a degree; originally a head covering, now worn over the shoulders. Color of band (red for theology) indicates type of degree; inside colors are those of institution conferring degree.

HOSANNA (From Hebrew, save now, we pray) An exclamation of praise and adoration to God.

HOST The bread or wafer consecrated in the Eucharist; in particular, the large, priest's host.

HUMERAL VEIL A large veil or scarf worn round the shoulders by the officiating minister while holding the sacrament in processions and in the benediction of the sacrament.

HYMN A religious song of adoration, praise, and appeal addressed to God.

HYMNAL A book of hymns or religious songs, often including psalms, chants, and responsive readings.

HYMNBOARD An especially constructed board, usually made of wood, attached to the wall of the nave of the church for the purpose of announcing the numbers of the hymns to be sung, Responsive Reading, Psalms, etc., to be used during the church service.

I

ICON An image, representation, painting, or mosaic of Christ, the Virgin, or a saint hung in Eastern or Greek Orthodox churches, where statues and crucifixes are forbidden.

I H C or I H S The first three letters (iota, eta, sigma) of the Greek spelling of Jesus. The first form (IHC) is the more ancient; the second form is the more common now.

IMMACULATE CONCEPTION Roman Catholic doctrine that the Virgin Mary was born free from the taint of original sin.

IMMANENT An attribute of God — the immanence of God; the essential presence of God in all the universe.

IMMERSION The submersion or dipping of a person down into the water in baptism.

IMMORTALITY The belief that the soul lives after the death of the body; "life everlasting" and the "life of the world to come" as in the creeds.

IMMOVABLE FEASTS Feasts and holy days of the church which always occur on the same date, as Christmas and Epiphany.

IMMERSION

IMPOSITION OF HANDS The ceremonial laying on of hands by a minister or a group of ministers, as in ordination, confirmation, etc. (See APOSTOLIC SUCCESSION)

INCARNATION (in the flesh) The action of God by which his Son (second person of the Trinity) was made flesh, took our nature upon him, and became the man Jesus.

INCARNATUS The part of the Nicene Creed beginning "And was incarnate by the Holy Ghost" and ending "was made man." In many churches people genuflect in honor of the Incarnation.

IMPOSITION OF HANDS

INCENSE A fragrant mixture of gums, resin, and spices, burned ceremonially in services of worship. See Psalm 141.2.

INFALLIBILITY A Roman Catholic doctrine (1870 A.D.) that the pope when speaking as head of the church (ex cathedra) cannot err in defining doctrines, faith, and morals.

I.N.R.I. The initials of the Latin version of the inscription written by Pilate and placed on the cross, "Jesus of Nazareth, King of the Jews."

INSPIRATION (breathing in) The divine influence received by writers of Scripture, which qualified them to receive and to communicate spiritual truth.

INCENSE

INSTITUTION The establishment of a sacrament by Christ, as the Eucharist; the words of Christ used in institution as in the consecration; the establishment of installation of a clergyman in a parish, etc.; an established law, organization, custom, or practice.

INTERCESSION (passing between) A type of prayer or a petition in behalf of another or others.

INTINCTION A method of administering the Eucharist by dipping or placing the bread or wafer in the wine and dispensing both at the same time — an ancient practice of the Eastern Church.

I.N.R.I.

239

INTINCTION

**INTINCTION
CUP**

JEHOVAH

**JESUS
(BAMBINO)**

INTINCTION INSERT or CUP A small metal container shaped to fit a portion of the inside of a chalice, to hold wine used for intinction purposes in the service of the Eucharist.

INTONE Chanting or reciting services (prayers, psalms, scripture) in monotone, with inflections of voice.

INTROIT (going in) A psalm or hymn which is sung before service while the minister enters the sanctuary.

INVOCATION (calling in) A solemn entreaty or prayer for aid or protection or blessing; the opening prayer in many worship services invoking the presence and blessing of God.

J

JEHOVAH — J H V H The Christian form of the name given to the Hebrew name of deity, consisting of the four letters J H V H, never spoken by the Jews. Translated "The Lord" in the King James version of the Bible.

JESUS (Gr. form of Hebrew name Joshua, Saviour) The human name of the Lord, given to him at his circumcision or name day (Jan. 1st). Jesu — poetical form of Jesus.

JOINING THE CHURCH Uniting with the fellowship of Christian believers. Usually the rite of membership is associated with baptism either by pouring (or sprinkling) or by immersion. In some churches, where infant baptism is practiced, the rite of confirmation (in later years) completes the formal membership.

JUBILATE DEO (be joyful in the Lord) The opening words of the 100th Psalm, arranged as a canticle appointed to be used in the service of Morning Prayer.

JUDAISM Pertaining to the religion and rites of the Jews. Symbol is that of six-pointed star.

JUSTIFICATION In theology the forgiveness of a sinner by reason of his faith in Christ, through which he is made acceptable to God as worthy of salvation.

K

KALENDAR Variation of calendar.

KINGDOM OF GOD or KINGDOM OF HEAVEN The dominion of God, which is represented in the world by the church; for Christians, the rule of God on earth.

JUDAISM

KISS OF PEACE An ancient custom of a mutual embrace by the faithful to testify to the existence of brotherly love. It has been discarded because of abuses. In the Roman High Mass the kiss is exchanged ceremonially between the celebrant and assistants.

KNEELER A board attached to back of chair or pew for kneeling; a cushion to kneel upon.

KNEELING The bodily posture appropriate for prayer, signifying humility and reverence. Christians kneel in the presence of God and Christ.

KALENDAR

KNEELING RAIL A rail extending across the front of the chancel.

KNELL The tolling of a bell at a death or at a funeral.

KYRIE ELEISON (Lord, have mercy) An ancient Greek petition, which is said or sung in services or worship of the Eastern and the Western churches.

L

LADY CHAPEL A chapel dedicated to St. Mary, the Virgin, often behind or beside the high altar.

KNEELER

LAITY Collective name for the people; members of the church apart from the ordained clergy. (LAY pertaining to laity)

LANTERN The tower located at the crossing or dome of a church; with windows for light; church light fixtures inside the church.

LAST GOSPEL The part of the fourth gospel silently or audibly read by the priest at the end of the Communion service (John 1:1-14).

LAST THINGS Death, judgment, heaven and hell.

KNEELING RAIL

LANTERN

LATIN CROSS

LAVABO

LECTERN

LATIN CROSS   The ordinary form of the Christian cross, with lower arm twice the length of the others.

LAVABO   (I will wash) The ceremonial washing of the celebrant's hands before the consecration, usually at the offertory; the small towel used; the bowl used for the water.

LAY READER   A layman who is licensed (by a bishop) to read certain of the church services and sermons in the absence of a clergyman.

LECTERN   The stand or desk upon which the Bible is placed and from which the Scripture lessons are read.

LECTERN BIBLE   The Bible kept on the lectern, from which the Scripture lessons are read in public worship.

LECTION   A lesson of appointed Scripture.

LECTIONARY   An authorized table of Scripture lessons and psalms to be read for each day of the church year.

LECTOR   A public reader of Scripture.

LENT   (Saxon Spring) (color: violet) A movable season of penitence, fasting, and sacrifice consisting of the forty days before Easter (not including the Sundays). It begins on Ash Wednesday and extends through Holy Week and Good Friday. The Sundays in Lent are: 1. Quadragesima; 2. Tribulation; 3. Exsurge; 4. Laetare or Refreshment or Mothering; 5. Passion; 6. Palm.

LESSON   A portion of the Scriptures appointed according to the lectionary to be read in divine services; usually both Old Testament and New Testament lessons are designated.

LICH GATE (LYCH GATE)   The roofed entrance or porch to a churchyard under which a bier is placed to await the arrival of the minister.

LITANY   (Gr. a prayer) A general or solemn supplication sung or said responsively by the minister and people kneeling; originally, sometimes now, sung in procession.

LITANY DESK   A kneeling desk from which the litany is read, located usually at the crossing in front center of the nave.

LITURGICAL   Procedure in accordance with the liturgy.

LITURGICAL COLORS   The colors used in the church during the course of the year: white, black, red, violet, green, rose. (See COLORS)

LITURGY   The prescribed public services of the Christian church, especially with reference to the celebration of the Eucharist.

LECTERN BIBLE

LOCUM TENENS   (hold the place) One who temporarily substitutes for another, especially a clergyman acting in lieu of a permanent minister.

LORD'S DAY   Sunday, the first day of the week, commemorating the Resurrection of Christ; not the Jewish Sabbath, which is the seventh day.

LORD'S PRAYER   The prayer which Christ taught his disciples ("Our Father who art in heaven" — Matthew 6:9 and Luke 11:12).

LICH GATE

LORD'S SUPPER   A common name used for the Eucharist.

LORD'S TABLE   A name used for the altar and for the Communion table.

LOW CELEBRATION   A plain or simple celebration of the Eucharist.

LOW CHURCH   A popular name for those in the Anglican Communion who emphasize the Protestant heritage of the church from the time of the Reformation — simple ceremonial and evangelical.

LITANY DESK

LOW SUNDAY   The first Sunday after Easter.

M

MAGNIFICAT   (magnify) A passage of Scripture (Luke 1:46ff) often said or sung as a canticle. It is the song of praise of Mary, the mother of Jesus, sung by her at the time of her visit to Elizabeth.

MANIPLE   A scarf or short stole, which hangs from the left arm as part of the Eucharistic vestments; originally a napkin.

MANIPLE

MARRIAGE

MANSE   The house assigned to and occupied by a clergyman.

MARRIAGE   The union of a man and a woman as husband and wife by mutual decision, to live together. In Christian marriage vows are exchanged and the marriage is solemnized by a clergyman and blessed.

MARTYR   One who sacrifices his life for his faith and principles.

MASS   (from "Ite, Missa est," — go, the congregation is dismissed) An ancient name for the Eucharist.

MATINS   (matutinus, of the morning) In the Anglican Communion another name for Morning Prayer.

MATRIMONY   (See MARRIAGE)

MARTYR

MAUNDY THURSDAY   (Latin mandare, to command; color: violet; white, for Communion) Thursday in Holy Week, commemorating the Last Supper and the institution of the Eucharist; the day when Jesus washed the feet of his disciples.

MEDITATION   An act of devotion, spiritual contemplation, by which the soul seeks a clear relationship with God.

MENSA   (table) A slab of stone used as the top of the altar; often used in reference to any altar top.

MISSAL

MID-LENT SUNDAY   The fourth Sunday in Lent, called also Laetare Sunday, Refreshment Sunday, and Mothering Sunday. (See LENT, SUNDAYS IN)

MINISTER-IN-CHARGE   A title sometimes given to the Vicar, Locum Tenens or any clergyman in charge of a chapel, mission, etc.

MISSAL   A book containing the service of the Eucharist, with the collects, epistles, and gospels; also called the altar book; loosely, a book of devotion.

MISSAL STAND

MISSAL STAND   The desk or stand on the altar upon which rests the missal or altar book; altar desk.

MISSION A church or congregation or district which is not self-supporting and receives aid from outside; a person or group of persons sent forth to places, peoples, and walks of life to witness to the gospel; a special program in a congregation for the revival of religious life.

MISSIONARY Anyone who is sent, whether clergyman or layman, to do the work of the church, either at home or abroad, where it has not been established.

MITRE

MISSIONARY BISHOP A bishop appointed to exercise episcopal duties in an area not organized into a diocese.

MITRE A traditional and ceremonial head-piece worn by a bishop or an abbot, representing symbolically the cloven tongues of fire which lighted on the heads of the apostles at Pentecost.

MONASTIC VOWS Traditional vows of obedience, poverty, and celibacy made by the members of religious orders.

MONK

MONKS Members of a religious community of men who have taken monastic vows.

MONSIGNOR An honorary title borne by certain clergy of the Roman Catholic church.

MONSTRANCE or OSTENSORIUM A transparent receptacle in which the Host is exposed to the congregation in certain churches.

MONSTRANCE

MORSE A metal clasp used to fasten a cope or cape in front.

MORTAL SIN A deliberate sin or act against God's will and divine law, involving and exposing to spiritual death.

MOTHERING SUNDAY (See LENT, SUNDAYS IN)

MOVABLE FEASTS AND FASTS Holy · days which are not observed on fixed dates but depend on the variable date of Easter.

MORSE

245

NARTHEX

NARTHEX A vestibule, usually a wide one across the front (west end) of a church and separate from the nave.

NAVE (Latin navis, ship) The body of the church building where the congregation assembles; called "nave" because the church is often symbolized in art as a ship, with pews, like benches in ancient galleys, and the people pulling together in service.

NICENE CREED The statement of the Christian faith set forth at the Council of Nicaea, A.D. 325, and reaffirmed at the Council of Constantinople in 381 A.D. It is used as an alternative to the Apostles' Creed, especially in the Eucharist. Its meaning is the same as that of the Apostles' Creed, but it is an extended form.

NAVE

NICHE A recess in a wall for a statue or similar ornament.

NONCONFORMIST Anyone who does not conform to established usage; a Protestant who is not of the Church of England.

NONLITURGICAL The procedure of public services of the Christian church which are not definitely prescribed.

NOVENA A devotion lasting nine days.

NOVICE One who is serving a period of trial before being professed to a religious order.

NUNC DIMITTIS Title from the two words beginning the Song of Simeon (Luke 2:29) often said or sung as an evening canticle.

NICHE

O

OBLATION A solemn offering to God; in plural, oblations refer to the elements of bread and wine.

OCTAVE (eight) The festival and seven days thereafter added for celebrating the great festivals such as Christmas, Epiphany, Easter, etc.

OFFERING That which is offered or presented at an altar, whether alms or Eucharistic elements of bread and wine.

OFFERTORY

OFFERING PLATE   (See ALMS BASIN)

OFFERTORY   The part of the service in which the alms or offerings of the people are received and presented. The singing of a hymn or anthem at this time is often called the Offertory, and verses of Scripture spoken by the minister are called OFFERTORY SENTENCES.

OFFICE   A prescribed form or act of worship, an older equivalent of the word "service."

OFFICE LIGHTS

OFFICE LIGHTS   Six candlesticks (three on each side of the cross) placed on the retable — symbolic of canonical hours of lauds, prime, tierce (morning prayer) and of sext, nones, and compline (evening prayer).

OILS, HOLY   Oil blessed by a bishop, traditionally on Maundy Thursday, in three kinds: for unction; for anointing catechumens before baptism, and for use by bishops in consecrations.

ORPHREY

ORATORY   (Latin, orare, to speak or pray) A small chapel or shrine for private devotions.

ORDER   The prescribed arrangement of a service; one of the orders of the ministry, as deacon, priest, bishop; a religious community or society.

ORDINAL   A book of forms used in the ordination of deacons and priests and in the consecration of bishops; a book of forms and directions for daily services.

**ORTHODOX
CROSS**

ORDINANCE   (Ordering) A religious decree or usage authoritatively enjoined by the church, such as the rite for the administration of the Communion.

ORDINARY   The bishop of a diocese or his deputy who has ordinary authority or jurisdiction; the nonvariable parts of the Eucharist or of the Mass.

ORDINATION   The act of setting apart to the sacred ministry by the laying on of hands by a presiding minister, a group of ministers, or by a bishop.

ORGAN   A musical instrument played from a keyboard producing tonal quality considered appropriate for use in services of public worship.

PALL, FUNERAL

**PALL,
COMMUNION**

ORPHREY   The embroidered band on an ecclesiastical vestment or hanging.

ORTHODOX CROSS   The Eastern Cross. The upper horizontal arm represents the place of the inscription over the head of the crucified Jesus. The lower slanting arm represents his footrest, since the Eastern church believes Jesus was crucified with his feet side by side and not crossed one over the other as usually pictured by the Western church.

OSTENSORY   (See MONSTRANCE)

P

PALM SUNDAY

PACE   A passageway between seats as in the nave, often incorrectly called aisle. (See AISLE)

PALL (FUNERAL)   A large cloth, usually black or purple, placed over a casket.

PALL, COMMUNION   A square piece of cardboard or metal covered with white linen, which is placed over the chalice.

PALM SUNDAY   The Sunday preceding Easter; the sixth Sunday in Lent; the first day of Holy Week, commemorating the triumphal entry of Christ into Jerusalem; traditionally symbolized by use of palm decorations and crosses on this day.

PARACLETE   (See HOLY GHOST)

**PARCLOSE
SCREEN**

PARADISE   (a park) Theologically, the abode or state after death where departed souls of the righteous await final judgment; often used as synonymous with the garden of Eden and heaven.

PARAMENTS   (Latin parare, to adorn) The rich ornamental furnishings, such as the antependium and other hangings which may decorate a pulpit or a lectern.

PARCLOSE SCREEN   A wooden screen used to separate a side chapel or altar from the nave.

PARISH   Originally the district of a parish church assigned to a clergyman; a self-supporting church (congregation) usually under charter or incorporation, including often chapels, schools, and other institutions.

**PARISH
REGISTER**

248

PARISH HOUSE   The building other than the church proper where the educational and social work of a parish is carried on.

PARISH REGISTER   The official record book of a parish in which all baptisms, confirmations, burials, and marriages are recorded.

PAROCHIAL SCHOOL   Pertaining to, supported by, or confined to a parish.

PARSON   A colloquial term designating any clergyman. The word probably came into use from the fact that the minister in the early parishes was the most prominent person.

PARSONAGE   The home of the parson, provided by a church.

PASCHAL CANDLE   A large, pure white candle, preferably of bleached wax, placed in a large candlestick in the sanctuary on the gospel side, symbolizing the risen Christ, and lit ceremonially on Easter Even, to remain lighted throughout the forty days of Eastertide until Ascension Day.

PASCHAL FEAST   The original name for Easter.

PASSION   (suffering) The sufferings, physical and spiritual, of Jesus Christ upon the cross; his sufferings between the Last Supper and the Crucifixion.

PASSION SUNDAY The fifth Sunday in Lent, so-called because in the gospel for that day Christ begins his sufferings by being stoned out of the temple.

PASSION TIDE   The last two weeks of Lent, during which Christ's passion and death are commemorated, being Passion Week following Passion Sunday and Holy Week following Palm Sunday.

PASSION WEEK   The fifth week of Lent, the week before Holy Week.

PASTOR   (shepherd) Name for a minister placed in charge of the spiritual care of a parish or congregation — a shepherd of souls.

PASTORAL STAFF   The official staff (a shepherd's crook) carried by or before a bishop, symbolic of his pastoral authority as a shepherd of Christ's flock.

PASCHAL
CANDLE

PATEN

PEAL

PECTORAL
CROSS

PEW

PATEN   A round flat plate, usually of silver, upon which the bread is consecrated and from which it is administered in the Communion service.

PEAL   A tuned set of bells, usually eight.

PECTORAL CROSS   A large cross of precious metal hanging from a chain around the neck upon the breast of a bishop. Smaller crosses now worn by other clergy are often thus termed.

PENANCE   The rite by which sins may be absolved; an act to show sorrow and repentance for sin.

PEW RACK

PENITENTIAL PSALMS   The 6th, 32nd, 38th, 51st, 102nd, 130th, and 143rd.

PENTECOST, THE FEAST OF   (color: red) The original name for Whitsunday. Pentecost is the Greek word for fiftieth. It was used to designate the Feast of Weeks, a Jewish festival which came seven weeks after the Passover. Since the Holy Ghost descended upon the apostles at Pentecost, Whitsunday superseded the Jewish feast of Pentecost or Weeks. It is about fifty days after Easter.

PEW   A bench or seat with a fixed back for use of members of a congregation.

PEW RACK   An enclosed shelf, open at the top, attached to the back of a pew and used to hold hymnbooks and Bibles. Smaller racks are sometimes used for cards and pencils.

PILLAR

PILLAR   A column placed to supply vertical support for a structure.

PISCINA   (fish pond) A basin and drain for disposing of ablutions and for cleansing of chalice and paten. It is often located in the south wall of the sanctuary or sacristy, and the drain carried to the ground outside.

PLAINSONG or PLAINCHANT   (See CHANT and GREGORIAN MUSIC)

PISCINA

PONTIFICAL   Pertaining to a pontiff (pope); the functions peculiar to bishops. When a bishop officiates at a service, as in the Eucharist, his function is a pontifical celebration.

POSTULANT (Latin *postulare*, to demand) One who desires to become a candidate for admission to a religious order preparatory to the novitiate.

POSTURES IN WORSHIP According to the Anglican order: stand for praise (canticles, hymns, creed); kneel for prayer; sit for instruction (lessons, sermon).

PRIE-DIBU

PREACHER One who preaches the sermon; often used as synonymous (incorrectly) with clergyman or minister.

PREACHING MISSION An intensive effort made in a church to arouse and quicken the people by special services, sermons, and instructions led by a missioner. (See REVIVAL)

PRECENTOR The leader of the choir in divine service; one who presents or intones the chants. (See CANTOR)

PREDELLA (See FOOTPACE)

PRIESTHOOD

PRESBYTER (Greek, meaning older) One who has been authorized or ordained to perform priestly functions — used as synonymous with priest; one whose function resembles that of a priest; in the Presbyterian church a teaching elder who assists in the service of the Communion.

PRESIDING BISHOP (Anglican) The president of the national council of the Episcopal Church, who also presides over the House of Bishops and the Triennial Convention.

PROCESSIONAL

PRIE-DIEU (pray God) A small desk constructed to support a book, and having a footpiece or kneeler, used for prayers and devotions.

PRIESTHOOD (priest, presbyter) Rank, character, and function of being a priest; the office of one ordained to perform priestly duties. A priest may celebrate the Eucharist and officiate at all sacraments and services, except those specifically reserved for a bishop, namely, confirmation, ordination, and consecration; a priest is one ordained to offer sacrifice and pronounce absolution.

PROCESSIONAL CROSS

PROCATHEDRAL (before the cathedral) A church serving as a cathedral but without cathedral organization, dean, or chapter.

PULPIT

PROCESSIONAL   The entrance of the choir and clergy at the beginning of a church service, often preceded by a crucifer with processional cross; the hymn sung while entering a church for divine service; a service book containing the offices for ecclesiastical processions.

PROCESSIONAL CROSS   A cross, usually of brass on a pole of wood, carried in front of a choir or ecclesiastical procession.

PROCESSIONAL TORCH   A lighted torch with a long wooden handle carried in an ecclesiastical procession. Processional torches can be either simple, dignified single candles at the top of brass bobeches or more elaborately designed torches with intricate craftsmanship, such as the sanctus torch and the processional lantern.

PULPIT BIBLE

PROPER   The office or Mass for a special day; e.g., the proper for Easter, the collect, epistle, and gospel appointed for the day; a prayer, antiphone, etc., for the day.

PROTECTOR   A heavy cloth, usually colored, placed on top of the fair linen of the altar when there is no service.

PROTESTANT   The collective name for those religious bodies or persons who are known as evangelical and reformed as opposed to Roman Catholic.

PROVINCE   A group of dioceses under the jurisdiction of an archbishop, whose bishops and clerical and lay deputies meet in a provincial synod annually or periodically.

PULPIT CHAIRS

PSALMS   Sacred poems or hymns of the Old Testament, frequently used in the worship and praise of God.

PSALTER   Name for the Book of Psalms, or a selection of Psalms, used in religious services. The Psalter is included in the Book of Common Prayer.

PULPIT   (platform) An elevated platform with a railing and a reading desk, from which the sermon is delivered; located at the front of the Chancel, either at one side or in the center.

PURIFICATOR

PULPIT BIBLE   The Bible kept and used on the pulpit when there is no lectern.

PULPIT CHAIRS   Usually two or three and of ecclesiastical design, situated near the pulpit and lectern for the use of the clergy.

PURGATORY   In Roman Catholic theology the place where faithful souls are purified or purged after death; referred to as the Intermediate State or Paradise.

PYX

PURIFICATOR   A small linen napkin used to wipe or cleanse the chalice after the celebration of the Eucharist; a mundatory.

PYX   A small receptacle or case used to carry the consecrated bread and wine of Communion to the sick. It is usually kept in the tabernacle or aumbry. (See CIBORIUM)

PYX, HANGING   A pyx of precious metal containing the reserved sacrament hung in the center of the chancel above the altar; most commonly used in England.

PYX, HANGING

Q

QUIET DAY   A day spent in meditations, instructions, and special devotions. The rules of silence and abstinence are sometimes observed.

QUINQUAGESIMA   The Sunday next before Lent, the word comes from fiftieth because it is the fiftieth day before Easter.

RABAT

R

RABAT   A neckband with a piece of cloth like a bib, worn by clergymen with the clerical collar.

RABAT VEST   A rabat extending down over the entire breast to the waist and around on the sides; used by clergymen when not wearing a vest.

REAL PRESENCE   The doctrine that the presence of the risen Christ in the Communion, although spiritual, is real.

RECESSIONAL   The retiring of the choir and clergy after a church service; a hymn sung while thus retiring called a recessional hymn.

RECESSIONAL

RECTOR

RECTOR   A priest who is in charge of a parish. He is the presiding officer at all its vestry meetings and is nominally ex officio head of all its organizations.

RECTORY The residence provided for the rector by the parish.

REDEMPTION   The deliverance from sin and its consequence through the atoning suffering and death of Christ.

REFORMATION   The religious movement of the 16th and 17th centuries which resulted in Protestantism and the elimination of many abuses in the medieval Roman Catholic Church.

RECTORY

REFRESHMENT SUNDAY   The fourth Sunday in Lent, so-named from the gospel for the day that tells of Christ feeding the multitude; called also Mid-Lent Sunday and Mothering Sunday. (See LENT, SUNDAYS IN)

REGENERATION   The spiritual rebirth of one entering into a new life of holy affections, purposes, and conduct according to the will of God; being born of water (baptism) and the spirit.

RELIGIOUS LIFE, THE   The life of persons living under vows in a religious order or community.

REPOSITORY

RENAISSANCE   The rebirth of the human intellect after the Dark Ages; the transitional period between the medieval and the modern eras (14th-16th centuries), marked by the revival of classical learning, the Reformation, the invention of printing, neoclassic architecture, geographical discovery, etc., in Europe.

REPENTANCE   Recognition and confession of sin and sorrow for the same, with a turning unto God.

REPOSITORY FOR BOOK OF REMEMBRANCE   A case or cabinet, usually placed in the narthex of the church, in which the Book of Remembrance is kept. The cover is of glass and the repository often has a fluorescent light inside to illumine the pages.

REREDOS

REQUIEM   The Communion with service when celebrated at a funeral or in memory of the departed; a musical setting of the Mass for the dead.

REREDOS   A screen or decorated wall, usually of carved wood or of stone, behind the altar.

RESERVATION   The retention of some of the consecrated elements of the Eucharist after an administration to the sick, or for adoration.

RESERVATION PEW CORD   A rope usually covered with velour or velvet which is laid across the tops of pews at the aisle end, to reserve a certain area for a special group, particularly at weddings and at funerals.

RESERVATION PEW CORD

RESPONSES   The answers made by the people in the services to the Psalms, the versicles, The Litany.

RESURRECTION   The rising of human beings from the dead; the rising of Christ after his death and burial.

RETABLE   A single shelf at the rear of the altar on which are placed the Cross, vases for flowers, and candlesticks. (See GRADINE)

RESURRECTION

RETREAT   A time of withdrawal and seclusion and refreshment spent entirely in devotional exercises consisting of periods of silence, meditation, instruction, and conference.

REVEREND, THE   A title of respect to clergymen. It is usually preceded by "the" and is used with the full name, or initials and surname — never as "Reverend Smith."

REVEREND, THE MOST   The customary title of address given to an archbishop.

RETABLE

REVEREND, THE RIGHT   The customary title of address given to a bishop.

REVEREND, THE VERY   The customary title of address given to a clergyman who has the position of dean, as of a cathedral, seminary, etc.

REVIVAL   A period or series of services designed to awaken and renew personal religious life and interest in the work of the church.

RIDDEL POSTS   Tall posts, usually of wrought iron, used to hold up the bars supporting the riddels; often decorated at the top with a symbol.

RIDDEL POSTS

RIDDELS

RIDDELS   Curtains suspended on bars at each side or end of the altar.

RITUAL   The mode of performing a rite of the church; a book of forms or rites of worship. (See CEREMONIAL) (See LITURGY)

RITUALISM   Religious worship according to a ritual; adherence to a prescribed and authorized form of procedure in worship, as in Anglican and Roman Catholic churches, with special emphasis upon symbolism; (derogatorily) excessive emphasis upon prescribed forms in worship.

ROCHET   A fine linen alb with full sleeves, worn by bishops under the chimere.

ROCOCO   An extravagant and fantastic style of ornamentation popular in 18th century Europe, characterized by curved lines, florid forms, and pierced decorative shellwork.

ROCHET

ROGATIONTIDE   The three days from Rogation Sunday (fifth after Easter) to Ascension Day (Thursday); a period of supplication for God's blessing upon the land and the crops.

ROMANESQUE   A pre-Gothic style of architecture characterized (after 1000 A.D.) by the round arch, substitution of piers for columns, decorative arcades, and elaborate ornament.

ROMAN USE   The ritual or liturgy of the Roman Catholic church.

ROOD   A cross or a crucifix above a beam or a chancel screen separating the chancel from the nave; a hanging rood dependent from the roof.

ROMANESQUE

ROOD LOFT   A narrow, long gallery over the rood screen of a cathedral or parish church, approached by a small stone staircase in the wall of the building.

ROOD SCREEN   A grill or open lattice of carved wood, stone, or wrought iron, between the nave and the chancel, surmounted by a crucifix or a rood; when without a rood often called the chancel screen.

RUBERICS   (red) Instructions or directions as to the conduct of the services, usually printed in italics, (originally printed in red ink).

S

SACRAMENT   An outward and visible sign of an inward and spiritual grace, instituted by Christ. The word sacrament is often used with reference to the Communion elements.

ROOD

SACRAMENTS OF THE CHURCH, IN THE LITURGICAL CHURCH   The seven are: baptism, the Eucharist, confirmation, penance, holy orders, matrimony, extreme unction. The first two are considered essential; the other five sacraments, for which there is warrant in the Scriptures, are voluntary for particular occasions. In the nonliturgical churches two only are recognized, baptism and the Eucharist.

ROOD SCREEN

SACRARIUM   A term which has been used for a variety of objects but always related to something regarded as sacred. It has been used to designate a sanctuary, a piscina, a receptacle for sacred objects, a wayside chapel, an altar stone, etc.

SACRIFICE, HOLY   Another name for the Eucharist emphasizing Christ's atonement.

SACRISTAN   One who has charge of the sacristy with its vestments, sacred vessels, and all things pertaining to the altar and sanctuary.

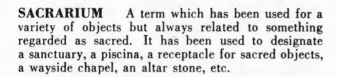

SACRISTY   The room in the church building where the vestments, sacred vessels, and altar appurtenances are kept.

SACRARIUM

SAINT   A person eminently pious and godly in thought and life; a consecrated and regenerated person canonized by the church.

SAINTS' DAYS   Holy days commemorating the lives of the saints of the church.

SALVATION   The gracious deliverance of God, especially redemption from sin and its consequences, realized for man in the life and death of Jesus Christ.

SANCTUARY

SANCTUARY   (holy place) The area around an altar, or portion of the chancel behind the altar rail; the main room for worship in evangelical churches.

SANCTUARY LAMPS   Lamps usually suspended in front of the altar. Lamps in churches probably antedate candles. A single lamp of red or white light in front of the reserved sacrament symbolizes the continual watchfulness of the church, three lamps symbolize the Trinity; seven lamps symbolize the Seven Churches of the Apocalypse (Rev. i-iii), or the seven gifts of the Holy Spirit.

SANCTUARY LAMP

SANCTUS BELL

SANCTUS (holy) The Tersanctus; the hymn beginning "Holy, Holy, Holy," which is said or sung in the liturgy of the Eucharist in Roman Catholic and in Anglican churches; a hymn in any church.

SANCTUS BELL A bell rung, usually by the acolyte, at the Sanctus and at the words of institution of the Eucharist.

SARUM USE The rites at one time peculiar to the diocese of Salisbury, England.

SEASONS There are nine major seasons of the Christian or church year: 1. Advent; 2. Christmastide; 3. Epiphany; 4. Septuagesima; 5. Lent, including Holy Week; 6. Eastertide; 7. Ascensiontide; 8. Whitsuntide; 9. Trinity season.

SEASONS

SEDILIA (a seat) A seat or series of seats, usually three, placed on the south side of the sanctuary for the use of the clergy.

SEE A diocese, the jurisdiction of a bishop.

SEPTUAGESIMA (seventieth) The third Sunday before Lent, seventy days before Easter; the beginning of the season of pre-Lent.

SERMON A religious address, usually by a clergyman, generally based on a text or passage of Scripture.

SERVER (See ACOLYTE)

SEDILIA

SEXAGESIMA (sixtieth) The second Sunday before Lent; sixty days before Easter.

SEXTON One who takes care of the church building and property, rings the church bell for services, etc.

SHRINE (chest) Originally a receptacle for sacred relics; the place or chapel where such relics are kept; a place of hallowed memory.

SOUNDING BOARD

SHROVE TUESDAY The day before Ash Wednesday. The people on that day went to the priest to be shriven (absolved) from their sins; Pancake Day.

SIN   Transgression, purposeful or through neglect, of the law of God; anything which separates man from God, or disturbs the relationship between man and God, man and his neighbor, or man and himself.

SIN, ORIGINAL   Man's inherent nature or inclination to sin, considered to be inherited from the original sin of Adam and Eve in the Garden of Eden.

SINS, SEVEN DEADLY   As shown in ecclesiastical art and literature: pride, anger, covetousness, lust, envy, sloth, and gluttony.

SOLOIST   A single voice, usually in the choir, singing a hymn or appropriate religious selection.

SOUND HOLES   Openings in the wooden shutters of a belfry or of tower windows which allow the sound of the bells to be heard.

SOUNDING BOARD   A board or canopy over a pulpit, so arranged as to keep the sound of the preacher's voice from ascending but impelling it ahead through the nave of the church.

SPIRE   (sprout) A tall slender pointed structure rising from a church tower and symbolically pointing to heaven. (See FLECHE)

SPONSORS   In baptism those who speak for the child until he can speak for himself. They are called godparents because their spiritual responsibility is almost parental. (See GODPARENT)

SPOON   In the Communion silver a spoon for recovering foreign matter; used also to aid in administering Communion to the sick.

STAINED GLASS   Pieces of colored glass which are put together to form colored windows in the church, with pictures or pleasing color designs, to beautify the interior of the church by the light shining through from the outside.

STALLS   Seats in the chancel for the clergy and choir. Sometimes a single stall is a dean's stall or a rector's stall.

STATIONS OF THE CROSS   Fourteen pictures, or images, ranged about a church, or along a way leading to a church or a shrine, portraying the Passion of Christ; a devotional service using these pictures.

SPOON

STAINED GLASS

STALL

STATIONS OF
THE CROSS

STEEPLE

STEEPLE A church tower; especially a tall structure of diminishing stories surmounted by a small spire and resting upon a church tower.

STOCK A metal container to hold the holy oils used in the services of the church.

STOLE A long narrow band of silk, fringed at the ends, and often embroidered, which a bishop or a priest wears about his neck, a deacon wears across his left shoulder and tied on the right side, and which is worn crossed on the breast with Eucharistic vestments. Its color matches the church season, and it symbolizes the yoke of Christ.

STOCK

STOOL OF REPENTANCE The cutty stool of old Scottish churches; a low seat on which guilty persons were compelled to sit as punishment for certain sins, especially unchastity.

SUB DEACON. One in holy orders below a deacon, who, in the Roman Catholic and the Eastern churches, prepares the holy vessels for the Mass, and who in Anglican churches reads the epistle at the Eucharist.

SUFFRAGAN BISHOP A bishop elected to assist the bishop of a diocese, but without the right of succession to his office. (See BISHOP)

SUNDAY SCHOOL (See CHURCH SCHOOL)

SUPERFRONTAL A cloth of lace or silk to cover the altar, hanging eight or ten inches over the frontal; in silk it has the color of the season.

STOLE

SUPERIOR The title for the head of a religious house; addressed as Reverend Father or Reverend Mother.

SURPLICE The outer vestment worn by the Roman Catholic and the Anglican clergy in various offices. It is of white linen, full, with wide, open sleeves, usually longer than the cotta worn by the choristers.

SUPERFRONTAL

SURSUM CORDA (lift up your hearts) The initial words of a versicle beginning the Preface of the Mass; the name for the responsive part of the Anglican Communion office.

SYNOD   An ecclesiastical council for consulting, advising, and deciding upon church matters; in the Anglican church a meeting of the clerical and lay deputies from the dioceses and missionary districts comprising a province.

SURPLICE

T

TABERNACLE   A small cupboard or receptacle, usually located at the center of the altar, holding the consecrated elements of the Eucharist.

TABERNACLE LAMP (See SANCTUARY LAMP)

TAPER   A waxed wick placed in a candle lighter from which the altar candles are lighted.

TARP   Abbreviation for "Take Ablutions Right Place;" i.e., immediately after Communion instead of at the end of the service.

TE DEUM LAUDAMUS   (We praise thee, O God) A canticle of praise, written about the 3rd century; often sung in anthem form.

TABERNACLE

TENEBRAE   (L. darkness) A church service for the last three days of Holy Week. It is a service of mourning observed in the evening in the darkness of the church, commemorating the suffering and death of Christ and symbolizing the darkness over the earth at the Crucifixion. A candelabra of 15 candles is used, which are progressively extinguished leaving only one lighted near the altar.

TESTER   A flat or shell-like canopy over a pulpit, altar, or tomb, etc.

THANKSGIVING   A type of prayer or worship; a prayer of appreciation or thanks to God; a festival of thanks.

TAPER

THREE HOURS, THE   A modern service usually from noon to 3 p.m. on Good Friday, commemorating the period of Christ's suffering on the Cross. The service is usually meditations on the Seven Last Words, interspersed with Passion hymns and prayers.

THURIBLE   A censer or vessel used for burning incense.

TENEBRAE

TESTER

THURIBLE

THURIFER

TIPPET

THURIFER   One who carries and swings the thurible or censer, formerly an acolyte, now an altar boy.

TIPPET   In the Church of England a long black scarf worn by the minister during the choir offices.

TITHE   The tenth part of the produce of the land, given to God; an offering of the tenth of one's income devoted to religious purposes.

TRACERY   Ornamental decorative supporting work with branching Lines in a (Gothic) window or vaulting.

TRACT   A brief religious treatise or leaflet.

TRANSEPT   The two wings of a cruciform church, representing the arms of the cross, usually intersecting the nave at the foot of the chancel called the crossing.

TRANSFER, LETTER OF   (See LETTER DIMISSORY)

TRANSLATION   (See BIBLE)

TRANSUBSTANTIATION   The Roman Catholic doctrine that the bread and the wine of the Eucharist are changed in substance to the body and the blood of Christ, the accidents or appearance and taste remaining the same.

TREASURER   The person who holds the money belonging to the church, pays the bills, and keeps an accurate record of receipts and expenditures.

TREFOIL   An ornamental design of three divisions or foils like a clover leaf, used in Gothic architecture in windows, tracery, paneling, etc.; a symbol of the Trinity.

TRIFORIUM   A gallery forming an upper story over an aisle, often with three openings to a bay.

TRINITARIAN FORMULA   The words "In the name of the Father and of the Son and of the Holy Ghost," a blessing or invocation used in baptism, before sermons, and at the beginning of official documents.

TRINITY, THE   The doctrine of the three-fold nature of God as three persons in one Godhead (the Father as Creator, the Son as Redeemer, the Holy Ghost as Sanctifier) — one in substance but three in individuality.

TRACERY

TRINITY SUNDAY   (color: white) A Sunday in honor of the Trinity and beginning the Trinity season; the Sunday after Whitsunday.

TRINITYTIDE   (color: green) The long season of the Christian year (June to November), from Trinity Sunday to Advent Sunday, varying from 22 to 27 Sundays.

TRIPTYCH   (Gr. threefold) A painting or carving on three panels on related subjects, usually the side panels hinged to fold together; often used behind an altar as a reredos.

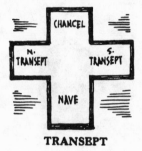

TRANSEPT

TROTH   (old Eng. for truth) Pledged faith; betrothal; (Anglican) the promise made in matrimony. (See BETROTHAL, MATRIMONY)

TRUSTEES   A group of people in the church who are elected to care for the buildings and property.

TUNICLE   A short vestment worn by the sub-deacon or epistler at a celebration of the Eucharist; similar to a dalmatic but simpler.

TWELVE APOSTLES   (See APOSTLES)

TREFOIL

U

UNCTION   The sacramental use of anointing the sick with oil as symbolic of the act of cleansing and healing; called extreme unction when death is imminent.

UNDERCROFT   A crypt, subterranean room, or chapel under a church.

USHER   A man appointed to greet and seat the congregation at the services of worship.

V

VASE   A vessel for flowers, usually of brass or silver, placed in pairs on the retable of the altar.

TRIPTYCH

TUNICLE

USHER

VASE

VAULTING

VAULTING   Arched construction of masonry supporting a ceiling.

VEIL, CHALICE   One of the fair linens that cover the Communion vessels after the Eucharist. The embroidered silk covering usually in the color of the season is generally called the Communion veil.

VENERABLE, THE   The title of an archdeacon.

VENI, CREATOR SPIRITUS   (Come, Creator Spirit) A hymn, probably from about the 8th century, used as a hymn in the breviary at Whitsuntide on solemn occasions, as at ordinations, coronations of kings, etc.

VENIAL SIN   In theology, a pardonable or slight sin, common to all mankind, in which there is no malice or premeditation.

VENITE, EXULTEMUS DOMINO   (Come, let us sing unto the Lord) The canticle derived from the 95th Psalm, said or sung in church services at matins.

VERGER   One who bears a staff (Fr. verge) as symbol of office in procession before a dignitary, such as a bishop, a dean; an official caretaker or sexton of a church.

VERSICLES   A series of sentences said or sung alternately by minister and people in services of worship.

VESPER LIGHTS   Seven-branch candelabra on the altar (originally lit at vespers) represent the sevenfold gifts of the Holy Spirit. (See OFFICE LIGHTS)

VESPERS   (evening) Originally one of the canonical hours (at sunset); now used for evening worship or evensong.

VESSELS, SACRED   The chalice, paten, ciborium, flagon, cruets, etc., used in Communion.

VESTIBULE   (See NARTHEX)

VESTMENTS   Any ecclesiastical garments used by clergy, acolytes, choirs, etc. (See EUCHARISTIC VESTMENTS)

VESTRY　1. In the Anglican church the official governing body of a parish, responsible for its temporal affairs. It is composed of the rector, two wardens, and several vestrymen. 2. A room in the church where the clergy and choir don their vestments.

VERGER

VIATICUM　(Latin: pertaining to a journey) Any rite or attention which gives spiritual comfort to the dying in preparation for the journey to the next life; a name sometimes given to the portable vessels for administering the Communion.

VICAR　One who has charge of a chapel or a mission (representing the rector of the parish or the bishop of the diocese.) The home provided for the vicar is the VICARAGE.

VIGIL　The eve of certain festivals, usually observed by a fast or preparation.

VESTIBULE

VIGIL LIGHTS　(See SANCTUARY LAMP)

VIRTUES, CARDINAL　The four virtues named in the Book of The Wisdom of Solomon (8:7): temperance, prudence, justice, and fortitude.

VIRTUES, THEOLOGICAL　The three virtues named by Paul (1 Cor. 13) faith, hope, charity.

VOCATION　The call to a life's work, especially the ministry or the religious life.

VOTIVE LIGHTS　Candles or tapers lighted before an altar or shrine in memory of someone, or for some particular intention.

VIATICUM

W

WAFER　A small, flat disk or square of unleavened bread for the Communion; also called people's host.

WARDEN, CHURCH　(See WARDENS)

WARDENS　Two lay officers of a parish vestry, called senior or rector's warden, usually appointed by the rector, and junior or people's warden, elected by the other vestrymen or by the people. Both wardens may be elected by the parish.

VIGIL LIGHT

VOTIVE LIGHT

WHITSUNDAY (color: red) The Anglo-Saxon name for Pentecost (fifty days after Easter), commemorating the Holy Spirit's descending on the apostles. It is a major feast of the Anglican church with an octave and a Proper Preface.

WORDS, SEVEN LAST Spoken by Christ from the cross: 1. "Father, forgive them; for they know not what they do" (Luke 23-34); 2. "Today, shalt thou be with me in Paradise" (Luke 23:43); 3. "Woman, behold thy Son," "Behold thy mother" (John 19:26-27); 4. "My God, my God, why hast thou forsaken me?" (Mark 15:34); 5. "I thirst" (John 19:28); 6. "It is finished" (John 19:30); 7. "Father, into thy hands I commend my spirit" (Luke 23:46) (See THE THREE HOURS)

WORSHIP The humble act of devotion to God. The self-expression of faith, love and gratitude to God through prayer, singing and meditation during a service in the church. A term often used to designate a church service (worship service).

WAFER

WORSHIP CENTER The area within the chancel containing the articles and furnishings conducive to worship; also the area within a church school appropriately arranged for worship by the children. (See ALTAR)

WORSHIP SERVICE (See WORSHIP)

Y

WORSHIP

YAH-WEH A modern translation of the Hebrew word translated "Jehovah" in the Bible, used by some critics to discriminate the tribal God of the ancient Hebrews from the Christian Jehovah. (See JEHOVAH)

YEW TREE In many churchyards, especially in the south of England, very old yew trees are found. Why this tree should be in Christian cemeteries is not clear, but it is known that the ancients considered the yew a symbol of death.

Z

ZUCCHETTO

ZUCCHETTO A small round skullcap worn by some Roman Catholic ecclesiastics. The color for a bishop is purple; for a priest, black.

LITURGICAL COLOURS

The earliest definite knowledge of the use of specific colour in the service of the Church is Clement of Alexandria's recommendation of white as suitable to all Christians. The Canons of Hippolytus assign white to the clergy as becoming their office. The medieval development of colour symbolism may be examined in the Rationale Divinorum Officiorum of Durandus. This 13th Century prelate explains the meanings of all colours but, interestingly enough, knows of no such thing as either a standard Use or a standard meaning.

The ancient Use of liturgical colours was relatively simple; the best, the second best, ordinary, and, in some places, black. The Eastern Orthodox Church still adheres to this practice. In so far as "the best" is concerned, it is still required by the Dominican Order's Rule to be worn on the highest feasts irrespective of its colour.

In the middle ages each Cathedral had its own Use, and although this Use was in no sense binding on the Diocese involved, it was inevitable that some sequences should become popular and that, ultimately, certain Cathedral Uses should grow wider even than diocesan in their influence. It must be remembered, however, that on an Ascension Day in the 16th Century, one could still have seen "the best" vestments used in Salisbury; white, in Westminster; blue, in the College of St. Bernard at Romans; yellow, in Prague; red, in Utrecht; and green, in Soissons.

The Use of Salisbury Cathedral (Sarum) has always had wide popularity, therefore, it is listed here — but it should be noted that the ancient Westminster Use, which was predominately white, red, and black, has always had considerable appeal to northern taste.

The best: Christmas, Epiphany, Easter, Ascension, Whitsunday, Trinity, Dedication, Patronal Festival, All Saints', Thanksgiving.

Second best: Weekdays in Epiphanytide, Trinitytide (if red be not used).

RED: In Octave of Epiphany, Sundays after Epiphany, Septuagesima to Ash Wednesday, Passiontide to Easter Eve, Sundays after Trinity, Holy Innocents; Martyrs, Apostles and Evangelists (except St. John).

WHITE: St. John the Evangelist, during Octave of Christmas, Circumcision, Eastertide, Rogation Days, Friday and Saturday before Whitsunday, during Octave of Trinity, Feasts of the B.V.M., Saints' days in Eastertide, Virgins, Michaelmas.

BLUE: Advent, and as alternative colour for Pre-Lenten Season, Nativity of St. John Baptist, All Souls' Day, Funerals and Requiems.

BLACK: All Souls' Day, Funerals and Requiems.

UNBLEACHED LINEN: Days of Lent until Passion Sunday.

The Lutheran rules on Paraments are strict and clear: the Altar vestments, hangings, Pulpit and Lectern falls, et cetera, are invariably of the Day or the Season irrespective of the Service involved. The colour Use is:

WHITE: Christmas Eve through Epiphanytide; Easter Day to Whitsun Eve; Feasts: Transfiguration, Presentation, Trinity Sunday through Octave, Annunciation, Visitation, and Michaelmas.

LITURGICAL COLOURS

RED: First Vespers of Whitsunday to First Vespers of Trinity Sunday; Festival of the Reformation (October 31) and the Sunday nearest it; Feasts: Apostles (except St. John), Martyrs, All Saints', Dedication of a Church, Church Anniversaries, Harvest Festival, and Thanksgiving Day.

GREEN: First Vespers of Septuagesima through Shrove Tuesday, II Trinity through to the First Vespers of I Advent.

VIOLET: First Vespers of I Advent to Christmas Eve, Vespers of Shrove Tuesday through to Vespers of Easter Even (excepting Good Friday).

BLACK: Good Friday, and for a Day of Humiliation.

The Fair Linen is required to be long enough to reach from one third to two thirds the distance from the top of the Altar to the floor, and wide enough to hang over the front (and back) a full span.

The Colour Sequence of the Roman Catholic Church is now very largely that common to the Court of Rome in the 16th Century. It is often referred to as the Western Use. It is as follows:

WHITE: Christmas and days of Octave; Circumcision, Epiphany and Octave; Maundy Thursday; Easter Even through the 5th Sunday after Easter; Ascension Eve through to Vigil of Pentecost; Trinity Sunday; Corpus Christi and Octave; Transfiguration; Christ the King; Feasts of the B.V.M.; All Saints' and Octave; Michaelmas; Confessors, Doctors, Virgins, and Holy Women.

RED: Pentecost and Octave; Apostles and Evangelists (except St. John, whose feast is a white one); Martyrs: (the Holy Innocents, only if that feast falls on a Sunday).

VIOLET: Advent Season—except the third Sunday, "Gaudette"; Septuagesima through to Maundy Thursday — except the Fourth Sunday, "Laetare"; Ember Days apart from the Octave of Pentecost; Rogation Days; Vigils, Holy Innocents, if not on a Sunday.

GREEN: The Sundays (and Ferias) after the Octave of the Epiphany through to the Eve of Septuagesima; the Sundays (and Ferias) after Pentecost (or, after Trinity) through to Advent.

BLACK: Good Friday; All Souls'; Requiems.

ROSE: The Third Sunday in Advent; the Fourth Sunday in Lent.

Chapter V
Symbols of the Church

SYMBOLS OF THE OLD TESTAMENT

STAR OF DAVID

Two interwoven equilateral triangles form a six-pointed star tradit!onally the shape of David's shield. Sometimes called "the Creator's Star", the six points recalling the six days of creation.

SERPENT

The serpent representing Satan is coiled about the trunk of a tree, with the apple as the object of temptation.

FLAMING SWORD

Symbolized by the flaming sword which guarded the path to the tree of life after the expulsion of Adam from the Garden of Eden.

SERPENT AND WORLD

The sinful nature of mankind everywhere as a result of Adam's fall is traditionally represented by a serpent coiled around the earth.

ARK

The most common symbol of the Flood. Also symbol of the Church, since in the Ark all living creatures found refuge from danger.

TOWER OF BABEL

This tower resembling somewhat a modern city set-back building is used in Old Testament symbolism.

APPLE

A symbol of the fall of man since sin is said to have entered the world when Eve tasted of the forbidden fruit.

DRAGON

Another symbol for Satan. Also, sin and pestilence. When shown underfoot it signifies victory over evil.

DOVE WITH OLIVE SPRIG

Sometimes used as a symbol for the Flood. It denotes peace, forgiveness, and anticipation of new life.

LASH AND BRICKS

Israel's captivity and forced labor under the taskmaster's lash.

ALTAR OF SACRIFICE

The altar with slain lamb on it indicates the sacrificial nature of Old Testament worship, and to the Christian suggests the sacrificial nature of Jesus' life and ministry.

LAMB

The blood of a lamb without blemish was commanded by God to be sprinkled on the doorposts of Hebrew homes in Egypt so His destroying angel might pass over and spare Israel. This was memorialized in the Passover Festival.

SCROLL AND SHEAF OF WHEAT

Symbols of the Feast of Pentecost, a festival which occurred at the close of the wheat harvest and later included the commemoration of the giving of the Law at Sinai.

DOORPOSTS AND LINTEL

The blood-sprinkled doorposts and lintel is a symbol of God's protection in Egypt at the passing over of the destroying angel, which is central in the Passover Festival.

TABLES OF STONE WITH THE TEN COMMANDMENTS

Represented by a two-fold stone tablet. The Roman Catholic Church and the Lutheran bodies show the first table with three commandments and the second with seven commandments.

TABLES OF STONE WITH THE TEN COMMANDMENTS

Other bodies of the church show four numbers for the first table and six on the second table. Sometimes five numbers on each table are used.

SCROLL

The scroll stands for the five Books of Moses, as the first five books of the Old Testament are commonly called. These are known as the Torah and constitute the most sacred Law of the Jews.

SEVEN-BRANCH CANDLESTICK

The seven-branch candlestick is a symbol for Old Testament worship, and known as the Menorah is used in Jewish synagogues today.

ALTAR OF BURNT OFFERING

The altar upon which the offerings of first-fruits and grains were made. Also a symbol for Old Testament worship.

ARK OF THE COVENANT

The Ark of the Covenant was the meeting place of God with the Israelites on the journey from Egypt and therefore was the symbol of the Presence of God among them.

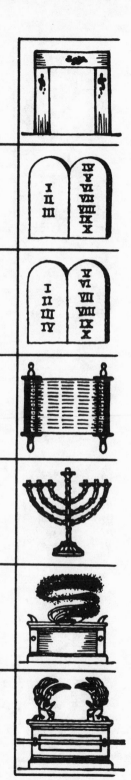

YOUNG BULLOCK AND CENSER

Symbol for Day of Atonement. In the ceremony of atonement for sin, the high priest at one point carried a smoking censer and the blood of a young bullock before the mercy-seat.

CLUSTER OF GRAPES

Signifies entry into Canaan. The spies reporting favorably on the Promised Land of Canaan brought back a large cluster of grapes borne on a staff between two men.

AARON

At the command of God Aaron threw down his rod before Pharaoh and it became a serpent, swallowing up the serpents produced by the magicians and sorcerers.

ABEL

Abel, the second son of Adam, was a shepherd and offered the firstlings of his flock as a gift to God.

ABRAHAM

The patriarch's symbol is the sacrificial knife, with God's promise to him indicated by a blue shield with many stars. One large star stands for the Messiah.

ADAM

Adam was told by God that because of his sin he must henceforth earn his food by the sweat of his brow.

AMOS

A herdsman of Tekoa who became the great prophet of righteousness whose written utterances are the earliest recorded in the Old Testament. (8th Century B.C.).

CAIN
The first son of Adam, Cain brought the result of his tilling the soil as an offering to God.

DANIEL
The ram with four horns signifies Daniel because it was a part of one of his visions (8:8).

DAVID
Symbolized by a harp because of his skill as a musician, while the lion recalls his exploits in protecting his sheep as a shepherd boy.

DEBORAH
Represented by a crown because she was gifted for leadership during the period of the Judges.

ELIJAH
The fiery chariot stands for Elijah because it appeared when he was carried to heaven in a whirlwind.

ESAU
A son of Isaac, and a skillful hunter, who through the deceit of his brother, lost his father's blessing due him as the first-born.

EVE
The symbol for Eve, the first woman according to the Biblical account, is a distaff.

EZEKIEL

A closed gate suggests Ezekiel's prophecy of the coming siege of Jerusalem which he was commanded to picture in a small model as a sign to the Israelites (4:3).

GIDEON

God commanded Gideon to attack the Midianites which he did with three hundred followers by concealing torches in pitchers and making a surprise blow.

HOSEA

This prophet of God's love is symbolized by a cast-off mantle representing Israel's unfaithfulness to God which Hosea daringly denounced.

ISAIAH

This prophet met his death reputedly by being sawn asunder. He was a great prophet who spoke for God at a critical time in the history of the Jews.

ISAAC

Isaac's symbol is bundles of wood arranged in the form of a cross, the wood recalling the near sacrifice of Isaac on the altar by his father, Abraham.

JACOB AND HIS FAMILY

Represented by a sun and full moon for Jacob and his wife, and twelve stars for their twelve sons.

JEREMIAH

Tradition says that the prophet Jeremiah was stoned to death because of his unpopular utterances in speaking for God against the rebellious Israelites.

JONAH

A great fish is the usual symbol for Jonah because of its part in the Bible narrative.

JOSEPH

The story of Joseph is familiar to all, and the many-colored coat has become his symbol, since it was one of the causes which greatly influenced his life.

JOSHUA

Under Joshua's leadership the walls of Jericho fell down to the accompaniment of the sound of trumpets, and the inhabitants were completely destroyed by his men.

MELCHISEDEK

The symbol for this very early priest-king is a loaf of bread and a chalice.

MICAH

Micah declared that the mountain of God's house would tower above every other mountain (4:1).

MOSES

Moses is symbolized by the basket made of bulrushes by which he was saved as a baby when the Pharaoh sought to kill all Hebrew babies.

THE CALL OF MOSES

The burning bush that was not consumed is the symbol for the call of the great Hebrew leader who recognized that God was speaking to him in that unusual place.

NAHUM

This symbol comes from the verse, "Behold, upon the mountains the feet of him that bringeth good tidings, that publisheth peace!" (1:15a).

NOAH

Noah is always associated with the Flood and the houseboat he built at God's command.

RUTH

The wisp of wheat recalls that Ruth was a gleaner in the fields of Boaz, where she was treated with kindness, though a foreigner.

SAMSON

Two of Samson's amazing feats are given as, slaying one thousand Philistines with the jawbone of an ass, and pushing down the pillars of a heathen temple by his own strength.

SETH

A thread wound three times around a thumb signifies Seth, the third son of Adam and Eve.

SOLOMON

This king is often represented by a model of the Temple which he built and which was the greatest of all the Hebrew temples.

ZEPHANIAH

The message of this prophet dealt with the Day of God's wrath which hung over Jerusalem and wherever wickedness was found in the land.

SYMBOLS OF THE NEW TESTAMENT

THE LATIN CROSS
The most commonly used form of cross.

THE CALVARY CROSS
Sometimes called the Graded Cross. The three steps, from the top down, stand for Faith, Hope, Love.

THE ST. ANDREW'S CROSS
Tradition says the apostle Andrew died on this form of cross, requesting that he be crucified on a cross unlike that of his Lord.

THE EASTERN CROSS
The upper horizontal arm represents the place of the inscription over the head of the crucified Jesus. The lower slanting arm represents his footrest, since the Eastern Church believes Jesus was crucified with his feet side by side and not crossed one over the other as usually pictured by the Western Church.

THE CELTIC CROSS
Or cross of Iona, dates back to early centuries of the Christian era. It was said to have been taken from what is now Ireland to the island of Iona by Columba in the 6th century.

THE TAU CROSS
So-called because of resemblance to the Greek letter T. This is the original form of cross.

THE ANCHOR CROSS

Which was used by the early Christians in the Catacombs. Ancient Egyptian in its origin.

THE GREEK CROSS

With all arms of equal length.

THE CROSS OF TRIUMPH

Symbolic of the triumph of the Gospel throughout the earth.

THE JERUSALEM OR CRUSADER'S CROSS

Usually has four small crosses between the arms, the five crosses symbolizing the five wounds of our Lord. Worn by Godfrey de Bouillon, first ruler of Jerusalem after the liberation from the Moslems.

THE MALTESE CROSS

Consisting of four spearheads with points together. Dates back to the days of the Crusades when the order of the Hospitallers used it for their emblem. Later they made their headquarters on the island of Malta.

THE CROSS PATTÉE

Resembles the Maltese Cross. A beautiful form of the cross used widely for decorative purposes.

THE CROWN AND CROSS

These symbolize the reward of the faithful in the life after death to those who believe in the crucified Savior.
Be thou faithful unto death and I will give thee the Crown of Life. (Rev. 2:10.)

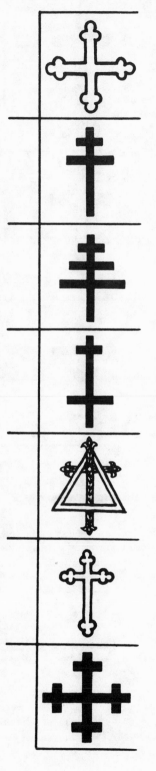

THE CROSS TREFFLÉE

A beautiful form with ends formed as trefoils. It is widely used wherever a decorative style of cross is needed. Also known as the Cross Botonnée.

THE PATRIARCHAL CROSS

Has two horizontal arms, the upper one slightly shorter than the lower. The upper represents the inscription over the head of our Lord on the cross.

THE PAPAL CROSS

Has three horizontal arms, each a little longer than the other, in descending order. The two upper cross bars are said by some to signify the crosses of the two crucified beside our Lord. This cross is used only in Papal processions.

THE CROSS OF LORRAINE

Has two horizontal arms, a short one near the top and a longer one near the base.

THE CROSS AND TRIANGLE

A symbol used mostly in church embroidery. Here the cross intertwined with the triangle emphasizes that Christ is one in the Holy Trinity.

THE CROSS BOTONNEE

Sometimes called the Budded Cross because of the moderate form of its trefoil ends. Hence it suggests the young or immature Christian, while the Cross Fleurée, or flowered cross, denotes by its more fully opened ends the adult Christian.

THE CROSS CROSSLET

Four Latin crosses joined at their bases. Represents Christianity spreading in the four directions and is especially appropriate when the missionary idea is expressed.

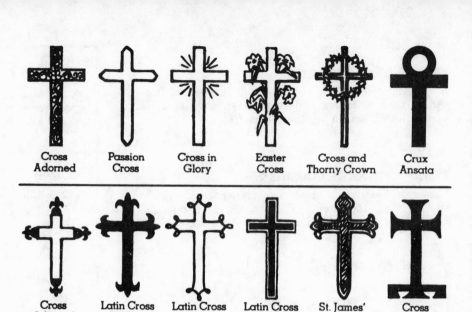

Cross Adorned	Passion Cross	Cross in Glory	Easter Cross	Cross and Thorny Crown	Crux Ansata

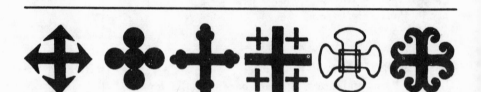

Cross Adorned	Latin Cross Fleurée	Latin Cross Clechée	Latin Cross Fimbriated	St. James' Cross	Cross Lambeau

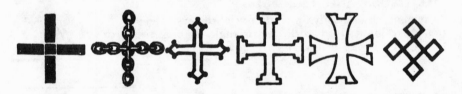

Cross Barbée	Cross Bezant	Cross Botonnée	Cross Cantonée	Canterbury Cross	Cross Cercelée

Cross Trononnée	Chain Cross	Cross Clechée	Cross Degraded	Demi Sarcelled	Cross Mascly

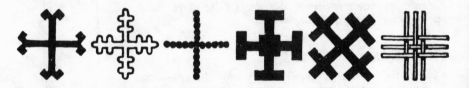

Cross Millrine	Cross Nebulée	Paternoster Cross	St. Chad's Cross	St. Julian's Cross	Triparted Cross

THE EQUILATERAL TRIANGLE

Symbol of the Trinity. The three distinct angles combine to make one complete figure.

THE CIRCLE AND TRIANGLE

Which suggests the eternity of the Trinity.

THE CIRCLE

Standing for eternity, because it is without beginning and without end.

THE THREE INTERTWINING CIRCLES

These indicate the doctrine of the equality, unity, and co-eternal nature of the three persons of the Trinity.

THE TRIQUETRA

Early symbol of the Holy Trinity. The three equal arcs express eternity in their continuous form, indivisibility in their interweaving, and their center is a triangle, ancient Trinity symbol.

THE TRIQUETRA AND CIRCLE

The Triquetra, denoting the Blessed Trinity, is combined with the circle of eternity producing a figure recalling several spiritual truths.

THREE FISH IN A CIRCLE

The fish is an ancient symbol for our Lord, and three fish in a circle signify that man's salvation comes from the Triune God.

THE CHI RHO

A monogram of the first two letters, Chi (X) and Rho (P), of the Greek word for Christ.

THE IHS

Are the first three letters (iota, eta, sigma) of the Greek spelling of Jesus. The upper form is the more ancient, though the lower is the more common now.

THE ALPHA AND OMEGA

The first and last letters of the Greek alphabet which signify that Jesus is the beginning and the end of all things. (See The Book of the Revelation, chapter I, verse 8.)

THE FYLFOT CROSS (OR SWASTIKA)

A pagan symbol used by early Christians in the catacombs. During the second and third centuries, some authorities say, the swastika was the only form of cross used by the Christians. It is made both clockwise and counter.

THE CHI RHO WITH THE ALPHA AND OMEGA IN A CIRCLE

Symbol for Christ is within symbol for eternity (circle), and so signifies the eternal existence of our Lord.

JESUS CHRIST CONQUERS

Consists of Greek cross with abbreviated Greek words for Jesus Christ (abbreviations indicated by horizontal lines), and "nika" meaning "conquers."

THE CORNERSTONE

The cornerstone with abbreviations of the Greek words for Jesus Christ symbolizes Him who was declared to be the chief cornerstone. (Ephesians 2:20.)

I X MONOGRAM

This symbol for our Lord consists of the initial letters for the Greek words for Jesus Christ arranged as a monogram.

GREEK CROSS AND X MONOGRAM

In this symbol for our Lord a Greek cross is superimposed on a X (Chi), first letter of the Greek word for Christ.

ALPHA-MU-OMEGA

Another symbol for our Lord consists of the initial letters of Greek words for "yesterday, today, and forever." (See Hebrews 13:8.)

CROSS FITCHÉE

Any cross whose lower arm is sharpened. This is said to have been used by the Crusaders who carried crosses with a pointed lower end so they could be thrust into the ground easily at the time of devotions.

CHI RHO WITH ALPHA AND OMEGA

This symbol for our Lord comes from the catacombs and indicates that he is the beginning, continuation, and end of all things.

CHI RHO MONOGRAM

Consists of the first two, and last letters of the word for Christ in Greek. The horizontal line in top center is the sign of abbreviation.

IESUS MONOGRAM

Formed by using the first two, and last letters of the word for Jesus in Greek, with abbreviation sign.

SWORD AND STAFF

These are the weapons which were in the hands of the "great multitude" that followed Judas into Gethsemane on the night of the betrayal of Jesus (Matt. 26:47).

SWORD, SCABBARD AND EAR

A symbol calling to mind the impulsive act of Peter in Gethsemane in cutting off the ear of the high priest's servant (John 18:10).

THE ROPE

A rope was used to bind Jesus when he was led away to the high priest; thus it is an emblem of the betrayal and arrest (John 18:12).

THE CROWN OF THORNS

A mockery crown, symbol of humiliation and suffering, plaited by the soldiers and imposed upon Jesus during his trial before Pilate (John 19:2).

THE NAILS

The great nails driven through the palms and the feet of Jesus at his crucifixion are symbols of the poignancy of his physical suffering (John 19:17, 18).

THE SEAMLESS COAT

One of the Passion symbols, referring to the garment of Jesus for which the soldiers at the foot of the cross cast lots (John 19:23, 24).

THE PALM LEAF

Branches of the palm tree, regarded as sacred from early Semitic times, were carried by the Jews as a sign of triumphant rejoicing (John 12:13).

I.N.R.I.

Initial letters for Latin superscription on the cross:
Iesus Nazarenus Rex Iudaeorum, Jesus of Nazareth,
King of the Jews (John 19:19).

LADDER CROSSED WITH
REED AND SPONGE

A symbol of our Lord's crucifixion, since the sponge
was used to provide him vinegar while on the cross.
(Matt. 27:48).

THE BURSTING POMEGRANATE

Symbol of the Resurrection and the power of our
Lord, who was able to burst the tomb and come
forth.

THE PHOENIX

A mythical bird which at death bursts into flame but
rises from its own ashes. Symbol of the Resurrection
and immortal life.

THE PEACOCK

Early symbol of the Resurrection. When the peacock
sheds his feathers, he grows more brilliant ones than
those he lost.

THE LILY

Symbol of Easter and immortality. The bulb decays
in the ground, yet from it new life is released.

MONEY BAG AND SILVER COINS

Emblem of the treachery of Judas in his conspiracy
between the chief priests and himself for the betrayal
of Jesus (Matt. 26:15).

THE BASIN AND EWER

Emblem of the footwashing ceremony recorded in John 13:5—evidence of the humility of Christ's love and his estimate of true greatness in his Kingdom.

THE COCK

The crowing of the cock is a warning to Peter as to his steadfastness of faith and as a rebuke to his weakness (Mk. 14:72).

THE CUP AND THE CROSS

In the Gospels the cup stands figuratively for the bitterness of the sufferings of Christ in Gethsemane and upon the Cross (Luke 22:42).

THE LANTERN

On the night of the betrayal and arrest of Jesus, Judas with a company of men and officers entered Gethsemane with lanterns and torches (John 18:3).

THE BUTTERFLY

Symbol of the resurrection and eternal life. As the butterfly leaves the pupa and soars upward with a new body, so through Jesus Christ are His followers borne to a new life.

THE CANDLESTICK

These suggest our Lord's words, "I am the light of the world", John 8:12. They also represent His two-fold nature — human and divine, when two candlesticks are used.

THE GRAPES

A bunch of grapes signifies the sacrament of the Holy Communion, and is most appropriately found about the Communion table.

THE MANGER

Suggestive of the simplicity and poverty surrounding the birth of Jesus and typical of his entire life.

THE STORK

Symbolizes chastity, prudence, and vigilance. Associated with the Annunciation because, as the stork announces the coming of spring, the Annunciation to Mary indicated the Advent of Christ.

THE HAWTHORN OR GLASTONBURY THORN

A thornwood tree which blossoms at Christmas. According to legend Joseph of Arimathaea struck his thornwood staff into the earth and it later miraculously blossomed at the time of Christ's birth. Symbol of the Nativity; named because of the ancient tree, offshoots of which still grow within the grounds of the ruined abbey of Glastonbury, England.

THE HERALD ANGEL

An angel floating in space with his right hand raised in benediction is a symbol of the Nativity.

MARY'S JOURNEY TO VISIT ELIZABETH

In the sixth month of Elizabeth's conception Mary journeyed into the hill-country to visit her kinswoman, and remained with Elizabeth for about three months (Luke 1:36-56).

THE FLEUR DE LIS

One of the most popular symbols for Mary. It was selected by the French Kings as their symbol and later was used in the banner of Jeanne d'Arc.

THE UNICORN

A familiar symbol of our Lord; early accepted as a symbol of purity and therefore especially related to the Virgin and the birth of Jesus.

THE ANGEL'S ANNOUNCEMENT TO THE SHEPHERDS

The angel of the Lord appeared before the shepherds and announced to them the birth of the Child Jesus in Bethlehem (Luke 2:8-14).

THE EPIPHANY STAR

The star of Jacob (Numbers 24:17) finds its fulfillment in the "manifestation" of Jesus to the Gentiles (Matthew 2:1,2).

THE MAGI

Gold, Frankincense, and Myrrh were given as gifts to the Infant Jesus by the Three Wise Men (Matthew 2:11, 12).

FLIGHT INTO EGYPT

"Arise, and take the young child and his mother, and flee into Egypt and be thou there until I bring thee word." (Matthew 2:13)

MASSACRE OF THE INNOCENTS

"Then Herod, when he saw that he was mocked of the wise men, was exceeding wroth, and sent forth, and slew all the children that were in Bethlehem," under two years of age (Matthew 2:16).

RETURN OF THE HOLY FAMILY

"Arise, and take the young child and his mother, and go into the land of Israel: for they are dead which sought the young child's life (Matthew 2:20).

THE DAISY

Conventionalized, symbol of the innocence of the Holy Child. Popular usage started towards the end of the fifteenth century.

THE OX

Suggestive of strength, patience, and sacrifice, and for this reason a symbol of our Redeemer ("For my yoke is easy, and my burden is light." Matthew 11:30).

THE CHRISTMAS ROSE

Symbol of the Nativity and of Messianic prophecy, a white hardy rose that blooms at Christmas.

THE HUGUENOT CROSS

Used by the French Protestants of the 16th and 17th centuries known as Huguenots. Worn today by many French Protestants.

THE WHEAT

Heads of wheat symbolize the Bread of Life (Mark 14:22). With clusters of grapes, appropriate for holy tables.

CROSS ON THE ROCK

The rock is a symbol of our Lord, based on I Cor. 10:4. With a cross, it suggests the words of the *Venite Exultemus,* "Let us make a joyful noise to the rock of our salvation."

THE SHIP

The Church sails unharmed through all perils. The word, "Nave," comes from the Latin word for "ship."

THE LAMP

Another symbol for the Word of God. Probably coming from "Thy word is a lamp unto my feet." (Psalm 119:105).

291

THE ALL-SEEING EYE

This all-seeing eye of God looks out from the triangle of the Trinity. It is found on some English and Greek churches.

THE HAND OF GOD

Symbol of the Father, as Blesser. The three extended fingers suggest the Holy Trinity, while the two closed fingers denote the two-fold nature of the Son.

THE HAND OF GOD

Symbol of the Father, with the idea of Creator. (Gen. 1:1.) The tri-radiant nimbus denotes the hand of the Divine.

SOULS OF THE RIGHTEOUS

Symbolizes a sentence in the Book of Wisdom, "The souls of the righteous are in the hand of God."

THE DOVE

The dove expresses innocence and purity. It signifies the Holy Spirit and the Presence of God as hovering over the water at Creation, and above Jesus at his baptism. The symbol must always include the three-rayed nimbus.

THE LAMB RECLINING ON THE BOOK OF THE SEVEN SEALS

The Revelation 5:1. Reclining because He is the Wounded Lamb. The three-rayed nimbus denotes deity.

THE LAMB STANDING WITH THE BANNER OF VICTORY

No longer wounded, but standing with the banner of victory, suggesting the victorious nature of His sacrifice.

THE OPEN BIBLE
Symbolizes the Word of God.

BELL
A bell calling to worship symbolizes the need of priority for the things of God over the secular. In general, the sounding forth of the Word.

SHIELD OF THE TRINITY
The three curving sides, each exactly equal in length, carry the Latin words, "is not". The short straight bands have the word "is". The outer circles bear the words, "Father", "Son", "Holy Spirit", while the inner circle is "God".

THE SUN
Made up of the Iesugram symbol placed in the circle of eternity and with flames shooting out in every direction. Suggests the "Sun of Righteousness" mentioned in Malachi 4:2.

THE GRIFFIN
The Griffin, an imaginary creature with the wings and beak of an eagle and the body of a lion, suggests the two-fold nature of Christ. The eagle portion recalls His Divine Nature and the lion portion denotes His humanity.

THE ASCENSION
This subject is usually pictured, though sometimes Elijah's chariot of fire is employed as a symbol.

THE PELICAN
Symbol of the Atonement. Pelican was believed to draw blood from its own breast to feed its young.

THE WINGED CREATURE
WITH A MAN'S FACE

The winged man represents Matthew because his Gospel narrative traces Jesus' human genealogy.

THE WINGED CREATURE
WITH A LION'S FACE

Is the symbol for Mark because his Gospel narrative begins with, "The voice of one crying in the wilderness", and this suggests the roar of a lion.

THE WINGED CREATURE
WITH THE HEAD OF AN OX

Luke is symbolized by the ox, the animal of sacrifice, since Luke stresses the atoning sacrifice of Jesus.

THE WINGED CREATURE
WITH AN EAGLE'S HEAD

The high-soaring eagle is the emblem of John because in his narrative he rises to loftiest heights in dealing with the mind of Christ.

THE NIMBUS

The nimbus has come to be emblematic of sanctity and to denote a person recognized for unusual piety, such as, apostles, martyrs, and saints.

THE THREE-RAYED NIMBUS

Signifies divinity and is used only with any Person of the Trinity. Rays of light were ancient emblems of divine power.

THE AUREOLE

An elongated nimbus used only as surrounding the entire body of our Lord, or the Virgin and Child.

THE SHEPHERD
This symbol, found in the catacombs, calls to mind the loving care of Jesus, the Good Shepherd.

CHRIST THE KING
(CHRISTUS REX)
When the Christ is depicted wearing Eucharistic vestments and as reigning from the Cross this is known as the Crucifix of Christ the King.

THE FISH
A secret sign used by the early persecuted Christians to designate themselves as believers in Jesus. The initial letters of the Greek words for "Jesus Christ, God's Son, Savior", spell the Greek word for fish.

NINE POINTED STAR
The nine points of this star stand for the nine fruits of the spirit as found in Galatians 5:22. Usually each point contains the name or initial of the Latin word of the gift it symbolizes.

ESCALLOP SHELL WITH
DROPS OF WATER
A symbol of our Lord's baptism.

CENSER
Symbol of prayer. As incense smoke wafts upward so prayer ascends before God (Revelation 8:4 and Psalm 141:2).

BURNING TORCH
As a Christian symbol it signifies witnessing for Christ. "Let your light so shine." (Matthew 5:1).

BALANCES

The symbol for justice. With tiny figure in one pan, or carried by St. Michael who is supposed to weigh the souls of men; balances signify the final Judgment Day.

BANNER

A banner is the symbol of rejoicing and of victory. The Lamb of God bearing a banner with a cross symbolizes the joyful victory over death won by our Lord.

BEEHIVE

Symbol for a community of those who work together for the benefit of all. Used modernly as a symbol for the Christian Church, and is one of the best.

HARP

The symbol for music, especially that rendered in praise of God.

OLIVE BRANCH

Since olive trees provide shelter and opportunity for rest, and the olive oil is used for ointments, the olive branch is the symbol for peace, harmony and healing.

CHI RHO IN JOINED RINGS

This is a fairly recent figure to symbolize matrimony. It signifies the joining of man and woman in unending union with the presence of Christ indicated by the Chi Rho monogram.

BIRDS AND GRAPES

From ancient classic times comes this motif often found on sarcophagi. It symbolizes the faithful feeding on the grapes, the blood of Christ.

CLOVER

The prominent three leaves make the clover an easily understood symbol of the Trinity. Legend says St. Patrick used the clover to explain the Trinity in his preaching.

COCKLE

The cockle is a weed that often grows among planted grain, and so symbolizes wickedness that may spring up in the fellowship of Christians.

COLUMBINE

The seven-petaled columbine blossom, or the seven-blossom stalk stand for the seven gifts of the Holy Spirit as given in Revelation 5:12: "power, and riches, and wisdom, and might, and honor, and glory, and blessing."

HOLLY

The thorny, prickly leaves of holly tree are regarded as a symbol of the crown of thorns, and so recalls the Passion of Christ.

IRIS

Frequently used instead of the lily in pictures of the Mother of our Lord.

LILY OF THE VALLEY

This sweet blossom signifies humility and purity, and is used most frequently with Mary the Mother of Jesus, or with Jesus Himself.

LOTUS

This blossom of exquisite beauty and purity, with its roots in the mud, suggests that the life of the Christian may rise through and above unlovely and evil influences.

MYRTLE

From early times myrtle has been the symbol of love. In Christian symbolism it is an allusion to the Gentiles who became followers of Christ.

VIOLET

St. Bernard describes the Virgin Mary as "the violet of humility." The violet is also used to evince the humility of the Son of God in assuming human form.

POPPY

The poppy signifies sleep, ignorance, and indifference. Sometimes shown with reference to the Passion of Christ because of the inference of sleep and death.

SKULL

A skull lying at the foot of the Cross represents the skull of Adam and symbolizes the sin of mankind where blood from the Lamb of God can drip upon it and wash away the believer's sin.

SKELETON

Obviously the symbol of death. Frequently shown with a scythe, since death is the cutting of this life, and/or an hourglass the symbol of the passing of time.

WINGS

Wings symbolize a divine mission, so angels and cherubim are shown with wings. The four evangelists are always shown as winged creatures.

SEVEN DOVES

Seven doves surrounding a circle containing the two letters SS (Sanctus Spiritus, Latin for Holy Spirit) symbolize the seven gifts of the Holy Spirit, as given in Revelation 5:12.

SEVEN LAMPS

The seven lamps burning before the throne of God (Revelation 4:5) symbolize the Holy Spirit. Occasionally seven flames alone are used.

THE PIERCED HEART

A symbol for Mary, the mother of Jesus, because of the prophecy uttered by the aged Simeon in the Temple, "Yea, and a sword shall pierce through thine own soul." (Luke 2:35).

FOOT

The human foot moves in the dust of the earth and so symbolizes humility and voluntary servitude.

SCOURGE AND PILLAR

The scourge is a symbol of the Passion and is sometimes accompanied by a pillar to which any unfortunate victim may have been tied.

SWAN

The swan is the symbol of a hypocrite because its beautiful white plumage covers its black flesh beneath.

TRUMPET

Symbol for the day of judgment, the resurrection, and the call to worship.

CYPRESS

The cypress has long been associated with death and is found in both pagan and Christian cemeteries. Once cut, it is said, the cypress never springs up again.

SYMBOLS OF
THE APOSTLES

PETER
The crossed keys recall Peter's confession and our Lord's gift to him of the keys of the kingdom. See Matt. 16:18, 19.

ANDREW
Tradition says that while Andrew was preaching in Greece he was put to death on a cross of this type.

JAMES (THE GREATER)
The scallop shell is the symbol of pilgrimage and stands for this apostle's zeal and missionary spirit.

JOHN, AS AN APOSTLE
Early writers state that John once drank from a poisoned chalice and was unharmed. Jesus once said that John should drink of His cup.

PHILIP
A cross and two loaves of bread, because of Philip's remark when Jesus fed the multitude. (John 6:7) ·

JUDE
This apostle traveled far on missionary journeys in company with Simon, according to tradition, hence the ship.

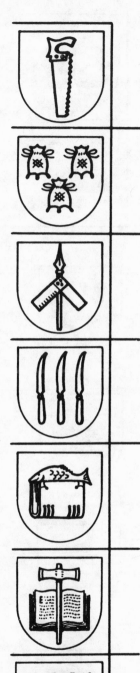

JAMES (THE LESSER)
Represented by a saw, since it is said his body was sawn asunder after a horrible martyrdom.

MATTHEW, AS AN APOSTLE
Is symbolized by three purses referring to his original calling as a tax collector.

THOMAS
A carpenter's square and a spear, because this apostle is said to have built a church with his own hands, in India. Later, he was persecuted there and was killed with a spear by a pagan priest.

BARTHOLOMEW
This apostle is said to have been flayed alive, hence he is usually represented by three flaying knives.

SIMON THE ZEALOT
This symbol is a book upon which rests a fish, because through the power of the Gospel Simon became a great fisher of men.

MATTHIAS
Chosen to take the place of Judas, he is symbolized by an open Bible and double bladed battle-axe. He is said to have been beheaded after his missionary work.

THE TWELVE APOSTLES
The apostles have been symbolized as a group as well as individually. In one place, twelve doves are used; in another, twelve men are shown, each with a sheep. Some very early carvings represent the apostles as twelve sheep.

PAUL

Referred to as the "Apostle to the Gentiles," but not one of the twelve apostles. Symbolized by an open Bible with the words "Spiritus Gladius" (sword of the Spirit), and behind the Bible the sword of the Spirit itself.

BARNABAS

Included among the apostles, although like Paul he was not of the Twelve. Tradition says he was especially successful as a preacher, hence the Gospel in the symbol.

OTHER SYMBOLS OF THE APOSTLES

Peter

Philip

Thomas

Andrew

Jude

Bartholomew

James the Greater

James the Less

Simon

John, An Apostle

Matthew, An Apostle

Matthias

This is a symbol of the Church, found in a church in Rome. From the Holy Spirit, symbolized by the dove, salvation comes through Christ's sacrificial death on the Cross into the Church, which is shown as a rock. From this rock flow the rivers of salvation from which drink the faithful, represented by the sheep and stags.

Beneath the rock is a symbol of Paradise where the faithful are enjoying their eternal reward guarded by an angel.

SYMBOLS OF
THE SAINTS

ST. AGATHA
Born in a noble Sicilian family, Agatha was famous for her beauty and gentleness. She refused to give up her Christian faith at the command of the governor, and was unspeakably tortured. She is the patroness of bell-founders. Died 251 A.D.

ST. AGNES
She was a devoted follower of Jesus who steadfastly refused all offers of marriage, claiming she was the "bride of Christ." She is now considered the patroness of chastity. Martyred about 304 A.D.

ST. AIDAN
An Irish monk of Iona who was sent to evangelize northern England and received the devoted help of Kings Oswald and Oswin. Died 651 A.D.

ST. ALBAN
He was a pagan who sheltered a persecuted priest, and was converted. He helped the priest escape, whereupon the fury of the pagans turned on Alban. He was beheaded in the city which now bears his name. Martyred about 303 A.D.

ST. ALFRED
At a time when England had been divided by various rulers, Alfred was accepted as the champion of England and of Christianity. He devoted himself tirelessly to the welfare of his people and to the relief of the poor against oppression. 849-899 A.D.

ST. AMBROSE
This famous Bishop of Milan, one of the four Doctors of the Western Church, was a great lover of music. He added to the richness of sacred services of the Church with it, and introduced the antiphonal chants bearing his name today. Died 397 A.D.

ST. ANNE

The mother of the Virgin Mary. From the Apocryphal Gospel records Anne has been honored, though nothing is known of her life. The book is a symbol of her careful instruction of Mary. First Century.

ST. ANSGARIUS (ANSKAR)

A missionary of the Faith to the Norsemen of Scandinavia. Long he labored amidst great discouragements and hostile tribes. Finally his self-denial and love for others made an impression and the savage people became Christian. Died 865 A.D.

ST. ANTHONY OF PADUA

A faithful and eloquent preacher against doctrinal errors and wickedness, he is usually referred to as the "hammer of heretics." A follower of St. Francis, he preached in France, Italy and Sicily until his death in Padua. Died 1231 A.D.

ST. ANTIPAS

He is venerated as the First Bishop of Pergamus (Asia Minor), and is by St. John in the Apocalypse (2:13) styled the "Faithful witness." Tradition avers that he was roasted to death in a brazen ox in the reign of the Emperor Domitian. Martyred 90 A.D.

ST. ASAPH

Distinguished for learning and piety, and for his earnest preaching. He was appointed Bishop in a newly formed See in North Wales, which later was named for him. Died about 595 A.D.

ST. ATHANASIUS

Athanasius was Bishop of Alexandria and an unusual student of Holy Scriptures. He was an authority on the ecclesiastical and canon laws of the Church and exerted a powerful influence in the Church. Died 373 A.D.

ST. AUGUSTINE

Known as the "Apostle of the English", Augustine and forty monks carried the Gospel to England. Received by the pagan king, Ethelbert, who soon was baptized with many others. Later Augustine was made Bishop. Died 604 A.D.

ST. AUGUSTINE OF HIPPO

His virtuous life and brilliant intellect caused him to be elected to the See of Hippo where he was recognized as the pillar of Orthodox Christianity. His "Confessions" and "City of God" have greatly influenced religious thinking. 354-430 A.D.

ST. BASIL

A bishop in Asia Minor, where he defended his province against the Arian heresy. He wrote many doctrinal works, founded the first recorded hospice for travellers, and wrote the Eucharistic Liturgy which bears his name. Died 379 A.D.

ST. BEDE

The Venerable Bede entered a monastery at the age of seven years for his education and remained there for the rest of his life. He spent his time reading, praying, teaching, and was a voluminous writer. Died 735 A.D.

ST. BERNARD

Early joined the Cistercians and later founded the Abbey of Clairvaux. Bernard was the adviser of popes and kings and wrote profusely, especially on the love of God. Died 1153 A.D.

ST. BONIFACE

This saint, a Benedictine monk, carried the Gospel to Germany and founded the Abbey of Fulda which was the center of German missionary activity. Martyred 755 A.D.

ST. BRIDE (ST. BRIDGET)

Baptized by St. Patrick, St. Bridget founded the first nunnery in Ireland. Legends stress her mercy and pity for the poor. Died 523 A.D.

ST. CECILIA

This Roman lady, educated as a Christian, converted her husband and shared martyrdom with him. Tradition says she wrote hymns and sang beautifully so she is regarded as the patroness of music. Martyred about 200 A.D.

ST. CHAD

Abbot of the Priory of Lastingham. Noted for his religious life. Preached as a missionary through all the Northumbrian territory. His church is considered the origin of Lichfield Cathedral. Died 673 A.D.

ST. CHARLES
(KING CHARLES THE FIRST)

The only person formally canonized by the English Church since the Reformation. Known as Charles the Martyr, he was beheaded in London in 1649.

ST. CHRISTOPHER

Legend says that Offero (bearer) once carried the Christ-child on his shoulders across a swollen stream, and so thereafter was known as Christopher (Christbearer). Patron saint of travel. Martyred about 250 A.D.

ST. CHRYSOSTOM

John, Bishop of Constantinople became the most eloquent preacher of the early Church, and so was called Chrysostom, or Golden-mouthed. Legend says that when he was a baby a swarm of bees settled on his mouth. Died 407 A.D.

ST. CLARE

Moved by the influence of St. Francis, she gave herself to monastic life and founded the order of the "Poor Clares." Her great charity and spiritual devotion have won the admiration of all. Died 1253 A.D.

ST. CLEMENT

Converted to the Christian faith by St. Paul. He became the Bishop of Rome, later he was martyred by being cast into the sea tied to an anchor. Martyred about 100 A.D.

ST. COLUMBA (ST. COLUM)

This saint founded many churches and monasteries in Ireland and Scotland, the most famous of which was on the island of Iona. One of the most consecrated and indefatigable of Christian missionaries. Died 597 A.D.

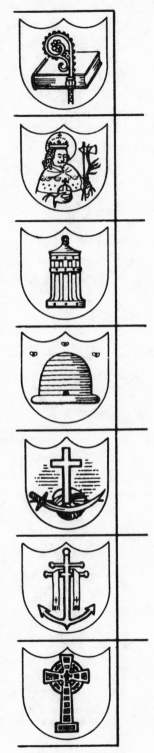

ST. CORNELIUS

A Pope of Rome 251-3 A.D. During his short episcopate he was harassed by religious controversies, and by the appearance of a rival pope. Martyred 258 A.D.

ST. CUTHBERT

A shepherd boy in Britain who embraced the monastic life. He became a faithful preacher and missionary to the wild and untamed mountain people of Scotland, and on Lindisfarne Island. Died 687 A.D.

ST. CYRIL OF JERUSALEM

Bishop of Jerusalem for many years. At one time was expelled because he sold ornaments of the church to provide food for the poor. Wrote instructions on Christian doctrine for catechumens which have been highly regarded ever since. Died 386 A.D.

ST. CYRIL OF ALEXANDRIA

A native of Alexandria and patriarch of the city. Gave much of his life to defense of the truth of Christ's divinity. Died 444 A.D.

ST. CYPRIAN

A lawyer, converted to Christianity, who became the bishop of Carthage. Wrote several important theological treatises, and became a pioneer of Christian literature writing. Martyred 258 A.D.

ST. DAVID

The patron saint of Wales, in which country he was born. He founded many monasteries, the most famous of which was in what is now St. David's. His monks followed a very austere rule. Died about 588 A.D.

ST. DENIS (DIONYSIUS) OF PARIS

A Roman missionary who penetrated far into Gaul and became the first bishop at Paris. Venerated as patron saint of France. Martyred 272 A.D.

ST. DOMINIC

Born a nobleman of Spain he resigned all worldly honors for his Master. He established the Dominican order of Preaching Friars, and did not spare himself in his work for the glory of God. Died 1221 A.D.

ST. DOROTHY

A virgin of Caesarea in Cappadocia noted for her beauty and piety. Refusing to sacrifice to idols, she was beheaded. Martyred about 300 A.D.

ST. DUNSTAN

The English-born Dunstan became Abbot of Glastonbury. Legend says the devil went to Dunstan's cell to tempt him, whereupon Dunstan caught the devil by the nose with red-hot pincers and caused him to flee. Died 988 A.D.

ST. EDMUND

At fifteen years of age Edmund became king of the East-Angles. He was very devout and religious. During a pagan invasion, Edmund refused to give up his Christian faith and was shot to death with arrows. Died 870 A.D.

ST. EDWARD THE MARTYR

King of England at the age of thirteen. He was stabbed to death by his stepmother, who wanted the throne for her own son Ethelred. Martyred 979 A.D.

ST. ELIZABETH

The mother of John the Baptist. All that is known of her is given in the first chapter of Luke. First Century.

ST. EUSTACE

Eustace was a Roman officer under the Emperor Trajan. He owed his conversion to the vision of a stag with a crucifix between its antlers which he saw while hunting. Died 118 A.D.

ST. FAITH

This beautiful young woman was very strong in her Christian belief and remained steadfast to her name when ordered to sacrifice to Diana. Burned to death. Died 290 A.D.

ST. FRANCIS

The well-born Francis resolved to devote his life to God. Founded the Franciscans, the members of which embrace complete poverty and help the sick and suffering. Died 1226 A.D.

ST. GABRIEL

This archangel was the angel sent to Mary to announce that she was to be the mother of Jesus. He is sometimes called the "Angel of the Annunciation." (Luke 1)

ST. GEORGE

St. George is the patron saint of England and venerated as the model of knighthood and protector of women. Also the patron of soldiers since he was long a military man engaged in warfare with the pagans. Martyred 303 A.D.

ST. GERALD

A Northumbrian monk who followed Colman from Lindisfarne to Ireland and became his successor in the English house built at Mayo for the English Monastic Colony. Died 732 A.D.

ST. GERALD OF AURILIAC

Gerald lived a very holy life "in the world" at a time of great moral degeneracy. He lived according to a very strict rule and founded a monastery for Benedictines. Died 909 A.D.

ST. GILES OF PROVENCE

Reputed to be a Greek cripple who refused to be cured of an accidental lameness in order that he might more completely mortify his pride. Lived as a hermit in a cave. Patron saint of cripples and beggars. Died 712 A.D.

ST. GREGORY

As Pope 590-604 A.D., Gregory reformed the services of the Church and arranged the music of the chants. One of the truly great popes. Died 604 A.D.

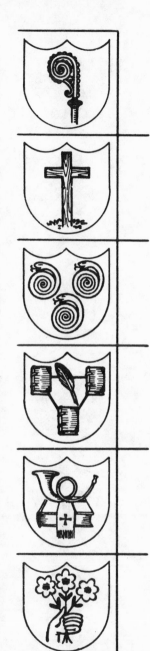

ST. HELENA (HELEN)

Mother of Constantine the Great and legendary discoverer of the true cross of Christ at Jerusalem. She built the Church of the Nativity at Bethlehem, the oldest Christian church in the world. Died 328 A.D.

ST. HILDA

Of royal blood, Hilda took the habit of a nun. Because of her piety and holy life she was soon appointed abbess. Her influence was a factor in securing unity in the English church. Died 680 A.D.

ST. HILARY OF POITIERS

Hilary was a student of rhetoric and philosophy and early became a convert to Christianity. He devoted his tongue and pen to fighting the Arian heresy and suffered banishment for his zeal. Died 368 A.D.

ST. HUBERT

According to legend, Hubert was converted while hunting and immediately won over to a better life a band of brigands he met in the forest. Became Bishop of Liege. Died 727 A.D.

ST. HUGH OF GRENOBLE

Appointed Bishop of Grenoble, he believed he was inefficient and retired to an austere abbey for discipline. The Pope, however, impressed by the Bishop's holy life, recalled him to his former high office where he served notably. Died 1132 A.D.

ST. IGNATIUS

Ignatius was Bishop of Antioch in Syria. When asked by the emperor for a sacrifice to heathen gods, Ignatius refused. He was condemned and thrown to the wild beasts. Martyred 107 A.D.

ST. JOHN THE BAPTIST
HE BAPTISED OUR LORD

"The man sent from God," the voice crying in the wilderness: "Prepare ye the way of the Lord," of whom Christ said "among those that are born of women there is not a greater prophet." First Century.

ST. JOSEPH

Joseph was the husband of Mary, the mother of Jesus. All that is known of Joseph is found in the first two chapters of Matthew and Luke. In Matthew he is described as "a just man". First Century.

ST. JULIA

Julia was a Christian slave girl with a pagan master who respected her faith and goodness. However, when visiting a foreign country the pagan governor ordered her to sacrifice to the gods. Her refusal brought swift crucifixion. Fifth Century.

ST. KATHERINE OF ALEXANDRIA
(CATHERINE)

Early converted to Christianity, she vanquished her pagan adversaries in a debate. This so enraged the Emperor that he ordered her put to death on a machine of spiked wheels. She was saved by a miracle but was later beheaded. Martyred 310 A.D.

ST. KATHERINE OF SIENNA
(CATHERINE)

From a child, Katherine was very religious, living at home in extreme self-mortification, spending much time in prayer and meditation. Later she felt called to leave home and devoted herself to the care of the sick and other good works. Died 1380 A.D.

ST. LAWRENCE

A deacon at Rome under Sixtus II. Three days after the latter was put to death, Lawrence was tortured on an iron bed over a fire. Martyred 258 A.D.

ST. LIOBA

Of English birth, Lioba early was called to Germany by St. Boniface, who gave her a convent there. She was outstanding in piety, humility and good works, and an honored friend of kings and queens. Died about 779 A.D.

ST. LOUIS

King of France, a brave warrior, very considerate to his people, especially the poor. In private life, more austere and prayerful than many a religious. Leader of two crusades. Died 1270 A.D.

ST. LYDIA

A seller of purple dyes. Lydia was converted through the preaching of Paul and was baptized with her whole household. She was the first recorded Christian convert in Europe. (Acts 16:14.). First Century.

ST. MARGARET

The daughter of a pagan priest of Antioch, she became a Christian. She endured much persecution because of her faith, but remained true. Patron saint of women in childbirth. Martyred about 306 A.D.

ST. MARTHA

Martha was the hostess of our Lord in her home in Bethany. Little is known of her beyond the accounts in the Gospels. She is the patroness of housewives and cooks. First Century.

ST. MARTIN

One day St. Martin saw a shivering beggar and shared his own cloak with the stranger. Later he entered the Church and while Bishop of Tours he converted his whole area to Christianity. Died 401 A.D.

ST. MARY

About fifty Marys are mentioned in the Book of Saints. The mother of Jesus is, of course, the outstanding character among them.

ST. MARY MAGDALEN

This Mary was the sinning and repentant woman forgiven through the love of Jesus. Appropriately, she is the patroness of penitent women. Died 68 A.D.

ST. MARY OF CLEOPHAS

The mother of the apostle, James the Less. She was one of the three Marys who stood at the foot of the cross on Calvary. First Century.

ST. MARY OF BETHANY

The sister of Martha and Lazarus, who won commendation from Jesus because of her eagerness to sit at His feet and learn of Him. First Century.

ST. MICHAEL

One of the archangels. St. Michael is regarded traditionally as guardian of the Church and its members against the evil one. It is he who is supposed to weigh the souls of men at the Last Day.

ST. MONICA

A Christian woman, she was married to a pagan husband whom she labored to convert, together with her eldest son, St. Augustine, who became the Bishop of Hippo. Died 387 A.D.

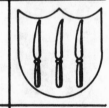

ST. NATHANIEL

Nathaniel is the name used for Bartholomew in the Fourth Gospel. He was the one whom Philip brought to Jesus and whose open-mindedness qualified him to receive additional revelations about his resurrected Lord. First Century.

ST. NICHOLAS

Bishop of Myra. Tradition says that St. Nicholas went secretly to the house of a destitute nobleman three nights in succession and threw a purse of gold in the window. Patron saint of children. Died about 326 A.D.

ST. OLAF

The son of the King of Norway. As a youth he lived a wild life. Accepted baptism and as king summoned missionaries from England to Christianize his country. Died 1030 A.D.

ST. OSWALD

First of the English Royal Saints. As King of Northumbria he diligently sought the complete evangelization of his country, and died fighting against a champion of paganism. Died 642 A.D.

ST. PATRICK

A captive British boy in Ireland, Patrick escaped and was educated in continental monasteries. Later he returned to Ireland preaching and teaching the Gospel and building churches. Patron saint of Ireland. Died about 465 A.D.

ST. RAPHAEL

The archangel who is the guardian angel of all humanity. He is called the "Healer of God" and is identified with the angel at the Pool of Bethesda.

ST. ROCH (ROCCO)

A citizen of France who devoted his life to the service of the plague-stricken, especially those who were abandoned. Patron of hospitals and prisons. Died about 1348 A.D.

ST. SIMEON

As a boy Simeon joined the community of St. John Stylites. For sixty-nine years he lived on the top of pillars within the monastery, in the exercise of religious contemplation. Died about 597 A.D.

ST. STEPHEN

The Deacon and first Christian martyr, called by Luke "a man full of faith and of the Holy Ghost." Stoned to death in the First Century.

ST. SYLVANUS

One of seven brothers who were persecuted as Christians under Marcus Aurelius. While his mother, St. Felicitas stood by exhorting him to remain faithful to Christ, he was cast from a cliff. Martyred Second Century.

ST. THADDAEUS

Also called Jude or Judas (not Iscariot). Thought by some to be the brother of James the Less and author of the epistle bearing his name. First Century.

ST. THEODORE TVRO

A soldier in the Roman army, Theodore set fire to the temple of Cybele, and suffered martyrdom for his deed. Martyred 306 A.D.

ST. THEODORE OF CANTERBURY

A Greek monk nominated by Pope Vitalian as Archbishop of Canterbury. He was the last foreign missionary to occupy the metropolitan See. Died 690 A.D.

ST. TIMOTHY

Companion of Paul on his missionary journeys, and referred to by Paul as "the beloved son in faith." Reputedly beaten and stoned to death for denouncing the worship of Diana. First Century.

ST. TITUS

A convert of St. Paul, and mentioned in the Pauline epistles as his brother and co-partner in his labours. Reputedly the first Bishop of Crete. First Century.

ST. URIEL

One of the archangels, his name means "God is my light." He is considered the interpreter of prophecy.

ST. VALENTINE

A priest who was active in assisting the martyrs in time of persecution. He was famous for the love and charity which he manifested. Martyred 269 A.D.

ST. VINCENT
At the age of twenty, Vincent was already an ordained deacon. With an unswerving Christian faith he underwent horrible tortures under Diocletian. Martyred 304 A.D.

ST. WENCESLAS
Duke of Bohemia. A Christian, he took over the reins of government at the time of a pagan reaction. He was murdered by his pagan brother. Patron saint of the Czechs. Martyred about 938 A.D.

ST. WILFRID (WILFRED)
A devoted Bishop who traveled widely on missionary labors, establishing, building and strengthening churches throughout England. Died 709 A.D.

ALL SAINTS
A rayed hand of God signifying divine care over the souls of the righteous.

WORLD COUNCIL OF CHURCHES
Ship with its mast in the form of a cross surrounded by the Greek Letters "OIKOUMENE." This symbol of the ship was selected by the World Council of Churches as representing its members engaged in a common and dangerous voyage. "OIKOUMENE" is an old Greek word meaning the universality of the Church and its world-wide mission.

GLOSSARY

Ablutions: The cleansing of the Chalice and Paten after the receiving of Holy Communion. Also the cleansing of the hands of the Priest at any time during the service.

Acolyte: One who serves the celebrant at the altar, sometimes called the server. In the non-liturgical church, one (usually a boy) whose principal function is to light and extinguish the candles on the altar.

Affusion: Baptism by pouring water upon the head of the person to be baptized.

Alb: A long white linen vestment with straight sleeves.

Alms Basin: A collection plate in which are collected the offerings of the people.

Altar: The Holy Table, the Communion Table.

Altar Rail: The railing which encloses the Sanctuary and at which communicants kneel to receive Holy Communion.

Altar Stone: A small flat stone (usually square, approximately 6″ x 6″ to 12″ x 12″) consecrated by the proper high church official, and on which the Sacrifice of the Mass may be said. It may be placed and used on an altar not yet consecrated and thus becomes the true altar.

Ambulatory: A passageway found in some churches around the chancel and behind the Altar.

Amice: A Vestment consisting of a linen neck-piece or collar, which is worn with the Alb. Originally a covering for the head, as well as the neck.

Antependium: The hanging or screen in front of an altar: frontal. Sometimes used in reference to the pulpit cloth.

Apse: A semi-circular or polygonal termination of a choir or chancel.

Aumbry: A receptacle made either in the wall or attached to the wall of the chancel or sacristy to contain the consecrated elements, holy oils, or sacred vessels; or a locked cupboard for storing altar books, vestments, or sacred vessels.

Aumbry Lamp: A light located near the aumbry to indicate the presence of the Sacred Elements.

Baguette: A long plain or decorated band of wood suspended from a cornice to enhance the beauty of a dossal.

Baldacchino: A canopy, which covers the altar.

Baptistry: In liturgical churches, wherever the font is located; in Baptist, or other churches which practice immersion, usually a large tank in the very front of the church, set into the platform or behind a communion table or altar.

Bier: The carriage upon which the coffin is placed in the church.

Biretta: A stiff four-sided cap worn by the clergy.

Bishop's Chair: The chair (cathedra) in a cathedral, reserved exclusively for the bishop of the diocese.

Boat: A vessel, named by its shape, for holding incense before it is put in censer or thurible.

Bread: Bread has long been the symbol for the means of sustaining life, as is evidenced in the sentence, "Bread is the staff of life."

Burse: The case for the corporal.

Candidate:	A Postulant who has been approved by the Bishop of Diocese on the recommendation of the Standing Committee is known as a Candidate for Holy Orders.
Candles:	See Eucharistic Lights, Office Lights, Paschal Candles.
Canon:	An ecclesiastical decree, code, or constitution. Also a clergyman who is connected with a cathedral.
Carillon:	An instrument comprised of at least two octaves of fixed cup-shaped bells (23 or more), arranged in chromatic series, and so tuned as to produce, when many such bells are sounded together, concordant harmony.
Cassock:	The long under garment worn by the clergy. It is usually black. There are two styles commonly in use. The Roman, which is buttoned down the front; and the Anglican, which is buttoned at the side. Also worn by choristers and acolytes.
Cathedra:	The seat of the bishop of a diocese.
Catholic:	Universal, world-wide ecumenical. The word refers to the ancient creeds of the whole Christian church, or the whole body of the church. The word is not the sole property of the Roman Catholic Church.
Cere-Cloth:	One of the three traditional cloths laid upon the top of the altar. It is a waxed cloth, designed to protect the fair linen from the dampness and moisture of the stone altar top.
Censer:	A brass or silver pot in which incense is burned.
Chalice:	The cup used at the Holy Communion.
Chancel:	The east end, so called, of a church.
Chapel:	A building or portion of one used for worship.
Chaplain:	A clergyman responsible for spiritual administration in a household, institution, or organization.
Chasuble:	A loose vestment with neck aperture and worn over the Alb.
Chimere:	A long garment of black or scarlet with armholes, but no sleeves, which is worn by Bishops over the Rochet.
Choir:	The choristers; also, the part of the chancel between the nave and the sanctuary.
Ciborium:	A covered cup to hold the Sacramental Bread; a canopy of wood or stone or marble, supported by four or more pillars covering an altar.
Cincture:	The girdle of a cassock.
Clerestory:	The wall above the arches and pillars in the church that has roofed-over side walls.
Cloister:	A covered passageway, usually open on one side into a court. The passageway connects the church with a parsonage or a school building or a parish house.
Collect:	A short prayer, more or less condensed in form, and aiming at a single point in behalf of a worshipping congregation.
Communion, The Holy:	The Sacrament of the Lord's Supper ordained by our Lord for the continual remembrance of the sacrifice of the death of Christ. Also called the Holy Eucharist.
Communion Table:	A table in the chancel or at the front of the church on which the elements for the Sacrament of the Lord's Supper are placed, and from which they are taken to the communicants.
Congregation:	An assembly of people gathered for the purpose of religious worship or instruction.

Cope:	A long cloak of rich material, varying in color according to the church season, worn over the Alb.
Corporal:	A square linen cloth used upon the altar at Communion.
Corpus:	The word means the body and refers to the representation of the Lord's body upon the cross.
Cotta:	A short white garment occasionally used by choristers over the cassock. It is not as long or as full as the surplice, although it is the same vestment.
Credence:	A shelf or table at the epistle side of the sanctuary upon which the Elements of the Holy Communion are placed until carried to the altar.
Crossing:	The place where the transept crosses the nave.
Crozier:	(Pastoral Staff) The staff of a bishop, patriarch, abbot, or prior.
Crucifer:	The one who carries the cross.
Crucifix:	A cross with a representation of our Lord's body (corpus) upon it.
Cruet or Ampulla:	The receptacle for wine and for water.
Crypt:	A vault beneath a church.
Curate:	Usually indicates a clergyman who assists the rector in a parish church.
Deacon:	In the Episcopal Church, the first and lowest Order in the Holy Orders of the Ministry. In other communions, a lay official working closely with the minister.
Deacon's Step:	The middle or second step approaching the altar.
Diocese:	The prescribed district in which a Bishop has jurisdiction.
Dossal or Dorsal:	A curtain of rich fabric behind the altar or communion table.
Doxology:	Any ascription of praise to God.
East End of a Church:	The end where the altar stands, even if not actually in the east.
Elder:	A layman in some churches who shares in the government of the local body.
Elements:	The materials used in the Sacraments appointed by Christ: water, wine, and bread.
Epistle Side:	The side of the altar at which the Epistle is read, the right as the congregation sees it.
Eucharist, The Holy:	The Holy Communion considered as a service of thanksgiving.
"Eucharistic Lights":	Two candles placed at either end of the top of the altar.
Eucharistic Vestments:	The Eucharistic Vestments differ from Choir Vestments in number and in ornateness. They are worn by a Bishop or a Priest for the celebration of the Holy Communion and include: alb, amice, chasuble, cassock, cope, girdle, maniple, and stole.
Even or Eve:	The day before a festival, i.e., Easter Even, Christmas Eve, designed to be a preparation for the feast it precedes.
Ewer:	The pitcher for holding the water for the font and for the lavabo basin.
Fair Linen:	The principal covering of the top of the altar. It hangs over the sides of the altar almost to the floor.
Flagon:	A large covered glass or metal container for a reserve of wine, or grape juice depending upon the church.

Font:	The receptacle of stone, metal, or wood, which holds the water for the Baptism.
Footpace:	The platform upon which the altar rests, where the priest stands to celebrate the Holy Eucharist; also called the predella. The highest of three steps is known as the Priest's Step; the other two being the Deacon's (second step) and the Subdeacon's being the bottom or first step.
Frontal:	A covering of cloth that hangs before the front of the altar, covering the entire front of the altar.
Frontlet or Superfrontal:	A short cover for the front of the altar, attached to linen on the altar top.
Genuflection:	A brief bending of the knee toward the altar when the Blessed Sacrament is present.
Girdle:	A cord, tied around the waist over the Alb.
Gloria Patri:	(Latin. Glory be to the Father) An ascription of praise to the Holy Trinity.
Gospel Side:	The side of the altar at which the Gospel is read, the left as the congregation sees it.
Gradine:	See retable.
Habit:	The special attire or garb worn by the clergy or by members of a religious community.
Hassock:	A stuffed cushion on which to kneel when praying.
Hell:	As used in the Apostle's Creed, the abode of all departed spirits.
Hood:	A shield-shaped hood or panel at the back of a cope; also, the academic vesture given by a college in token of a degree.
Host:	The bread or wafer of the Holy Communion.
Immersion:	Baptism when the recipient is completely immersed in the water.
Intinction:	Receiving the Holy Communion when the Wafer is dipped into the Wine of the Chalice and thus administered to the recipient both together.
Intone:	To chant or recite in monotone with inflections of the voice at pre-determined places.
Jubilate Deo:	(Latin: O be joyful in the Lord) The one hundredth Psalm arranged as a canticle appointed to be used in the Service of Morning Prayer.
Lantern:	The open tower above the crossing in a church.
Lavabo:	The ceremony of cleansing the celebrant's hands before the offertory oblation in the Holy Eucharist. The word is also used to denote the bowl containing the water, and for the small towel accompanying it.
Lectern:	A stand near the chancel on which rests the Bible.
Lectionary:	A selected list of Scripture passages for daily readings throughout the Christian year.
Litany:	(Greek: a prayer) The name applied to a General Supplication found in the Prayer Book of the Episcopal Church in which minister and people join responsively. In other communions, any form of prayer with alternate responses shared by clergy and congregation.
Litany Desk:	A kneeling desk, sometimes called a faldstool from which the litany is read. Its customary place in the church is on the floor of the nave in front of the chancel steps. Similar in shape to the prie-dieu.

Liturgical Colors:	The colors used in the church during the course of the year; white, black, red, violet, green, rose, ash and blue.
Liturgy:	Prescribed public services of the Christian Church, especially with reference to the celebration of the Holy Communion.
Maniple:	A scarf which hangs from the left arm over the Alb as part of the Eucharistic Vestments.
Mensa:	The top of the altar.
Minister:	In the Episcopal Church one who is ordained by the Bishop and hence is in Holy Orders; or one who is licensed by the Bishop to read certain specified services in the Book of Common Prayer. In other communions one who has been ordained to preach.
Missal:	Altar Book. The book containing the Communion Service, Collects, Epistles and Gospels.
Missal-Stand:	The desk on the altar upon which the Missal rests.
Mitre:	A traditional headpiece worn by some Bishops, emblematic of the highest order of the ministry.
Morse:	A metal clasp, usually elaborate, for use in fastening the cope.
Narthex:	The vestibule or closed-in porch across the building at the rear of the nave.
Nave:	The central division of the church in which the congregation is seated.
Oblation:	The act of offering the elements to God in the Holy Eucharist. The "offertory oblation" when the unconsecrated bread and wine are placed on the altar.
Office:	An authorized form of worship: Daily offices of Morning or Evening Prayer; an occasional office: Burial office.
Office-Lights:	All lights used on the altar, other than the two Eucharistic Lights, are office lights.
Order:	A religious fraternity.
Orders:	In the Anglican and Eastern Church these three orders of the ministry — Bishop, Priest, and Deacon; in the Roman Church — Priest, Deacon and Subdeacon.
Orders, Holy:	The three orders in the ordained Ministry, namely, Deacon, Priest, Bishop.
Orphrey:	A wide band of decorated material originally used for covering seams of vestments. Now mostly used for decorative use on vestments and to embellish the dossal.
Pall:	The linen cover for the Chalice; also, the cover for a coffin.
Paraments:	A word commonly used to designate the frontal of the altar and other hangings which may decorate a pulpit or lectern.
Paschal Candle:	A candle lighted on Easter Even and extinguished on Ascension.
Pastor:	(Latin: shepherd) The clergyman who accepts responsibility for the spiritual welfare of a parish.
Pastoral Staff:	(Crozier) Staff of a bishop, patriarch, abbot or prior.
Paten:	The silver or gold plate for the Bread at the Holy Communion.
Pectoral Cross:	A cross which hangs on the breast of a bishop.
Piscina:	A basin with drain-pipe leading directly to the ground for disposal of water from liturgical ablutions.

Postulant:	One approved by the Bishop of a Diocese as the first step towards becoming a Candidate for Holy Orders.
Predella:	See Footpace.
Presbyter:	In the Episcopal Church, a priest. In the Presbyterian Church, an elder, one of several who is elected to administer the affairs of the particular church.
Prie-Dieu:	The prie-dieu is more commonly called a prayer desk.
Processional Cross:	A cross affixed to the end of a staff which is carried at the head of a procession.
Protecting Cloth:	A cloth placed over the fair linen when there is not a service, designed to protect the linen from dust and dirt.
Purificator:	A small linen napkin used to wipe the Sacred Vessels after Holy Communion.
Pyx:	A covered receptacle of precious metal for the Sacrament used to carry the Consecrated Elements of the Holy Eucharist to the sick.
Pyx, Hanging:	A pyx of precious metal containing the Reserved Sacrament hung in the center of the chancel above the altar. Most commonly used in England.
Rabat:	A neck-band with cloth hanging down over the breast used by clergy wearing an ordinary vest.
Rabat, Vest:	A neck-band with cloth hanging down over the entire breast and to the waist, used by clergy when not wearing a vest.
Rail:	The altar rail between the choir and the sanctuary.
Rector:	(Latin: to govern) A priest in the Episcopal church permanently in charge of a parish.
Reredos:	A decorated panel behind an altar. It is usually of wood or stone. The reredos is often made elaborate with sculpture, carvings and painting.
Retable:	A shelf at the rear of the altar on which are placed the altar cross, vases, and candlesticks. Also called the gradine.
Riddels:	Curtains at either side of an altar.
Rochet:	A long white linen vestment.
Rood:	A cross or crucifix above the entrance to the chancel, usually resting on a beam or screen.
Rood Screen:	A grille or lattice between the nave and chancel, surmounted by a cross or crucifix.
Sacrament:	"An outward and visible sign of an inward and spiritual grace given unto us; ordained by Christ himself."
Sacrarium:	Another name for the piscina.
Sacristan:	The person in charge of the Sacristy and its contents.
Sacristy:	The room in the church building where the vestments, books, and sacred vessels are kept.
Sanctuary:	The sacred portion of the church in which the altar stands.
Sanctuary Lamp:	The lamps suspended in front of the altar. One, three, or seven.
Sarum Use:	The missal at one time peculiar to the Diocese of Salisbury in England.
Screen:	Carved open woodwork, or stone.
Sedilia:	The seats for the clergy within the sanctuary, on the south side.

Server:	An acolyte.
Sexton:	A layman of the parish appointed to care for the church buildings.
Shell:	A scallop-shell, or metal vessel of this shape, used for taking water from the font to pour over the head of a person to be baptized.
Stall:	Individual seats in the choir are usually called Stalls.
Steward, Communion:	A lay person in the Methodist Church who cares for the vessels and the elements used in Holy Communion, similar to the Sacristan.
Stole:	A long narrow band of silk or brocade worn over the shoulders of the clergy.
Stoup:	A basin usually on the wall or on a stand as one immediately enters the door of the liturgical church to hold holy water.
Subdeacon's Step:	The first of the three steps to the altar.
Superfrontal:	See frontlet.
Surplice:	A white linen vestment worn by the clergy over the cassock.
Tabernacle:	A locked safe used for the reservation of the Sacrament.
Tester:	A flat canopy or covering over a pulpit, altar, or tomb.
Thurible:	A vessel in which incense is burned. A censer.
Tippet:	A black scarf worn by the clergy.
Transepts:	The arms of a cruciform church.
Triptych:	A three-paneled painting or carving, usually behind the altar.
Undercroft:	A subterranean room or chapel under a church; a crypt.
Veil:	A covering for the Chalice.
Verger:	One who carries the Verge or Staff before a Cathedral or Collegiate Dignitary. A custom in the Church of England. In the American Church usually an usher who is paid by the church, oftentimes the Sacristan.
Vestment:	An ecclesiastical garment worn for church services; also, coverings for the altar.
Viaticum:	(Latin: pertaining to a journey) Any rite or attention which gives spiritual comfort to the dying in preparation for the journey to the next life. A name sometimes given to the portable vessels for administering Holy Communion.
Vicar:	A priest in the Episcopal Church in charge of a dependent chapel or mission under the Bishop of the Diocese or the rector of the parish.
Vigil Light:	A lamp, other than that before the Reserved Sacrament, which burns perpetually before a shrine, image, or altar.
Votive Lights:	Candles lighted before an altar or shrine to honor the memory of some loved one, or for some special request in prayer.
Votive Ship:	A ship model seen mostly in churches and cathedrals in Europe representing the belief that an unseen Deity protects all seafaring people.
Wardens:	Two lay officers of the vestry of a parish in the Episcopal Church, one known as the Senior Warden and the other as the Junior Warden.
Wafer:	A thin disk of unleavened bread used in the Communion.

FORMS OF SALUTATION

MEMBERS OF THE ORDAINED CLERGY

OFFICIAL TITLE	ADDRESS—Written Forms	INTRODUCTION—Speaking Forms
		1. Formal Address ⎱ Nos. 1 & 2 are 2. Formal by Title ⎰ often combined 3. Informal Address
PRESIDING BISHOP	The Most Reverend John Smith 1. Most Reverend and Dear Sir: 2. Dear Bishop Smith: 3. Dear Bishop:	1. The Most Reverend John Smith 2. The Presiding Bishop of .... 3. Bishop Smith
BISHOP Coadjutor Suffragan	The Right Reverend John Smith 1. Right Reverend and Dear Sir: 2. Dear Bishop Smith: 3. Dear Bishop	1. The Right Reverend John Smith 2. The Bishop of .... 3. Bishop Smith
MINISTER Rector Vicar Curate Priest-in-Charge Pastor Priest	The Reverend John Smith 1. Reverend and Dear Sir: 3. Dear Sir: 2. Dear Mr. Smith: (Low Churchmen Prefer) 2. Dear Father Smith: (High Churchmen Prefer) 2. Dear Dr. Smith: (Only if he has that degree)	1. The Reverend John Smith 2. The Rector of .... 3. The Reverend Mr. Smith 3. Mr. Smith 3. The Reverend Father Smith 3. Father Smith 3. The Reverend Dr. Smith 3. Dr. Smith
DEAN Of a Cathedral Of a Seminary	The Very Reverend John Smith 1. Very Reverend and Dear Sir: 2. Dear Dean Smith: 3. Dear Dean:	1. The Very Reverend John Smith 2. The Dean of .... 3. Dean Smith

(Continued)

325

CANON Precentor, Pastor Chancellor, Missioner Archivist, Almoner, Burser, Prebendary, Residentiary, Sacrist.	The Reverend John Smith Canon of .... 1. Reverend and Dear Sir: 2. Dear Canon Smith: 3. Dear Canon:	1. The Reverend John Smith 2. The Canon............of........ 3. Canon Smith
ARCHDEACON	The Venerable John Smith 1. Venerable and Dear Sir: 2. Dear Archdeacon Smith: 3. Dear Archdeacon:	1. The Venerable John Smith 2. The Archdeacon of .... 3. Archdeacon Smith
DEACON	The Reverend John Smith 1. Reverend and Dear Sir: 2. Dear Mr. Smith:	1. The Reverend John Smith 3. The Reverend Mr. Smith 3. Mr. Smith

MEMBERS OF RELIGIOUS COMMUNITIES

SISTER
 	
Superior
	Sister Mary Joan, O.S.M.
	   Dear Sister Mary:
	The Reverend Mother Mary Joan,
	   O.S.M.
	2. Reverend and Dear Mother:
	
	3. Dear Sister Superior:
		1. Sister Mary Joan
		3. Sister Mary
		1. The Reverend Mother Mary
		   Joan, O.S.M.
		2. The Reverend Sister Superior
		   of ....
		3. Sister Mary

BROTHER Superior	Brother John Joseph, O.S.B. 1. Dear Brother John Joseph: 2. Dear Brother: 1. The Reverend Father Superior: 2. Dear Father:	1. Brother John Joseph 3. Brother John 1. The Reverend Father Superior 2. Reverend Father Superior of .... 3. Father
DEACONESS	Deaconess Mary Smith 1. Dear Deaconess Smith: 2. Dear Deaconess:	1-3. Deaconess Smith

Chapter VI
Facts About Christmas

A CHRISTMAS CAROL One of the world's most famous Christmas stories written in 1843 by the great English novelist Charles Dickens.

ADAM, ADOLPHE CHARLES Professor, at the Paris Conservatory of Music, who wrote the tune for the Christmas song "O Holy Night" in 1856.

ADESTE FIDELES

ADESTE FIDELES A Latin Christmas hymn, often attributed to St. Bonaventure in 1274, existing in several versions. The popular English form, "O come, all ye faithful, joyful and triumphant," is from the translation by Frederich Oakeley in 1841.

ADORATION The act of worship of a Divine being. Adoration was expressed by the shepherds when they worshiped the Christ Child in the manger at Bethlehem. Adoration was shown by the Wisemen when they knelt before the infant Jesus and presented their gifts of gold, frankincense and myrrh. We express adoration when we participate in services of worship during the Christmas season.

ADORATION

ADORATION, THE A painting of the Virgin Mary and Child with two angels by Fra Lippo Lippi, who lived in Florence, Italy during the early Renaissance period. This painting of quiet grace and beauty hangs in the Uffize Gallery in Florence.

ADORATION OF THE MAGI, THE The title of several paintings of Christmas including:
  1. A painting by Albrecht Durer (1471-1528), a German artist, finished in 1524, four years before his death. It is one of his best Christmas pictures, with strong lines and rich colors, showing the worship of the Kings from the east before the Christ Child. It is preserved in the Vienna Albertina Museum in Munich, Germany.
  2. A painting by Peter Paul Reubens, Flemish artist of the seventeenth century, housed presently in the Metropolitan Museum of Art, New York City.
  3. A painting by the famous Italian Renaissance painter, Botticelli. It is a masterpiece of color and detail.
  4. A painting by Leonardo da Vinci, Italian artist (1452-1519), contemporary of Christopher Columbus.

ADORATION OF THE MAGI

ADORATION OF THE SHEPHERDS, THE The name of a group of paintings by various famous artists including:
  1. A painting by El Greco (1541-1614), a Spanish artist noted for the elongation of his painted figures.
  2. A masterpiece by Georgione (1478-1511), an Italian artist who was a fellow student of Titian.
  3. A painting by Rembrandt (1607-1669), famous Dutch painter and resident of Amsterdam.
  4. A painting by Bartolome Murillo, a Spanish painter, in 1682.

ADORATION OF THE SHEPHERDS

ADVENT WREATH

ANDERSON, HANS CHRISTIAN

ANGELS

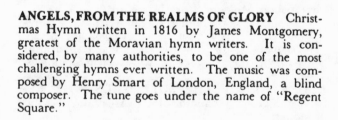

ANNA

ADVENT The season of the Church year which is a preparation for Christmas. The beginning of Advent is usually described as the Sunday nearest to St. Andrew's Day, which is November 30, the close of Advent comes on Christmas Eve. It is of four weeks duration. The origin of Advent seems to have developed from the need of the congregations of early local churches to make spiritual preparations for the true celebration of the festival of Christmas.

ADVENT WREATH A wreath of holly or other evergreen with four candles placed in the center to represent the four weeks of Advent. The custom began in Germany in the Lutheran Church a few hundred years ago. The word Advent means "coming" and signifies the coming of Christ. Thus the Advent Season is that time just prior to the coming of Christ in His birth at Bethlehem. On each of the four Sundays preceding Christmas, one of the four candles in the Advent Wreath is lighted, and the family joins together in prayer. Symbolically it represents the Light of the World who came as a fulfillment of the promise of God.

ANDERSON, HANS CHRISTIAN Born in Denmark, April 2, 1805. Famous poet and story-writer. He wrote the noted Christmas story "The Fir Tree."

ANGELS The word angel means "a messenger." They are represented in the Bible as messengers from God to man. The angel, Gabriel, announced to Mary that she was to give birth to the Christ Child. The angels proclaimed the good news of Christ's birth to the shepherds tending their flocks outside the city of Bethlehem. Luke 1:26-35, Luke 2:9-14.

ANGELS, FROM THE REALMS OF GLORY Christmas Hymn written in 1816 by James Montgomery, greatest of the Moravian hymn writers. It is considered, by many authorities, to be one of the most challenging hymns ever written. The music was composed by Henry Smart of London, England, a blind composer. The tune goes under the name of "Regent Square."

ANGELS WE HAVE HEARD ON HIGH Traditional French carol. Melody first sung in England by the Westminster Abbey Choir. It is often called the "Westminster Carol." "Gloria in excelsis Deo" (glory to God in the highest) is the Latin translation of the song the angels sang on the night of the Nativity.

ANNA A prophetess of Jerusalem who was present at the dedication of the baby Jesus and declared Him to be the expected Messiah. Luke 2:37.

ANNUNCIATION The announcement to Mary by the angel Gabriel that she was to be the mother of a son to be called Jesus. Luke 1:30-31.

ANNUNCIATION

ANSGAR, SAINT Introduced the tradition of celebrating Christmas to the Scandinavian countries in the year 865.

ANTHEM A sacred choral composition sung by a Church choir. The Christmas anthem is an important part of the religious celebration of the birth of Christ.

ARMENIA Celebration of Christmas in Armenia is primarily religious in nature with not so much of the spirit of carnival that marks the traditions of many other countries. On Christmas Eve, the children sing songs of rejoicing from the housetops, after which they are presented with cookies, fruit, candy, and other gifts.

ARRIVAL OF THE SHEPHERDS A famous Christmas painting by the French artist Henri Lerolle, who was born in Paris in 1848. He was noted for his unusual effects with evening light. "The Arrival of the Shepherds" has a quiet, worshipful beauty that is in complete harmony with the dignity of the Holy Nativity.

AUGUSTUS CAESAR

AUGUSTUS CAESAR Ruler of Rome at the time of the birth of Christ. From Caesar Augustus came the decree that a census of the Roman Empire should be taken. It was this decree that forced Joseph and Mary to go to Bethlehem, the city of their fathers, and subsequently it determined the location of the birthplace of the Saviour. Luke 2:1-7.

AUSTRIA From a little Austrian village came the song of Christmas, "Silent Night, Holy Night." In Austria, Christmas is a time of neighborliness. On Christmas Eve, high in the Austrian Alps, each mountaineer lights a fagot and makes his way to a neighbor's home; joined by others with lighted torches, they proceed to the village to welcome the birth of the Saviour.

AUSTRIA

AUGUSTINE OF CANTERBURY Introduced the tradition of celebrating Christmas to England in the year 604.

AWAY IN A MANGER Often called Luther's "Cradle Hymn." A Christmas hymn frequently attributed to Martin Luther but more recently thought to be of German Lutheran origin in early Pennsylvania.

AZALEA A Christmas plant with large, green leaves and brilliant, variegated flowers. Although there are more than one hundred species native to North America and Asia, it is the Chinese azalea that is cultivated in the greenhouses of Europe and America for the popular Christmas plant.

AZALEA

BACH

BALSAM FIR

BAY

BEACON HILL

BABE OF BETHLEHEM The central figure in the celebration of Christmas. The Christ Child born in the manger in the city of Bethlehem, to whom the shepherds and wisemen came in worship, and of whom the angels said, "Unto you is born this day a Saviour which is Christ the Lord." Luke 2:11.

BABUSHKA A legendary old lady gift-bearer in Russia. It was said that she misguided the wisemen on their way to Bethlehem and has been wandering around ever since trying to find the Christ Child on Christmas eve. As she goes she distributes gifts to the children.

BACH, JOHANN SEBASTIAN German composer born in 1685, famous for his contribution in the field of music to the Christian Church. The Christmas Oratorio is one of the greatest of his religious works, and includes many of the better known Christmas chorales.

BALLAD A series of words spoken or sung with the accompaniment of a musical instrument. Many of the early Christmas carols were ballads, and were sung by wandering minstrels or troubadours.

BALSAM FIR An American evergreen tree also called fir balsam. This tree is one of the most popular choices for the Christmas tree. Its branches are extraordinarily green and symetrical.

BALTHAZAR According to ancient legend, Balthazar, King of Chaldea, was one of the wisemen who brought gifts to the Christ Child in the manger at Bethlehem. His gift was incense.

BAROCCI, FEDERIGO Italian artist (1528-1612) who painted "The Nativity."

BAY A laurel tree which has lance-like leaves and rich purple berries. It is one of the traditional Christmas plants. The branches of laurel from the bay-tree have been considered a mark of honor both in secular and religious life for centuries. There is a legend which claims that lightning will never strike a bay-tree because it once gave shelter to the holy family during a thunder storm.

BEACON HILL The first organized Christmas eve carol singing was in Boston, Massachusetts, on Beacon Hill in 1908. Here also were the first lighted windows on Christmas eve.

BEFANA An old lady of Italian legendry who, on January fifth, the eve of Epiphany, leaves gifts from her pack to all good children, and birch rods and ashes to all bad children. The tale says that she is in constant search for the Wisemen and the Baby Jesus.

BEGONIA The Christmas Begonia is fast becoming a very popular Christmas plant. It is a native of the East and West Indies and South America. It is prized as a Christmas flower because of the brilliant red of its under leaves and grace and beauty of its flowers.

BEFANA

BELGIUM In Belgium the children expect St. Nicholas to make two appearances. The first is a sort of "check up," to find out whether they have been good or bad. Then, on the night before the feast day, they place their shoes, baskets or other containers where they can be filled from his never empty sack. Just to be on the safe side, they put water and hay nearby so to attract St. Nicholas' white horse. The next morning all the good children find candy, fruit and toys in their shoes or baskets; the bad ones, according to the story, will find switches.

BELLS About the year 400 A.D. an Italian Bishop, Paulinus, had a bell hung in the tower of his church. This was the first Christian bell calling people to worship. Since that time, from century to century, and country to country, bells have been used more and more to stimulate public worship. Christmas especially is a time when the air is filled with the joyous notes of vibrating bells, proclaiming the birth of the Saviour. Bells became so closely associated with the Christmas season that they were used as the designs for the first Christmas cards and tree decorations. Special true-toned hand-bells have been made so that bell ringing can be accomplished manually as well as from great Church towers. In America, groups of hand-bell players heralding the Christmas season with joyful carol music, were introduced at Beacon Hill in Boston. Henry W. Longfellow expressed, perhaps better than anyone, the part bells have to play in the celebration of Christmas in his great hymn "I Heard the Bells on Christmas Day."

BEGONIA

BELSNICKLE An early Pennsylvania Dutch person of "frightening character" who visited the homes of the community on Christmas Eve to check up on the behavior of all the children. If questions on the catechism, school work, and home life, were answered untruthfully, the children received raps on the knuckles from Belsnickle, who always carried a hickory stick with him for that purpose. If the questions were answered truthfully, then Belsnickle took candies and nuts from mysterious folds in his robe and scattered them freely on the floor.

BELL

BETHLEHEM A city in Judea, and the birthplace of Jesus. As it was the birthplace and ancestral home of David, it was called the City of David. As a village it existed as early as the time of Jacob. Rachel died and was buried in its vicinity. (Genesis 35:16, 19) It was prophesied as the place where the Messiah should be born. (Micah 5:2) It was the city to which Joseph and Mary traveled at the time of the

BETHLEHEM

BIBLE

BISHOP OF ANTIOCH

BLITZEN

BOAR'S HEAD

census-taking in the rule of Augustus Caesar. (Luke 2:4) Near Bethlehem the annunciation to the shepherds took place (Luke 2:1-20); and to this city the wisemen from the east came with their gifts, guided by the great star. Geographically the city is located five miles south of Jerusalem and about fifteen miles west of the Dead Sea. Bethlehem is a familiar word in many of the Christmas hymns, with one, "O Little Town of Bethlehem" by Phillips Brooks, taking it as its main theme.

BETHLEHEM, NEW HAMPSHIRE A town and summer resort of Grafton County, New Hampshire, that has the same name as the city of Judea where Jesus was born.

BETHLEHEM, PENNSYLVANIA A city in Pennsylvania bearing the same name as the birthplace of Jesus. It has a population in the vicinity of 60,000 residents. Every year special festivities are held to commemorate the birth of Christ in Bethlehem. The city was founded by a group of Moravian missionaries on Christmas Eve in 1741.

BIBLE The sacred scriptures where the beautiful story of the first Christmas is recorded in the Gospels of Matthew and Luke.

BIRTH The act or fact of coming into life, or being born. It is the birth of Jesus, the Messiah, which is celebrated on Christmas day.

BIRTHS ON CHRISTMAS DAY Christmas day is the birthday of many noted people of the world including:
1. Sir Isaac Newton, natural philosopher, in 1642.
2. Rebecca West, novelist, in 1892.
3 Maurice Utrillo, artist, in 1883.
4. Gladys Swarthout, mezzo-soprano, in 1904.

BISHOP OF ANTIOCH In the second century, Theophilus, Bishop Of Antioch, refers to December 25 as the day when Christians celebrate Christ's birth.

BISSELL, EMILY Introduced Christmas Seals to America at Wilmington, Delaware in December, 1907, because of the inspiration received from reading an article by Jacob Riis, friend of Theodore Roosevelt, advocating their sale. See CHRISTMAS SEALS.

BLITZEN The name of the eighth of Santa Claus' reindeer according to the poem "A Visit From St. Nicholas" by Clement Moore.

BOAR'S HEAD CAROL, THE The oldest secular carol in existence. (1521) The carol commemorates the ancient English Christmas custom of serving the head of the wild boar. The words of the song are regarded as traditional, but the music is credited to a Wynkyn de Worde.

BONIFACE, SAINT He introduced the tradition of celebrating Christmas to Germany in the year 754. He is credited, by many, with originating the Christmas use of the fir tree.

BONAVENTURE, SAINT A Franciscan priest (1274), later a Cardinal, to whom is often attributed the authorship of the Christmas hymn "O Come, All Ye Faithful."

BOUGHS

BOTTICELLI Italian Renaissance painter (1444-1510). Among his works is the famous "Adoration of the Magi."

BOUGHS The branches of evergreen trees used in the making of wreaths and other Christmas decorations.

BOXING A popular Christmas custom in England. On the 26th of December gifts are distributed and exchanged. It is called "boxing," and is patterned after the medieval custom of breaking open the alms boxes on the feast of St. Stephen, December 26, and distributing the contents among the poor of the parish.

PHILLIPS BROOKS

BRING A TORCH, JEANNETTE, ISABELLA A traditional French carol tracing back to the seventeenth century. It is based on the custom of carrying torches at Christmas eve.

BROOKS, PHILLIPS Famed Episcopal Bishop and author of the popular Christmas carol "O Little Town of Bethlehem." This famous carol was first sung in the Church of the Holy Trinity at Philadelphia, Pennsylvania, December 25, 1868. It was written at the request of the Church School children, who had asked Bishop Brooks, while he was rector of this church, to compose a Christmas song. The words were inspired by a previous pilgrimage to the Holy Land, where Phillips Brooks worshiped in the Church of the Nativity at Bethlehem. The music was composed by the Church organist, Lewis H. Redner, who received the melody in a dream on Christmas Eve. The entire Christmas Carol was completed in less than a single day.

CAESAR

C

CAESAR Title given to all the Roman Emperors. See AUGUSTUS.

CAMEL Beast of travel often called "the ship of the desert," upon which, it is generally believed, the wisemen came from the east in search of the new-born King.

CAMEL

CANDLE

CANDLE A common Christmas season decoration used from the time the first lighted candle was placed on the Christmas tree by Martin Luther in the 13th century. In recent years, the idea of lighted candles on the Christmas tree has been replaced by electricity. The first candles are believed to have been used by the Romans to burn on the altars of their gods, and to light the great festive halls. The early Christians adopted the candle readily because of its appropriate relationship to the words of Jesus: "I am the light of the world."

CANDLELIGHT SERVICE A religious service, usually held on Christmas eve or the evening of Christmas Sunday, where the birth of Christ is celebrated through worship, prayer and song. The part of the candles in the service is symbolic of the gift of the Light of the World from God's love and the sharing of that gift with one another. The act of the candle lighting takes place as the Minister lights his candle from the Church Altar, gives the light to the deacons, vestrymen, or ushers, who in turn give the light to the congregation. In this quiet moment, by candlelight, together they pay homage, in the spirit, to the Christ, Messiah, given at Bethlehem.

CAROL SINGING

CANTIQUE DE NOEL See O HOLY NIGHT.

CAROL The singing of Christmas carols began in Italy in the thirteenth century. From Italy the carol spread into Spain, France, Germany, England and other European countries. The original, true carol was a mixture of folksong, legendary lore and mirthful simplicity. The transition to the more serious Christmas hymn came later in the eighteenth century.

CAROL OF THE DRUM A delightful, old Czech carol in which a little drummer boy plays on his drum for the Christ Child. A drum-like effect "pa-rum-pa-pum-pum" is repeated after each stanza.

LEBANON CEDAR

CAROL SINGING Often called "caroling." A delightful practice of group Christmas carol-singing either indoors or outdoors The more picturesque custom, originating with the European medieval minstrels, is where the group goes from house to house serenading the occupants with gay, festive Christmas music.

CEDAR An evergreen tree selected by many as their choice for a Christmas tree. It is native, in one form or another, to almost every continent in the world.

CENSUS An enumeration and registration of a people. A census was ordered by the emperor Augustus for the Roman Empire shortly before the birth of Christ. This census, which was taken every fourteen years in the Empire, forced Joseph to travel with Mary to Bethlehem, their ancestral home. It took place during the reign of Herod the Great, King of Judea, in the year 4 B.C.

CENSUS

336

CHERRY It is a custom in Central Europe to place a branch of the cherry tree in a container of water at the beginning of Advent. By Christmas it is in full bloom, adding beauty to the holiday decorations, and a sign of good luck.

CHERRY TREE

CHERRY TREE, THE An ancient Christmas legend. On the way to Bethlehem, Mary asked Joseph to pick some cherries from a tree which had bloomed miraculously by the wayside. When Joseph, tired and weary from the journey, refused, the cherry tree bent down its branches so Mary could pick its fruit. Joseph saw this as a sign of the Son of God who was soon to be born, and bowed in worship and adoration before it.

CHERRY TREE CAROL, THE An old Christmas ballad, popular in the Appalachian highlands, originating in fifteenth century England. The legend of the carol is taken from the Apocryphal book of Pseudo-Matthew and tells of how a cherry tree bent down to the ground at the command of the infant Jesus, so his mother Mary could pluck cherries from its boughs.

CHESTNUTS

CHESTNUTS One of the traditional nuts of Christmas.

CHICKEN One of the modern choices for Christmas dinner. It came on the end of a line of traditional dinners: peacock, goose, turkey, and chicken.

CHILD A young or recently born human being. The term is used in reference to the Christ Child. Luke 2:17.

CHIMNEY The place where tradition says Santa Claus enters the home laden with toys for all the good children. This tradition was made popular in the poem "A Visit from St. Nicholas" by Dr. Clement Moore.

CHILD

CHINA Christmas came to China as an import from the Western world. It is called Sheng Dan Jieh, which when translated, means the Holy Birth Festival. Paper flowers, chains, banners, and cotton snow are the decorations placed on the Christmas tree, called the "Tree of Light."

CHRIST The anointed one. A name conferred upon Jesus meaning Messiah. Luke 2:11. See JESUS.

CHRIST BUNDLES In Germany, during the seventeenth century, Christmas presents were called "Christ-bundles."

CHIMNEY

CHRISTMAS An annual Church Festival, kept on December 25 in memory of the birth of Christ. It is celebrated generally by a particular church service, and by special gifts, greetings, and hospitality, and in most Christian communities is a legal holiday.

CHRISTMAS CANDY

CHRISTMAS BELLS One of the American Christmas carols that never seems to lose its popularity. It was written by the eminent poet, Henry Wadsworth Longfellow in 1863, a year when our country was locked in the death struggle of the civil war. Longfellow's own son, a lieutenant in the Army of the Potomac, had been seriously wounded. It is easy to understand why he and hundreds of others were anxious for "peace on earth, good will to men!"

CHRISTMAS BELLS The orange-colored flowers of an Australian lily.

CHRISTMAS BERRY The bright, scarlet berry of the toyon bush, grown on the American west coast. See TOYON.

CHRISTMAS BUSH A tree, native to Australia, often used in Christmas decorations.

CHRISTMAS CACTUS A South American cactus with red flowers, also called Crab Cactus. It is a native of Brazil, and grows, like mistletoe, on the trunks and branches of trees. It never fails to blossom at Christmas time.

CHRISTMAS CARD

CHRISTMAS CANDY Candy has long been one of the gifts left by traditional gift-bearers, such as Santa Claus, St. Nickolas, Befana and others, to all good children on Christmas eve. There have been numerous shapes, flavors, and sizes, from home-made sweets of ancient days to striped candy canes and chocolate figures of Santa Claus of the present.

CHRISTMAS CARD Christmas greeting cards were first published in England by Joseph Cundall of London in 1846. The first card was designed by J. C. Horsley, following a suggestion by Sir Henry Cole.

CHRISTMAS CLUB An association for saving, as by bank deposits, to help meet the financial needs of the Christmas season.

CHRISTMAS CLUB

CHRISTMAS COVE A beautiful finger of the sea located on the southern coast of Maine in New England.

CHRISTMAS DAISY An American aster cultivated in England. It blooms in the late autumn. The daisy was adopted as a Christmas symbol towards the end of the fifteenth century. It symbolizes the innocence of the Holy Child.

CHRISTMAS EVE The evening before Christmas day.

CHRISTMAS EVERGREEN The festoon pine, a creeping evergreen plant native to eastern North America.

CHRISTMAS DAISY

CHRISTMAS FERN A North American evergreen fern used for winter decoration.

CHRISTMAS ISLAND Two different islands of British possession located in the Indian Ocean and the Pacific Ocean.

CHRISTMAS MAN The gift-bearing personality at Christmas substituted by many countries for St. Nicholas after the Reformation. See SANTA CLAUS.

CHRISTMAS NAMES The following are some of the names for Christmas around the world: "Dies Natalis Domini," one of the original Latin forms; "Il Natale" in Italy; "La Navidad" in Spain; "Noel" in France; "Weihnacht" in Germany; "Boze Narodzenie" in Poland; "Rozhdestvo Khrista" in Russia; "Nadolig" in Wales; "Genethlia" in Greece. The English "Christmas" comes from the old feast day "Cristes Maesse" dating from the year 1038.

CHRISTMAS PAGEANT A symbolic religious service reenacting the spirit of the first Christmas in Bethlehem.

CHRISTMAS PIE Traditional pie immortalized by the nursery rhyme, "Little Jack Horner." The Christmas pie was not what is conceived of as pie today. For instance, here are the ingredients of a pie ordered in 1770 for Christmas by a London nobleman: two bushels of flour, twenty pounds of butter, forty fowl, including, geese, turkeys, ducks, pigeons, woodcocks, partridges, and blackbirds, two beef tongues, and two rabbits. The pie was nine feet across and had to be wheeled into the dining table.

CHRISTMAS PLAY A play or pantomime presented in churches during the Christmas season commemorating the birth of Christ.

CHRISTMAS PRESENTS The tradition of giving presents at the Christmas season symbolizes the first great gift of the Messiah given at Bethlehem.

CHRISTMAS ROSE A European herb having white or purplish flowers like single roses. They grow wild in the mountainous areas of central Europe and bloom in mid-winter. In ancient days it was considered a cure for melancholy. Symbolically, its green stalks and white flowers sent forth each Christmas, are significant of the purity and strength of the Christmas Child.

CHRISTMAS SEALS Christmas seals were originated by Einar Holboll, a kindly Danish postmaster, in 1903. His idea was to issue stamps for letters at Christmas and use the proceeds in the support of some worthy cause. The next year, the first Christmas seals, carrying a portrait of Queen Louise of Denmark, went on sale in the post office of Denmark. More than four million stamps were sold. By the time of Holboll's death, in 1927, he had

CHRISTMAS PIE

CHRISTMAS PRESENTS

CHRISTMAS ROSE

CHRISTMAS SEAL

CHRISTMAS STOCKING

seen his idea travel all around the world. In the United States, as well as in most of the other countries of the world, Christmas seals are sold to raise revenue to fight tuberculosis.

CHRISTMAS STOCKING "Their stockings all hung by the chimney with care, In hopes that St. Nicholas soon would be there," so writes Dr. Clement C. Moore in his famous poem, "A Visit from St. Nicholas." The custom of "hanging stockings" is based on a Dutch tradition of placing all types of receptacles, including wooden shoes and baskets, for the toys and good things brought by the benevolent St. Nicholas, "Sinter Klaas," on Christmas eve.

CHRISTMASTIDE The festive season from Christmas eve until after New Year's.

CHRISTMAS TREE

CHRISTMAS TREE The origin of the Christmas Tree is believed to have been in Germany. The Germans imported the idea of decorated trees from the old Roman festival called "Saturnalia," where it was customary to have evergreen trees covered with gifts and decorations. Martin Luther is credited with decorating the first tree. Some authorities feel that the ancient worship of the evergreen as a symbol of immortality developed into the Christian practice of "setting up a Christmas tree" at the time of the celebration of the birth of Christ. However, the Christmas Tree, as we think of it today, is thought to have had its beginning from the medieval "miracle plays." They were called miracle plays because they depicted the miracles of Christ and the early saints. One of the most popular plays told the story of creation. The only stage decoration used was a so-called "paradise tree," a fir tree hung with apples. Because the play closed with the promise of the coming of Christ, it was presented during the Advent Season as a means of preparing Christians for Christmas. About the 16th century the fir tree began to be used by the people in their personal celebration of Christmas. From Germany the idea spread to other countries and was brought to America by German immigrants.

CHURCH

CHRISTMAS TREES Among the many kinds of the most popular wild trees selected for the home to be decorated during the Christmas season are Spruce, Balsam, Fir, Cedar, Hemlock, and Pine.

CHRIST'S BIRTHDAY By a strange coincidence the birthday of Jesus is recorded as four years before Christ (4 B.C.). This unusual phenomenon resulted as an error in early calculation. The writers of gospel history were concerned with facts and events but not days and dates. When Biblical scholars first approached the problem in the sixth century there was so little data that they made a mistake of about four years. A learned monk by the name of Dionysius conceived the idea of a Christian calendar. After careful investigation of history, he assigned the year one, the year of Christ's birth, to the year 754

CITY OF DAVID

after the founding of Rome. It turned out, through the agreement of most Biblical scholars subsequently, that he was in error of at least four years. It is a known, established fact that at Herod's death, Jesus was with Mary and Joseph in Egypt. Historians agree that this death occurred in the year 4 B.C. As Jesus was from six months to three years old at the time, his birth had to be either 4 B.C. or earlier.

CLEMENT OF ALEXANDRIA

CHURCH A place of worship where the spiritual services associated with the observance of Christ's birth are held.

CITY OF DAVID Bethlehem of Judea. Because Bethlehem, the place of Christ's birth, was the birthplace and ancestral home of King David, second king of Israel, it was called the "City of David." Luke 2:4.

CLEMENT OF ALEXANDRIA One of the early Church Fathers of Alexandria, Egypt, who made the first recorded reference, in 200 A.D., to the observation of the Christmas celebration. According to tradition Christmas was first celebrated in 98 A.D.

COUNSELLOR

COLE, SIR HENRY Suggested the idea for the first Christmas card in 1846. See CHRISTMAS CARD.

COMET The name of the fifth of Santa Claus' reindeer according to the poem, "A Visit From St. Nicholas" by Clement Moore.

CORREGGIO, ANTONIO Italian artist (1494-1534) who painted the Christmas picture, "The Holy Night."

CRACKER

COUNSELLOR One of the terms used by the prophet Isaiah to describe the coming child who was to be born in the future of Israel's history. Isaiah 9:6.

CRACKER The name of one of the goats that, in folk lore, pulled the cart of Thor. See GNASHER.

CRECHE A representation of the stable at Bethlehem with the infant Jesus surrounded by Mary, his mother, Joseph, the adoring Shepherds, and gift-bearing wisemen, together with an ox, donkey, and sheep. Creches are hand-carved from fine quality woods by expert craftsmen in all parts of the world. They are made also from glass, bronze, plastic, china, porcelain, plaster, cardboard, and paper-mache.

CRÈCHE

CYCLAMEN

CYRENIUS

DAVID

DA VINCI

CRIB The place where Jesus lay as a new-born child. See MANGER.

CUMMINGS, WILLIAM HAYMEN Adapted the music from Mendelssohn in 1856 for the Christmas hymn, "Hark the Herald Angels Sing."

CUNDALL, JOSEPH The first publisher of Christmas cards in 1846. See CHRISTMAS CARD.

CUPID The name of the sixth of Santa Claus' reindeer according to the poem, "A Visit From St. Nicholas" by Clement Moore.

CYCLAMEN A strange flower, member of the primrose family, which grows abundantly in the Holy Land. Because of its "red throat" in the center, the flower was dedicated to Mary, the mother of Jesus. The Arabs call the cyclamen "Cock of the Mountains."

CYRENIUS The Greek name for Quirinius, who was the Roman governor of Syria in A.D. 6. He was ruler of Syria at the time of Joseph's and Mary's visit to Bethlehem during the great census of the Empire. Luke 2:2.

CZECHOSLOVAKIA Christmas is a time for carol singing in the streets and homes, dancing and eating following the fasting which ends on Christmas Eve. It is a time for visiting friends and relatives. Carolers carrying small Bethlehem scenes, and little boys dressed as three kings, go from house to house giving small concerts for treats and sweets.

D

DANCER The name of the second of Santa Claus' reindeer according to the poem, "A Visit From St. Nicholas" by Clement Moore.

DASHER The name of the first of Santa Claus' reindeer, according to the poem, "A Visit From St. Nicholas" by Clement Moore.

DAVID Son of Jesse, and second king of Israel. His connection with Christmas lies in the fact that he was an important ancestor of Jesus (Matthew 22:41-45), and that the "City of David" where he was buried became the birthplace of the Saviour.

DA VINCI, LEONARDO A famous Italian artist (1452-1519) noted for his many Madonna paintings. See MADONNA OF THE ROCKS.

342

DEATHS ON CHRISTMAS DAY Christmas is in celebration of the world's most famous birth; however, it is a day, as well, each year, when some one dies. Here are a few of world renowned people who died on Christmas day:

1. Adrian I, Pope of Rome, died on Christmas day in 795 A.D.
2. Persieus, Greek Poet, died on Christmas day in 62 A.D.
3. Emperor Leo V, Armenian, was slain in Constantinople on Christmas day in 820 A.D.

DECEMBER 25,
1492

DECEMBER 25 The official day for Christmas Celebration. It is generally accepted by the Christian world, since about 400 A.D., as the day to honor the birth of the Christ Child in Bethlehem of Judea.

December 25, 1492 Christopher Columbus joined with the men of the Santa Maria in singing Christmas hymns and kneeling in prayers of joy and thanksgiving on strange soil, celebrating the first Christmas in America.

December 25, 1607 Captain John Smith of the colony of Jamestown celebrated Christmas as a captive of savage Indians, but wrote in his journal of their kindness and said, "We were very grateful to God for His goodness to us on this Christmasse Day."

December 25, 1620 1620 was the year the Pilgrims landed at Plymouth Rock in New England. Their records show that on Christmas Day of that year they began together to build the first house for their new colony.

December 25, 1743 In Bethlehem, Pennsylvania, on Christmas Day, viols, flutes and French horns "were played for the first time in the house of God."

December 25, 1764 Patrick Henry, Virginian Patriot, inspired the sending of a message to the King of England establishing the idea of "no taxation without representation."

December 25, 1776 On Christmas Day George Washington crossed the Delaware. Braving the cold and dangers of floating ice, Washington crossed and recrossed the river, capturing vast stores of arms, munitions and prisoners, turning the tide of the Revolutionary War.

December 25, 1917 The battle of Caporetto ended on Christmas day.

December 25, 1936 Generalissimo Chiang Kai-Shek was released on Christmas day after being kidnapped by forces of Marshall Chang, War Lord of China.

December 25, 1941 The city of Hong Kong, China, fell to the armies of Japan on Christmas day.

December 25, 1943 General Dwight D. Eisenhower was named to command the invasion forces of Europe, on the day before Christmas.

DECEMBER 25,
1764

DECEMBER 25,
1776

DECK THE HALLS A favorite English carol based on an old Welch tune. There is no mention of the Nativity in the song, only reference to the customs of the Yuletide season. The words and jolly music indicate that this song was used as a song for dancing.

DECORATIONS

DECREE

DELLA ROBBIA

DICKENS

DONKEY

DECORATIONS Objects used to beautify home and hearth during the Christmas season. Evergreen boughs, holly, mistletoe, laurel, ribbon, paper, cloth, tinsel, ornaments, pine cones, berries, flowers, and crepe are but a few of the many Christmas decorations. See ORNAMENTS.

DECREE An order or decision from one having authority declaring what is or is not to be, done. Augustus Caesar sent a decree throughout the Roman Empire stating that there was to be a kingdom-wide census or "tax," just prior to the birth of Christ. Luke 2:1.

DELLA ROBBIA Luca Della Robbia, an Italian sculptor, born in 1400, was the first of a family of artists famed for their process of glazed terra cotta sculpturing. Their skill and technique has never been equaled. The appeal of the Della Robbia plaque is in its gentle grace of the madonnas, its portrayal of the Christ child, and the frame of garlands made of fruits and flowers that gracefully encircles it.

DE LORENZO, FIORENZO An artist of the Italian Renaissance who painted Christmas themes. See NATIVITY, THE.

DENMARK Christmas customs in Denmark are similar to those of Norway and Sweden because of their common ancestry. Denmark is remembered at Christmas for its contribution, by Einar Holboll, a postal clerk, for his idea of creating Christmas seals to be sold to raise money for the fight against tuberculosis.

DICKENS, CHARLES One of the world's greatest novelists. (1812-1870) Author of many literary classics including the immortal Christmas story, "A Christmas Carol" written in 1843.

DOLCI, CARLO A noted Florentine painter of the 17th century. See MADONNA.

DONDER The name of the seventh of Santa Claus' reindeer according to the poem, "A Visit From St. Nicholas" by Clement Moore.

DONKEY One of the animals associated with Christmas, traditionally present at the manger at the time of the birth of Christ, and the beast of burden upon which Mary traveled from Nazareth of Galilee to Bethlehem of Judea.

DRUIDS Members of a religious order of ancient Britain. They were "readers of the stars" and "workers of magic." From the Druids many of the customs of Christmas, including the use of mistletoe, have come.

DURER, ALBRECHT Famed German artist born on May 21, 1471, who painted, in 1524, the famous Christmas subject "The Adoration of the Magi."

EAST The place from which the Wisemen came to search for the new-born King. (Matthew 2:1) East, in this case, is considered by many authorities to be part of the territory of Media. The Greek historian Heroditus, living in the 5th century B.C., refers to the Magi as a priestly caste belonging to one of the six tribes of Media. Media later became part of the great empire of Persia.

DURER

EGYPT A large and very fertile country, southwest of Palestine, through which flows the river Nile. To Egypt fled Joseph and Mary with the infant Jesus to escape from King Herod, and there they remained until the king died. Matthew 2:14, 15.

ELF A make-believe being of the fairy world. They are pictured as small and frail and ready to be helpful or full of mischief toward the human world. At Christmas it is customary in many countries to think of them as Santa's helpers as he gets ready to deliver toys and gifts to children all over the world.

EGYPT

EL GRECO A Spanish painter (1547-1614). See ADORATION.

ELIZABETH A relative of Mary, and Mother of John the Baptist. It was while she was entertaining Mary as a visitor in her home that Elizabeth, inspired by the Holy Spirit, welcomed Mary as the mother of the Lord. It was at the home of Elizabeth that Mary voiced the Magnificat. Luke 1:40-56.

EMMANUEL A term referring to the Messiah, and meaning God with us. Matthew 1:23. See IMMANUEL.

ELF

ENGLAND In England Christmas means friendship and food, wassails and waits, carols and community plays, holly and mistletoe, steamed Christmas puddings and roast goose. It is rich with Christmas custom and tradition and filled with Christmas music from the hundreds of ringing bells to the great Cathedral choirs. Here the first Christmas card was designed; here is the home of the great Christmas author Charles Dickens who wrote "A Christmas Carol;" here is the birthplace of the Yule log and its friendly fire; here originated such lively carols as "God Rest You Merry Gentlemen," "Good King Wenceslas," and "Deck the Halls."

EPIPHANY Originally a ceremony of the Eastern Church commemorating the baptism of Jesus. Later it was associated with the Nativity, with special reference to the visit of the Magi to Bethlehem. It has been called "Old Christmas." Epiphany has the popular designation "Twelfth Day."

ELIZABETH

EVERGREENS

EVERGREENS The tree or bush, or branches of the trees, shrubs, or bushes, which belong to the conifer (cone bearing) family. The berry-growing shrubs are also included, as a rule.

EVERLASTING FATHER One of the terms used by the prophet Isaiah, in his prophetic foretelling of the birth of Jesus, to describe the coming Saviour of Israel. Isaiah 9:6.

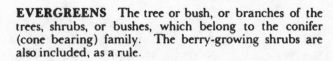

F

FATHER CHRISTMAS One of the names of Christmas' gift-bearing personality. See SANTA CLAUS.

FEAST OF ST. ANDREW November thirtieth. This day determines the beginning of Advent, as Advent starts on the Sunday nearest St. Andrew's day.

FESTIVAL A time of feasting or celebration. An anniversary day of joy, civil or religious. Christmas may be called properly a religious festival, for it is a time of joyous celebration of the birth of the Messiah, the King of Kings.

FATHER CHRISTMAS

FIELD, EUGENE American poet and journalist (1850-1895), and author of delightful Christmas stories for children, including "The Sugar-Plum Tree" and "The Fir Tree."

FINLAND In Finland Christmas begins with a bath. After the Finnish bath or "sauna," the night-before Christmas festivities begin. A light meal is enjoyed with the replica of the manger suspended from the ceiling over the dining table. After the supper there used to be wrestling matches by the men on floors of straw. Later the children would sleep on these floors in imitation of the first Christmas when Jesus slept on a bed of straw. Christmas day is one of religious worship and family gatherings. "Father Christmas" brings the children their toys and presents.

FIRECRACKERS

FIR An evergreen tree which is a very popular choice for the Christmas tree. It is also called balsam fir and fir balsam. Fir trees used for Christmas decorations were mentioned as early as 1604 in authentic Strassburg manuscripts.

FIRECRACKERS AT CHRISTMAS In parts of our own southland, and in China and Japan, firecrackers are used to celebrate the birth of Christ.

FIREPLACE

FIREPLACE One of the common areas for Christmas decorations. Here the mantle is dressed with holly, mistletoe, and other flowers of Christmas; here the stockings are "hung with care;" here the crèche is set with loving hands; and here the "yule" log burns with warmth and cheer.

FIRST NOEL, THE A popular Christmas carol printed for the first time in a collection of carols published in 1833. However, it was handed down from generation to generation by word of mouth long before this 19th century date. Some authorities believe it to have either French or Latin origin; others feel that "Nowell" is a contraction of the phrase "Now all is well", and that it has early English beginnings.

FLEUR-DE-LIS One of the most popular symbols for Mary. It was selected by the French Kings as their symbol and later was used in the banner of Jeanne d'Arc.

FLEUR DE LIS

FLIGHT INTO EGYPT, THE The name of several paintings by famous artists including:
1. A painting by Giotto, early Renaissance artist and friend of Dante, showing the dramatic escape into Egypt by the Holy Family. This classic painting is located in Padua, Italy.
2. A painting by Bartolome Murillo, seventeenth century Spanish painter, who devoted his life to painting religious themes.
3. A painting by Anthony Van Dyck (1599-1641), famous Dutch painter, who was considered the foremost European artist of his day.

FLIGHT INTO EGYPT

FLOCKS The term used to identify the assembly of sheep guarded and protected by the shepherd. It was while the flocks were being guarded by night that the angels appeared unto the shepherds announcing the birth of Christ in Bethlehem. Luke 2:8.

FLY AND THE SPIDER, THE An ancient legend which tells of the escape of Jesus to Egypt. Once on the long, tired journey, the Holy Family stopped by the wayside and went to sleep in the grass. The soldiers of Herod were marching near by, and coming close. A little fly landed on Joseph's face and woke him up. Joseph rose quickly and led Mary and Jesus to the safety of a near-by cave. When they were inside a little spider quickly wove a web across the front of the cave. When the soldiers of Herod passed by, they took only a fleeting glance at the cave, because if anyone were inside, they would certainly have broken the web. Thus the Holy Family was saved by a spider and a fly.

FLOCK

FRANCE French customs at Christmas are a blend of those of her neighbors north and south, in addition to her own. The traditional midnight Mass is held on Christmas Eve; special foods are served in restaurant and side-walk cafe; the yule-log tradition is observed, especially in rural communities; and the children are visited by "Le Pere Noel" bearing gifts, and by "Le Pere Fouettard" bearing spanks if they have been bad children.

FLY AND THE SPIDER

FRANKINCENSE

FRA ANGELICO An early Italian painter (1387-1455) who painted the Christmas theme. See NATIVITY.

FRANKINCENSE A sweet-scented gummy substance which exudes from certain trees. It is imported from Arabia and India and was used by the Hebrews in worship to make fragrant smoke at the altar. It was one of the gifts of the Wisemen to the new-born King at Bethlehem. Matthew 2:11.

FRA LIPPO LIPPI Fra Filippo Del Carmine (1406-1469), an Italian painter of masterpieces. See NATIVITY, ADORATION.

FRANCIS OF ASSISI

FRANCIS OF ASSISI, SAINT On Christmas Eve, in 1224 A.D., Francis of Assisi assembled the world's first living Creche in Greccio, Italy. Local villagers played the parts of Mary, Joseph, the Shepherds and Kings. Real animals were used to enhance the setting. The story of the first Holy Night was reenacted to remind the people of the first Christmas.

FRIENDLY BEASTS, THE A 17th century English ballad carol. It tells of the gifts made by the beasts to the Holy Child. The donkey carried his Mother to Bethlehem; the cow gave him the manger to sleep in; the sheep gave him wool for his blanket; and the doves in the rafters cooed him to sleep so he would not cry. Thus every beast "was glad to tell of the gift he gave Emmanuel."

FRIENDLY BEASTS

FROM HEAVEN ABOVE TO EARTH I COME A Christmas hymn written in 1535 by Martin Luther of Germany. The music is an arrangement of the famous composer Johann Sebastian Bach.

G

GABRIEL A high ranking angel who visited Mary and hailed her as the Mother of Jesus. Luke 1:11-22.

GALILEE

GALILEE The northern section of Palestine, about sixty miles long by twenty-five miles wide, extending from the Jordan river to the Mediterranean sea. It is a picturesque area, generally mountainous with fertile valleys in between. Mary and Joseph lived in Galilee in the city of Nazareth, and traveled from this city to Jerusalem at the time of the Roman census just before Christ's birth. Jesus spent most of his life in this area.

GARLAND The Christmas garland is similar to the Christmas wreath except that it is a rope of evergreen instead of a circle of evergreen. It is made of balsam, white pine, cedar, hemlock, or spruce, and decorated with cones, berries, ribbon, nuts, and fruits and makes very attractive Holiday decorations.

GASPAR The same as Jasper. One of the traditional names of a wise man who visited Jesus. See JASPER.

GESU BAMBINO A recent Christmas musical composition, words by Frederick Marten and music by Pietro Yon, in 1943.

GIFT Something given to another, a present. The Wisemen brought gifts of gold, frankincense, and myrrh to Jesus at the time of his birth in Bethlehem. Jesus, himself, was a gift to the world, from God's love.

GIORGIONE, GIORGIO An Italian painter (1478-1511), one of the foremost of the Venetian school. See ADORATION OF THE SHEPHERDS.

GLASTONBURY THORN A hawthorn or black thorn which blossoms during the Christmas season. According to ancient legend, Joseph of Arimathea traveled to England from Palestine and became the first settler of Glastonbury. Upon arrival he stuck his thorn staff into the ground and celebrated the first Christmas around it. The next year, upon his return, he found that the staff had taken root and was in full bloom. For many years after, the tree continued to grow and provide cheer to multitudes of Christmas visitors. The tree was later destroyed in the great wars, but many other trees were grown from cuttings of the original. It is claimed that all thorn bushes of this species originate from the first Glastonbury thorn.

GNASHER The name of one of the two goats which folk-lore says pulled the cart of Thor. Clement Moore used this as a background for his poem, "A Visit From St. Nicholas."

GOD The supreme Creator and Ruler of all the Universe. It was from God the angels came to make the annoucement to Mary and to the shepherds of the birth of the Messiah.

GOD REST YOU MERRY, GENTLEMEN The most popular carol in England. It is an English traditional melody, harmonized by Sir John Stainer in 1867. The outstanding feature of the hymn is its unusual expression of simple, cheerful, almost boisterous Christian joy in the tidings of Christmas.

GARLAND

GASPAR

GIFT

GLASTONBURY THORN

GOLD

GOLD A precious metal. It was used lavishly, in ancient days, for the overlaying of Temple furniture, and in the making of crowns, idols, rings, chains, and earrings. It was one of the gifts brought by the Magi to the Christ Child at Bethlehem. Symbolically it speaks of genuine worth and great value.

GOOD KING WENCESLAS A Christmas carol founded on the ancient Bohemian legend of the kindness of King Wenceslas the Holy, ruler of Bohemia in A.D. 928-935. He is famed for his consideration of the poor and needy, especially at Christmas. This arrangement by Sir John Stainer has a melody from Sweden, a story from Czechoslovakia, and a poem from England.

GOOD KING WENCESLAS

GOOD WILL Benevolence, well wishing, kindly feeling, good intention. Good will was part of the message of the angels in their announcement of the birth of Christ, "Glory to God in the highest, and on earth peace, good will toward men." Luke 2:14.

GOOSE One of the traditional Christmas dinners.

GOSPELS The four written histories of Jesus Christ, Matthew, Mark, Luke and John. They are the first part of the New Testament in the Bible. The gospels of Matthew and Luke give the details of the birth of Christ.

GOOSE

GOVERNOR One who governs, a chief ruler or magistrate. Cyrenius was Governor of Syria at the time of the Roman census. See CYRENIUS.

GRAIN To represent the well-being that each person enjoys and shares at Christmastime, it is the custom in northern European countries, to provide extra food for the animals. Sheaves of grain are tied on poles for the birds. Extra grain is given to the cattle with the words, "Eat well, keep well; this is Christmas Eve."

GREECE In Greece a special loaf of bread is prepared for Christmas. A cross is marked on the top and a coin is placed inside. The bread is broken into small pieces and shared by the whole family. There are four main pieces in the loaf. The first is for the Mother of Jesus, the second is for the home, the third is for the farm animals, and the fourth symbolizes material wealth; the remainder is shared by all the members of the household from the oldest to the youngest. The Christmas log, games and story-telling, and mysterious elf-like creatures known as "karkantzari" also play an important part in the Christmas season which continues until Epiphany.

GOVERNOR

GROUND JOY A dainty, little ground ivy, with fragrant, heart-shaped leaves, very popular with the early Christians, who used it to garnish their Christmas wreaths.

GRUBER, FRANZ Composer of Christmas' most popular carol, "Silent Night, Holy Night." See SILENT NIGHT.

HAM

H

HALLELUJAH CHORUS A stirring section of the famous sacred oratorio, Messiah, written in 1741 by George Frederic Handel. See MESSIAH.

HAM One of the early traditional Christmas dishes. Roast beef, peacock, goose, turkey and chicken became more popular as time went on.

HANDBELLS The custom of playing Christmas carols with handbells on Christmas Eve in the United States had its beginning on picturesque Beacon Hill overlooking Boston bay in Massachusetts.

HANDBELLS

HANDEL, GEORGE FREDERIC The famed composer of the Sacred Oratorio, Messiah, in 1741. He was born in Halle, Germany in 1685, but lived most of his life in England. He died in 1759. See THE MESSIAH.

HARK! THE HERALD ANGELS SING Immortal Christmas hymn written by Charles Wesley of England in 1739. The melody was adapted from the music of Mendelssohn by William Haymen Cummings in 1856.

HARP A stringed musical instrument upon which early minstrels and troubadours played many of the first Christmas carols.

HARP

HAY The soft bedding of the manger upon which Jesus could have lain as a babe in swaddling clothes. Hay is used generously in reconstructing creche scenes of the original Nativity.

HEAVEN The upper area of the universe. The Hebrews divided heaven into three parts: the lower, where clouds are; the firmament, in which are the sun, moon, and stars; and the upper, the dwelling-place of God and Hisangels, where the children of God go after death. The gospel historian, Luke, reports that the host of angels that proclaimed Jesus' birth were from heaven. Luke 2:13.

HEMLOCK An evergreen tree found especially in eastern and western North America which is one of the popular choices for a Christmas tree.

HEMLOCK

351

HEROD

HEROD AND THE COCK

HOLLAND

HOLLY

HEROD Known as Herod the Great, King of Judea (37-4 B.C.) at the time of Christ's birth. The gospel of Matthew speaks, at some length, of the dramatic part Herod played in the unfolding drama of the Christmas story. It relates that the Wise Men from the east came to Herod at Jerusalem seeking information concerning the birth of the new King. Herod immediately sought the advice of his priests and scribes and discovered that such an event had been prophesied to take place in Bethlehem. With malice in his heart, he encouraged the Wise Men in their search for the infant, making known to them his own desire to discover the identity of the new King, that, as he said, "I may come and worship him also." (Matthew 2:8.) However, after the Wise Men found the baby Jesus, they were warned in a dream to return to their homes via another route. Meanwhile, Joseph was also warned to flee with the Christ Child to escape the wrath of the Judean King. Matthew reports that Herod was so insane with rage that he ordered all of the male children two years old and under to be destroyed. Jesus, however, was safe in Egypt, where he remained until after the death of Herod.

HEROD AND THE COCK An old legend that tells of how when King Herod was questioned by the Wisemen concerning the birth of a new King which no other king would be able to destroy, he scoffed, and said that if such a preposterous story were true the roasted cock on the dish before him would stand up and crow; whereupon, the cock burst out in feathers, stood up, and crowed clearly three times.

HE SHALL FEED HIS FLOCK An aria by Handel based on Isaiah 40:11. It is part of "The Messiah," and a favorite solo during the Christmas season.

HILARY OF POITIERS, SAINT Writer of the earliest known Nativity hymn, "Jesus, Light of all the Nations," in 368.

HOLBOLL, EINAR A kindly Danish postmaster who originated the idea of Christmas seals. See CHRISTMAS SEALS.

HOLLAND In Holland, gift-giving takes place on December sixth, when St. Nicholas comes to each member of the family telling them of their good deeds and bad deeds for the year. Christmas Eve and Christmas Day are times of religious observance.

HOLLY A Christmas evergreen used in the making of wreaths and other Christmas decoration. There are over three hundred kinds of holly found in one form or another in almost every country in the world. In ancient times holly was believed to have the power of protection against witches, thunder and lightning. The burning bush, from which God spoke to Moses, was thought by some to be holly. Ancient legend reports that holly was the crown of thorns worn by Christ. The berries were white, but with the flowing of His blood turned to red.

HOLY FAMILY A term often used to identify the three members of the Christmas family: Jesus, the Christ Child; Mary, His mother; and Joseph, His earthly father.

HOLY FAMILY

HOLY FAMILY, THE The title of a number of paintings of the Holy Family by renowned artists including:
1. A painting by the famous artist of Rome, Carlo Maratta. It shows Mary, Joseph and the Christ Child surrounded by angels. It is an exceptional study of love and devotion. (1625-1713)
2. A painting by the great Italian artist and sculptor, Michelangelo. (1475-1564)
3. A painting by the noted Renaissance painter Titian. (1477-1576) Its colors are unusually bright and lustrous.
4. A painting by the famed Spanish artist El Greco (1548-1625)

HOLY LAND

HOLY NIGHT, THE The name of a number of famous Christmas paintings by noted artists including:
1. A painting by Carlo Maratta (1625-1713) Italian artist, showing Madonna and Child surrounded by children. It is a painting having unusual effect with light and shadow contrast.
2. A painting by Antonio Correggio (1494-1534). Italian painter, called the creator of harmony in coloring.

HOLY LAND Palestine, the land of Jesus' birth, life, and death, is often called the "Holy Land."

HOLY SPIRIT One of the manifestations of God in the Trinity, whereby He has fellowship with men. One of the memorable acts of the Spirit is the miraculous conception of Jesus, by which God entered into the material world through a human infant Matthew 1:18-20.

HOLY SPIRIT

HOPKINS, JOHN HENRY, JR. Episcopalian minister, outstanding in the field of literature and music, who at the age of thirty-seven in 1857, wrote the Christmas carol "We Three Kings of Orient Are." Based on the story of the magi visiting the Christ Child in Matthew 2:1-12, "We Three Kings" has become one of the most popular of the later Christmas songs.

HORSE In Holland the traditional mode of travel for St. Nicholas is a white horse. In Hungary, also, Kris Kringle makes his rounds on a white horse. In Belgium, St. Nicholas rides on a gray horse or a white donkey.

HORSE

HUNGARY

ICELAND

INCENSE

INN

HORSLEY, J. C. The designer of the first Christmas card. See CHRISTMAS CARD.

HOW THE GREAT GUEST CAME A famous poem by Edwin Markham, born April 23, 1852, about a cobbler who had a dream that the Lord was coming as a guest to his shop the next day. He decorated the place with evergreen boughs to make ready for his arrival. The next day, while he was waiting, he gave shoes to a beggar, bread to an old lady, and milk to a young child who came seeking help at his door. At the end of the day, he was disappointed because the Lord had not come as his guest. Then he heard a soft voice say, "I was the beggar with bruised feet; I was the woman you gave to eat; I was the child on the homeless street."

HUNGARY Many of the Christmas traditions are based on agricultural magic. Ashes from the yule log are scattered at the foot of fruit trees insuring good harvest. Cutting an apple in two indicated the health of a person for the coming year. If a clear star appeared he would have good health, if a broken pattern resulted he would have poor health. In Hungary, Kris Kringle appeared as a man dressed in white riding on a white horse. Because of Hungary's geographical location, her customs are a mixture of east and west.

I

ICELAND Because trees are scarce in Iceland, the natives make their own. A center pole is erected and sticks are fastened on as branches. If the snow melts enough, pieces of ground shrubs are tied on. Then the paper ornaments and candles are attached and lo! a synthetic Christmas tree.

I HEARD THE BELLS ON CHRISTMAS DAY First line of a popular carol by Henry W. Longfellow. See CHRISTMAS BELLS.

IMMANUEL A Hebrew word meaning "God is with us." The name given to Jesus by the prophet Isaiah as he looked ahead to His birth. See EMMANUEL.

INCARNATION The word means "to be made flesh." The incarnation took place when the Son of God became man in a true human body. John 1:14.

INCENSE Gums and spices which burned with a fragrant odor, used as a part of the ritual of worship. It was one of the gifts brought to Jesus by the Magi and symbolized his divinity.

IN EXCELSIS GLORIA! One of the oldest Christmas carols, written by Thibaud, French King of Navarre, who lived in the 13th century.

INFANT A child in the first period of life, a babe. Jesus was the infant of Christmas, born of Mary, laid in a manger in Bethlehem.

INN The lodging place at Bethlehem which could not accommodate Joseph and Mary on the night of Jesus' birth. The city was crowded with people from all over Palestine who had come at the request of Caesar's decree, and rooms were hard to find. It was necessary for Mary to wrap her new born infant in swaddling clothes and lay him in a manger. Luke 2:7.

IRELAND Christmas in Ireland is essentially a religious celebration of the birth of Christ and the crèche is the center of every home. It is one of the few countries that have never officially adopted the Christmas tree as a tradition. The popular custom of placing lights in the window on Christmas eve originated in Ireland.

IRVING, WASHINGTON American author of the literary classics, "Rip Van Winkle" and "The Legend of Sleepy Hollow." In his popular "Sketch Book" are three vivid essays on Christmas called "Christmas Eve," "Christmas Day," and "The Christmas Dinner." Irving was born in New York City just at the close of the Revolutionary War in 1783.

ISAIAH The great prophet of the Old Testament who foretold the birth of Jesus. He spoke of the child who would be born, centuries before it happened, who would be known as the Prince of Peace, and upon whose shoulders would rest the justice and order of the world. Isaiah 9:6-7.

I SAW THREE SHIPS A traditional English carol at least 500 years old. It is based on an English legend that three ships, carrying members of the holy family, sail by on Christmas morning.

ISRAEL The name used to designate the peoples of the twelve tribes and later to include the whole company of Hebrews. (Genesis 32:22-32) The birth of Christ was a fulfillment of the prophecy of Isaiah concerning the advent of a great spiritual leader of Israel. (Isaiah 9:6)

ITALY Christmas lasts three weeks in Italy. Beginning eight days before Christmas, it lasts until Epiphany. Christmas Eve is for the family, a festive supper, church at midnight, and merrymaking. Presents are given only to the very young and the very old.

IT CAME UPON THE MIDNIGHT CLEAR An American Christmas hymn written by Edmund Hamilton Sears, Unitarian minister, in 1850. Mr. Sears was born in the year 1810 in the Berkshires, Massachusetts, and spent most of his life as the Pastor of a church in Wayland, Massachusetts.

IRVING

ISAIAH

I SAW
THREE SHIPS

ITALY

IVY

IVY Because it was a symbol of the Roman wine-god, Bacchus, ivy was opposed as a Christmas plant in England, and allowed to grow outside the house only. However, the small "ground ivy" was later accepted and became a popular Christmas decoration.

J

JAPAN Christmas came to Japan from the western world, but many of their own customs enhance the beauty of the holiday season. The little wind chimes found all over Japan make pleasant ornaments hanging on the Christmas tree. Japanese cookies containing little paper messages are favorites. And, of course, the Japanese lanterns are famous the world over.

JAPAN

JASPER King of Tarshish, an Ethiopian, and the largest of the three Kings who brought gifts to the newborn King at Bethlehem in Judea, according to ancient legend. His gift was myrrh.

JERUSALEM The major city of Palestine at Jesus' birth. It was called the city of Zion and was located about six miles north of Bethlehem. In this city was the palace of King Herod to whom the wise men came in search of the new-born King.

JERUSALEM CHERRY A Christmas flower with bright red berries about the size of cherries. It was introduced to England in the 16th century from Madeira, a Portuguese island of the Atlantic Ocean. The name Jerusalem was given to it to indicate that it was a foreign and not native plant.

JERUSALEM CHERRY

JESOUS AHATONHIA One of the first American Christmas carols called the "Huron Indian Carol." It was supposedly written by a Jesuit missionary to the Hurons named Father de Brebeuf in 1641. It speaks of the choir of angels sent by Gitchi Manitou to announce the birth of Christ who was born in "a lodge of broken bark."

JESUS The central figure of Christmas. The gift of God's love to the world. Of Him it was said by the angels, "Unto you is born this day in the city of David, a Saviour, which is Christ the Lord." The name Jesus was given to Him by the angel to Joseph (Matthew 1:21) and to Mary (Luke 1:31). He was born in Bethlehem, according to leading authorities, about the year 4 B.C. The nature of His divinity was attested by the homage of the shepherds on the first Christmas eve, and the Magi from the east who brought him gifts of gold, frankincense, and myrrh symbolic of his power, purity, and future sacrifice on the cross. His birth was a fulfillment of prophecy by Isaiah and Micah in the Old Testament (Isaiah 9:6; Micah 5:2).

JESUS

JESUS LIGHT OF ALL THE NATIONS The earliest known hymn in honor of the Nativity, written by St. Hilary of Portiers in 368 A.D.

JINGLE BELLS Strictly speaking, this is not a Christmas song, but it is very popular during the Christmas season. It was written by John Pierpont (1785-1866).

JINGLE BELLS

JOHN THE BAPTIST A cousin of Jesus, and son of Elisabeth, a relative of Mary.

JOSEPH The husband of Mary, mother of Jesus. He was a carpenter living in Nazareth of Galilee when the angel told him of the coming Messiah who was to be named Jesus (Matthew 1:21). He guided Mary to Bethlehem where Jesus was born, and he fled with Mary and Jesus to Egypt to protect his family from King Herod (Matthew 2:13). He returned to Nazareth after the death of Herod, where he established a home for the Lord's early years of childhood.

JOSEPH

JOURNEY OF THE MAGI A painting by the Italian Renaissance painter, Sassetta, showing the colorful representation of the pilgrimage of the Wisemen to Bethlehem. It is presently in the Metropolitan Museum of Art, New York City.

JOY TO THE WORLD! A great hymn of the Nativity written in 1719 by the "father of English hymnody," Isaac Watts. It is based on the ninety-eighth psalm, "Make a joyful noise unto the Lord, all the earth: make a loud noise, and rejoice, and sing praise." The tune is considered by many authorities to be an arrangement by Lowell Mason from Handel's Messiah.

JUDEA The southern portion of Palestine in which Bethlehem and Jerusalem were major cities. Its northern boundaries extend from Joppa on the Mediterranean Sea to a point on the Jordan about ten miles north of the Dead Sea. Its southern boundary is a line drawn from the Mediterranean Sea to the bottom of the Dead Sea. It is an area about 55 miles long and wide.

JUDEA

JUGOSLAVIA In Jugoslavia there is a type of yule log called "badniak," which is brought into the house on Christmas Eve, poured over with brandy, and burned. Usually a pig is roasted for supper on Christmas eve, and the meal is eaten on the floor, covered with straw, instead of on the table.

JULE-NISSE The Christmas elf in Danish legendry who is given a bowl of rice pudding on Christmas eve so that he will not play a thousand tricks on those who live in the household.

JULE-NISSE

K

KINGS

KING A male sovereign given supreme authority over a kingdom. The Magi were three kings from the east who followed the star to Bethlehem. Herod, who tried in vain to destroy the Christ Child, was King of Judea. Jesus was called the new-born King and was spiritual leader of all men.

KRISS KRINGLE One of the names for Santa Claus. The name was developed from the German "Christkindl" or Christ Child. Among the early European customs was the belief that not only St. Nicholas left gifts at Christmas, but angels, and also, in some areas, the Christ Child. Eastern European countries also believed that the Wise Men would leave gifts in wooden shoes if hay was put in them for the camels. "Christkindl" soon became Kriss Kringle, and as this was the gift-bearing person at Christmas, he soon was thought of as Santa Claus.

L

LAGERLOF

LAGERLOF, SELMA Swedish author born in 1858, and writer of "The Legend of the Christmas Rose." Her exquisite and artistic treatment of Christmas legends is considered one of the finest in literature.

LAMB

LAMB One of the traditional animals of Christmas. It is presumed that if shepherds were present at the manger on Christmas eve that probably a lamb was there as well. Symbolically it would be fitting for a lamb to be present at the birth of Christ, for he was later known as the "Lamb of God" and the "Good Shepherd."

LAUREL

LAUREL Laurel is alleged to have been the first plant ever used as a Christmas decoration. Early Christians decorated their homes with laurel in honor of the birth of Christ. The presence of a laurel wreath on the outside of their door meant a friendly greeting to all who passed by. This plant, also called bay laurel and bay tree, has been highly prized by many civilizations. The ancient Greeks and Romans hung it over their doors as a protection against evil. A story is told of how the Emperor Tiberius wore a laurel crown during a severe lightning storm and crawled under his bed until it was over. Laurel was a badge of victory in war, and a trophy of triumph in sports. Poets have been crowned with laurel, hence, the term "poet laureate." Laurel is a native of southern Europe and at Christmas is a symbol of victory, glory, joy, and celebration.

LEGEND A story or collection of stories coming down from the past, especially one that is popularly taken for historical truth though not verifiable. There are many legends associated with Christmas, some interesting, some strange, some amusing, some doubtful, but all part of the tradition of the celebration of the Christmas season. Each makes its own contribution and each plays its own dramatic role.

LEROLLE, HENRI A French painter born in Paris in 1848. He painted the beautiful Christmas picture, "The Arrival of the Shepherds." See ARRIVAL OF THE SHEPHERDS.

LIGHTS

LIGHTS The first Christmas lighting is usually attributed to Martin Luther in Germany. According to the legend, one Christmas Eve as Luther was walking home through white fields, he glanced at the stars shining through the snow-covered branches of a fir tree. He hurried home to tell his family of its beauty. Cutting a small fir, he took it into his house and placed lighted candles on its branches to illustrate what he meant: A candle-lighted Christmas tree became a permanent part of the annual Christmas ritual in the Luther home from that time on. Paris, France has the credit for the first lighted community Christmas tree in Tuileries about the turn of the 19th century. In 1909 the citizens of Pasadena, California illuminated a tall evergreen on the top of Mt. Wilson. Madison Square, New York, and the Common in Boston, Massachusetts were lighted with Christmas trees in 1912. Philadelphia, Pennsylvania, erected its first lighted tree in Independence Square in 1914. The custom of placing colorful lights in the windows of private homes originated on Beacon Hill in Boston, Massachusetts.

LILY

LILY A symbol, developed in the early church, used to represent Mary the mother of Jesus.

LITHUANIA In Lithuania, Christmas eve dinner is served on a table covered with straw to remind them of the manger where Christ was born. The menu consists of twelve courses symbolizing the twelve apostles. It is a time of peace, good will, and intimate family relationship. On Christmas day the time is spent at home or visiting neighbors. Gifts are given only to the children.

LITTLE CHRISTMAS

LITTLE CHRISTMAS Celebrated in the Scandinavian countries twelve days before Christmas on December 13. It is the time of the first light when the Christmas season is ushered in by "Lucia." See SWEDEN.

LITTLE STRANGER, THE An ancient legend that tells the story of a woodsman and his family. One Christmas eve they sat before their meager meal in a poor cottage deep in the forest. They didn't have much, but they were kind people and cheerful. Suddenly they heard a weak knock on their door. When the woodsman opened it, he saw a tired, shivering child dressed

LITTLE STRANGER

359

LOG

in rags standing in the cold snow. Without hesitation they brought him, dressed him in warm clothes, and fed him the hot food from their own table. After supper they put him in the bed where their son usually slept. In the middle of the night, the whole family awoke to the sound of heavenly music from a great angelic choir. When they could not find the little stranger, they ran outdoors. There they saw him standing in the snow, dressed in splendid garments, and radiating in a golden glow. They knew then that this was the Christ Child and they bowed down in reverence before Him. The Christ Child broke off a fir branch, stuck it in the ground, and said, "Because you have been so kind to me, this tree will always be green, and bear fruit at Christmas, and you will always have plenty at that season."

LONGFELLOW

LOG The tree drawn from swamp or forest for the fireplace at Christmas. The custom of the yule log originated in Europe and is still observed in one form or another. It is a symbol of warmth and cheer. See YULE LOG.

LONGFELLOW, HENRY WADSWORTH Distinguished American poet who in 1863 wrote the words to the famed Christmas song, "Christmas Bells." See CHRISTMAS BELLS.

LORD A term of authority referring to God or Jesus. In announcing the birth of Jesus, the angels referred to Him as "Christ the Lord."

LOVE The benevolence attributed to God as being like a father's affection for his children. In one of the few references to the birth of Christ by the gospel-writer John, he said, "For God so loved the world that he gave his only son . . ." (John 3:16). Thus love was the spirit of the first Christmas and has been the spirit of Christmas ever since.

LUKE

LUKE A Christian physician and close companion of the Apostle Paul. He was the author of a history of the life of Christ, known as the Gospel of Luke, where he records in great detail the manner of His birth. The second chapter of the Gospel of Luke is the scriptural account of the beautiful story of the first Christmas.

LUTHER

LUTHER, MARTIN German Reformer, born November 10, 1483, one of the most important Christmas personalities in relation to custom and tradition. To Luther goes the honor of decorating and lighting the first Christmas tree. Many of the customs of Christmas were introduced to America through the Lutherans settling in Pennsylvania and the east coast. He is also the author of the Christmas hymn, "From Heaven Above to Earth I Come" and some authorities believe "Away in a Manger." See CHRISTMAS TREE.

M

MADONNA A designation of the Virgin Mary. An original Italian word for Mary, the mother of Jesus.

MADONNA, THE A painting of Madonna and Child by Carlo Dolci, a Florentine painter of the seventeenth century. He was noted for his fresh, glowing colors and his dedication to detail. The Madonna is located presently in the Galleria Arte Antica, Rome, Italy

MADONNA

MADONNA OF THE CHAIR, THE A famous Madonna painting by the great Italian artist, Raphael (1483-1520).

MADONNA OF THE ROCKS A famous Madonna painting by the great artist, Leonardo da Vinci (1452-1519).

MAGI Another name for the Wise Men who followed the star to Bethlehem in search of the new-born King. They were men of a priestly caste from the East, who made a special study of astrology and mysterious natural sciences. Legend gives them names: Melchior, King of Nubia; Balthazar, King of Chaldea; and Jasper, King of Tarshish; and it was believed that they represented the three great races, European, Asian, and African. The Magi brought gifts of gold, frankincense and myrrh to the Manger.

MAGI

MAGNIFICAT The beautiful words of praise and humility spoken by Mary upon her realization of the fact that she was to become the mother of Jesus (Luke 1:46-55).

MANGER An open box or trough from which cattle ate their food. At Jesus' birth he was wrapped in swaddling clothes and "laid in a manger" because there was no room in the inn. Luke 2:7.

MANGER

MANTLE OF FIRE An ancient Christmas legend which tells the story of Joseph and the shepherds. According to the legend, when Joseph reached Bethlehem and found no room in the inn, he had to take refuge in a stable. There Christ was born and laid carefully in a manger. Joseph went out into the night to find fire to keep Mary and the baby warm. He found some shepherds on the hillside keeping warm by their fire, and he asked them if he might have some coals. When he picked up the coals, neither his hands nor his mantle were burned. While the shepherds spoke to each other of this strange miracle, the angels came and told them of the birth of the new king, and asked them to go to Bethlehem. They went, and saw the Christ Child, now being kept warm by the coals from their fire, still burning and remaining unburned.

MANTLE OF FIRE

MARY, MOTHER OF JESUS

MARY The mother of Jesus, and one of the main figures of the first Christmas. Of Mary, the angel Gabriel said, "Blessed art thou among women," for she was to become the mother of the Messiah, the Saviour of the world. (Luke 1:28) From Mary's lips came the words of the beautiful Magnificat, "My soul doth magnify the Lord, and my spirit hath rejoiced in God my Saviour." (Luke 1:46, 47) With Joseph she shared the responsibility of bringing up Jesus in Nazareth of Galilee.

MASON, LOWELL Medfield, Massachusetts man who composed, in 1872, the music for the carol "Joy to the World" using tunes from Handel's Messiah.

MATTHEW One of the twelve apostles, and writer of the Gospel in the New Testament bearing the same name. Matthew writes in detail concerning the visit of the Wise Men to Bethlehem, and the drama of the escape of the Holy Family from the wrath of King Herod. Matthew 2.

MATTHEW

MELCHIOR One of the Three Wisemen, according to ancient legend. Melchior, King of Nubia, was considered to be the smallest of the three, and brought the gift of gold.

MENDELSSOHN, FELIX A famous German composer, born in 1809, who wrote the music for the Christmas carol, "Hark, the Herald Angels Sing."

MERRY CHRISTMAS! A warm greeting of friendliness used in the United States during the Christmas season.

MESSIAH Jesus was named the Messiah because he is believed to be the one sent by God to fulfill the great expectation of the Jews for a Deliverer and Saviour.

MELCHIOR

MESSIAH, THE An immortal classic in Christmas music created by the genius of George Frederick Handel. This tremendous oratorio is without doubt the greatest in the world. The composition was completed within a span of twenty-four days in August of 1741, at which time Handel was completely withdrawn from everything in the world. The first performance of Handel's Messiah was given in Dublin, Ireland in 1742. Since that time, its glorious, sublime music has entertained and inspired the whole world.

MEXICO From Mexico came the Christmas flower, the poinsettia. They call it Flor de la Noche Buena, "the flower of the Holy Night." One story of its origin says that a young girl died of a broken heart on Christmas eve, because she was separated from her lover. The blood drops which fell to the earth became the poinsettia.

MENDELSSOHN

MICAH One of the minor prophets of the Old Testament who foretold of the birth of the new-born King in Bethlehem. Micah 5:2.

MICAH

MIGHTY GOD One of the words used by the prophet Isaiah to describe the coming Messiah. Isaiah 9:6.

MINCE PIE A traditional Christmas dessert. They were frequently baked in the form of a Manger to be reminded of the place of Christ's birth. At one time the baking of mince pies was forbidden as a heathen practice. See QUEER CHRISTMAS CUSTOMS No. 8.

MINCE PIE

MIRACLE PLAY Medieval church plays showing the miracles of Christ and His disciples. It was from the miracle play that the Christmas tree is believed to have had its origin. See CHRISTMAS TREE.

MIRACULOUS HARVEST, THE An ancient legend concerning the escape of Jesus into Egypt. According to the story, King Herod was greatly frightened when he heard the news of a new king being born. "Show me the King that I may worship him," he had said; but secretly he had planned to kill the baby. The Wise Men, warned, had returned to their country by another way. King Herod, greatly angered, ordered all boys under two years be slain. When Mary and Joseph heard the news, they hurried away with Jesus toward the land of Egypt. The journey was more than three hundred miles, and much could happen on the way. One day they came to a farmer plowing a field and getting ready to sow his wheat. The child Jesus spoke to him and told him to get ready for the harvest that very day. The farmer recognized Jesus and bowed down before him. Jesus told him that someone would come by and ask him if he had seen a man, woman and child pass by. He was to tell them, yes, while he was sowing the seed. Very soon a troop of Herod's soldiers came rushing into the field, waving their spears, and asking the farmer and his men if they had seen a man, woman, and child pass that way. "Yes," the farmer said quickly, "While I was sowing the wheat." As they were now harvesting the wheat, the captain ordered his men to turn back, for it must have been many weeks since they passed. So the Holy Family was saved by a miraculous harvest, and went on to Egypt.

MIRACULOUS HARVEST

MISTLETOE A green shrub with thick yellowish leaves and waxy-white berries that clings to the branches of other trees such as oak or apple. It is one of the most interesting of the Christmas plants because of the many colorful legends associated with it. The pagan Druids of ancient Britain considered the mistletoe a sacred plant. They used it in all manner of ways to heal diseases and prevent evil. Dignified ceremonies were

MISTLETOE

MISTLETOE

enacted in the gathering of the mistletoe each year. The custom of kissing under the mistletoe originated in the Scandinavian countries and was taken from an ancient myth. In France amulets of mistletoe were worn to prevent illness; and in Sweden mistletoe rings were worn for the same purpose. The early Church in England barred the use of mistletoe as a church decoration because of its pagan importance.

MOHR, JOSEPH Author of the carol, "Silent Night, Holy Night." See SILENT NIGHT, HOLY NIGHT.

MONTGOMERY, JAMES A talented English hymn writer (1771-1854) and composer of the Christmas hymn "Angels from the Realms of Glory."

MYRRH

MOORE, CLEMENT CLARKE American educator and poet, author of the popular Christmas classic, "A Visit From St. Nicholas." It was written in 1822, while a professor at the General Theological Seminary in New York, for his own children, and printed anonymously, without his knowledge, in the Troy Sentinel, December 23, 1823. This poem, more than any other force, has perpetuated the traditions associated with Santa Claus in this country.

MYRRH A Palestinian shrub with fragrant wood and bark. Its sap-like, yellowish gum was used as a perfume, in medicine, anointing oil and cosmetics, and as a part of the preparation for the burial of bodies. It was one of the gifts brought by the Wise Men at the time of Christ's birth. Symbolically it represented the future death of Christ at the Crucifixion.

N

**NATIONS
CHRISTMAS
TREE**

NATION'S CHRISTMAS TREE In 1926, a giant sequoia tree in King's Canyon National Park, California, known as General Grant Tree, was officially dedicated as the Nation's Christmas Tree. The massive sequoia is forty feet thick at the base and towers two-hundred and sixty-seven feet into the sky. It is thousands of years old, and was standing when the star guided the Wisemen to the Manger at Bethlehem.

NATIVITY Birth, the coming into life or into the world, the circumstances attending birth, such as time, place, and manner, especially of the Birth of Christ. Nativity refers to Christ's birth or the day of His birth.

NATIVITY, THE The name of several famous Christmas paintings among which are:
1. A painting by Bernardino Luini, a pupil of

NATIVITY

Leonardo da Vinci, showing the adoration of the shepherds on the night of the Nativity. It is now part of a collection in the Isaac Delgado Museum of Art in New Orleans, Louisiana.

2. A painting by the famous Italian renaissance painter, Fiorenzo de Lorenzo. He was known as a painter of frescoes, and his nativity is a calm, serene study of the Holy Birth. It is preserved in the Metropolitan Museum of Art, New York City.

3. A painting by the Italian artist, Federigo Barocci (1528-1612). It stresses the rustic manger setting of the first Christmas.

4. A painting by the Italian Artist Fra Lippo Lippi, great teacher of Botticelli. This early renaissance painting is in the National Art Gallery at Washington D.C.

5. A painting by Fra Angelico (1387-1455), early Italian artist.

NAZARETH

NAZARETH   A small village in southern Galilee which was the home city of Joseph and Mary. It was here that Jesus grew from boyhood to manhood.

NEW TESTAMENT

NEALE, JOHN M.   Author of the words to the English carol, "Good King Wenceslaus" in 1866.

NEW TESTAMENT   The last 27 Books of the Bible beginning with Matthew and ending with Revelation. It contains the Gospels of Matthew and Luke which tell the story of the first Christmas in detail.

NIGHT   The time of Jesus' birth, and the time of the announcement by the angels to the shepherds tending their flocks. As the popular carol says, "While shepherds watched their flocks by night . . ."

NIGHT

NIGHTINGALE, THE   An old Christmas legend which tells the story of the nightingale and Jesus. In the stable at Bethlehem, on the night of Jesus' birth, the baby was restless. Mary sang sweet lullabys, but nothing she could do would comfort him. A nightingale on the roof had been listening to Mary's song. Now he flew in the door and perched unafraid on Mary's shoulder and joined in the lullaby with her. The baby Jesus closed his eyes softly and went to sleep. In gratitude for the nightingale's song, Mary told him that from then on all nightingales would be endowed with her own voice. From that time forward the nightingale's song became the lovliest of all the birds, and when he sang in field or forest, all the other birds stopped in wonder to listen to the beauty of his notes.

NOEL   A name for Christmas of French origin.

NIGHTINGALE, THE

NORTH POLE

NORTH POLE The imaginary home of Santa Claus. The place popular legend holds as being the abode and workshop where Santa, with the help of his elves, gets ready each year for his annual trip around the world laden with toys for girls and boys.

NORWAY Preparation for Christmas comes long before Christmas day in Norway. The traditional foods of sausage, cheese, bread, cookies, and special dishes are made for the big Christmas dinner. A thin bread made from oat flour is made in great quantities. Special attention is given to the animals at Christmas, with sheaves of grain hung out for the birds and extra food for the barn animals. Christmas trees have long been a tradition in this land where evergreen trees grow in profusion. On the very top of the Norwegian Christmas tree are placed three candles representing the three wisemen.

NORWAY

O

OAKELY, DR. FREDERICK Anglican Clergyman who wrote the English version of "O Come, All Ye Faithful" in 1880

O CHRISTMAS TREE! The most popular carol about the Christmas tree. The melody is an old Medieval folk song of Germany. Called "O Tannenbaum," it is rivaled only by "Silent Night" as the most popular carol in modern Europe today.

O COME, ALL YE FAITHFUL An exalting, majestic Christmas hymn which has been translated into more than 125 different languages. Recent research has identified the author as John Francis Wade, an Englishman by birth, but a resident of France when he wrote the hymn in 1744.

OFFERING

O COME, O COME, EMMANUEL An old Christmas hymn coming directly from the Latin, which was sung originally in the Roman Church at vespers on the seven days before Christmas during the ninth century or earlier. The translation was by Dr. John Mason Neale (1818-1866), an eminent Cambridge scholar and renowned hymnologist.

OFFERING The collection of money in a church service. At Christmas most churches have a special Christmas Offering to honor the birth of the Saviour.

O HOLY NIGHT! (Cantique de Noel) A beautiful, haunting French carol, the melody of which was written by Adolphe Adam, composer, born in Paris in 1803. There is a story which relates that during the Franco-Prussian war in 1870 on Christmas Eve, the French and German soldiers were facing each other in trenches near the city. Suddenly a young soldier of France leaped from his trench and surprised the Germans with

O HOLY NIGHT

a loud, clear renditon of Adam's "Cantique de Noel." The Germans were so smitten by his singing that not a shot was fired; in fact, at the conclusion a German soldier stepped forward and responded with Luther's noted Christmas hymn, "From Heaven Above to Earth I Come."

OLD TESTAMENT The first 39 Books of the Bible beginning with Genesis and ending with Malachi. It contains the prophecies of Isaiah and Micah concerning the coming of the Messiah.

O LITTLE TOWN OF BETHLEHEM A Christmas hymn written by Philips Brooks in 1868. (See BROOKS for more detail.)

ORANGES

ORANGES Fruit used frequently to decorate Christmas trees and Christmas candy boxes.

ORNAMENTS Decorating and trimming the tree with brightly colored ornaments had its origin in old Roman customs. Egyptians also honored their gods with decorated trees. The decorated Christmas tree, however, goes back to the renaissance period in 16th century Germany. Small trees were taken indoors and trimmed with paper roses, apples, nuts, sweets, and ornaments. The first decorated Christmas trees in America were set up by Hessian soldiers during the Revolutionary war. The Christmas tree ornament industry had its beginning in central Germany. Here the ancient art of glassblowing was used in their manufacture. The ornaments varied in size, shape, brilliance, and color. What began as a simple hand-made industry developed to the point where recently one ornament manufacturer was able to offer a variety of 13,000 different ornaments.

ORNAMENTS

OTHER WISE MAN, THE An imaginative story, by Henry Van Dyke, of the Fourth Wise Man who finally found the Christ after many wanderings and probations.

OX One of the traditional Christmas animals. Usually included with the figures of a creche scene. Because of its strength, patience, and use for sacrifice, the ox has been adopted as a symbol for the Redeemer.

OX

P

PACK The bag carried by Santa Claus which holds all the toys for girls and boys.

PACKAGE A bundle made up for Christmas mailing or for placing under the Christmas tree.

PAGEANT A play or exhibition. Most churches have a group or groups of its members or young people re-enact the story of the first Christmas in play or pantomime as an act of commemoration and devotion during the Christmas season.

PACK

ST. PATRICK

PALESTINE A small country, 150 miles long and 40 miles wide, located on the eastern shores of the Mediterranean Sea. In this area Jesus was born and lived and completed his ministry.

PARADISE TREE A fir tree hung with apples used in the medieval "miracle plays." It is thought to be a forerunner of the Christmas tree.

PATRICK, SAINT He is said to have introduced the tradition of celebrating Christmas in Ireland in the year 493.

PAULINUS, BISHOP An Italian Bishop who rang the first Christmas bells in Nola, Campina, Italy in 300 A.D.

PEACE A mental or spiritual state in which there is freedom from that which is disquieting or perturbing, such as fears, agitations, or anxieties. Peace was part of the message of the angels at the birth of Christ as they proclaimed, "Glory to God in the highest, and on earth peace, good will toward men." Luke 2:14.

PARADISE TREE

PHILIPPINES On Christmas eve a traditional supper of cooked root crops and fruit called "colacion" is eaten by everyone over twelve. To eat anything else is considered an invitation to disaster.

PILGRIMS On December 25, 1620, the Pilgrims started building the homes for their new settlement in Plymouth, Massachusetts.

PINE An evergreen tree sometimes selected as the choice for the Christmas tree, usually in areas where the thicker branched evergreens are not native. Some species of pine grows in almost every part of the world.

PILGRIMS

PITTI MADONNA RELIEF A famed sculptured relief of Mary and Child by the great Florentine artist and sculptor, Michelangelo. It was finished in 1504. The name Pitti is taken from the man who commissioned the work, Bartolommeo Pitti.

PLUM PUDDING A favorite English Christmas food containing plums, flour, raisins, currants and other fruits, suet, eggs, and spices. Often it is boiled in a bag. According to ancient legend, an early English King became lost in a blizzard while hunting the day before Christmas. One of the hunting party, assuming the responsibility of cook, did the best he could to prepare a meal with the few ingredients he could find. He threw everything there was into one mess, including the remains of a recently killed deer, dried plums, apples, eggs, flour and sugar, along with anything else he had at hand. Tying the whole mixture into a bag, he boiled it into a pudding. The lost King

PINE

was so pleased with the strange concoction that he made it an annual Christmas festive food. Thus a famous Christmas recipe was born.

PLUM PUDDING

POINSETTIA The most popular of the Christmas plants. Its beautiful, flaming star-shaped blossom reaches its peak of exquisite perfection just at the Christmas season, making it extremely popular for decoration in the private home and public building. It derives its name from Dr. Joel Roberts Poinsett, American Ambassador to Mexico in 1829, who discovered the plant growing wild on the Mexican hillsides. He brought some with him when he returned to his Charleston, S.C. home, and it became a Christmas favorite immediately. Actually, what is considered the flower of the poinsettia is not a flower at all, but the bracts, or a sort of inner leaf, which are generally small and unnoticed in most flowers, but large and developed in the poinsettia. It is a distinctively American plant.

POINSETTIA

POLAND In Poland, Christmas is a time for special activity in helping nature raise good crops. One way is to show an apple tree an ax and warn it that it will be cut down if it does not bear fruit. Another way is to take a whip and beat the trunk, or tie a stone to one of the branches. Inside the house, straw is spread under the table to be reminded of the Manger where Christ was born, and a chair is left empty for the Holy Child.

POPCORN A tasty filling for Christmas candy boxes, and a colorful decoration for the Christmas tree when laced together in long strings.

PRANCER The name of the third of Santa Claus' reindeer according to the poem, "A Visit From St. Nicholas," by Clement Moore.

POPCORN

PRANG, LOUIS A Boston lithographer who introduced the printing of Christmas cards to America in 1875.

PRINCE OF PEACE One of the names used by Isaiah in his prophecy concerning the coming of the Messiah. Isaiah 9:6.

PROPHECY A declaration of things to come, a foretelling, a prediction. Isaiah foretold the birth of the new-born King (Isaiah 9:6, 7). Micah predicted the place of Messiah's birth (Micah 5:2).

PUTZ A Moravian version of the Christmas tree. It is a miniature portrayal of the nativity, made of tiny scenes with little figures of paper-mache or wood, and decorated with sand, earth, rocks, and wee fences, and so arranged as to show the Holy Family in a cave or thatched stable. Almost every Moravian home has a "putz" which will vary according to the imagination of the individual family.

PUTZ

#3 YORKSHIRE

#5 DEVONSHIRE

#11 DENMARK

#13 GREECE

Q

QUEER CHRISTMAS CUSTOMS Through the centuries, there have been many strange ideas and beliefs associated with Christmas. Here are a few of the hundreds of legends and tales of an unusual nature related to the Yuletide season.

1. At Drewsbury, in England, on Christmas Eve, upon the stroke of twelve the age of the year is tolled as on the death of a person. This custom called the "devil's passing bell" comes from the belief that the devil died when Christ was born.

2. In Czechoslovakia, a twig of the cherry tree is placed in water on December 4, and if it blossoms by Christmas Eve, the young girl tending it will marry before another Christmas.

3. In Yorkshire, England, on Christmas day, it is customary for singing boys to bring large baskets of bright red apples into the church and pass them out, with a sprig of rosemary, to each member of the congregation.

4. In Slavic countries, children often sleep on beds of straw and hay on Christmas Eve, so that they may share in Jesus' humble birth.

5. On Christmas Eve, in Devonshire, England, if an unmarried girl goes to the door of a hen-house and raps, her future can be foretold. If a hen cackles, her future is not encouraging; but if a rooster crows, she will be married before the end of the year.

6. Dutch children filled their wooden shoes with straw for Santa Claus' white horse. In Italy, children set out their shoes for the female Santa Claus, La Befena, to fill with gifts.

7. An old European legend says that at one o'clock on Christmas morning, the cattle would all turn their heads to the east, and get down on their knees to worship the King that was born in a stable.

8. In 1644, the Puritans of England forbade the observance of Christmas. They passed a law making December 25 a market day. The making of plum puddings and mince pie was illegal because it was a heathen custom.

9. If a girl walks backward to a pear tree on Christmas Day, and walks around the tree three times, she will see the image of her future husband. This is an old English legend.

10. The use of fireworks to celebrate Christmas has been common in Italy, France, Spain and China. It was introduced in New Orleans, Louisiana, by French settlers.

11. On New Year's eve in Denmark, it is the custom to throw old crockery, which has been saved all year just for this occasion, against the door of a friend, and then run fast, but not too fast, for he is to catch you and invite you in his home.

12. In Finland, a dessert of rice pudding with a single almond is served on Christmas day, the one who finds the almond in his portion can expect good luck during the coming year.

13. In Greece, it is a custom to burn old shoes in the fire during the Christmas season to prevent misfortunes from falling upon you.

REINDEER

R

REDEEMER   One who sets free, buys back, delivers, or saves.   This title is used for Jesus, who came to redeem people from sin and spiritual bondage and to restore them to sonship with God.

REINDEER   According to popular legend, the animals used by Santa Claus to carry his sleigh all over the world on Christmas eve.

RIBBON   A long, narrow piece of fabric of varied widths, made of silk, satin, velvet, or nylon, used at Christmas for trimming Christmas presents or other Christmas decorations.

RIBBON

ROBIN, THE   An ancient Christmas legend concerning the robin and his red breast.   According to the tale, the fire was burning low in the stable where Joseph, Mary, and the infant Jesus lay in that first, cold Christmas night.   They stirred restlessly in their sleep as the cold Judean breezes chilled their weary bodies. But the Heavenly Father would let no harm come to them and sent a little brown bird to help.   The little bird flew in the window and perched on a log near the fire.   He flapped his wings and fanned the coals until they caught fire and were blazing once again.   The little bird's breast became redder and redder but he would not leave until the fire was safely burning and the Holy Family warm and dry.   The robin's breast has remained red ever since, and is a constant sign of his devotion to the new-born King.

ROBIN, THE

ROMANIA   In Romania, following an ancient Christmas custom, the men and boys carry a wooden star called a "steaua" on a long pole from house to house while they sing carols and recite poems and legends. The star, covered with colored paper or gilt, brightly trimmed with bells, ribbons and tinsel, is lighted by candles from within and reflects a picture of the Nativity.   It is often referred to as the "heavenly lantern."

ROSE   See CHRISTMAS ROSE.

ROSEMARY   A fragrant shrub of southern Europe and Asia Minor. Rosemary is associated with Christmas through the tale of ancient legend.   According to the story, the branches of the Rosemary held the tiny garments of the Christ Child placed there by his mother Mary, as they rested on their flight from the wrath of King Herod.   Originally the flowers were white, but they were supposed to have changed to lavender to match the color of Mary's cloak.

ROSEMARY

RUDOLPH

ST. NICHOLAS

SANTA CLAUS

SCOTLAND

ROSE OF JERICHO Legend says that during the flight of Joseph, Mary and Jesus to Egypt, wherever Mary stepped, a little flower sprang up out of the desert soil. It was called the Rose of Jericho, and is one of the many Christmas roses.

ROSSETTI, CHRISTINA Often called the "Poet of Christmas." She was born in London, England, and wrote the famed poem, "A Christmas Carol," in which were contained the lines: "What can I give Him, Poor as I am? If I were a shepherd I would bring a lamb, If I were a Wise Man I would do my part, Yet what can I give Him, Give my heart."

RUDOLPH Rudolph, the red-nosed reindeer, by modern song and story, is the lantern-nosed little reindeer who was able to guide Santa's team through the foggy Christmas night.

RUSSIA It was the custom, at one time, in Russia to put stockings and shoes outside the door, at Christmas, for Old Man Winter. Whatever was dreamed by maidens on Christmas eve was believed by them to come true. Traditional gifts are red boots for the boys and golden slippers for the girls.

S

SAINT NICHOLAS Bishop of Myra in Asia Minor, who died in that city about 350 A.D. The legend built around his life speaks of him as a kindly person, born of a rich family, who used to ride by the windows of the poor and toss money in the window. He gave all his possessions to the sick and the suffering, the needy and the destitute. Through the years following his death, the belief grew that he still appeared each year at the beginning of Advent laden with gifts and good things, preparing the hearts of children for the coming of Christ at Christmas. He was usually impersonated by a man in long white beard, dressed in the garments of a Bishop. Many of the characteristics of Saint Nicholas were incorporated into the figure of Santa Claus. See SANTA CLAUS.

SANTA CLAUS The American name for the gift-bearing Christmas personality. The name was developed from the Dutch "Sinter Klaas." The image of Santa Claus as he is seen today the jolly, round, be-whiskered gentleman with the big pack came as a combination of three gift-bearers of the past; St. Nicholas, kindly Bishop who gave presents to the children at Christmas; the Christmas Man, whose home and factory for toys was at the North Pole and who traveled by sleigh and reindeer; and Father Christmas, who dressed in bright, red garments. The tradition of Santa Claus was made widely popular with the publication of Clement Moore's "Visit from St. Nick."

SANTA CLAUS, INDIANA A city in the state of Indiana bearing the same name as the legendary American Christmas gift-bearing personality.

SATURNALIA An ancient Roman festival where it was customary to have evergreen trees covered with fruit and decorations.

SAVIOUR A term applied to Jesus because of his redeeming work in saving people from their sins. Luke 2:11.

SCRIBES

SCOTLAND In Scotland there is a custom called "first-footing." The first person to enter the house on Christmas morning calls, "first footing!," and brings a gift with him to introduce good luck to the household for the year. It is considered a sign of good fortune if the "first-footer" is a dark-haired man.

SCRIBES A group of people who copied the sacred Scriptures. They were consulted, together with the chief priests, by King Herod to determine the location of Jesus' prophesied birth. Matthew 2:4.

SCROOGE Famed character in Charles Dickens' "A Christmas Carol."

SCROOGE

SEALS See CHRISTMAS SEALS.

SERMON A spiritual message delivered by a clergyman to a congregation. Special Christmas sermons are presented each year to commemorate the birth of Christ.

SERVICE A religious ceremony held in a church. Special Christmas Services are held each year in honor of the birth of Christ.

SHAKESPEARE, WILLIAM Famous English poet who recorded many of the ancient Christmas customs and superstitions in his poetry; for example, from Hamlet: "Some say that ever 'gainst that season comes Wherein our Saviour's birth is celebrated, The bird of dawning singeth all night long: And then, they say, no spirits dare stir abroad; The nights are wholesome; then no planets strike, No fairy takes, no witch has power to charm, So hallowed and so gracious is the time."

SHAKESPEARE, WILLIAM

SHEAF A bundle of grain. In many European countries sheaves are placed on the end of poles for the birds during Christmas.

SHEEP One of the Christmas animals, associated with the Shepherds outside Bethlehem.

SHEAF

SHEPHERDS

SHEPHERDS On the night of the Nativity there were certain shepherds watching their flocks of sheep outside Bethlehem. To them the angels made the proclamation of Jesus' birth. They hurried to Bethlehem and found where the young child lay, wrapped in swaddling clothes, and in a manger. They bowed down in worship before the new-born King and then returned to their flocks telling everyone on the way about the birth of the Saviour. Luke 2:8-17.

SILENT NIGHT, HOLY NIGHT! Probably the best known, most widely sung Christmas song the world over. This beautiful, simple carol was written on the 24th of December, 1818, in the little village of Oberndorf, near Salzburg, Austria, by Joseph Mohr, the Vicar of the Church of Saint Nicholas. The dramatic story centered around the Christmas Hymn is almost unbelievable. Joseph Mohr gave the simple poem to his organist Franz Gruber the day before Christmas with the request that he compose the music for the Christmas Eve Service. The church organ had broken down and thus the first rendition of "Silent Night" was a duet by the author and composer in a quiet church by simple guitar accompaniment.

SILENT NIGHT, HOLY NIGHT

The drama of the story does not end there. Because the organ was broken, "Silent Night, Holy Night" received its chance for fame. It seems that later when the organ was being repaired that Gruber played the new carol as a means of testing the newly-tuned instrument. The repair man was enchanted. He requested a copy which he took with him to his own village of Zillerthal where it caught on very quickly. Four sisters by the name of Strasse, daughters of a Zillerthal glove maker, used the song in their concerts given from town to town while their father sold gloves. The catchy carol passed from mouth to mouth until it became almost a legend. Thus, because a church organ was broken at Christmas, the world's most popular Christmas song was written and gained glory never dreamed by its authors.

SIMEON

SIMEON A just and devout man of Jerusalem who held the baby Jesus in his arms, blessed him, and predicted glorious things of his life. Luke 2:25-35.

SINTER KLAAS Dutch name for St. Nicholas. See SANTA CLAUS.

SKETCH BOOK Famous Christmas Literature by Washington Irving. See IRVING, WASHINGTON.

SLEIGH

SLEIGH The vehicle which tradition says is used by Santa Claus as he makes his rounds with toys for the children on Christmas Eve.

SMART, HENRY (1813-1879) Composer of the music for the Christmas Hymn, "Angels, from the Realms of Glory." The music was composed in 1867 when Smart was blind. All the notations were made through dictation.

SPAIN After Christmas Eve, there is much gaiety and laughter, dancing and singing, in celebration of the Nativity. All through Christmas week, friends and relatives visit freely. The children are excited looking forward to the night of Epiphany when the Wise Men, journeying on their way to the Holy Land, will leave gifts in the wooden shoes filled with straw for their camels.

SPIRIT OF CHRISTMAS, THE A famous message by Henry Van Dyke, written in 1905, with the challenge that "there is a better thing than the observance of Christmas Day, and that is keeping Christmas."

SPRUCE An evergreen tree often selected as the choice for the Christmas tree.

STABLE A shelter for the housing and feeding of donkeys and cattle. Jesus was born in a stable in Bethlehem.

STAR The luminous, celestial body seen in the skies by the Wisemen of the east which they interpreted as a sign of the birth of a King. They followed the star to Jerusalem where they inquired of King Herod the whereabouts of the new-born King of the Jews. They continued to follow the star to Bethlehem where they discovered the Baby Jesus lying in the manger. They knew their destination had been reached when they observed the great shining star directly over the Manger where Jesus lay. Matthew 2:2-10.

STEPHEN, SAINT December 26, the day after Christmas, is the feast of St. Stephen. In Great Britain it is the day for "boxing," or giving of gifts.

STOCKING See CHRISTMAS STOCKING

STRASBOURG A city in Germany where the Christmas tree was first used in any large degree. A manuscript dated 1605 gives a detailed description of its use. From here the Christmas tree slowly became popular in other parts of Germany.

STRAW Used for the floors of creche scenes in the reproduction of the original Nativity.

SUGAR PLUMS A kind of candy or sweet meat made up in small balls or disks. Usually associated with Christmas, especially in "A Visit From St. Nicholas" by Clement Moore.

SPRUCE

STABLE

STAR

SUGAR PLUMS

**SWADDLING
CLOTHES**

SUGARPLUM TREE, THE   A delightful poem by Eugene Field. The custom of making sugarplum trees at Christmas has developed in many areas.

SWADDLING CLOTHES   The method of wrapping up newborn and very young babies.   The baby was placed diagonally upon a square piece of cloth and the corners were folded over the body and the feet and under the head.   Then the whole bundle was wrapped around with bands of cotton or of silk.   When Jesus was born he was wrapped in swaddling clothes.   Luke 2:7.

SWEDEN   In Sweden the Christmas season is ushered in by St. Lucy on December 13.   Some young girl is chosen to represent this early Christian martyr who was burned at the stake because she refused to give up her faith to marry a pagan.   When the gifts are presented at Christmas, a small rhyme is always given with them. Grot, a rice, cooked in milk, and decorated with cinnamon, is served on Christmas eve.   There is one almond in the grot, and the one who finds it, will be the first to marry, according to tradition.

SWEDEN

SWITZERLAND   Because of the mixed cultures in the land of the Alps, Christmas is observed in varied ways. In most parts St. Nicholas arrives on December 6 and distributes candy and toys.   In some regions "Samichlaus," wearing a mask, furs, and a big white beard, comes with his big bag of toys on the eve of December 5. In other places, it is "Father Christmas" and his wife, Lucy, giving out toys and goodies on December 13. Still in other areas, it is the "Christ Child," traveling with a sleigh pulled by six reindeer, who brings gifts.

SWITZERLAND

T

TALKING ANIMALS, THE   An ancient Christmas legend relates that on the stroke of midnight, Christmas eve, the animals talk among themselves about the glorious birth of Christ. Some of them kneel in devotion, while others stand in their stalls out of reverence to the new King, and others foretell the happenings of the coming year.

TATE, NAHUM   Writer in 1703 of the popular Christmas hymn "While Shepherds Watched Their Flocks By Night."

TAXING   A process of numbering and counting in ancient days.   A census taking.   Luke 2:1-3.

TELESPHORUS   Seventh Bishop of Rome, 128-139 A.D., who ordered Christmas to be celebrated as a solemn feast in 137 A.D.   He died later as a martyr, the observance of the anniversary of Christ's birth being one of his offenses.

TELESPHORUS

TEMPLE The holy place in Jerusalem where Jesus was brought to be presented to the Lord. Luke 2:22, 27.

THOR The Yule-god, among ancient tribes of north European countries, from which the custom of the yule-log originated.

THORN See GLASTONBURY THORN.

TINSEL A shining, metallic, or metal coated material used for decorating the Christmas tree and other Christmas trimming.

TINY TIM Brave, lovable, little character in Charles Dickens' Christmas classic, "A Christmas Carol."

TOYON One of the loveliest of all the Christmas plants. It has delicate, fragrant white blooms and exciting red-colored berries which glow like fire when used in Christmas wreaths. A native of the American west coast, Toyon is called frequently "California Holly."

TOYS Traditional gifts for children at Christmas.

TREASURES The gifts of the Wisemen; gold, frankincense, and myrrh.

TREE See CHRISTMAS TREE.

TURKEY A traditional Christmas dinner very popular in modern times.

TURKEY The baptism of Christ is celebrated in Turkey at the Christmas season. The cross is carried from door to door and many presents are received.

'TWAS THE NIGHT BEFORE CHRISTMAS See VISIT FROM ST. NICHOLAS.

TWELVE DAYS OF CHRISTMAS, THE A traditional English carol celebrating the Christmas season between Christmas day and Epiphany.

TEMPLE

TINY TIM

TURKEY

U

UKRAINE A twelve-course dinner is served on Christmas eve, following a forty-day fast. Christmas is a three-day holiday filled with Church services, visiting friends, singing, and dancing. Although the Ukraine is part of the Union of Soviet Socialist Republics, many of its Christmas customs are patterned on those of Lithuania and Poland by whom they were controlled during the thirteenth century.

TWELVE DAYS OF CHRISTMAS

UNICORN

UNICORN A familiar symbol of our Lord; early accepted as a symbol of purity and therefore especially related to the Virgin and the birth of Jesus.

UNITED STATES Most of the Christmas customs in the United States were imported from European nations; however, there are a few contributions made exclusively from this country. Electric lights on the tree, indoors and outdoors, are an American innovation. The spraying of entire trees with silver, pink, blue, gold and other colors, originated in this country. The present idea of Santa Claus, a combination of St. Nicholas and the Christmas Man, is an American contribution.

V

VIXEN

VAN DYKE, HENRY American Presbyterian Clergyman (1852-1933) born in Germantown, Pennsylvania. Among his many books, he was the author of the Christmas story "The Other Wise Man."

VIRGIN A young unmarried woman. A term used especially in connection with Mary the mother of Jesus. Matthew 1:23.

VIXEN The name of the fourth of Santa Claus' reindeer according to the poem, "A Visit From St. Nicholas" by Clement Moore.

W

WAITS

WADE, JOHN FRANCIS A music copyist, in Douay, France about 1740, considered by some authorities as the author and composer of "O Come, All Ye Faithful."

WAITS A group of street or rustic serenaders who play and sing at night, especially at Christmas, for a few small coins. They are of English origins and up until 1800 they wore a special uniform of blue gowns with red sleeves and caps.

WALES Wales is noted at Christmas for its great choirs of trained voices and its succulent plum puddings. Contests are held all over the country to find the best original Christmas music; and the plum puddings are so well made that they will keep for years.

WASHINGTON

WASHINGTON, GEORGE George Washington made his famous crossing of the Delaware river on Christmas day in 1776. See DECEMBER 25.

WASSAIL An English Christmas drink served in a large bowl, and consisting of roasted apples, ale, sugar, eggs, nutmeg, ginger, and cloves. It was served while hot.

WASSAILING An English phrase used to describe the act of going from house to house singing Christmas carols. Also used to describe any boistrous activity at Christmas.

WASSAIL

WATCHMAN, TELL US OF THE NIGHT A Christmas hymn written by Sir John Bowring (1792-1872), one time a distinguished member of the English Parliament, also Governor of Hong-kong.

WATTS, ISAAC English Congregational Clergyman and hymn writer (1674-1748). Among his over 600 hymns, are the Christmas classics, "Joy to the World" and "Hush, My Dear, Lie Still and Slumber."

WESLEY, CHARLES English Methodist Clergyman, brother of John Wesley, and famous hymn-writer. He was born in 1707, seven days before Christmas. Among the 6,500 hymns which Charles Wesley has written is the Christmas favorite "Hark! the Herald Angels Sing."

WESLEY

WE THREE KINGS OF ORIENT ARE One of the most popular of the recent Christmas carols. Words and music were written in 1857 by Rev. John Henry Hopkins, Jr., rector of Christ Church, Williamsport, Pennsylvania, and son of John Henry Hopkins, the first Episcopalian Bishop of Vermont. See HOPKINS for more detail.

WHILE SHEPHERDS WATCHED THEIR FLOCKS A popular Christmas hymn written in 1703 by Nahum Tate, Poet Laureate of England, as part of a volume entitled "A New Version of the Psalms of David, Fitted to the Tunes Used in Churches" and "Supplement to the New Version."

WHY
CHIMES RANG

WHY THE CHIMES RANG A Christmas classic by Raymond Macdonald Alden. A story of Pedro and Little Brother and the church with a chime of bells that had not rung for many years.

WISEMEN The Kings who came from the East bearing gifts to the Infant Jesus. See MAGI.

WONDERFUL One of the terms for the coming Messiah used by Isaiah in his famed prophecy. Isaiah 9:6.

WORSHIP Reverence paid to someone of merit. The shepherds and the Wisemen came to the manger to worship Jesus.

WISEMEN

WREATH

WREATH A circle of evergreen branches used to decorate the home during the Christmas season. Wreaths are usually made from fir, pine, cedar, hemlock, balsam, or holly and often trimmed with berries, cones, bright leaves and ribbons. They are believed to have developed from the pagan, pre-Christian custom of the use of evergreens to symbolize immortality.

X

XMAS A term for Christmas. The letter "X" is similar in form to the Greek letter "Chi," which is the initial letter of "Christ" or "Christian." Thus "X" is often used alone to symbolize Christ, or with other letters such as Xian for Christian, and Xmas for Christmas.

Y

YEW

YEW An evergreen tree native to Europe, Asia, and Africa, with rich, dark evergreen branches, used as one of the primary Christmas decorations in England and Europe. It is pronounced like the word "you."

YODELING In some parts of Austria, Christmas yodeling is considered a natural way to pay homage to the Christ Child.

YON, PIETRO Composer of Gesu Bambino in 1943. See GESU BAMBINO.

YULE LOG

YULE LOG The oak log, or gnarled stump, brought from the woods on Christmas Eve for the great fireplace. The custom originated in England and was a symbol of warmth and light.

YULETIDE Christmas time or Christmastide.

Z

ZACHARIAS

ZACHARIAS Father of John the Baptist, who prophesied at the birth of his son, about the coming Redeemer of Israel, and how his son would go before him to prepare the way. Luke 1:67-76.

CHRISTMAS IN THE OLD TESTAMENT

6 For unto us a child is born, unto us a son is given: and the government shall be upon his shoulder: and his name shall be called Wonderful, Counsellor, The mighty God, The everlasting Father, The Prince of Peace.

7 Of the increase of *his* government and peace· *there shall be* no end, upon the throne of David, and upon his kingdom, to order it, and to establish it with judgment and with justice from henceforth even for ever. The zeal of the LORD of hosts will perform this. Isaiah 9:6, 7

2 But thou, Beth-lehem Eph-ra-tah, *though* thou be little among the thousands of Judah, *yet* out of thee shall he come forth unto me *that is* to be ruler in Israel; whose goings forth *have been* from of old, from everlasting. Micah 5:2

MARY'S MAGNIFICAT
Luke 1:46-55

46 And Mary said, My soul doth magnify the Lord,

47 And my spirit hath rejoiced in God my Saviour.

48 For he hath regarded the low estate of his handmaiden: for, behold, from henceforth all generations shall call me blessed.

49 For he that is mighty hath done to me great things; and holy *is* his name.

50 And his mercy *is* on them that fear him from generation to generation.

51 He hath shewed strength with his arm; he hath scattered the proud in the imagination of their hearts.

52 He hath put down the mighty from *their* seats, and exalted them of low degree.

53 He hath filled the hungry with good things; and the rich. he hath sent empty away.

54 He hath holpen his servant Israel, in remembrance of *his* mercy;

55 As he spake to our fathers, to Abraham, and to his seed for ever.

NATIVITY SCRIPTURES

Luke 2:1-16

1 And it came to pass in those days, that there went out a decree from Caesar Augustus, that all the world should be taxed.

2 (*And* this taxing was first made when Cy-re-ni-us was governor of Syria.)

3 And all went to be taxed, every one into his own city.

4 And Joseph also went up from Galilee, out of the city of Nazareth, into Judaea, unto the city of David, which is called Bethlehem; (because he was of the house and lineage of David:)

5 To be taxed with Mary his espoused wife, being great with child.

6 And so it was, that, while they were there, the days were accomplished that she should be delivered.

7 And she brought forth her first-born son, and wrapped him in swaddling clothes, and laid him in a manger; because there was no room for them in the inn.

8 And there were in the same country shepherds abiding in the field, keeping watch over their flock by night.

9 And, lo, the angel of the Lord came upon them, and the glory of the Lord shone round about them: and they were sore afraid.

10 And the angel said unto them, Fear not: for, behold, I bring you good tidings of great joy, which shall be to all people.

11 For unto you is born this day in the city of David a Saviour, which is Christ the Lord.

12 And this *shall be* a sign unto you; Ye shall find the babe wrapped in swaddling clothes, lying in a manger.

13 And suddenly there was with the angel a multitude of the heavenly host praising God, and saying,

14 Glory to God in the highest, and on earth peace, good will toward men.

15 And it came to pass, as the angels were gone away from them into heaven, the shepherds said one to another, Let us now go even unto Bethlehem, and see this thing which is come to pass, which the Lord hath made known unto us.

16 And they came with haste, and found Mary, and Joseph, and the babe lying in a manger.

SCRIPTURE OF THE MAGI

Matthew 2:1-12

1 Now when Jesus was born in Bethlehem of Judaea in the days of Herod the king, behold, there came wise men from the east to Jerusalem,

2 Saying, Where is he that is born King of the Jews? for we have seen his star in the east, and are come to worship him.

3 When Herod the king had heard *these things*, he was troubled, and all Jerusalem with him.

4 And when he had gathered all the chief priests and scribes of the people together, he demanded of them where Christ should be born.

5 And they said unto him, In Bethlehem of Judaea: for thus it is written by the prophet.

6 And thou Bethlehem, *in* the land of Judah, art not the least among the princes of Judah: for out of thee shall come a Governor, that shall rule my people Israel.

7 Then Herod, when he had privily called the wise men, inquired of them diligently what time the star appeared.

8 And he sent them to Bethlehem, and said, Go and search diligently for the young child; and when ye have found *him*, bring me word again, that I may come and worship him also.

9 When they had heard the king, they departed; and, lo, the star, which they saw in the east, went before them, till it came and stood over where the young child was.

10 When they saw the star, they rejoiced with exceeding great joy.

11 And when they were come into the house, they saw the young child with Mary his mother, and fell down, and worshipped him: and when they had opened their treasures, they presented unto him gifts; gold, and frankincense, and myrrh.

12 And being warned of God in a dream that they should not return to Herod, they departed into their own country another way.

A CHRONOLOGICAL LIST OF CHRISTMAS
CAROLS AND THEIR DATES

Year	Composer	Title
368	St. Hilary	Jesus Light of All the Nations
1250	Thibaud	In Excelsis Gloria!
1274	St. Bonaventure	O Come, All Ye Faithful
1400	Traditional	I Saw Three Ships
1521	Traditional	The Boar's Head Carol
1535	Luther	From Heaven Above to Earth I Come
1641	de Brebeuf	Huron Indian Carol
1703	Tate	While Shepherds Watched Their Flocks
1719	Watts	Joy To The World
1741	Handel	The Messiah
1816	Montgomery	Angels From the Realms of Glory
1818	Mohr	Silent Night! Holy Night!
1825	Bowring	Watchman Tell Us of the Night
1833	Traditional	The First Noel
1850	Sears	It Came Upon the Midnight Clear
1856	Adams	O Holy Night
1856	Wesley	Hark! The Herald Angels Sing
1857	Hopkins	We Three Kings of Orient Are
1863	Longfellow	Christmas Bells
1867	Stainer	God Rest You Merry, Gentlemen
1868	Brooks	O Little Town of Bethlehem
1943	Martin & Yon	Gesu Bambino

CHRISTMAS STORIES AND THEIR AUTHORS

Author	Title
Alden	Why the Chimes Rang
Anderson	The Fir Tree
Dickens	A Christmas Carol
Field	The Sugar Plum Tree
Irving	Christmas Sketch Book
Lagerlof	Legend of the Christmas Rose
Moore	A Visit From St. Nicholas
Rossetti	Poem A Christmas Carol
Van Dyke	The Other Wise Man

CHRISTMAS PAINTINGS AND THEIR ARTISTS

Artist	School	Title
Barocci	Italian	The Nativity
Botticelli	Italian	Adoration of the Magi
Correggio	Italian	The Holy Night
Da Vinci	Italian	Madonna of the Rocks
		Adoration of the Magi
Dolci	Italian	Madonna
Durer	German	Adoration of the Magi
El Greco	Spanish	Adoration of the Shepherds
		The Holy Family
Fra Angelico	Italian	The Nativity
Fra Lippo Lippi	Italian	The Adoration
		The Nativity
Georgione	Italian	Adoration of the Shepherds
Giotto	Italian	Flight Into Egypt
Lerolle	French	Arrival of the Shepherds
Lorenzo	Italian	The Nativity
Luini	Italian	The Nativity
Maratta	Italian	The Holy Family
		The Holy Night
Michelangelo	Italian	The Holy Family
		Pitti Madonna Relief
Murillo	Spanish	Adoration of the Shepherds
		Flight Into Egypt
Raphael	Italian	Madonna of the Chair
Rembrandt	Dutch	Adoration of the Shepherds
Reubens	Dutch	Adoration of the Magi
Sassetta	Italian	Journey of the Magi
Titian	Italian	The Holy Family
Van Dyke	Dutch	Flight Into Egypt

"MERRY CHRISTMAS" ALL OVER THE WORLD

Country	Merry Christmas!
Armenia	"Schenorhavor Dzenount"
Belgium	"Vrolijke Kerstmis"
Czechoslovakia	"Vesele Vanoce"
Denmark	"Glaedelig Jul"
England	"Merry Christmas"
Finland	"Hauskaa Joulua"
France	"Joyeux Noel"
Germany	"Froehliche Weinachten"
Greece	"Kala Christougena"
Holland	"Zalig Kerstfeest"
Hungary	"Boldog Karacsony"
Ireland	"Nodlaig Nait Cugat"
Italy	"Bono Natale"
Lithuania	"Linksmu Kaledu"
Mexico	"Feliz Navidad"
Norway	"Gledelig Jul"
Poland	"Wesolych Swiat"
Russia	"S Rozhestvom Khristovym"
Spain	"Felices Pascuas"
Sweden	"Glad Jul"
Ukraine	"Chrystos Rozdzajetsia Slawyte Jeho"
Yugoslavia	"Sretan Bozic"

A VISIT FROM SAINT NICHOLAS
by Clement C. Moore

'Twas the night before Christmas, when all through the house
Not a creature was stirring, not even a mouse;
The stockings were hung by the chimney with care,
In hopes that St. Nicholas soon would be there;

The children were nestled all snug in their beds,
While visions of sugar-plums danced in their heads;
And Mamma in her kerchief, and I in my cap,
Had just settled our brains for a long winter's nap,

When out on the lawn there arose such a clatter,
I sprang from my bed to see what was the matter.
Away to the window I flew like a flash,
Tore open the shutters and threw up the sash.

The moon, on the breast of the new-fallen snow,
Gave a luster of mid-day to objects below;
When, what to my wandering eyes should appear,
But a miniature sleigh, and eight tiny reindeer,
With a little old driver, so lively and quick,
I knew in a moment it must be St. Nick.

More rapid than eagles his coursers they came,
And he whistled, and shouted, and called them by name:
"Now, Dasher! now, Dancer! now, Prancer and Vixen!
On, Comet! on, Cupid! on, Donder and Blitzen!
To the top of the porch, to the top of the wall!
Now, dash away, dash away, dash away, all!"

As dry leaves that before the wild hurricane fly,
When they meet with an obstacle, mount to the sky,
So, up to the house-top the coursers they flew,
With a sleigh full of toys--, and St. Nicholas, too.

And then in a twinkling I heard on the roof
The prancing and pawing of each little hoof.
As I drew in my head, and was turning around,
Down the chimney St. Nicholas came with a bound.

He was dressed all in fur from his head to his foot,
And his clothes were all tarnished with ashes and soot;
His droll little mouth was drawn up like a bow,
And the beard on his chin was as white as the snow.

The stump of a pipe he held tight in his teeth,
And the smoke it encircled his head like a wreath;
A bundle of toys he had flung on his back,
And he looked like a peddler just opening his pack.

His eyes how they twinkled! His dimples how merry!
His cheeks were like roses, his nose like a cherry;
He had a broad face and a little round belly
That shook when he laughed, like a bowlful of jelly.

He was chubby and plump--, a right jolly old elf;
And I laughed when I saw him, in spite of myself.
A wink of his eye, and a twist of his head,
Soon gave me to know I had nothing to dread.

He spoke not a word, but went straight to his work,
And filled all the stockings; then turned with a jerk
And laying his finger aside of his nose,
And giving a nod, up the chimney he rose.

He sprang to his sleigh, to his team gave a whistle,
And away they all flew like the down of a thistle;
But I heard him exclaim ere he drove out of sight,
Happy Christmas to all, and to all a goodnight!"

CHRISTMAS CHRONOLOGY

DATE   EVENT

4 B.C.	The birth of Jesus at Bethlehem
368	First hymn of the Nativity written
400	The first ringing Church bell
604	Christmas introduced to England by St. Augustine of Canterbury
754	Christmas introduced to Germany by St. Boniface
865	Christmas introduced to Scandinavian countries by St. Ansgar
1224	St. Francis of Assisi assembles first living creche on Christmas Eve
1274	"O Come All Ye Faithful" "Adeste Fideles" written by St. Bonaventure
1400	Della Robbia plaques first painted
1492	Columbus celebrates first Christmas in America
1521	Boar's Head Carol written in England
1604	Ancient Strassburg manuscript mentions use of Christmas trees
1620	Pilgrims begin erection of colony on Christmas day
1641	First American Christmas hymn written. Hymn to the Huron Indians
1685	Christmas Oratorio composer Johann Sebastian Bach born
1710	First Christmas trees set up in America by Germans
1719	Joy to the World written by Isaac Watts
1741	Bethlehem, Pa. founded on Christmas Eve
1741	"Messiah" written by Handel
1776	George Washington crosses the Delaware on Christmas day
1818	Silent Night, Holy Night written in Austria
1822	Clement Moore writes A Visit From St. Nicholas
1843	"A Christmas Carol" written by Charles Dickens
1846	First Christmas card published by Joseph Cundall
1875	Louis Prang creates first American Christmas card
1896	"The Other Wiseman" written by Henry Van Dyke
1903	Christmas seal conceived in Denmark
1907	Christmas seal introduced to America
1908	Christmas carol singing organized at Boston
1909	First lighted Community tree in Pasadena, California
1926	Red Wood tree made Nation's Christmas tree
1943	"Gesu Bambino" composed by Martin and Yon

Part III—Hymns of The Church

Chapter VII
Who's Who of Hymn Writers

ADAMS, John Quincy (ăd'amz), 1767-1848, Unitarian. The son of the second President of the United States was born in Braintree, Massachusetts, in 1767. He graduated from Harvard University, and during a period of seven years was appointed minister to the Netherlands, England and Prussia successively. In 1806 he was made professor of Rhetoric at Harvard, and in 1809 appointed minister to Russia. He declined an appointment to the Supreme Court, and in 1817 became Secretary of State under President Monroe. Ultimately he was elected to the office of President of the United States, where he served for one term from 1825 to 1829, and in 1831 was elected to the House of Representatives from Massachusetts. He wrote, among other things, "Poems of Religion and Society" and "Version of the Psalms" as well as hymns. He died very suddenly on February 21, 1848.

> **Sure to the Mansions of the Blest** **1803**
> **Alas! How Swift the Moments Fly** **1839**

ADAMS, Mrs. Sarah Flower (ăd'amz), 1805-1848, Unitarian. Born Sarah Flower in Harlow, England, February 22, 1805, Sarah Adams lost her mother very early through consumption. Both she and her sister Eliza grew up with frail health, and were always very close, even after Sarah moved to London when she married William Bridges Adams, inventor and civil engineer. In 1837 Sarah very successfully played Lady MacBeth in London, but ill health forced her to abandon the theatre and  she concentrated on a literary career. Her personality was charming, and both mentally and physically she was considered remarkable. When Eliza was stricken with tuberculosis in 1847, Sarah nursed her and contracted the same sickness. She died August 11, 1848, twenty months after the death of Eliza.

> **Nearer, My God to Thee** **1841**
> **Part in Peace** **1841**

ADDISON, Joseph (ăd'ĭ-s'n), 1672-1719, Anglican. Born May 1, 1672, in Milston, Wiltshire, England, Joseph Addison was the son of the Dean of Lichfield and nephew of the Bishop of Bristol. He attended Charterhouse and Magdalen College, Oxford, receiving his B.A. in 1691 and his M.A. two years later. Having studied law and politics at Oxford, he held the positions of Commissioner of Appeals, Undersecretary of State, Secretary to the Lord Lieutenant of Ireland, and Chief Secretary of  Ireland successively. In a long literary career he became famous for his contributions to the "Tatler" and the "Spectator" as well as "The Guardian" and the "Freeholder." He also wrote dramas, including his tragedy "Cato." When he married the Countess of Warwick in 1716 his literary career was terminated. He suffered from asthma, dropsy, and the ill will of the Countess' son, the Earl of Warwick. Three years after his marriage he died in Kensington, on June 17, 1719.

> **The Spacious Firmament on High** **1712**
> **When All Thy Mercies, O My God** **1712**

ALEXANDER, Mrs. Cecil F. (ăl-ĕg-zăn′dẽr), 1818-1895, Anglican. Cecil Frances Humphreys was born in Ireland in 1818. At thirty-two she married the Rev. William Alexander, an outstanding worker for the Church of Ireland, who eventually became Archbishop of Armagh, Primate of Ireland. Mrs. Alexander was a faithful churchgoer and a supporter of many public benefits, such as the Home for Fallen Women. An expert in child psychology, she wrote most of her 400 hymns for children. She died at the age of 77, on October 12, 1895.

    There Is a Green Hill Far Away.............1848
    Jesus Calls Us! O'er the Tumult 1852

ALFORD, Dean Henry (ăl′fẽrd), 1810-1871, Anglican. Henry Alford, born in London, England on October 7, 1810 and educated at Trinity College, Cambridge, was probably one of the most gifted men of his day. During his very active lifetime he served as Dean of Canterbury; wrote fifty religious books, including four volumes of the Greek Testament; founded the influential "Contemporary Review" which he edited for a number of years; became a successful poet, artist and musician. Through his untiring devotion to the Christian cause he made many worthwhile contributions both to a better understanding of the Bible and to Christian Hymnody. Because of his strenuous efforts and unlimited activities he suffered a physical breakdown in 1870, and died on January 12, 1871.

    Come, Ye Thankful People, Come...........1844
    Ten Thousand Times Ten Thousand...........1867

AMBROSE, of Milan (ăm′brōz), 340-397, Early Christian. Born in Trier, a city in the Roman provinces, Ambrose was the son of a Roman noble, governor of Gallia Narbonensis. After the death of his father, Ambrose moved to Rome, where he was educated. Later he went to Milan to practice law, and moved steadily up in governmental positions, eventually becoming governor of Upper Italy. When Bishop Auxentius died, Ambrose was made Bishop by acclamation, despite the fact that he had not been baptized. His personality was magnetic and confidence-inspiring, and his generosity such that upon becoming Bishop he sold his property and distributed the profits among the poor. In 384 Ambrose revised the music of the church, thereby earning the title of "Father of Church Music." His hymns spread through western Europe, and soon even those who held unorthodox religious views were singing them. He died on Easter Eve, 397.

    O Splendor of God's Glory Bright........4th Cent.
    Savior of the Nations, Come............4th Cent.

BABCOCK, Rev. Maltbie Davenport (băb'cŏk), 1858-1901, Presbyterian. Maltbie Babcock was born August 3, 1858 in Syracuse, New York of a socially prominent family. He was graduated from Syracuse University and later went to Auburn Theological Seminary, after which he became an ordained minister of the Presbyterian Church. A skilled musician, he played organ, piano and violin; and many of his verses were set to music  after his death. He enjoyed writing poetry, but all of his works were published posthumously, under the title "Thoughts for Everyday Living." In the midst of a Mediterranean cruise, he died in Naples at the age of 43, on May 18, 1901.

> Gaily the Bells Are Ringing 1899
> This Is My Father's World 1901

BACON, Rev. Leonard (bā'kŭn), 1801-1881, Congregationalist. Leonard Bacon was born February 19, 1802 and spent his first years on an Indian reservation in Detroit, Michigan, where his father was a missionary. At the age of 9 he went to live with an uncle in Hartford, Connecticut, and later attended Yale College, from which he graduated in 1820. From Yale, Bacon continued on to Andover Theological Seminary, to become a clergyman. This dedicated man of letters was a pastor  for 41 years, and spent an additional 15 years as a professor at Yale Divinity School. He was well known for his writings and lectures against slavery, and while still a theological student he had his first book published, "Hymns and Sacred Songs for the Monthly Concert." After a long and active life he died at his home in New Haven, Conn., on December 23, 1881.

> O God, Beneath Thy Guiding Hand 1833
> Hail, Tranquil Hour of Closing Day 1845

BAKER, Rev. Sir Henry Williams (bā'kẽr), 1821-1877, Anglican. The son of Admiral Henry Loraine Baker, Henry Williams Baker was born in London in 1821. He attended Trinity College, Cambridge, receiving his B.A. in 1844 and his M.A. in 1847. He was ordained a priest in 1846 and made Vicar of Monkland (near Leominster) in Herefordshire in 1851. He was editor of "Hymns Ancient and Modern" and wrote thirty-three hymns of his own. In 1859 he succeeded to his father's baronetcy, and died 18 years later, in 1877.

> Praise, Oh, Praise, Our God and King 1861
> The King of Love My Shepherd Is 1868

BARING-GOULD, Rev. Sabine (bâr'ing-gŏŏld), 1834-1924, Anglican. Born in Devonshire, England in 1834, Sabine Baring-Gould was raised in an aristocratic atmosphere. As eldest son he inherited a large estate and lived well as lord of the manor, and respected clergyman. Despite his social position, he fell in love with a beautiful young mill-hand, had her educated, and then married her. They had fifteen children. One of the most prolific of the English writers, he was successful as poet, translator, prose and fiction writer (his works include "Lives of the Saints" in 15 volumes), composer of two books of hymns and two valuable collections of English folk songs. The catalog of the British Museum lists more titles by him than by any other author of his era. He died on January 2, 1924.

Onward, Christian Soldiers.................**1865**
Now the Day Is Over......................**1865**

BARLOW, Joel (Bär'lō), 1755-1812, Presbyterian. The "ingenious Mr. Barlow of Connecticut" as he was called, was born in Reddington, Connecticut. He received his B.A. degree from Yale University in 1778 and intended studying for the law. The American Revolution was in progress at the time of his graduation, and he took a short cut to the ministry by becoming an Army Chaplain. At the end of the war he returned to Hartford, Connecticut and was admitted to the bar in 1786. This proved unsuccessful and in 1788 he went to France. He moved to London, where he met Thomas Paine and gradually became a political and religious radical. He returned to America in 1795, and was sent to Algiers as consul, proving himself to be a statesman as well as a writer. In 1811, President Madison appointed him Minister to France, a post he held until his death in December, 1812. He was buried in Poland.

Awake, My Soul, to Sound His Praise........**1786**
Lord, Thou Hast Scourged Our Guilty Land....**1786**

BATES, Katherine Lee (bāts), 1859-1929, No Denominational Affiliation. Born in Falmouth, Massachusetts, the daughter and granddaughter of clergymen, Katharine Lee Bates received her earliest education at a village school. When her family moved to Wellesley Hills in 1871 her schooling was continued at Wellesley High School, Newton High School, and finally Wellesley College. In 1880, after earning her B.A. degree she began a teaching career at Natick High School; then Dana Hall; and eventually Wellesley College. After studying at Oxford University she became head of the English department at Wellesley College. The degree of Litt.D. was conferred on her by Middlebury, Oberlin and Wellesley Colleges. Approximately two dozen of her works were published, including books of poetry, a school textbook, and a modern "Canterbury Tales." She died at Wellesley in March, 1929.

O Beautiful for Spacious Skies.............**1893**
Dear God, Our Father, at Thy Knee Confessing..**1926**

BAXTER, Rev. Richard (băk'stẽr), **1615-1691, Presbyterian.** Born in the small village of Rowton in Shropshire, England in 1615, Richard Baxter received an erratic education from private tutors and his own love for books. He was unable to realize his desire to attend a University, and instead obtained a position in the Court of Charles I. This was short lived, however, for he was by nature a serious man and soon returned to his studying. At twenty-three he was ordained. During the Great Rebellion he served as Chaplain in Cromwell's army, and wrote his first work, the success of which encouraged him to later literary efforts. After the Restoration in 1660 he was made Chaplain to King Charles II. As leader of the Presbyterian party he was asked to reform the traditional Prayer Book, and within 14 days created a replacement instead of a mere revision. He died in December, 1691.

> **Ye Holy Angels Bright** **1672**
> **Lord, It Belongs Not to My Care** **1681**

BENSON, Rev. Louis FitzGerald (bĕn's'n), **1855-1930, Presbyterian.** Louis FitzGerald Benson was born in Philadelphia, Pennsylvania in 1855, and graduated from the University of Pennsylvania in 1874 at the age of nineteen. He practiced law for a number of years, but eventually turned to the ministry and became pastor of the Presbyterian Church of the Redeemer in Germantown, Pennsylvania, in 1888. He remained at this church until 1894, at which time he began to devote his energies to literary and church work in Philadelphia. He edited several hymnbooks, becoming one of the leading American authorities of his day on hymnology. Dr. Benson lectured and wrote on his subject, and collected a hymnological library of 8,000 volumes, the largest in the country. His own hymns reflect the spirit of the times. He died in 1930.

> **O Thou Whose Feet Have Climbed Life's Hill** . . **1894**
> **The Sun Is on the Land and Sea** **1897**

BERNARD OF CLAIRVAUX (bẽr-närd', klẽr-vō), **1091-1153, Early Christian.** Bernard, the future Abbott of Clairvaux, was born at Fontaine in Burgundy, France in 1091, of a noble family. At the age of twenty-two he joined the new Cistercian monastery at Citeaux, Burgundy, and through his influence it was filled to overflowing within three years. He led a colony into a barren valley known as the "Valley of Wormwood," changed the name to Clairvaux (Bright Valley), and it flourished. He was offered many high offices and rewards, but remained in his valley influencing and inspiring the Pope, the German Emperor, and the kings of both France and England. Martin Luther called him "The best monk that ever lived, whom I love beyond all the rest put together . . ." He died in 1153, at the age of sixty-two.

> **Jesus, the Very Thought of Thee** . . . . . . **ca. 1091-1153**
> **O Sacred Head, Now Wounded** . . . . **ca. 1091-1153**

BERNARD OF CLUNY (bĕr-närd', kloo'ny), 12th century, Early Christian. Bernard of Cluny, sometimes referred to as Bernard of Morlaix, was born of English parentage in what is variously called Murles, Morlas or Morval, in France. Very little is known about his life, partly due to the fact that he was overshadowed by a famous contemporary, Bernard of Clairvaux. He spent most of his life at Cluny, then a splendid and well-known abbey in France. There he wrote his 3,000-line satire "De Contemptu Mundi" from which many of his hymns came, as well as sermons and various other works including the poem "Mariale." He lived and died in the 12th Century A.D.

Brief Life Is Here Our Portion . . . . **ca. 1140**
Jerusalem the Golden . . . . **ca. 1145**

BICKERSTETH, Rev. Edward Henry (bĭk'ĕr-stĕth), 1825-1906, Anglican. Born in London, England on January 25, 1825 of a family prominent in various fields, Edward Henry Bickersteth was educated at Trinity College, Cambridge, where he received his B.A. and M.A. degrees. In 1848 he was ordained, and became curate, successively, of Banningham, Norfolk, and Christ Church (Tunbridge Wells); next he became rector of Hinton-Martel, then vicar of Christ Church, Hampstead, then Dean of Gloucester; and from 1885 until 1900, the year of his retirement, he was Bishop of Exeter. He authored 12 books including sermons, hymnals, and a good deal of widely-discussed poetry. Many of his hymns are in use today. He died in London on May 16, 1906.

O God, the Rock of Ages **1860**
Peace, Perfect Peace **1875**

BLANCHARD, Rev. Ferdinand Quincy (blăn'-ch'd), 1876-19—, Congregationalist. Dr. Blanchard was born on July 23, 1876 in Jersey City, New Jersey; educated at New High School (Massachusetts) and Amherst College, where he received his B. A. in 1898, and Yale University, where he received his B.D. in 1901. In 1918 Amherst conferred a D.D. on him, and the following year Oberlin College conferred on him the same degree. He was ordained as a Congregational minister in 1901, the same year that he was married. Apart from his ministry, Dr. Blanchard served as trustee of Fisk University; member of the executive committee of the American Missionary Association; member of the Prudential Committee of the American Board of Commissioners for Foreign Missions; moderator of the Congregational Christian churches for the term ending 1944. He has written several books, not all of which deal with religion, in addition to a number of hymns.

O Child of Lowly Manger Birth **1906**
Before the Cross of Jesus **1928**

BLISS, Philip Paul (blĭs), 1838-1876, Congregationalist. Born at Rome, Pennsylvania, in 1838, Bliss was raised in a Christian atmosphere. He was always a lover of music, and at the age of 26 went to Chicago and became associated with the Root and Cady Music house. There he wrote Sunday-school songs and melodies, and conducted musical institutes. By the age of 36 he was doing successful evangelical work with Major Whittle. He was an uncommonly handsome man, with a good  physique, a moving bass voice, and strength of character coupled with sensitivity and tenderness. His most valuable hymns were works of inspiration rather than of studied deliberation. He gained his ideas for the hymns from incidents, conversations and sermons, often thinking of hymn words and melodies simultaneously. On Christmas Day, 1876, he and his wife made a trip to his old home in Rome. Returning to Chicago four days later, the train on which they were traveling was wrecked and both Bliss and his wife were killed. The people of Rome erected a monument to his memory in the Rome cemetery.

      Almost Persuaded **1871**
      Brightly Beams Our Father's Mercy **1874**

BODE, Rev. John Ernest (Bōd), 1816-1874, Anglican. Clergyman, educator and poet, John Ernest Bode was born in London, England, on February 23, 1816. He was educated at Eton, Charterhouse, and at Christ Church, Oxford, where he received his B.A. and M.A. degrees. At Oxford he was the winner of the Hertford Scholarship, and from 1837 to 1843 was Tutor of Christ Church. Ordained in 1841, he became rector of Westwell, Oxfordshire in 1847 and of Castle Camps, Cambridgeshire  thirteen years later. Invited to give the Bampton lectures at Oxford in 1855, he wrote and published in addition to the lectures 3 books of hymns and poems. He died in Castle Camps on October 6, 1874.

      Sweetly the Sabbath Bell **1860**
      O Jesus, I Have Promised **1868**

BONAR, Rev. Horatius (bō'när), 1808-1889, Presbyterian. One of a long line of ministers, Horatius Bonar was born in Edinburgh, Scotland, on December 19, 1808. He studied at the Edinburgh High School under Thomas Chalmers, who had a great effect on his intellectual and spiritual outlook. After attending the University of Edinburgh he began pastorate work at Leith, was ordained at the age of 30 and placed in charge of the North Parish at Kelso. During a zealous  career of church work he was active in organizing the Free Church of Scotland, and in 1883 was elected moderator of the General Assembly, a great honor. A Calvinist, he was known for his unwavering devotion to his work. He died on July 31, 1889, in Edinburgh.

      Go, Labor On; Spend and Be Spent **1843**
      I Heard the Voice of Jesus Say **1846**

BOWIE, Rev. Walter Russell (bōo'ē), 1882-19—, Episcopalian. Born in Richmond, Virginia, October 8, 1882, Walter Russell Bowie attended Harvard University, where he received his B.A. degree in 1904 with Phi Beta Kappa honors, and his M.A. degree in 1905. In 1908 he received his B.D. degree from the Theological Seminary in Virginia, and was ordained deacon of the Protestant Episcopal Church. The following year he married Jean Lavarack, (by whom he eventually had four children), and was ordained a priest. Feeling he had work to be done he declined his election to the episcopacy and in 1939 became professor of Practical Theology at Union Theological Seminary in New York, a position he still holds. Dr. Bowie is the author of many religious books.

O Holy City Seen of John.................1909
God of Nations, Who From Dawn...........1913

BOWRING, Sir John bou'rĭng), 1792-1872, Unitarian. Born October 17, 1792 at Exeter, England, the son of a woolen goods manufacturer, John Bowring left school at the age of fourteen to help his father in business. As most of the business was carried on abroad, he set himself to studying languages and by the time he was sixteen was proficient in five. By the end of his life he had studied two hundred languages, and could speak one hundred. His cultural achievements include translations into English from twenty-two languages and dialects. He was also a biographer, naturalist and financier, having great interest in the decimal system of money. Sir John Bowring's social and political accomplishments were numerous, including service in Parliament for two terms, consular appointments in seven different countries, governorships of Hong Kong, minister plenipotentiary and envoy extraordinary to Europe for the kingdoms of Siam and Hawaiian Islands. He was knighted in 1854 by Queen Victoria. His death occurred at Exeter, November 23, 1872.

In the Cross of Christ I Glory...............1825
Watchman, Tell Us of the Night............1825

BRIDGES, Matthew (brĭj'ĕz), 1800-1894, R. C. Matthew Bridges was born at Malden, Essex, England on July 14, 1800. He was brought up in the Church of England, and at the age of twenty-eight wrote the controversial "The Roman Empire under Constantine the Great," attacking the Roman Catholic Church. In later years, however, influenced by the Oxford Movement, he himself became a Roman Catholic. His main interests were history and literature, and among his published works are three books of religious poetry, from which his more popular hymns were taken. He spent his last years in the province of Quebec, Canada, but died in England at Sidmouth, Devon., October 6, 1894.

Behold the Lamb of God.....................1848
Crown Him With Many Crowns.............1851

BRONTE, Anne (brŏn'tāy), 1820-1849, Anglican.
The youngest of the three famous Bronte sisters, Anne was born in Yorkshire, England in 1820. With her sisters she attended a boarding school for clergymen's daughters, and later taught as a governess. In 1846 her poems were published under the pseudonym "Acton Bell." Anne Bronte wrote "Agnes Grey" with material based on her experiences as a governess; and her second novel, published three years later in 1848, was "The Tenant  of Wildfell Hall." Both novels were unsuccessful at the' time of their publication, but showed a decided talent. Her hymns were published posthumously. She died at the age of 29.

> Spirit of Truth, Be Thou My Guide............1873
> My God, O Let Me Call Thee Mine..........1879

BROOKS, Rev. Phillips (brŏoks), 1835-1893, Episcopalian. This very remarkable man was born in Boston on December 13, 1835. He attended Boston Latin School and Harvard University, where he received his B.A. degree in 1855. After an unsuccessful attempt at teaching Latin, he began his studies for the ministry at the Episcopal Theological Seminary in Virginia. In 1869, after a 10-year period in Philadelphia, he returned to  Boston to the start of a long and distinguished career. He declined several professorships at Harvard, but finally was prevailed upon to become Bishop of Massachusetts in 1891, a position in which he served less than two years. He wrote several hymns for Easter and Christmas, and is known for his Yale "Lectures on Preaching," 1877. He died on January 23, 1893.

> O Little Town of Bethlehem.................1868
> God Hath Sent His Angels..................1877

BRYANT, William Cullen (brī'ant), 1794-1878, Baptist. Born in Cummington, Massachusetts on November 3, 1794, William Cullen Bryant was the son of a cultured, educated country physician, who occasionally wrote poetry. He grew up in an atmosphere of literature and religion. His first poem was written when he was eight; a satirical poem was published when he was thirteen; his famous "Thanatopsis" came off the press when he  was but eighteen. He studied at Williams College, and was admitted to the bar in 1815. For ten years he practiced law in Great Barrington, Mass., then gave it up to devote himself to writing. He had always held deep religious convictions, though shrinking from the strict theology of New England, and in 1858 while spending the winter in Italy, he formally joined the Baptist church. Throughout his life he made many contributions to various churches; contributed verse and prose to many newspapers; wrote many hymns that have enjoyed wide circulation both in America and England. He died July 12, 1878, on Long Island, New York.

> Thou, Whose Unmeasured Temple Stands......1835
> All That in This Wide World We See.........1836

BUNYAN, Rev. John (bŭn'yan), 1628-1688, Baptist. John Bunyan was born November 30, 1628, in Elstow, England, the son of a tinker. He was trained in his father's craft, but in 1644 was drafted into military service. After two years of service he was discharged and married a very pious woman. His religious experiences described in his "Grace Abounding" were taking place about this time, and in 1653 he joined a Christian fellowship in Bedford, England. He moved to Bedford in 1655, and by popular demand became the pastor of the Baptist church, which led to his preaching in various villages around Bedford. A gifted speaker, he became so powerful that the government arrested him in 1660, and during his imprisonment he wrote 6 books as well as some smaller works. Released from prison in 1672 by the Declaration of Indulgence, he was granted a license to preach, but was imprisoned again 3 years later when the Declaration was withdrawn. During this second imprisonment he wrote the first part of "The Pilgrim's Progress," which was published in 1678. He died on August 31, 1688, and was buried in Bunhill Fields.

He That Is Down Need Fear no Fall.........1684
Who Would True Valour See...............1684

BURNS, Rev. James Drummond (bûrnz), 1823-1864, Presbyterian. James Drummond Burns was born in Edinburgh, Scotland on February 18, 1823. After receiving his M.A. degree from the University of Edinburgh he followed his theological teacher, Dr. Thomas Chalmers, into the Free Church of Scotland in 1843. Despite some trouble in his opening sermon at Dunblane, Scotland, he served there until 1847, when he was forced to resign because of a lung condition. He traveled to Madeira, where his health improved enough for him to take over the newly organized church in Hampstead, England. He wrote 40 original hymns, and authored the article on "Hymns" for the eighth edition of the Encyclopedia Britannica. He died in Mentone, France on Nov. 27, 1864, and was buried at Highgate Cemetery, London.

Still With Thee, O My God................1857
Thou, Lord, Art Love, and Everywhere......1858

BYROM, John (bī'rŭm), 1691-1763, Anglican. John Byrom was born in the Old Shambles, Manchester, England. He attended King's School; Merchant Taylors' School; Trinity College, Cambridge, where he received his B.A. in 1711 and his M.A. in 1715; the medical college at Montpelier University, France. In 1715, offered a fellowship at Cambridge that would necessitate his ordination, he declined and went instead to live in France, where he studied mysticism. Upon returning to London he decided against practicing medicine, and began to write poetry. His writings included religious studies, poems, and hymns, as well as humorous verse. He died in 1763.

Christians, Awake! Salute the Happy Morn....1750
My Spirit Longs for Thee...................1773

CARY, Alice, 1820-1871; Phoebe, 1824-1871 (kâr'y), Universalist. The two sisters were born on a farm near Cincinnati, Ohio—Alice in 1820 and Phoebe in 1824. From the beginning they had to struggle for an education, as they were discouraged by their stepmother, who forbade the use of candles for night study, and there was a dearth of books available to them. Their first attempts to write poetry were successful, and many appeared in magazines and papers. They moved to New York in 1852, where they lived economically with Alice doing most of the writing that kept them alive. Eventually their lives became more comfortable through their published work, but still Alice kept on writing until her weak constitution collapsed under the strain and she died in 1871, leaving only one memorable hymn for posterity. Phoebe, always in perfect health, declined steadily after her sister's death, and died the same year.

Phoebe

Alice

    One Sweetly Solemn Thought........1852 (Phoebe)
    A Crown of Glory Bright.........1868 (Alice)

CENNICK, Rev. John (sĕn'ĭk), 1718-1755, Moravian. Born December 12, 1718 in Berkshire, England of Quaker stock, John Cennick was brought up in the Church of England. He was converted to Methodism at the age of 19, became a preacher, and was eventually given charge of the school founded by Wesley for the children of coal miners. He joined out-of-door evangelistic tours with Howell Harris, the Welsh revivalist, and by 1741, having discovered his talent for poetry, had written enough hymns to make a small book. Soon his religious views changed again, and he became a Moravian. On July 4, 1755 he died in London, at the age of 37.

    Children of the Heavenly King..............1742
    Cast Thy Burden on the Lord.................1745

CHISHOLM, Thomas O. (chĭz'm), 1866-1960, Methodist. Thomas Chisholm was born in the back woods of Kentucky in 1866, and grew up there on a small farm. At the age of 16 he became a country schoolteacher and six years later co-editor of a weekly paper, "The Franklin Favorite." He was talented at writing poetry, and many of his first attempts were published in the Louisville Courier-Journal. At the age of 27, on a reporting assignment, he heard the evangelist, H. C. Morrison, preach, and within a short time thereafter was converted. He wrote approximately 1200 hymns. Mr. Chisholm died in a Methodist Home at Vineland, New Jersey, March 2, 1960.

    Living for Jesus a Life That Is True.........1917
    Great Is Thy Faithfulness....................1923

CLARKE, Rev. James Freeman (klärk), 1810-1888, Unitarian. This Unitarian clergyman of the 19th century was born April 4, 1810 in Hanover, New Hampshire. He was raised in a quiet and conservative atmosphere on the Newton, Massachusetts estate of his maternal grandfather, James Freeman, who gave him his early education. At the age of 10 he entered Boston Latin School, and at 15 entered Harvard, graduating at the age of 19. He was pastor of the Church of the Disciples in Boston from 1841 to 1850, and again from 1854 to 1888. Though basically a conservative man, he was called a heretic for offering free pews to the public, and was the first Christian minister to preach on non-Christian religions to a theological school. He wrote a book on the subject, called "Ten Great Religions." He was an astronomer, inventor, poet, reformer and teacher; a moralist and an idealist; a remarkably warm, sympathetic broad-minded man, whose greatness is somewhat overshadowed by the fame of his contemporaries and close friends, Emerson and Holmes. He died June 8, 1888.

Father, to Us Thy Children.................1833
Brother, Hast Thou Wandered Far............1844

CLEMENT of Alexandria (klĕm′ĕnt), ca. 170-ca. 220, Early Christian. Though it is uncertain, it is believed that Titus Flavius Clemens, called Clement of Alexandria, was born in the year 170 A.D. in Athens. He eventually became converted to Christianity under Pantaenus, the founder and head of the Catechetical School of Alexandria, after first drifting from Stoicism to Eclecticism. In 190 he succeeded Pantaenus as head of the school, where the developers of Greek theology were educated. Clement remained at the school until about 202, at which time he fled from Alexandria at the beginning of the nine-year persecution of the Christians by the Emperor Septimus Severus. He wrote ten works, the most famous of which is "The Tutor." Most authorities state that he died in the year 220.

Shepherd of Tender Youth...............2nd Cent.
Sunset to Sunrise Changes Now..........2nd Cent.

CLEPHANE, Elizabeth Cecilia Douglas (klĕf′ān), 1830-1869, Presbyterian. Born in Edinburgh, Scotland on June 18, 1830, Elizabeth Clephane and her sister grew up in Melrose, near the home of Sir Walter Scott. Although of delicate health, she served the sick and poor of Melrose and was known by the people as "The Sunbeam." Both she and her sister gave more than generously to charities, on one occasion selling their horse and carriage in order to help a needy family. Her hymns were first published under the title "Breathings on the Border." She died February 19, 1869, and in 1872 at least eight of her hymns were published anonymously in a Scottish magazine called "Family Treasury."

Beneath the Cross of Jesus.................1868
There Were Ninety and Nine................1874

COGHILL, Mrs. Anna Louisa (kŏg'hĭl), **1836-1907, Anglican.**  Described variously as "striking-looking," "very English, very dignified" and "of charming manners," Anna Louisa Walker was born in Staffordshire, England in 1836, the youngest of three daughters of Robert Walker, a civil engineer. About 1857 the family moved to Canada, where the three sisters conducted a private school for girls until the two older sisters died and the school had to be closed. Returning to England in 1863, Anna Louisa became a governess, reviewed books, and edited an autobiography of her cousin, Mrs. Margaret Oliphant. In 1883 she married a wealthy merchant, Harry Coghill, and they moved to Coghurst Hall near Hastings, England. She wrote her best-known hymn while living in Canada, and is claimed by that country as well as by England. She died in 1907 at Bath.

> **Work, for the Night Is Coming**...............**1854**

COWPER, William (koo'pẽr), **1731-1800, Anglican.**  William Cowper was born on November 26, 1731 in Berkampstead, Hertfordshire, England, the son of the chaplain to King George II. His mother died when he was six, which was unfortunate for the shy and timid child. He attended Westminster School, and as a grand-nephew of the Lord Chancellor, was forced to study law. At 18 he left school and was articled to a solicitor, becoming a barrister three years later in 1754. From 1759 until 1763 he was Commissioner of Bankrupts, then became Clerk of the Journals in the House of the·Lords. He so dreaded addressing the House that he suffered a temporary insanity, spending a year in an asylum at St. Albans. Upon his discharge he took up a life of quiet retirement with the Morley Unwins at Huntingdon, and when Mr. Unwin died Cowper moved with the widowed Mary Unwin to Olney, where he developed a friendship with John Newton. This friendship led ultimately to the "Olney Hymns," 67 of which Cowper wrote. His hymns have been called "part of the prized treasures of the Christian Church." He died on April 25, 1800.

> **O for a Closer Walk With God**..............**1772**
> **God Moves in a Mysterious Way**..............**1774**

COXE, Rev. Arthur Cleveland (kŏks), **1818-1896, Episcopalian.**  Born into the Cox family of an eminent Presbyterian minister in Brooklyn, New York in 1818, Arthur Cleveland Coxe changed both the spelling of his name and his denomination upon completing his studies at the New York University. In 1841, after studying at the General Theological Seminary in New York, he was ordained and became rector of St. John's Episcopal Church in Hartford, Conn. In 1865 he was consecrated Bishop of Western New York, and made his home in Buffalo, the center of the diocese. Bishop Coxe was intensely devoted to his ideals and to the church, and was militant and spirited in ecclesiastical affairs. He died July 20, 1896 at Clifton Springs, New York.

> **O Where Are Kings and Empires Now**........**1839**
> **We Are Living, We Are Dwelling**...........**1840**

CROLY, Rev. George (krō'ly), 1780-1860, Anglican. This poet, novelist, dramatist, historian, satirist and clergyman, George Croly, was born in Dublin, Ireland on August 17, 1780. Graduating from the University of Dublin with his M.A. in 1804, he went to live in London to devote his energies to writing, a field in which he was quite successful. Three years after moving to London he was given an LL.D. by the University of Dublin. In 1835 he became rector of St. Bene't Sherehog and St. Stephen's, Walbrook, where he reopened a pulpit that had been closed for more than 100 years, and attracted large congregations through his strong preaching. Theologically a fundamentalist and politically a conservative, he opposed all liberalism in these fields. For his own congregation he published "Psalms and Hymns for Public Worship," which included ten metrical psalms and fifty hymns which he himself wrote. He died very suddenly on November 24, 1860, while walking in Holborn, London.

Spirit of God, Descend Upon My Heart......1854
Teach Us, O Lord, This Day................1854

CROSBY, Fanny J. (krŏz'by)—Mrs. Frances Van Alstyne, 1820-1915, Methodist. Fanny J. Crosby was born in South East, New York, on March 24, 1820. At six weeks of age, she became blind, due to improper treatment from a country doctor, and entered the New York City School for the Blind at the age of twelve. She taught at the school from 1847 to 1858, and during this time met the future President of the United States, Grover Cleveland (who was a secretary at the school), and they became good friends. In 1858 she married a blind musician, Alexander Van Alstyne. She showed a talent for poetry early in life, her first poem appearing in print when she was only eight. Fanny Crosby became the best-known gospel song writer of the day. She died on February 12, 1915, almost 95 years old.

Blessed Assurance 1873
Rescue the Perishing......................1880

CROSS, Rev. Allen Eastman (krŏs), 1864-1943, Congregationalist. Allen Eastman Cross, born in Manchester, New Hampshire on December 10, 1864, was educated at Amherst College (B.A. 1886) and at Andover Theological School (B.D. 1891). In 1906 he received a D.D. degree from Dartmouth College. He was ordained on December 29, 1892, and served successively at the following churches: Congregational Church in Cliftondale (1891-1896), Park Church, Springfield (1896-1901), associate at Old South Church, Boston (1901-1911), Milford (1914-1925), all of the pastorates being in Massachusetts. His literary works include two books and 17 hymns now in standard hymnals. He died in Manchester, New Hampshire, on April 23, 1943.

Jesus, Kneel Beside Me....................1907
America, the Shouts of War Shall Cease........1918

CROWELL, Mrs. Grace Noll (krō'wĕll), 1877-19—, Methodist. One of America's most prolific verse writers, Mrs. Crowell, née Grace Noll, was born October 31, 1877 at Inland, Iowa. On September 4, 1901 she married Norman H. Crowell, and five years later began to write her verse. Since that time she has written 21 books and no less than 3,500 poems. The mother of three sons, Mrs. Crowell was chosen American Mother of the Year in 1938, and was named the same year as one  of the ten outstanding women of America. She holds an honorary degree of Litt.D. from Baylor University, and has been a resident of Texas for many years.

Because I Have Been Given Much 1936

DAVIS, Rev. Ozora Stearns (dā'vĭs), 1866-1931, Congregationalist. Ozora Stearns Davis was born in Wheelock, Vermont on July 30, 1866. He attended Dartmouth College (where he was a member of Phi Beta Kappa), receiving his B.A. in 1889; Hartford Theological Seminary; University of Leipzig, from which he received his M.A. and Ph.D. degrees. In 1896 he was ordained, and that same year married Grace Emeline Tinker  of Vermont. He served churches in Vermont, Massachusetts and Connecticut until 1908, when he was made president of the Chicago Theological Seminary. Dartmouth granted him a D.D. in 1909 and Colorado College an LL.D. in 1921, the year after he resigned his presidency of the Theological Seminary. In 1927 he was moderator of the National Council of Congregational Churches. During his career Dr. Davis wrote and had published some 13 works. He died March 15, 1931.

We Bear the Strain of Earthly Toil 1909
At Length There Dawns the Glorious Day 1909

DEARMER, Rev. Percy (dẽr'mẽr), 1867-1936, Anglican. The son of Thomas Dearmer, an artist, Percy Dearmer was born February 27, 1867 in London. He attended Westminster School, and Christ Church, Oxford, from which he received his B.A. and M.A. degrees. In 1891 he became a deacon and the following year a priest, and served as curate at four successive churches until 1901. He was made vicar of St. Mary's, Primrose Hill in 1901 and remained there until 1915.  Beginning in 1919 he was professor of Ecclesiastical Art in King's College, London, and in 1931 was made Canon of Westminster. In a long career as churchman he lectured in various countries and wrote or contributed to at least 61 works, including novels, books on social questions, and hymn collections. He married twice. His first wife, Mabel White, whom he married in 1891, died in Serbia during the First World War while Dearmer was chaplain to the British Red Cross there. His second wife, Mary Knowles, he married in 1916. He died in 1936, having greatly influenced contemporary English hymnody.

Father, Who on Man Dost Shower 1906
God, We Thank Thee, Not in Vain 1906

DIX, William Chatterton (dĭks), 1837-1898, Anglican. William Chatterton Dix, the son of a surgeon and writer, was born June 14, 1837 in Bristol, England. After an education at the Bristol Grammar School he entered the insurance business, and was soon made manager of a marine insurance company in Glasgow, Scotland. A student of both Ethiopian and Greek, he translated a number of hymns from those languages into English, as well as writing many original hymns in English. This author of four books of verse died at Clifton, England, on September 9, 1898.

As With Gladness, Men of Old...............1859
To Thee, O Lord, Our Hearts We Raise.......1864

DOANE, Rev. George Washington (dōn), 1799-1859, Episcopalian. Born in Trenton, New Jersey on May 27, 1799, George Washington Doane lived and was educated in New York City and Geneva, New York. He later attended Union College, New York, from which he received his B.A. with high honors in 1818. For a short time following this he studied law in New York City, but soon became interested in theology and gave up the legal profession to take up ecclesiastical studies. In 1821 he was ordained deacon and became assistant rector of Trinity Church, New York, where his ordination as priest took place two years later. When he was 25 his first book of hymns was published. He was made assistant rector of Trinity Church in Boston in 1828, and two years later became rector. In 1829 he married, and in 1832 moved to Burlington, New Jersey, after accepting his election as Bishop of New Jersey. During the following years he established a church school for girls, founded Burlington College, and was responsible for a tremendous growth of his diocese. On April 27, 1859 Bishop Doane died after a brief illness, in Burlington.

Softly Now the Light of Day.................1824
Fling Out the Banner, Let It Float...........1848

DOANE, Rev. William Croswell (dōn), 1832-1913, Episcopalian. Born March 2, 1832 in Boston, Massachusetts, William Croswell Doane received his B.A. and M.A. degrees from Burlington College (founded by his father, Bishop George Washington Doane) in 1850 and 1852 respectively, and an M.A. degree from Trinity College in 1863. He was ordained a deacon in 1853, and a priest of the Protestant Episcopal Church in 1856. From 1853 to 1869 he was rector of three churches successively, and on February 2, 1869 became Bishop of Albany, New York. His career included service as teacher of English Literature at Burlington College, lecturer on English Literature at Trinity College, and chancellor of the University of the State of New York. He died on May 1, 1913, in Albany, New York.

Ancient of Days, Who Sittest Throned in Glory..1886
To Thee, O Father, Throned on High...(not known)

DODDRIDGE, Rev. Philip (dŏd'rĭj), 1702-1751, Congregationalist. Philip Doddridge, the twentieth child of his parents, was born in London, England on June 26, 1702, the son of a merchant and grandson of a Bohemian Lutheran minister. His early religious training was given him by his mother, but at an early age he was orphaned. Refusing an offer from the Duchess of Bedford to educate him for the ministry in the Church of England, he joined an institution of non-conformist  reputation at Kibworth, and at 21 began his preaching. In 1729 he began his 22-year pastorate at the Castle Hill Congregational Chapel in Northampton, at the same time taking charge of a seminary there. A brilliant scholar, he received a D.D. from Aberdeen University in 1736, and his most famous theological work, "The Rise and Progress of Religion in the Soul" was published in seven languages. When it was discovered that he was tuberculous some friends sent him to Portugal for his health, but it was too late and he died in Lisbon on October 26, 1751. He was the author of more than 400 hymns.

    O Happy Day, That Fixed My Choice........1735
    Awake, My Soul, Stretch Every Nerve........1755

DUFFIELD, Rev. George, Jr. (dŭf'fēld), 1818-1888, Presbyterian. George Duffield, Jr., born September 12, 1818 in Carlisle, Pennsylvania, was from a long line of Duffields prominent in the Presbyterian Church. He studied at Yale University and Union Theological Seminary, and in 1840 began his pastorate work in Brooklyn, New York. He served churches in New Jersey, Pennsylvania, Illinois and Michigan before his retirement in 1884. For seven years he was on the Board of  Regents for the University of Michigan, and he received a D.D. degree from Knox College. Dr. Duffield died in Bloomfield, New Jersey on July 6, 1888 at the home of his son, the Rev. Samuel Willoughby Duffield, an excellent hymnologist.

    Blessed Saviour, Thee I Love................1851
    Stand Up, Stand Up for Jesus................1858

DWIGHT, Rev. Timothy (dwīt), 1752-1817, Congregationalist. Timothy Dwight was born in Northampton, Massachusetts on May 14, 1752. He graduated from Yale in 1769, and remained there to tutor for six years. After serving as chaplain in the U.S. Army for eight years, he became pastor at the Congregational Church in Fairfield, Connecticut, where he taught school at the same time, resigning in 1796 to become president of  Yale University. He revised Isaac Watts' "Psalms and Hymns," wrote a seven-book epic, a seven-part poem, and other works. Though only 43 when assuming the presidency of Yale, he taught metaphysics, literature, theology, oratory, logic and ethics, besides acting as president and college chaplain. He is considered one of the most important of the early American hymnologists. On January 11, 1817 he died in Philadelphia, Pennsylvania.

    I Love Thy Kingdom, Lord................1800
    How Pleasing Is Thy Voice................1800

EBER, Rev. Paul (ā'bĕr), 1511-1569, Lutheran.
Paul Eber, the son of a tailor, was born in Kitzingen, Bavaria on November 8, 1511. At 12 he was sent to the Ansbach Gymnasium, but because of illness had to return to Kitzingen. Two years later he attended the St. Lorenz School in Nurnberg, and at 21 graduated from the University of Wittenberg. While there he studied under Martin Luther, and in later life was second only to Luther of the Wittenberg poets. He served as tutor on the Philosophical Faculty, and as professor of Latin, Physics, and Hebrew, successively. He was preacher at Castle Church in Wittenberg, secretary to Melanchthon at the Colloquy of Worms, and after returning from Worms became municipal preacher and superintendent of the electoral circuit. He died December 10, 1569, at Wittenberg.

> **When in the Hour of Utmost Need . . . . ca. 1560**
> **Lord Jesus Christ, True Man and God 1565**

ELLERTON, Rev. John (ĕl'ĕr-tŭn), 1826-1893, Anglican. John Ellerton was born in London, England on June 15, 1826 of a strongly Evangelical family. During his years at Trinity College, Cambridge, he came under the influence of Frederick D. Maurice, and changed his views to a broader position. From Cambridge he received both his B.A. and M.A. degrees, and following his ordination in 1850 he was at different times curate of Easebourne, Sussex; curate of Brighton; vicar of Crewe Green; chaplain to Lord Crewe; rector of Hinstock and of Barnes and of White Roding. Always generous and unselfish, he devoted much of himself to public service, and refused to copyright his hymns, feeling that they were the property of Christian hymnody. He was so devoted to hymns that on his death-bed he repeated many favorites to himself. Matthew Arnold called him "the greatest of the living hymn-writers." The year before he died he was appointed Canon of St. Albans, but was not well enough to take the position. Nevertheless, he is referred to as "Canon" by most writers. He died in 1893.

> **Saviour, Again to Thy Dear Name We Raise . . 1866**
> **The Day Thou Gavest, Lord, Is Ended 1870**

ELLIOTT, Charlotte (ĕl'ĭ-ŭt), 1789-1871, Anglican. Charlotte Elliott was born in Clapham, England on March 18, 1789. There she lived for 32 years, writing light verse. When she met Cesar Malan, an evangelist from Geneva, her life was completely transformed and she devoted herself thereafter to religious and philanthropic pursuits. She corresponded with Malan for 40 years, celebrating the date of their meeting as her soul's birthday. Her first hymns were published in 1834, her last in 1869, for though an invalid from around 1820 to her death, she continued a prolific literary career that produced 150 hymns. She lived in Brighton for a number of years, and died there on September 22, 1871 at the age of 82.

> **My God and Father, While I Stray 1834**
> **Just as I am Without One Plea 1836**

FABER, Rev. Frederick William (fā'bĕr), 1814-1863, R. C. Born June 28, 1814 in Yorkshire, England and raised in a traditionally Calvinistic background, Frederick William Faber received his education at Shrewsbury, Harrow, and Oxford (where he was made a Fellow of University College). He was at first strongly anti-Roman Catholic, and published a sharp criticism of the Church, in which he asked God's mercy for that Church.  Later, however, more and more influenced by John Henry Newman, he became a Roman Catholic, even though he had already served three years as rector of his own parish. In 1854 the Pope created him a Doctor of Divinity. His hymns were written to give to the Roman Catholic Church music comparable to that of the Protestant church. He died September 26, 1863.

> Faith of Our Fathers........................1849
> There's a Wideness in God's Mercy..........1854

FAWCETT, Rev. John (fŏ'sĕt), 1740-1817, Baptist. John Fawcett was born in January, 1740 in Lidget Green, Yorkshire, England. At the age of 11 he was left without a father, but with several brothers and sisters, which caused hardship to his mother, and at the age of 13 he was apprenticed to a tradesman in a nearby town. During the six years of his apprenticeship he became influenced by the preaching of George Whitefield and became a Methodist, but in 1758  left them to become a Baptist. He began to preach at 23, and in 1764 took control of a Baptist church in Yorkshire and was ordained there on July 31, 1765. Between 1772 and 1811 his important works were published, including a collection of 166 hymns in 1782. He wrote a hymn to go with every one of his sermons. He suffered a paralytic stroke in 1816, and died on July 25, 1817.

> Lord, Dismiss Us With Thy Blessing..........1773
> Blest Be the Tie That Binds.................1782

FOSDICK, Rev. Harry Emerson (fŏs'dĭk), 1878-19—, Baptist. Harry Emerson Fosdick, a descendant of the remarkable pioneer John Spencer Fosdick, was born May 24, 1878 in Buffalo, New York. At Colgate University (B.A. 1900)' he was class poet, cheer leader, and recipient of five major awards. After attending Colgate Divinity School for an additional year, he went on to Union Theological Seminary (B.D. 1904) and Columbia (M.A. 1908). From 1915 to 1934  he was professor of Practical Theology at Union Theological Seminary; he has served as exchange preacher in both England and Scotland; he has written innumerable books (the first of which was published in 1908), many of which have been translated into ten foreign languages; has also written a number of hymns. Dr. Fosdick retired from the active ministry in 1956, on his 68th birthday.

> God of Grace and God of Glory..............1930
> The Prince of Peace His Banner Spreads......1930

FRANCIS of ASSISI (ă-sē′zē), 1182-1226, Early Christian. Giovanni Bernardone was born in Assisi, Italy in 1182. After a self-indulgent youth as a soldier he was struck with a serious illness at 25, from which he recovered with a new philosophy. He gave up his wealth and devoted himself to social reform and religion. He founded the Franciscan order of friars in 1210, and in 1223 went to Egypt and preached before the Sultan, gaining for the Franciscans the privilege of guardians of the Holy Sepulchre. He retired as a hermit to Monte Alverno, where it is said he experienced the miracle of the stigmata in September, 1224. A great lover of nature, he wrote "Canticle of the Sun" from which his hymn, "All Creatures of Our God and King" is translated. His death occurred October 4, 1226, and on the same date in 1228 he was canonized by Pope Gregory IX.

> **All Creatures of Our God and King......13th Cent.**
> **O Most High, Almighty, Good Lord God..13th Cent.**

GERHARDT, Rev. Paul (gâr′härt), 1607-1676, Lutheran. Born on March 12, 1607 at Grafenhainichen, Germany, Paul Gerhardt experienced much suffering in his early life due to the Thirty Years' War and the loss of his father. For five years he went to school in Grimma, then to the University of Wittenberg to study theology. He remained at Wittenberg from 1628 to 1642, at which time he settled in Berlin as a private tutor. Here his first hymns were published. In 1651 he became provost at Mittenwalde, and in 1657 he returned to Berlin to become third assistant pastor at the Church of St. Nicholas. He was well-loved in the city, and the most popular of the pastors. In 1669 he became archdeacon of Lubben, remaining in this position until his death in 1676. He wrote altogether 132 hymns.

> **Jesus, Thy Boundless Love to Me............1653**
> **O How Shall I Receive Thee.................1653**

GILKEY, Rev. James Gordon (gil′ky), 1889-1964, Congregationalist. Author of 15 books on religious topics, James Gordon Gilkey was born September 28, 1889 in Watertown, Massachusetts. He attended Boston Latin School, Harvard University (B.A. 1912, M.A. 1913) and Union Theological Seminary (B.D. 1916). He did graduate work at Berlin University and Marburg University in Germany; was a member of Phi Beta Kappa, Delta Upsilon, and the International Society of Theta Phi. He served as first assistant minister of the Bryn Mawr (Pennsylvania) Presbyterian Church, then as pastor of the South Church (Congregational) in Springfield, Mass., where his ministry began, in 1917. He also was professor of Biblical Literature at Amherst from 1923 to 1930. Dr. Gilkey's earliest religious affiliation was with the Baptist Church; in his student days he was connected with the Presbyterian Church; after 1917 he was a Congregationalist.

> **O God, in Whose Great Purpose............1912**
> **Outside the Holy City.....................1915**

410

GILMORE, Rev. Joseph Henry (gĭl'mōr), 1834-
1918, Baptist. Joseph Henry Gilmore was born on
April 29, 1834 in Boston, Massachusetts. He attended Brown University, where he was an exceptional student and received his B.A. in 1858 with
high honors. He went on to the Newton Theological Seminary, from which he graduated in 1861.
The following year he was ordained, and spent a
year in a Baptist church at Fisherville, New Hampshire. Following this he acted as private secretary
to his father, who was governor of the state of New Hampshire. He
then spent two years as pastor of the Second Baptist Church in Rochester,
New York, followed by a year as professor of Hebrew at the Theological Seminary in that city. In 1868 he took the post of professor of
English Literature, Logic and Rhetoric at the University of Rochester,
where he remained until his retirement in 1911. He died in Rochester,
New York on July 23, 1918.

> **Tenderly the Father Greets Us**................**1855**
> **He Leadeth Me, O Blessed Thought**..........**1861**

GLADDEN, Rev. Washington (glăd'n), 1836-1918,
Congregationalist. Born on February 11, 1836 in
Pottsgrove, Pennsylvania, Dr. Gladden attended
Williams College, where he received his B.A. in
1859, and in 1860 took over the ministry of a
church in Brooklyn, New York. This pastorate was
followed by one at Morrisania, N. Y. (1861-
1866) and another in North Adams, Mass. (1866-
1871). In 1871 he began a 3-year service on the
editorial staff of the "Independent" in New York
City, where as religious editor he fought the notorious Tweed Ring.
On his resignation in 1874, he became pastor at the North Church in
Springfield, Mass., and after 8 years there became minister of the First
Congregational Church in Columbus, Ohio, where he remained for 32
years. He wrote not less than 32 works in addition to his famous hymns.
He died on July 2, 1918 in Columbus.

> **O Master, Let Me Walk With Thee**..........**1879**
> **Forgive, O Lord, the Doubts That Break**......**1879**

GRANT, Robert (grănt), 1779-1838, Anglican.
Robert Grant was born in 1779 in India, the son
of a Scotsman who was secretary of the Board of
Trade in India and a member of the East India
Company. Having made a fortune in India the
father returned to his native Inverness, Scotland,
and sent his son to Magdalene College, Cambridge.
Robert graduated in 1806, and a year later became a barrister. In 1826 he was elected to Parliament to represent four towns. After being knighted
in 1834 he returned to India as governor of Bombay. The following
year his hymns entered two collections, (his complete works being
published posthumously by his older brother, Lord Glenelg). A popular
and benevolent philanthropist, he died on July 9, 1838 in Bombay,
where a medical college has been erected as a memorial to him.

> **Saviour, When in Dust to Thee**..............**1818**
> **O Worship, the King, All-Glorious Above**....**1833**

GREGORY I, Pope (greg'o-ry), 540-604, R. C.
Gregory the Great, as he is called, was born in
Rome in 604, of an influential and wealthy sena-
torial family, and received the best possible education. In his first position, as Praetor of Rome,
he was known both for his great administrative
ability and his love of finery. Following his father's death he devoted his time and wealth to
founding seven monasteries, one at his own palace
where he himself became a monk of the Benedic-
tine order at the age of 35. His monastery years were lived in simplicity
and hard work, which proved detrimental to his health. He became a
Cardinal Deacon, and in 590 was drafted into the Papacy, with great
reluctance on his part. His fourteen years of service as Pope are marked
by great achievements, including the famous Gregorian Chants. He
died March 12, 604 of rheumatic gout.

Father, We Praise Thee, Now the Night Is Over. .6th Cent.
O Christ, our King, Creator, Lord . . . . .6th Cent.

**GURNEY, Rev. Archer T. (gûr'ny), 1820-1887,
Anglican.** Archer Thompson Gurney was born in
1820, educated with the law in mind, and had
already been received at the bar in the Middle
Temple in London when he decided for the ministry rather than the law. He took Holy Orders
in 1849, and was curate for four years at Buckingham. In 1858 he became chaplain at the Court
Church in Paris. He wrote a good deal of poetry,
and in 1862 contributed 147 of his own hymns
to the "Book of Praise." He died March 21, 1887 in Bath, England.

Christ Is Risen, Christ Is Risen 1862
Memory of the Blest Departed 1867

**HANAFORD, Rev. Phebe A. (han'a-ferd), 1829-
1921, Universalist.** Phebe A. Coffin, the first
woman preacher ordained in New England, was
born on Nantucket Island (off Massachusetts) on
May 6, 1829. She was educated by the rector of
the Episcopal Church in her village. Married in
1848 to Joseph H. Hanaford, she had two children.
In 1868 she was ordained, and served as pastor of
the Universalist Church in Hingham, Mass. for two
years; a church in New Haven, Conn. for four
years; the Church of the Good Shepherd in Jersey City, N. J. from
1874-1884; then back to New Haven as Pastor of the Holy Spirit (Universalist) Church. In her long career she was chaplain in the Connecticut legislature, minister for the marriage of her own daughter, and a
polific writer of both prose and poetry. She died in 1921.

Cast Thy Bread Upon the Waters 1884

HANKEY, Katherine (hăn′ky), 1834-1911, Independent. Arabella Katherine Hankey, better known as Kate Hankey, was born in Clapham, England in 1834. Her father was a banker and member of the "Clapham Sect," a group of wealthy, aristocratic philanthropists and evangelists. While still in school, Kate taught Sunday-school, promoting Bible study among working girls and girls of her own social level. A great interest in missions grew in her after a trip into South Africa to bring home an invalid brother. The royalties from her publications—several books and many hymns—she contributed to missions. She died in London in 1911.

> Tell Me the Old, Old Story 1866
> I Love to Tell the Story 1874

HARKNESS, Georgia Elma (härk′nĕs), 1891-19—, Methodist. Born near Lake Champlain in the Adirondack town of Harkness on April 21, 1891, Georgia Harkness received her education at Cornell University and Boston University, where she earned two Masters degrees and a Ph.D. Dr. Harkness taught French and Latin at the high school level following her graduation from Cornell, and later taught at Boston University, Elmira College, Mount Holyoke, Garrett Biblical Institute, and the Pacific School of Religion. Among the many honors conferred on her were her selection by the "Christian Century" as one of the six most influential Church women in the U.S.A. in 1952, and being named Church-woman of the Year in 1958 by Religious Heritage of America, Inc. Dr. Harkness has written more than twenty books and a hymn—"Hope of the World"—which was selected by the Hymn Society of American for the Evanston Assembly of the World Council of Churches.

> Hope of the World 1954
> God of the Fertile Fields 1955

HASTINGS, Thomas (hās′tĭngz), 1784-1872, Presbyterian. Born in Litchfield County, Connecticut on October 15, 1784, the son of a farmer and doctor; Thomas Hastings achieved early success in his country school education by ability and hard work. When he was 12 the family moved to Clinton, N. Y., where he continued to excel. He became choir leader in Clinton at the age of 16, and edited and published "The Western Recorder," a religious periodical, in Utica. He trained choirs, composed music and wrote hymns, and in 1858 was given a Doctorate in Music by the University of the City of New York. He was unusual both physically and in ability, in that he was a pure albino and was able to read a printed page held upside down. Before his death on May 15, 1872, he had written more than 600 hymns and composed more than 1,000 hymn-tunes.

> Gently, Lord, O Gently Lead Us 1831
> Hail to the Brightness of Zion's Glad Morning . . 1832

HAVERGAL, Frances Ridley (hăv′r-gāl), 1836-1879, Anglican. Frances Ridley Havergal was born on December 14, 1836 in Astley, Worcestershire, England, into a cultured, religious family. Daughter of a minister, at four she could read the Bible, and memorized the New Testament as well as part of the Old. She received private instruction in her own country and in Germany, and learned five languages besides English. Excelling in music, she sang beautifully, composed, and could play on the piano from memory much of the great masters' work. She was active in the work of the Sunday-school, gave Bible readings to servants, concerned herself with the needs of the poor, and answered all correspondence coming to her, which assumed voluminous proportions. She died at 42 on June 3, 1879, in Swansea, Wales.

> **True-Hearted, Whole-Hearted** **1874**
> **Who Is on the Lord's Side?** **1877**

HAWKS, Mrs. Annie Sherwood (höks), 1835-1918, Baptist. Born in Hoosick, New York, on May 28, 1835, Annie Sherwood began contributing poems to newspapers at the age of 14. In 1857 she married Charles H. Hawks, and two years later they moved to Brooklyn, N. Y. She became a member of the Hanson Place Baptist Church, and in 1868 the pastor, Dr. Robert Lowry, discovered her talent for poetry and encouraged her to continue her writing. During the period from 1868 to 1876 Mrs. Hawks wrote most of her 400 hymns, the majority of which were written for Sunday-school use. In 1888, on the death of her husband, she went to live at the home of her daughter in Bennington, Vt., and there she died on January 3, 1918.

> **I Need Thee Every Hour** **1872**
> **Thine, Most Gracious Lord** . . . . **(not known)**

HEBER, Rev. Reginald (hē′bẽr), 1783-1826, Anglican. Born in Malpas, Cheshire, England on April 21, 1783, Reginald Heber was educated by his father until he was seven. He attended local school until the age of 17, when he went to Brasenose College, Oxford, there receiving the Chancellor's prize for his Latin verse, the Newdigate poetry award, and the University Bachelor's prize for prose essay. In 1807, after taking Holy Orders, he became rector of the village church in Hodnet, where he had accepted the living from his half-brother, and remained there for 16 years. He continued a prolific literary career, contributing to magazines, writing poetry, essays and hymns, yet never losing sight of his work as a pastor, and it was during this period that he started a collection of hymns, including many of his own. This collection was not published until after his death, as his Bishop did not give it approval until 1827. In 1823, after twice refusing the bishopric of Calcutta, he accepted and went to India where he labored energetically for three years. He succumbed to a sudden stroke on April 3, 1826.

> **The Son of God Goes Forth to War** **1827**
> **Holy, Holy, Holy! Lord God Almighty** **1827**

**HERBERT, Rev. George (hûr'bẽrt), 1593-1632,
Anglican.** Born in Montgomery Castle, Wales,
April 3, 1593, George Herbert entered Trinity
College, Cambridge at the age of 15 and received
his M.A. from there in 1611. He was made University Orator, and elected a Fellow in 1619.
He was in favor with several royal persons, including King James I, but when the latter died he was
forced to give up thoughts of advancement through
this means. He went to Kent, entered the Church,
and was appointed to Leighton Bromswold, Hunts. in 1626. He resigned
in 1629 because of poor health, and the following year became rector
of Bemerton in Wiltshire. During his four years at Bemerton he devoted
a great deal of his time and energy to the poor, at the same time
writing verse and prose. Most of his poems were published in 1633 in
"The Temple," and it is from this that the majority of his hymns were
taken. He died in February, 1632 at the age of 39.

    Teach Me, My God and King...............**1633**
    Let All the World in Every Corner Sing......**1633**

**HOLMES, Rev. John Haynes (hōmz), 1879-1964,
Unitarian.** John Haynes Holmes was born in
Philadelphia, Pennsylvania on November 29, 1879,
and attended Harvard University, where he received his B.A. in 1902 summa cum laude, and his
S.T.B. two years later. Ordained a Unitarian minister in 1904, he began service at the Church of
the Messiah in New York City in February, 1907,
and from that time was appointed to several posi-
tions in the Unitarian Church, including Chairman
of the General Unitarian Conference (1915-1917). In 1919 he resigned
from his denomination to become an Independent. He collaborated in
1935 with Reginald Lawrence in producing a play, "If This Be Treason,"
with the New York Theatre Guild. He retired from his church in 1949
and lived in New York City until his death.

    O God, Whose Love Is Over All.............**1909**
    O God, Whose Law From Age to Age........**1910**

**HOLMES, Dr. Oliver Wendell (hōmz), 1809-1894,
Unitarian.** Oliver Wendell Holmes, the father of
the future Justice of the U.S. Supreme Court,
was born August 29, 1809 in Cambridge, Massachusetts. Graduating from Harvard in 1829, he
gave up law for medicine and received his M.D.
from Harvard in 1836. He began medical prac-
tice in Boston, and two years later a three-year
service as professor of Anatomy at Dartmouth,
followed by the same position at the Harvard
Medical School from 1847 to 1882. He was given a Doctor of Laws
degree by Harvard and Edinburgh Universities, a Doctor of Letters by
Cambridge, and a Doctor of Civil Law by Oxford. He wrote poems,
novels, essays, biographies and various miscellaneous works including
hymns. He died in Boston, October 7, 1894, and was buried at Mt.
Auburn Cemetery. He is listed in the American Hall of Fame.

    Lord of All Being, Throned Afar.............**1848**
    Thou Gracious Power, Whose Mercy Lands....**1869**

HOPPER, Rev. Edward (hŏp'ĕr), 1816-1888, Presbyterian. Born February 17, 1816 (or 1818) in New York City, Edward Hopper graduated from New York University and Union Theological Seminary. He held pastorates at Greenville, N. Y. and at Sag Harbour, Long Island, N. Y., for a total of 11 years, after which he returned to New York City to serve at the Church of Sea and Land, a mission for sailors. In 1871 Lafayette College awarded him a D.D. degree. His hymns and poems were written anonymously, or under an assumed name. He died suddenly of a heart attack on April 23, 1888, in the midst of writing a poem.

Jesus, Saviour, Pilot Me.....................1871
They Pray the Best Who Pray and Watch......1874

HOSMER, Rev. Frederick Lucian (hŏz'mĕr), 1840-1929, Unitarian. A descendant of the early settlers in Concord, Massachusetts, Frederick Hosmer was born in nearby Framingham on October 16, 1840. Graduating with a B.A. from Harvard in 1862 and completing a course at the Harvard Divinity School in 1869, he was ordained to the ministry in 1872. He served successively at Unitarian churches in Northboro, Mass. and Quincy, Ill., (1872-1877) at which time his "Way of Life" was published; at Cleveland, Ohio (1878-1892), where he collaborated with W. C. Gannet in writing "The Thought of God in Hymns and Poems"; in St. Louis, Missouri (1894-1899). A student of hymnody, he gave lectures on the subject at Harvard Divinity School in 1908 and at the Pacific Unitarian School in 1912. His final ministry was in Berkeley, California. He died there on June 7, 1929.

"Thy Kingdom Come," on Bended Knee......1891
Forward Through the Ages.................1908

HOW, Rev. William Walsham (hou), 1823-1897, Anglican. "The Poor Man's Bishop" as he was called by his followers, was born on December 13, 1823 in Shrewsbury, England. Graduating from Wadham College, Oxford with a B.A. in 1845, he was ordained and was curate of Kidderminster and Holy Cross (Shrewsbury) from 1845 to 1851; rector of Whittington from 1851 to 1853; rural dean of Oswestry from 1853 to 1860. In 1860 he was appointed honorary canon of St. Asaph, and later rector of St. Andrew Undershaft and Bishop Suffragan of Bedford. In 1888 he became Bishop of Wakefield. His hymns, sermons, poems and essays were published, and approximately 60 of the hymns came into general use. At one time he collaborated with a Congregationalist (Thomas Baker Morrell) in compiling "Psalms and Hymns" and edited with Sir Arthur Sullivan "Church Hymns." He died while vacationing in Ireland, on August 10, 1897.

O Jesus, Thou Art Standing.................1867
O Word of God Incarnate..................1867

HOWE, Mrs. Julia Ward (hou), 1819-1910, Unitarian. Julia Ward was born on May 27, 1819 in New York City. Brought up in a strongly evangelical Episcopalian atmosphere, she rebelled and easily fit into the liberal atmosphere in which she found herself after marrying the great humanitarian, Dr. Samuel Gridley Howe. She joined the Radical Club, studied the modern philosophies, and became a member of James Freeman Clarke's Church of the Disciples in Boston. She was violently anti-slavery, and once received John Brown in her home. Inspired by a visit to a Washington fortified for the Civil War, she wrote "The Battle Hymn of the Republic" one night, and received $5.00 for its publication in the Atlantic Monthly. Later in life she was a leader in woman suffrage and in the movement of international peace. She wrote several books, including the biography of her husband, and several volumes of poetry. She died on October 17, 1910, twelve days after receiving the Doctor of Laws degree from Smith College.

Battle Hymn of the Republic 1861

HUGHES, Thomas (hūz), 1823-1896, Anglican. The author of "Tom Brown's School Days" is remembered primarily for his famous book, but he was also a biographer and hymn-writer. Born at Donington Priory, Newbury, Berkshire, England in 1823, he attended Rugby and Oriel College, Oxford and in 1848 took up the practice of law. He became a supporter of the Christian Socialism movement, and after making a lecture tour in the United States founded Rugby, Tennessee in 1880 —a colony of Englishmen named after Rugby College. A Liberal, he held seats in Parliament from 1872 to 1883, and in 1882 became a county court judge. He died at Brighton, March 22, 1896.

O God of Truth, Whose Living Word 1859

HUNTINGDON, Lady Selina Shirley (hŭn'ting-dŭn), 1707-1791, Calvinistic Methodist. The second daughter of a family that traced its lineage back to Edward the Confessor, Selina Shirley Ferrers was born in England on August 24, 1707. As a child, and all through womanhood, she was serious and prayerful. She married Theodolphus, the Earl of Huntingdon, in June, 1728, and was thereafter Lady Huntingdon, or the Countess of Huntingdon. On her husband's estates she performed philanthropic works and engaged in public worship. Presented at Court, she was unable to join fully in court festivities because of her seriousness of purpose. She was caused to sympathize with the Wesleys and with Whitefield by her sister-in-law, Lady Margaret Hastings, and in 1739 joined the Methodists and entered even more zealously into good works. She founded several chapels, for which a hymn-book was published in 1764, several of her own hymns appearing in the book. In November, 1790 she broke a blood-vessel, and died the following June. The two hymns listed are generally attributed to Lady Huntingdon.

When Thou, My Righteous Judge ....ca. 1774
We Soon Shall Hear the Midnight Cry ......ca. 1774

HYDE, Rev. William de Witt (hīd), 1858-1917, Congregationalist. William de Witt Hyde was born in Winchendon, Massachusetts, in 1858, graduated from Harvard in 1879, and from the Andover Theological Seminary in 1883. The year of his graduation from the latter he became pastor at a church in Paterson, N. J., but within three years he was made a professor of Philosophy and President at Bowdoin College in Maine. He was called "the Boy President." He successfully filled the position, writing educational and religious books and acting as University preacher at Harvard, University of Chicago, and Yale at the same time. He was a Fellow of the American Academy of Arts and Sciences. He continued as president at Bowdoin College until his death in 1917.

Creation's Lord, We Give Thee Thanks........1903

JOHN OF DAMASCUS (da-măs'kŭs), ca. 676-ca. 754, Early Christian. John Damascene was born in Damascus about 676, and educated by the cultured Sicilian monk, Cosmas. After holding a position under the Mohammedan Caliph, he and Cosmas the Younger, his foster brother, entered St. Sabas, a monastery near Jerusalem. At a late age he became a priest in the Church of Jerusalem, and is considered by some to be the greatest of the Greek church poets. He wrote hymns, an encyclopedia of Christian Theology, and other works, among which is "Barlaam and Joasaph," considered to be a disguised version of Buddha's life. He died about 754, after devoting a long life to furtherance of orthodox religion.

The Day of Resurrection................8th Cent.
Come, Ye Faithful, Raise the Strain......8th Cent.

JONAS, Rev. Justus (yō'nŭs), 1493-1555, Lutheran. The son of Jonas Koch, the Burgomaster at Nordhausen, Germany was born on June 5 1493. He obtained his M.A. from Erfurt in 1510, and his LL.B. from Wittenberg. Returning to Erfurt in 1517, he was made Canon of St. Severus Church and professor at the University in 1518, and in 1519 became rector of the University. He changed his name to Jonas when at the rectorate he was referred to as "Just Jonas," accepting the prefix "Justus" as a Christian name. In 1527 he was made Probst of All Saints, Wittenberg, and professor of Church Law at the University of Wittenberg. For 20 years he was assistant and friend to both Luther and Melanchthon. After considerable difficulties, he became head pastor of Eisfield in 1553, and there he died on October 9, 1555.

If God Were Not Upon Our Side............1524

JUDSON, Rev. Adoniram (jŭd's'n), 1788-1850, Baptist. Adoniram Judson was born August 9, 1788 in Malden, Massachusetts, and in 1808 entered the Andover Theological Seminary. Four years later, with Ann Haseltine, his bride of only a month, he was sent by the London Missionary Society as a missionary to Calcutta, at his own request. On shipboard, however, the Judsons' sentiments changed, and they became Baptists upon arriving in Calcutta. Unwelcome among their former associates, they traveled to the Isle of France, to Madras, to Burma, until in 1814 the American Baptists formed a missionary society that would support them. For years they lived a difficult but rewarding life. In 1826 Ann Judson died in Amherst, India and Judson married Mrs. Sarah Hall Boardman and moved to Maulmain. When her health failed, they started a voyage back to America with their children, but she died enroute. On June 2, 1846 he married the famous literary figure, Emily Chubbuck, and they returned to Maulmain. Four years later, with failing health, he started out for the Isle of France and died on the way there on April 12, 1850. He was given a sea burial.

> Our Father God, Who Art in Heaven........1825
> Come, Holy Spirit, Dove Divine..............1832

JUDSON, Mrs. Emily Chubbuck (jŭd's'n), 1817-1854, Baptist. Emily Chubbuck, alias Fanny Forester (her nom de plume), was born in Eaton, New York on August 22, 1817. At eight she developed a conviction that she would be a missionary. Because of her family's financial circumstances she was forced to work in a woolen factory, and later she taught in a small village school. At twenty she contributed her poems to the town newspaper, and eventually wrote her way to a high place in literary circles. In January, 1846 she met Adoniram Judson. She became Judson's third wife five months later, and they set off for Burma. After the death of her husband at sea in 1850 Mrs. Judson returned to the U. S. She died at Hamilton, N. Y., June 1, 1854.

> Mother, Has the Dove That Nestled....(not known)

KEBLE, Rev. John (kĕ'b'l), 1792-1866, Anglican. Born in Fairfield, Gloucestershire, England on April 25, 1792, John Keble entered Corpus Christi College, Oxford, on scholarship at the age of fifteen. In his fifth year there he won both the English and Latin essay prizes. He was ordained in 1815, and spent most of his life living quietly in a small parish in Hursley (near Winchester), but had great influence on affairs outside of his parish through his correspondence and writing, which included essays, religious poetry, sermons and a variety of other subjects. His greatest work was the "Christian Year," published in 1827. For ten years he was professor of Poetry at Oxford, and in 1869 Keble College was founded there as a tribute to him. He died on March 29, 1866 at Bournemouth.

> Blessed Are the Pure in Heart...............1812
> New Every Morning Is the Love..............1822

KEN, Rev. Thomas (kĕn), 1637-1711, Anglican.
Thomas Ken, one of the most famous bishops of all time, was born in July, 1637 at Little Berkhamstead, Hertfordshire, England. He was educated at Winchester, Hart Hall, Oxford and New College, Oxford, where in 1657 he was elected a Fellow. In 1669 he was made a Fellow in Winchester College, and domestic chaplain to the Bishop of Winchester, and during the following years wrote his most widely-known hymns. He was chaplain to Princess Mary, wife of William of Orange, at the Hague for a short time, but was forced to resign his post when he incurred the latter's displeasure because of his frank criticisms. On June 29, 1865, he was consecrated Bishop of Bath and Wells, and was one of the "Seven Bishops" who refused to read the "Declaration of Indulgence." True to his independent spirit, after the revolution he also refused to take the oath to William and Mary, the new monarchs, and was subsequently forced to resign his bishopric. He spent the last twenty years of his life at Longleat, Wiltshire, where he died on March 19, 1711. Of him Macaulay wrote ". . . his moral character approaches, as near as human infirmity permits, the ideal perfection of Christian virtue."

Praise God, From Whom All Blessings Flow....1692
Awake, My Soul, and With the Sun............1692

KETHE, Rev. William (kēth), 15— ca.-1593, Presbyterian. A Calvinist, William Kethe was probably born in Scotland, although there is no definite evidence of the fact. He, with many who shared his beliefs, was exiled by Queen Mary and spent from 1555 to 1559 in Frankfurt and Geneva, where he wrote countless letters to other refugees on the Continent. Twice, in 1563 and again in 1569, he was chaplain of the Earl of Warwick's soldiers at Havre; later, he was pastor of Childe Okeford in Dorsetshire. He was active as a scholar, being one of the translators of the Geneva Bible (The Breeches Bible), the author of several religious ballads, and the holder of a reputation as "no unready rhymer." There is a dispute as to the year of his death. One authority maintains it to be 1608, but the year 1593 is generally agreed upon.

All People That on Earth Do Dwell..........1561

KEY, Francis Scott (kē), 1779-1843), Episcopalian
Francis Scott Key, son of a distinguished Revolutionary War officer, was born on August 1, 1779 in Frederick, Maryland. After studying for the legal profession he began his practice in Frederick in 1801. The following year he moved to Georgetown, D. C. and there served at a later date as the District Attorney, for three terms. In 1814 his "Star Spangled Banner" was published in the Baltimore American. In Washington he spent much time in public service, visiting invalids, teaching Sunday-school, improving negro conditions, and as a lay reader in the Protestant Episcopal Church, reading service. He died January 11, 1843.

The Star Spangled Banner...................1814
Lord, With Glowing Heart I'll Praise Thee....1823

420

KILMER, Joyce (kĭl'mẽr), 1886-1918, R. C. Alfred
Joyce Kilmer was born in New Brunswick, New
Jersey, on December 6, 1886 of German-English-
Scottish ancestry. He attended Rutgers College,
and received his B.A. from Columbia in 1908.
For one year thereafter he taught Latin at the
Morristown, N. J. High School, then joined the
staff of the "Standard Dictionary," where he re-
mained until 1913 when he went to work for the
Sunday Magazine and Book Review of the New
York Times. At 22 he married Aline Murray, also a poet, and when
one of their daughters contracted infantile paralysis he turned from the
Episcopal Church in which he was a member, to Roman Catholicism.
During the First World War he served with the 165th Regiment of the
famed Rainbow Division. He was killed in action on July 30, 1918
and awarded a posthumous Croix de Guerre. He is buried near
Seringes, France.

Trees 1914
No Longer of Him Be It Said 1918

KINGSLEY, Rev. Charles (kĭngz'ly), 1819-1875,
Anglican. The son of a country gentleman and
vicar, Charles Kingsley was born at Holne Vicarage, Dartmoor, Devonshire, England on June 12,
1819. He was educated at Clifton and at Helston,
then at King's College in London, and finally at
Magdalen College, Cambridge, graduating with
highest honors in the classics. After his ordination
in 1842 he was curate at Eversley; rector of Eversley, 1844-1875; canon of Chester, 1869-1873;
canon of Westminster, 1873-1875. He was be-
loved by his parishioners for his fine character and disposition, as
well as for the welfare agencies he established for them. In all, he
wrote 35 books, including historical novels, sermons, lectures and
poetry. He died at Eversley on January 23, 1875.

The Day of the Lord Is at Hand, at Hand 1858
From Thee All Skill and Science Flow 1871

KIPLING, Rudyard (kĭp'lĭng), 1865-1936, Angli-
can. Rudyard Kipling was born in Bombay, India
in 1865 and educated at the United Services
College at Westward Ho, England. Returning to
India at fifteen, he joined the staff of the "Civil
and Military Gazette" in Lahore. In 1889 he
returned to England, where he was acclaimed for
his writing, and settled in London. He married
Miss Caroline Balestier of Vermont, U.S.A. in
1892, and spent several years in America, where
he wrote "Captains Courageous" and other stories reflecting American
backgrounds. He became an ardent imperialist, as reflected in his work
after the turn of the century. His verses were not intended to be used
as hymns, but some have survived as such, i.e. "The Recessional,"
which was written to commemorate Queen Victoria's Diamond Jubilee.

God of Our Fathers, Known of Old 1897
(The Recessional)
Father in Heaven, Who Lovest All 1906

KLOPSTOCK, Friedrich Gottlieb (klŏp'stŏk), 1724-1803, Lutheran. Friedrich Gottlieb Klopstock, the oldest of 17 children, was born July 2, 1724 at Quedlinburg, Germany and attended the school in Schulpforta from 1739 to 1745. He was a student of Theology in 1745 at the University of Jena, and in 1746 at the University of Leipzig. It was during these two years that he started his "Messiah," a work which was not completed until 27 years later. While a private tutor in Langensalza he fell in love with his cousin, who became his "Fanny" in several of his poems. From 1751 to 1770 he lived on pension in Copenhagen at the court of King Frederick V of Denmark, and in 1771 retired to Hamburg where he continued to work on the "Messiah," completing it in 1773. He helped to inaugurate the Golden Age of German Literature with his lyrics and odes, and was considered in his day to be one of the great religious poets. He died at Hamburg on March 14, 1803.

Saviour! by Thy Holy Birth..................1758
Grant Us, Lord! Due Preparation............1758

KNIGHT, Rev. William Allen (nīt), 1863-1957, Congregationalist. William Allen Knight was born in Milton, Missouri on October 20, 1863. He attended the Oberlin Graduate School of Theology, and held the following pastorates: First Church in Saginaw, Michigan 1894-1897; Central Church, Fall River, Mass. 1897-1902; Brighton Church, Boston, Mass. 1903-1919; Plymouth Church, Framingham, Mass. 1919-1934. He was well-known for his book "The Song of Our Syrian Guest," which was published in at least five languages and two systems for the blind, and sold more than five million copies. He died in Framingham on February 11, 1957.

Come, My Heart, Canst Thou Not Hear It....1915

LANIER, Sidney (la-nēr'), 1842-1881, Presbyterian. Born in Macon, Georgia in 1842, Sidney Lanier prepared himself for college and entered Oglethorpe College in Georgia at the age of fourteen. Following his graduation he tutored at the college for a time, and then joined the Confederate Army as scout, blockade runner and signal officer, but was captured and imprisoned. Not until the end of the war was he released, and then with impaired health. He moved to Texas and became greatly interested in music. In 1873 he became flutist in the Peabody Orchestra of Baltimore and eventually, in spite of tuberculosis, was the most prominent flutist in the country. Chosen in 1879 as lecturer of English Literature at Johns Hopkins University, he suffered a health breakdown and went to live in the mountains in North Carolina, where he died at the age of 39, in 1881. He wrote and published 10 volumes of poetry and 14 of prose. His bust is to be found in New York University's Hall of Fame.

Thou God, Whose High Eternal Love........1865
Into the Woods My Master Went.............1880

LARCOM, Lucy (lär'kŭm), 1826-1893, Episco-palian. Lucy Larcom was born on March 5, 1826, in Beverly, Massachusetts. When only a child she lost her sea-captain father, and moved with her mother and sisters to Lowell where she got a job in a clothing factory. At seven she had begun to write poetry, and while still in the mill was noticed by John Greenleaf Whittier, with whom she had a life-long friendship. Her position in the factory  advanced, and always she contributed to the "Lowell Offering," a magazine of the literary works of the factory girls. She found time to study English, German, mathematics, grammar, and eventually secured a teaching position in Looking Glass, Illinois. She then attended and graduated from the Monticello Female Seminary in Alton, Illinois and returned to teach in Massachusetts, continuing her studies at Wheaton Seminary in Norton. Failing in health, she retired to write exclusively, and to edit anthologies with Whitfier. She continued her writing up until her death on April 17, 1893.

> Heavenly Helper, Friend Divine..............1885
> O God, Thy World Is Sweet With Prayer......1892

LATHBURY, Mary Artemisia (Lăth'bĕr-y), 1841-1913, Methodist. Mary Lathbury's father was a Methodist minister, as were her two brothers. She herself was an artist by profession, but devoted most of her energy to religious work and to writing. Born on August 10, 1841 in Manchester, New York she taught drawing and painting at Newbury Academy, Vermont and in New York City. She was general editor of the 'Methodist  Sunday-school religious papers, and with Bishop Vincent started the Chautauqua Movement. She started the Look-Up Legion of the Methodist Sunday-school, and was called "The Poet Laureate of Chautauqua," becoming well known in the United States for her poetry. She died on October 20, 1913 at East Orange, New Jersey.

> Break Thou the Bread of Life...............1877
> Day Is Dying in the West...................1877

LONGFELLOW, Henry Wadsworth (lŏng'fĕl-ō), 1807-1882, Unitarian. Born on February 27, 1807 at Portland, Maine, Henry Wadsworth Longfellow graduated from Bowdoin College in 1825. He studied abroad from 1826 to 1829, at which time he took the chair of Modern Languages at Bowdoin, remaining there until 1836 when he moved to Boston to become professor of Modern Languages and Literature at Harvard, a post he held for 18 years. In 1854 he retired, to devote  himself exclusively to his writing. His works were widely acclaimed during his lifetime, and are still read with pleasure today. He died October 3, 1882, and a bust was placed in Westminster Abbey in his honor.

> I Heard the Bells on Christmas Day..........1863
> Ah, What a Sound.........................

LONGFELLOW, Rev. Samuel (lŏng'fĕl-ō), 1819-1892, Unitarian. Samuel Longfellow, the younger brother of Henry Wadsworth Longfellow, was born on June 18, 1819 in Portland, Maine. He graduated from Harvard College in 1839 and from Harvard Divinity School seven years later. In collaboration with a classmate, Samuel Johnson, he brought out the "Book of Hymns," which proved to be such a success that in 1848, only two years after its first publication, it had to be reprinted. In 1864 he and Samuel Johnson again collaborated in producing "Hymns of the Spirit." After preaching for a short time in a Unitarian church in Germantown, Pa., he retired to write his brother's biography in 1882. He lived in retirement at Cambridge, Mass. until 1892, when his death occurred on October 3rd at his native Portland. He wrote 27 original hymns, and it was he who introduced the custom of vesper services.

> **God of the Earth, the Sky, the Sea**..........**1864**
> **Holy Spirit, Truth Divine**..................**1864**

LOWELL, James Russell (lō'ĕl), 1819-1891, Unitarian. Born in Cambridge, Massachusetts on February 22, 1819, James Russell Lowell graduated from Harvard in 1838 and from Harvard Law School in 1840. After an unsuccessful attempt at law practice he discovered his talent for writing, and started on a literary career. He wrote various poems and essays until 1855, when he gave a series of lectures for the Lowell Institute, which resulted in his appointment to the chair of Modern I anguages and Literature at Harvard, succeeding Henry Wadsworth Longfellow. He served as U. S. minister to Spain (1877-1880) and to Great Britain (1880-1885), and was given honorary degrees by Harvard, Oxford, Cambridge, St. Andrews, Edinburgh, and Bologna. He died on his estate in Cambridge on August 12, 1891, and was elected posthumously (1905) to the American Hall of Fame.

> **Once to Every Man and Nation**.............**1844**
> **What Means This Glory Round Our Feet?**....**1874**

LOWRY, Rev. Robert (lou'ry), 1826-1899, Baptist. Robert Lowry was born in Philadelphia, Pennsylvania on March 12, 1826. He attended Lewisburg University (now Bucknell) and was ordained a Baptist minister soon after his graduation. He served churches in West Chester, Pa., New York City, and Brooklyn, N. Y. until in 1876 he was made professor of Rhetoric at Bucknell. In 1882 he resigned this post to become pastor at the Second Baptist Church in Plainfield, N. J., where he remained until his death. Having a great interest in hymnody, Lowry wrote many hymns, but he preferred preaching to writing. His sentimental "Where Is My Wandering Boy Tonight," for which he wrote both the words and the music, was widely sung at the time of its publication. He died in Plainfield on November 25, 1899.

> **Shall We Gather at the River**...............**1864**
> **One More Day's Work for Jesus**.............**1869**

LUKE, Mrs. Jemima Thompson (lōk), 1813-1906, Congregationalist. Born Jemima Thompson in Colebrook Terrace, Islington, London on August 19, 1813, Mrs.  Luke early showed a talent for writing when she contributed anonymously to the "Juvenile Magazine" at the age of thirteen. She planned to do missionary work in India, but was prevented because of poor health. She married a Congregational minister, the Rev. Samuel Luke, in 1843 and began her literary career. She was always very interested in schools and in children as well as missions, and edited "The Missionary Repository," a missionary magazine for children. She died February 2, 1906.

I Think When I Read That Sweet Story of Old. . 1841

LUTHER, Rev. Martin (lōō'thĕr), 1483-1546, Lutheran. Martin Luther, son of a poor Saxon miner, was born on November 10, 1843, the Eve of St. Martin, for which he was named. During  his lifetime he started a movement that was to make his name practically synonymous with the Protestant Reformation. Though Luther is remembered primarily for this, he was also a man of great culture, and a devoted musician. Shortly after his ordination as a priest in 1507, he became a doctor of Philosophy at Wittenberg, although this career was interrupted by the famous Diet of Worms in 1521. Luther was brought up in a religious background and applied this to his musical ventures. He believed strongly in congregational singing, even for women. Believing also that "the devil should not have all the best tunes," he wrote more than 30 hymns in his lifetime, designed to renew in the people an enthusiasm for religious music. An avid musician, he played both the lute and the flute, and enjoyed accompanying himself to his own hymns. He died on February 18, 1546 in Eisleben, his birthplace.

A Mighty Fortress Is Our God **1529**
From Heaven Above to Earth I Come **1535**

LYTE, Rev. Henry Francis (līt), 1793-1847, Anglican. Life was not easy for this hymnist, born June 1, 1793 in Ednam, Scotland. Although his childhood was plagued with poverty, Henry Francis Lyte managed to finish training for the ministry at Trinity College, Dublin (where he won  three times the prize for writing the best English verse), take Holy Orders, and settle down as curate in a small parish near Wexford, Ireland in 1815. In 1819 he served a parish at Lymington, Hampshire and in 1823 was appointed perpetual curate of Lower Brixham, a fishing village in Devon where he remained until 1847. It was here that he wrote many of his hymns, set up a Sunday-school of some eight hundred children, and trained seventy teachers for it, eventually effecting a great change in the moral and religious tone of the village. In September, 1847 he took up residence wih his family in Nice, France, where he died one month later.

Jesus, I My Cross Have Taken **1824**
Abide With Me **1847**

MARKHAM, Charles Edwin (märk'am), 1852 1940, No Denominational Affiliation. Called variously "the greatest poet of the century," "the poet of humanity" and "not more poet than prophet," Charles Edwin Markham was born in Oregon City, Oregon in 1852 but moved to California with his family at the age of five. Educated at the San Jose Normal School, he was variously teacher, principal and school superintendent in California. He moved to New York in 1899, where he devoted himself to lecturing and writing. His works, mostly books of poetry, met with great success. A copy of the most famous, his "Man with a Hoe," is exhibited in Millet's studio at Barbizon, France, to supplement the artist's great landscape. Markham is also called "the poet of democracy." He died in 1940.

The Crest and Crowning of All Good..........1899

MARLATT, Earl Bowman (mär'lät'), 1892-19—, Methodist. Dr. Marlatt was born in Columbus, Indiana on May 25, 1892. After attending various public schools he went to DePauw College, graduating with a B.A. degree in 1912. He started his career with a teaching position at the high schools in Raleigh and Rushville, Indiana and became an associate editor of the Kenosha, Wisconsin, Evening News. With one interruption to serve as 2nd Lieutenant in the U. S. Field Artillery in World War I, Dr. Marlett worked on the Evening News until 1917. He has taught at Southern Methodist University in Dallas, Texas and at Boston University School of Theology; has written a number of books, including a volume of biography, "Protestant Saints"; served on the official committee of the Interchurch Center in New York City, (and wrote the dedication hymn which was sealed into the cornerstone); is a member of four fraternities and several literary and philosophy societies. He retired in 1946 from his chair of Philosophy of Religion at Southern Methodist University. His poetic works have received high praise from others in his field, as well as from critics.

Spirit of Life in This New Dawn.............1924
"Are Ye Able," Said the Master.............1926

MARTIN, Mrs. C. D. (mär'tin), 1867-1948, Disciples of Christ. The initials "C. D." stand for Civilla Durfee, the maiden name of the wife of the Baptist preacher, Rev. Walter Stillman Martin. Mrs. Martin was born August 21, 1867 in Nova Scotia. She taught school for a while, then married Dr. Martin and traveled with him on his evangelistic campaigns. Dr. Martin and his wife collaborated in writing their famous hymn "God Will Take Care of You." It was written at New York in 1904, she writing the words, he composing the music. In 1916, they changed their denomination and became members of the Disciples of Christ church. Mrs. Martin died at Atlanta, Georgia on March 9, 1948.

God Will Take Care of You.................1904
His Eye Is on the Sparrow..................1906

MATHESON, Rev. George (măth'ĕ-s'n), 1842-1906, Presbyterian.  Born in Glasgow, Scotland on March 27, 1842, the son of a prosperous Scottish merchant, George Matheson was handicapped from childhood by exceedingly poor vision. In spite of this he attended Glasgow University and graduated with his M.A. with honors in 1862. In 1866 he began his ministry at Sandyford Church in Glasgow as assistant preacher, and two years later received a parish of his own at Innellan, Argyllshire. There his fame as a preacher spread, and in 1886 he began a 13-year service at the 2,000-member St. Bernard's Parish Church in Edinburgh. Because of his blindness (he was almost completely blind at 18) he was unable to do the kind of research he wanted to do, but he did write at least seventeen works, and during his life was given B.D., D.D., LL.D. and F.R.S.E. degrees He died on August 28, 1906 at the Firth of Forth

      O Love That Wilt Not Let Me Go............1882
      Gather Us in, Thou Love That Fillest All......1890

MEDLEY, Rev. Samuel (mĕd'ly), 1738-1799, Baptist.  Born in Cheshunt Hertfordshire, England, on June 23, 1738, Samuel Medley received a good education at the hands of his father, who ran a school. Apprenticed to an oil-dealer for a while, he soon became dissatisfied and joined the Royal Navy, from which he was forced to retire in 1759 after being wounded. In critical condition, he went to live with his grandfather, who effected his conversion by prayer and the reading of an Isaac Watts sermon. In London, Medley joined a Baptist Church, and in 1767, after preaching a short while, he became pastor of the Baptist Church in Watford. Five years later he was made pastor of the Baptist Church in Liverpool, where he remained until his death on July 17, 1799.

      I Know That My Redeemer Lives............1775
      O Could I Speak the Matchless Worth........1789

MELANCHTHON, Philip (mĕ-lăngk'thŭn), 1497-1560, Lutheran.  Philip Melanchthon was born February 16, 1497 at Bretten, Germany. He was educated at the Latin School in Pforzheim from 1507 to 1509, at the University of Heidelberg, and at Tubingen (where he transferred from Heidelberg because of his youth), receiving his M.A. in 1514. Born Philip Schwarzerd, he adopted the name Melanchthon (being the Greek word for Schwarzerd, or Black Earth) at Heidelberg. After his graduation, he remained at Tubingen as lecturer in Philosophy and in 1516 was appointed professor of Greek at Wittenberg, where he became a close associate of Martin Luther. He worked closely with Luther during the Reformation, contributing to the work through his writing. He composed the Augsburg Confession (1530) and wrote the first great work in Protestant dogmatic theology, "Loci Communes." Melanchthon died on April 19, 1560. His hymns, written in Latin were collected in 1842.

      Lord God, We Give All Praise to Thee........1543

MERRILL, Rev. William Pierson (měr'il), 1867-1954, Presbyterian. William Pierson Merrill was born January 10, 1867 in Orange, New Jersey, and attended Rutgers (B.A. 1887, M.A. 1890) and Union Theological Seminary (B.D. 1890). When he was 11 years old he became a member of a Congregational Church, and in 1880 joined a Dutch Reformed Church, but in 1890 he was ordained into the Presbyterian ministry. His first church was in Philadelphia, where he served for five years; his second was in Chicago, from 1895 to 1911; his third and last was the Brick Presbyterian Church in New York City, from which he retired in 1938. He was a member of Phi Beta Kappa, and received degrees from New York University, Rutgers, Columbia and Rollins. He authored a number of books and several hymns. He died in 1954.

Not Alone for Mighty Empire.................1909
Rise Up, O Men of God!....................1911

MILMAN, Rev. Henry Hart (mil'man), 1791-1868, Anglican. Henry Hart Milman was born in London on February 10, 1791, the son of a physician to King George III. He was educated at Greenwich, Eton, and Brasenose College, Oxford. At Oxford he won first place in classics, and several prizes for scholastic achievement. He received his B.A. in 1813 and his M.A. in 1816 when he was ordained as vicar of St. Mary's in Reading. He served at this post until 1835. He was professor of Poetry at Oxford for 10 years; Canon of Westminster (1835); dean of St. Paul's Cathedral (1849). He wrote plays, hymns, poems, theological studies, and history, among which works is his "History of the Jews" and his greatest, "History of Latin Christianity." He died September 24, 1868.

Ride On! Ride on in Majesty.................1823
When Our Heads Are Bowed With Woe.......1827

MILTON, John (mil'tŭn), 1608-1674, Congregationalist. England's mighty bard, John Milton, was born on December 19, 1608 in London, the son of a scrivener who early recognized his son's genius. He attended St. Paul's School, and Christ's College, Cambridge, where he was called the "Lady of Christ's" because of his fastidious morals and manners. He was poet, essayist, tutor, politician, and served for some years as Latin secretary to the Council of State. Though blind from 1652, he continued writing and after 1660 devoted his entire time to this effort. There were three marriages—in 1643 to Mary Powell, who died in 1652; in 1656 to Catherine Woodcock, who died 15 months later in childbirth; in 1662 to Elizabeth Minshull, a girl with 25 years to his 55, who outlived him. One of England's greatest poets, Milton is not considered a "people's poet," and while he wrote several poems which are used as hymns, he had little influence on hymnology. He died on November 8, 1674.

Let Us With a Gladsome Mind..............1623
How Lovely Are Thy Dwellings Fair..........1648

MOHR, Rev. Joseph (mōr), 1792-1848, R. C. The son of Franz Mohr, a roving mercenary and musketeer in the archbishop's army, Joseph Mohr was born on December 11, 1792 in Salzburg, Austria. Since Franz Mohr was away from home a good part of the time, Domvikar J. N. Hiernle, a Roman Catholic priest, became the boy's foster father, and Joseph was ordained in the Roman Catholic Church in 1815. He served at several parishes around Salzburg until 1828, when he was appointed vicar at Hintersee. In 1837 he became vicar at Wagrein, and here he remained until his death on December 4, 1848. It was while he was assistant at the Church of St. Nicholas in Oberndorf (near Salzburg) in 1818 that he wrote the hymn that is his only claim to world-renown, "Silent Night, Holy Night."

Franz Gruber, composer, is shown above Joseph Mohr

    Holy Spirit, Hear Us........................1816
    Silent Night! Holy Night!..................1818

MONSELL, Rev. John Samuel Bewley (mŏn-sĕl'), 1811-1875, Anglican. The son of the archdeacon of Londonderry, John Samuel Bewley Monsell was born on March 2, 1811 at St. Columb's, Londonderry, Ireland. He attended Trinity College, Dublin, receiving his B.A. in 1832, and was ordained in 1834. He served as chaplain, chancellor, rector and vicar at various dioceses in Ireland and England, his last post being that of rector of St. Nicholas in Guildford, England. He wrote 11 books of poetry, in which his 300 hymns were contained. He died on April 9, 1875, as the result of an accident that occurred while he was watching workmen making repairs on his church.

    Light of the World, We Hail Thee............1863
    Fight the Good Fight With All Thy Might....1863

MONTGOMERY, James (mönt-gŭm'ĕry), 1771-1854, Moravian. James Montgomery was born at Irvine Scotland, on November 4, 1771. Sent to school in Yorkshire, he was forced to leave because of poor marks, and became a baker's apprentice. He ran away, however, in 1787 as he did not like the work, and after trying two more jobs that he found equally as boring, went to London in the hope of publishing the poems which he had started writing at the age of ten. There he became co-editor of the radical "Sheffield Register," achieving full ownership when the original owner fled England for his life. As editor of the "Sheffield Iris" (the name he used for the paper) he was several times imprisoned and fined, and during the terms in prison he wrote poems. He received a royal pension in 1833, giving him 200 pounds per year. He died April 30, 1854 in Sheffield. James Montgomery was the author of not less than 400 hymns, more of which are in use today than those of any other hymn-writer except Charles Wesley and Isaac Watts.

    Angels, From the Realms of Glory..........1816
    O Spirit of the Living God..................1823

MUHLENBERG, Rev. William Augustus (mū'lĕn-bûrg), 1796-1877, Episcopalian. William Augustus Muhlenberg was born on September 16, 1796 in Philadelphia, one of a family of illustrious Americans and Lutherans. Because he attended Christ Episcopal Church in his youth, he grew up to become an Episcopal clergyman. At that time the Episcopalians were lacking hymns, and a committee was chosen to prepare a hymnal. Muhlenberg was on the committee, and contributed four of his own hymns. Later, in New York City, he became well-known as a church leader and rector of the Church of the Holy Communion, as well as the head of a boys' school and founder of St. Luke's Hospital. He died April 6, 1877.

Saviour, Who Thy Flock Art Feeding........1826
Shout the Glad Tidings, Exultingly Sing........1826

NEALE, Rev. John Mason (nēl), 1818-1866, Anglican. Born the son of an Anglican clergyman in London on January 24, 1818, John Mason Neale attended Trinity College, Cambridge and there won the Seatonian prize for sacred poetry eleven times. Moved by the Oxford Movement to High Church principles, he was unable to hold an influential position in the Church of England. Always of poor health, he spent from 1843 to 1844 at Madeira, Spain and then had to refuse a position at Perth because of the unfavorable climate. A brilliant scholar, Neale had a knowledge of 20 languages; he authored books on church history, church architecture, etc.; he translated many hymns from the Latin, and more from the Greek than any other hymnologist; he wrote some hymns of his own. He was honored with only one degree—that of D.D.—and received it not from his own alma mater, but from an American University. Dr. Neale died at East Grinstead on August 6, 1866.

Around the Throne of God a Band............1842
Blessed Savior, Who Has Taught Me..........1842

NEANDER, Rev. Joachim (nā-ăn'dĕr), 1650-1680, Reformed. "The first poet of the Reformed Church in Germany" and "the greatest of the Reformed hymn-writers" as he has variously been called, Joachim Neander (the Greek form of the German name, Neumann) was born in Bremen, Germany in 1650. He was educated at the Paedogogium and the Gymnasium Illustre in Bremen, where he entered into the riotous and boisterous life of the students most heartily. He tutored at Heidelberg and Frankfurt for a number of years, then in 1674 became headmaster of the Reformed grammar school in Dusseldorf and an assistant pastor of the Reformed Church there. Neander was a scholar, equally as well accomplished in theology, literature, music and writing. He wrote 60 hymns, and composed many tunes. He died in 1680 of tuberculosis at the age of thirty.

Praise Ye the Lord, the Almighty............1679
Wondrous King, All-Glorious................1680

NEWMAN, Rev. John Henry (nū'man), 1801-1890, R. C. John Newman was born February 21, 1801 in London, the son of a wealthy banker.  He spent some lonely school years at Great Ealing and Trinity College, Oxford where he studied for a church career in opposition to his father's hopes for the law. He was ordained in 1824, becoming curate of St. Clement's, Oxford and the following year vice-principal of Alban Hall. For two years (1826-1828) he was tutor at Oriel College. Then, in 1828, he was made vicar of St. Mary's, Oxford. Although he had originally been decidedly Anglican, he moved steadily toward the Church of Rome, and in 1845 he was received into the Roman Catholic Church (which never fully trusted him). In 1864 he published his well-received autobiography—called "Apology for His Life" and considered one of the best in the English language— and finally, in 1879, was made Cardinal of St. George in Velabro. The last years of his life were probably his happiest, as he had at last been honored by the Vatican, which had once labeled him "the most dangerous man in England." He died at his Oratory on August 11, 1890.

Lead, Kindly Light, Amid the Encircling Gloom . 1833
Praise to the Holiest in the Height 1868

NEWTON, Rev. John (nū't'n), 1725-1807, Anglican. John Newton was born on July 24, 1725 in London. His mother, a religious woman, died when he was seven and he went to sea with his father at the age of eleven. Forced to enter the British Navy as a midshipman, he deserted and  became a slave trader. He had spells of being religious, and on a trading voyage read the book "The Imitation of Christ," which deepened his religious interests. Through this study, his acquaintanceship with a truly Christian sea-captain, and an experience of facing death one night at sea in 1748, he became truly converted. Upon returning to England he took up the study of Greek and Hebrew. After six years he was ordained at Olney, and began a brilliant and influential career. He remained at Olney as curate (1764-1779), counting among his intimate friends William Cowper, with whom he wrote the "Olney Hymns." 283 of the hymns were written by Newton. He died in London, December 21, 1807.

Glorious Things of Thee Are Spoken 1779
How Sweet the Name of Jesus Sounds 1779

NORTH, Rev. Frank Mason (nörth), 1850-1935, Methodist. Frank Mason North was born in New York City on December 3, 1850. He was educated at private schools in New York and at Wesleyan University. He began studies for the Methodist ministry at Middletown, Connecticut.  From 1873 to 1892 he was pastor at churches in Florida, New York and Connecticut. In 1892 he began his 20 years as corresponding secretary for the New York Church Extension and Missionary Society. He died on December 17, 1935.

Where Cross the Crowded Ways of life 1903
Thou Lord of Light, Across the Years 1917

OATMAN, Rev. Johnson, Jr. (ōt'man), 1856-1926, Methodist. The most prolific gospel song writer of his day, Johnson Oatman, Jr. was born on April 21, 1856 near Medford, New Jersey. He was educated at Herbert's Academy in Vincentown, New Jersey and at New Jersey Collegiate Institute in Bordentown. He joined the M. E. Church at 19, was licensed to preach and was eventually ordained, although he never actually had a church of his own. Until his father's death, Johnson, Jr. worked in the mercantile business of Johnson Oatman and Son, and then went into the life insurance business. In 1892 he wrote his first hymn, his average yearly output being 200 from then on. Altogether, he wrote approximately 3,000 hymns. Oatman died in 1926.

I'm Pressing on the Upward Way.............1925
Count Your Blessings................(not known)

OCCOM, Rev. Samson (ŏk'ŭm), 1732-1792, Presbyterian. Born at Norwich, Connecticut in 1732 into the Mohican Indian tribe, Samson Occom was converted at the age of 17, on hearing a sermon of Whitefield's. He lived and studied for four years at the home of the Rev. Eleazer Whealock in Lebanon, Conn. and was ordained in 1759. He began work with the Montauk Indians on Long Island, and in 1766-1767 made fund-raising trips to England, where he raised more than 10,000 pounds for his Indian school (later part of Dartmouth College). In 1774 he published "Choice Collection of Hymns and Spiritual Songs." The last years of his life were spent on Long Island, where he died in 1792.

Now the Shades of Night Are Gone...........1799
Awaked by Sinai's Awful Sound..............1802

OXENHAM, John (ŏk's'n-hăm), 1852-1941, Congregationalist. Oxenham was born William Arthur Dunkerley on November 12, 1852 at Manchester, England. He took his nom de plume from a character in Kingsley's "Westward Ho!", a book he read as a child. (Later he also used the nom de plume Julian Ross in his contributions of a serialized fiction story to a newspaper.) Upon graduating from Victoria University in Manchester, he took charge of the French branch of his father's wholesale provision business, and went to live in Rennes, Brittany. Traveling in America in 1877 he became interested in publishing, and after two years returned to London. He published "Today" and "The Idler" and wrote novels until 1913, when he moved to Ealing to write verse and religious books, and raise his six children. The identity of Oxenham was kept secret for many years, his correspondence being handled through an agent. He died on January 24, 1941, having written some 62 books.

In Christ There Is No East or West..........1908
'Mid All the Traffic of the Ways............1917

PALMER, Rev. Ray (päm'ĕr), 1808-1887, Congregationalist. Dr. Palmer was born in Little Compton, Rhode Island on November 12, 1808, the son of a judge. He spent his youth in Boston, where he was a clerk in a dry-goods store and a very active member of the Park Street Congregational Church. He attended Phillips Academy in Andover for three years, and Yale University, where he graduated in 1830. For five years following his graduation he studied theology, while
teaching at a New York girls' school. Upon his ordination in 1835 he began a 30-year service as pastor, divided equally between the Central Congregational Church in Bath, Maine and the First Congregational Church in Albany, New York. In 1865 he became corresponding secretary of the American Congregational Union, and remained there until his retirement to Newark, New Jersey in 1878. Dr. Palmer led a busy life, but managed to write a number of hymns (for which he refused payment) and translate many hymns from the Latin to English. He died March 29, 1887.

> My Faith Looks Up to Thee.................1830
> Take Me, O My Father, Take Me............1864

PARK, Rev. John Edgar (pärk), 1879-1956, Congregationalist. This son, grandson, and great-grandson of Presbyterian preachers, was born in Belfast, Ireland on May 7, 1879. He was educated at the Royal University of Ireland; Queen's College, Belfast; Edinburgh; Leipzig; Munich; Oxford; Princton. He was ordained to the ministry in 1902 and served in the ministry for 22 years (19 years in the Second Congregational Church in Newton, Mass.). In 1926 he became president
of Wheaton College in Norton, Massachusetts. Dr. Park wrote a number of books as well as several hymns, and contributed to leading magazines. His death occurred at his home in Osterville, Massachusetts on March 4, 1956.

> O Jesus Thou Wast Tempted.................1913
> We Would See Jesus, Lo, His Star............1913

PARKER, Rev. Theodore (pär'kĕr), 1810-1860, Unitarian. The youngest of 11 children, Theodore Parker was born August 24, 1810 in Lexington, Massachusetts. Admitted to Harvard College at the age of 20, he received only an honorary M.A. degree in 1840. After teaching school for some time, he became a minister in Boston in 1846, having been ordained in 1837. He was very well-read, an intense patriot and champion of anti-slavery, and a hard worker for the causes in
which he believed. He was considered one of the most prominent and pronounced extremists of the Unitarian Church in America. In 1859 he went abroad for reasons of health, and died in Florence, Italy on May 10, 1860, and was buried there in the Protestant cemetery.

> In Darker Days and Nights of Storm....(not known)
> O Thou Great Friend of All the Sons of Men..1846

PERRONET, Rev. Edward (pĕr-ō-nā'), 1726-1792, Independent. Edward Perronet, son of the "Archbishop of Methodism" (so named because of strong support of the Wesleys), was born in 1726 in Kent, England. In 1749 he accompanied John Wesley on a tour of Northern England, and for eight years worked hard as an itinerant evangelistic preacher. Because of Peronnet's attacks on the Church of England, and because of his satire "The Mitre" against the church, the association with the Wesleys was broken off entirely in 1771, and he became a chaplain of the Countess of Huntingdon. His attacks against the church were too strong for the Countess, also, and he wandered among different groups until he finally took charge of a Congregational chapel in Canterbury. He died there on January 2, 1792. He published three volumes of religious verse, from which his hymns were taken.

> All Hail the Power of Jesus' Name............1779
> Hail, Holy, Holy, Holy Lord..................1785

PHELPS, Rev. Sylvanus Dryden, (fĕlps), 1816-1895, Baptist. S. Dryden Phelps, born May 15, 1816 in Suffield, Connecticut, attended the Connecticut Literary Institute, Brown University, and the Yale Divinity School. After a short time at the Baptist Church of Bristol, Conn., he began a pastorate at the First Baptist Church in New Haven which lasted from 1846 to 1874. During his service, the church received 1,217 new members including 615 baptisms. In 1874 he went to the Jefferson Street Baptist Church in Providence, R. I. and resigned in 1876 to edit "The Christian Secretary" in Hartford. In 1879 he became a trustee of Brown University, which in 1854 had given him a D.D. degree. Dr. Phelps' literary efforts extended back to the temperance hymns of his college days, and in later life much of his poetry, sermons and other works were published. He died in New Haven on November 23, 1895.

> Saviour, Thy Dying Love.....................1862
> Sweet Is the Hour of Prayer.................1862

PHILLIPS, Philip (fĭl'ĭps), 1834-1895, Methodist. Philip Phillips was born on a farm in Chautauqua County, New York on August 13, 1834. He did not, however, remain on the farm for very long. Musically talented, he became a singing evangelist, traveling all over the English-speaking world giving concerts, singing at meetings, writing and composing hymns. His book "Hallowed Songs" was for a time used by the evangelists Sankey and Moody in their meetings. He died in Delaware, Ohio on June 25, 1895.

> I Have Heard of a Saviour's Love............1862
> I Will Sing the Story.......................1866

PIERPONT, Folliott Sandford (pēr'point), 1835-1917, Anglican. Folliott Sandford Pierpoint was born in Bath, England on October 7, 1835. Graduating from Queens College, Cambridge in 1857, he was first classical master at Somersetshire College, and then independent writer. Besides contributing to "Lyra Eucharistica" he wrote several collections of his own poems, most of which were of a religious nature. He died at Newport, Mon. in 1917.

    For the Beauty of the Earth.................**1864**
    O Cross, O Cross of Shame.................**1864**

PIERSON, Rev. Arthur Tappan (pēr's'n), 1837-1911, Presbyterian. Arthur Tappan Pierson was born on March 6, 1837 in New York City. He graduated from Hamilton College in 1857, and at the age of 23 began his ministry as pastor of the Congregational Church in Binghamton, New York. This was followed by a pastorate at the Presbyterian Church in Waterford, New York and in 1869 by one at the Fort Street Presbyterian Church in Detroit, Michigan. At the latter church

he instituted the custom of free evening services, in order to draw outsiders into the congregation. After several years in Detroit, he went to Philadelphia to the mission congregation at Bethany Presbyterian Church, and after several more years gave up a fixed pastorate to become a missionary, evangelist and lecturer, as well as an author of pamphlets and books. In 1892, however, he went to London to succeed the Reverend Charles Spurgeon at the Metropolitan Tabernacle. When he was baptized by immersion in 1896, he forfeited his connection with the Philadelphia Presbytery, and thereafter had no formal ministerial standing in any denomination. His death occurred in 1911.

    Once I Was Dead in Sin.....................**1873**
    To Thee, O God, We Raise.................**1874**

PLUMPTRE, Rev. Edward Hayes (plŭm'tĕr), 1821-1891, Anglican. Born in London on August 6, 1821, Edward Hayes Plumptre attended King's College and went on to Oxford, where he graduated summa cum laude from University College and became a Fellow of Brasenose College. He was ordained in 1846, and the following year received his M.A. degree. He served in a variety of positions at King's College, Lincoln's Inn, Oxford University, St. Paul's, the Theological School

(Oxford), Pluckley in Kent, and Brickley. He became dean of Wells Cathedral in 1881, remaining in that position until his death. A member of the Old Testament Company for the Revision of the Authorized Version of the Holy Scriptures, he also wrote a biography; translated Dante, Aeschylus and Sophocles; edited the "Biblical Educators" and two collections of poems; authored several volumes of poetry. He died February 1, 1891.

    O Light, Whose Beams Illumine All..........**1864**
    Rejoice, Ye Pure in Heart.................**1865**

POLLOCK, Rev. Thomas Benson (pŏl'ŭk), 1836-1896, Anglican. Thomas Benson Pollock was born on the Isle of Man on May 28, 1836. He attended Trinity College, Dublin, there winning the Vice-Chancellor's Prize for English verse in 1855. He was ordained in 1861, and was curate of St. Luke's, Staffordshire; St. Thomas', London; St. Alban's, Birmingham. At the latter church he worked for thirty years as his brother's assistant, succeeding him as vicar. It was a poor parish, and the overwork told on both brothers. They labored faithfully, and in the course of three years raised approximately 150,000 pounds to promote their work, maintaining a large staff to assist in their educational and welfare programs. Pollock wrote several hymns and litanies, and his "Metrical Litanies for Special Services and General Use" was published in 1870. He died at the age of 60, on December 15, 1896.

Jesus, With Thy Church Abide...............1871
Great Creator, Lord of All.................1876

POTEAT, Rev. Edwin McNeil (pō-tēt'), 1893-1956, Baptist. Born November 20, 1893 in New Haven, Connecticut, Edwin Poteat was the son of the pastor of the Calvary Baptist Church there. He attended and graduated from Furman University and Southern Baptist Theological Seminary. From 1917 to 1927 he was a missionary to China, then held two successive pastorates—the Pullen Memorial Baptist Church in Raleigh, North Carolina and the Euclid Avenue Baptist Church in Cleveland, Ohio. Later he became president of Colgate-Rochester Divinity School in Rochester, New York, leaving this post to return to Raleigh, where he died on December 16, 1956.

Light of the World, How Long the Quest....(not known)
Eternal God Whose Searching Eye Doth Scan..(not known)

PRENTISS, Mrs. Elizabeth Payson (prĕn'tĭs), 1818-1878, Presbyterian. Elizabeth Payson was born on October 26, 1818 in Portland, Maine. At 16 she became a contributor to the "Youth's Companion," a magazine of high spiritual and literary standards. Until her marriage she taught school in Portland, in Ipswich, Massachusetts, and in Richmond, Virginia. At the age of 27 she married the Rev. George L. Prentiss, a Presbyterian minister who became professor of Homiletics and Polity at Union Theological Seminary. Never in good health, Mrs. Prentiss continued to write and publish stories and poems, most of which were of a religious nature, and attained considerable success. One of her books sold more than 70,000 copies in the U. S. alone, and her hymn "More Love to Thee, O Christ" was translated into many languages, including Arabic and Chinese. She died in 1878 at her summer home in Dorset, Vermont.

More Love to Thee, O Christ...............1869
As on a Vast Eternal Shore................1869

RANKIN, Rev. Jeremiah Eames (răng′kĭn), 1828-1904, Congregationalist.  Jeremiah Rankin was born in Thornton, New Hampshire in 1828 and studied for the ministry at the Andover Theological Seminary in Andover, Massachusetts. After pastorates at a number of Congregational Churches, he became president of Howard University in 1889. He attracted large congregations with his powerful and effective preaching, and in the evenings held evangelistic services. He wrote much verse (little of which has lasted) and edited several gospel-song type hymnals. He died in 1904.

> Laboring and Heavy Laden...................1855
> God Be With You 'Till We Meet Again........1880

RINKART, Rev. Martin (rĭng′kärt), 1586-1649, Lutheran.  Martin Rinkart was born April 23, 1586 in Eilenburg, Saxony, Germany. He attended school in Eilenberg and later St. Thomas' School in Leipzig and the University of Leipzig, both on scholarship. In 1617 he became archidiaconus—a position tantamount to bishop—at his native Eilenburg, and remained there for the rest of his life. During the Thirty Years' War the town suffered severely from pestilence, and eight thousand people, including Rinkart's wife, died. He shared his food with the people, and when all the other clergy fled, read the burial service for as many as forty or fifty persons a day. Weak and prematurely aged by the time the peace was signed in 1648, this dedicated humanitarian, fruitful writer, and fine musician, died. One hundred and thirty-five years later a tablet was placed on his house in Eilenburg in memory of the great man.

> Hallelujah, Love, Thanks and Praise.........1642
> Now Thank We All Our God.................1648

ROBERTS, Rev. Daniel Crane (rŏb′ẽrts), 1841-1907, Episcopalian.  Daniel Crane Roberts was born on November 5, 1841 in Bridgehampton, Long Island, New York. He graduated from Kenyon College, Ohio in 1857 and served in the Union Army during the Civil War. Ordained to the Episcopal ministry in 1866, he was rector of churches in Vermont and Massachusetts, and for many years was vicar of St. Paul's in Concord, New Hampshire. He was also president of the New Hampshire Historical Society, president of the State Normal School in Vermont, and Chaplain of the National Guard of New Hampshire. His famous hymn, listed below, was written for the people of Brandon, Vermont in 1876, to be used in celebration of the 100th Anniversary of the Declaration of Independence. It was not published until 1894. Dr. Roberts died in Concord, New Hampshire, on October 31, 1907.

> **God of Our Fathers, Whose Almighty Hand...1876**

ROBINSON, Rev. Richard Hayes (rŏb'ĭn-sŭn), 1842-1892, Anglican. Richard Robinson was born in London in 1842. He was educated at King's College, London and after his ordination as a minister in the Church of England became the 24-year-old curate of St. Paul's, Penge. From 1870 to 1872 he was in charge of Octagon Chapel in Bath (it closed as a place of worship in 1894, and is now a public hall), and then of St. Germain's in Blackheath. He died November 5, 1892.

Holy Father, Cheer Our Way................1871

ROBINSON, Rev. Robert (rŏb'ĭn-sŭn), 1735-1790, Baptist. Born in Swaffham, Norfolk, England on September 27, 1735, Robert Robinson lived for eight years in Swaffham, then for six years in Scarning. At 14 he went to London as apprentice to a hairdresser-barber, and while there partially educated himself by reading. At 17 he attended a sermon by George Whitefield, mostly to scoff at the "poor deluded Methodists" as he called them. However, he received a profound impression, and two years later made a confession of faith and entered the ministry at Mindenhall, Suffolk. After a short time he went to Norwich and organized an Independent congregation. Another year passed before he again changed his affiliations, this time to become pastor at a Baptist church in Cambridge, where he moved in 1761. In a town critical of the clergy he won the respect of the students, and even convinced his parish to adopt open communion, a practice contrary to Baptist belief. Due to his ability as a preacher, the small Baptist parish grew steadily, and he came to be regarded as an able theologian. A versatile man of many talents, Robinson wrote many theological works, and some hymns. Influenced by a friendship with Joseph Priestley in later life, he turned toward Socinianism. He died at Priestley's house in Birmingham on June 9, 1790.

Come, Thou Fount of Every Blessing..........1758
Mighty God, While Angels Bless Thee........1774

ROSSETTI, Christina Georgina (rō-sĕt'y), 1830-1894, Anglican. Born December 5, 1830 in London, Christina G. Rossetti was educated at home. In 1862 she published her first book of poetry, "Goblin Market and Other Poems." This was followed by three other collections of poems, in 1866, 1875, and 1881; a "Book of Prayers for Every Day of the Year" in 1874; and "Letter and Spirit of the Decalogue" in 1883. Before her death in 1894 she wrote various other books of poems, some of which were later made into cantos, and some hymns.

The Shepherds Had an Angel.................1856
In the Bleak Mid-Winter....................1872

438

SANKEY, Ira David (săn'ky), 1840-1908, Methodist. Born in Edinburgh, Pennsylvania in 1840, Ira David Sankey joined the Methodist Episcopal Church at the age of sixteen. He lived in New Castle, Pennsylvania from 1860-1870 and was in charge of a large Sunday-school there. Dwight L. Moody heard Sankey sing at the International Convention of the Y.M.C.A. at Indianapolis, and persuaded him to join in the evangelistic work Moody was carrying on in Chicago. Sankey
worked with Moody there from 1870-1873, at which time the two set out for England to begin their famous crusades—Moody doing the preaching, Sankey the singing. Together they carried on their evangelistic meetings in America (returning again to England in 1883) and published a book called "Sankey and Moody's Songs."

Rejoice, Rejoice 1888
Home at Last, Thy Labour Done......(not known)

SCRIVEN, Joseph Medlicott (skrĭv'ĕn), 1819-1886, Congregationalist. The eccentric and remarkable Joseph Scriven was born at Seapatrick, County Down, Ireland in 1819, and was educated at Trinity College, Dublin. His family was well-off, and Scriven might have pursued a prosperous career had he remained in Ireland. There are two theories to explain why, at the age of twenty-five, he migrated to Canada—the first is that he was influenced by the Plymouth Brethren, thereby
slightly estranging his family, and the second is that the tragic death by drowning of his fiancee on the eve of their wedding produced in him a deep melancholia and he wished to remove himself from the scene. At any rate, he became a private tutor at Rice Lake, Ontario, later moving to Hamilton and eventually to Port Hope. He believed in living the Sermon on the Mount literally, and never refused a request for help. Finally, burdened by failing health, near-poverty, and chronic melancholia, he was taken ill and friends who came to watch over him found him on August 10, 1886, drowned in a brook near the home he had once had at Rice Lake.

What a Friend We Have in Jesus............1857

SEARS, Rev. Edmund Hamilton (sērs), 1810-1876, Unitarian. Born April 6, 1810 in Sandisfield, Mass., Edmund Sears attended Westfield Academy and then Union College in Schenectady, N. Y., from which he graduated in 1834. After studying the law for a brief period he joined the faculty of a Brattleboro, Vt. academy, studying theology while he worked. He finally attended Harvard Divinity School, graduating in 1837, and was ordained February 20, 1839. He wrote
books as well as hymns, and was well-known enough to take a successful preaching tour through England in 1873. Although a Unitarian, he leaned toward the Swedenborgian tenets. He died on January 16, 1876.

Calm on the Listening Ear of Night..........1834
It Came Upon the Midnight Clear............1849

439

SHURTLEFF, Rev. Ernest Warburton (shurt'lĕf), 1862-1917, Congregationalist. Born in Boston, Mass. on April 4, 1862, Ernest Shurtleff was educated at the Boston Latin School, Harvard University, the Swedenborgian New Church Theological Seminary, and Andover Theological Seminary, where he graduated in 1888. After being ordained, he served pastorates in California, Massachusetts and Minneapolis, leaving the latter in 1905 to go to Germany. At Frankfort-on-the-Main he organized the American Church, and in 1906 moved to Paris to direct student activities at the Academy Vitti in the Latin Quarter, remaining there until his death. Dr. Shurtleff wrote several books of poetry, four of which were published before he had graduated from Andover Theological Seminary. He died on August 29, 1917.

Lead On, O King Eternal.....................1887

SMITH, Rev. Samuel Francis (smith), 1808-1895, Baptist. Samuel Francis Smith was born in Boston, Mass. on October 21, 1808. After graduating from Harvard in 1829 and Andover Seminary in 1832 he became editor of the "Baptist Missionary Magazine" and started contributing to "Encyclopedia Americana." Two years later he was made pastor at a church in Waterville, Maine and professor of Modern Languages at what is now Colby College, holding both positions until 1842. Moving to Newton, Mass. he became pastor of the First Baptist Church (1842-1854) and for six years edited the "Christian Review" in Boston. He was an accomplished linguist (15 languages); published "The Social Psalmist" (1844), "Lyric Gems" (1844), "The Life of Rev. Joseph Grafton" (1848), "Missionary Sketches" (1879), "History of Newton, Massachusetts" (1880), "Rambles in Mission Fields" (1884); served as Secretary of the Baptist Missionary Union for 15 years. He died suddenly in 1895, at the age of 87.

My Country, 'Tis of Thee....................1832
The Morning Light Is Breaking..............1832

SPURGEON, Rev. Charles Haddon (spûr'jŭn), 1834-1892, Baptist. Editor, psalmist, hymnist and (somewhat) nonconformist clergyman— Charles Haddon Spurgeon was born on June 19, 1834 in Kelvedon, Essex, England. His early schooling was at Colchester and at Agricultural College at Maidstone. At the age of 16 he gave his first sermon at Waterbeach, in a small Baptist church, where he became pastor a year later. He moved to London in 1854, and his preaching attracted such large crowds that eventually the great Metropolitan Tabernacle was erected, and he remained there through the rest of his ministry. Somewhat of a nonconformist, he became a controversial figure among English clergymen, but he remained exceedingly popular with his congregation. During the last years of his life his health failed, and he died in Mentone, France on January 31, 1892.

Lord, I Would Dwell With Thee.............1866
O God, Be Thou No Longer Still..............1866

440

STENNETT, Rev. Samuel (stĕn'ĕt), 1727-1795, Baptist. Samuel Stennett was born in 1727 at Exeter, England. At an early age he moved to London, where his father was minister at a Baptist Church on Little Wild Street, and at the age of 20 he became assistant pastor there. At 31 he was elected by the congregation to succeed his father after the latter's death in 1758, and in 1767 was asked to serve at the Seventh Day Baptist Church in London, a church once served by his grand-
father. Never accepting formally, he nevertheless gave a sermon there each Saturday morning for 20 years, at the same time serving his own church on Little Wild Street. He might have been high in the Church of England, but preferred to remain a Dissenter as had his grandfather. He used his influence among the statesmen of the time in support of religious freedom, and ranged high among the non-conformist clergy of his day. In 1787 his 38 hymns were published in the "Selection" of Dr. John Rippon. He died on August 24, 1795 in London.

> **On Jordan's Stormy Banks I Stand**............**1787**
> **Majestic Sweetness Sits Enthroned**..........**1787**

STITES, Rev. Edgar Page (stīts), 1836-1916, Methodist. Very little is known about the author of the world-renowned "Beulah Land," Edgar Page Stites. He was born on March 22, 1836 in Cape May, New Jersey and was a local preacher of the Methodist Episcopal Church. His inspiration for the hymn came from reading Bunyan's description of Beulah. Ira D. Sankey's "Sacred Songs and Solos" lists the author as being "Edgar Page" but in Sankey's "My Life and Sacred Songs" he attributes it to "E. P. Stites."

> **Simply Trusting Every Day**.................**1876**
> **I've Reached the Land of Corn and Wine**
> **(Beulah Land)** **1878**

STOCK, Harry Thomas (stŏk), 1891-1958, Congregationalist. Harry Thomas Stock was born November 10, 1891 in Springfield, Illinois. He attended Knox College (B.A. 1915); Chicago Theological Seminary (B.D. 1916); University of Chicago (M.A. 1917). He later received a D.D. degree from both Knox and the University of Chicago, as well as from Piedmont College. He was associate professor of Church History at Chicago Theological Seminary for 5 years, followed
by 16 years (1922-1938) as Secretary of Student Life Young People's Work of the Congregational Education Society. Dr. Stock had a great interest in young people; wrote many books for and about them, and was offered the directorship of the young people's program of the International Council of Religious Education. He served as an executive of the Congregational Christian Churches in America from 1938 until his death in 1958. Dr. Stock wrote only one hymn.

> **O Gracious God, Whose Constant Care**.......**1939**

STOCKING, Rev. Jay Thomas (stŏk'ĭng), 1870-1936, Congregationalist. Jay Thomas Stocking, born April 13, 1870 in Lisbon, N. Y. was educated at Amherst (B.A. 1895) and Yale (B.D. 1901). A member of Phi Beta Kappa, he was given a D.D. by Amherst in 1913 and later the degree of Litt.D. by Rollins. In a varied career, he taught English at a preparatory school in New Jersey from 1895-1898; studied at the University of Berlin in 1902-1903; was ordained a Congregational minister in 1901; served pastorates in Vermont, Massachusetts, District of Columbia, New Jersey, and Missouri from 1903-1935, and in the Congregational Church in Newton Center, Mass. for a brief time before his death on January 27, 1936. Dr. Stocking served on numerous boards and commissions, was the author of many children's stories, and wrote several volumes of sermons and studies.

O Master-workman of the Race 1912

STONE, Rev. Samuel John (stōn), 1839-1900, Anglican. Samuel John Stone was born at Whitmore Rectory, Staffordshire, England on April 25, 1839. After an education at Charterhouse and Pembroke College, Oxford (B.A. 1862, M.A. 1872), he was curate of Windsor for eight years beginning in 1862. In 1870 he started a 21-year service at his father's parish, Haggerston, the most poverty-stricken in London, succeeding his father as vicar in 1874. In 1890 he became rector of All-Hallows-on-the-Wall in London. He wrote seven books of verse, the last of which was published posthumously. He died November 19, 1900 at the Charterhouse.

The Church's One Foundation 1866
Round the Sacred City Gather 1866

STOWE, Mrs. Harriet Beecher (stō), 1812-1896, Congregationalist. Harriet Beecher was born into the eminent Beecher family on June 14, 1812 in Litchfield, Conn. At the age of four she lost her mother and went to Guilford, Conn. to live with her grandmother, later returning to Litchfield to attend the Academy there. While at the Academy she wrote an essay titled "Can the Immortality of the Soul Be Proved by the Light of Nature?", which won her acclaim for her writing talent and depth of thought. In 1832 she moved with the family to Cincinnati, Ohio, and here she met and married the Rev. Calvin E. Stowe, who was professor of Languages and Biblical Literature at the Seminary. The couple moved eventually to Brunswick, Maine, and there Mrs. Stowe wrote her famous "Uncle Tom's Cabin." When the book was finally published, it was translated into more than twenty languages. She died in Hartford on July 1, 1896.

Still, Still With Thee, When Purple
Morning Breaketh 1855
When Winds Are Raging O'er the Upper Ocean . . 1855

STRONG, Rev. Nathan (strŏng), 1748-1816, Congregationalist. Born October 16, 1748 in Coventry, Conn., Nathan Strong graduated from Yale University in 1769 with highest honors. After studying for the law for a short time he devoted himself to theology, tutored at Yale in 1772, and two years later, on January 5, 1774, was ordained to serve at the First Congregational Church of Hartford, Conn. An army chaplain during the Revolutionary War, he returned to his Hartford Church after the  war and remained there for the rest of his life. An essay written in 1796 won him fame, and he was given an honorary D.D. degree by Princeton. In 1799 he edited "The Hartford Selection," the following year founded the "Connecticut Evangelical Magazine," and helped establish the Connecticut Home Mission Society in 1801. He died in 1816.

> **Swell the Anthem; Raise the Song**............**1799**
> **Almighty Sovereign of the Skies**..............**1799**

STUDDERT-KENNEDY, Rev. Gregory Anketell (stŭd'ert-kĕn'ĕdy), 1883-1929, Anglican. Celtic in origin, the Rev. Studdert-Kennedy was born in 1883, graduated from Trinity College, Dublin, and was ordained a clergyman in the Church of England in 1908. In addition to doing service in the Great War (MC) and being Chaplain to the King (in which capacity he often preached at Buckingham Palace), he was also vicar of St.  Paul's, Worcester from 1914-1921 and rector of St. Edmund's, King and Martyr, Lombard Street from 1922 until his death. He was a powerful speaker, with what is known as "the common touch" and had a passion for the truth. His publications were "Rough Rhymes of a Padre" (under the pseudonym Woodbine Willie), "The Hardest Part," "Lies," "Food for the Fed-Up," "The Wicket Gate," and "The Word and the Work." In 1929 he made a journey to Liverpool to deliver Lenten lectures, and there he died of influenza at St. Catherine's Vicarage, Abercrombie Square, on March 8th.

> **Awake, Awake to Love and Work**.............**1921**

TAPPAN, Rev. William Bingham (tăp'an), 1794-1849, Congregationalist. William Bingham Tappan was born on October 24, 1794 in Beverly, Mass. Apprenticed to a Boston clock-maker at 16, he moved to Philadelphia in 1815 and was engaged in the business of clock-repairing for some time. At 28 he became superintendent of the American Sunday School Union, and remained with them until his death. In 1840 he became a licensed  minister for the Congregational denomination, and traveled about the country advocating Sunday-schools. The first of his ten books was published in 1819—"New England and Other Poems"; the last—"Gems of Sacred Poetry"—in 1860. He wrote eight hymns which appeared in various hymn collections. He died on June 18, 1849 in Needham, Mass. of cholera.

> **There Is an Hour of Peaceful Rest**............**1818**
> **'Tis Midnight, and on Olive's Brow**..........**1822**

TARRANT, Rev. William George (tăr′ant), 1853-1928, Unitarian. William George Tarrant was born July 2, 1853 in Pembroke Dock, South Wales, and orphaned at the age of six (his father was killed in the Crimean War in 1854 and his mother died six years later). He grew up in the Free Industrial School, a Birmingham orphanage, and was educated there. While serving as an apprentice to the silver trade, he attended evening classes at Midland Institute, and went on to the Unitarian Home Missionary College in Manchester and then to Manchester New College in London where he received his B.A. degree in 1883. He wrote 3 devotional manuals, several song books, hymn texts and hymn tunes. His death occurred at Wandsworth on January 5, 1928.

> With Happy Voices Ringing 1888
> Come, Let Us Join With Faithful Souls 1892

TATE, Nahum, tāt), 1652-1715, Anglican. Born in Dublin, Ireland in 1652, the son of the Rev. Faithful Tate, Nahum Tate attended Trinity College in Dublin. After receiving a degree he went directly to England to pursue the profession of a writer. His first stage play was produced in London in 1678, and he did several "improved versions" of Shakespeare's tragedies. Also, with the help of Dryden, he wrote a second part to the satire "Absalom and Achitophel" and with Nicholas Brady produced a "New Version of the Psalms of David." In 1690 he became Poet Laureate of England, and twelve years later was made Historiographer Royal. He lived a highly intemperate life, and died August 12, 1715 at a debtor's refuge in Southwark, London. He was buried in an unmarked grave in the churchyard of St. George the Martyr (illustrated) at Southwark.

> As Pants the Hart for Cooling Streams 1696
> While Shepherds Watched Their Flocks
>   by Night 1700

TENNYSON, Alfred (Lord) (tĕn′i-sŭn), 1809-1892, No Church Affiliation. Born August 6, 1809 at Somersby, Lincolnshire, England, Alfred Tennyson was the eldest son, though the fourth child, in a family of twelve. He attended Trinity College, Cambridge from 1828-1831, and won the Chancellor's Medal for English Poetry. He left Trinity after only three years and in 1832 toured Europe with his close friend, Arthur Hallam, who was engaged to one of his sisters. In 1833 his first volume of "Poems" was published, and unfavorably received. However, in 1842 he became famous when the volume was published and brought a civil pension of 200 pounds a year. Other books of poetry followed rapidly, and in 1850 he became Poet Laureate of England, receiving a degree of D.C.L. from Oxford. Twice he refused a baronetcy, finally accepting a peerage offered him at the express wish of Queen Victoria, in 1884. Lord Tennyson died on October 6, 1892 in Aldworth, England.

> Strong Son of God, Immortal Love 1849
> Sunset and Evening Star 1849

TIPLADY, Rev. Thomas (tip'la-dy), 1882-19—,
Methodist. Born of "saintly Methodist working
folk" (to quote his own words) on January 1,
1882 at Gayle in Wensleydale, England, Thomas
Tiplady spent his first five years in the place of his
birth. He was raised in Lancashire, where he interspersed an education at the Methodist Day School
with working at the local mill. At 13 he began
a period of working 56 hours a week at the mill
and studying nights at the Evening Technical
School. He joined the Methodist Church at 15, only to reject this for
the Church of England, and then return to Methodism in 1905. After
training in the Methodist Theological College at Richmond, Surrey,
at the start of his ministry he inaugurated the Guild Hall services at
Portsmouth. In 1919 he preached and lectured in forty-three of the
United States in the course of five months. He has more verse in modern hymnals, mainly American and Canadian, than any of his contemporaries, and is an active member of the British Hymn Society.

      Beyond the Wheeling Worlds of Light.........**1932**
      O Men of God, Go Forth to Win.............**1937**

TOPLADY, Rev. Augustus Montague (tŏp'lā-dy),
1740-1778, Anglican. Augustus Toplady was born
November 4, 1740 at Farnham, England. His
father, a major in the British Army, was killed
in 1741, and his mother enrolled him at the
Westminster School in London. He received his
M.A. from Trinity College, Dublin and in 1762
was ordained by the Church of England. He was
vicar of Broadhembury, Devonshire and in 1775
became a preacher in the French Calvanist Chapel
at Leicester Fields, London. He was a powerful and zealous preacher,
but having a frail constitution, he died of over-work in 1778, at the
age of thirty-eight.

      Great God, Whom Heaven and Earth and Sea..**1759**
      Rock of Ages, Cleft for Me..................**1776**

TRENCH, Richard Chenevix (trĕnch), 1807-1886,
Anglican. Archbishop Trench of Dublin was born
in that city on September 19, 1807 while his
parents were on an extended visit there. He grew
up in Elm Lodge near Southampton, and was
educated at Twyford School, Harrow, and Trinity
College, Cambridge. He left Cambridge in 1829,
undecided between the law and theology, and
joined his father at Elm Lodge. He married his
cousin, Frances Mary Trench, on May 31, 1832,
and was ordained as deacon later that same year. In 1835 he was
ordained a priest, and became Archbishop of Dublin in 1864. He wrote
a great number of essays, sermons and poems (a few of which were
later used as hymns). His book "Sacred Latin Poetry" opened
the way for John Mason Neale's translation of hymns, and it was at
his suggestion that the Oxford English Dictionary was begun. Resigning
his archbishopric in 1884, he died in London two years later.

      High Thoughts at First, and Visions High......**1835**
      Let All Men Know That All Men Move........**1835**

TWEEDY, Rev. Henry Hallman (twēd'y), 1868-1953, Congregationalist. Henry Hallam Tweedy was born of Scottish ancestry on August 5, 1868 at Binghamton, New York. There he grew up and received most of his early education. Later he attended Phillips Andover Academy, Yale University (B.A. 1901, M.A. 1909), Union Theological Seminary, and the University of Berlin. His career, starting with his ordination in 1898, included a pastorate at the Plymouth Church in Utica, N. Y. (1898-1902); a pastorate at South Church in Bridgeport, Conn. (1902-1909); professorship of Practical Theology at Yale Divinity School (1909-1937). Dr. Tweedy edited and compiled a number of hymnbooks and wrote many hymns of his own. In 1928 he received first prize from the Hymn Society of America for a hymn "Eternal God, Whose Power Holds," which was selected from more than a thousand submitted. Dr. Tweedy died September 11, 1953.

    O Gracious Father of Mankind. **1925**
    O Spirit of the Living God. **1933**

UFFORD, Rev. Edward Smith (ŭf'fĕrd), 1851-1929, Baptist. Edward Smith Ufford was born in Newark, N. J. in 1851. He was educated at Stratford Academy in Connecticut, and at Bates Theological Seminary in Maine. He held several Baptist pastorates, and edited, compiled or wrote various song-books and Sunday-school song-manuals. "Converts' Praise," "Life-Long Songs," "Wonderful Love," and "Gathered Gems" are his work. Inspiration for his well-known hymn "Throw Out the Life-Line" came spontaneously after he had witnessed a coast guard unit throwing life-lines to a wrecked ship off of Point Allerton, near Boston. Mr. Ufford died in 1929.

    Throw Out the Life-Line. **1884**
    On the Shore of the Blue Galilee. **1915**

VAN DYKE, Rev. Henry (văn-dīk'), 1852-1933, Presbyterian. Henry Van Dyke was born November 10, 1852 in Germantown, Pennsylvania. After graduating from the Polytechnic Institute in Brooklyn, N. Y. he attended Princeton University (B.A. 1873, M.A. 1876), graduated from the Princeton Theological Seminary in 1877, and was ordained in 1879. A Presbyterian, he served as minister of the United Congregational Church in Newport, R. I. at the start of his career, then went to the Brick Presbyterian Church in New York City in 1883, remaining there until 1900. He became professor of English at Princeton in 1900 and retained that position until 1923, with two interruptions—the first in 1908 and 1909 when he was American lecturer at the Sorbonne in Paris, the second when he was appointed by Woodrow Wilson as U. S. Minister to the Netherlands and Luxembourg in 1913 (to 1917). He spent his last ten years in retirement at Princeton, N. J., and died there on April 10, 1933.

    Joyful, Joyful, We Adore Thee. **1907**
    Jesus, Thou Divine Companion. **1909**

WALTER, Rev. Howard Arnold (wŏl'tẽr), 1883-1918, Congregationalist. Howard Walter was born in New Britain, Conn. on August 19, 1883 and educated at Princeton (graduating in 1905), Hartford Theological Seminary (1905-1906 and 1907-1909), continuing his studies in Edinburgh, Glasgow and Goettinggen in 1909-1910). In the interval of 1906-1907 he taught English at Waseda University in Tokyo, Japan. In 1910 he became assistant pastor of Asylum Hill Congregational  Church in Hartford, and that same year married Marguerite B. Darlington, of Brooklyn, N. Y. Three years later he joined the executive staff of the Y.M.C.A. in India and Ceylon, specializing in work with the Mohammedans. In spite of physicians' warnings about a weak heart, he nurtured his enthusiasm for evangelical work in the Far East by establishing evangelistic headquarters at Lahore, India and carrying on his work from there. He died suddenly of a heart attack on November 1, 1918.

> I Would Be True...........................1906

WARING, Anna Laetitia (wär'ĭng), 1823-1910, Anglican. This "gentle.spirit" with "a merry, quiet, humor" was born April 19, 1823 at Neath, Glamoganshire, Wales. Although she was raised a Quaker, she joined the Church of England by baptism in 1842. Wishing to read the original Old Testament, she learned Hebrew and from then on read the Hebrew Psalter daily. In her teens she started writing hymns, and by the age of 43 had written 39, all of which had been published.  Philanthropic-minded, she devoted much energy in her later years to visiting prisons (especially Bristol Gaol) and working for the Discharged Prisoners' Aid Society. All who knew her loved her, and she made friends easily. She had one outstanding dislike—her hatred of publicity. She died at the age of 87 at Bristol, on May 10, 1910.

> In Heavenly Love Abiding....................1850
> Jesus, Lord of Heaven Above.................1854

WARNER, Anna Bartlett (wôr'nẽr), 1827-1915, Presbyterian. Anna Warner, known also as Amy Lothrop, was born near New York City in 1827. She was the sister of Susan B. Warner, well-known authoress (under the pen-name of Elizabeth Wetherell) of "The Wide, Wide World." Anna wrote "Say and Seal," "Wych Hazel," "Stories of Vinegar Hill" and others of a similar nature, as well as editing and publishing books of hymns to which she contributed many of her own. She also wrote  books on gardening and translated hymns into English. Living on Constitution Island, very near West Point, Anna and her sister conducted Bible classes for the cadets, being in such close contact with the Academy that at their funerals they were given military honors. Anna Warner died in 1915.

> We Would See Jesus.......................1852
> Jesus Loves Me, This I Know...............1859

WATTS, Rev. Isaac (wŏts), 1674-1748, Congregationalist. The eldest of nine children, Isaac Watts, was born on July 17, 1674 in Southampton, England. He was taught Latin, Greek and Hebrew by the rector of All Saints Church in Southampton. In 1690 he went to the nonconformist Stoke Newington Academy, and while there became a member of the Independent congregation at Girdlers' Hall in preference to the Church of England. Dissatisfied with the traditional hymns of the day, he spent two years (1694-1695) in Southampton writing his own hymns, published 1707-1709 as "Hymns and Spiritual Songs." In 1702 Watts became pastor of an Independent church in Mark Lane, but in 1712 was stricken by a fever that left him an invalid. For the last thirty-six years of his life he lived at the home of Sir Thomas Abney. He wrote essays, catechisms, textbooks and a variety of other works. He died in 1748, and a monument in his honor was erected in Westminster Abbey.

Joy to the World! the Lord Is Come..........1719
When I Survey the Wondrous Cross..........1719

WESLEY, Rev. Charles (wĕs'ly), 1707-1788, Methodist. This hymn-writer and evangelist, the 18th child of the Rev. Samuel Wesley, rector of Epworth, was born December 18, 1707 at the Epworth Rectory. He was educated in his early years by his mother, then at Westminster School, and later at Christ Church, Oxford, where he graduated in 1729 and remained as a tutor. While at Christ Church he formed a small group which was derisively called the "Oxford Methodists." He is considered one of the greatest hymn-writers of all ages, having written more than 6,500 hymns using almost entirely biblical language. He died on March 29, 1788 in London and was buried in Marylebone Churchyard, having remained in the communion of the Church of England.

Christ the Lord Is Risen Today...............1739
Love Divine, All Loves Excelling...........1747

WHITE, Henry Kirke (hwīt), 1785-1806, Anglican. Poet and hymnist, Henry Kirke White, son of a butcher, was born in Nottingham, England on March 21, 1785. Apprenticed to a weaver of stockings at the age of fourteen, he found the work intolerable and took up the study of law. He made remarkable progress in his studies, mastering languages as well as other subjects. He composed poetry and contributed articles to the periodicals of his day, and at seventeen was encouraged to publish a volume of his poetry. He became a devout Christian through the arguments and appeals of an intimate friend, and then chose to become a preacher. Before he had taken the orders of the English Church, however, he died of consumption on October 19, 1806 in the midst of his education at Cambridge University.

When, Marshaled on the Nightly Plain........1804
Oft in Danger, Oft in Woe..................1806

WHITING, William (hwīt'ing), 1825-1878, Angli-can. William Whiting was born November 1, 1825 in London. He was educated at Clapham and Winchester, and held the position of Master of Winchester College Choristers' School for several years. He published a book of poems, "Rural Thoughts," in 1851, and wrote other poetry as well as some hymns, which he contributed to several collections. He died at Winchester, in 1878.

Eternal Father, Strong to Save..............1860
Now the Billows, Strong and Dark...........1872

WHITTIER, John Greenleaf (hwit'i-ẽr), 1807-1892, Quaker. Born on December 17, 1807 in Haverhill, Massachusetts, John Greenleaf Whittier was very much affected in health by the hard farm work he was forced to perform. The family was desperately poor, but eventually, at the age of nineteen, Whittier had earned enough by shoemaking to study at Haverhill Academy for two years. Inspired by the poetry of Robert Burns, he himself began to write and his older sister sent

some of his poetry to the abolitionist, William Lloyd Garrison, who became an interested friend. Whittier, too, was an abolitionist (though not as radical as Garrison) and his anti-slavery sentiments led to violent opposition in New England. He joined the editorial staff of several publications successively, all the while continuing to write his poetry. A Quaker, not raised in the musical tradition, he nevertheless wrote hymns that were widely used by all denominations. In fact, he wrote more poems that are used as hymns than any other American poet. He died at Hampton Falls, New Hampshire on September 7, 1892.

Immortal Love, Forever Full................1866
Dear Lord and Father of Mankind...........1872

WILLIAMS, Rev. William (wil'yamz), 1717-1791, Calvinistic Methodist. William Williams, son of a prosperous farmer, was born February 11, 1717 in Carmarthenshire, Wales. He started to prepare for a career as a physician, but switched to the ministry and was ordained deacon in the Established Church in 1740. After serving as curate because of his evangelical views, he left the Established Church and for three years, on being denied priest's orders became an itinerant preacher,

traveling nearly 96,000 miles during the following forty-three years. At first a follower of the Wesleys, he eventually came to identify himself with the Calvinist Methodists. His first work, "Alleluia," was published in 1744 and his last, "Gloria in Excelsis, or, Hymns of Praise to God and the Lamb," in 1771. He was the author of approximately 800 hymns in Welsh, as well as about 100 in English, and is called the "Watts of Wales." He died January 11, 1791, at Pantycelyn, Wales.

Guide Me, O Thou Great Jehovah...........1745
My God, My God, Who Art My All...........1759

WOLFE, Aaron Robarts (wŏolf), 1821-1902, Presbyterian. Aaron Wolfe was born at Mendham, New Jersey on September 6, 1821. He attended Williams College, receiving his B.A. in 1844, and Union Theological Seminary in New York. In 1851 he became a minister, licensed by the Third Presbytery of New York. Pursuing his career in the educational field, rather than the ministry, he conducted a woman's school in Tallahassee, Florida for three years until 1855, and in 1859 founded his own school (The Hillside Seminary for Young Ladies) in Montclair, New Jersey. He was principal at the school until his retirement in 1872. Under the signature "A.R.W." he contributed several hymns to Hastings' "Church Melodies," published in 1858. He died in 1902, at the age of eighty-two.

A Parting Hymn We Sing....................1858
Draw Near, O Holy Dove, Draw Near........1858

WORDSWORTH, Rev. Christopher (wûrdz'wirth), 1807-1885, Anglican. The son of a rector, Christopher Wordsworth was born in the town of his father's parish, Lambeth, England, on October 30, 1807. He attended Winchester, and held distinguished records for both studies and athletics. Entering Trinity College, Cambridge in 1826, he earned a very unusual number of prizes and awards and when he graduated in 1830 was elected a Fellow of Trinity. He was college lecturer for some time, and in 1836 became public orator for Cambridge and head master of Harrow School. He was appointed canon at Westminister in 1844, became parish priest at Stanford-in-the-Vale cum Goosey in Berkshire in 1850, and in 1869 was made Bishop of Lincoln. He resigned the bishopric in 1885, just before his death on March 20th. He was a voluminous writer on subjects concerning the church, but still found time to write 127 hymns, many of which are still used.

O Day of Rest and Gladness.................1862
O Lord of Heaven and Earth and Sea........1863

ZINZENDORF, Count Nicolaus Ludwig (tsĭn'tsĕn-dôrf), 1700-1760, Moravian. Born at Dresden, Germany on May 26, 1700, Count von Zinzendorf was educated at Halle and Wittenberg (1716-1719) and at the age of twenty-one became Counselor of State at the Court of Saxony in his native city. His heart set on becoming a clergyman instead of continuing his career in public life, he received a license to preach from the Theological Faculty of the University of Tubingen in 1734, and in 1737 was made Bishop of the Moravian Brethren's Unity at Berlin. He used his considerable fortune to further his Church, and had little money in his last years, which were spent in Hernhut, a settlement of refugee Moravians living on his estate since 1722. He died there on May 9, 1760, the author of more than 2,000 hymns.

Jesus, Still Lead On........................1721
Jesus, Thy Blood and Righteousness..........1739

Chapter VIII
Stories of Favorite Hymns

A CHARGE TO KEEP I HAVE
Charles Wesley, 1707–1788

An 18th century hymn by Charles Wesley. Sung to the tune of "Old Kentucky" by Jeremiah Ingalls, this revival hymn could be heard swelling from tent and camp ground all over America. About a hundred years after it was written, Lowell Mason composed the music which is used presently.

A charge to keep I have, A God to glorify,
A never dying soul to save, And fit it for the sky.

A Charge To Keep

A MIGHTY FORTRESS IS OUR GOD
Martin Luther, 1483–1546

Martin Luther, one of the outstanding figures in the history of the Protestant Church, in no greater way served his fellow Christians than in the writing and composing of one of the world's best loved hymns, "A Mighty Fortress Is Our God." It was written in the late summer of 1529. The famed German theologian, after a long period of deep depression, had found spiritual comfort in the strength of Psalm 46. He repeated over and over the words, "God is our refuge and strength, a very present help in trouble." With this thought in mind, he hurled his defiance at all his foes, physical and spiritual, the struggles of mind and body, the opposition of pope and people, and penned these words never to be forgotten by mortal men:

A mighty fortress is our God,
    A bulwark never failing;
Our helper He, amid the flood,
    Of mortal ills prevailing.
For still our ancient foe,
    Doth seek to work us woe;
His craft and power are great,
    And armed with cruel hate.
On earth is not his equal.

A Mighty Fortress

A PARTING HYMN WE SING
Aaron R. Wolfe, 1821–1902

This simple communion hymn was written by Aaron R. Wolfe in 1858. A graduate of Union Theological Seminary, New York, Wolfe spent his life in educational work, one of his major accomplishments being the founding of the Hillside Seminary for Young Ladies at Montclair, New Jersey, in 1859. When asked why he wrote his hymn, Wolfe had this modest reply, "I looked over the topics in the hymn book and thought something of this kind might be suitable in rising from the Lord's table."

A parting hymn we sing
    Around Thy table, Lord;
Again our grateful tribute bring,
    Our solemn vows record.

A Parting Hymn

453

A SHELTER IN THE TIME OF STORM
Ira David Sankey, 1840–1908

A Shelter In Time
Of Storm

The great song-leader and musician Ira David Sankey had a knack of recognizing a good potential gospel hymn in poetry written in remote areas of the world. He found "Shelter in the Time of Storm" in a little paper published in London, called the "Postman." Written by V. J. Charlesworth, it was said to have been a favorite of fishermen in the northern part of England. They could often be heard singing it together as they approached their harbors during the threat of a storm. The tune they used was a strange, weird minor sound. Sankey composed a more workable, practical melody for church use; and this is the way it has been sung in every singing generation since.

ABIDE WITH ME
Henry Francis Lyte, 1793–1847

Abide With Me

This famous hymn, written September 4, 1847, by Henry Francis Lyte, nearly was not written at all. Life had not been easy for him, and at the age of 54, this famed English Clergyman, serving as Vicar of Lower Brixham in Devonshire, was advised by his doctor to save his health by wintering in Italy. He was determined to administer Holy Communion once more to his congregation. And on the first Sunday of September in 1847 he did exactly that, even though the ravages of tuberculosis left him weak and exhausted. After the service he strolled by the sea until sunset thinking of the abiding presence of God and working on a hymn poem started many years before in the early days of his ministry. He was really too tired to complete the poem and thought of putting it aside until his return from Italy. However, some inner compulsion pressed him to finish the last line. That evening he placed the completed hymn "Abide With Me" in the hands of his family. He never returned from Italy, dying two months later on Nov. 20th. If he had waited until he returned, one of the world's most famous hymns would not have been written.

ALAS AND DID MY SAVIOUR BLEED
Isaac Watts, 1674–1748

Alas And Did My
Saviour

Written by Isaac Watts, one of the greatest hymn writers of all time (he wrote over 600 hymns), "Alas and Did My Saviour Die" appeared in a volume of poems published in 1705 entitled "Hymns and Spiritual Songs." A very unusual man, Watts served as minister of the English Congregational Church, preaching his first sermon when 24 years of age. History says that though he was a charming man, his stature was small and his physical appearance hard to believe. Only five feet in height, his face was sallow with a hooked nose, small beady eyes and deathlike pallor. One lady, a Miss Elizabeth Singer, who had fallen in love with his poetry and thought she had met her soul-mate at last, refused his hand in marriage when she finally saw him, with the remark, "I admired the jewel but not the casket!" However, his hymns have been jewels admired by all generations of Christians.

ALL CREATURES OF OUR GOD AND KING
St. Francis of Assisi, 1182–1226

All Creatures Of
Our God

In July 1225, one of the great Christians of all times, St. Francis, ill, blind and lonely, came to a little group of buildings called St. Damian just outside the village of Assisi in Italy. Depressed and tired he found peace in this quiet little refuge with the sounds of birds and animals, which he always loved, and the kind care of a group of women called the Poor Clares. It was here, just one year before his death, St. Francis wrote a simple, beautiful hymn which has stood the test of ages. It praised the wonder of God's creation and reflects St. Francis' love of the simple things of life:

> All creatures of our God and King,
> Lift up your voice and with us sing
>   Alleluia, alleluia!
> Thou burning sun with golden beam,
> Thou silver moon, with softer gleam;
> Thou rushing wind that art so strong,
> Ye clouds that sail in heaven along,
>   O praise Him, alleluia!

ALL GLORY, LAUD AND HONOR
Theodulph of Orleans, Ninth Century

All Glory,

"All Glory, Laud, and Honor" written by Theodulph Bishop of Orleans in the 9th century, one time freed its author from death in the dungeon. The story is told that on Palm Sunday, 821, King Louis the Pious, son of Charlemagne, while celebrating the day with his people, glimpsed the radiant face of Theodulph through the bars of the prison where he had been confined. The King had experienced trouble with his relatives and had suspected Theodulph of supporting them. Thus he had cast him into the dungeon. Now as he passed by, he saw the brave saint and heard his voice singing with joy "All Glory, Laud, and Honor," a song he had written himself. The king was so pleased at the evidence of religious devotion that he released Theodulph at once and restored him to his ecclesiastical position.

ALL HAIL THE POWER OF JESUS' NAME
Edward Perronet, 1726–1792

All Hail The Power

Edward Perronet, born in 1726 in the quaint village of Shoreham, was the son of a minister, who served as vicar of this village. A giant cross stood facing the hill where Vincent Perronet enjoyed a long and holy ministry. Young Perronet received profound inner inspiration not only from his father, but also from John Wesley who frequently visited their parish.

All The Way My Saviour

Perronet and Wesley remained friends, even though they differed in the question of lay administration of the Sacraments. Eventually he became a minister of an independent church in Canterbury. It was in 1779 while serving as vicar at the Canterbury Cathedral that "All Hail the Power of Jesus' Name" was written. The majesty of the words:

And Crown Him,
Crown Him, Crown Him,
Crown Him Lord of all

has reflected the power and glory of Christ to Christians the world over.

ALL THE WAY MY SAVIOUR LEADS ME
Fanny J. Crosby, 1820–1915

There is no end to the unusual stories told about Fanny J. Crosby, the blind poetess author of this hymn and scores of other gospel songs. "All the Way My Saviour Leads Me" is the outcome of one of those dramatic moments. One day in 1874, Miss Crosby, who was short of money and with no time to reach her publishers for advance payments, simply knelt in her home and prayed for five dollars, which was her immediate need. She had hardly finished her prayer when the doorbell rang. Upon opening the door she was greeted by a stranger, an admirer of her hymn tunes. According to Miss Crosby, when the stranger left he shook her hand and pressed something into it. It was five dollars! From this experience she wrote:

All the way my Saviour leads me,
What have I to ask beside?

All Things Bright And Beautiful

ALL THINGS BRIGHT AND BEAUTIFUL
C. Frances Alexander, 1818–1895

A hymn for children written in 1848 by C. Frances Alexander and taken from her volume called "Hymns for Little Children." Sung to the tune of an old English melody, this hymn emphasizes the eternal truth that God is the author of all beauty, all wisdom, and all creation. Each little flower that opens, each little bird that sings, each purple mountain, running river and ripe fruit in the garden, all are a product of His everlasting majesty.

ALMOST PERSUADED
Philip Paul Bliss, 1838–1876

Almost Persuaded

Gospel hymn written by Philip Bliss in 1870 while waiting for a train in Ohio. The famed gospel hymn writer had slipped into an Ohio church, one Sunday night, a few moments before his train was scheduled to leave. While here he heard the minister read from the Book of Acts: "Then Agrippa said unto Paul, almost thou persuaded me to be a Christian." Bliss recognized immediately a good theme for a hymn, and thus one of the outstanding gospel hymns was born.

AMAZING GRACE
John Newton, 1725–1807

John Newton wrote "Amazing Grace" in 1779; and only he could write this hymn with such meaning. Amazing Grace was the story of his life. Every word was pulled with pain from the dark days and the treacherous times of his early sea-faring youth to the wondrous joy of his discovery of the love of God. His epitaph, written by his own hand, tells more eloquently than any other words the extent of depth and height he experienced: "John Newton, clerk, once an infidel and libertine, was by the rich mercy of our Lord and Saviour, Jesus Christ, preserved, restored, pardoned and appointed to preach the faith he had long labored to destroy." Every line of his hymn is filled with tears of remorse because of the greatness of his sin, and expressions of joy because of the discovery of God's grace:

Amazing Grace

Amazing grace, how sweet the sound,
    That saved a wretch like me;
I once was lost but now am found,
    Was blind but now I see.

AMERICA THE BEAUTIFUL
Katherine Lee Bates, 1859–1929

Katherine Lee Bates, author of "America the Beautiful," daughter of a clergyman, was born in Falmouth, Massachusetts, in the year 1859. After graduating from Wellesley College she became a full professor of English literature of that college in 1891. While on her way to Colorado Springs to teach in a summer school, she stopped in Chicago during the Columbian Exposition in 1893. The tremendous beauty of the Colorado fruited plains and the "alabaster city" of the World's Fair became the inspiration for writing this hymn. These words have been sung in every corner of the world substituting "Australia" for "America," or when sung in Canada, the refrain reads, "O Canada, O Canada;" even in Africa the missionaries sing, "O Africa, O Africa." But all nations can join and sing together:

America The
Beautiful

God shed His grace on thee,
And crown Thy good with brotherhood,
From sea to shining sea.

ANCIENT OF DAYS, WHO SITTEST THRONED IN GLORY
William Croswell Doane, 1832–1913

In Albany, New York, in 1886, "Ancient of Days" was written for the bicentennial celebration of the city by Bishop William Croswell Doane. The 54 year old Doane (he was born in Boston, 1832) conducted the singing of his own hymn at its first public demonstration at this celebration in the Cathedral Church in Albany. It proved very successful and was widely acclaimed. "Ancient of Days" can be found in most American hymnals and is labeled by critics as being noble and stately.

Ancient Of Days,

ANGELS, FROM THE REALMS OF GLORY
James Montgomery, 1771–1854

Angels, From The
Realms Of Glory

This Christmas hymn is one of James Montgomery's favorite compositions. Montgomery, one of the greatest of the Moravian hymn writers, wrote the hymn in 1816 and it is considered one of the most challenging hymns ever written. The tune going under the name "Regent Square" was written by Henry Smart a blind composer of London, England. His physical vision may have been impaired, but Smart could see as few men are able to see. From the combined vision of these two men has come one of the immortal Christmas classics.

Angels, from the realms of glory,
  Wing your flight o'er all the earth;
Ye who sang creation's story,
  Now proclaim Messiah's birth:
Come and worship, Come and worship,
  Worship Christ, the new-born King!

ART THOU WEARY, HEAVY-LADEN
John Mason Neale, 1818–1866

Art Thou Weary,

This ancient Latin hymn, translated into English by John Mason Neale in 1862, was President Franklin D. Roosevelt's favorite hymn. The original text can be traced back as far as John of Damascus whose nephew Stephen, in the 8th century A.D., then choirmaster of the community of monks in the famous Marsaba Monastery of the Eastern Church in the Kidron Valley of Palestine, composed this hymn which proved to be his masterpiece. The eloquence and influence of this song of the church is attested by the fact that it has lived over a thousand years after its author has died.

Art thou weary, heavy laden;
  Art thou sore distressed?
"Come to me," He saith, "and coming
  Be at rest!"

AS WITH GLADNESS MEN OF OLD
William Chatterton Dix, 1837–1898

On January 6, 1860, an insurance agent named William Chatterton Dix lay ill in his bed at Bristol, England. It was Sunday, the feast of the Epiphany; and because he was unable to attend church, Dix read to himself from the Epiphany gospel, Matthew 2:1–12. As he pondered over the passage the significance of the journey of the Wisemen to Bethlehem made itself more clearly known than ever before. He saw with inspirational clarity the relationship between the experience of the Magi and the destiny of our own lives. Before the night's darkness had surrendered to dawn, Dix had penned the lines long since made immortal:

As with gladness men of old
Did the guiding star behold;

As With Gladness

AWAY IN A MANGER
author unknown

This quiet little Christmas song is often called "Luther's Cradle Hymn" and is considered by many authorities to have been written by him sometime during the early 16th century. More recently it is thought to be of German Lutheran origin in early Pennsylvania. No matter who the author may have been, this lovely carol lullaby is sung over and over again to children of every land and language during the Christmas season. It is one of their first encouragements to learn and to love "the little Lord Jesus."

Away In A Manger

BEAUTIFUL ISLE OF SOMEWHERE
Jessie Brown Pounds, 1861–1921

This hymn of heaven was written by Jessie Brown Pounds, wife of a cleryman of the Christian Church (later affiliated with the Congregational Church). In 1896 The Rev. John E. Pounds, then serving as pastor of the Central Christian Church of Indianapolis, was informed by his newly married bride Jessie that she did not feel well enough to attend church services. After conducting the service in the usual manner he returned to find that his wife had composed a complete hymn poem on heaven. Not satisfied with the usual poems of heaven which she felt were "selfish" and "Sickly sentimental," Mrs. Pounds wrote upon the theme that heaven depended upon her faith in the existence of God and in His goodness. She felt that we should "leave the present to God's love and care" and "heaven will thereby almost take care of itself." Inspired by this thought Jessie Brown Pounds had been able to complete her poem during part of a Sunday morning, and had been able to hand it to her husband upon his return from service with the words, "My hymn is written!"

Beautiful Isle Of Somewhere

Somewhere the sun is shining,
    Somewhere the songbirds dwell;
Hush then thy sad repining,
    God lives, and all is well.
Somewhere, somewhere,
    beautiful isle of somewhere;
Land of the true, where we live anew,
    Beautiful isle of somewhere.

BENEATH THE CROSS OF JESUS
Elizabeth Cecilia Clephane, 1830–1869

This hymn of Christian experience so popular as a solo for the male voice was written by a woman. Elizabeth Cecilia Clephane was about 35 years old when she wrote the hymn near Scott's Abbotsford Abbey in England in 1865. Four years later she was dead. Although she lived to be but thirty-nine, most people could live to be a hundred and not accomplish half what she did in the writing of two of the world's beloved hymns: "Beneath the Cross of Jesus" and "There Were Ninety and Nine."

Beneath The Cross Of Jesus

BE STILL MY SOUL
Katharina von Schlegel 1697–1765

Be Still My Soul

Katharina von Schlegel, born in Germany in 1697, was the author of this hymn of Christian experience. Very little is known of its origin or of its author save that it was discovered and translated by Jane L. Borthwick (1813–1897). It is thought that Katharina von Schlegel was head of a Woman's House of the Evangelical Lutheran Church at Gothen, Germany. No doubt one of the reasons for the great popularity of this hymn is its music. It is set to the famous melody of Sibelius, "Finlandia," one of the most stirring and beautiful melodies ever written.

BEULAH LAND
Edgar Page Stites, 1836–1916

I've reached the land of corn and wine,
And all its riches freely mine.

This old gospel hymn written by E. P. Stites was first sung at Ocean Grove, New Jersey, at a great conference of Methodists. It became an immediate favorite the world over and was sung not only by Methodists but by congregations of every denomination since the time of its origin. Ira Sankey, the famed song leader who teamed up with Dwight L. Moody to make one of the most famous evangelistic duos of American Church history speaks of this hymn as being one of the most requested at funerals in his experience as a gospel singer.

Beulah Land

BEYOND THE SUNSET
Virgil and Blanche Brock 1888–1958

The most popular gospel song produced by the "singing Brocks," came as the result of a colorful evening sky and the chance remark of a blind man. Virgil P. Brock and his wife Blanche Marie Kerr Brock were one of the most outstanding teams in gospel hymn-writing history. Their ability to conceive themes, write and compose music together is legendary. Frequently they rose in the middle of the night or at early sunrise to compile and complete hymn themes that were spontaneously inspirational. "Beyond the Sunset" was written in 1936 at Rainbow Point, Winona Lake, Indiana, at the home of Homer Rodeheaver. On a particular summer evening the two Brocks with other guests were watching a beautiful sunset across the lake. One of the guests, Horace L. Burr, a blind man, said, "I never saw a more beautiful sunset!" Being curious, Virgil Brock inquired, "I wonder why you always talk about seeing." Burr answered, "I do see through the eyes of others. I even see beyond the sunset." On the spot, Brock, inspired by the sunset and even more by the remark of Burr, began to hum the tune and sing the words that came to his mind. Catching the feeling of her husband, Blanche Brock excused herself quietly and went to a nearby piano, picking out the melody her husband was singing.

Beyond The Sunset

BLESS THIS HOUSE, O LORD WE PRAY
Helen Taylor, 1890–1957

Written in 1927 by Helen Taylor (also author of "Come to the Fair"), "Bless This House" rightfully should not be called a hymn; however, it has received great popularity as a favorite hymn throughout English speaking countries, especially around Thanksgiving. In recent years the word "house" has been changed to "church" and the song has been used as a special church anthem. Whether or not the song fits the requirements of the definition of a hymn, the words have been cherished by a great many hymn singing people all over the world.

Bless This House,

BLESSED ASSURANCE, JESUS IS MINE
Fanny J. Crosby, 1820–1915

Fanny Crosby's contribution to the Christian world through music is enhanced by another favorite, "Blessed Assurance, Jesus is Mine," a song of true salvation. Her personal faith in Christ shines like a light in every verse. The stirring tune to this hymn which arouses many congregations to sing with great power and emotion was written by Mrs. Joseph F. Knapp (Fanny Crosby), born in 1820.

Blessed Assurance,

BLEST BE THE TIE THAT BINDS
John Fawcett, 1740–1817

The drama of this famous hymn centers around a loving congregation, a woman who spoke her mind, and a Baptist minister who refused a call to one of the largest churches in England. In the summer of 1772, the Rev. John Fawcett, whose family had "increased faster than our income," was overjoyed with the receiving of a "call" to the famous Carter's Lane Baptist Church in London. Immediately, preparations were made to transfer to this greater opportunity. A great loyalty and devotion had developed between Pastor and People, and although they gave their time and strength willingly to help him pack, they did not hide their reluctance about letting him go. When the final day of moving came, the wagons arrived early and loading of boxes and bundles began. Finally only one box remained, in the middle of the dining room. Rev. Fawcett noted that his wife stood near it in deep thought. "What's the matter?" he asked. Her reply was slow and thoughtful, "Do you think we are doing the right thing?" she asked, "Where will we find a congregation with more love and help than this?" The minister was silent a moment, then he replied, "I think you are right, dear. I have acted too hastily. I was so overjoyed to think that I would have a better home and a larger salary for you and the children that I did not really pray about it." Together they walked to the porch and explained to their people that they had decided to remain.

Blest Be The Tie That Binds

BREAK THOU THE BREAD OF LIFE
Mary A. Lathbury, 1841–1913

Break Thou The Bread

Mary A. Lathbury, talented artist and writer, became associated with the famous "Chautauqua Movement" in 1877, when she was hired as an assistant to Dr. John H. Vincent, secretary of the Methodist Sunday School Union. She spent the summer of her 35th year at the assembly grounds on the quiet shores of beautiful Lake Chautauqua in the Finger Lakes region of western New York. One day as she and Dr. Vincent were standing by the lake watching the sunset, the Methodist Bishop asked her if she would write a hymn to be used by the Chautauqua Literary and Scientific Circle. Miss Lathbury agreed and began to think of a possible theme. As she meditated about the blessing that had been received at the summer conference she related the thought to the multitude that had been fed with bread on the hillside by Galilee. Thus came to life the words which Christians have come to know and to love.

BREATHE ON ME, BREATH OF GOD
Edwin Hatch 1835–1889

Breathe On Me,

The beauty of Edwin Hatch's hymn poem "Breathe On Me, Breath of God" was not discovered until after his death in 1889. His early years had been spent in Canada, first as professor of classics in Trinity College, Toronto, and then as Rector of the High School, Quebec. Even though later at Oxford, England, he received fame as church historian and theologian, it was while he was among the peaceful lakes and beautiful rivers of eastern Canada that he was moved to write this little gem of prayer to God.

BRIGHTLY BEAMS OUR FATHER'S MERCY or LET THE LOWER LIGHTS BE BURNING
Philip Paul Bliss, 1838–1876

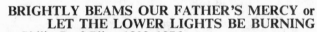

Popular gospel song written by Philip Paul Bliss in 1867. One night while he was listening to the famous Evangelist Dwight L. Moody, Bliss was so inspired by the message that he wrote both words and music to this hymn which proved to be one of the most popular of his song-writing career. Moody told the story of a captain of a boat approaching the harbor at Cleveland on a dark and stormy night. The lighthouse blinked but one light. "Where are the lower lights?" the captain asked. "Gone out, sir," was the reply he received from the pilot. "Can we make the harbor?" he inquired. "We must or we perish!" was the terse reply. The eloquent preacher related dramatically the subsequent crashing and destruction of the ship on the craggy rocks, and concluded with the challenging exhortation, "The Master will take care of the great lighthouse; let us keep the lower lights burning."

Brightly Beams Our Father's Mercy

Philip Bliss was so deeply moved that he immediately transformed, with the inherent, natural musical ability that was a God-given gift, the whole emotional, spiritual experience into one of the most widely popular evangelistic hymns of all time.

CHRISTIANS, AWAKE, SALUTE THE HAPPY MORN
John Byrom 1691–1763

On Christmas morning, 1749, Dolly Byrom, daughter of hymn-writer John Byrom, found in her breakfast plate a new Christmas hymn written especially for her by her father. It was "Christmas Day, for Dolly," later called "Christians, Awake, Salute the Happy Morn." It had been composed on Christmas Eve the night before and placed with tender, loving care where it could be found by his daughter at the break of Christmas day. It is said that on that same morning a group gathered outside Byrom's home and sang his new carol to music composed within an hour by the village organist.

Christians, Awake

CHRIST THE LORD IS RISEN TODAY
Charles Wesley 1707–1788

"Christ the Lord Is Risen Today" a resurrection hymn written by Charles Wesley, one of the famed Methodist Wesley brothers, appeared first in 1739 in a volume called "Hymns and Sacred Poems." Wesley's inspiration for this hymn came from a 14th century Latin composition "Jesus Christ Is Risen Today." It was first called "Hymn for Easter," and has known wide popularity from the time it was written. Of all of Wesley's hymns this one is sung the most:

Christ the Lord is risen today, Alleluia!
Sons of men and angels say, Alleluia!
Raise your joys and triumphs high, Alleluia!
Sing, ye heavens, and earth reply, Alleluia!

Christ The Lord

COME, THOU ALMIGHTY KING
author unknown

This hymn, one of the most popular in the English language, first appeared in a half-penny leaflet about the year 1757 along with one other hymn, "Jesus, Let Thy Pitying Eye" by Charles Wesley. As a result, for over a hundred years the authorship was attributed to Wesley; however, it is now believed that the author is unknown. It is thought that because it is an imitation of the English National Anthem, "God Save Our Gracious King," that the author did not want to have his name associated with it. A story is told that during the Revolutionary War a British military force invaded a colonial church and commanded the congregation to rise and sing "God Save the King," whereupon the fast-thinking group immediately stood up and sang different words to the same tune—, it was this great hymn that they sang!

Come, Thou Almighty King

COME, WE WHO LOVE THE LORD
Isaac Watts, 1674–1748

Come, We Who Love

Isaac Watts probably wrote more hymns than any other person who has ever lived, but "Come, We Who Love the Lord," which he wrote in 1709, is no doubt, the only hymn that he or anyone else wrote, which was used to end the threatened strike of an unhappy choir. It is told that a New England church was experiencing a difference of opinion within the congregation. The argument had progressed to such an extent that the choir had become rebellious. Dr. Samuel West, the pastor, received word that the choir was going to express its displeasure by refusing to sing on the following Sunday. The minister averted any trouble, cleverly and uniquely, by rising on the Sabbath morning in the Church Service and announcing the opening hymn as "Come, We Who Love the Lord." After reading the first verse through very slowly, he turned to the choir and requested that they lead in the singing of the second verse:

    Let those refuse to sing
        Who never knew our God.

It goes without saying, that the choir could do nothing but abide by their pastor's resourceful request!

COME, YE THANKFUL PEOPLE, COME
Henry Alford, 1810–1871

Come, Ye Thankful

Of all the harvest hymns, "Come, Ye Thankful People, Come," written by the Reverend Henry Alford, Dean of Canterbury Cathedral, is the most popular. It was first published in his Psalms and Hymns in 1844. To describe Alford as precocious as a child is an understatement. He started writing at the age of six, and by eleven had compiled a collection of hymns. At sixteen these were his words: "I do this day as in the presence of God and my own soul renew my covenant with God, and solemnly determine henceforth to become His, and do His work as far as in me lies." "Come, Ye Thankful People, Come" may not have been his most scholarly effort, but it will always remain the most popular writing of his career.

DAY IS DYING IN THE WEST
Mary A. Lathbury, 1841–1913

Day Is Dying

One of the favorite hymns of evening praise written in 1877 by Mary A. Lathbury, at the request of Bishop John H. Vincent founder of the Chautauqua Assembly on Lake Chautauqua, western New York. Considered to be one of the finest and most distinctive hymns written in the 19th century, "Day is Dying in the West" was composed as a study hymn for the Chautauqua Literary and Scientific Circle. William F. Sherwin, director of music, at the Chautauqua Assembly, composed special music entitled "Chautauqua—Evening Praise." There is no finer example of a perfect wedding of words and music found in the whole file of Christian hymns.

464

DEAR LORD AND FATHER OF MANKIND
John Greenleaf Whittier 1807–1892

Only a poet of John Greenleaf Whittier's depth and understanding could so successfully challenge the world to forget for a while the stress and strain, the hurry and hustle, of every day life and responsibility and find in the quietness of meditation, a renewal of strength and faith in God. His hymn "Dear Lord and Father of Mankind" is one of the strongest voices leading men to the truth that in the still silence of our inner mind is found the beauty of God's loving care.

Dear Lord And Father

Dear Lord and Father of mankind,
    Forgive our feverish ways;
Reclothe us in our rightful mind;
    In purer lives thy service find,
In deeper reverence praise.

ETERNAL FATHER, STRONG TO SAVE
William Whiting, 1825–1878

This hymn is the national hymn of the Navy and is used at the United States Naval Academy in Annapolis and on English ships. In addition a beautiful French translation is a standard part of the hymn book of the French Navy.

FACE TO FACE
Mrs. Frank A. Breck, 1855–1934

This popular gospel hymn originated in a manner which defies the imagination. In 1898, the Rev. Grant C. Tullar, famous composer and publisher, was visiting a Methodist minister and his wife in Rutherford, New Jersey. One afternoon they had visited the sick and were late returning to the parsonage. They sat down to a hasty supper, just before the service. Everything seemed to be in order except the dish of jelly, which was almost empty. Knowing Tullar's love for jelly, the host and hostess left the little bit of it for him. Dr. Tullar, lifting the jelly, said with a smile, "All for me; it's all for me!" Immediately the words appealed to him. "What a theme for a song," he shouted. Jumping to the piano, he amazed his hosts by writing and singing a hymn before their eyes."

Eternal Father,

All for me the Saviour suffered;
    All for me He bled and died.

When urged to incorporate it into the evening service, Tullar thought it should be polished, and promised it for the next day. However, fate has strange ways, and the next morning there occurred one of the oddest happenings in hymn writing history. In Dr. Tullar's mail there was a letter from Mrs. Frank A. Breck, a native Vermont Presbyterian, containing several original hymn poems, one of which was "Face to Face with Christ My Saviour." He could hardly believe his eyes. The words of her poem fitted perfectly the tune he had composed the previous night. Somehow he knew it was meant to be; and substituting her words for his, one of the great evangelistic songs of all time was born!

Face To Face

FAIREST LORD JESUS
author unknown

Fairest Lord Jesus

This famous hymn had its origin in Germany in the 17th century, and was discovered in America in the year 1850 by Richard Storrs Willis, a musician and newspaper man, who wrote books on church music and other musical subjects. The tune is an ancient Silesian folk song derived from legend and story, which is a ballad picturing common life with its interests and enthusiasm. It was said to have been sung by the German Knight Crusaders on their way to Jerusalem in the 12th Century and is still referred to as The Crusaders' Hymn, although no proof of this has been established. This hymn telling of the beauty of Nature is often called "The Marching song of the out-of-doors" and is a favorite of young people. It is also interesting to note that pianist Franz Liszt made large use of this tune in his oratorio "St. Elizabeth."

FAITH OF OUR FATHERS
Frederick William Faber, 1814–1863

Faith Of Our Fathers

There is no Christian hymn that lifts the soul more or stirs the imagination more than "Faith of Our Fathers" written in approximately 1850, by Frederick W. Faber, Anglican clergyman of England. Yet the strange fact is that very few people realize the reason for his writing the hymn. Record shows that all his hymns were written after being received into the Roman Catholic Church in 1846. One of Faber's views was that the true Church of England was continued through the Roman Catholic Church. This is what he meant when he spoke of the "faith of our fathers." However, this was a case of what he had written far exceeding the boundaries of what he had intended; and thus, Protestants sang the hymn with equal meaning and fervor as Catholics. It proves, once again, that the mass singing of hymns is one of the strongest expressions of faith in Christendom.

FIGHT THE GOOD FIGHT
John Samuel Bewley Monsell, 1811–1875

Fight The Good Fight

This martial hymn was written in 1863 by John Samuel Bewley Monsell an English Episcopal Clergyman. A prolific hymn-writer (there are over three hundred accredited to his name) Monsell's "Fight the Good Fight" is the one that time has proven to be the most popular. It is based on I Timothy 6:12 and was written for the nineteenth Sunday following Trinity Sunday. Always popular in the English speaking world, the hymn was introduced to the American public during the Spanish-American war. Monsell himself "fought the good fight" during his entire ministry. His death came by accident when as a Vicar he fell from the roof of his church while inspecting some reconstruction work which was being finished at the time.

466

FLING OUT THE BANNER! LET IT FLOAT
George Washington Doane, 1799–1859

This stirring militant hymn was written in December, 1848, for a flag-raising at St. Mary's School, Burlington, New Jersey. The author, Bishop George W. Doane, then living at Riverside, Massachusetts, had founded the girls' school 11 years before the writing of this hymn; but their interest was always primary in his heart. It takes little imagination to realize the pride that was surging through the beings of both author and school members as on this particular day the bright colors of the Christian flag unfurled in the morning wind:

Fling Out The
Banner!

Fling out the banner, Let it float
Skyward and seaward, high and wide;
The sun that lights its shining folds,
The Cross on which the Saviour died.

FOR THE BEAUTY OF THE EARTH
Folliott Sanford Pierpont, 1835–1917

Folliott Sanford Pierpoint was twenty-nine years old when he sat on the green hillside late in the spring of 1864 outside his native city of Bath, England. The violets and primroses were in full bloom and the world was a beautiful place to see. As he sat down to rest and meditate he could not help but feel the wonder and glory of God around him. His glad fingers had wings of joy as he wrote word after word, inspired by the spreading spring-time beauty:

For The Beauty Of
The Earth

For the beauty of the earth,
For the glory of the skies,
For the love which from our birth
Over and around us lies;
Lord of all, to Thee we raise
This our hymn of grateful praise.

FROM GREENLAND'S ICY MOUNTAINS
Reginald Heber, 1783–1826

This famous missionary hymn was written in fifteen minutes by Reginald Heber, then 36 years of age, in 1819 at the request of his father-in-law. The King of England had ordered a special offering for the Propogation of the Gospel in Foreign Parts to be taken on Whitsunday of that year. It was the custom to have a special hymn accompany the special offering. Heber, who was then a minister at Hodnet, England, was visiting his father-in-law, Dean Shipley at Wrexham, England. On Saturday afternoon before Whitsunday a group had gathered in the library. It was here that the Dean asked his talented son-in-law if he could provide something special for the next day's offering. Heber said he could, and moved to the end of the table where he started to write the famous lines to his great hymn. In fifteen minutes he had completed it. It was so well liked that not a stanza was added or changed. We sing it today as he wrote it then.

From Greenland's
Icy Mountains

GLORIOUS THINGS OF THEE ARE SPOKEN
John Newton, 1725–1807

Glorious Things Of
Thee

This joyous hymn is considered to be the greatest ever to come from the pen of the Reverend John Newton, close friend of William Cowper. It was part of a collection by Newton and Cowper called "Olney Hymns" which included two hundred and eighty of Newton's and sixty-eight of Cowper's, and was in use in England at about the time of the American Revolution. Newton also wrote "How Sweet the Name of Jesus Sounds."

GOD BE WITH YOU TILL WE MEET AGAIN
Jeremiah Eames Rankin, 1828–1904

An emotional hymn of prayer written in 1882 by Jeremiah Eames Rankin, a Congregational minister of New England. His purpose for writing the hymn was to find a way for the Christian to say good-bye which was not contradictory to his faith and belief. He finally settled for the phrase "God be with you," which he felt was the Christian way of saying "good-bye until we meet again." The story is told that Rankin invited two composers to write music for the words. One composer was well known, the other unknown. He chose the work of the unknown composer, William G. Tomer. He certainly must have been inspired in his choice for there is no finer example of the harmony of words and music than in this hymn. Without doubt, the popularity of "God be With You Till We Meet Again" has been augmented considerably because of the melody.

God Be With You

GOD MOVES IN A MYSTERIOUS WAY
William Cowper, 1731–1800

This hymn, written by William Cowper in 1774, might never have been written at all if a London cab-driver had not lost his way in the thick English fog. The story is told in the memoirs of William Cowper, that the great English poet, who often had dark moments of doubt and despair, was seized by an urgent impulse to drown himself in the river Thames. He hailed a cab and asked the driver to take him to the river; but a sudden appearance of thick, heavy fog prevented the cabman from finding the river. After driving around and around in complete confusion, the cabman refused to continue and ordered his passenger out of the cab. As Cowper stumbled along the dark street, he suddenly found himself in front of his own door. After Cowper recovered his senses, he sat down and wrote the words to "God Moves in a Mysterious Way" completely convinced that God had caused the coming of the fog to save his life.

God Moves In
Mysterious Ways

GOD OF OUR FATHERS, KNOWN OF OLD
Rudyard Kipling, 1865-1936

It was the thought of Rudyard Kipling that of all the poems and stories he had written that two pieces would last as long as literature lasted. His "Just So Stories" was one, and the other,—"God of Our Fathers, Known of Old." The famed British poet, grandson of a Methodist minister, wrote the hymn in 1897 at the height of the colorful British Empire during Queen Victoria's Diamond Jubilee. There has never been a more soul-searching national hymn written by the hand of man:

God Of Our
Fathers,

God of our fathers known of old,
　　Lord of our far-flung battle line,
Beneath whose awful hand we hold
　　Dominion over palm and pine;
Lord God of Hosts, be with us yet,
　　Lest we forget, lest we forget!

GOD OF GRACE AND GOD OF GLORY
Harry Emerson Fosdick, 1878-19—

God of grace and God of glory,
　　On Thy people pour Thy power;
Crown Thine ancient Church's story;
　　Bring her bud to glorious flower.

This hymn was written by the Reverend Harry Emerson Fosdick for the opening services of the new Riverside Church in New York City, October 5, 1930. It first appeared in a published hymnal "Praise and Service" in 1932. Two different hymn tunes are frequently used; a Welch hymn melody by John Hughes, 1873-1932, and Regent Square, a tune by Henry Smart, 1867, first sung in the Regent Square Presbyterian Church of London, England.

God Of Grace

GUIDE ME O THOU GREAT JEHOVAH
William Williams, 1717-1791

In 1785 Selina, Countess of Huntingdon, founded a college in South Wales to train "godly and pious young men" for the Christian ministry. Tradition says that she was not only a beautiful woman, but one who had a sense of the dramatic. She acquired the "sweet singer" of Wales to celebrate the opening of the college with a new, original hymn. William Williams, as he was called, sang and played for the first time his own hymn poem "Guide Me O Thou Great Jehovah." Not only did it inspire the potential men of the cloth in great fashion, but it became a favorite hymn of generations to follow.

Guide Me

Guide me, O Thou great Jehovah,
　　Pilgrim through this barren land;
I am weak, but Thou are mighty,
　　Hold me with Thy powerful hand;
Bread of heaven, Feed me till I want no more;
Bread of heaven, Feed me till I want no more.

469

HALLELUJAH, WHAT A SAVIOUR
Philip Paul Bliss, 1838–1876

Hallelujah,

Philip P. Bliss wrote words and music to this hymn in 1876 just a short time before his death. He had visited the State prison at Jackson, Michigan, where he heard a stirring address on the subject of "Jesus, the Man of Sorrows." Bliss was deeply moved and chose "Hallelujah, What a Saviour" as his solo for the day. It is said that the presentation was so dramatic that scores of the prisoners were converted on the spot. This is the last known time that Bliss ever sang a song.

HARK! THE HERALD ANGELS SING
Charles Wesley, 1707–1788

Hark! The Herald Angels

Charles Wesley of England is without doubt one of the two most productive hymn writers of all time,—the other being Isaac Watts. Yet, strangely enough, Wesley was able to get but one Hymn poem into the Church of England's Book of Common Prayer,—and that one by error! An eighteenth century printer didn't know that the "established Church" of England frowned with disapproval upon Wesley's hymns. He had need of material to fill an empty space in the Book of Common Prayer and took it upon himself to insert a Christmas poem called "Hark, How All the Welkin Rings!" by an Anglican clergyman named Charles Wesley. When the error was discovered attempts were made to have it removed, but it proved so popular that it was allowed to remain. This is not the end of the story. "Hark! the Herald Angels Sing" still might not have reached its tremendous Christmas popularity if it hadn't been for other twists of fate. Wesley had called his poem "Hymn for Christmas Day" and it was sung with mild enthusiasm for over a hundred years. It might have slipped gradually into the mist of oblivion if it had not been for a tenor William Haymen Cummings, who when vocalizing on a bit of Felix Mendelssohn's "The Festgesang" noticed how the arrangement was perfect for Wesley's "Hymn for Christmas Day." Retitled "Hark! the Herald Angels Sing" and strengthened by the powerful music of Mendelssohn, Wesley's hymn became one of the greatest Nativity songs ever composed. Written in 1738, one of the first of Wesley's hymns became one of his greatest.

HAVE THINE OWN WAY
Adelaide A. Pollard, 1862–1934

"Have Thine Own Way" was written in 1902; the music, composed by George Cole Stebbins, was not written until five years later. Although Miss Pollard wrote many hymns and poems, "Have Thine Own Way" was the only one to survive the tests of time. However, this alone would justify her claim to fame; for this hymn became a favorite throughout all the Christian world.

470

HE LEADETH ME O BLESSED THOUGHT
Joseph Henry Gilmore, 1834–1918

In March 1862, during the Civil War, twenty-eight year old Reverend Joseph H. Gilmore, son of a New Hampshire governor, was supplying in an historic old Philadelphia church, the First Baptist Church at Broad and Arch Streets. Because of the dark depression of the war between the states, Gilmore selected as a theme the Twenty-Third Psalm, emphasizing God's leadership during dark days. Over and over again he repeated the phrase, "He Leadeth Me." Later at the home of one of the deacons, Gilmore was so filled with the thought of his theme that he was unable to contain himself. Seizing a piece of paper, he jotted down these lines: "He leadeth me! O blessed thought; O words with heavenly comfort fraught." When he finished there were four stanzas and a chorus. Gilmore promptly forgot all about what he had written; but his wife, recognizing something good, sent a copy to a Boston periodical. It was here that William Bradbury, famous composer and publisher of Church music, discovered it and set it to music.

He Leadeth Me

HIS EYE IS ON THE SPARROW
Mrs. C. D. Martin, 1867–1948

This beautiful gospel hymn was written because of the courage and faith of a woman bedridden for more than 20 years. Mrs. C. D. Martin and her husband were visiting Mr. and Mrs. Doolittle of Elmira, New York. Both of the Doolittles were "incurable cripples," but in spite of their handicaps carried on their business in a courageous manner. Greatly impressed by the faith of the saintly couple Dr. Martin commented upon the spirit and joy of his host and wife. Mrs. Doolittle's reaction was simple and direct. "His eye is on the sparrow and I know he watches me," she said. Mrs. Martin, who wrote many hymns and poems immediately recognized the potentiality of the phrase, and before the day ended she had arranged and incorporated it into one of the most touching hymns of all time.

His Eye Is On The Sparrow

HOLY, HOLY, HOLY!
LORD GOD ALMIGHTY
Reginald Heber 1783–1826

One of the greatest hymns of all ages, "Holy, Holy, Holy" was written in 1826 by Bishop Reginald Heber. It was based on the meter of the Apocalypse as found in Revelation 4:8–11: "Holy, Holy, Holy, Lord God Almighty, which was, and is, and is to come." The famed English poet-bishop wrote the hymn especially for Trinity Sunday as a tribute to the Trinity. It is one of the few hymns written for a specific Sunday of the Church Year, yet equally adaptable for every other Sunday. It is said of this hymn that it is found in more hymn books than any other hymn written.

Holy, Holy,

471

HOLY SPIRIT, TRUTH DIVINE
Samuel Longfellow, 1819–1892

The Reverend Samuel Longfellow shared the distinguished talent of poet with his famous brother Henry W. Longfellow. An ardent theist and devoted pastor, he spent his life in active service to others. Ill health was the reason for his early retirement from the ministry, as well as his desire to write the life of his beloved brother. Earnest devotional emotion is evidenced in his hymn "Holy Spirit, Truth Divine," which was published in the year 1864. Deep mysticism pervades in every stanza of this great hymn and opens the channels toward God for our prayers.

Holy Spirit,

HOW FIRM A FOUNDATION
author unknown

One of the truly great hymns of the church which has the unusual distinction of being absolutely anonymous. Most of the experts of hymnody agree that this hymn was written in 1787, most of them agree that it is one of the outstanding hymns of Christendom,—but most of them also agree that the author is unknown. This hymn joins the long line of Christian hymns which remain anonymous, but whose blessings are shared by the whole church.

How Firm A
Foundation

HOW GREAT THOU ART
authorship doubtful

Strangely enough, this truly impressive contemporary hymn received its present popular form through two different countries and two different translations. The original form was a Swedish poem "O Mighty God" by Carl Boberg written in 1886 and translated by Professor E. Gustav Johnson, of North Park College in 1925. The poem, based on the everlasting wonders and eternal powers of God had a metrical pattern that was easily identified with an old Swedish folk song and soon the words became a permanent part of that song. Before his death, Boberg had the joy of knowing his poem had become a cherished contribution to Swedish music. "O Mighty God" spread beyond Sweden and its native tongue. Soon it was popular in other countries, and sung in Russian, Polish, German and other tongues. In 1923, Reverend Stuart K. Hine, London missionary to the Ukraine, heard the song for the first time in Russia. Unaware of the fact that the song had originated in Sweden, Hine attributed it to a Russian prisoner and credited him with writing it in 1921. He was so impressed with the song that he made an English translation in 1948 which he called, "How Great Thou Art." The interesting fact of the story of this great hymn is that although two translations were made through three different languages, over thirty years apart, the might and grandeur of the hymn is preserved. "How Great Thou Art" inspires the human heart to the wonder and majesty of God.

How Great Thou
Art

I AM SO GLAD
Philip Paul Bliss, 1838–1876

Popular hymn for little children written by Philip P. Bliss after he had heard another hymn for children, "Oh, How I Love Jesus." While singing the chorus over and over again about his love for Jesus, the thought came to Bliss that there should be a hymn written about Jesus' love for him. He returned immediately to his home and wrote the lines:

I am so glad that our Father in Heaven
Tells of His love in the Book He has given;
Wonderful things in the Bible I see,
This is the dearest, that Jesus loves me.

I Am So Glad

I AM THINE, O LORD
Fanny J. Crosby, 1820–1915

This gospel hymn written by Fanny Crosby has been a favorite of Christian Endeavor societies the world over. It was written on an occasion of the famed blind poetess' visit to Cincinnati, Ohio at the home of W. H. Doane who has composed scores of popular gospel songs. They were sitting together in the still hush of the evening twilight hour talking about the nearness of God. The close fellowship of these two great Christians so impressed Miss Crosby that before retiring she had written the complete hymn. The next morning Mr. Doane fitted the music to the words and thus was born a special favorite of gospel hymn lovers wherever gospel hymns are sung.

I am Thine, O Lord, I have heard Thy voice,
And it told thy love to me;
But I long to rise in the arms of faith,
And be closer drawn to Thee.

I Am Thine, O Lord

I GAVE MY LIFE TO THEE
Frances Ridley Havergal, 1836–1879

Frances Ridley Havergal was sitting in the study of a German minister, January 10, 1858. On the wall a Cross of Christ hung with the inscription: "I did this for thee; what hast thou done for Me?" As Miss Havergal sat there looking at the cross, a thought flashed through her mind. Seizing a piece of paper she wrote rapidly:

I gave My life for thee,
  My precious Blood I shed,
That thou might'st ransomed be,
  And quickened from the dead.
I gave my life for thee;
What hast thou given for Me.

Not satisfied with the words, she crumpled the paper and threw it into the fireplace. Fortunately, she missed and the paper was only singed and charred. When her father, Reverend William Havergal saw the poem, he not only encouraged her to finish it, but wrote the tune to which it has been sung since that day.

I Gave My Life To Thee

I HEARD THE BELLS ON
CHRISTMAS DAY

Henry Wadsworth Longfellow, 1807–1882

I Heard The Bells

This lovely Christmas Carol, written at the turn of
the Nineteenth Century, was one of the few hymns
authored by the eminent poet, Henry Wadsworth
Longfellow. The phrase "Peace on earth, good-will
to men" was the inspiration for this poem. The famed
New England poet truly believed that God was
powerful and strong enough to overcome the strife
on earth and had vision far beyond his time of the
day when all nations would live together in peace.
> And in despair I bowed my head;
>   There is no peace on earth, I said,
> For hate is strong, and mocks the song
>   Of peace on earth, good will to men.

Its ringing tune was written by John Baptiste Calkin.
"Waltham" is also used as hymn tune in Doane's
popular Missionary hymn, "Fling Out the Banner."

I HEARD THE VOICE OF JESUS SAY

Horatius Bonar, 1808–1889

I Heard The Voice
Of Jesus

"I Heard the Voice of Jesus Say" was published by
Dr. Horatius Bonar, eminent Scottish hymn-writer
and preacher, in 1846. It is one of a long line of
hymns encouraging the singer to hear the clear voice
of God speaking out in a world of weariness to find
rest, in a world of darkness to find light, in a world
of fear to find faith. Bonar adds his voice to the many
other clarion voices crying out in the cloudiness of a
confused world to be assured that the truth of God
is free to all who can hear and see; that the voice of
Jesus cuts through like a bright beacon on a foggy
shore.

I LOVE THY KINGDOM LORD

Timothy Dwight, 1752–1817

I Love Thy Kingdom

Timothy Dwight, D. D., President of Yale College,
wrote "I Love Thy Kingdom, Lord" just after the
American Revolutionary War. Critics of early American hymnody say that the use of Watts' "Psalms and
Hymns" did not become general throughout New
England because of the reference to English characteristics. Something had to be added and changed to
make it palatable to the newly liberated American
patriots. Timothy Dwight was the one to do it, with
alterations to Isaac Watts' hymnal and new versifica-
tions. "I Love Thy Kingdom, Lord" was part of the
new arrangement.
> I love Thy kingdom, Lord,
> The house of Thine abode,
> The Church our blest Redeemer saved
> With His own precious blood.

I LOVE TO TELL THE STORY
Katherine Hankey, 1834–1911

Katherine Hankey was thirty-two years old when she wrote the hymn "I Love to Tell the Story." It arose out of a deep desire in her heart to tell the simple gospel story wherever she was in life. First, it was in the Sunday School of Clapham, England, where she became a devoted, refined consecrated woman. Then, it was in the heart of Africa, where she spent the most of her life, giving the sales of all her writings to missions. Finally, it was in the hospitals of London, where she spent the last minutes of her life telling lonely patients of God's beautiful love. When Katherine Hankey wrote "I Love to Tell the Story" in 1866, she was doing more than expressing a feeling in her own being, she was projecting that same feeling into the minds of thousands of people through the years who would sing her song and receive the same challenge.

I Love To Tell The Story

I love to tell the story Of unseen things above,
Of Jesus and His glory, Of Jesus and His love,
I love to tell the story, Because I know 'tis true
It satisfies my longings, As nothing else can do.

I NEED THEE EVERY HOUR
Annie Sherwood Hawks, 1835–1918

Annie Sherwood Hawks, a thirty-seven year old Brooklyn, New York, housewife, wrote the words to this gospel hymn one morning in 1872 while she was doing her housework. On the following Sunday she showed her simple poem to the pastor of her church, Reverend Robert Lowry, minister at the Hanson Place Baptist Church, who himself was a composer as well as a preacher. Lowry took them home, set them to music, added a chorus of his own, and a famous hymn was born.

I Need Thee Every Hour

I need Thee every hour, Most gracious Lord;
No tender voice like Thine Can peace afford.
I need Thee, O I need Thee,
     Every hour I need Thee;
O bless me now, my Saviour, I come to Thee.

I THINK WHEN I READ THAT
SWEET STORY OF OLD
Mrs. Jemima Thompson Luke, 1813–1906

This familiar children's hymn was written in 1841 by Miss Jemima Thompson, while riding on a stage coach from London to Wellington in England. Miss Thompson, aged 28 at the time, had discovered a Greek song that she felt would make a good hymn for the children if only the right words could be found. She searched through Sunday School books and hymn books but could not find the proper words. While riding on the stage coach, the rythmic motion of the wheels inspired her, and before the hour's journey's end she had written the words on the back of an old envelope. (See The Sweet Story of Old)

I Think When I Read

I WILL SING THE WONDROUS STORY
Francis H. Rowley 1854–1921

I Will Sing The
Wondrous Story

A gospel hymn written in one evening by Francis H. Rowley while he was conducting Revival meetings at the First Baptist Church, North Adams, Massachusetts, in 1886. He was being assisted in the services by a young Swiss musician named Peter Bilhorn, who suggested that he write a hymn for the following evening's services to which Bilhorn would compose the music. In the author's own words, "It came to me with no particular effort on my part." For a long time the hymn was very popular, and still is, although an old Welch tune by Rowland Hugh Pritchard, 1855, is used for music rather than the original Bilhorn composition.

I WOULD BE TRUE, FOR THERE ARE THOSE WHO TRUST ME
Howard A. Walter, 1883–1918

I Would Be True,

In July, 1906, Howard A. Walter, a Congregational Minister, was teaching English at Waseda University in Japan. He sent his mother a poem he had written called "My Creed." In the poem he expressed the feeling that motivated him as a Christian:

I would be true,
for there are those who trust me;

His mother was so impressed with the sincerity of the poem that she submitted it to the editors of Harper's Bazaar, who published it in 1907. Three years later it was seen by Joseph Peek who saw its possibility as a hymn. Although a tune was running clearly in his mind, Peek was unfamiliar with the techniques of musical composition and got an organist friend to write it down while he whistled. "I Would Be True," one of the outstanding youth songs of all time, is one of the few hymns that mention the word "laughter" as a Christian attribute.

IN CHRIST THERE IS NO EAST OR WEST
John Oxenham, 1852–1941

In Christ There Is
No East Or West

In the year 1908, Winston Churchill made the opening speech at a great missionary exhibition in London called "The Orient in London." Part of the exhibition was a pageant depicting the triumphs of the missionary cause. In charge of the pageant was a minister named Reverend Dugald Macfadyen, nephew of John Oxenham. Macfadyen persuaded his famous uncle to provide the music for the pageant; and part of the music was "In Christ There is No East or West." This hymn which was so widely acclaimed in that day has never lost its significance; its plea for the fellowship of love has even more profound meaning in our world of today.

In Christ there is no East or West,
In Him no South or North;
But one great Fellowship of Love
Throughout the whole wide earth.

IN HEAVENLY LOVE ABIDING
Anna L. Waring, 1823–1910

Anna L. Waring was thirty years old when she published, in 1850, a little volume of nineteen hymns called "Hymns and Meditations." Included among the poems was a hymn of meditation called "In Heavenly Love Abiding." Although her poetry could not be classified as literary, Anna Waring had a simple, sincere and refreshing expression of the wonder and power of God. The genuine piety of the Welsh woman is witnessed in these lines of her hymn:

Wherever He may guide me,
  No want shall turn me back;
My Shepherd is beside me,
  And nothing can I lack.

In Heavenly Love
Abiding

IN THE CROSS OF CHRIST I GLORY
Sir John Bowring, 1792–1872

The real inspiration of the hymn "In the Cross of Christ I Glory" came from the words of the Apostle Paul, "Far Be It From Me to Glory, Save in the Cross of Our Lord Jesus Christ, Through Which the World Hath Been Crucified Unto Me, and I Unto the World," Gal. 6:14. The author, Sir John Bowring, published this hymn in 1825 and uses only the first line of the scripture, although altered a bit, tries not to emphasize the experience of being crucified with Christ, but instead wants to bring forth the joy and cheer which fills the heart of the believer who realizes what is really meant by the redeeming work of Christ. On his gravestone are engraved the words of this his best known hymn:

In the Cross of Christ I glory,
  Towering o'er the wrecks of time;
All the light of sacred story
  Gathers round its head sublime.

In The Cross Of
Christ

IN THE GARDEN
C. Austin Miles 1868–1946

"In the Garden" is one of the favorite gospel hymns of all times. Its author and composer, C. Austin Miles, was born in 1868 in Lakehurst, New Jersey, and died in 1946, 32 years after the writing of this hymn. His musical career started at the age of twelve, at which time he played for his first funeral at the local Methodist Church. In 1912 he was asked to write a hymn poem that would "breathe tenderness" and bring hope and rest for the weary. Miles visualizing Mary Magdalene at the Garden of the Resurrection brought forth the words:

And He walks with me, and He talks with me
  And He tells me I am His own,
And the joy we share as we tarry there,
  None other has ever known.

In The Garden

477

IN THE HOUR OF TRIAL
James Montgomery, 1771–1854

In The Hour Of Trial

James Montgomery born in 1771 in Ayrshire, Scotland, was the son of a Moravian minister and was educated in a Moravian school at Fulneck, near Leeds, England, for the Christian ministry. He spent more of his time writing poetry than in his studies. After leaving school in 1787 he spent four years in very precarious and doubtful modes of living, and was even twice imprisoned for his outspoken political opinions. He was classed by the literate as a minor English poet, but the church ranks him with Wesley, Watts and Doddridge. From the four hundred hymns he wrote more than three hundred are widely sung today. Montgomery wrote "In the Hour of Trial" on October 13, 1834. He drifted away from the church and at the age of forty-three, like the prodigal son who was lost but found again, returned to the old Moravian church of his boyhood, and later peacefully died in his sleep in 1854.

INTO THE WOODS MY MASTER WENT
Sidney Lanier, 1842–1881

Into The Woods

The hymn poem "Into the Woods My Master Went" was written by Sidney Lanier, who devoted his life to poetry, flute playing and music writing after serving in the Confederate Army. The scene of this hymn takes place on the Mount of Olives and the antique and mysterious flavor of its melody brings us close to the loneliness of the Saviour in His hour of trial:

> Into the woods my Master went,
>   Clean forspent, forspent;
>   Into the woods my Master came,
>   Forspent with love and shame.
> But the olives they were not blind to Him,
>   The little gray leaves were kind to Him,
>   The thorn tree had a mind to Him,
>   When into the woods He came.

IT CAME UPON THE MIDNIGHT CLEAR
Edmund Hamilton Sears, 1810–1876

It Came Upon A Midnight

A popular Christmas hymn written in 1850 by a Unitarian minister Edmund Hamilton Sears, born at Sandisfield, Massachusetts, April 6, 1810. Although most of his life was spent in the ministry (twenty-seven years at Wayland, Massachusetts), for twelve years he was associated with Reverend Rufus Ellis in the editorial work of the Monthly Religious Magazine. It was here that most of Sear's poetical works were published.

> It came upon the midnight clear,
>   That glorious song of old,
>   From angels bending near the earth,
>   To touch their harps of gold.

IT IS WELL WITH MY SOUL
Horatio Gates Spafford, 1828–1888

Tragedy was associated with the writing of the words of this famous gospel hymn, and followed closely the composing of the music. H. G. Spafford wrote the poem in the mid-Atlantic over the exact spot where his four children had drowned a few days before. His wife and children were sailing to France on the "Ville du Havre," one of the largest ships afloat. It was rammed by an English iron sailing vessel and sank to the bottom of the ocean within two hours, killing 226 people. Mrs. Spafford lived, but the four children were lost. Just weeks before this tragic drowning, Spafford had lost everything he owned in the great Chicago fire. And now, if not tested enough, he lost all of his beloved children. As soon as it could be arranged he sailed to Europe to join his wife. On the way, December 1873, the Captain of his ship pointed out to him the spot where the tragedy had occurred. Here in the dark of night, with a heart heavy with grief and pain, but yet surging with faith and hope, Spafford wrote these words:

It Is Well With My Soul

When peace like a river attendeth my way,
   When sorrow like sea-billows roll,
Whatever my lot, Thou hast taught me to say,
   It is well, it is well with my soul!

Philip Paul Bliss, great song leader and composer, wrote the music for this hymn in November, 1876. Two weeks after it had been written, Bliss and his wife were killed in a tragic train crash in Ashtabula, Ohio. It was said by witnesses that Bliss could have escaped, but chose to die by the side of his wife, who was caught in the flaming wreckage.

JERUSALEM THE GOLDEN
Bernard of Cluny, 12th Century

Jerusalem The Golden

J. M. Neale translated "Jerusalem the Golden" from a poem by Bernard of Cluny, a 12th century mystic. 700 years separated the writing of the poem and its translation, but truth and beauty are not altered by the passing of the years. The original poem, written in 1145, was 2,966 lines long, a bitter satire on the corruption and degeneration of his age in comparison to the glories of heaven which were to come. Neale, in his translation shortened (and many critics say improved) the original to achieve the hymn in its present form.

JESUS CALLS US! O'ER THE TUMULT
Mrs. Cecil F. Alexander 1818-1895

This beautiful gospel hymn was written in 1852 by Mrs. C. Frances Alexander. Based on Matthew 4:18-19 which contains the verse, "Follow me and I will make you fishers of men" this hymn is written in the simple, unadorned, emotional but refined style so typical of Mrs. Alexander. Used by some denominations as a hymn for St. Andrew's day "Jesus Calls

Jesus Calls Us!

Us! O'er the Tumult" is a favorite in the hymnal of every church.

JESUS, KEEP ME NEAR THE CROSS
William H. Doane, 1832-1915

Jesus, Keep Me

In 1869, William H. Doane, famed composer of gospel music, wrote a hymn tune and handed it to the equally famed blind hymn writer Fanny J. Crosby with the request that she write words to fit it. She did, promptly, and there came into being "Near the Cross" a gospel hymn popular in every decade since. A shadow of fate fell upon this hymn as it was being written. The words of the chorus said, "In the cross, in the cross, Be my glory ever, Till my raptured soul shall find Rest beyond the river." Strangely enough, 46 years later, in the year 1915, both Doane and Crosby found their eternal rest,—in the same year.

JESUS, LOVER OF MY SOUL
Charles Wesley, 1707-1788

Jesus, Lover Of My Soul

The famed clergyman Henry Ward Beecher said of "Jesus, Lover of my Soul" that he had rather have written that hymn than have the fame of all the kings that ever sat upon the earth. Written by the master hymn writer, Charles Wesley in 1740, it was not considered by the author as one of his better hymns. In fact, it was not published until nine years after Wesley's death. However, the singing public has not agreed with Wesley's opinion and has made his hymn an all-time popular favorite. Many stories have circulated concerning the origin of the hymn. One tale tells of a flock of birds who flew in the window and found refuge under Wesley's coat. Other stories speak of savage storms at sea which prompted the author to pen his famous words. Still another source says that the hymn-poem resulted because of an angry mob which threatened Wesley's life forcing him to flee. The truth, however, is that the noted Methodist clergyman was simply praising God with one of the thousands of hymns which he left as a legacy to the world.

Jesus, lover of my soul,
    Let me to Thy bosom fly,
While the nearer waters roll,
    While the tempest still is high.

JESUS LOVES ME, THIS I KNOW
Anna Warner, 1827-1915

Jesus Loves Me,

The hymn "Jesus Loves Me, This I Know" is an international favorite among children, written in 1859. It has been taught and sung in many tongues by missionaries the world over. The author, Anna Warner, wrote many hymns for her Bible Class at West Point, and when she died a military funeral was held in her honor by the cadets whom she loved and taught for many years. The composer of this hymn, William Bradbury, developed the "Sunday-School song" form, which was a single ballad style verse with a refrain. It may be said that this was a true American contribution to hymnody.

JESUS SAVIOUR PILOT ME
Edward Hopper, 1818-1888

This seafaring hymn was written by Reverend Edward Hopper who was born in 1818 and a graduate from Union Theological Seminary. His last pastorate was at the Church of Sea and Land in New York, a favorite place of worship for sailors and men of the sea. Although this song was composed for seamen, and imitated the tossing of a boat by the ocean waves, its rhythm also accents the motion of a mother rocking her child. This gospel hymn has found its place in hymnology as a hymn of spiritual trust. It first appeared as a poem in the Sailor's Magazine in 1871 and was published that same year in the "Baptist Praise Book."

Jesus Saviour Pilot Me

> Jesus, Saviour, pilot me
> Over life's tempestuous sea;
> Unknown waves around me roll,
> Hiding rocks and treach'rous shoal;
> Chart and compass come from Thee,
> Jesus, Saviour, pilot me.

JESUS SHALL REIGN WHERE'ER THE SUN
Isaac Watts, 1674-1748

The first hymn of significance written on the theme of world missions was in 1719 by Isaac Watts, "Jesus Shall Reign Where'er the Sun." Strangely enough this theme of Jesus' Kingship was taken from the Old Testament, Psalm 72: "He shall have dominion also from sea to sea. . .They shall fear thee as long as the sun and moon endure . . . .All nations shall call Him blessed. . .Let the whole earth be filled with His glory."

Jesus Shall Reign

> Jesus shall reign where'er the sun
> Does His successive journeys run;
> His kingdom stretch from shore to shore,
> Till moons shall wax and wane no more.

JESUS, THE VERY THOUGHT OF THEE
Bernard of Clairvaux, 1091-1153

David Livingstone, famed missionary of the dark continent Africa, had these words to say about this fine old hymn of the middle ages, "The hymn of St. Bernard on the name of Christ pleases me so that it rings in my ears as I wander across the wide, wide wilderness." Dr. Livingstone believed as many believed after him that "Jesus, the Very Thought of Thee" was penned by the saintly Bernard of Clairvaux early in the 12th century. However, most authorities conclude that it was written much later than that and by author unknown. Whatever the case, it is done with the same devout spirit and inspired style as used by the noted cleric of the middle ages. Translated in 1849 by John B. Dykes, "Jesus, the Very Thought of Thee" has

Jesus, The Very Thought

481

long held a sacred place in the hearts of the lovers of hymnody.

> Jesus, the very thought of Thee,
>   With sweetness fills my breast;
> But Sweeter far Thy face to see,
>   And in Thy presence rest.

Joyful, Joyful

JOYFUL, JOYFUL WE ADORE THEE
Henry Van Dyke, 1852-1933

The joyous music in this famous hymn is an arrangement from the famed composer Beethoven's "Ninth Symphony." Many hymn writers had tried their hand at creating verse which would measure up in some degree to this which was some of the world's greatest music. It wasn't until a few years before the first World War, about 1911, that Dr. Henry Van Dyke, while on a preaching visit to Williams College, finally succeeded in writing words that caught the fulness of the joy of Ludwig von Beethoven's music. Together, the words and music of this hymn combine to make one of the outstanding pieces of hymnody in the Church.

> Joyful, joyful, we adore Thee,
>   God of glory, Lord of love;
> Hearts unfold like flowers before Thee
>   Hail Thee as the sun above.

Joy To The World

JOY TO THE WORLD
Isaac Watts, 1674-1748

There could be no hymn which can boast of such famous parenthood as this 250-year old Christmas carol. The words were penned by that master of English hymns, that giant of sacred verse, that most famous of hymn writers, Isaac Watts. The music was composed by that wonder of divine sound, that leader of choral interpretation, that most famous of song writers George Frederick Handel (An adaption from the Messiah). Who can say which one has been more responsible for the continued popularity of "Joy to the World"? Contemporaries, Handel died (1759) some eleven years after Watts. But what they created together has never died,—and probably never will!

JUST AS I AM
Charlotte Elliott, 1789-1871

Just As I Am

At the age of 33, Charlotte Elliott, because of the pressure of a musical education, had become a helpless invalid. She developed a bitter and rebellious spirit. One evening at her home, while being visited by Dr. Cesar Malan, a noted Swiss minister and musician, the frustrated woman enquired of the noted clergyman with despair, "How do you become a Christian"? He replied, "You pray this prayer: O God, I come to you just as I am." Fourteen years later in 1836, Miss Elliott, reminiscing about the evening with Dr. Malan, wrote her famous seven-stanza poem which began:

> Just as I am, without one plea,
> But that Thy blood was shed for me,

LEAD KINDLY LIGHT
John Henry Newman, 1801-1890

John Henry Newman, 32-year old Anglican Clergyman wrote this hymn while pacing impatiently upon the deck of a becalmed, little sailing vessel bound for Marseilles with a cargo of oranges, but stricken at the Strait of Bonifacio between the Islands of Corsica and Sardinia in June of 1833. To pass the time away during the week of waiting for the winds to fill the sails that would take them home, Newman penned the words that would mean so much to millions seeking the light of the heavenly home:

Lead, kindly light! amid the encircling gloom;
    Lead Thou me on.
The night is dark and I am far from home;
    Lead Thou me on!
Keep Thou my feet;
    I do not ask to see
The distant scene.
    One step enough for me.

Lead Kindly Light

LEAD ON, O KING ETERNAL
Ernest W. Shurtleff, 1862-1917

This militant hymn was written for the graduating class of a theological school in 1888 by one of its members. Twenty-six year old Ernest W. Shurtleff wrote this hymn expressly for the graduation of his Andover Theological Seminary Class, Andover, Massachusetts. It was first publicly sung on this occasion. Little did his classmates realize as they joined in singing this remarkable hymn that they were voicing words and thoughts which would far out-live any one of them present on that day.

Lead on, O King Eternal,
    The day of march has come;
Henceforth in fields of conquest
    Thy tents shall be our home.
Through days of preparation
    Thy grace has made us strong,
And now, O King Eternal,
    We lift our battle song.

Lead On O King

LEANING ON THE EVERLASTING ARMS
Anthony Johnson Showalter 1857-1927

A gospel hymn written in 1887 by A. J. Showalter, composer-publisher-teacher as a result of deaths in the families of two of his former pupils. While he was writing letters of consolation to them reminding them that "The Eternal God is Thy Refuge, and Underneath are the everlasting Arms," the thought occurred to him that this would be a good theme for a hymn. With the help of Elisha Hoffman, author of "Glory to His Name" and two thousand other hymn-poems, "Leaning on the Everlasting Arms" was written and published;

What a fellowship, what a joy Divine,
    Leaning on the Everlasting Arms!

Leaning On The Everlasting Arms

LORD FOR TOMORROW AND ITS NEEDS
Sybil F. Partridge (Sister Mary Xavier) 1842-1910

The simple, heart-felt prayer "Lord for Tomorrow and Its Needs" was written in the year 1877 by a Roman Catholic nun, Sybil F. Partridge of Liverpool. Sister Mary Xavier wished to have this hymn remain anonymous, but the beauty of its words and significance of its theme were too great to be hidden from Christians who would have need of its strength to sustain them in their daily tasks. The prominent American musician, Horatio R. Palmer, composed the music to this prayer.

Lord For Tomorrow

LORD I'M COMING HOME
William J. Kirkpatrick 1838-1921

One of the strangest experiences that ever occurred in the history of hymnody is related to this hymn. One evening in 1921, Professor William J. Kirkpatrick, who had written the music to "We have heard the joyful sound, Jesus saves, Jesus saves!" "Tis so sweet to Trust in Jesus" and many others, told his wife that a song had been running through his mind all day and that he was going to retire to his study to put it on paper before he forgot it. Mrs. Kirkpatrick was accustomed to the fact that her husband often worked late in his study and retired for the evening thinking nothing of it. Later, after midnight, she awoke; and seeing the lights in her husband's study still burning, went in to investigate. She found him at his desk,— dead! The pencil was still clutched in his lifeless hand. Spread before him were pieces of paper upon which were the lines of his newly completed hymn:

Lord, I'm Coming Home

Coming home, coming home,
  Never more to roam,
Open wide Thine arms of love,
  Lord, I'm coming home.

Strangely enough, here was a hymn written with a dying man's last breath which spoke of man's last message of "coming home to God."

LOVE DIVINE, ALL LOVE EXCELLING
Charles Wesley, 1707-1788

Again, the immortal the Reverend Charles Wesley gives the world an exalted spiritual power in the writing of "Love Divine, All Love Excelling." Written in 1756, it was part of his collection entitled "Hymns for Those That Seek and Those That Have Redemption in the Blood of Jesus Christ." The first tune was written by John Zundel, noted organist in America. He served for nearly 30 years as organist of the Plymouth Church, Brooklyn, New York, where he and the famous preacher, Henry Ward Beecher, pastor of that church were intimate friends. Both their names were held in high esteem by church goers. The last words of this hymn, "Lost in wonder, love and praise," have been the inspiration of innumerable sermons and hymns.

Love Divine,

MINE EYES HAVE SEEN THE GLORY or BATTLE HYMN OF THE REPUBLIC
Julia Ward Howe 1819-1910

In 1861 Julia Ward Howe was riding through the Union Army camps as a guest of President Lincoln. Everywhere she went the Federal troops were singing the very popular southern tune "John Brown." The catchy tune appealed to the gifted Boston writer. When she returned to her Washington hotel and tried to sleep the music stayed in her mind. Finally, she got up, and with her bathrobe still on, she wrote some words of her own to the tune;

Mine eyes have seen the glory
Of the coming of the Lord;

Strangely enough, this tune which had been written originally by John W. Staffe of Richmond, Virginia, ended up as the Union Army marching song and was sung by the northern troops as they marched with Sherman through Richmond on their way to the sea.

Mine Eyes Have Seen

MORE LOVE TO THEE, O CHRIST
Mrs. Elizabeth Payson Prentiss, 1818-1878

As in so many cases, this popular revival hymn, was written from the depth of great sorrow. Experience is a thorough teacher and tragedy is an unyielding instructor. Elizabeth Prentiss, author of this hymn, had lived a happy life,— from the time of her birth in Portland, Maine, in 1818, through the marriage to her Presbyterian preacher husband, the Reverend George L. Prentiss, and the birth of her healthy children. But ten years after her marriage tragedy struck with a hammer blow. While in New York one child died. Soon after, their youngest child was taken. In a moment of despair, Mrs. Prentiss expressed her grief with a cascade of bitter tears. Her husband comforted her with the words, "In times like these God loves us all the more, just as we love our children in their distress." Later, when Mrs. Prentiss was alone, with the words of her husband still in mind, she wrote these lines:

More love to Thee, O Christ, More love to Thee;
Hear Thou the prayer I make, on bended knee.

More Love To Thee,

MY COUNTRY 'TIS OF THEE
Samuel Francis Smith, 1808-1895

The most famous patriotic hymn in the history of America was written by a twenty-three year old student preparing for the Baptist ministry. In 1832, Reverend Samuel F. Smith, studying theology at Andover Theological Seminary, Andover, Massachusetts, penned the immortal words with the moving sentiment:

My country 'tis of thee,
Sweet land of liberty,
Of thee I sing;

My Country 'Tis Of Thee

485

MY FAITH LOOKS UP TO THEE
Ray Palmer, 1808-1887

My Faith Looks Up

In the fall of 1830, just having graduated from Yale University, Ray Palmer sat down in the evening and wrote his first and finest hymn. He wrote six stanzas with such feeling and emotion that he finished the closing lines with tears streaming from his eyes. He placed it in his pocket-book and carried it around with him for two years not thinking any more about it. In the autumn of 1832, he met his good friend Dr. Lowell Mason in Boston who asked him if he knew of any new hymns that could be used in a "Hymn and Tune Book" soon to be published. Palmer, with some reluctance, gave him the words of his poem written two years previously. Mason was so impressed that he composed an original tune which he named "Olivet." Later, when Mason met Palmer, he remarked, "Mr. Palmer, you may live many years and do many good things, but I think you will be best known as the author of "My Faith Looks Up to Thee."

MY HOPE IS BUILT ON NOTHING LESS
Edward Mote 1797-1874

My Hope Is Built

Before Edward Mote became a Baptist Minister in England, he was an ordinary laborer in London. Here are his words regarding the writing of his hymn, "One morning as I went to work I thought I would write a hymn on the experience of being a Christian." Before the day was finished, he had not only completed his hymn, but had sung it at a neighbor's house where much spiritual comfort was received from its content. Later, in 1836, it was published in a volume called "Hymns of Praise."

MY JESUS I LOVE THEE
Adoniram Judson Gordon, 1836-1895

My Jesus I Love Thee

Dr. Adoniram Judson Gordon, D.D. will be remembered as pastor of Clarendon Street Baptist Church of Boston, Massachusetts; as a founder of the famous theological college, Gordon Theological and Divinity School, Beverly Farms, Massachusetts, and as the originator of the Coronation Hymnal, but none of his accomplishments will ever equal the lasting influence of his great and touching hymn "My Jesus, I Love Thee." While preparing the Coronation Hymnal, he came across an old anonymous English hymn. Changing words and music, he gave to the world "My Jesus, I Love Thee." It is interesting to note that Dr. A. J. Gordon, a great theologian and cleric of his century and the centuries to follow, although famous for his inspired understanding of the holy scriptures, will be held in grateful reverence for the writing of a simple hymn.

NEARER MY GOD TO THEE
Sarah F. Adams, 1805-1848

Sarah F. Adams wrote hundreds of hymns; only one was remembered! In 1841, at the request of her pastor, Reverend William J. Fox, English Unitarian minister, Mrs. Adams wrote "Nearer My God To Thee." During a personal conversation, Fox revealed to Mrs. Adams that he was going to preach about Jacob. "Is there a hymn about Jacob's dream with which to end the service," she is reported to have said. When Fox replied no she sat down immediately and wrote "Nearer My God To Thee." Little did she dream that this song, written so suddenly, would be so cherished by the whole world. The influence of this simple hymn is attested in part by the fact that President William McKinley requested that it be sung at his funeral as his favorite hymn, and that hundreds of voices were singing these words as the great ship Titanic was swallowed up by the sea.

Nearer My God To Thee

NOW THANK WE ALL OUR GOD
Martin Rinkart, 1586-1649

This joyous Thanksgiving refrain was written by the Reverend Martin Rinkart, minister in the little town of Eilenburg, Saxony, at the close of the Thirty Years' War in 1648. Rinkart was the only surviving clergyman in the town, which was so crowded with refugees and so ravaged with plague and pestilence, famine and fury, that often 50 to 100 funerals were held each day. When news finally arrived that the Peace of Westphalia had ended the great and terrible war, a decree was circulated ordering Thanksgiving Services to be held in every church. Ministers were requested to preach on the text, "Now bless ye the Lord of all, Who everywhere doeth great things." Martin Rinkart was so moved by the thought of this text that he sat down and wrote these words for his own Thanksgiving Service:

Now Thank We All

> Now thank we all our God,
>> With hearts, and hands, and voices,
> Who wondrous things hath done,
>> In Whom His world rejoices;

NOW THE DAY IS OVER
Sabine Baring-Gould, 1834-1924

In the quaint village of Calder Valley of Yorkshire, Sabine Baring-Gould, a young 31-year old curate, wrote this hymn especially for his own created "night school." The children of the valley would join in with their parents in asking Gould to tell them stories after their day's labor in the mill. Tirelessly he would tell stories and lead them in songs in his crowded two rooms. Through the chinks in the floor the voices of children would ring out the hymn written for them:

Now The Day Is Over

> When the morning wakens,
>> Then may I arise
> Pure, and fresh, and sinless
>> In Thy holy eyes.

O BROTHER MAN, FOLD TO THY HEART THY BROTHER
John Greenleaf Whittier, 1807-1892

John Greenleaf Whittier believed in the simplicity of worship and felt that the true worship of man, recognized by God, is when he loves his fellowman. In 1848 he wrote a poem entitled "Worship" based on James 1:27: "Pure religion and undefiled before God and the Father is this, To visit the fatherless and the widows in their affliction, and to keep himself unspotted from the world." From this poem developed one of the Church's finer brotherhood hymns:

O Brother Man,

O brother man, fold to thy heart thy brother;
    Where pity dwells, the peace of God is there;
To worship rightly is to love each other,
    Each smile a hymn, each kindly deed a prayer.

O COME ALL YE FAITHFUL
author unknown

One of the most popular Christmas hymns, "O Come All Ye Faithful" might never have been known by the English speaking world if it had not been for the chance work of a wandering scribe. In 1750, John Francis Wade, who made his way in life as a professional copy writer, included an "original" Christmas poem, called "Adeste Fideles" in a manuscript compiled for the English Roman Catholic College at Lisbon, Portugal. Thirty-five years later a copy of the hymn was sent to the Portuguese Chapel in London, from which its popularity spread throughout the world. Many critics say that Wade "borrowed" the words and and tune of this beautiful Nativity hymn from an old French chorale. But, whether or not Wade originated the hymn, the fact that he included it in the manuscript copied for the Catholic College in Lisbon has meant that the world received one of its most loved Christmas songs. "O Come All Ye Faithful" received its title from a translation into English by Frederick Oakley, an English Canon, in 1852.

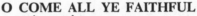

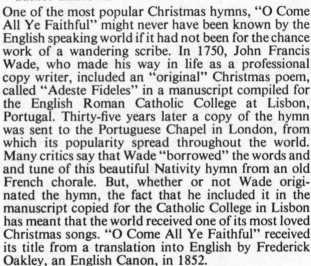

O Come All Ye
Faithful

O COME, O COME EMMANUEL
author unknown

A 12th century Latin hymn popular during the Advent season, translated into English during the middle 19th century by the Reverend John M. Neale. The Latin hymn was used originally as a short musical response to be sung at vesper services. The song tells us that Advent is a joyous season because it is the time when God draws near to men to deliver them from bondage with the coming of Emmanuel.

O Come, O Come,
Emmanuel

O come, O come, Emmanuel,
And ransom captive Israel,
That mourns in lonely exile here
Until the Son of God appear.

O DAY OF REST AND GLADNESS
Christopher Wordsworth, 1807–1885

Classified as a teaching hymn, "O Day of Rest and Gladness" was written in 1862 by Christopher Wordsworth, nephew of the famed English poet Wordsworth. Young Wordsworth was serving as country parish minister at the time, but was later appointed Bishop of Lincoln. This hymn is one of the most outstanding examples of the meaning and purpose of the Sabbath Day that can be found in the history of hymnody.

O Day Of Rest

> O day of rest and gladness,
>   O day of joy and light,
> O balm of care and sadness,
>   Most beautiful, most bright;
> On Thee, the high and lowly,
>   Through ages joined in tune,
> Sing Holy, Holy, Holy
>   To the great God Triune.

O FOR A CLOSER WALK WITH GOD
William Cowper, 1731–1800

The son of a clergyman, William Cowper, was born at Berkhampstead, Hertfordshire, England, on November 15, 1731, and lived for sixty-nine years. The burden of his mental affliction and at times partial insanity was lightened by his desire and ability to write. Most of his hymns were written when he resided with his fellow hymnist John Newton in Olney, and at one time they issued a volume of hymns under the title, "Olney Hymns." This suffering man was loved by many and known to be a true Christian. He was able to produce some of our sweetest and most spiritual hymns such as:

O For A Closer Walk

> O for a closer walk with God,
>   A calm and heavenly frame;
> A light to shine upon the road
>   That leads me to the Lamb.

O FOR A THOUSAND TONGUES TO SING
Charles Wesley, 1707–1788

Charles Wesley wrote this hymn on the first anniversary of his conversion to God, which occurred on Sunday, May 21, 1738. It is said that the opening lines came as a result of a conversation between Wesley and Peter Bohler, the Moravian. On the subject of praising Christ Bohler had said, "Had I a thousand tongues I would praise Him with them all." From this chance remark Wesley conceived the idea of his hymn.

O For A Thousand Tongues

> O for a thousand tongues to sing
>   My great Redeemer's praise,
> The glories of my God and King,
>   The triumphs of His grace!
> My gracious Master and my God,
>   Assist me to proclaim,
> To spread thro' all the earth abroad
>   The honors of Thy name.

O GOD, OUR HELP IN AGES PAST
Isaac Watts, 1674–1748

O God, Our Help

This international hymn written by one of the greatest hymn masters, Isaac Watts, leads the list as a favorite of many Christians. It was written early in the Eighteenth Century and its words have been a comfort to many in moments of crisis. It is universal in appeal and lends celestial beauty and strength through its words:

A thousand ages in Thy sight
  Are like an evening gone;
Short as the watch that ends the night
  Before the rising sun.

The original title "Our God, Our Help In Ages Past" was substituted with "O God, Our Help In Ages Past," by John Wesley in 1738.

O HOLY NIGHT
Adolphe Adam, 1803–1856

O Holy Night

A beautiful, haunting French carol whose melody was written by Adolphe Adam, composer born in Paris in 1803. A story is told that on Christmas Eve in 1870 during the Franco-Prussian War, the French and German soldiers were facing each other in opposite trenches. Suddenly a young French soldier leaped from his trench and startled the Germans by singing in a loud, clear voice, the "Cantique de Noel" or "O Holy Night." The Germans were so surprised that not a shot was fired. Not to be outdone, a German soldier stepped forward and sang Luther's "From Heaven Above to Earth I Come."

O JESUS, I HAVE PROMISED
John E. Bode, 1816–1874

A hymn of consecration written by John E. Bode, an English Rector and poet of the nineteenth century. He was born in London in 1816, educated at Eton, Fellow and Tutor of Christ Church, Oxford, for six years, Rector at Westwell, Oxfordshire, and Rector of Castle Camps, Cambridgeshire. "O, Jesus, I Have Promised" was written on the occasion of the confirmation of his own two sons and daughter at Castle Camps in 1869. The hymn tune was written in 1881 by Arthur H. Mann, who at one period in his life served as Organist and Choirmaster at Kings College, Cambridge, England, famous for its superb choral music.

O JESUS, THOU ART STANDING
William Walsham How, 1823–1897

O Jesus, I Have
Promised

It is said by many hymn critics that William Walsham How's hymn-poem "O Jesus, Thou Art Standing" is one of the noblest hymns ever given to the world. Written in 1867 by How, then an Honorary Canon of St. Asaph's Cathedral in England, it is not known whether its inspiration came from a famous painting

490

or a country sermon in an English fishing village. About thirteen years before the hymn was written Holman Hunt's famous painting, "The Light of the World," was exhibited for the first time. The words of the hymn are a perfect reflection of the beauty and message of the Hunt masterpiece.

O Jesus, Thou Art Standing

O LITTLE TOWN OF BETHLEHEM
Phillips Brooks, 1835–1893

The dramatic birth of this popular Christmas hymn was as sudden as the announcement of the angelic host, concerning the birth of Christ, to the shepherds in the fields outside Bethlehem. The seeds of the hymn were sown in 1865 when on Christmas Eve in Bethlehem, Phillips Brooks, noted Episcopal Bishop, attended services in the ancient basilica claimed to have been built by Emperor Constantine in the 4th century. He was a young minister, at the time, and the beauty of the simple service made a permanent impression on his heart. Three years later, while rector of Holy Trinity Church, Philadelphia, at the request of the children of the Church School, Phillips Brooks wrote a new Christmas song. His trip to the Holy Land came back to mind vividly and he penned these beautiful words:

O little town of Bethlehem,
    How still we see thee lie;

The thought of the little town of Bethlehem was so strong in his mind, that Brooks completed the entire hymn in one evening. The next day when Lewis Redner, Organist and Church School Superintendent, came into his study, Phillip Brooks gave him the poem and asked if he could write some music for it so that it could be sung during the Christmas season. Redner waited for inspiration, but none came. On the night before Christmas he woke up suddenly, in the middle of the night, the melody of the song ringing in his ears like happy bells. Seizing the nearest piece of paper he wrote down the music that was so clear in his mind, and went back to sleep. In the morning he harmonized the melody, and that same day the little children of Holy Trinity Church sang for the first time one of the most loved Christmas carols.

O Little Town Of Bethlehem

O LOVE THAT WILT NOT LET ME GO
George Matheson, 1842–1906

This great hymn of courage and faith was written, strangely enough, under circumstances of tragic inner conflict and severe mental suffering as a release from personal tragedy. Dr. George Matheson, beloved clergyman in the Church of Scotland, and totally blind since the age of fifteen, composed this strong hymn in 1882. The courage and fortitude of Dr. Matheson was evidenced by the dramatic fact that from this deep sorrow and heartache he could write:

O love that wilt not let me go,
    I rest my weary soul in thee;

O Love That Wilt Not

O MASTER, LET ME WALK WITH THEE
Washington Gladden, 1836–1918

O Master, Let Me
Walk

Dr. Washington Gladden did not think of himself as a hymn writer; yet in 1879 he wrote a poem for the publication "Sunday Afternoon," which has become one of the world's most cherished devotional hymns.

O Master, let me walk with Thee
In lowly paths of service free;
Tell me thy secret; help me to bear
The strain of toil, the fret of care.

This hymn reflected Gladden's religious philosophy which was in a sentence, "Religion is nothing but friendship; friendship with God and with man." It is no wonder that in this world, which so needs the intimate relationship of man to God and man to man, that his hymn has found such a warm response.

ONCE TO EVERY MAN AND NATION
James Russell Lowell, 1819–1891

Once To Every Man

In the year 1845, at the same time Abraham Lincoln was opposing in Congress the agitators for a war with Mexico, the famed poet James Russell Lowell was using his talent to speak out against what he thought was the plan of the slave-holding states to gain more territory. It was a 90-line poem, later reduced to 32 lines, which became one of the strongest hymns challenging national righteousness ever printed:

Once to every man and nation
Comes the moment to decide,
In the strife of truth with falsehood,
For the good or evil side.

Legend says that the tune used for this hymn can be traced back to its discovery in a bottle washed up on the shores of Wales.

ONWARD CHRISTIAN SOLDIERS
Sabine Baring-Gould, 1834–1924

Onward Christian
Soldiers

"Onward Christian Soldiers," written in 1865 by Reverend Sabine Baring-Gould an English clergyman, is one of the most popular hymns ever composed for children. It was created originally as a processional for singing Sunday School children marching between villages. It is said that Baring-Gould was deeply disappointed in what he considered many of its imperfections and never imagined that it would reach the height of popularity that later it attained. A humorous incident is reported concerning the last line of the hymn. Many objected to the children's carrying processional crosses while they were marching,—in a moment of whimsey, the last line "going on before" was changed to "left behind the door." "Onward Christian Soldiers" is, without doubt, the greatest marching hymn of all Christendom.

O SACRED HEAD NOW WOUNDED
Bernard of Clairvaux, 1091–1153

The theme of "O Sacred Head Now Wounded" had its origin in the solitude of a lonely monk's cell in the mind of Bernard of Clairvaux, famous 12th Century monk. The story of this medeval monk is one of the most beautiful and romantic of all times. So wonderful was his spirit and leadership that the monastery that first housed only eleven monks, increased to one hundred twenty-five. A dedicated person, St. Bernard refused many high posts in the church and continued on as Abbott of Clairvaux. It was in his cell that he would meditate upon the suffering of the Saviour on the cross, and penned the Passion Hymn, which is used particularly for Passion Sunday. It was first translated into German from the Latin by Paul Gerhart in 1656. Then later for the Anglican Church, by Dr. James W. Alexander, in 1830.

O Sacred Head

O WHERE ARE KINGS AND EMPIRES NOW
Arthur Cleveland Coxe, 1818–1896

One of the great hymns of the church, "O Where are Kings and Empires Now" was written by Bishop Arthur Cleveland Coxe in 1839. A tremendous hymn of faith and power, the story is told how it once saved a religious group from possible dissolvement. The incident took place at the General Conference of the Evangelical Alliance in New York a short time after the writing of the hymn. There had been a theological dispute in the Alliance concerning the purpose and place of prayer, and the whole assembly was filled with a stormy skepticism. The president of the group in making the opening address quoted from Bishop Coxe's hymn:

O where are kings and empires now
Of old that went and came?
But, Lord, Thy Church is praying yet,
A thousand years the same.

O Where Are Kings

It is said that such a round of instantaneous applause occurred that there was hardly any ceasing, and the effect was to draw everyone together in a close, harmonious bond of prayerful fellowship.

O WORSHIP THE KING, ALL GLORIOUS ABOVE
Robert Grant, 1779–1838

One day in the 1830's approximately eight years before his death, Sir Robert Grant, who became Governor of Bombay in 1834, was glancing through the Anglo-German Psalter written in 1561. He was greatly impressed and inspired by a translation of the 104th Psalm by William Kethe. Immediately he began to write an original poem about the omnipotence of God, guided by the theme of the classic Hebrew Psalm.

O worship the King, all glorious above,
O gratefully sing His power and His love;
Our Shield and Defender, the Ancient of Days,
Pavilioned in splendor, and girded with praise.

O Worship The King,

It received public acclaim in 1833, when it was first published in Bickersteth's "Christian Psalmody." The tune most frequently used is called Lyons, an adaptation from Johann M. Haydn.

O ZION HASTE, THY MISSION HIGH FULFULLING
Mary Ann Thomson, 1834–1923

O Zion Haste,

One night in 1868 Mary Ann Thomson sat with her young child who was ill with typhoid fever. While she was sitting there the thought came to her mind that she would like to write a missionary hymn. She had written many hymns before, but never one on the theme of missions. She wrote most of the hymn that very evening, but it wasn't until two years later that the song was complete.

PASS ME NOT, O GENTLE SAVIOUR
Fanny J. Crosby, 1820–1915

If ever a hymn writer used a theme which was indicative of his or her life, it was the blind Fanny Crosby when she wrote, in 1868, "Pass Me Not, O Gentle Saviour." Of a truth, God certainly did not pass her by. She turned a tragedy at six weeks of age into a triumph of a life time. She overcame a terrible, personal adversity, and contributed a life of power and purpose to the world. Fanny Jane Crosby was a little baby girl of six weeks, in May, 1820, when she caught a common cold. A country doctor of Putnam County, New York, unwittingly prescribed a hot mustard poultice. She was blinded for life! At the age of five, sympathetic neighbors and friends pooled their money and sent her to a noted New York surgeon, Dr. Valentine Mott. After a careful examination, the specialist said sadly, that there was nothing he could do. Looking toward her, he said, "Poor little blind girl!" Fanny Crosby always remembered these words and turned the sympathetic remark of a kindly physician into the purposeful pattern of a truly remarkable personality.

Pass Me Not,

The world may have thought of her as the "poor little blind girl," but not Fanny Crosby! She once told a friend that her blindness had proved a blessing, because it enabled her to be more alone where the writing of her poetry became easy. And she told another that if she had a choice she still would remain blind, for when she died the first face she ever would see would be the face of her "blessed Saviour."

Saviour, Saviour, Hear my humble cry;
While on others Thou art calling, Do not pass me by.

PEACE, PERFECT PEACE
Edward Henry Bickersteth, 1825–1906

The Reverend E. H. Bickersteth was Vicar of Christ Church, Hampstead, England, when he wrote the hymn "Peace, Perfect Peace, In This Dark World of Sin." It came about in a rather strange and unusual way. On a Sunday in August 1875, Bickersteth, who was a guest at Harrogate, heard the Vicar, a Canon Gibbon, preach from the text "Thou wilt keep him in perfect peace, whose mind is stayed on Thee." He was

Peace, Perfect Peace

greatly impressed by the way the Canon treated the text. On that same afternoon Bickersteth visited a dying relative who lived near the church. Finding him in a somewhat troubled state, the words of the Canon's text came to mind. Taking a sheet of paper, Bickersteth wrote, without any hesitation, the complete hymn poem, afterwards reading it to the dying man, who found comfort for his confused mind in the quietness of its message.

PRAISE TO THE LORD, THE ALMIGHTY
Joachim Neander, 1650–1680

Praise To The Lord

A hymn of praise written by Joachim Neander shortly before his death at 30 years of age in 1680, in Bremen, Germany, the city of his birth. It is said that the hymn developed out of a difficult situation experienced in Dusseldorf in the Rhineland, Germany, while he was schoolmaster there. When Neander refused to conform with the rules of the elders of the Reformed Church who controlled the school, he was forced to seek retreat in a wild cave where this and many other poems were written down.

Praise to the Lord, the Almighty,
the King of creation!
O my soul, praise him,
for He is thy health and salvation!
All ye who hear, Now to His temple draw near;
Join me in glad adoration!

REJOICE, THE LORD IS KING
Charles Wesley, 1707–1788

Rejoice, The Lord

One of the six favorite hymns of Charles Wesley. The great Methodist hymn writer compiled thousands of hymns during his lifetime of 81 years and this one was written somewhere in the vicinity of 1750. It is difficult to realize that one man could write such all-time favorites as "Jesus Lover of My Soul," "Love Divine All Love Excelling," "O For a Thousand Tongues to Sing," "O Thou Who Camest From Above," "Ye Servants of God" and "Rejoice, the Lord is King." But he did, and many, many others. Perhaps it suffices to say that here was a man so filled with the joy of the Spirit of God that it continuously manifestered itself with the glad sound of music and psalm!

REJOICE YE PURE IN HEART
Edward Hayes Plumptre, 1821–1891

Rejoice Ye Pure

In May of 1865 a great choir festival was held in Peterborough Cathedral in England. A new and stirring hymn, written especially for the festival by the Reverend Edward Hayes Plumptre, was introduced:

Rejoice ye pure in heart,
Rejoice, give thanks and sing:
Your glorious banner wave on high,
The cross of Christ your King.

RESCUE THE PERISHING
Fanny J. Crosby, 1820–1915

Rescue The Perishing

In 1869, Fanny Crosby wrote the words for "Rescue the Perishing" while riding between Brooklyn and the Bowery in a hired horse-drawn hack. She had just attended a service in the Bowery Mission where she had been asked to address an audience made up of New York's lowest derelicts. While traveling home after the service the blind poetess' mind could not help but dwell upon the experience through which she had just passed. Lines of a poem began to form in her mind. Before she reached her home the poem was completed and a new hymn was born.

Rescue the perishing
Care for the dying,
Snatch them in pity from sin and the grave;
Weep o'er the erring one,
Lift up the fallen,
Tell them of Jesus the Mighty to save.

RIDE ON, RIDE ON IN MAJESTY
Henry Hart Milman, 1791–1868

Ride On, Ride On

The hymn, "Ride on, Ride on in Majesty" is the most well-known of the Palm Sunday hymns. It was written by the very Reverend Henry Hart Milman, dean of St. Paul's in London. Dean Milman, born in 1791, also won world acclaim as a historian. Reverend John Bacchus Dykes wrote the music to this hymn and was famous in his own right for such favorites as "Lead, Kindly Light," and "Ten Thousand Times Ten Thousand."

Ride on, ride on in majesty!
Hark! all the tribes Hosanna cry;
O Saviour meek, pursue thy road,
With palms and scattered garments strewed.

RING THE BELLS OF HEAVEN
William Orcutt Cushing 1823–1902

Ring The Bells Of Heaven

The author of "Ring the Bells of Heaven," William O. Cushing, says of his old-time popular hymn, "It was written to fit a beautiful tune sent me by George F. Root. After receiving the melody, it ran in my head all day long, chiming and flowing in its sweet musical cadence. I wished greatly that I might use the tune in Sunday School and for other Christian purposes. I got to thinking how the bells of heaven would ring when one person believed in God. All at once the words flowed into the melody. It was a beautiful and blessed experience, and the bells seem ringing yet!"

Ring the bells of heaven! there is joy today
For a soul, returning from the wild.

RISE UP, O MEN OF GOD
William Pierson Merrill, 1867–1954

In the year 1911, William Pierson Merrill was aboard a Lake Michigan steamer on his way to Chicago. As he watched the waves lapping around the boat, he thought of a remark made to him by Nolan R. Best, an editor, just a short while before, "What we need, Dr. Merrill, is a good brotherhood hymn!" Suddenly the words came to him, quickly and without any effort he wrote them down:

Rise up, O men of God!
    Have done with lesser things;
Give heart and mind and soul and strength
    To serve the King of Kings.

Immediately the hymn was widely acclaimed and developed the reputation as a hymn that challenged men to do something, and to do it without delay.

Rise Up, O Men Of God

ROCK OF AGES
Augustus Montague Toplady, 1740–1778

The writing of Rock of Ages by the Reverend Augustus M. Toplady, an English Vicar in 1775, is one of the strangest stories in the history of hymns. The words, "Rock of ages, cleft for me, Let me hide myself in Thee; Let the water and the blood, From Thy riven side which flowed, Be of sin the double cure, Clense from wrath and make me pure," were first written on the back side of a playing card, the six of diamonds. It came about one day when Toplady was walking some distance from his home and was caught in a sudden, violent storm. There was no shelter nearby, but the Vicar spied a huge cleft running down a ledge beside the road. He took refuge here and was protected from the storm. He thought, while there, of the spiritual significance of his experience. God is a refuge from the storms of life. Reaching down to the ground, he picked up a playing card, which he found lying there, and upon this surface, the famous words were penned.

Rock Of Ages

Rock of Ages, cleft for me,
    Let me hide myself in Thee;
Let the water and the blood,
    From Thy riven side which flowed,
Be of sin the double cure,
    Save from wrath and make me pure.

SAFE IN THE ARMS OF JESUS
Fanny J. Crosby, 1820–1915

One of Fanny Crosby's most popular hymns. It was written in less than 30 minutes, at the request of William H. Doane who had composed a new tune to be used at a Sunday School Convention in Cincinnati in 1868. Doane, trying to catch a train to the Convention, had rushed in to Fanny Crosby's home, requesting words for his new tune. Hurriedly he played the tune for her, saying with impatience that he had only 35 minutes to catch his train. Fanny Crosby listened intently while he played, and said at the conclusion without hesitation, "Your tune is saying "Safe in the Arms of Jesus." In a matter of minutes she had penned these famous lines:

Safe In The Arms Of Jesus

Safe in the arms of Jesus, Safe on His gentle breast;
    There by his love o'ershaded,
        Sweetly my soul shall rest.

SAVED BY GRACE
Fanny J. Crosby, 1820–1915

Saved By Grace

A gospel hymn written in 1894 by Fanny J. Crosby, one of hymnody's most dramatic authors. Ira D. Sankey, D. L. Moody's song leader, lists this hymn as one of his five favorites to sing as solos. It was first heard by the public, as a recitation by Miss Crosby, at a summer conference in Northfield, Massachusetts, conducted by Dr. Adoniram Judson Gordon in 1894. An English reporter was present and requested a copy to be taken to London, where it was published in his paper. Sankey discovered the poem in the English paper and requested George C. Stebbins, famed gospel tunesmith, to compose music for it. Not only did this hymn remain one of Sankey's favorites during his lifetime, but it became the favorite of hundreds of thousands throughout the world.

And I shall see Him face to face,
And tell the story, saved by grace.
And I shall see Him face to face,
And tell the story, saved by grace.

SAVIOUR, AGAIN TO THY DEAR NAME WE RAISE
John Ellerton, 1826–1893

Saviour, Again

This majestic church hymn was written in a moment of inspiration by the Reverend John Ellerton, an English Vicar, in 1866. He was responsible for providing the hymn at the annual Hymn Festival held in Cheshire. On the night before, Ellerton seized his last Sunday's sermon and scribbled these words on the back:

Saviour, again to Thy dear name we raise
With one accord our parting hymn of praise;
We stand to bless Thee 'ere our worship cease;
And now, departing, wait Thy word of peace.

Ellerton's hastily penned hymn proved to be one of the most popular that he wrote and was translated into many languages.

SAVIOUR LIKE A SHEPHERD LEAD US
Dorothy Ann Thrupp, 1779–1847

Saviour Like A
Shepherd

In 1859 William D. Bradbury gave the Christian world the great and peaceful hymn "Saviour Like a Shepherd Lead Us." It is believed that this hymn poem had been written by Reverend Henry F. Lyte, author of "Abide With Me," while others say it first appeared in a book by Dorothy Ann Thrupp. Bradbury was a protege of the talented religious composer Lowell Mason and was instrumental in influencing and encouraging blind Fanny Crosby to turn her talents from writing secular songs to hymns for the church. Though poverty stricken in his childhood, he was able to contribute great wealth through his immortal music to such hymn poems as "Just As I Am," "Sweet Hour of Prayer," and "He Leadeth Me."

SAVIOUR THY DYING LOVE
Sylvanus Dryden Phelps, 1816–1895

A hymn of consecration written in 1862 by Dr. S. Dryden Phelps, an American Baptist minister. Published in Sankey's "Gospel Hymns" under the title "Something for Jesus," the music was written by another prominent American Baptist Clergyman, Robert Lowry, in 1872. On his 70th birthday Dr. Phelps received a telegram from Lowry which expressed the sentiment of all who knew him, "It is worth living seventy years, even if nothing comes of it but one such hymn as this one. Happy is the man who can produce one song which the world will keep on singing after its author shall have passed away."

Saviour Thy Dying Love

    Saviour, Thy dying love thou gavest me;
      Nor should I aught withhold, Dear Lord, from
        Thee;
    In love my soul would bow, My heart fulfil its vow,
    Some off'ring bring Thee now, Something for Thee.

SHALL WE GATHER AT THE RIVER
Robert Lowry, 1826–1899

Dr. Robert Lowry wrote this "Hymn of the Hereafter" as the result of a raging epidemic, July 1864, in Brooklyn, New York. He had just accepted a call to the Baptist Church of Brooklyn. It was an unusually hot and humid summer. When the epidemic struck hundreds were left dead and dying in its wake. Everywhere Lowry went comforting his people he heard the words, "Pastor, we have parted at the river of death; shall we meet again at the river of life?" Filled with this thought, Lowry wrote down the words:

Shall We Gather

    Shall we gather at the river,
      Where bright angel feet have trod,
    With its crystal tide forever
      Flowing by the throne of God?

SHEPHERD OF TENDER YOUTH
Clement of Alexandria 2nd Century

Shepherd of Tender Youth is the earliest known hymn in Christian history. Written in the second century by Clement of Alexandria, its present form is a translation in 1846 by Henry Dexter. Its translation came about when the Reverend Dexter was preaching in the Congregational Church, Manchester, N. H., on a topical theme of "Remember the Days of Old" dealing with characteristics of the early Christians. He thought that there might be more interest shown in the subject if he had an early hymn to be sung at the close of his message. The music usually used with this early Christian hymn is "Come Thou Almighty King."

Shepherd Of Tender Youth

    Shepherd of tender youth, Guiding in love and truth
      Through devious ways;
    Christ, our triumphant King, We come thy name to
      sing,
    And here our children bring,
      To sound thy praise!

Silent Night

SILENT NIGHT, HOLY NIGHT
Joseph Mohr, 1792–1848

This most beautiful of Christmas hymns was written on the night before Christmas in 1818 at the little village of Oberndorf, Austria, by Joseph Mohr, the Vicar of the Church of St. Nicholas. Mohr gave the words of the simple poem to his organist Franz Gruber, who composed the music in time for the Christmas Eve service. The drama of the first rendition of "Silent Night, Holy Night" was augmented by the fact that the organ broke down, and the first public presentation of Christmas' most famous hymn was a simple duet between the author and the composer with voice and plain guitar accompaniment. The breaking down of the organ was instrumental in popularizing the new hymn. Later when it was being repaired, Gruber played the new carol on the organ as a means of testing the tone of the instrument. The repair man was fascinated and enchanted. He requested a copy and took it back with him to his own village of Zillerthal where it was received joyously. Four daughters of a Zillerthal glove maker named Strasse used this song in concerts from town to town and village to village while their father sold gloves. Soon everyone was singing "Silent Night, Holy Night," and so they have through the generations up to now, and so they will as long as Christmas is a part of the human life.

SING THEM OVER AGAIN TO ME
Philip Paul Bliss, 1838–1876

Sing Them Over Again

"Sing Them Over Again to Me," a popular gospel hymn, also called "Wonderful Words of Life," with words and music written by Philip P. Bliss in the middle 19th century. Although it is classified in that group of hymns considered by most critics as being "sentimental" or "emotional" it has been well received by congregations who love to sing songs with spirit and feeling. Philip Bliss, born in 1838, was the author of many gospel hymns similar to "Wonderful Words of Life" including "Let the Lower Lights be Burning" and "I am So Glad that Jesus Loves Me."

SOFTLY AND TENDERLY
Will L. Thompson, 1847–1909

Softly And Tenderly

When the famed Evangelist Dwight L. Moody lay dying, Will Thompson, the author and composer of "Softly and Tenderly," visited him to give spiritual strength in his hour of greatest need. Taking the composer's hand in his own Moody said, "Will, I would rather have written 'Softly and Tenderly,' than anything I have been able to do in my whole life." They were prophetic words, for this most famous composition of Will Lamartine Thompson the "Bard of Ohio" has been one of the "all-time" influential hymns of history. It's tender words have reached more needy hearts than almost any other:

Softly and tenderly Jesus is calling,
Calling for you and for me;

SOFTLY NOW THE LIGHT OF DAY
George Washington Doane, 1799–1859

Bishop George Washington Doane, famed Episcopal clergyman, was 25 years old when he wrote "Softly Now the Light of Day" in 1824. Originally titled "Evening" the author had these words to say concerning the writing of his hymn-poem: "Let my prayer be set forth before Thee as incense; and the lifting up of my hands as the evening sacrifice."

Softly Now

Softly now the light of day
Fades upon my sight away;
Free from care, from labor free,
Lord, I would commune with Thee.
Thou, whose all-pervading eye
Naught escapes, without, within,
Pardon each infirmity
Open fault, and secret sin.

SOLDIERS OF CHRIST ARISE
Charles Wesley, 1707–1788

Charles Wesley was one of the master hymn writers. "Soldiers of Christ Arise" was one of the master hymns of Christian action. Written in 1749, it was first published in a book called "Hymns and Sacred Poems" under the title of "The Whole Armour of God." Based on the text Ephesians 6:10–17, this martial hymn with the spiritual connotation is a challenging admonition to wrestle against the powers of evil with the weapons of full faith and certain knowledge that the power of God is invincible. Wesley's gift of inspiring action in Christian living is unmatched by the hymnwriters of all time.

Soldiers Of Christ

Soldiers of Christ, arise, And put your armor on,
Strong in the strength which God supplies
 Through his eternal Son;
Strong in the Lord of hosts,
 And in His mighty power,
Who in the strength of Jesus trusts
 Is more than conqueror.

SPIRIT OF GOD, DESCEND UPON MY HEART
George Croly, 1780–1860

"Spirit of God, Descend Upon My Heart" was written by an Irish priest George Croly who was born in 1780 and lived to be eighty years old. The original title to this hymn was "Holiness Desired." It is interesting to note that any ten-syllable tune is adaptable for this hymn. The comforting words and reassuring faith, stressed especially in the second and third verses make this hymn a favorite.

Spirit Of God,

I ask no dream, no prophet ecstasies.
 No sudden rending of the veil of clay,
No angel visitant, no opening skies;
 But take the dimness of my soul away.
Hast Thou not bid me love Thee, God and King?
 All, all Thine own—soul, heart, and strength, and
  mind.

Stand Up, Stand Up

STAND UP, STAND UP FOR JESUS
George R. Duffield, 1818–1888

This famous church hymn, one of the outstanding men's choruses ever written, originated as a result of the dramatic and unusual death of Reverend Dudley A. Tyng, a young Episcopalian minister of Philadelphia 1858. In a letter dated May 29, 1883, Dr. George Duffield, author of the hymn, revealed to a friend the unusual occurrence that led to the writing of "Stand Up for Jesus." Tyng had preached to a Young Men's Christian Association group with Duffield present on the text of Exodus referring to the "slain of the Lord." Within one week Tyng himself had been slain and the hymn had been written. The Wednesday following Tyng's sermon, the young Episcopalian had gone into the barn where a mule was pulling on a wheel-power corn-shelling machine. Patting the mule's neck, Tyng's sleeve caught in the cogs of the wheel and his arm was completely severed from his body. Within two hours he was dead. The following Sunday Duffield, using the dramatic death as an illustration, preached on the text in Ephesians 6:14 which speaks of putting on the whole armour of God and standing in the truth. He closed his sermon with the words he had written the previous Friday which had been inspired by Tyng's tragic death:

Stand up, stand up for Jesus,
　　Ye soldiers of the cross,

STILL, STILL WITH THEE WHEN PURPLE MORNING BREAKETH
Harriet Beecher Stowe, 1812–1896

Still, Still With Thee

This beautiful morning hymn based on Psalms 139:18 was written in the middle 19th century by Harriet Beecher Stowe, author of Uncle Tom's Cabin. Although Mrs. Stowe wrote a number of hymns this one proved to be the most popular. The tune is taken from Felix Mendelssohn's collection of forty-eight pieces known as "Song Without Words."

Still, still with Thee
When purple morning breaketh,
When the bird waketh,
And the shadows flee;
Fairer than morning,
Lovelier than daylight,
Dawns the sweet consciousness,
I am with Thee.

SUN OF MY SOUL, THOU SAVIOUR DEAR
John Keble, 1792–1866

Sun Of My Soul

This hymn, written by John Keble in 1820, was part of a famed collection of hymns and poems entitled "The Christian Year" which sold over 300,000 copies in forty-six years. Based on Luke 24:29 the hymn represents a lone traveler, after sundown, continuing his darkened way in the trust and confidence that God will care for his needs. The simple, delightful sincerity of the hymn has made it a favorite through the years.

SUNSET AND EVENING STAR
Alfred Lord Tennyson, 1809–1892

Sunset and evening star,
    And one clear call for me,
And may there be no moaning of the bar
    When I put out to sea,
For though from out our bourne of time and place
    The flood may bear me far,
I hope to see my Pilot face to face
    When I have crossed the bar.

Sunset And Evening Star

It was the immortal English poet, Alfred Lord Tennyson who penned this sublime prayer three years before
his death in 1892. The deep sense of real "Presence"
was characterized in all his mature spiritual life and
such faith made no room for dying terrors. His prayer
was answered, for his death was serene and dreadless.
His "Pilot" guided him gently "across the bar."

SWEET BY AND BY
Sanford Filmore Bennett, 1836–1898

It is said that this entire hymn, including words by
S. F. Bennett and music by J. P. Webster, was written
and composed in less than 30 minutes. Webster, who
was subject to moods of melancholy and depression,
once visited his friend Bennett who was writing at his
desk. Walking to the fire, Webster turned his back to
his friend without a word. When Bennett asked him
what the matter was, he received the curt reply that
"it would be alright, by and by." Seizing upon the
last three words Bennett exclaimed, "The sweet by
and by! That would make a good title for a hymn!"
Whereupon, he wrote without stopping, covering the
paper as fast as his pen could go. When he finished he
handed the manuscript to Webster, who immediately
sat down and composed a melody to fit the stirring
words. From this union in the village of Elkhorn,
Wisconsin, almost a hundred years ago, the gospel
hymn was born:

Sweet By and By

There's a land that is fairer than day
    And by faith we can see it afar,
For the Father waits, over the way,
    To prepare us a dwelling-place there.

SWEET HOUR OF PRAYER
William W. Walford 1800–1875 (approximate dates)

"Sweet Hour of Prayer" one of the world's most
popular prayer hymns was written by a man who
could not see. In 1842, the Reverend William W.
Walford, a blind English Clergyman, dictated his
inspirational poem of prayer to the Reverend Thomas
Salmon, minister at the Congregational Church,
Coleshill, England. Salmon took it with him on a
journey to New York City, where it was published
in September of 1845. Without doubt, Walford's
physical blindness gave him a spiritual sight to see,
where many others could not see the tremendous
significance of the power of illumination in prayer.

Sweet Hour Of Prayer

TAKE MY LIFE AND LET IT BE
Frances Ridley Havergal, 1836–1879

Take My Life

Challenging Gospel hymn written by Frances Ridley Havergal in 1874, four years before her death. The words were conceived while visiting the home of a friend where the author helped to convert ten people. She was so happy and excited that she could not sleep until the words which were forming in her mind were written down. Throughout her life, Miss Havergall considered this hymn a measure of her own consecration to God and constantly reviewed the verses to renew her own spiritual life.

Take my life and let it be
Consecrated, Lord, to Thee;
Take my moments and my days,
Let them flow in ceaseless praise.

TAKE TIME TO BE HOLY
William Dunn Longstaff, 1822–1894

Time To Be Holy

Although "Take Time to be Holy" was written by an Englishman, William Dunn Longstaff after listening to a sermon on the text, "Be ye holy; for I am holy," it was an American musician, George Stebbins who brought it into being. Stebbins, who was at one time choir leader in Tremont Temple, Boston, Massachusetts, and who wrote the music for such hymns as "True-Hearted, Whole Hearted," "Jesus is Tenderly Calling," "Have Thine Own Way, Lord" and many, many more for such hymn writers as Frances Havergal, Adelaide Pollard and Fanny Crosby, was in India in the autumn of 1890 when someone mentioned the need for a hymn on Holiness. Stebbins remembered a poem on the subject by William Longstaff which he he had cut out and saved. He searched among his papers, found it, and set the stanzas to music. Thus in distant India, "Take Time to be Holy" began a popular career that has continued in every generation.

TELL ME THE OLD, OLD STORY
Katherine Hankey, 1834–1911

Tell Me The Old, Old Story

In January, 1866, Kate Hankey, daughter of a London banker was told that if she did not go to bed for at least a year, she would die. So Kate Hankey went to bed; but she took with her a stack of writing papers. While confined, the thirty-year old woman wrote a fifty stanza poem called "The Story Wanted" and a fifty stanza sequel called "The Story Told." From these poems came the hymn "Tell Me the Old, Old Story." The tune was written by William Howard Doane while riding on a stage coach one afternoon to the White Mountains of New Hampshire. He had heard a reading of the poem for the first time that morning by Major General Russell of England to a YMCA delegation at Montreal, Canada.

TEN THOUSAND TIMES TEN THOUSAND
Henry Alford, 1810–1871

A majestic processional hymn written by Henry Alford and sung for the first time at Canterbury Cathedral in England where Alford reigned as Dean from 1857 to 1871. It is said that the great nave of the cathedral with its wondrous beauty, its brightly lighted chancel, and its long, colorful processions of saints on the Sabbath Sunday was the inspiration behind the hymn.
Ten thousand times ten thousand,
   In sparkling raiment bright,
The armies of the ransomed saints
   Throng up the steeps of light.

**Ten Thousand
Times**

THE CHURCH'S ONE FOUNDATION
Samuel John Stone, 1839–1900

Bishop Gray was the one who stirred Samuel John Stone, born in 1839, then a curate at Windsor, to write the hymn "The Church's One Foundation." Bishop Gray was defending the name of Bishop Colenso of Natal whose name stood for heresy and disloyalty. His treatment of the Atonement and the Sacraments were considered unorthodox. It is claimed that Bishop Colenso was before his time. Is it not ironic that the great hymn that his "heresies" inspired has become a magnificent statement about the church?
The Church's one foundation
   Is Jesus Christ her Lord;
She is His new creation By water and the word;
From Heaven He came and sought her
   To be His holy bride;
With His own blood He bought her,
   And for her life He died.

**The Church's One
Foundation**

THE GOD OF ABRAHAM PRAISE
Daniel Ben Judah, 14th century

A 14th century Hebrew melody written by Daniel Ben Judah. Although it has been translated from the original many times, it is based on the Hebrew Yigdal or Doxology which is part of the morning and evening ritual of Jewish worship. In 1770, Thomas Oliver, a Methodist minister, while attending a Synagogue service in London, heard the haunting Hebrew tune for the first time. Its depth of beauty in the minor key enraptured him so completely that he was inspired immediately to secure it for Christian worship. After acquiring the tune he wrote the stanzas of "The God of Abraham Praise" and it has been used widely as a recessional and processional hymn through the years,
The God of Abraham praise,
   All praised be His name,
Who was, and is, and is to be, And still the same!
The one eternal God, Ere aught that now appears;
The First, the Last: beyond all thought
   His timeless years!

**The God Of
Abraham**

505

THE LIGHT OF THE WORLD IS JESUS
Philip Paul Bliss, 1838–1876

In the summer of 1875 P. P. Bliss was passing through the hall of his room in his home at Chicago, Illinois, when the words and music of this favorite gospel hymn came to his mind in sudden inspiration. Immediately he sat down and wrote the hymn as the Spirit spoke in his heart. As has happened so many times in the experience of hymn writers the complete song, melody, harmony and words, were written in a matter of moments,—as if the Spirit himself was guiding the hand that penned the immortal phrases.

The Light Of The World

THE MORNING LIGHT IS BREAKING
Samuel Francis Smith, 1808–1895

Samuel Francis Smith was twenty-four years old at the time Adoniram Judson, one of the first famous five missionaries from Tabernacle Congregational Church, Salem, Massachusetts, commissioned by the American Board for Foreign Missions, was dramatically active in Burma. Smith was so stirred by reports being sent back to the home church, that he wrote this hymn which has been a favorite of missionaries ever since:

The morning light is breaking,
The darkness disappears;
The sons of earth are waking To penitential tears;
Each breeze that sweeps the ocean
Brings tidings from afar
Of nations in commotion, Prepared for Zion's war.
Some years later, one of Smith's own sons went to Burma as a missionary.

The Morning Light

THE NINETY AND NINE
Elizabeth Clephane, 1830–1869

It is said of this hymn that it is the only one in hymnody written and composed while the author was singing it to the congregation for the first time. The great evangelist Dwight L. Moody was conducting services in Edinburgh, Scotland. The equally famed song leader Ira David Sankey was responsible for the song leading and solos during the services. While riding on the train with Moody from Glasgow to Edinburgh, Sankey spotted a little poem in the local paper written by a Scottish girl named Elizabeth Clephane. He tore the poem out and stuck it in his pocket. Now at the opening service in Edinburgh, it was time for Sankey's solo. Moody's sermon subject was the Good Shepherd but Sankey had not been told and had no appropriate song. He had not even planned to sing alone. Suddenly he thought of the poem in his pocket. It fitted the theme of Moody's sermon perfectly. But there was no music! Quickly, in a seizure of inspiration Sankey whipped out the poem, placed it on the piano, and composed the music, note for note as it is today, singing for the very first time as he composed.

The Ninety And Nine

THERE IS A FOUNTAIN FILLED WITH BLOOD
William Cowper, 1731–1800

William Cowper was born in 1731 and lived to the edge of the 19th century. He was a strange man driven by deep and emotional phobias. Four times he was committed to insane asylums; many times he attempted suicide. His sixty-nine years of life were physical torture and mental anguish. However, there was one bright spot in this holocaust of torture,— the peaceful home of the Reverend John Newton. Newton, who wrote hundreds of hymns, provided a place where Cowper could write his literary masterpieces. When Cowper spoke, his words were twisted and impaired by lisping and stammering; but when he wrote they tumbled forth shining cataracts of verbal beauty. It was here in this haven, the home of Newton, that Cowper wrote "There is A Fountain Filled With Blood." Hundreds of people have sung this grand old favorite through the years. They are unaware of the struggle Cowper had in his life; they see only the beauty and feeling reflected in this hymn. God truly works in mysterious ways his wonders to perform.

There Is A Fountain

THE SHADOWS OF THE EVENING HOURS
Adelaide Anne Proctor, 1825–1864

"The Shadows of the Evening Hours" was written by Adelaide Anne Proctor, friend of Charles Dickens, in 1858. Musically inclined and skilled in many languages, she was also the author of the familiar and popular composition "The Lost Chord." That she was a woman of exceedingly great compassion and kindness is attributed by Dickens' description of her life, "Perfectly unselfish, swift to sympathize, and eager to relieve, she wrought at such designs with a flushed earnestness that disregarded season, weather, time of day or night, food, rest."

The Shadows Of The Evening

THE SWEET STORY OF OLD
Mrs. Jemima Thompson Luke, 1813–1906

I think when I read that sweet story of old,
When Jesus was here among men.

This sweet little children's hymn was written by chance in 1841 by Mrs. Jemima Luke. While she was riding on a stage coach, she scribbled the words on the back of an old envelope. Later in one of her Sunday School classes she was teaching the children her song when her father, the Sunday School superintendent, asked where it had come from. "Oh, Jemima made it," was the reply. The next day he asked for a copy and sent it to the Sunday School Times magazine where it got into print for the first time. Mrs. Luke regarded her hymn writing ability with modest humility. In her own words, "It was a little inspiration from above, and not in me, for I have never written other verses worthy of preservation." (See I Think When I Read That Sweet Story of Old)

The Sweet Story

THERE IS GREEN HILL FAR AWAY
Mrs. Cecil F. Alexander, 1818–1895

There Is A Green
Hill

This hymn, picturing the crucifixion of Jesus, was written in 1848 by Mrs. Cecil Frances Alexander, wife of Reverend W. Alexander, D.D., Bishop of Derry, Ireland. Written for children with the purpose of making the Scripture more understandable, Mrs. Alexander conceived the idea for the song while driving on a shopping expedition to Derry. Outside the city walls there was a little green-covered hill which always made her think of Calvary. Therefore, when she explained the meaning of the death and resurrection of Christ, this little hill came into mind and she wrote:

There is a green hill far away
    Without a city wall,

THERE'S A WIDENESS IN GOD'S MERCY
Frederick William Faber, 1814–1863

There's A Wideness

It was said of Frederick William Faber, Anglican Clergyman, the author of this hymn, that his vivid, unusual imagination was almost without compare. "There's a Wideness In God's Mercy" written in the vicinity of 1846 is a good example of his remarkable talent. Comparing God's love to the wideness of the sea demonstrates not only an extraordinary ability to choose the right metaphor, but a deep insight in the boundlessness of the mercy of the Almighty. This hymn was one of one hundred and fifty written by Faber, all of them composed after being converted to Roman Catholicism in 1846. Protestants have used his hymns freely, however, finding in them a true expression of living faith.

There's a wideness in God's mercy
    Like the wideness of the sea;

THIS IS MY FATHER'S WORLD
Maltbie Davenport Babcock, 1858–1901

This Is My Father's
World

One of Hymnody's most beautiful nature poems, this hymn was written by Reverend Maltbie D. Babcock, prominent Presbyterian minister, during his first pastorate in Lockport, New York. Filled with a deep devotion to his calling, the learned clergyman would often say to his people, "I am going out to see my Father's world." Whereupon he would run to the summit of a hill about two miles outside the city and gaze upon the panorama of the combination of Lake Ontario, natural life, and a bird sanctuary where there were forty different varieties of birds. Speaking of the birds, he would say, "I like to hear them raise their carols in praise to God." Upon the return of one of his morning pilgrimages he wrote down his feelings with these lines:

This is my Father's world, And to my listening ears
    All nature sings, and round me rings
        The music of the spheres.

THROW OUT THE LIFE LINE
Edward Smith Ufford, 1851–1929

In 1886, the Reverend Edward Smith Ufford, Baptist
Minister, preached a sermon beside the sea in Boston,
Massachusetts. At the scene of his sermon was an old
ship-wrecked vessel blown in from sea many years
before which had become a permanent part of the
rock-bound coast. That afternoon as he preached,
using the vessel as an object in his sermon, he con-
templated the writing of a hymn based on the theme
of saving men who had been wrecked at sea. At the
time he could not put the lines together, but a little
later while visiting a lifesaving station at Nantasket
Beach an attendant showed him a slender lifeline and
explained its purpose. "This is how we throw out the
lifeline," he said as he twirled it around his head. This
was just the phrase Ufford had been looking for. His
mind began to vibrate with thought and ideas. Upon
returning home he wrote the four stanzas of the hymn
in less than fifteen minutes.

Throw Out The Life Line

'TIS MIDNIGHT AND ON OLIVE'S BROW
William Bingham Tappan, 1794–1849

This beautiful hymn picturing the suffering and devotion of Jesus in the Garden of Gethsemane was written
in 1822 by a Congregational minister, William Bingham Tappan. The author was born in Beverly, Massachusetts, in 1794, and spent many years of his life
associated with the American Sunday School Union.
First published in a volume called "Gems of Sacred
Poetry," "Tis Midnight and On Olive's Brow" has
long been a favorite of congregations of every denomination, especially during Holy Week in the Easter
season.

'Tis Midnight

'Tis midnight, and on Olive's brow,
    The star is dimmed that lately shone;
'Tis midnight in the garden, now,
    The suffering Saviour prays alone!

TRUST AND OBEY
J. H. Sammis, 1850–1919

During a series of meetings conducted by the famous
D. L. Moody in Brockton, Massachusetts, a young
man rose in the congregation and said, "I am going
to trust, and I am going to obey." Present in the group
that evening was a professor of Music by the name of
D. B. Towner. The young man's statement appealed
to the professor and he wrote it down and sent it
together with the story to a Presbyterian minister,
Rev. J. H. Sammis. Sammis, recognizing the appeal of
the young man's sentence, wrote the well known
chorus which has been a favorite through the years:

Trust And Obey

Trust and obey
For there's no other way
To be happy in Jesus
But to trust and obey.

WATCHMAN, TELL US OF THE NIGHT
John Bowring, 1792–1872

Watchman, Tell Us

An Advent hymn written by John Bowring in the early 19th century. Proficient in five different languages before the age of sixteen, Bowring uses English in this hymn to ask the question first asked in Isaiah 21:11: "Watchman, what of the night?" Before his death, November 23, 1872, Bowring had served as a government official, British consul at Canton, China, and governor at Hong Kong, but he will be remembered far longer for his hymns "Watchman, Tell Us of the Night" and "In the Cross of Christ I Glory."

WHAT A FRIEND WE HAVE IN JESUS
Joseph Medlicott Scriven, 1819–1886

What A Friend We Have

Without question this is one of the ten most popular of all the four hundred thousand Christian hymns published in Church history. Written in 1855 by Joseph Scriven, Irish by birth but Canadian by adoption, this Gospel hymn has been in more constant use by Christian congregations than almost any other imaginable. The hymn was discovered in a very dramatic manner. When Scriven, who lived an extremely tragic life, was in his last days, a friend who was sitting with him during a time of severe illness came upon the manuscript. The friend was very impressed and wondered why it never had been published. Scriven replied, "What A Friend We Have In Jesus has been written by God and me to comfort my mother during a time of great sorrow." He explained that he never intended that it be used by anyone else. Strange are the ways of fate; a song written only for the life and need of one person became the inspiration of millions! There are conflicting reports about the death of Joseph Scriven. Some authorities say he died of natural causes; others that he took his life in a fit of melancholia. However, they all agree as to the humility and kindness that ruled his days from the great tragedy on the eve of his marriage when his bride-to-be accidently drowned to the day of his death in 1886. The hymn tune usually associated with this song was written in 1868 by Charles G. Converse, born in Warren, Massachusetts. Converse studied in Germany and was acquainted with Franz Liszt.

WHEN I SURVEY THE WONDROUS CROSS
Isaac Watts, 1674–1748

When I Survey

The noted critic Matthew Arnold said of the two and a half century old Christian hymn "When I Survey the Wondrous Cross" that it was "the greatest hymn in the English language." He held such admiration for it that he sang and quoted it on his death bed. Written in 1707 by Isaac Watts the hymn was inspired by the words of the Apostle Paul as recorded in Galatians 6:14, "God forbid that I should glory, save in the cross of our Lord Jesus Christ, by whom the world is crucified unto me, and I unto the world."

WHEN MORNING GILDS THE SKIES
Edward Caswall, 1814–1878

A famous old German folk song hymn translated into English by Edward Caswall in 1853. One of the first churches to use this hymn was St. Paul's Episcopal Church in London, England, where leaflets were printed and distributed so all the congregation could share in the singing of this beautiful music. One of England's eminent ministers of the 19th century, Canon Liddon, considered this one of the greatest of all the Church hymns and requested that it be sung at his funeral service.

When Morning Gilds

When morning gilds the skies,
    My heart awaking cries,
May Jesus Christ be praised!

WHEN THE ROLL IS CALLED UP YONDER
J. M. Black 1840–1910 (approximate dates)

J. M. Black wrote the words and music to this gospel hymn in less than fifteen minutes. At a consecration meeting in his church when members were answering the roll call with verses from the Bible, a little fourteen year old girl, who had been previously taken in off the streets, failed to respond. The following are the author's own words, "I spoke of what a sad thing it would be, when our names are called from the Lamb's Book of Life, if one of us should be absent." According to Black, he wanted something appropriate to sing just at that time, but could find nothing in the hymnal. The thought came to him, "Why don't you write it yourself?" When he went home that evening, just as he went in the door the words suddenly came to him. Seizing a pen, he wrote them down in a frenzied flourish. Going to the piano, he played the music just as it is found in the hymn books today, note for note! Black was so amazed at the speed and ease of his own creation that he dared not change a single word or note from the moment it was written.

When The Roll Is
Called

WHERE CROSS THE CROWDED WAYS OF LIFE
Frank Mason North, 1850–1935

The influence of a hymn on the philosophy of an age cannot be under-estimated. It was with this in mind that in 1903, Dr. Frank Mason North wrote the most famous of his hymns "Where Cross the Crowded Ways of Life." He based his hymn on Matthew 22:9: "Go ye therefore into the highways" and hoped that the singing of this song would express the social content of the gospel.

Where Cross The
Crowded

Where cross the crowded ways of life,
    Where sound the cries of race and clan,
Above the noise of selfish strife,
    We hear Thy voice, O son of man!

The problem of race and strife is still with us in the modern age; and the message of North's stirring hymn is profoundly appropriate.

511

WHILE SHEPHERDS WATCHED THEIR FLOCKS BY NIGHT
Nahum Tate, 1652–1715

A beautiful, pictorial Christmas hymn written by Nahum Tate in the late 17th century. It first appeared in the Supplement to the New Version of the Psalms in 1700, and was one of six hymns written for Christmas, Easter and Communion. Only the Christmas hymn, "While Shepherds Watched" based on St. Luke's version of the Nativity in Luke 2:8–14, survived. It has become so permanent a part of the celebration of the holy season that it will last as long as Christendom exists.

While Shepherds Watched

WORK FOR THE NIGHT IS COMING
Annie Louise Coghill, 1836–1907

This hymn which emphasizes the joy and the dignity of work and Christian service was written in 1854 by a young girl only eighteen years old. Known then as Annie Louise Walker (later as Annie Louise Coghill) she first published her poem in a Canadian newspaper, and later in her own book called "Leaves from the Back Woods." Philosophers have made profound statements about the intrinsic value of labor; authors have written paragraphs of prose phrases painting the purpose of labor; poets have sung the praises of the beauty of labor; but none have been able to state more simply and meaningfully the joy of labor in love than has Annie Louise Coghill in her hymn "Work for the Night is Coming."

Work For The Night

YIELD NOT TO TEMPTATION
Horatio R. Palmer 1834–1907

This gospel hymn, written by H. R. Palmer, is said to have quelled a prison riot in Sing Sing. According to the story, a lady was visiting the women's department one Sunday afternoon. (At one time Sing Sing housed women prisoners as well as men.) The inmates were allowed to sit in the corridor and hear her talk, and sing hymns with her. A matron gave an order which the women rebelled against, and a terrible uprising filled with screams, threats, ribaldry and profane curses curdled the Sabbath air. It was well known that a revolt by the women prisoners was more difficult to contain than a revolt by the men. The matron, in desperation, sent to the men's department for help. Suddenly a clear, strong voice rose above the clamor and crying of the rebellious prisoners, "Yield not to temptation, For yielding is sin; Each victory will help you Some other to win. Fight manfully onward, Dark passions subdue; Look ever to Jesus, He'll carry you through!" A hush stilled the riot. One by one the inmates joined in the song until as one they formed a line and marched quietly back to their cells.

Yield Not To Temptation

Yield not to temptation, For yielding is sin;
Each vict'ry will help you Some other to win;
Fight manfully onward, Dark passions subdue:
Look ever to Jesus, He'll carry you through.

512

INDEX

INDEX

Part I — Names (Persons and Places)

Aaron 15, 79, 274
Abagtha 15
Abednego 15
Abel 15, 79
Abelard, Peter 143
Abiathar 15
Abigail 15
Abimelech 16
Abner 16
Abraham 16, 79, 274
Absalom 16, 79
Adam 17, 79, 274
Adam, Adolphe Charles 329
Adams, John Quincy 391
Adams, Mrs. Sarah Flower 391
Addison, Joseph 391
Agabus 17
Agatha, St. 304
Agnes, St. 304
Ahab 17
Ahaz 18
Ahaziah 18
Alban, St. 304
Albright, Jacob 143
Alexander 19
Alexander, Mrs. Cecil F. 392
Alexandrians, 19
Alford, Dean Henry 392
Alfred, St. 304
Alphaeus 19
Amaziah 19
Ambrose (of Milan) 143, 304, 392
Ammiel 19
Ammonites 20
Amnon 20
Amok 20
Amos 20, 80, 274
Anammelech 20
Ananias 20
Anderson, Hans Christian 330
Andrew 21, 80, 300
Andrews, C. F. 144
Andrews, Lancelot 143
Andronicus 21
Angels 21, 80
Anna 21, 80, 331
Annas 21, 80
Anne, St. 305
Anthony 144

Anthony of Padua, St. 305
Antipas 21, 305
Apollos 21, 80
Apostles (symbols of) 302
Appian Way 80
Aquila 22
Aquinas, Thomas 144
Aramaic 81
Ararat 81
Archelaus 81
Areopagus 81
Ariel 22
Aristarchus 22
Arius 145
Armenia 331
Arndt, Johann 145
Artemas 22
Asa 22
Asaph, St. 305
Asbury, Francis 145
Asherah 81
Assyria 81
Athaliah 23
Athansius 145, 305
Athenians 23
Augustine 146, 305
Augustine of Canterbury 331
Augustine of Hippo, St. 306
Augustus Caesar 23, 331
Axton, John T. Sr. 146
Azariah 23
Baal 24, 82
Baalzebub 24
Babcock, Maltbie Davenport 393
Babe of Bethlehem 332
Babel, Tower of 82
Babylon 24, 82
Bach, Johann Sebastian 146, 332
Backus, Isaac 146
Bacon, Leonard 393
Baker, Henry Williams 393
Balaam 24
Balch, William 147
Ballou, Hosea 147
Balthazar 332
Bar-Jona 25
Barabbas 25, 83
Barak 25
Baring-Gould, Sabine 394

Barlow, Joel 394
Barnabas 25, 83, 302
Barocci, Federigo 332
Bartholomew 25, 301
Bartimaeus 25
Basemath 25
Basil The Great 147, 306
Bates, Katherine Lee 394
Bathsheba 25
Baxter, Richard 147, 395
Bede 148, 306
Beecher, Henry Ward 148
Beelzebub 26
Belshazzar 26, 83
Ben-Hadad 26
Benedict of Nursia 148
Benjamin 26
Benson, Louis FitzGerald 395
Bernard of Clairvaux 148, 395
Bernard, St. 306, 396
Bernice 26
Bethany 84
Bethel 84
Bethesda 84
Bethlehem 84, 333, 334
Beza, Theodore 149
Bickersteth, Edward Henry 396
Bildad 27
Bissell, Emily 334
Blair, James 149
Blanchard, Ferdinand Quincy 396
Bliss, Philip Paul 397
Boaz 27, 85
Bocskay, Stephen 149
Bode, John Ernest 397
Bohme, Jakob 149
Bonar, Horatius 397
Bonaventura 150
Bonaventure, St. 335
Bonhoefer, Dietrich 150
Boniface 150, 306, 335
Booth, William 150
Bossuet 151
Botticelli 335
Bowie, Walter Russell 398
Bowring, John 398
Brainered, David 151
Brent, Charles H. 151
Bresse, Phineas F. 151
Bridges, Matthew 398
Bridget (Bride) St. 306
Bronte ,Anne 399
Brooks, Phillips 152, 335, 399
Browne, Robert 152
Browning, Robert 152
Bryant, William Cullen 399

Bunyan John 152, 400
Burns, James Drummond 400
Bushnell Horace 153
Butzer (or Bucer), Martin 153
Byrom, John 400
Caesar 27, 86, 335
Caesarea Philippi 86
Caiaphas 27, 86
Cain 27, 275
Caleb 27
Calvary 86
Calvin, John 153
Campbell, Alexander 153
Canaan 28, 86
Capernaum 86
Carey, William 154
Carmel, Mount 87
Carroll, John 154
Cartwright, Peter 154
Cartwright, Thomas 154
Cary, Alice 401
Cary, Lott 155
Cecilia, St. 306
Cennick, John 401
Chad, St. 307
Chaldeans 28, 87
Chalmers, Thomas 155
Channing, William Ellery 155
Charles, St. 307
Chisholm, Thomas O. 401
Chloe 28
Christ 28, 295, 337
Christian 28, 88, 221
Christopher, St. 307
Chrysostom 155, 307
Church 88, 222, 341
Clare, St. 307
Clark, Francis B. 156
Clarke, James Freeman 402
Clarke, John 156
Claudius 28
Clement 28, 307
Clement of Alexandria 156, 341, 402
Cleophas 29
Clephane, Elizabeth Cecilia Douglas 402
Coghill, Anna Louisa 403
Coke, Thomas 156
Cole, Sir Henry 341
Colet, John 157
Coligny, Gaspard De 157
Constantine the Great 157
Corinthians 29, 89
Cornelius 29, 89, 308
Correggio, Antonio 341
Cotton, John 158

Coverdale, Miles 158
Cowper, Williams 403
Coxe, Arthur Cleveland 403
Cranmer, Thomas 158
Croly, George 404
Cromwell, Oliver 158
Crosby, Fanny J. 404
Cross, Allen Eastman 404
Crowell, Grace Noll 405
Cummings, William Haymen 342
Cundall, Joseph 342
Cusa, Nicholas of 159
Cuthbert, St. 308
Cyprian 159, 308
Cyrenius 342
Cyril of Alexandria, St. 308
Cyril of Jerusalem, St. 308
Czechoslovakia 342
Da Vinci, Leonardo 342
Damascus 91
Daniel 30, 91, 275
Dante, Alighieri 159
Darby, John N. 159
Darius 30
David 30, 91, 275, 308, 342
Davis, Ozora Srearns 405
De Lorenzo, Fiorenzo 344
Dead Sea 91
Dearmer, Percy 405
Deborah 30, 275
Decapolis 92
Delilah 31
Della Robbia 31
Demetrius 31
Denis of Paris, St. 308
Desmet, Pierre Jean 160
Deuteronomy 92
Diana 31
Dickens, Charles 344
Dix, William Chatterton 406
Doane, George Washington 406
Doane, William Croswell 406
Doddridge, Philip 407
Dolci, Carlo 344
Dominic 160, 309
Donne, John 160
Dorcas 31, 92
Dorothy, St. 309
Dostoevsky, F. M. 160
Duffield, George, Jr. 407
Dunstan, St. 309
Durer, Albrecht 161, 344
Dwight, Timothy 407
Dyer, Mary 161
Eber, Paul 408
Eckhart, Johannes 161

Eddy, Mary Baker 161
Eden, Garden of 93
Edmund, St. 309
Edward the Martyr, St. 309
Edwards, Jonathan 162
Egypt 32, 93, 345
El Greco 345
Eli 32
Eliakim 32
Eliezer 32
Elihu 32
Elijah 33, 93, 275
Eliot, John 162
Eliphaz 33
Elisha 33, 93
Elisheba 33
Elizabeth 33, 93, 309, 345
Elizabeth, Queen 162
Ellerton, John 408
Elliott, Charlotte 408
Emerson, Ralph Waldo 162
Emmanuel 33, 93, 345
Emmaus 93
Enoch 33
Epaphras 34
Ephad 94
Ephraim 34
Epicureans 34
Erasmus 163
Erastus 34
Esau 34, 94, 275
Esdraelon 94
Essenes 34, 94
Esther 34, 94
Ethiopia 35, 94
Eunice 35
Euphrates 94
Eusebius of Caesarea 163
Eustace, St. 309
Eutychus 35
Eve 35, 94, 275
Ezekiel 35, 95, 276
Ezra 35, 95
Faber, Frederick William 409
Faith, St. 310
Farel, Guillaume 163
Fawcett, John 409
Felix 35, 96
Fenelon 163
Festus 36
Field, Eugene 346
Finney, Charles G. 164
Fosdick, Harry Emerson 409
Fox, George 164
Foxe, John 164
Fra Angelico 164, 348

517

Fra Lippo Lippi 348
Francis of Assisi 165, 310, 348, 410
Francis of Sales 165
Francke, August Hermann 165
Frazier, John B. 165
Frederich, William Brandenburg
  166
Gabriel 36, 97, 310, 348
Gaius 36
Galilee 36, 97, 348
Gallio 36
Gamaliel 36
Gandhi, Mohandas 166
Genesis 98
Gentiles 36, 98
George, St. 310
Georgione, Giorgio 349
Gerald, St. 310
Gerald of Aurilias, St. 310
Gerhardt, Paul 410
Gesu Bambino 349
Gethsemane 98
Gibbons, James 166
Gideon 36, 98, 276
Giles of Provence, St. 300
Gilkey, James Gordon 410
Gilmore, Joseph Henry 411
Gladden, Washington 166, 411
God 37, 99, 349
Golgotha 99
Goliath 37, 99
Good Samaritan 37
Grant, Robert 411
Grebel, Conrad 167
Gregory I, Pope 167, 311, 412
Grenfell, Sir Wilfred 167
Grotius, Hugo 167
Gruber, Franz 351
Grundtvig, N.F.S. 168
Grunewald, Matthias 168
Gurney, Archer T. 412
Gustavus Adolphus 168
Habakkuk 37
Hagar 37
Haggai 37
Hanaford, Phebe A. 412
Handel, George Friedrich 168, 351
Hankey, Katherine 413
Harkness, Georgia 413
Harnack, Adolp 169
Hastings, Thomas 413
Hauge, Hans Nielsen 169
Havergal, Frances Ridley 414
Hawks, Annie Sherwood 414
Herber, Reginald 414
Hebon 100

Henry of Navarre (Henry IV) 169
Herbert, George 415
Herod 39
Herod the Great 101, 352
Hezekiah 39, 101
Hicks, Elias 169
Hilary of Poitiers, St. 311, 352
Hilda, St. 311
Hildebrand 170
Hiram 39, 101
Hobart, John Henry 170
Holboll, Einar 352
Holmes, John Haynes 415
Holmes, Oliver Wendell 415
Hooker, Richard 170
Hooker, Thomas 170
Hopkins, John Henry Jr. 353
Hooper, Edward 416
Horeb, Mount 102
Hosea 40, 102, 276
Hosmer, Frederick Lucian 416
How, William Walsham 416
Howe, Julia Ward 417
Hubert, St. 311
Hubmaier, Balthasar 173
Hugel, Baron Friedrick Von 173
Hugh of Grenoble, St. 311
Hughes, Thomas 417
Huntingdon, Selina Shirley 417
Huss, John 173
Hyde, William de Witt 418
Ignatius 173, 311
Immanuel 40, 103
Innocent III 174
Irenaeus, St. 174
Irving, Wasington 355
Isaac 40, 276
Isaiah 40, 104, 276, 355
Iscariot 40
Israel 41, 104, 355
Jackson, Sheldon 174
Jacob 42, 104, 276
James 42, 300, 301
Jehoiachin 43
Jehoshaphat 43
Jehovah 43, 105
Jephthah 43
Jeremiah 43, 105, 276
Jericho 105
Jeroboam 44
Jerome 174
Jerusalem 105, 356
Jesse 44
Jesus Christ 44, 105, 240, 284, 285,
  356
Jethro 44

518

Jew 44, 105
Jezebel 44
Joab 45
Joan of Arc 175
Joash 45
Job 45
Joel 45
John 45, 300
John of Damascus 175, 418
John of the Cross 175
John the Baptist 45, 105, 312, 357
Johnson, Samuel 176
Jonah 46, 277
Jonas, Justus 418
Jonathan 46, 105
Jones, Rufus M. 176
Joseph 46, 277, 312, 357
Joshua 46, 105, 277
Josiah 46
Judah 47, 106
Judas 47, 106
Jude 47, 300
Judea 47, 357
Judson, Adoniram 176, 419
Judson, Emily Chubbuck 419
Julia 47, 312
Jupiter 47
Justin Martyr 176
Kagawa, Toyohiko 177
Kant, Immanuel 177
Katherine of Alexandria 312
Katherine of Sienna, St. 312
Keble, John 419
Ken, Thomas 420
Kethe, William 420
Key, Francis Scott 420
Khomiakov, Alexy 177
Kierkegaard, Soren 177
Kilmer, Joyce 421
Kingsley, Charles 421
Kipling, Rudyard 421
Klopstock, Friedrich Gottlieb 422
Knight, William Allen 422
Knox, John 178
Lagerlof, Selma 358
Lanier, Sidney 422
Larcom, Lucy 423
Las Casas, Bartholomas 178
Lathbury, Mary Artemisia 423
Latimer, Hugh 178
Laud, William 178
Law, William 79
Lawrence, St. 312
Lazarus 48
Lee, Jason 179
Lefevre D'Etaples 179

Lerolle, Henri 359
Levi 49, 108
Lincoln, Abraham 179
Lioba, St. 312
Livingstone, David 180
Longfellow, Henry Wadsworth 360, 423
Longfellow, Samuel 424
Louis, St. 313
Lowell, James Russell 424
Lowry, Robert 424
Loyola, Ignatius 180
Luke 49, 109, 360
Luke, Jemima Thompson 425
Lull, Raymond 180
Luther, Katherine von Bora 180
Luther, Martin 181, 425, 360
Lydia 49, 109, 313
Lyte, Henry Francis 425
Maccabees 109
Macedonia 50, 110
Magi 50, 110
Makemie, Francis 181
Malachi 50
Marcion 181
Margaret, St. 313
Markham, Charles Edwin 426
Marlatt, Earl Bowman 426
Marquette, Jacques 181
Martha 51, 111, 313
Martin, Mrs. C. D. 426
Martin of Tours 182, 313
Mary 51, 362
Mary Magdalene 111, 313
Mary of Bethany 111, 314
Mary of Cleophas, St. 314
Mary, The Mother of Jesus 111, 289, 313
Mason, Lowell 362
Mather, Cotton 182
Matheson, George 427
Matthew 52, 111, 301, 362
Matthias 52, 111, 301
Maurice, J. F. D. 182
McKendree, William 182
McPherson, Aimee Semple 183
Mediterranean Sea 112
Medley, Samuel 427
Melanchthon, Philip 183, 427
Melchior 362
Melchisedek 52, 277
Mendelssohn, Felix 362
Menno, Simons 183
Merrill, William Pierson 428
Micah 53, 277, 363
Micaiah 53, 113

Michael 53, 314
Miller, William 183
Mills, Samuel J. 184
Milman, Henry Hart 428
Milton, John 428
Miriam 53
Moab 54, 113
Moffat, Robert 184
Mohammed 184
Mohr, Joseph 429, 364
Molech 54, 113
Monica, St. 314
Monsell, John Samuel Bewley 429
Montgomery, James 364, 429
Moody, Dwight L. 184
Moore, Clement Clarke 364
Mordecai 54
More, Thomas 185
Moses 54, 114, 277
Mott, John R. 185
Muhlenberg, Henry M. 185
Muhlenberg, William Augustus 430
Muller, George 185
Murray, John 186
Naaman 54, 115
Naboth 55
Nahum 55, 278
Naomi 55
Nathan 55
Nathaniel 55, 314
Nazareth 56, 115, 365
Neale, John Mason 365, 430
Neander, Joachim 430
Nebuchadnezzar 56, 116
Nehemiah 56, 116
New Testament 116, 365
Newman, John Henry 186, 431
Newton, John 431
Nicholas, St. 314
Nicodemus 56, 116
Noah 57, 117, 278
North, Frank Mason 431

Oakley, Dr. Frederick 366
Oatman, Johnson, Jr. 432
Oberlin, John Frederick 186
Occom, Samson 432
Olaf, St. 314
Olives, Mount of 118
Onesimus 57, 118
Origen 186
Oswald, St. 315
Otterbein, Philip William 187
Oxenham, John 432

Palestine 119, 368
Palestrina, G. P. 187

Palmer, Ray 433
Park, John Edgar 433
Parker, Theodore 433
Pascal, Blaise 187
Patrick 187
Patrick, St. 315, 368
Paul 59, 220, 302
Paul III, Pope 188
Paulinus, Bishop 368
Peck, John Mason 188
Penn, William 188
Perronet, Edward 434
Peter 59, 120, 300
Peter the Hermit 188
Petri, Laurentius 189
Petri, Olaus 189
Pharaoh 59, 120
Pharisees 59, 121
Phelps, Sylvanus Dryden 434
Philemon 59, 121
Philip 59, 300
Philippi 60, 121, 368
Phillips, Philip 434
Pierpont, Folliott Sandford 435
Pierson, Arthur Tappan 435
Pilate 60, 121
Pius IX 189
Plumptre, Edward Hayes 435
Pollock, Thomas Benson 436
Polycarp 189
Poteat, Edwin McNeil 436
Potiphar 60, 122
Prang, Louis 369
Prentiss, Elizabeth Payson 436
Priscilla 61
Raikes, Robert 190
Rameses 126
Rankin, Jeremiah Eames 437
Raphael, St. 315
Rauschenbusch, Walter 190
Rebekah 62, 126
Rehoboam 62, 126
Rembrandt 190
Reuben 62, 127
Ricci, Matteo 190
Rich Young Ruler 63
Rinkart, Martin 437
Roberts, Daniel Crane 437
Robertson, Frederick W. 191
Robertson, John 191
Robinson, Richard Hayes 438
Robinson, Robert 438
Roch, St. 315
Rossetti, Christina 372, 438
Russell, Charles Taze 191
Ruth 63, 128, 278

Sadducees 63, 129
Saint Nicholas 372
Salome 64
Samaritans 64, 129
Samson 64, 129, 278
Samuel 64, 129
Sankey, Ira David 439
Sarah 64, 129
Sargon 65, 129
Saul 65, 129
Savonarola, Girolamo 191
Schaff, Philip 192
Schlatter, Michael 192
Schleiermacher, Friedrich
  Ernst Daniel 192
Schmucker, Samuel Simon 192
Scriven Joseph Medlicott 439
Seabury, Samuel 193
Sears, Edmund Hamilton 439
Sennacherib 65, 131
Servetus, Michael 193
Seth 65, 278
Shakespeare, William 373
Sheldon, Charles M. 194
Shurtleff, Ernest Warburton 440
Silas 67, 132
Simeon 67
Simeon Stylites 194
Simon 67, 315, 374
Simon the Zealot 301
Sinai, Mount 132
Smart, Henry 375
Smith, Joseph 194
Smith, Samuel Francis 440
Smyth, John 194
Socinus, Faustus 195
Soderblom, Nathan 195
Solomon 68, 132, 278
Spener, Philip Jacob 195
Spurgeon, Charles H. 195, 440
Stennett, Samuel 441
Stephen 68, 134, 315, 375
Stites, Edgar Page 441
Stock, Harry Thomas 441
Stocking, Jay Thomas 442
Stone, Samuel John 442
Stowe, Harriet Beecher 442
Strong, Nathan 443
Studdert-Kennedy,
  Gregory Anketell 443
Swedenborg, Emmanuel 196
Sylvanus, St. 315
Tappan, William Bingham 443
Tarrant, William George 444
Tarsus 135
Tate, Nahum 376, 444

Taylor, J. Hudson 196
Temple, J. Hudson 196
Temple, William 196
Tennent, Gilbert 196
Tennyson, Alfred 197, 444
Tertullian 197
Tetzel, Johann 197
Thaddaeus 70, 316
Theodore of Canterbury, St. 316
Theodore Tvro, St. 316
Theophilus 70, 197
Theresa of Avila 198
Thomas 70, 301
Thomas a Becket 198
Timothy 70, 136, 316
Tiplady, Thomas 445
Titus 71
Tolstoy, Leo N. 198
Toplady, Augustus Montague 445
Torquemada, Thomas De 198
Trench, Richard Chenevi 445
Tweedy, Henry Hallman 446
Tyndale, William 199
Ufford, Edward Smith 446
Uriah 71
Uriel, St. 316
Uzziah 72
Valentine, St. 316
Van Dyke, Henry 378, 446
Vincent De Paul 199
Vincent, St. 317
Wade, John Francis 378
Waldenstrom, P. P. 199
Walter, Howard Arnold 447
Walther, Carl F. W. 199
Waring, Ann Laetitis 447
Warner, Anna Bartlett 447
Washington, George 378
Watts, Isaac 200, 448
Weil, Simone 200
Wenceslas, St. 317
Wesley, Charles 200, 379, 448
Wesley, John 200
Wesley, Susanna 200
White, Henry Kirke 448
White, William 201
Whitefield, George 201
Whiting, William 449
Whitman, Marcus 201
Whittier, John Greenleaf 201, 449
Wilfrid, St. 317
William of Nassau,
  Prince of Orange 201
Williams, George 202
Williams, Roger 202

Williams, William 449
Wolfe, Aaron Robarts 450
Woolman, John 202
Wordsworth, Christopher 450
Wren, Sir Christopher 202
Wycliffe, John 202
Xavier, Francis 203
Yon, Pietro 380
Young, Brigham 203

Zacharias 73, 140, 380
Zebedee 73
Zechariah 73
Zeisberger, David 203
Zephaniah 278
Zinzendorf, Count Nicolaus
    Ludwig 203, 450
Zwingli, Huldreich (or Ulrich) 203

Part II — Topics (Church and Theological)

Abbey 207
Ablution 207
Abomination 79
Absolution 207
Abstinence 207
Acolyte 207
Acts of the Apostles 79
Adoration 207, 329
Advent 207, 330
Adversary 79
Affusion 207
Alabaster 79
All Saints 217
All Saints' Day 208
Alms 79, 208
Alpha and Omega 79, 208, 284
Altar 79, 209, 273
Altar of Sacrifice 272
Ambassador 19
Ambulatory 209
Amen 79, 210
Ampulla 210
Anathema 80, 210
Angels 289, 290, 330
Angelus 210
Anglican Church
    (or Communion) 210
Anglo-Catholic 210
Annunciation 80, 331
Anoint 80, 210
Anthem 210, 331
Antichrist 80
Apocrypha 80
Apostles 21, 80, 210, 301
Apostles' Creed 211
Apostolic Succession 211
Apple 80, 272
Archaeology 81
Archangel 211
Archbishop 211
Archdeacon 211

Archers 81
Ark 81, 271, 273
Armor 81
Arrival of the Shepherds 331
Ascension 211, 293
Ash Wednesday 211
Athanasian Creed 212
Atonement 82, 212
Ave Maria 212
Avenger 82

Balances 82, 296
Balm 82
Banners 212, 296
Banns 212
Baptism 83, 213
Barbarian 25, 83
Basilica 213
Basin and Ewer 288
Bay 213, 332
Beatitude 83
Belfry 213
Bell 214, 333, 293
Benediction 214
Betrothal 214
Bible 84, 214, 293, 334
Bier 84, 214
Birthright 84
Births on Christmas Day 334
Bishop 27, 84, 214, 215
Bishop of Antioch 334
Blasphemy 84
Blessing 84
Blindness 84
Blood 84
Bondage 85
Book of Remembrance 215
Books 85
Brambles 85
Bread 85, 215
Breastplate 85

522

Broad Church 216
Bulrush 85
Burning Torch 295
Burnt Offering 85
Buttress 216

Caldron 86
Calendar 216
Camel 86, 335
Campanile 216
Candle 216, 217, 336
Candlestick 86, 273, 288
Canon 217
Canon of Scripture 86
Canonization 217
Canticles 86, 218
Cantique De Noel 336
Captive 86
Captivity of the Jews 87
Cardinal 218
Carillon 218
Carol 218, 336
Catechism 218
Cathedral 218
Catholic 87, 219
Catholic Epistles 87
Cedar 87, 336
Celebrant 219
Celibacy 219
Censer 87, 295
Census 336
Centurion 87
Chalice 219
Chancellor 219
Chapel 220
Chapter 220
Chariot 87
Chasten 88
Cherubim 88
Chest of Joash 88
Chi Rho 284, 285, 296
Child 337
Children of God 88
Children of Israel 88
Chimes 220
Choir 220, 221
Chrism 221
Christ 295, 337, 340
Christ Bundles 337
Christen 221
Christian 221
Christian Year (or Church Year) 221
Christmas Carol 329
Christmas Customs 337, 338, 339,
    340, 383, 384, 385, 386, 387, 388
Christmas Day 221, 222, 362

Christmas Paintings and
    Their Artists 385
Church 222, 341
Church School 222
Churching (of Women) 222
Cincture 222
Circumcision, The Feast of the 222
City of David 341
Clay Tablets 88
Clergy 223
Cloister 223
Cloud, Pillar of 88
Coat (The Seamless) 286
Collect 223
Color, Liturgical 223
Comforter 88, 224
Common Prayer, Book of 224
Communion, Holy 224
Communion of Saints 224
Community, Religious 225
Confirmation 225
Confiteor 225
Conquest of Canaan 88
Consecrate 89, 225
Constantine Cross 225
Consubstantiation 226
Conversion 89, 226
Convocation 226
Cornerstone 89, 284
Cornice 226
Corpus 226
Council 226
Counsel 89, 341
Covenant 89
Covet 89
Creation 89
Crèche 227, 341
Credo or Creed 227
Crosier or Crozier 227
Cross 89, 227, 248, 279, 280, 281, 282
    (full page of various types) 285
Cross Section of a Church
    (drawing) 237
Crossing, The 227
Crown 90, 227, 286
Crucifix 227
Crucifixion 90
Crypt 227
Cuneiform Writing 90
Curate 227
Cure 228
Curse 90
Cymbals 90

Dancer 91, 342
David, Star of 91

Deacon 91, 228
Deaconess 228
Dean 228
Decalogue 91, 228
Decorations 344
Decree 92, 344
Dedication 92, 228
Demon 31, 92
Deposition 228
Desert 92
Devil 92
Devout 92
Diaconate 228
Dimissory Letter 228
Diocese 229
Disciples 31, 92
Dispersion 92
Doctor 229
Dogma 229
Donkey 92, 344
Doorpost and Lintel 273
Dossal, Dorsal or Dosser 229
Dove 272, 292, 298
Doxology 229
Dragon 272
Druids 344
Dungeon 93
Dyeing 93

Eagle 93
East 229, 345
Easter 229, 230
Elder 93, 230
Elements 230
Embalming 93
Ember Days 230
Encampment 94
Engine 94
Epiphany 345
Epiphany, The Feast of the 230, 290
Episcopacy 230
Episcopal Church, The 230
Epistles 94, 230
Eschatology 231
Eternal Life 94
Ethiopian Eunuch 35
Eucharist 231
Evangelist 94, 231
Eve (or Even) 231
Evensong 231
Everlasting Father 346
Evil 94
Excommunicate 95, 231
Exodus 95
Exorcist 95

Famine 95

Farthing 95
Fasting 95, 232
Father 232
Fear of the Lord 95
Feast of St. Andrew 346
Feasts and Festivals 95, 232
Festal 232
Festival 346
Fetters 96
Fire 96
Firmament 96
First-Born 96
First Fruit 96
Fishing 96
Flag, Christian 232
Flagon 233
Flight into Egypt 290, 347
Flock 96, 347
Flood 96
Fly and the Spider, The 347
Font 233
Fool 96
Forerunner 96
Fountain 96
Fowl 96, 97
Frankincense 97, 348
Friendly Beasts, The 348
Frontal 233
Frontlets, or Phylacteries 97

Galatians, Epistle of Paul to the
    36, 97
Garland 349
Generation 98
Genuflexion 233
Ghost, Holy 233
Giant 98
Gift 349
Gleaning 98
Gloria in Excelsis 233
Glory 99
Goad (Ox-goad) 99
God 37, 99, 349, 363
Godless 99
Godly 99
Godparent 233
Gold 350
Good Friday 234
Goodwill 350
Gospel 99, 234, 350
Gothic 234
Governor 99, 350
Grace 99, 234
Granary 99
Grapes 99
Grasshoppers or Locusts 100

Gregorian Music 234

Habit 235
Hades 235
Hallow 100
Hand of God 292
Handmaiden 100
Harp 100, 296, 351
Hassock 235
Heart, The Pierced 299
Heathen 100
Heaven 100, 235, 351
Hell 101, 235
Helmet 101
Hemlock 351
Herald 101
Herdsmen 101
Heresy 235
Heritage 101
High Celebration 235
High Church 235
High Priest 101
Hireling 101
Holly 297, 352
Holy Days of Obligation 235
Holy Family 290, 353
Holy Ghost (or Holy Spirit) 39
Holy Land 353
Holy Night 353
Holy of Holies 101
Holy Spirit 102, 353
Holy Week 235
Homily 235
Hosanna 102, 238
Hospitality 102
Host 102, 238
Husbandman 102
Hymns 1 03, 238
Hypocrite 103
Hyssop 103
I.C.S. (or I.H.S.) 238, 284
Icon 238
Idol 103
Idolatry 103
Images 103
Immaculate Conception 238
Immanuel 354
Immersion 238
Immortality 103, 239
Immovable Feasts 239
Imposition of Hands 239
Incarnation 103, 239, 354
Incense 103, 239, 354
Infallibility 239
Infant 355
Inheritance 103

Iniquity 103
Inn 103, 355
I.N.R.I. 239, 287
Inspiration 104, 239
Intercession 104, 239
Introit 240
Invocation 240

Jacob's Well 104
Javelin 104
Jehovah (JHVH) 240
Jesus 240, 284, 285, 295, 337, 340
Jewess 44
Joining the Church 240
Journey of the Magi 357
Jubilee, Year of 106
Judaism 240
Judges 47, 106
Justification 240

Kalendar 241
King 48, 358
Kingdom of God (Heaven) 106, 241
Kinsmen 106
Kiss of Peace 241
Kneeling 241
Knell 241

Laity 241
Lamb 107, 272, 292, 358
Lamentation 107
Lamp 107, 291, 299
Lantern 241, 288
Last Gospel 241
Last Things 241
Latin Cross 242
Laurel 358
Law 107
Lay Leader 242
Laying on of Hands 107
Leather 107
Leaven 107
Legend 358
Legion 108
Lent 242
Lentil 108
Lepers 48
Leprosy 108
Lesson 242
Leviticus 108
Libraries 108
Light 108, 359
Lily 108, 287, 359
Lily of the Valley 297
Litany 242
Liturgical 243, 267

Loaf 108
Locust 108
Log 360
Lord 108, 360
Lord's Day, The 109, 243
Lord's Prayer, The 109, 243
Lord's Supper, The 109, 243
Lotus 297
Love 360
Low Church 243
Lyre 109

Madonna 361
Madness 110
Magi 290, 361
Magic 110
Magician 50
Magnificat 110, 243, 361
Magnify 110
Malefactor 110
Mammon 110
Man 110
Manger 110, 289, 361
Manna 110
Manse 244
Mantle 110
Mantle of Fire 361
Mark 51, 111
Marriage 244
Martyr 111, 244
Mary's Journey to Visit Elizabeth
  289
Mass 244
Massacre of the Innocents 290
Matins 244
Matrimony 244
Maundy Thursday 111, 244
Mediator 112
Mediation 244
Mercy 112
Messiah 53, 112, 362
Minister 113
Minister-in-Charge 244
Minstrel 113
Miracle Play 363
Miracles 113
Missal 244
Mission 245
Mitre 245
Monastic Vows 245
Money 114, 287
Monks 245
Monsignor 245
Monstrance (or Ostensorium) 245
Mortal Sin 245
Most High 114

Mote 114
Mourning 114
Multitude 115
Music 115
Mustard Seed 115
Myrrh 115, 364
Myrtle 115, 298

Narthex 246
Nativity 364
New Moon 116
New Testament 116, 365
Nicene Creed 246
Night 116, 365
Nightingale, The 365
Noel 365
Nonconformist 246
Nonliturgical 246
Novena 246
Novice 246
Nun 57
Nunc Dimittis 246

Oath 117
Obeisance 117
Oblation 117, 246
Offering 246
Offerings 117, 366
Oils, Holy 247
Ointment 117
Old Testament 118, 367
Olive Branch 296
Olive Tree 118
Omnipotent 118
Oracle 118
Oratory 247
Order 247
Ordinary 247
Ordination 118, 247
Organ 247
Ornaments 367
Other Wise Man, The 367
Ox 119, 291, 367

Pageant 367
Palm Leaf 286
Palm Sunday 248
Palsy 119
Papyrus 119
Parable 119
Paradise 119, 248
Parental Blessing 119
Parish 248
Parochial School 249
Paschal Candle 249
Passion 119, 249

Passover 119
Pastoral Epistles 120
Patriarch 59, 120
Paul 59, 120, 302
Peace 368
Pennance 250
Pentateuch 120
Pentecost 120
Pentecost, The Feast of 250
Pestilence 120
Petition 120
Phylacteries 121
Pilgrimage 121
Pilgrims 368
Plague 122
Plowshare 122
Poetry 122
Polytheism 122
Pontifical 250
Postures in Worship 251
Pottage 122
Potter 122
Praise 123
Prayer 123
Precentor 251
Precept 123
Presbyter 251
Presiding Bishop 251
Press 123
Priest 60, 123, 251
Prince of Peace 369
Processional 252
Procurator 123
Prodigal 123
Prophecy 369
Prophet 61, 123, 124
Proselyte 124
Protector 252
Protestant 252
Proverb 124
Provinces 124, 252
Psalms, Book of 124, 252
Publican 61, 124
Pulpit 252
Purgatory 253
Purge 124
Purification 124
Purim, Feast of 125
Purse 125

Quarternion 125
Quartus 61
Queen 61
Queen of Heaven 61
Queen of Sheba 61
Queer Christmas Customs 370

Quiver 125

Rabbi 62, 125
Raiment 125
Rainbow 125
Real Presence 253
Receipt of Custom 126
Recessional 253
Reconciliation 126
Rectory 254
Redeemer 62, 126, 371
Redemption 254
Reformation 254
Refuge 126
Regeneration 254
Religious Life, The 254
Remnant 126
Renaissance 254
Repentance 126, 254
Requiem 254
Reredos 255
Responses 255
Restitution 127
Resurrection 127, 255
Retreat 255
Reverend 255
Revival 255
Righteous 127
Ritual 127, 256
Rod, Shepherd's 127
Rogationtide 256
Romanesque 256
Rose of Jericho 372
Ruler 63

Sabbath 128
Sackcloth 128
Sacrament 128, 256, 257
Sacrifice 128, 257
Sacristy 257
Saints 129, 257
Salutation, Forms of 325
Salvation 257
Samuel, I and II 129
Sanctuary 129, 257
Sanctus 258
Sanhedrin 64, 129
Satan 65
Saviour 65, 130, 373
Scapegoat 130
Scepter 130
Scourge 130
Scribes 65, 130, 373
Scrip 130
Scripture 130
Scroll 130, 272, 273

Scrolls, The Dead Sea 130
Seasons 258
See 258
Septuagint 131
Sepulchre 131
Sermon 258, 373
Sermon on the Mount 131
Serpent 271
Service 373
Sexagesima 258
Sheaf 131, 373
Sheepfold 131
Shekel 131
Shema 66, 131
Shepherds 66, 290, 295, 374
Shewbread 131
Ship 291
Shrines 131, 258
Shrove Tuesday 258
Siege 132
Sin 132, 259
Skull 298
Slaves 68
Sling 132
Sluggard 132
Snare 132
Sojourn, The 132
Son of Man 132
Song of Degrees 133
Sons of God 133
Soothsayer 133
Sorcerer 133
Soul 133
Souls of the Righteous 292
Sponsors 259
Stable 133, 375
Staff 133
Stained Glass 259
Star 271, 295, 375
Stations of the Cross 259
Stewards 68, 134
Stoning 134
Stork 289
Straw 134, 375
Suffer 134
Sun 293
Sunday 134
Sunday School 260
Superscription 134
Surplice 260
Swaddling Clothes 376
Swine 134
Sword and Staff 286
Sword, Flaming 271
Symbols of the Church
    (full page) 303

Symbols of the Saints 304
Synagogue 134
Synod 261
Synoptic Gospels 135

Tabernacle 135, 261
Tables of Stone with the
    Ten Commandments 273
Tables of the Law 135
Talent 135
Talmud 135
Tanner 135
Tares 135
Tax 135
Temple 135, 377
Ten Commandments, The 136
Tenebrae 261
Tents 136
Testament 136
Tester 261
Testimony 136
Tetrarch 69
Thank Offering 136
Thanksgiving 261
Thessalonians 70
Thief 70
Three Hours, The 261
Threshing 136
Throne 136
Tidings 136
Tilling 136
Timbrel 136
Tithe 136, 262
Tittle 137
Tongue 137
Tongues of Fire 137
Torah 137
Tower of Babel 271
Tract 262
Transept 262
Transfer, Letter of 262
Transfiguration 137
Transgression 137
Translation 262 (see Bible)
Transubstantiation 262
Trespass 137
Tribe 137
Tribulation 137
Tribute 137
Trinitarian Formula 262
Trinity, The 263
Troth 263
Trumpet 299
Trustees 263
Twelve Days of Christmas, The 377
Twelve, The 137, 263

528

Unction 263
Undercroft 263
Unicorn 289, 378
Unleavened 137
Upper Room, The 137
Usher 263
Usury 138

Vale 138
Vase 263
Vaulting 264
Veil 138
Venerable, The 264
Vengeance 138
Veni, Creator Spiritus 264
Venial Sin 264
Venite, Exultemus Domino 264
Verger 264
Versicles 264
Vespers 264
Vessels 138, 264
Vestible (see Narthex) 264
Vestments 264
Vestry 265
Via Dolorosa 138
Viaticum 265
Vicar 265
Vigil 265
Vine 138
Virgin 378
Virtues, Cardinal 265
Vision 138
Vixen 378
Vocation 265
Votive Lights 265

Vow 138
Vulgate 139

Wafer 265
Wallet 139
Warden, Church 265
Wassail 379
Watches of the Night 139
Waterpots 139
Wayfaring Man 139
Wedding 139
Well 139
Whitsunday 266
Why the Chimes Rang 379
Wilderness 139
Winepress 139
Winged Creatures 294
Wings 298
Winnowing 140
Wiseman 72, 140, 379
Woman at the Well 72
Words, Seven Last 266
World Council of Churches 317
Worship 140, 266, 379
Wreath 380
Writing 140

Xerxes 72

Yah-Weh 266
Yew 380
Yew Tree 266
Yoke 140
Yuletide 380

Zion 140

Part III—Hymns and Carols

A Charge to Keep I Have 453
A Mighty Fortress Is Our God 453
A Parting Hymn We Sing 453
A Shelter in the Time of Storm 454
Abide with Me 454
Adeste Fideles 329
Alas and Did My Saviour Bleed 454
All Creatures of Our God and King 455
All Glory, Laud and Honor 455
All Hail the Power of Jesus' Name 455

All the Way My Saviour Leads Me 456
All Things Bright and Beautiful 456
Almost Persuaded 456
Amazing Grace 457
America the Beautiful 457
Ancient of Days, Who Sittest Throned in Glory 457
Angels, from the Realms of Glory 330, 458
Angels We Have Heard on High 330
Art Thou Weary, Heavy-Laden 458

529

As with Gladness Men of Old 458
Away in a Manger 331, 459

Be Still My Soul 460
Beautiful Isle of Somewhere 459
Beneath the Cross of Jesus 459
Beulah Land 460
Beyond the Sunset 460
Bless This House, O Lord We Pray 461
Blessed Assurance, Jesus Is Mine 461
Blest Be the Tie That Binds 461
Boar's Head Carol, The 334
Break Thou the Bread of Life 462
Breathe on Me, Breath of God 462
Brightly Beams Our Father's Mercy 462
   (Let the Lower Lights Be Burning)
Bring a Torch, Jeannette, Isabella 335

Cherry Tree Carol, The 337
Christ the Lord Is Risen Today 463
Christians, Awake, Salute the Happy Morn 463
Come, Thou Almighty King 463
Come, We Who Love the Lord 464
Come, Ye Thankful People, Come 464

Day Is Dying in the West 464
Dear Lord and Father of Mankind 465
Deck the Halls 343

Eternal Father, Strong to Save 465

Face to Face 465
Fairest Lord Jesus 466
Faith of Our Fathers 466
Fight the Good Fight 466
First Noel, The 347
Fling Out the Banner! Let It Float 467
For the Beauty of the Earth 467
From Greenland's Icy Mountains 467
From Heaven Above to Earth I Come 348

Glorious Things of Thee Are Spoken 468
God Be with You Till We Meet Again 468
God Moves in a Mysterious Way 468
God of Grace and God of Glory 469
God of Our Fathers, Known of Old 469

God Rest You Merry, Gentlemen 349
God King Wenceslas 350
Guide Me O Thou Great Jehovah 469

Hallelujah Chorus 351
Hallelujah, What a Saviour 470
Hark! The Herald Angels Sing 351, 470
Have Thine Own Way 470
He Leadeth Me O Blessed Thought 471
He Shall Feed His Flock 352
His Eye Is on the Sparrow 471
Holy, Holy, Holy! Lord God Almighty 471
Holy Spirit, Truth Divine 472
How Firm a Foundation 472
How Great Thou Art 472

I Am So Glad 473
I Am Thine, O Lord 473
I Gave My Life to Thee 473
I Heard the Bells on Christmas Day 354, 474
I Heard the Voice of Jesus Say 474
I Love Thy Kingdom Lord 474
I Love to Tell the Story 475
I Need Thee Every Hour 475
I Saw Three Ships 355
I Think When I Read That Sweet Story of Old 475
I Will Sing the Wondrous Story 476
I Would Be True, for There Are Those Who Trust Me 476
In Christ There Is No East or West 476
In Excelsis Gloria! 254
In Heavenly Love Abiding 477
In the Cross of Christ I Glory 477
In the Garden 477
In the Hour of Trial 478
Into the Woods My Master Went 478
It Came upon the Midnight Clear 355, 478
It Is Well with My Soul 479

Jerusalem the Golden 479
Jesus Calls Us! O'er the Tumult 479
Jesus, Keep Me Near the Cross 480
Jesus Light of All the Nations 357
Jesus, Lover of My Soul 480
Jesus Loves Me, This I Know 480
Jesus Saviour Pilot Me 481
Jesus Shall Reign Where'er the Sun 481
Jesus, the Very Thought of Thee 481

Joy to the World 357, 482
Joyful, Joyful We Adore Thee 482
Just As I Am 482

Lead Kindly Light 483
Lead On, O King Eternal 483
Leaning on the Everlasting Arms
483
Lord for Tomorrow and Its Needs
484
Lord I'm Coming Home 484
Love Divine, All Love Excelling 484

Mine Eyes Have Seen the Glory 485
(Battle Hymn of the Republic)
More Love to Thee, O Christ 485
My Country 'Tis of Thee 485
My Faith Looks Up to Thee 486
My Hope Is Built on Nothing Less
486
My Jesus I Love Thee 486

Nearer My God to Thee 487
Now Thank We All Our God 487
Now the Day Is Over 487

O Brother Man, Fold to Thy Heart
Thy Brother 488
O Christmas Tree! 366
O Come All Ye Faithful 366, 488
O Come, O Come Emmanuel
366, 488
O Day of Rest and Gladness 489
O For a Closer Walk with God 489
O For a Thousand Tongues to Sing
489
O God, Our Help in Ages Past 490
O Holy Night 366, 490
O Jesus, I Have Promised 490
O Jesus, Thou Art Standing 490
O Little Town of Bethlehem 367, 491
O Love That Wilt Not Let Me Go
491
O Master, Let Me Walk with Thee
492
O Sacred Head Now Wounded 492
O Where Are Kings and Empires
Now 493
O Worship the King, All Glorious
Above 493
O Zion Haste, Thy Mission High
Fulfilling 494
Once to Every Man and Nation 492
Onward Christian Soldiers 492

Pass Me Not, O Gentle Saviour 494

Peace, Perfect Peace 494
Praise to the Lord, the Almighty
495

Rejoice, the Lord Is King 495
Rejoice Ye Pure in Heart 495
Rescue the Perishing 496
Ride On, Ride On in Majesty 496
Ring the Bells of Heaven 496
Rise Up, O Men of God 496
Rock of Ages 497

Safe in the Arms of Jesus 497
Saved By Grace 498
Saviour, Again to Thy Dear Name
We Raise 498
Saviour Like a Shepherd Lead Us
498
Saviour Thy Dying Love 499
Shall We Gather at the River 499
Shepherd of Tender Youth 499
Silent Night, Holy Night 374, 500
Sing Them Over Again to Me 500
Softly and Tenderly 500
Softly Now the Light of Day 501
Soldiers of Christ Arise 501
Spirit of God, Descend upon My
Heart 501
Stand Up, Stand Up for Jesus 502
Still, Still with Thee When Purple
Morning Breaketh 502
Sun of My Soul, Thou Saviour Dear
502
Sunset and Evening Star 503
Sweet By and By 503
Sweet Hour of Prayer 503

Take My Life and Let It Be 504
Take Time to be Holy 504
Tell Me the Old, Old Story 504
Ten Thousand Times Ten
Thousand 505
The Church's One Foundation 505
The God of Abraham Praise 505
The Light of the World Is Jesus 506
The Morning Light Is Breaking 506
The Ninety and Nine 506
The Shadows of the Evening Hours
507
The Sweet Story of Old 507
There Is a Fountain Filled with
Blood 507
There Is a Green Hill Far Away 508
There's a Wideness in God's Mercy
508
This Is My Father's World 508

531

Throw Out the Life Line 509
'Tis Midnight and on Olive's Brow
  509
Trust and Obey 509

Watchman, Tell Us of the Night
  379, 510
We Three Kings of Orient Are 379
What a Friend We Have in Jesus
  510
When I Survey the Wondrous Cross
  510

When Morning Gilds the Skies 511
When the Roll Is Called Up Yonder
  511
Where Cross the Crowded Ways of
  Life 511
While Shepherds Watched Their
  Flocks by Night 379, 512
Work for the Night Is Coming 512

Yield Not to Temptation 512